# The Korean Cookbook
한식

# The Korean Cookbook
# 한식

By Junghyun Park
and Jungyoon Choi

# Contents

| | |
|---|---|
| 6 | Prefaces |
| 10 | Introduction |
| 14 | A History of Korean Cuisine |
| 18 | Hansik |
| 22 | Korea's Regional Foods |
| 27 | Korean Bapsang & Bansang |
| 32 | The Korean Pantry |
| 40 | Glossary |
| **42** | **Fermentation** |
| 44 | Jang Fermented Soybean Sauces |
| 54 | Kimchi Fermented Vegetables |
| 78 | Jangajji Fermented Vegetables in Jang |
| 84 | Jeotgal Fermented Seafood |
| **90** | **Bap** Cooked Rice |
| 96 | Bibimbap Mixed Rice |
| 112 | Ssambap Wrapped Rice |
| 118 | Gukbap Rice in Soup |
| 126 | Bokkeumbap Fried Rice |
| 130 | Gimbap Gim Rice Rolls |
| 136 | Sotbap Pot Rice |
| 142 | Deopbap Rice Bowls |
| **150** | **Banchan** Dishes to Accompany Rice |
| 152 | Namul Seasoned Vegetable Dishes |
| 186 | Muchim Seasoned |
| 202 | Hwe Raw |
| 208 | Ssam Wrapped |
| 216 | Pyunyuk & Suyuk Pressed & Boiled Meats |
| 224 | Muk Starch Jelly |

**Icon Legend**

| | |
|---|---|
| dF | Dairy-free |
| gF | Gluten-free |
| vg | Vegan |
| vE | Vegetarian |
| -5 | 5 ingredients or fewer |
| -30 | 30 minutes or less |
| [◻] | Photography |

목차

| | |
|---|---|
| 230 | **Jeon & Buchimgae** Savory Pancakes |
| 250 | **Bokkeum** Stir-Fried |
| 258 | **Gui** Grilled |
| 276 | **Jorim** Braised |
| 296 | **Jjim** Steamed |
| 302 | **Twigim** Deep-Fried |
| | |
| 312 | **Yuksu** Broths |
| 316 | **Guk & Tang** Soups |
| 346 | **Jjigae** Stews |
| 356 | **Jeongol** Hotpot |
| | |
| 364 | **Guksu** Noodles |
| 386 | **Mandu** Dumplings |
| 394 | **Juk** Porridge |
| 404 | **Tteok** Rice Cakes |
| | |
| **410** | **Husik** Desserts |
| | |
| **422** | **Master Artisans** |
| 424 | Hee Sook Cho |
| 430 | Mal Soon Lee |
| 434 | Soon Do Ki |
| 440 | Kwang Hee Park |
| 446 | Yeong Geun Park |
| 452 | Myeong Hwan Seo |
| 458 | Jung Yoo Huh |
| 464 | Ji Soon Kim |
| 472 | Jeong Kwan |
| 476 | Gyung Kyun Shin |
| | |
| 482 | Index |

# Preface 서문
## From Junghyun Park

I always consider it a blessing that I am able to work through the medium of food, which I have long been interested in, and have found joy in, since I was a child. In particular, I feel grateful to be able to deliver *hansik*, Korean cuisine, the very food that I grew up eating, the food that has essentially made me who I am, to the world.

While I believed that I had studied and deeply considered *hansik* for a long time in my life, in the process of writing this book I realized how little I really knew. Working on this book not only taught me how to write a cookbook—a process that allowed me to dive deeply into the identity of *hansik*—but, more important, it taught me the true value of exchanging my thoughts with many different people around the world.

I was born in Korea, and it was in Korea that I first began studying the culinary arts. When I took on my first professional role in the kitchens of The Ledbury restaurant in London, I was more interested in French cuisine than Korean cuisine. My dream then was to further my studies in France or the United States, and eventually become a chef-owner of a famous restaurant. But as I continued to gain experience and to learn more about different cuisines, I realized that what I would be best at, was best suited for, and loved the most was actually my own cuisine: *hansik*.

Returning to Korea after working in England and Australia, I was able to pursue my philosophy of the tradition of *hansik* at the restaurant Jungsikdang in Seoul, where I experienced *hansik* through the lens of new ingredients, techniques, and its combinations. I then moved to New York City, where I worked at Jungsik New York. Through that experience I built the confidence in my vision of what was possible through *hansik*, especially in a city like New York, one unlike any other in its diversity, open-mindedness, and continuous growth.

After three years of working in New York, I opened my first restaurant, Atoboy, in 2016. At Atoboy, I hoped to convey the culture of *hansik* through the focus of *hansang* (the complete set of essential components for a proper meal) and *banchan* (side dish) culture, in which diverse dishes are shared and enjoyed alongside *bap* (rice). In 2018, I opened my second restaurant, Atomix, a fine-dining restaurant with the intention of sharing another facet of Korea's food culture in a new way befitting of New York. Atomix honed in on our focus of storytelling about the role of cuisine in culture, about my faith in food as the living and evolving record of our humanity and history.

Through Atoboy, we were able to exchange ideas and our vision with New York's dining community; through Atomix, we garnered recognition and understanding of the global dining community. As the understanding and interest in *hansik* has grown, we opened Naro in 2022 in the historic Rockefeller Center. Naro, with its roots in traditional *hansik*, aims to showcase my personal vision and reinterpreted memories of Korean cuisine. The intention is to showcase the most foundational flavors, techniques, and philosophies of *hansik*—basically an homage to deeply rooted traditional dishes, some of which are explored here in the book.

Despite my professional work over the last fifteen years having focused on *hansik*, the process of writing this book made me realize how much more I had to learn. Often, the more you learn, the more you realize how much more there is to learn and explore. This is the true charm of food: There are no set answers. The study of food and cuisine is endlessly evolving and growing. Cooking is a way of constant creation, and I am excited to continue my life's work in food with renewed delight.

I hope that the readers of this book will be able to experience the deep joy that has lived on for thousands of years in *hansik*, to find it in themselves and their daily lives, and to evolve together for the many years to come. Instead of a book of references for recipes, I hope that this book helps you to learn the story of *hansik*—about how Koreans eat and what our cuisine means to the Korean culture. I hope that *hansik* can become another medium for us to communicate and share together in the journey of life.

# From Jungyoon Choi

Food is the nourishment to the roots of life. As long as I can remember, my parents have taught me that the joy of living lies in culture, and in particular, the importance of culture through food, from the careful preparation to its enjoyment. I was taught to cultivate a curiosity about the world, observing and questioning, endlessly and deeply. As a curious person, there is nothing like the joy of cooking, which allows for the creation of something new every day. Thanks to my parents' teachings, cooking became the foundation and the root of my life.

Throughout my life, I was fortunate to work in many places around the world, including Korea, Australia, Spain, China, and the United States. I was exposed to diverse food cultures, and the more I learned about the rich cultures of other nations, the more I became curious about *hansik*, the Korean food culture that raised and fed me throughout my life.

After working as a chef in the kitchen for more than twelve years, I wanted to begin a new challenge. At the time, I was inspired by how Spain moved the focus of global gastronomy from France to Spain. In 2009, I joined chef Ferran Adrià's culinary science research center Fundació Alícia (Alícia Foundation), established in partnership with the Catalan government, as a research chef. Up until then my career had been focused on learning culinary techniques and applying them in the kitchen. When I learned the mission of the foundation, I realized that the purpose of my work was to learn and develop techniques and skills, but also to learn how to enrich the quality of people's lives, to spark joy and happiness, through cuisine.

During my time at the Alícia Foundation, I learned three big lessons. The first was cooking techniques. The second was how to apply scientific methods of research to cuisine. The third was the power of a team, how solidarity and exchange allow for a more powerful, faster development of knowledge. I evolved from a chef who executed recipes in the kitchen to a chef who researched and developed recipes, and I found that culinary research was an ideal fit for me. The culinary research method allowed me to observe deeply, to continue asking questions and to seek answers: a process that brought me continued joy.

After returning to Korea, I was inspired to apply the culinary research method to *hansik*, to research the foundations of Korean cuisine through the lens of science. In sharing my experiences and lessons with friends in Korea's culinary world, I met Jinsun Park, the CEO of Sempio, who agreed with my vision to establish a research institute to study *hansik*. Sempio established the first and only research institute to conduct foundational Korean food research using a scientific methodology centered on cuisine.

I began finding the answers to my questions on Korean cuisine through my work. I am Korean, and I am a Korean chef, but ultimately, there was so much more to learn about Korean food. The main topics of my research centered around Korea's fermentation, Korea's vegetables, and Korea's *jang* (fermented soybean sauces), the foundation of Korean cuisine.

Through the world of *hansik* culinary science, by formulating the questions and in my pursuit of their answers, I have had the opportunity to meet and converse with countless people. I have been able to meet experts in food culture and culinary research in Korea and around the world, as well as many world-class chefs. It has been more than a decade since I began asking the question, "what is *hansik*?"

In 2019, I received a call from chef Junghyun (JP) Park, asking for me to join him in writing a book to introduce *hansik* culture to the world. I had first met him more than twenty years previously through a young cooks' gathering in Korea. As aspiring cooks, we shared time to study together, cooked together, and shared ideas. Many of our conversations were about our dreams, to work hard in our respective places to spread the story of *hansik* through our work. Years later, the proposition of writing this book together felt like a youthful dream coming true at last.

Chef JP has created restaurants in New York beloved by people all over the world. I applied the culinary science methodology to Korean cuisine, resulting in unprecedented research of Korean food, and I have become the Vice President of Korea and China for the World's 50 Best Restaurants, sharing my experiences with gourmets around the world. We have done our best in our respective places through the years, and I am so grateful to be able to create this book on Korean cuisine together from where we are today.

The making of this book took more than three years, and during this time JP and I had weekly calls with Jinah Rhee, our project manager and translator. We spent countless hours discussing, questioning, researching, reflecting, and editing the contents of this book. Discussing *hansik* at length was a difficult yet extremely joyful process.

My guiding philosophy in collaborating on this book was that it be a collection of recipes, but also that it tells the story of Korea and of the lives of Koreans. Food tells the story of each nation; *hansik* tells the rich and diverse story of Korean life, and I hope this book conveys that beauty.

## 소개글 Introduction

Food is a culture that expresses the essential characteristics of humans, and a language that allows connection. A nation's food culture at once conveys the country's unique climate and geographic factors, its sociocultural factors, and tells the story of its history and is an expression of its people. This is the reason that traditional food culture and cuisine are so important to a nation.

*The Korean Cookbook* aims to tell the stories of Korea through *hansik*, or Korean cuisine. It tells the story of how Koreans eat, and how food figures in the Korean lifestyle.

The book has three objectives. First, it seeks to tell the story of how Koreans celebrate food, and how they came to find their specific cooking methods and food cultures. Second, it shares the everyday dishes that you would find in home kitchens across the nation. Third, it showcases the most important cultural aspects of *hansik* through the prized recipes of master artisans who have dedicated their lives to furthering *hansik*.

## Hansik's Identity

In evoking *hansik*, the dishes that first come to mind include kimchi, *bulgogi*, and *bibimbap*. Yet, in addition to these iconic dishes, this book includes a huge variety of recipes that have been developed over thousands of years by countless people and that highlight the depth and breadth of Korean cuisine.

The best way to understand a nation's food culture is to observe the humble, common dishes that appear on the tables of home kitchens, and to venture into the bustling markets to see its ingredients and its street food.

A Korean dining table is set with various dishes made from seasonal ingredients as defined by the twenty-four seasons of the traditional solar calendar, which was used when Korea was an agricultural society. The common thread among most dishes is that the ratio of the vegetable ingredients to meat ingredients is 7:3. Of the ingredients used in *hansik*, 70 percent are plant-based. Furthermore, the main flavoring method in *hansik* is fermentation. Aside from a handful of dishes, including rice, it is difficult to find dishes in which fermentation has not played a part.

## Korea's Plant-Based Foods & Fermentation

The two most important factors in *hansik* food are plant-based foods and the practice of fermentation.

Throughout their history, Koreans have developed many different and delicious ways to eat vegetables. As a result, in order to introduce the culture of vegetables in *hansik* cuisine, more than 60 percent of the recipes in this book are plant-based or are vegetable-centric. Along with traditional vegetarian recipes, you will also find many vegetable-oriented recipes that use meat or seafood broths or fermented foods to achieve balance and depth of flavor. This showcases the *hansik* wisdom on how to maximize the flavor potential of animal products. Of course, such recipes can easily be made vegetarian by replacing meat-based ingredients, such as beef or anchovy broth or salted shrimp, with plant-based counterparts, such as vegetable broth or soy sauce.

There are three main characteristics that make Korean's plant-based cuisine unique. First is the diversity of vegetables used from the sea, field, and mountains. Second is the application of fermentation methods to its vegetables. Third is the seasoning of vegetables with *jang* (fermented soybean sauces). Not only do these three factors make *hansik* an extremely diverse world of plant-based food, but they also contribute to the extremely rich and balanced flavors in its dishes.

Korea's mainland is 70 percent mountainous lands, where countless herbs and vegetables grow in abundance. Fragrant plants that are used as herbs in other countries are often used as a main vegetable in *hansik*. The vegetables and herbs that grow wild in the Korean mountains possess not only strong fragrance (in the case of herbs), but also have a savoriness and high moisture content that makes them perfect for cooking.

In addition to eating vegetables (raw or cooked) in season, *hansik* also has a long history of preserving seasonal vegetables through dehydration and fermentation. The diversity and wealth of preserved foods, such as kimchi and *jangajji* (Korean pickles), showcase this tradition and history.

Recipes for kimchi, perhaps the most iconic food of Korea, are said to be as diverse as the number of households in Korea—and, indeed, the recipes that exist are countless. At the heart of kimchi's history was the deep need to find a delicious way to preserve its abundance of seasonal vegetables, through fermentation. Even now, more than two thousand years after the first iteration of kimchi, this category of food is still evolving. Korea's determination to find better methods in kimchi is showcased by the modern development of kimchi refrigerators, engineered specifically to ferment and store kimchi at an optimal temperature. What's more, what was once a newfangled invention is now a standard part of the modern Korean household.

The importance of fermentation in Korean vegetable food culture cannot be overstated. *Jang*, a category of seasoning made from fermented soybeans, defines *hansik* and, moreover, is of great importance in the way that Koreans enjoy vegetables. *Jang*, when used as a seasoning ingredient in vegetable recipes, reduces any bitterness found in vegetables while enhancing their inherent fragrance and flavors. The richness and depth that come from fermentation allows a satisfying balance of flavors even when no animal products or oils are used.

In Korean culture, the standard of judging one's skill in *hansik* cuisine is through the making of kimchi and *namul* (vegetable dishes). It is interchangeable to say one is skilled in *hansik* cuisine or that one is skilled at making kimchi, *namul*, and *jang*. Even as a home cook becomes more accomplished in *hansik* cuisine, it is often said that it's difficult to mimic the flavors achieved by grandmothers and mothers in kimchi and *namul*.

## Pairing & Balance in Hansik

When foreigners arriving in Korea first take a seat at a Korean table, a moment of confusion arrives when the numerous *banchan* (side dishes) arrive at the table. How, and in what order, does one eat the *banchan*? In the kitchen where the food is prepared, and at the table where the food is eaten, people are busy with the question of how to harmonize the many different dishes in different combinations. This question is the essence of *hansik*.

The ultimate charm of a *hansik* dining experience is that even though everyone is drawing from the same set of *banchan* on the communal table, each person has a unique eating experience composed of different flavors and textures. Korean cuisine is made complete in the mouth of the eater, who makes choices to create their personalized combination of flavors. A curious eater will find a Korean table setting to be like a canvas, where each *banchan* provides a different palette of texture, flavor, and temperature to create a unique experience in each bite.

When Koreans are enjoying *hansik*, the most important factor is balance and harmony. Each ingredient and dish should complement the others, without converging or all sharing a singular flavor profile. When dining, it is up to each person to find the balance of a meal by curating the pairings of various *banchan* and *bap* (rice) set on the table.

This book aims to share not just the recipes that show how to make Korean food, but also how to eat these foods like Koreans. Moreover, we hope to shed light on why Koreans cook and eat in these ways.

## Universality & Identity

Until recently, the complete story of Korean cuisine was not much known outside of Korea. When writing this book, as authors, we were most concerned about properly expressing the Korean food language, *hansik*, and its essence. We concluded that the two most important defining elements of *hansik* were found in these universal and foundational aspects of Korean cooking: vegetables and fermentation. From the everyday dishes that are enjoyed in homes throughout Korea, to the traditional regional recipes from Seoul to Jeju Island to a small city in North Korea, to even the popular contemporary recipes that some may consider "Korean-ish." Although Korean food culture has deep roots, with long-standing traditions and identity, the cuisine continues to evolve, maintaining a balance between tradition and innovation.

Our aim as authors has been to showcase the multifaceted nature of Korean cuisine and the many ways it is enjoyed. This book was written with home cooks in mind, with recipes that can be easily made in the home kitchen. We have also included the recipes and stories of master artisans who have spent their lives contemplating the aspects of cuisine that make up the identity of *hansik*—namely kimchi, *jang*, *hanwoo* (Korean beef), temple food, noble food, ceramics, and more.

We authors first met nearly two decades ago and became good friends through our shared love of cuisine and, in particular, of our cuisine, *hansik*. Throughout the years since, we have continued to study *hansik* together in our cooking and in our conversations. We never imagined that one day we would co-author a book together. Writing this book has been an opportunity for us to delve more sincerely and deeply into *hansik*. The process has been a priceless gift that has revealed to us the immeasurable value of *hansik* anew.

It is our hope that the readers of this book will discover the delicious and joyful world of *hansik*, as we did in the writing of it, and that the recipes and stories found in these pages will make you want to begin to cook Korean food in your kitchens.

# A History of Korean Cuisine
## 한식의 역사

The history of humankind is not defined in complete terms, but in evolving, contextual forms as time progresses and new cultures are created. Korean food culture continues to develop on the Korean peninsula, as it has for thousands of years, through the collective creative efforts of generations of Koreans who strive for a better life. As with most food cultures, Korea's cuisine was first defined by its geography and climate. From there, a variety of historic and social influences, ranging from politics, wars, religion, and the evolution of social and cultural life, shaped the way that Koreans eat and drink today.

Korean cuisine is defined by the staple food of rice, and the format of *bap* (rice dishes) and *banchan* (side dishes), along with the development of *jang* (fermented soybean sauces), fermentation, and plant-based cuisine, evolved over time to become the foundational factors of a Korean cuisine that continues to this day.

## Neolithic Period (8000–1500 BCE)

Agriculture first began on the Korean peninsula, starting with grains, such as millet and sorghum, and expanding to legumes, such as soybeans and red beans (adzuki beans). There was a parallel development of functional agricultural tools, and human dwellings migrated from the hills to form villages. Primitive grain-processing tools, such as grindstones, evolved into stone grinders, and pottery developed from the early Neolithic Jeulmun period to the prevalence in the Mumun pottery period of undecorated or plain cooking and storage vessels.

Grains were boiled in earthenware, kneaded to make rice cakes, cooked on stone plates, or buried in the coals of a fire to roast. Grains were also roasted to remove hard hulls and then ground to create cooked grain flour.

## Bronze Age (3300–1200 BCE)

Agriculture continued to develop, significantly the beginning of rice farming. Korea's natural landscape and climate conditions were ideal for rice, and settlements arose in Pyongyang, Yeoju, Gimpo, and Buyeo (all now cities), defining the framework of agricultural society and the formation of larger settlements. By the third century bce, the development of iron pushed forward agricultural technology, establishing the foundation of an agricultural society with rice farming as the main crop. Rice is a crop with a high yield, a great energy source with good taste and digestibility, and can be transformed into flour and other forms. Rice quickly became the staple food of Korean cuisine and culture and continues to be so today.

In primitive agricultural societies, villages were formed based on blood ties and totemism. As agriculture and trade developed, interactions between villages increased and naturally created power relations.

Federated kingdom societies, such as Buyeo, Goguryeo, Okjeo, and Samhan, were formed during the Iron Age. In this era of kingdoms, collective harvest traditions, ceremonies, and festivals continued to develop an agriculture-oriented society.

## Three Kingdoms Era (57 BCE–668 CE)

With the formation of kingdoms, the formation of a centralized government system developed in which the land was maintained as state-owned property, and agricultural policies were established and promoted through rice farming. During this period, new crops were introduced and cultivated widely, including *mu* (Korean radish) and lettuce. Significant development in shipbuilding technology and fisheries further established the foundations of Korean cuisine, and dehydrated and preserved foods, such as *jang* (fermented soybean sauces), *meju* (dried fermented soybeans), salt-preserved vegetables, and dried seafood, become a large part of the food culture.

In the later part of this era, cast-iron pots became widespread cooking utensils and rice was cooked daily. Along with cooked rice, *banchan* (side dishes) made from *jang*, preserved foods, and dried seafood became the foundations of meals, establishing the basic framework of *bap* and *banchan*. *Tteok* (rice cakes) and *sool* (alcohol) become established as ceremonial or festive foods.

The Three Kingdoms Era was the period when the basic structure of Korean food culture was established. Skills, such as brewing *sool*, steaming *tteok*, and preserving vegetables, crossed over to Japan in the process of a cultural transmission that included a writing system (Hanja), religion (Buddhism), and architectural techniques, forming the basis of the ancient food culture in that country.

## Goryeo Dynasty (918–1392)

The early Goryeo dynasty was a period marked by widespread adherence to Buddhism, which influenced the great development of rice and vegetable production as Buddhists refrain from meat consumption. This improved the land system and actively promoted farmland reclamation.

As Buddhism and temples became concentrated sources of funds, the alcohol and vegetable industry became popularized and salt production became a national monopoly. In the palace, there was a *yangonseo*, a place for brewing and storing alcohol, and large-scale government-sponsored brewing was carried out in temples. The Goryeo dynasty can be said to be the period of settlement of brewing technology and the development of traditional grain wine.

In the mid-Goryeo dynasty, after the establishment in 1271 of the Won (a Mongol imperial dynasty), the influence of the carnivorous Mongol diet restored meat to the diet. Still, the influence of Buddhist culture remained and shaped the practices of utilizing every part of the animal once it is butchered, from its hide to its feet. These developments during the Goryeo dynasty further built on the dietary structures formed in the Three Kingdoms Era.

A History of Korean Cuisine

## Joseon Dynasty (1392–1910)

In the early Joseon dynasty, research in medicine and agriculture were published as books and distributed by the government. Irrigation techniques, planting techniques, and facility support for rice farming expanded. This had a positive influence in life expectancy and domestic lives.

Korean familial structure solidified into a strict patriarchal, eldest-inheritance system, and multigenerational families composed of various age groups became common. To provide the daily meals, food management skills, including *jang* making, and preservation skills, such as salting and dehydrating, became necessary. The knowledge of festive foods and table setting etiquette became required as essential virtues.

In the late Joseon dynasty period, the fishery industry further developed and began to become commercialized. Trade centers, such as Yukuijeon in Seoul and Hyangsi in Hyangchon, were formed, and the distribution of processed seafood food expanded.

Joseon society was built on an agricultural economy, which required the mobilization of collective labor. A communal culture naturally took place as people lived and worked together in close proximity, and communal rituals and festivals that were built around harvests became important virtues and societal duties. These rituals included making a large amount of cooked white rice to share with one hundred families, and sharing *banchan* at ancestral rites and festivals with neighbors.

Defined home kitchens appear in drawings from the Goryeo dynasty, where proper meals were prepared on dining tables. It was during the Joseon dynasty when the table setting and manners became solidified, with the placements of individualized *bap* and *guk* (soup) as well as the setting of the *banchan* became defined, and our modern table manners developed.

## Modern Day (1910–Present)

The history of Korean cuisine of the most recent century, from 1900 to the present, can be divided into three distinct periods: the Korean enlightenment movement into the Japanese colonial rule (1890–1945), the post-liberation period in the 1960s (1945–1966), and the period of economic development (1967–present).

In the Joseon dynasty of the 1890s, 80 percent of the total population of Korea were farmers. While the Korean nation suffered widespread food shortages due to continuous years of war, it was also a time when Korea began to import the food products and cultures of other nations as it opened international trade in 1876 and began signing trade treaties. After 1910, processed food products were imported, and food manufacturing industries developed, spanning across mills and breweries.

After 1945, which marked the Korean liberation, and later the Korean War (1950–1953), there was a big shift in the food culture with the import of wheat, increased consumption of snacks and bread, and the development of the processed food industry.

After the 1970s, Korea experienced multiple cultural shifts, including rapid economic growth, the shift to nuclear families, and the advancement of industrial technology. The development of rice varieties expanded, and the Korean diet evolved from a grain-based diet to one that included more animal foods, such as meat, eggs, and milk. Various foreign cuisines began to be imported into the country, and restaurant and dining culture began to take root. As the traditional multigenerational living formats shifted to the nuclear family units, averaging at four members, the amount of *banchan* set at the table also shrank.

# 한식 Hansik

By Hae Kyung Chung, professor at Hoseo University

A nation's cuisine and food culture condense the nation's climate, geography, and characteristics into one essence. *Hansik*, Korean cuisine, is a cultural symbol that contains the essence of Korea's history and culture, as well as the emotions of Korea's identity as a nation.

*Hansik* is a food culture that contains a universe. Its dishes contain various colors and diverse ingredients, colorful garnishes, and many different seasonings and sauces. This is rooted in the theory of yin and yang and the five elements, which was a defining philosophy of the Eastern culture in understanding the cosmos. This philosophy lives on in the principle of *hansik*. The ideal harmony of heaven and earth is represented through Korean food. The principles of yin and yang, represented by animal products and plant products, are harmonized in balance when making a recipe. Following the four seasons and their products are of key importance, and the balancing of the five colors and five tastes are embodied in its dishes.

The philosophy of interchangeability between entities, that I can become you and you can become me, is represented in *hansik* through the harmonization of its ingredients. Instead of highlighting or emphasizing one main ingredient, a balance of ingredients and flavors is the ideal. This principle in taste comes alive in each dish, even those that may seem simple or disorderly. For example, neatly prepared kimchi, which may seem like simply prepared vegetables, contains the deep flavor of fermented animal products invisible to the eye, revealing a profound, complex flavor profile unimaginable at first glance.

## Harmony of Bap & Banchan

The basic composition of *hansik* is made of *bap* (rice) and *banchan* (side dishes). Most food that accompanies the rice is categorized as *banchan*. For each meal, cooked rice is served with an array of *banchan* made of soup, vegetables, meat, fish, and even rice cakes and *sikhye* (sweet rice punch) all at once. When the *bap* harmonizes with the *banchan*, it becomes a meal. This is a different system and philosophy from Western food culture, where the concept of a main dish prevails.

There is a modern development of table setting in *hansik* where the food is served in a coursed method as in Western or Chinese cuisine, but this is more often in restaurants or when entertaining guests. The traditional *hansik* format of setting all courses at once is called *bansang* in which there is the main *bap* and *banchan*. *Banchan* are prepared with a portion of meat but are mostly composed of vegetables. In a meal, the ratio of plant-based ingredients to animal ingredients is 7:3. The focus on plant-based dishes is the key reason why *hansik* is considered a healthy cuisine. The *banchan* made with plant-based ingredients have been called *namul* since ancient times.

## Characteristics of Korean Banchan Culture

These are the key points that define *banchan* culture:

1. While *bap* and *guk* (soup) are served in individual portions, the *banchan* are served family-style, as an array of dishes in the middle of the table.

2. Typically, fresh, in-season ingredients are used to create the main *banchan*, and these *banchan* determine the remainder of the *banchan* to serve along with.

3. About two-thirds of Korea's *banchan* are made with plant-based ingredients, with the majority of them being vegetables. To make these *banchan*, the vegetables are cooked and seasoned with *jang* (fermented soybean sauces) and salt.

4. *Banchan* can be largely categorized into freshly made *banchan*, prepared just before eating, and preserved *banchan*, which are stored and easily eaten year-around. Kimchi is the most representative of the latter category and is rarely absent in a *banchan* spread. *Jeotgal* (preserved seafood), *jangajji* (pickles), *bugak* (battered vegetables) are other examples of *banchan* that apply preservation techniques, such as dehydration, fermentation, and salt preservation.

5. As the saying "the last step of *hansik* cooking is in the mouth" goes, the *banchan* culture allows the diner to determine the final combination of *banchan* to enjoy as the finished dish. The joy of creating customized bites, and the endless combinations that a spread of well-prepared *banchan* can create, is the key characteristic of *banchan* culture and the essence of Korean cuisine.

6. Although *guk*, *jjigae* (stews), and *jeongol* (hotpots) all officially fall under the category of *banchan*, they are often categorized separately from *banchan* when discussing Korean cuisine.

## Vegetables: The Main Star of Banchan

Korea's food culture has traditionally been centered around vegetables, and it has developed a deep knowledge and many techniques for enjoying vegetables.

Korea is located above 35 degrees north latitude, and thus has four distinct seasons. More than two-thirds, about 70 percent, of the nation is composed of mountainous terrain. This leads to an abundance of mountain vegetables and mushrooms in addition to field vegetables. Because it is a peninsula nation, there is also an abundance of sea vegetables along with seafood. Korean *banchan* developed around these readily available ingredients, developing kimchi, *namul* (vegetable dishes), and *ssam* (wraps). To season these ingredients, fermented foods, such as *ganjang* (Korean soy sauce), *doenjang* (fermented soybean paste), and *gochujang* (red chili paste), were developed. The long-standing food traditions of dehydration, fermentation, and salt preservation are all contained in *banchan*. It is difficult to find any other food culture that enjoys such a wide variety of vegetables prepared in so many different ways. It is for this reason that the Korean people can be called the "Namul People," with Koreans recording among the highest consumption of vegetables per capita.

## Namul People: Diverse Methods of Preparing Vegetables

As "Namul People," Koreans boast a wide range of vegetable recipes. From rice to dessert, there is not a type of dish that cannot be made with vegetables. Vegetable rice and *juk* (porridge) fed our ancestors when there were periods of famine. In modern times, when obesity-related health concerns abound, the same recipes are consumed as health foods.

Most edible vegetables are ingredients for soups and *banchan*, and when the nutrients of vegetables are married with the fermented *ganjang* and *doenjang* the dish can be considered medicinal, because of the known health benefits of fermented foods. Each recipe for *saengchae* (raw vegetable dishes) and *sukchae* (cooked vegetable dishes) calls for different seasonings in order to highlight the inherent flavors and color of each vegetable, ranging from salt to a specific *jang* or a combination of seasonings.

Because of the importance of vegetables in Korea's diet, different methods were developed to preserve the vegetables so they could be enjoyed during the cold winter. In-season fresh vegetables were enjoyed fresh or cooked, and the remaining harvest was preserved: either sun-dried or preserved in salt, vinegar, *jang*, or lees from alcohol. Sea vegetables, such as *gim* or *dasima*, were dried as they were or with a layer of glutinous rice paste, so they could be eaten as deep-fried *bugak* (battered vegetables). All kinds of vegetables were made into *jangajji* (Korean pickles) in a *jang* and vinegar. Vegetable scraps were saved and recycled into new prized ingredients to last the winter. Green radish tops, for example, were dried to make *siraegi* and the tough outer layers of napa cabbage (Chinese leaf) were boiled to make *ugeoji*; both were used to make various *namul* and *guk* dishes, providing vitamins and minerals over the winter months. In 2013, Korea's "kimjang culture" (the tradition of communal kimchi making) was registered as a UNESCO Intangible Cultural Heritage of Humanity.

## Fermented Food

Without fermentation, Korean food cannot exist.

Preservation originally stemmed from a need to preserve food for lean times, such as winter or natural disasters, including drought and severe weather damage. The main preservative is salt. Some of the classic fermented foods include *jang* (made by adding salt to soybeans), salted vegetables like kimchi, and salted fish. Eventually, these same preservation methods were turned to making other products. For example, rice, barley, and other grains are fermented with yeast and water to make products such as *makgeolli* (Korean rice wine) and vinegar.

## Hansik: Considering the Future of the Earth

The world currently faces climate change, energy inefficiencies, urbanization, and hunger. Many of the problems are heavily influenced by the excessive production and consumption of meat.

Many chronic illnesses are caused by unhealthy diet. Shifting into a conscious plant-based diet is not only beneficial to one's individual health but the health of the world. Even in considering the use of fossil fuels or energy usage, the same amount can produce a much larger quantity of plants than animals. A shift toward plant consumption is a shift toward a conservation of a healthier environment.

*Hansik* is a food culture based on vegetables above all else. Within *hansik*, a delicious vegetarian or plant-based diet is possible through its *namul* culture. The *namul* culture that the Korean people have passed down for generations is a recipe for an alternative future of the earth through cuisine. This book showcases the *namul* culture of Korea, and its world of possibilities.

# Korea's Regional Foods
## 지역음식

Korea is a peninsula located in the northeastern part of Asia, bordered by China to the west and Russia to the north. Its topography is composed of approximately 70 percent mountainous terrains, with relatively few arable plains. The northern and eastern regions of Korea are marked by high-elevation mountain terrain; the southwest has a lower elevation, in which farmable lowlands and river valleys are found. Because of this, the southwest regions became the center of rice farming, and the central and eastern regions were mainly developed for field crops and the cultivation of various wild vegetables, because of its abundance of forests.

One of the results of the Korean peninsula's location is its seasonal climate, which produces very distinct climate patterns for each season. These seasons manifest in a unique way, depending on the region, which in turn has a distinct impact on the development of regional foods. For example, in regions where temperatures run high, food tends to spoil easily, so foods will be more heavily salted or strongly seasoned. In the mountainous north, the temperature is low, so the seasoning of food is mild. In the south, where it gets hot, the seasoning is stronger, and being surrounded by the sea, salted fish is used more.

Because the region is surrounded on three sides by the sea, Korea's fishing industry is well developed. Each coast provides distinct conditions, yet all provide an abundance of a variety of seafood. The east coast has a smooth coastline, with deep waters with cold water temperatures. The west coast has shallower waters and wide mud flats. The southern coast has a lacy coastline dotted with many islands.

Before the development of the modern infrastructure, transportation and communication was difficult between the regions, because of Korea's mountainous terrain. As a result, each region of Korea has developed its own unique cuisine based on local food supply. Today, with the ease of transportation and the development of modern technology, there is a convergence of food cultures and dishes, with regional specialties becoming available nationwide. Yet, the unique food cultures and traditional dishes of each region remain distinct and popular today.

Regional foods can be classified by the characteristics of its northern, central, and southern regions. For example, kimchi production will vary by season and region based on available crops. In Jeolla-do and Gyeonsang-do, where no Korean version of napa cabbage (Chinese leaf) was grown, a type of kimchi called *bibim kimchi* was developed made of bean leaves, perilla leaves, *minari* (a celery-like vegetable), mustard greens, and scallion (spring onion).

## Seoul

Although there are not many foods native just to Seoul, as the capital of Korea for more than five hundred years since the early Joseon dynasty, it is where various ingredients, dishes, and cultures from all over the country came together.

The food culture of the royal court developed and continues in Seoul, and the historic concentration of *yangban*, the aristocratic noble class, in the capital had a great impact on the food culture. The prevailing influence of Confucianism established a food culture with an emphasis on formality and decorum. Yet, the frugal nature of Seoul native culture led to a preference for a large number of smaller dishes with a focus on delicate, artful plating over larger banquet-style plating. The culture of fine dining extended beyond the noble class; it is documented that those with economic wealth through trade enjoyed gourmet dining as well.

The food cuisine of Seoul is characterized by milder flavors with a restrained use of spiciness. Ingredients are often finely julienned or diced, and food is often served in neat white porcelain vessels in small amounts, just enough for the meal. Meat, seafood, and vegetables are all widely used with various seasonings in Seoul cuisine. Of *jeotgal* (preserved seafood), salted shrimp is the most common, and long-simmered soups, such as *seolleongtang* (ox bone soup) and *gomtang* (beef bone soup), are popular. Seoul's famous *banchan* are those that are fanciful and often painstaking to make. Dried fish is enjoyed grilled or pan-fried, and *mit-banchan*, such as jerky and *jangajji* (pickles), are a mainstay in traditional Seoul meals.

## Gyeonggi-do

Gyeonggi-do boasts a well-developed agricultural culture centered around the rice paddy field and field farming, making the region abundant in its rice, vegetable, and soup culture. Seafood, such as fish and clams, are caught on the west coast in abundance, and freshwater fish and crabs are found in the Imjin River. Wild vegetables and mushrooms abound in the mountains. Gyeonggi-do's rice has long been famous for its high quality, with famous varieties of rice, such as *rhee-chun* and *yeoju* rice, still popular today.

The abundance of resources in Gyeonggi-do led to diverse ingredients used in its cuisine and has also led to the development of more complex and labor-intensive dishes, including snacks. Instead of plain white rice, mixed-grain and five-grain rice are popular in this region, and the noodle and *guk* (soup) dishes feature heavier, savory broths rather than light *jang*-based broths. Fresh and dehydrated vegetables are mainstay *banchan*, and vegetables are often made into *bugak* (battered vegetables), soybeans into tofu, and mung beans into *muk* (jelly).

Its most famous meat *banchan* include *suyuk* (boiled meat), *pyunyuk* (pressed meat), and *sundae* (Korean blood sausage). Famous meat-based dishes such as *jong galbijjim* (braised pork ribs), *Soowon gabi* (Soowon-style braised beef ribs), chicken *jeot guk* (chicken and salted shrimp soup), and *jokpyeon* (beef trotter terrine) originate here. With fresh seafood from the western coast, dishes such as simmered webfoot octopus, clam fritters, and fresh oysters are commonly enjoyed. Its freshwater fish makes for a long history of white fish *guk* (soups) and *bungeo jjim*. The region is also famous for its *tteok* (rice cakes): The common *sirutteok* (steamed rice cakes with red beans), *injeolmi* (steamed rice cakes coated in roasted soybean flour), and *jeolpyeon* (steamed rice cake molded into shapes) are specialties here while each micro-region has their specialty regional *tteok*. For example, Yeoju is famous for its "mountain *tteok*," Ganghwa Island for its "military *tteok*," and Gapyeong for buckwheat *tteok*.

## Chungcheong-do

Chungcheong-do is an agricultural region known for its rice, barley, *mu* (Korean radish), and cabbage production. While its western coast produces an abundance of seafood, because inland transportation was historically difficult, much of its seafood cuisine is based on preserved or dried fish. From its mountains, mushrooms and mountain vegetables are key ingredients throughout the region. Like the local culture, the regional cuisine is characterized by simplicity. Dishes are often unadorned, with focus on natural flavors using minimal seasoning.

White rice, barley rice, and glutinous rice are commonly eaten and *doenjang*-based *guk* are common, such as mung bean *guk* and flounder chard *guk*. Popular *banchan* include *jang-tteok* (pancake made with *gochujang* and sometimes *doenjang*), *oiji* (salt-pickled cucumbers), and stir-fried *muk* (starch jelly), and its famous drinks include grain-based drinks, such as the glutinous rice *misu*, and fruit drinks, such as the peach *hwachae*. Famous regional delicacies include *eoriguljeot* (spicy salted oysters) and *mu cheonggukjang* (a stew made from extra-strong fermented soybeans). In Chungcheongbuk-do, special dishes are made with freshwater snails, blowfish, catfish, and loach. Chungcheong province has delicacies made with *ungeo* (a type of anchovy) and *hwangbok* (a type of blowfish).

## Gangwon-do

Gangwon-do is divided by mountain ranges into Yeongseo and Yeong-dong, and each region produces distinct crops. Its coastal regions also yield a completely different range of produce. In its highlands, field farming produces corn, buckwheat, and potatoes. Acorns and the roots of the arrowroot plant are also foraged. In the East Sea, a wealth of seafood, such as pollock, squid, and seaweed, are caught or harvested, and many dishes are based on these.

Main dishes such as corn rice, potato rice, buckwheat noodles, and potato *sujebi* (hand-torn noodles) are popular. *Namul banchan* or *saengchae* (raw vegetable dishes) made from mountain vegetables and mushrooms are a significant part of its cuisine. *Banchan* made from grilled squid, braised or roasted pollock, and dried and braised blowfish are popular. Fish innards and roe are preserved and used to prepare dishes, such as *myeongranjeot* (salted pollock roe) and *changranjeot* (salted pollock innards). Due to its large production of potatoes, they are often eaten simply steamed or made into starch bases to make *sujebi*, *songpyeon* (half-moon-shaped rice cakes), and *buchim* (pan-fried dishes). Delicacies include *juk* (porridge) made with cornstarch, *chodang-ri* tofu made with seawater, and *makguksu* (noodles) made from buckwheat dough.

Korea's Regional Foods

## Jeolla-do

Jeolla-do produces an abundance of produce from land, sea, and mountains, making for a well-developed, rich food culture boasting a wide range of ingredients. In particular, because of the fertile land and its long history of wealthy populations, the Gwangju region is famous for a cuisine of cultural importance, with many family recipes that have been passed down through generations.

Jeolla-do's food is characterized by its stimulating, strong seasoning with a healthy use of salted fish, *gochugaru* (red chili flakes), and sauces. The region's cuisine is marked by a strong development of fermented foods: There are dozens of distinctly different kimchis and *jeotgal* (preserved seafood), with a diversity of *jang* (fermented soybean sauces) and *jangajji* (pickles) used commonly. Beyond the common *mu* (Korean radish) and napa cabbage (Chinese leaf), mustard greens, *daepa* (Korean scallion), and radish greens are often made into kimchi, and its heavy use of different types of *jeotgal* and *gochugaru* creates a complex, strong, sweet-and-savory flavor profile. *Jangajji* are made from *mu*, muskmelon, persimmon, chili leaves, bellflower root, and more—all based on regional produce. The Sunchang area has been known for its *gochujang* (red chili paste) since ancient times.

While white rice and barley rice are common, *juk* (porridge) culture is also well developed here, including sesame, octopus, and clam *juk*. Seafood-based *banchan* including loach *tang* (long-simmered soup), grilled skewered octopus, and raw dishes made with skate, jeoneo (a type of fish), and cockle, with skate dishes being a delicacy often reserved for prized guests. Vegetable-based *banchan* such as shredded bamboo shoot, mustard *japchae* (glass noodles), and *jang tteok* (rice cakes) are famous dishes.

Other popular dishes include the original Jeonju *bibimbap* (mixed rice) served in traditional brass bowls. Bean sprout *gukbap* (rice soup) made with salted shrimp and rice is one of the nation's favorite morning hangover soups. *Hongtak samhap* is a dish of fermented skate eaten with pork slices and red kimchi. In addition, Gwangyang gulbi (a type of fish), Boseong river loach, Haenam octopus, Gokseong *ayu hwe* (raw sweetfish), and Gwangyang charcoal-grilled pork *bulgogi* are famous in each region.

## Gyeongsang-do

Gyeongsang-do is famed for its quality and abundance of seafood due to the fertile fishing grounds in both the South Sea and the East Sea. The Nakdong River, which curves through Gyeongsang-do, further provides lush farmland that produces abundant agricultural products.

The regional foods of Gyeongsang-do are marked by spicy, strong seasoning with a simple, rustic preparation. The common addition of wild pepper or millet leaves in signature dishes impart a unique regional flavor as well.

In addition to white rice, *mu* (Korean radish), rice, soybean noodles, clam noodles, and chicken *kalguksu* ("knife-cut" noodle soup) are popular main meals. Its popular soups include *jaecheop guk* (clear freshwater clam soup), seaweed mussel soup, cod soup, and more. Famous seafood dishes include seafood and scallion (spring onion) *jeon* (fritters), anchovy *hwe* (raw fish), and fish *sikhae* (salted fermented fish and grain). Vegetable dishes include the simply prepared steamed zucchini (courgette) *seon*, steamed *minari*, and *baechu jeon* (napa cabbage/Chinese leaf fritters). Popular regional *jangajji* include variations of *mu mallengi* (dried strips of Korean radish) including *mu mallengi* kimchi, and those made with bean leaves and angelica. Its kimchi is marked by higher levels of spiciness and saltiness, and regional produce, such as bean leaves, chives, and perilla, are used.

Compared to other regions, *doenjang* (fermented soybean paste) is eaten more commonly, and various shortcut versions of *doenjang* are enjoyed, including *jipjang*, *makjang*, and *dambukjang*—all made with slightly different methods, but usually fermented for only a week to 10 days. The Masan region is famous for steamed sea squirt and blackmouth angler, and the Jinju *bibimbap* is distinct in the usage of mung bean sprouts and diced clams, served with cow blood soup. Andong is a region famed for its great pride and preservation of traditional culture. Andong *sikhye* is a rice drink made by adding chili pepper powder and diced radish in fermentation, giving it a unique sweet and spicy taste. Dongnae *pajeon* is a signature regional *jeon* (fritter) made with *daepa* (Korean scallion) and *minari*, along with shellfish, such as clams and oysters, batter fried.

## Jeju-do

In the past, Jeju island was known as a barren and rugged island but now it is a global destination famed for its natural beauty. Because it's a volcanic island, there is little to no rice production; soybeans, buckwheat, barley, and sweet potatoes are its main specialties. Citrus, abalone, and the horsehead tilefish are famous regional ingredients. Being an island, seafood and sea vegetables are used in abundance in its cuisine and *doenjang* (fermented soybean paste) is its main seasoning ingredient. *Juk* (porridge) and other broth-based dishes are well developed, and its *banchan* are also marked by dishes made with broth.

Mixed-grain rice and buckwheat-based dishes are the main carbohydrates in Jeju-do. Its representative *juk* include abalone, shiitake mushrooms, and seaweed. *Guk* (soups), such as *mom-guk* made from pork and seaweed, fiddlehead *guk*, beltfish and zucchini (courgette) *guk*, and *yukgaejang* (spicy pork soup) are popular. Its fresh seafood is mostly consumed raw; raw abalone and cod made with *doenjang* are delicacies. Horsehead tilefish and hairtail are often grilled or long simmered.

Jeju-do's delicacies include Jeju black pork, ginger shoot *muchim* (a seasoned dish), and shiitake fritters. *Bingtteok*, thin cakes made by kneading buckwheat flour with radish greens, is a food that is common at ancestral rites or banquets.

# 한식 밥상과 반상
# Korean Bapsang & Bansang

A formal Korean meal, known as *bansang*, is composed of *bap* (rice) and *banchan* (side dishes). *Bapsang*, which translates to "meal table," is the informal version of *bansang* and refers to the traditional daily meal spread.

In Korean tradition, each diner has an individual table setup with the main rice dish along with a set of *banchan* to supplement the rice. In a proper *bansang*, it is important to not overlap ingredients or seasoning in *banchan*, because each is intended to provide a different combination with the rice while working harmoniously together. The *banchan* are selected centered around a main *banchan*. Kimchi is a *banchan* that is always present, and other *banchan* selected can include *saengchae* (raw vegetables), *sukchae* (cooked vegetables), *gui* (grilled dishes), *jorim* (simmered dishes), *jeon* (fritters), *hwe* (raw seafood/meat), *jeotgal* (preserved seafood), and dehydrated foods. In the past, there were more formalities and rules to follow in what should be served together and how it should be eaten. Today, there is more creative freedom.

Korean meals are composed of *bap* and *banchan*, in which *banchan* includes *guk* (soup) and *jjigae* (stew). The table is set with the *bap* dish and *guk* dish in front of the diner, with the *bap* on the left, the *guk* on the right, and a spoon and a pair of chopsticks to the right of the *guk*.

At a communal table, each diner is set with their own *bap* and *guk* and the other *banchan* are set in the middle of the table, to be shared. Kimchi is a *banchan* that's rarely missing at a table setting. In a common home meal, three or four *banchan*, including kimchi, are prepared. Of the four, one will consist of animal protein, such as beef, pork, or fish, and the rest will usually be vegetable-based.

There are various ways to enjoy *bap* and *banchan* together. The basic way to eat *bap* and *banchan* is to top each spoonful of rice with a different *banchan* to pair. After eating a richer *banchan*, such as meat, an acidic *banchan*, such as kimchi or *jangajji* (pickles), is often eaten to cut the heaviness. In a *hansik bapsang* setting, even as one shares the same table spread, there's a distinct style of pairing or preferences that is revealed among the diners.

For example, with a simply grilled fish, eating the fish by itself versus eating it atop a spoonful of freshly made white rice, followed by a sip of cold, refreshing *yeolmu* (young summer radish) kimchi broth is a completely different experience. Or take the common *banchan gyeranjjim* (Korean steamed eggs): It can be eaten on its own, but mashed on top of a bowl of rice creates a completely different flavor and texture. Eating *bap* and *guk* separately is distinct from eating the rice folded directly into the *guk* to make *gukbap*; adding some fresh napa cabbage (Chinese leaf) kimchi or the deeply flavored mustard green kimchi to a spoonful of this *gukbap* creates a new flavor. With a large bowl, one can most often create an impromptu *bibimbap* by combining rice and the desired *banchan* from the table spread.

To enjoy a Korean meal, to enjoy *bap* and *banchan* in the many ways possible, it's important to know the composition of the Korean table. Here, we introduce the basics of *bansang* and examples of two popular meals in Korean cuisine.

## The Basics of Bansang

The most important facet of a Korean table is the pairing with vegetables. Even in the carnivorous Korean food culture, the defining characteristic is that it always incorporates vegetables.

Most often when consuming meat, it's prepared on a tabletop grill in the middle of a communal table, cooked à la minute and shared. In a typical Korean meat-based meal, more than 50 percent of the array of dishes will consist of vegetables. Grilled meat is often accompanied by grilled vegetables. Typical *banchan* that are served with meat include kimchi, *jangajji* (pickles), *saengchae muchim* (seasoned raw vegetables), *ssam* (wrap) vegetables, and vegetable *doenjang* (fermented bean paste) stew. When eating the meat itself, it's enjoyed paired with bites of rice and these vegetable *banchan*.

After the meats have been grilled, they are dipped into prepared condiments made of salt, pepper, and sesame oil, as well as dipping sauces such as *gochujang* (red chili paste) and *ssamjang* (soybean paste). These accompaniments allow for a diverse eating experience full of different flavors, even with one cut of meat.

The pairing of meats and different types of *banchan* is a fun experience, especially when put together in a *ssam*. The main vegetable wraps are large leaves of lettuce. A personalized wrap with a combination of rice, meat, *ssamjang*, kimchi, and *jangajji* makes for a bite that's full of different textures—soft, crunchy, juicy—and temperatures—cold and hot—as well as the flavors that each ingredient adds. The satisfaction of all the combined ingredients is the ultimate charm of the Korean *ssam* culture.

*Bap* is always served along with a meat spread and is an important part of the Korean meat culture. In addition to being eaten directly with the meat, any leftover rice is often fried on the meat grill at the end of the meal. Any remaining grilled meats or kimchi are cut into bite-size pieces and incorporated into the final fried rice with sesame oil and crushed *gim* (seaweed). Another option is to fold the leftover rice into the *doenjang jjigae* (stew) to finish. While it's more difficult to prepare at home, at restaurants it's very typical to finish a meat-based meal with refreshing noodle dishes such as *naengmyun* (a North Korean noodle dish) and *bibimguksu*.

## How to Eat Like a Korean: Samgyupsal (Grilled Pork Belly)

**Step 1: Eat the first bite simply seasoned with a light dip in the salt.** Follow with bites of pork belly dipped in *ssamjang* (soybean paste), *gochujang* (red chili paste); pair bites with preserved anchovies, seasoned oysters, and other *jeotgal* (preserved seafood) as available. Trying the different seasoning pairings and dips allows a multicourse like experience using just one grilled meat.

**Step 2: Combine the meat with the vegetable side dishes,** including *namul* (vegetable dishes), *muchim* (seasoned dishes), and *jangajji* (pickles). Pairing the bites of meat and vegetables together creates new "dishes" of pork belly.

**Step 3: Make ssam (wraps).** Lettuce, perilla, squash leaf, napa cabbage (Chinese leaf), various seasonal vegetables, or seaweed, such as *dasima*, can all be used as the wrap. Top with grilled pork, a dollop of *ssamjang*, kimchi, and *jangajji* in preferred combinations for a personalized experience. Like fireworks exploding in your mouth, you can feel the contrasts of cold and warm temperatures, of crunchy and soft textures, the richness of the pork and the freshness of vegetables, cut with acidity or supplemented savoriness. A *ssam* provides a completely different charm from the pure taste of grilled meats seasoned with sauces or eaten paired with *banchan*.

**Step 4: Grill the fresh vegetables directly on the meat grill in the pork fat.** Spring herbs and vegetables such as *naengi* (shepherd's purse) and *minari* (a vegetable similar to celery and watercress); hearty summer vegetables, such as eggplants (aubergines), potatoes, and squash; fall harvest of *deodeok* (ginseng-like plant) and mushrooms; and winter vegetables, such as scallions (spring onions) and roots, are all great.

**Step 5: Pair with kimchi.** Well-fermented kimchi and its acidic, bright flavors pair great with the rich, savory meat.

**Step 6: Finish the meal with rice, the Korean way.** The end of a pork belly meal is always with rice, stir-fried on the grill using the rendered pork fat. Add any leftover *banchan*, kimchi, and vegetables as desired to create the ultimate fried rice. Top with a fried egg and eat along with *doenjang jjigae* for a real Korean dining experience.

## How to Eat Like a Korean: Fish Hwe Bapsang

When eating fish *hwe* (raw), the dipping condiments accompanied are made of *ganjang* (soy sauce), *gochujang* (red chili paste), and *ssamjang* (soybean paste). The fish is dipped directly in the sauce to begin, to enjoy the flavors and textures of the fish.

Even when eating a raw fish dish, vegetables are always present. *Ssam* (wraps) always accompany fish *hwe*; *ssam* vegetables, such as lettuce, perilla and *dasima*, are rarely missing, and large-leaved kimchi, such as *mugeunji* and white kimchi, are also commonly used to make *ssam*.

In the springtime, when there is an abundance of herbs, it is unique to Korean food culture to include these in the spread to add to the joy of eating fish *hwe*.

Any parts of the fish that are leftover after making the *hwe* appear at the table as well. The head, tail, and bones of the fish are used to create fish-based *jjigae* (stew). Oftentimes, while eating the *hwe*, a pot of *jjigae* will be simmering on the table, finished with noodles at the end of the meal or eaten with rice. Any remaining *hwe* is often combined with rice and the remaining *ssam* vegetables, cut to bite-size pieces, and *cho-gochujang* (vinegared *gochujang*) and made into a *hwe bibimbap*. When fish *hwe* is eaten along with alcohol, it's mostly eaten without rice, finishing with the broth and rice or noodles.

# The Korean Pantry
# 기본식재료

## Grains

### White Rice
### Hinssal 흰쌀
The main staple food in Korea's diet is white rice. The word *bap* (rice) refers to white rice. In Korean, there are two types of white rice used: *mepssal*, short-grain nonglutinous rice, and *chapssal*, glutinous rice. *Mepssal* (see below) is the rice typically eaten at meals. White rice is cooked by boiling with water until the grains have fully absorbed the water and is cooked throughout.

### Short-Grain Rice (Nonglutinous)
### Mepssal 멥쌀
*Mepssal*, nonglutinous short-grain white rice, is the main type of rice grown and consumed in Korea. The grains have a round shape, almost as wide as they are long, and are translucent with a glossy finish. Because of their high starch content, the cooked grains cling together.

### Glutinous Rice
### Chapssal 찹쌀
*Chapssal* is a short-grain rice rich in a type of starch called amylopectin. This high starch content gives the grains an opaque, milky white color and when cooked produces a very sticky consistency. *Chapssal* is used to make rice cakes or sticky rice.

### Brown Rice
### Hyunmi 현미
Rice is classified by how much of the outer layers of the grain are milled off. The most common classifications are white rice, which is 100 percent milled rice, 70 percent milled rice, 50 percent milled rice, and *hyunmi*, brown rice. The higher the percentage of milling, the whiter the rice, resulting in a softer, more easily digestible cooked rice. The bran and germ of the rice grains do contain important nutrients, so *hyunmi*, brown rice, which only has the very outer husk of the grain removed, is much more nutritious than the other milled rices, but it is also not as easily digested.

### Barley
### Bori 보리
Barley, along with rice, wheat, and corn, is one of the most important grain crops around the globe. In Korea, it was historically used as the substitute grain for when rice supplies ran out, because barley is sown in the winter and harvested in the summer, before the harvest of rice in fall. In addition to its role as a food grain in Korean cuisine, malted barley (dried sprouted grain) is used to make *jocheong* (rice syrup) and *gochujang* (red chili paste).

### Millet
### Jo 조
*Jo*, also called *jopssal*, is millet. It is one of the oldest grains consumed on the Korean peninsula and was the staple grain crop prior to the development of irrigation technology that allowed the large-scale cultivation of rice. During times of poor harvest or economy, millet acted as the famine crop. In the modern age, Korea's consumption of millet has dramatically decreased and is most often used as an secondary ingredient in mixed-grain rice.

### Beans
### Kong 콩
The most important bean in Korean cuisine is the soybean. Other beans that are consumed include red beans, mung beans, black beans, and kidney beans.

### Red Beans
### Pat 팥
Red beans—known in English-speaking countries by their Japanese name, adzuki—are rich in fiber and starch and are lower in protein than many other beans. In Korean cuisine, red beans are mainly used to make porridge or are boiled with sugar to make red bean paste, which is a main ingredient in desserts.

### Soybeans
### Kong 콩
The protein-rich soybean plays a very important role in Korean cuisine; it is used to make *jang* (fermented soybean sauces), oil, tofu, soy milk, and more. The category of *jang* is discussed in depth in the Jang section (pages 44–53) of the Fermentation chapter. Soybeans are also used to make sprouts (Soybean Sprouts, page 35).

### Mung Beans
### Nokdu 녹두
The mung bean is similar in shape to the red bean (adzuki bean) but has green skin. Because of the bean's high starch content, it is often turned into a flour that is used to make glass noodles. The whole beans are cooked into *juk* (porridge) and enjoyed as *bindaetteok* (savory mung bean pancakes). The beans are also used to make sprouts (see Mung Bean Sprouts, page 35).

## Vegetables

### Napa Cabbage
### Baechu 배추
*Baechu*, which in English-speaking countries is called napa cabbage, Chinese cabbage, or Chinese leaf, is most famous as the main ingredient in common kimchi. The modern form of Korean cabbage was developed around 1900 and has a unique crispy texture with a mild savory/sweetness. In addition to kimchi, napa cabbage is widely used in all areas of Korean cuisine, such as in *ssam* (wraps), in broth-based dishes, and *jeon* (fritters).

### Lettuce
### Sangchu 상추
Lettuce is the most popular vegetable used to make *ssam* (wraps). Compared with other common *ssam* vegetables, it has a mild flavor and soft texture. It is also often enjoyed lightly dressed in *geotjeori* (fresh kimchi) seasoning or made into salads.

### Spinach
### Sigeumchi 시금치
In modern Korea, although spinach is available year-round in markets, the local spinach season is from the end of November to the end of March. The spinach native to southern coastal regions of Korea, namely Pohang, Namhae, and Sinan, are considered to be the best quality. Quality Korean spinach is marked by large, wide leaves with robust stems that are a reddish-purple color at the root ends.

### Perilla Leaf
### Kkaennip 깻잎
The leaf of the perilla plant is considered the national herb of Korea. Perilla leaves have a minty, grass-like aroma with a slightly rough texture and can be challenging to unaccustomed palates. Perilla leaves pair very well with pork or fatty dishes. The highest quality perilla leaves should be green on the top with a dark purple underside, with a subtle cotton-like fuzzy texture.

### Korean Chrysanthemum
### Ssukgat 쑥갓
The chrysanthemum plant is most often used as an ornamental plant in the West, but in the East it is cultivated as an edible plant. Korean chrysanthemum is used as a leafy vegetable in *namul* (vegetable dishes), as a vegetable for *ssam* (wraps), or added as an herb garnish to many soups or stews to add fragrance to the dish.

### Minari 미나리
*Minari* is a vegetable with a refreshing fragrance similar to celery and watercress. It is eaten raw or blanched as a *namul* (vegetable dish), added to fish-based broth dishes to reduce fishy flavors, or boiled and wrapped around ingredients.

### Daepa 대파
*Daepa*, which translates to "large green onion," is the main native variety of green onion used in Korea. It looks like a large scallion (spring onion) or small leek, although it is a separate variety. When Koreans just say *pa*, they typically mean *daepa*, which is the mature form of the plant. For the thinner and younger form see Silpa (below). *Daepa* is used widely in all manner of Korean dishes, including soups, stir-fries, grilled dishes, and more. The moderate pungency of *daepa* is softened by being cooked, but it loses its flavor if cooked too long, so it's often added at the end of the cooking process. *Daepa* is also commonly used as a broth ingredient or long-cooked until softened.

### Silpa 실파
*Silpa*, which translates to "green onion thread," is the tender young green onion plant, which if not harvested would mature into the *daepa* (see above). It is milder and softer than *daepa*, and as such is often used as a raw ingredient and in seasonings or sauces.

The Korean Pantry

### Jjokpa 쪽파
*Jjokpa* is a hybrid green onion made by crossing green onions with shallots. It is smaller than *daepa* (see above) and has a bulbous, round root. *Jjokpa* has a mild flavor and a good crunchy texture, making it a popular choice for *pajeon* (onion fritter) or as a kimchi ingredient.

### Garlic Chives
### Buchu 부추
*Buchu* historically was used in specific regional cuisines but today is used across all Korean cuisine. Some of its most popular uses are as a *muchim* (seasoned dishes), as garnish to rice soup, as a bed on which meats are steamed, in *jeon* (fritters), in *japchae* (stir-fried vegetables and glass noodles), and in kimchi—either as a supplemental ingredient such as in *oi sobagi* (stuffed cucumber kimchi) or as a main ingredient. Because chives do not release much moisture, they're a popular choice for adding onion flavor to the filling for *mandu* (dumplings).

### Garlic
### Maneul 마늘
Garlic is widely used across seasonings and dishes in Korean cuisine. It is one of the most used ingredients in Korean cuisine, with an estimated 15 pounds (7 kg) of garlic consumed annually per person—this is about seven times the amount consumed in North America. While Koreans do eat raw garlic in *ssam* (wraps), more often, because of its pungency, it is used as a background ingredient in seasonings or in broths. It is often used in fermented products, including kimchi.

### Ginger
### Saenggang 생강
Ginger is used to add refreshing spiciness to dishes in Korean cuisine and is also used as a medicinal ingredient. Because ginger's flavor is so strong, it is typically used in small amounts, either minced or juiced, and is often used in meat dishes to balance strong or gamey flavors. Dried ginger is also enjoyed in teas.

### Korean Zucchini
### Aehobak 애호박
*Aehobak* is a Korean variety of green zucchini (courgette). It is light green in color with a fuzzy stem and has a mild sweet flavor when cooked. *Aehobak* is a popular ingredient in stews and soups, and is enjoyed as a vegetable dish as well.

### Old Pumpkin
### Neulgeun Hobak 늙은호박
The "old pumpkin" is squat with a tough orange-yellow skin, and its flesh is nutty and sweet. In Korea, the pumpkin is most often used to make the sweet *hobak-juk* (pumpkin porridge) and is popular in its processed juice form as well. Its natural sweetness makes it a popular ingredient to make syrup, or as a flavoring in desserts, such as *sikhye* (sweet rice punch).

### Chili Pepper
### Gochu 고추
*Gochu*, or chili pepper, is one of the most iconic of aromatic vegetables in Korean cuisine. Korean chili peppers are long and turn from green to red as they ripen. Cheongyang chili is the most common varietal. Ripe red chili peppers are harvested and dried to make *gochugaru* (red chili flakes or powder), which is a main ingredient in Korean seasonings. Many modern varieties of chili are mild enough to be eaten raw dipped in *ssamjang* or made into *banchan* (side dishes).

### Cucumber
### Oi 오이
Korea's cucumbers have a high water content and are long in shape. They are enjoyed raw, in *namul* (vegetable dishes), in *naeng-guk* (chilled soups), in kimchi, and as pickles. They are sometimes used in stir-fried dishes as well.

### Korean Radish
### Mu 무
*Mu*, along with *baechu* (napa cabbage/Chinese cabbage), is one of Korea's most representative vegetables. This radish has an oval shape and a firm, crunchy texture, and is mostly white with light green shoulders. Raw *mu* has a slight spiciness and a markedly crisp texture, but it becomes sweet and soft when cooked. When added to broth-based dishes, it imparts a refreshing taste, so is popular in many fish-based brothy dishes and other broth dishes. It is also popular in steamed or simmered dishes, because it absorbs the seasoning well while adding a balanced sweetness to the dish. Young *mu* (called *yeolmu*) and *altari-mu*, which is a smaller *mu* varietal, are popular kimchi ingredients.

### Bellflower Root
### Doraji 도라지
*Doraji*, bellflower root, is a common vegetable that grows all throughout Korea. It is peeled and made into *namul* (vegetable dishes) or stir-fried. Bellflower root is known to have health-giving properties, especially for the throat, and is often used medicinally or as a medicinal tea.

### Deodeok 더덕
*Deodeok* is a wild mountain plant native to Korea. Its roots are similar in shape to ginseng and it also has an herbal and slightly bitter taste similar to ginseng. While it used to be a precious foraged root, these days it is cultivated and distributed widely. In the most common dish made with *deodeok*, it is pounded and

grilled and seasoned with *gochujang* (red chili paste).

### Fiddlehead Fern
### Gosari 고사리
The bracken fern is a perennial plant that grows all over the world. Called *gosari* in Korea, it has long been part of Korean cuisine. Mostly available in dried form, it is rehydrated before cooking. *Gosari* is popular as a vegetable dish, as a staple ingredient in *bibimbap* (mixed rice), as a stir-fry, and goes particularly well with pork. It is also used in broth-based dishes, such as *yukgaejang* (shredded beef soup with vegetables), perilla seed soup, and more.

### Soybean Sprouts
### Kong Namul 콩나물
While mung bean sprouts (see below) are a common ingredient across Asia, soybean sprouts are much rarer. However, in Korean cuisine, they are a common ingredient in *namul* (vegetable dishes), in rice, and in many broth-based dishes.

### Mung Bean Sprouts
### Sukju Namul 숙주나물
Mung bean sprouts, a popular ingredient across much of Asia, are also a common ingredient in Korean cuisine. It is more fragile than the hardier soybean sprout, and it loses its texture easily, so it is often just lightly cooked. It's mainly used to make *namul* (vegetable dishes) and as one of the ingredients in the filling for *mandu* (dumplings).

### Mushrooms
### Beoseot 버섯
Korea boasts more than two hundred varieties of mushrooms due to its ideal terrain and soil. The technology for mushroom cultivation is well developed in Korea, and many varieties are readily available and consumed.

### Shiitake Mushrooms
### Pyogo Beoseot 표고버섯
*Shiitake* mushrooms, known as *pyogo* in Korea, boast a strong, balanced fragrance and flavor. *Pyogo* mushrooms grow at the base of broadleaf trees and are widely cultivated. Although the mushrooms are produced in quantity and are readily available at low prices, its fragrance is still comparable to any rare mushroom. Dried *pyogo* mushrooms are also widely used in Korean cuisine and are a staple ingredient in Korean broths. Its pleasantly chewy texture is often compared to that of meat.

### Oyster Mushrooms
### Neutari Beoseot 느타리버섯
*Neutari* mushrooms have a shape similar to oysters, with a wide cap ranging from 2–8 inches (5–20 cm), in colors that range from white to brown, to gray. It's the second most produced mushroom in Korea, after the shiitake mushroom. When cooked, it has a soft mouthfeel and a balanced mushroom fragrance, making it a popular ingredient in vegetable dishes, stir-fries, and hotpots.

### Songyi Mushrooms
### Songyi Beoseot 송이버섯
The *songyi* mushroom is the most rare and prized mushroom in Korea. It grows under pine trees and boasts a strong fragrance reminiscent of pine, and the aroma intensifies when grilled or cooked in broth. In English-speaking countries, it is often called the pine mushroom or by its Japanese name, matsutake. It is difficult to cultivate and is in season for only one month at the beginning of fall. To eat *songyi* mushrooms in season is considered one of the most precious fine-dining experiences.

### Wood Ear Mushrooms
### Mogi Beoseot 목이버섯
*Mogi beoseot*, which translates directly to "wood ear mushroom," was so named because the mushrooms look like ears on a tree. This mushroom is mainly used in stir-fry dishes such as *japchae* (stir-fried vegetables & glass noodles). While similar in shape, *seoki* mushrooms are another type of thin, ear-shaped mushroom that grow on rocks. Because *seoki* mushrooms are difficult to cultivate and grow slowly, they are usually only used as a garnish instead of as a main ingredient.

### Enoki Mushrooms
### Paengi Beoseot 팽이버섯
Enoki mushrooms, known as *paengi* in Korea, are widely cultivated. They are well known for their small caps and stringy, lengthy stems, but wild *paengi* mushrooms can have caps as large as 1½–2 inches (4–8 cm) across. Compared to other mushrooms, it has almost no taste or fragrance, yet its signature chewy texture makes it a popular mushroom even for those who are typically averse to mushrooms. It is most often used in stews, hotpots, and other broth-based dishes, and are also enjoyed grilled.

## Fruits

### Korean Pear
### Bae 배
Known in English-speaking countries as Asian pear or apple pear (among other names), *bae* is one of the most popular fruits in Korea due to its crispy texture, refreshing sweet taste, and high juice content. Among the many varieties of pear grown around the world, the Korean pear is unique in its large round size and distinct texture and flavors. In addition to being enjoyed as is, the Korean pear

is also a popular ingredient in kimchi seasoning and meat marinades, and it is also enjoyed poached as a dessert.

### Apple
### Sagwa 사과
There are countless variations in taste, texture, and color, considering all the apple cultivars grown globally. In Korea, there are about fifteen varieties of apples cultivated, with *busa* being the most common. Koreans prefer apples that have a sweet-acidic taste with a crunchy, juicy texture. While most commonly eaten raw, apples are also used to add sweetness to sauces or marinades, or in broths.

### Mandarin Orange
### Gamgyul 감귤
*Gamgyul*, Mandarin orange, is round and flat with an orange skin. It is most popular in the wintertime, and it is enjoyed for its sweet flavor and high juice content. The most prized Korean varieties are *hallabong* and *cheonryehyang*, but there are many cultivated hybrids as well. While Jeju-do is the main producing region, it is also cultivated in southern parts of Korea.

### Yuzu
### Yuja 유자
*Yuja* (yuzu) is a citrus fruit with a bright yellow, thick, and lumpy peel that boasts a strong aromatic citrus fragrance. Despite its strong fragrance, the yuzu fruit is sour in taste and has a small amount of edible flesh with low moisture content. Instead of being eaten as is, it's typically made into tea, syrup, or punch. Along with *mogwa*, Korean quince, it is one of the most common fruits used to make beverages.

### Red Magnolia Berry
### Omija 오미자
*Omija* means "five flavors," and the red magnolia berry is so named because it expresses five flavors: sweet, bitter, sour, spicy, and salty. The *omija* tree bears its berries in July through August, and they turn red when ripe. Red magnolia berries are widely used in Korean cuisine to infuse alcohol, to make tea, and in beverages such as sweet punch, and the berries are also used medicinally, because they are believed to improve blood circulation and strengthen the respiratory system.

### Pomegranate
### Seongnyu 석류
The pomegranate is a fruit with a hard, waxy skin filled with droplet-shaped kernels of juicy seeds. Its sour-sweet taste and jewel tones makes it popular as a garnish for *hwachae* (punches) and other beverages, salads, and raw seafood. Pomegranate is also made into syrup form to be enjoyed as tea.

### Jujube
### Daechu 대추
The jujube is a small fruit also known as Chinese red date. Fresh jujubes are green and taste somewhat like an apple, with a nice balance between sweetness and acidity. The most popular form of the fruit, however, are dried jujubes, which are a deep red-brown. Dried jujubes are used as natural sweeteners in soups, porridges, and steamed dishes, or as garnish, and they are also used widely to flavor tea and *sool* (Korean alcohol).

### Persimmon
### Gam 감
The persimmon is an orange waxy-skinned fruit. Some sweet varieties are eaten raw, and the fruit has a crunchy texture with a deep natural sweetness. More astringent persimmon varieties are peeled and sun-dried to make *gotgam*, or dried persimmons.

## Seaweed

### Gim 김
*Gim* is the name for dried sheets of seaweed and can be made of a number of similar red seaweeds. *Gim* can be eaten as is, or pan-roasted or grilled with sesame oil and salt. It is often served as a *banchan* (side dish) to eat with rice or eaten simply as a snack. Crushed *gim* is also a popular garnish for many dishes including broth-based dishes.

### Miyeok 미역
Korea has been consuming seaweed for more than a thousand years, and *miyeok* has been the most widely consumed variety of seaweed. It is often sold outside Korea by its Japanese name, wakame. The most common dish made with *miyeok* is *miyeokguk* (seaweed soup), which was traditionally eaten postpartum because of to its high iron and calcium content. It has also long been a popular Korean tradition to eat *miyeokguk* to celebrate birthdays.

### Dasima 다시마
*Dasima*, a seaweed in the kelp family, is one of the most common seaweeds, along with *gim* and *miyeok* (see above) consumed in Korea. It is eaten raw in the form of salad or as a *ssam* (wrap) ingredient, or braised to make *banchan* (side dishes). The most common use of *dasima* is in its dried form to flavor broths. It is mainly farmed, with most of the production centered in Wando county, the southernmost region of Korea.

## Seafood

### Pollock
### Myungtae 명태
Pollock is a member of the cod family and is one of the most important fish in Korean cuisine; it has many different

names, depending on its form. Young pollock is called *nogari*, semidried is called *kodari*, and fully dried it is called *bugeo*. Pollock that undergoes a specific drying process of freezing and thawing repeatedly in the wintertime is called *hwangtae*. Its use is as varied as its preparations across many categories of food, including soup, steamed dishes, grilled foods, *jeotgal* (preserved seafood), and *twigak* (deep-fried but not battered food). Because the high levels of demand outpace the supply, a large amount of pollock is imported into Korea from overseas.

## Mackerel
### Godeungeo 고등어
Mackerel is one of the most well-known fatty fish in the world, and it is one of the most common fish in Korea. It is both affordable and delicious, and is often served grilled, as well as in *jorim* (simmered dishes) and *jjigae* (stews). Although it is not often eaten raw (it has a strong fishy smell), in regions where they are caught fresh, such as Jeju-do and Toyong, mackerel eaten as *hwe* (raw seafood) is considered a delicacy. Recently, restaurants in Seoul have also begun to serve mackerel in raw dishes.

## Korean Seerfish
### Samchi 삼치
*Samchi*, or Korean seerfish, is larger and pointier than mackerel. It is usually caught off the southern coast of Korea. While it is a fatty fish, compared to other fish in the category, its flesh is softer and has a less pronounced fishy smell, so there are many who prefer *samchi*. Its use is similar to the mackerel, and it is mainly grilled or used in *jorim* (simmered dishes). In Jeollanam-do, it is eaten as a thick-cut *hwe* (raw seafood), eaten with *gim* and *mugeunji* (aged kimchi) as a *ssam* (wrap).

## Cod
### Daegu 대구
Cod has been long used in Korean cuisine. Today, because of overfishing, it is considered a rarer fish. The most popular cod dish is a long-simmered soup called *daegu tang* and is a common dish available in restaurants (but these are often made with imported cod). Traditionally, when making *tang*, the cod used is semidried, because this results in a deeper, more concentrated flavor in the broth. *Daegu jjim* (steamed cod) is popular, too. Cod is also dried and used as a main ingredient in other dishes, either simply steamed or grilled and eaten as a snack or *anju* (drinking food), or used in soups.

## Beltfish
### Galchi 갈치
*Galchi*—beltfish or largehead hairtail in English—boasts a lengthy body and a pearly silver color. Today, it is considered a high-quality fish with a premium price, but even as recently as the 1980s, it was considered a common fish. Beltfish has a high oil content and a savory flavor, and it is often enjoyed simply salted and grilled or made into *jorim* (simmered dishes) or *jjigae* (stews). It is also used in fermented foods: It can be chopped and added to kimchi, and in Jeju-do the innards are used to make *jeotgal* (preserved seafood), classically enjoyed with grilled pork.

## Octopus
### Muneo 문어
Octopus is widely distributed around the world including Korea, and it is famous for its unique body structure and intelligence. In the East Sea, *pi-muneo*, the large red common octopus (*Enteroctopus dofleini*), is mainly caught, and off the southern coast, *dol-muneo* (*Octopus vulgaris*) is mainly caught. Since ancient times, the octopus has been regarded as a valuable ingredient for ceremonial occasions, such as weddings. In Korea, octopus is usually lightly blanched and sliced to be eaten semiraw, or sliced and dried.

## Long-Arm Octopus
### Nakji 낙지
*Nakji*, sometimes called the long-arm octopus, is a small-bodied octopus species native to Korean seas. It is distinct from the larger Pacific octopus. It is sweet and has a good texture, and is commonly enjoyed raw, stir-fried, or in broth. *San-nakji*, live octopus, is a famous dish of Korean cuisine in which a live octopus is chopped into bite-size pieces and eaten with sesame oil or *cho-gochujang* (vinegared *gochujang*). It is known for the unique experience of eating the still-moving octopus pieces with active tentacles.

## Korean Blue Crab
### Kkotge 꽃게
The Korean blue crab has a diamond shape and is 3–4 inches (7.5–10 cm) wide. It is the most popular and common crab of Korea, especially along Korea's west coast, where referring to crab, it means the blue crab. With the rise of popularity of *ganjang gaejang* (raw crab marinated in soy sauce), it has become known globally. In Korea, crabs are often used in broth-based dishes, and when in season it is delicious enjoyed simply steamed. Other crabs native to Korea include red crab, snow crab, and hairy crab.

## Shrimp
### Saeu 새우
Shrimp (prawns) are globally beloved for their fragrance and flavor. In Korea, there are about ninety different types of

shrimp, but the most common are the Asian shrimp from the West Sea (Yellow Sea), the heavily farmed whiteleg shrimp, the *ttak-saeu* (red shrimp) native to Jeju-do, and the Dokdo shrimp (also known as *dohwa* shrimp), and the southern rough shrimp. Shrimp are used in a variety of dishes, including deep-fried dishes, fried rice, long-simmered soups, and in *jang* (fermented soybean-based sauces). Seasonal shrimp are often enjoyed grilled over a bed of coarse salt, resulting in a delicious, steamed-like texture.

## Clams
### Jogae 조개
Clams have long been an excellent source of protein for humans, because they reproduce abundantly where there is water and are easy to harvest, not being mobile. There are various types of clams in Korea, and the most popular and common is the Manila clam. In addition, cockles, scallops, orient clams, hard clams, blood clams, and pen shell clams are widely used.

## Anchovies
### Myeolchi 멸치
Korean anchovies are categorized and named according to their size. Small anchovies are stir-fried to make *banchan* (side dishes) or pressed and dried as sheets. Larger anchovies are dried and used in making broths. Broth made from anchovy is one of the most foundational elements of Korean cuisine and is the base of countless dishes. Anchovy-based broths are so common that it's often simply called "broth." While fresh anchovies during the height of their season are eaten as *hwe* (raw seafood) as a delicacy, anchovies are mostly available in dried form.

# Seasonings

## Korean Chili Flakes or Powder
### Gochugaru 고춧가루
*Gochugaru* is ground up dried red chili pepper. Stemmed and seeded fresh red chilies are fully dried and then ground to flakes or a powder. Which coarseness of *gochugaru* is needed depends on where it will be used. Fine *gochugaru* powder is used to make *gochujang* (red chili paste) or *jeotgal* (preserved seafood), and medium *gochugaru* flakes are used in making sauces and seasonings. Coarse *gochugaru* is used primarily in kimchi. Depending on the desired effect, a mixture of different coarsenesses can be used. While it has quickly become one of the most well-known spices of Korean cuisine, its history is relatively short, because the red chili pepper wasn't imported to Korea until about five hundred years ago, and it has only become a main ingredient in the last hundred years or so.

## Sesame Oil
### Cham gireum 참기름
Sesame oil is one of the most utilized in Korean cuisine. It is not generally used to cook ingredients, but instead used as an aromatic oil added at the end of the cooking process. Sesame oil is made by pressing roasted sesame seeds, and the process and temperature of roasting or pressing determines the quality of the final oil. Nowadays, there are many high-quality sesame oils produced using low-temperature processes. The distinct nutty fragrance of sesame oil can be imparted to dishes using just a small amount; using too much sesame oil will overpower the dish, so it is important to be careful of the amount used.

## Perilla Oil
### Deul gireum 들기름
Perilla oil is made from pressing perilla seeds. In October, as the perilla flowers fall and produce seeds, the seed pods are harvested, processed, and roasted before pressing for the oil. Along with sesame oil, perilla oil is one of the native oils of Korean cuisine; however, because of its strong fragrance and volatility, it's used less frequently than sesame oil. With the development of modern production and packaging processes, it has become easier to obtain high-quality perilla oil and the product is rising in popularity.

## Vinegar
### Sikcho 식초
Vinegar is made by fermenting alcohol brewed from grains or fruits. Naturally made vinegar contains 3 to 5 percent acetic acid. However, these days, vinegars are made by starting with a 95 percent alcohol base that then undergoes acetic acid fermentation by adding brown rice or apple extract. Adding a small amount of vinegar to fish-based dishes or strongly flavored meat dishes can result in a more balanced flavor. Vinegar is a popular ingredient in summertime dishes, such as *muchim* (seasoned dishes), cold noodles, or chilled soups to boost appetite. The most popular types of vinegars available in Korea include rice vinegar, barley vinegar, and apple vinegar.

## Honey
### Kkul 꿀
Honey is the product of bees collecting and storing the nectar of flowers. The documented history of honey in Korea traces back to the Three Kingdoms period (see page 15), suggesting that it may have been in use even before that time. Depending

on the flower the nectar is collected from—such as acacia, rapeseed, chestnut, or buckwheat—the color and taste of the honey differs accordingly. In Korea, honey is used for food, as well as a medicinal folk remedy, because it is good for blood circulation. It's often used in desserts, in tea, or as topical treatment for rough skin.

**Rice or Grain Syrup**
**Jocheong 조청**
*Jocheong* is a sweet syrup made by boiling starchy grains and fermenting the resulting mash with the enzyme in malt powder. It can be made of a number of grains, such as rice, barley, or corn, but is most commonly made with rice. *Jocheong* made using traditional methods is brown (because of the fiber remaining from the grains) and has a sweet, savory flavor profile. It has a thick consistency and it is used to add sweetness to simmered savory dishes such as *jorim* and also adds luster to sweets. *Jocheong* can be cooked down to make *yeot*, a Korean confection.

**Hot Mustard**
**Gyeoja 겨자**
*Gyeoja*, Korean hot mustard, is thought to have been in use beginning around the first century BCE. It is made from the seeds of the mustard plant. Ground mustard seeds are combined with warm water to make a paste that is then fermented, which produces it signature spicy taste. While it has a slight bitterness as well, adding vinegar to the water to make it slightly acidic reduces the bitterness. In Korean cuisine, hot mustard is usually used to make salad dressings, and hot mustard oil (oil infused with mustard) can be added to taste when making mixed noodles.

**Chopi 초피**
*Chopi*, also called *jepi* or *jenpi*, depending on regional dialect, is a native Korean plant that's is the same as the Japanese sanshō pepper. *Chopi* berries are ground to a powder and used as a spice to impart a lightly numbing sensation. Before the chili pepper was introduced to Korea, *chopi* was the main source of spiciness in food. Today, it is mainly used as a garnishing spice for soups such as *chueo tang* (loach soup) or *maeuntang* (cod soup) and it is delicious paired with grilled pork either as an addition to *ssamjang* (dipping sauce for wraps) or as garnish. The leaves of the *chopi* plant are also great as *jangajji* (pickles).

**Fish Sauce**
**Aekjeot 액젓**
Fish sauce, a product of salt-fermented fish or shellfish, is a staple ingredient in Southeast Asian cooking, but it's also a staple in Korean cuisine and is known as *aekjeot*. The two most commonly used *aekjeot* are one made from a small fish called a sand lance and one made from anchovies. *Aekjeot* is used in making kimchi and is also used for seasoning such mixtures as marinades. It adds saltiness, umami, and depth in flavor to a widely variety of dishes, including *guk* (soup) and *jjigae* (stew).

**Sesame Seeds**
**Chamkkae 참깨**
The sesame seed is one of the most popular garnishes in Korean cuisine. They are also used to make sesame oil. The seeds are often used in stir-fried dishes or as a finishing garnish. Roasted and ground sesame seeds are called "sesame salt" in Korean (although there is not necessarily any salt in the mixture) and it is often called for in Korean recipes to add nutty, savory flavors to dishes.

The Korean Pantry

# Glossary 사전

**aehobak**: Korean zucchini (courgette)
**aekjeot**: Korean fish sauce

**bae**: Korean pear, aka Asian pear or apple pear
**baechu**: napa cabbage (Chinese leaf)
**banchan**: side dishes
**bansang**: traditional structure of a traditional Korean meal
**bap**: rice
**beoseot**: mushroom
**bibimbap**: mixed rice
**bokkeum**: stir-fry or stir-fried
**bokkeumbap**: fried rice
**bomdong**: spring napa cabbage (Chinese leaf)
**bori**: barley
**buchim**: pan-fried ingredients
**buchimgae**: pancake / pan-fried fritter
**buchu**: garlic chives
**bugak**: rice- or flour-battered vegetables
**bulgogi**: thinly sliced meat

**chae**: shredded, julienned
**cham gireum**: sesame oil
**chamkkae**: sesame seeds
**chapssal**: glutinous rice
**cheongjang**: light Korean soy sauce
**chopi**: peppery berries (peppercorns) used as a spice; aka sanshō

**daechu**: jujube (Chinese red date)
**daegu**: cod
**daepa**: a Korean variety of large scallion (spring onion)
**dasima**: a variety of seaweed
**deodeok**: a Korean plant similar to ginseng
**deopbap**: rice bowl
**deul gireum**: perilla oil
**doenjang**: fermented soybean paste
**dolsot**: traditional stone pot
**dongji**: flowering napa/Chinese cabbage
**doraji**: bellflower root
**dosirak**: packed meal
**dubu**: tofu

**eomuk**: Korean fish or seafood cake

**galbi**: ribs or short ribs
**galchi**: beltfish
**gam**: persimmon
**gamasot**: traditional iron pot
**gamgyul**: mandarin orange
**gan**: to season
**ganjang**: Korean soy sauce
**geotjeori**: fresh kimchi
**gim**: dried sheets of seaweed
**gimbap**: rice rolled in *gim*
**gochu**: chili pepper
**gochugaru**: Korean chili flakes or powder
**gochujang**: red chili paste
**godeungeo**: mackerel
**gomtang**: beef bone soup
**gosari**: fiddlehead fern
**gotgam**: dried persimmons
**gui**: grilled
**guk**: soup
**gukbap**: rice in soup
**guksu**: noodles
**gyeoja**: Korean hot mustard

**hansik**: Korean cuisine
**hanwoo**: breed of cattle native to Korea; Korean beef
**husik**: dessert
**hwachae**: Korean punch
**hwe**: a dish with raw seafood; raw sliced seafood or meat
**hyunmi**: brown rice

**jang**: fermented soybean sauces
**jangajji**: Korean pickles
**jeon**: fritters
**jeongol**: Korean hotpot dish
**jeot** or **jeotgal**: preserved seafood
**jinjang**: dark Korean soy sauce
**jjigae**: stew
**jjim**: steamed
**jjokpa**: a Korean variety of scallion (spring onion) crossed with a shallot
**jo**: millet
**jocheong**: grain syrup (often rice syrup)
**jogae**: clam
**jorim**: simmered
**juk**: porridge
**jungjang**: medium Korean soy sauce

**kimchi**: salted and fermented vegetables
**kimjang**: traditional communal process of making kimchi

**kkaennip**: perilla leaf
**kkotge**: Korean blue crab
**kkul**: honey
**kkwari**: shishito peppers
**kong namul**: soybean sprouts
**kong**: soybean

**makgeolli**: Korean rice wine
**mandu**: Korean dumplings
**maneul**: garlic
**meju**: block of dried fermented soybeans
**mepssal**: short-grain rice
**minari**: a vegetable similar to celery and watercress
**mit-banchan**: Korean preserved side dish
**miyeok**: a variety of seaweed; aka wakame
**mogi beoseot**: wood ear mushroom
**mu**: Korean radish
**muchim**: a dish mixed with seasoning
**mugeunji**: aged kimchi
**muk**: a gelatin- or jelly-like food made from the starches found in grains, nuts, and beans
**muneo**: octopus
**myeolchi**: anchovy
**myungtae**: pollock

**nakji**: long-arm octopus
**namul**: vegetable side dishes or greens
**neutari beoseot**: oyster mushroom
**nokdu**: mung bean

**oi**: cucumber
**omija**: red magnolia berry

**paengi beoseot**: enoki mushroom
**pat**: red beans (adzuki beans)
**pyogo beoseot**: shiitake mushroom
**pyunyuk**: pressed meat

**saengchae**: raw vegetable dishes
**saenggang**: ginger
**saeu**: shrimp (prawns)
**sagwa**: apple
**samchi**: Korean seerfish
**samgyupsal**: pork belly
**sangchu**: lettuce
**seolleongtang**: ox bone soup

**seon**: traditional Korean dishes made from steamed vegetables
**seongnyu**: pomegranate
**sigeumchi**: spinach
**sikcho**: vinegar
**sikhye**: Korean sweet rice punch
**silpa**: young *daepa*
**siraegi**: dried radish tops
**soju**: Korean clear distilled sprit
**somyeon**: very thin wheat flour noodles
**songpyeon**: half-moon-shaped *tteok* (rice cakes)
**songyi beoseot**: songyi mushroom; aka pine mushroom or matsutake
**sool**: general category of Korean alcohol
**sotbap**: pot rice
**ssam**: wrap
**ssambap**: rice wrap
**ssamjang**: Korean *jang* (fermented soybean paste) for dipping *ssam* (wraps)
**ssukgat**: chrysanthemum
**sujebi**: Korean hand-torn noodles
**sukchae**: cooked vegetable dishes
**sukju namul**: mung bean sprouts
**sundae**: Korean blood sausage
**suyuk**: boiled meat

**tang**: long-simmered soup
**tteok**: rice cakes
**tteokbokki**: stir-fried rice cakes
**twigim**: deep-fried dishes

**ugeoji**: outer leaves or stems of cabbage, radish, and other greens

**yangjo ganjang**: naturally brewed soy sauce with wheat
**yeolmu**: young summer Korean radish
**Yondu**: a Korean plant-based and fermented seasoning sauce
**yuja**: a citrus fruit also known as yuzu
**yuksu**: broth

Glossary

# Fermentation

발효

To find the essence of each country's food culture, one should look to the foods that are consumed daily as part of a common table spread. There, one would find the ingredients that are used the most, what the most common method of cooking is, and how one eats.

When one is seated at a typical Korean meal, aside from the white rice, almost all the dishes incorporate some aspect of fermentation: Either the ingredient is fermented itself, such as kimchi, or incorporates some form of fermented ingredient or sauce as a part of its seasoning. One may even wonder if it is possible to have a complete Korean meal without fermentation?

The key flavors in Korean cuisine derive from fermentation, and a meal is created by designing a complementary spread. Without understanding fermentation and how deeply rooted it is in Korean cuisine, one cannot truly understand Korean cuisine or culture.

Korea applies fermentation to diverse ingredients, following the natural rhythms of nature. The four distinct seasons in Korea are each busy with preparing delicious fermented food to the extent that it can be said that there is a "ferment calendar." Vegetables are made into kimchi and *jangajji* (pickles) at the height of their season. Simply following the life cycle of a soybean in Korea covers the whole year—from its growth, harvest, and drying to the process of creating *jang*: salting and brining, drying and grinding, fermenting and aging. Pantry staples, such as *gochugaru* (red chili powder) or vinegars, are also a year-round process.

Of the countless types of fermented foods in Korea, this chapter will focus on *jang*, the historical mother recipes that for more than two thousand years have been made from fermented soybeans, as well as kimchi and *jangajji* (pickles), the expansive category of fermented vegetables dishes. *Jang*, kimchi, and *jangajji* all tell the story of Korea's history, climate, and topography as the ingredients and methods used were the most accessible to its people.

# 장 Jang Fermented Soybean Sauces

*Jang* refers to the category of basic Korean seasonings based on fermented soybeans. The category encompasses three basic *jangs*: *ganjang* (Korean soy sauce), *doenjang* (soybean paste), and *gochujang* (red chili paste). All *jang* begins with the primary fermentation of soybeans to create *meju*, a traditional brick-like block of dried fermented soybeans. The *meju* is combined with salt and water to create the foundational base of *jang*.

While the simple combination of *meju*, salt, and water is the most prevalent, many variations exist, depending on the regional traditions or the end use of the recipe. Grains, such as barley, wheat, or glutinous rice, can be added to this base. The *meju* block can be ground to powder and mixed with *gochugaru* (red chili flakes) or other vegetables. Even fish or meat can be added to this secondary fermentation process to add robust flavoring.

The history of Korean *jang* began more than two thousand years ago and its practice is still alive, not only on a commercial, industrial level but also in home kitchens. Records of making *ganjang* can be found in *Jurye*, a book written in the second century BCE, and this is a tradition that continues today as *jang* is still the foundational seasoning of Korean cuisine and defines its central flavors.

The *jang* is the most important factor in the final taste of a dish, enriching the taste of vegetables, seafood, meat, broth, and more without masking the inherent taste of the ingredients. Especially when cooking vegetables, it reduces any astringent, bitter, or vegetal tastes or flavors. At the same time, the body and deep, savory flavors that only fermentation can provide add richness to dishes, especially when there is minimal or no use of animal products, oils, or fats.

# Types of Jang

*Jang* can be a liquid, such as *ganjang*, or a paste, such as *doenjang*, *gochujang*, and *ssamjang*.

### Ganjang (Korean Soy Sauce)

*Ganjang* is a liquid seasoning made by fermenting soybeans with salt and water. *Gan* is a Korean word that means "to season," and this dark, salty brown liquid is a primary seasoning for all foods. The most traditional, common version is made with just soybeans, salt, and water. Each region of Korea has included common ingredients in the fermentation process to create an entirely separate category of *ganjang*. The traditional *ganjang* is gluten-free because no barley or wheat is added. Other types of *ganjang* made with different types of beans, such as black beans or *pureun kong* (green soybeans), also exist. A subcategory of *ganjang* called *eoyukjang* exists, in which fish and meat are cofermented in the process. Up until the 1960s, with the Korean Industrialization, each household made their own *ganjang* at home using traditional methods.

Korean soy sauce has a delicious, deep, and balanced flavor that comes from the length of the soybeans' fermentation process, and that complements an ingredient's natural flavor without overpowering it. As the length of the fermentation is one of the key determining factors of its flavors, each type soy sauce has its own name. *Cheongjang* is a light and clear *ganjang* that is fermented for just a year. *Jinjang* is a dark *ganjang* that has a deeper umami and sweetness that comes from a longer fermentation period.

### Cheongjang

This is a light soy sauce. The *cheong* in *cheongjang* translates to "clear." This category of *ganjang* is aged for one year and is indeed clear with a light brown color, and when used in cooking it elevates the savory flavor of the ingredient without discoloring the food. Compared to salt, *cheongjang* has an additional layer of deep flavoring to enhance the salty flavor, and it adds to the body of the dish. *Cheongjang* has a similar flavor impact in cooking to the combination of salt, broth, and fish sauce. It is the ideal seasoning to use when cooking vegetables, where it's important to preserve the vivid colors of the ingredients. It reduces any bitterness, balances sweetness, and adds savory flavors that do not compete with the inherent flavor and fragrance of the vegetables. It's also a base ingredient in broths and soups, because it adds body and subtle savory notes without the need for animal products, such as fish sauce or meat-based broths. For this reason, the common name for *cheongjang* is *guk ganjang*, which translates to "soup soy sauce."

### Jinjang

A dark soy sauce, the *jin* in *jinjang* is rooted in the word *jin-hada*, which means "deep." It refers to the age of the soy sauce, which is a minimum of five years. *Jinjang* is widely used as the base in sauces, such as marinades and dipping sauces, as well as directly in stir-fried, stewed, and grilled dishes. *Jinjang* has a deep color and a rich profile of savory and sweetness to match, all from the patient fermentation of the soybeans over many years. It pairs particularly well with vegetables with richer textures and flavors, such as mushrooms, and it is the most commonly used soy sauce in cooking fish and meat dishes, because the strong flavors of the ingredients harmonize well together.

**Yangjo Ganjang**
After the Korean Industrialization began in the 1960s, companies began a large-scale production of soy sauce that incorporated wheat into the fermentation. With the rise of industrialization and mass commerce, this type of soy sauce quickly became a common pantry staple and is now widely used. Compared to the traditionally made soy sauce with just soybeans, *yangjo ganjang* has a sweeter flavor with distinct acidic notes, along with a darker color and fragrance.

The *yangjo* soy sauce, which is often marketed as "naturally brewed soy sauce" in Western markets, can be used in a wide variety of dishes due to its balanced sweet-acidic profile. Its stronger and rounded profile can also help overcome any unwanted flavors or fragrances of ingredients. It is especially good for making dressings for raw seafood or meat, *twigim* (deep-fried dishes), or salads, and it can be used universally for most dishes except those that call for a lighter broth. It can easily be substituted in any recipe that calls for the darker flavors of *jinjang*.

**Choosing Ganjang**

Just as different wines are chosen based on their varietal or vintage, to pair with different dishes, Koreans will use different types of soy sauce for different dishes and keep several types of soy sauce in the pantry. A home cook will instinctively know to reach for *cheongjang* when creating a *miyeok guk* (seaweed soup), a dish that highlights the clean, savory flavors inherent in seaweed, the same way the cook will reach for *jinjang* when cooking meat dishes, such as *bulgogi* (thinly sliced meat), to create a robust seasoning to match the heartiness of beef.

If you want to enjoy the taste of Korean food like Koreans do, it is recommended that you have at least the two distinct traditional soy sauces: *cheongjang* and *jinjang*. In recipes where it really makes a difference which is used, and to demonstrate their typical use in Korean cuisine, the specific type will be called for. If it doesn't matter which soy sauce is used, the recipe will simply call for *ganjang* (Korean soy sauce).

A note of importance is the salinity levels. The commercially common Korean *yangjo ganjang* measures at 16 percent. *Cheongjang* (light soy sauce), *jungjang* (medium soy sauce), and *jinjang* (dark soy sauce) begin at 16 percent and can measure up to 21 to 23 percent. If using traditional brands of Korean soy sauce, you can check the salinity level on the label and adjust as needed.

**Doenjang**
*Doenjang*, which is fermented soybean paste, comes from the same process used to make *ganjang* (Korean soy sauce). *Ganjang* is the liquid that results from the fermentation of soybeans; *doenjang* is the solid paste. The word *doenjang* comes from the Korean word *doen*, which translates to "without water," and when combined with the word *jang* translates to "solid paste," referring to the *meju* (the fermented soybean solids) that remain after skimming off the soy sauce.

While soy sauce is used for seasoning in cooking, *doenjang* is used as not only a seasoning ingredient but also as a base ingredient, highlighting the rich texture and flavor of the fermented soybeans themselves.

**Tojang**
*Tojang* is a special hybrid *jang*. It starts with the fermentation of soybeans, but after the initial fermentation, when the *ganjang* and *doenjang* ordinarily would be separated to continue fermenting separately, for *tojang*, solid and liquid parts are mixed together to create a looser paste. It is characterized by savory, deep flavors of soybeans. It can be used as a substitute for *doenjang* when seeking a richer, denser flavor.

**Gochujang**
*Gochujang* is a paste made by cofermenting *meju* with rice, glutinous rice, barley, and other grains along with the distinctive Korean red chili powder called *gochugaru*, hence the name *gochujang*. The combination of the savory, deep flavor of the fermented soybeans, the sweetness of the grains, and the heat from the *gochugaru* make a well-balanced condiment. In Korean cuisine, *gochujang* is a pantry staple used in all types of dishes.

# Choosing Jang Ingredients

Each *jang* has a different flavor that adds contrast and character to dishes, amplifying ingredients' flavors in totally different ways. Each *jang* contains salty, sweet, savory, sour, spicy, and fruity flavors, all resulting from fermentation. Like an artist's palette, the combination of these different flavors can "paint" totally different results, opening a world of possibilities.

**Soybeans**

One important factor in selecting soybeans for *jang* is their moisture content, because it will impact the feeding of the microorganisms required for fermentation. Ideally, only soybeans harvested that year should be used, selecting only the round, smooth soybeans to avoid any unwanted impurities.

**Salt**

In Korea, sun-dried salt with a high mineral content is traditionally used to make *jang*. However, other types of salt may also be used, but avoid sea salt that contains any bitterns (minerals extracted from seawater), because the unwanted bitter flavors will transfer to the *jang*.

**Water**

Water is the ingredient that is used in the largest quantity to make *jang*, and thus its purity and flavor is also of the utmost importance. Avoid using any water that has been processed with or contains chlorine, because it will interfere with the growth of the microorganisms.

**Microorganisms**

The microorganisms at work to make the *jang* include:

*Aspergillus oryzae*: It breaks down the soybeans' proteins and carbohydrates into amino acids and glucose

*Bacillus subtilis*: It breaks down the soybeans' proteins into amino acids

Yeast: These organisms ingest sugar to produce alcohol and carbon dioxide flavor components

*Lactobacillus*: These bacteria produce lactic acid and flavor components by ingesting sugar

**Additional Ingredients**

It's common to see dried red chili pepper or charcoal in the *hangari* (fermentation vessel) when making *jang*. This is a tradition that signifies the maker's intent in creating a beautiful *jang* without impurities, with the red pepper signifying fortune and the charcoal clarifying any impurities or bad fortune. In actuality, they have no measurable impact on the final taste. Another common addition is jujubes (Chinese red dates), which also signify good fortune and do not impact the taste. Although some say that they add a note of sweetness, it's really more of a ceremonial or aesthetic choice.

# Meju
메주

dF gF vg vE –5

The building blocks of *jang* are literally that: *Meju* are the brick-like blocks of fermented cooked soybeans that are used as the starting point for all *jangs*. While it is unlikely that most home cooks will go to the trouble of making their own *meju*, anyone who would choose to do so should seek to source some hay in order to make it in the traditional manner.

**Preparation time: 30 minutes, plus 6 hours soaking time and 30–40 days drying time**
**Cooking time: 1 hour**
**Makes: 1 block (about 1½ lb/ 650–700 g)**

4 cups (700 g) dried soybeans
12 cups (96 fl oz/2.8 liters) spring water
7 oz (200 g) straw, traditionally rice or wheat (optional)

Pick over the soybeans and remove any cracked or rotten beans. In a large bowl or sieve, wash the soybeans under cold running water.

In a large bowl or pot, combine 4¼ cups (34 fl oz/1 liter) of the spring water and the soybeans and let soak for 6 hours at room temperature.

Drain the soaked soybeans and place in a pressure cooker along with the remaining 7¾ cups (61 fl oz/1.8 liters) spring water. Lock the pressure cooker and bring to pressure over medium heat. Once at pressure, adjust the heat to maintain even pressure and cook for 1 hour. Let the pressure release naturally for 20 minutes, then release the remaining pressure and remove the lid. The soybeans should be a dark brown color, and when lightly pressed with the fingers should easily crumble. (This can also be done in an electric pressure cooker. Cook at high pressure for 1 hour, natural release for 20 minutes, then quick-release any remaining pressure.)

Drain the cooked soybeans and pour them into a large bowl while still warm. Using a large wooden spoon, gently mash until the soybeans are uniformly crushed.

Tip the soybeans onto a work surface and mold them into rectangular blocks about 4¾ × 6¼ × 3 inches (12 × 16 × 7.5 cm). The texture of the soybeans should be enough for them to stick together.

Set out some well ventilated fabric, such as netting, to dry the outer surface of the meju block. If making it in the traditional manner, evenly distribute the straw over the fabric (this also helps with the growth of the microorganisms) and lay the meju block on top. Keep in a cool, dry place, preferably with ongoing air ventilation, such as a fan, for 2–3 days or until the outer layer of the block is dry to the touch.

Once dry on all four sides, either wrap the meju block with cloth (or straw) to hang or dry on a straw mat until the outer layer of the block is fully dry with no hint of moisture, 30–40 days.

The meju is now ready for using. It will keep well for 1 year in the freezer.

# Ganjang & Doenjang
## 간장 & 된장

dF gF vg vE -5

*Ganjang* is a liquid seasoning made by fermenting soybeans with salt and water. *Gan* is a Korean word meaning "to season," and this dark, salty brown liquid is historically the primary ingredient used to season all foods; it translates loosely to Korean soy sauce.

*Doenjang* is another product that is made with the identical process as *ganjang*. When soybeans are fermented, the *ganjang* is the liquid that results from the fermentation and *doenjang* is the solid paste. *Doenjang* loosely translates to fermented soybean paste.

**Preparation time:** 2 hours, plus 8–12 months fermentation (and up to 5 years)
**Makes:** 4½ quarts (4.2 liters) ganjang and 26 lb 7 oz (12 kg) doenjang

9 lb 4 oz (4.2 kg) sea salt
13¼ quarts (12.6 liters) spring water
9 lb 4 oz (4.2 kg) meju blocks

In a large bowl, mix the salt and water together until well dissolved.

In a sterilized ongi hangari (Korean clay fermentation vessel) or a 32¾-quart (30 liter) airtight opaque plastic container, combine the dried meju blocks and salt water. Cover with a tight net or cheesecloth (muslin) and cover with a lid.

Keep in a dry, sunny environment of 59–68°F (15°–20°C). Ferment for 40–60 days. Leave the lid open during the day to receive sunlight, taking care to leave it covered with the cloth or net to block any foreign substances, and close it at night.

After fermentation, the liquid and solids should be fully separated and ready to be fermented separately as ganjang and doenjang.

For the doenjang, carefully remove the meju blocks, place in a large container, and break into an even paste using your hands. Depending on the region, sometimes some liquid is added to the paste or layered with salt before storing, but the main way is simply just with the container cover.

For the ganjang, strain the liquid through a cheesecloth or fine filter and move to a separate fermentation container.

Both are aged for a minimum of 8–12 months. Depending on how long the ganjang is aged, it will be either light soy sauce (cheongjang) after 1 year of age, medium soy sauce (junjang) after 3 years, or dark soy sauce (jinjang) after 5 or more years. The ganjang will keep well for 10 years in the refrigerator, while the doenjang will keep well for 3 years in the refrigerator.

# Gochujang
## 고추장

dF vg vE -5

*Gochujang* is a Korean fermented chili paste made by cofermenting *meju* with rice, glutinous rice, barley, and other grains and, of course, the distinct Korean red chili powder, *gochugaru*. As a result the *gochujang* has a savory, deep flavor from the fermented soybeans, sweetness from the grains, and heat from the *gochugaru*.

**Preparation time:** 30 minutes, plus 1 month fermentation
**Makes:** 11 lb (5 kg)

1 lb (450 g) sea salt
2¼ lb (2 kg) water
2 lb 10 oz (1.2 kg) malted barley syrup
14 oz (400 g) meju powder
2¼ lb (1 kg) fine gochugaru (red chili powder)

In a large bowl, combine the sea salt and water until fully dissolved.

Add the barley syrup, meju powder, and gochugaru and stir until it's uniformly combine and there are no lumps.

Transfer the final mixture to a sterilized fermentation vessel and cover with a net or cloth. Store at room temperature or around 77°F (25°C) for 1 month. It's ideal to store in a dry, ventilated area with access to sunlight and wind. After 1 month, the gochujang is ready for consumption.

The gochujang will keep well for 3 years in the refrigerator.

# Vinegared Gochujang
## Cho-Gochujang
## 초고추장

*Cho* means "vinegar," and *cho-gochujang* refers to the sweet and sour condiment that is made from *gochujang* mixed with vinegar along with a sweetener, such as *jocheong* (rice syrup), corn syrup, or sugar. It is the main condiment used to dip *hwe* (raw seafood or meat) or to dress *saengchae namul* (raw vegetable dishes).

dF vg vE -3o

**Preparation time:** 10 minutes
**Serves:** 4

10 tablespoons (5 oz/140 g) gochujang (red chili paste)
2½ tablespoons sugar
1 tablespoon corn syrup
4 teaspoons mirin
4 tablespoons rice vinegar
½ teaspoon ginger juice
¼ teaspoon minced garlic

In a bowl, combine all the ingredients until blended.

The vinegared gochujang will keep well for 3 days in the refrigerator

---

# Stir-Fried Gochujang
## Yak-Gochujang
## 약고추장

*Yak-gochujang* is *gochujang* that has been stir-fried with ground meat. While it can be eaten as a *banchan* (side dish), it is most often used in *ssam* (wraps) or as a sauce for *bibimbap* (mixed rice).

dF -3o

**Preparation time:** 10 minutes
**Cooking time:** 20 minutes
**Serves:** 4

1 teaspoon ganjang (Korean soy sauce)
½ teaspoon minced garlic
1 teaspoon minced scallion (spring onion)
½ teaspoon sugar
¼ teaspoon freshly ground black pepper
1½ teaspoons sesame oil
1¾ oz (50 g) ground (minced) beef
⅔ cup (150 g) gochujang (red chili paste)
7 tablespoons (100 ml) Korean pear juice

In a large bowl, combine the soy sauce, garlic, scallion, sugar, black pepper, and ½ teaspoon of the sesame oil. Fold in the beef and let marinate for 5 minutes.

In a pan, stir-fry the marinated beef over low heat for 5 minutes. Add the gochujang and pear juice and stir-fry until the excess moisture is gone, about 10 more minutes. Add the remaining 1 teaspoon sesame oil and stir-fry over medium-low heat for 2–3 minutes. Remove from the heat.

Once cooled, transfer to an airtight container. Store in the refrigerator. The stir-fried gochujang will keep well for 3 days in the refrigerator

## Vegan Stir-Fried Gochujang
## Vegan Yak-Gochujang
## 비건 약고추장

dF vg vE -5 -3o

**Preparation time:** 10 minutes
**Cooking time:** 15 minutes
**Serves:** 4

1 tablespoon sesame oil
1½ cups (9 oz/250 g) minced onions
4 teaspoons gochujang (red chili paste)

This vegan version of *yak-gochujang* is made with minced onions. The depth from the cooked onions makes it a great sauce for *bibimbap* and *ssam*.

Heat a small pot over low heat, add the sesame oil and minced onions, and stir-fry until the onions are semitranslucent, 2–3 minutes. Add 1 cup (8 fl oz/240 ml) water and boil over low heat until the onions have a jammy texture, 5–7 minutes. Add the gochujang and cook over medium heat for 3–4 minutes to blend the flavors. Remove from the heat.

Once cooled, transfer to an airtight container. It keeps well for up to 2 weeks in the refrigerator.

## Ssamjang
## 쌈장

dF vg vE -3o

**Preparation time:** 10 minutes
**Cooking time:** 10 minutes
**Makes:** 12 oz (340 g); 4 servings

2 teaspoons sesame oil
3½ tablespoons doenjang (fermented soybean paste)
4 teaspoons gochujang (red chili paste)
Scant 1 cup (5 oz/150 g) minced onion
2 teaspoons minced garlic
1 tablespoon minced scallion (spring onion)

*Ssamjang* combines the savory depth of *doenjang*, the spice of the *gochujang*, and the flavors of the alliums to create a balanced *jang*. As its name suggests, it is the main *jang* used when eating *ssam* with meat and it is a great sauce for simply dipping vegetables.

In a pan, combine the sesame oil, doenjang, and gochujang and stir-fry for 3 minutes over medium heat. Add the onion, garlic, scallion, and 7 tablespoons water and simmer over medium heat until the ssamjang thickens, 4–5 minutes. Remove from the heat.

Once cooled, transfer to an airtight container. It keeps well for up to 3–4 days in the refrigerator.

# Ssamjang with Nuts
## Gyungwaryu Ssamjang
## 견과류 쌈장

DF VG VE -30

The nuts add a nutty, savory profile to *ssamjang* and balance the strong flavors of *doenjang* and *gochujang*. While best when eating *ssam* (wraps), it's also great eaten simply with rice and vegetables.

**Preparation time: 15 minutes**
**Cooking time: 10 minutes**
**Makes: 14 oz (400 g);
   4 servings**

2 teaspoons sesame oil
3½ tablespoons doenjang
   (fermented soybean paste)
4 teaspoons gochujang
   (red chili paste)
Scant 1 cup (5 oz/150 g)
   minced onion
2 teaspoons minced garlic
2½ teaspoons minced scallion
   (spring onion)
3 tablespoons minced toasted
   walnuts
3 tablespoons minced roasted
   almonds

In a pan, combine the sesame oil, doenjang, and gochujang and stir-fry for 3 minutes over medium heat. Add the onion, garlic, scallion, and 7 tablespoons water and cook over medium heat for 4–5 minutes. Add the minced nuts and stir until uniformly thickened and remove from the heat.

Once cooled, transfer to an airtight container. It keeps well for up to 3–4 days in the refrigerator.

# 김치 Kimchi Fermented Vegetables

There are more than two hundred types of recognized Korean kimchi made with seasonal vegetables. There is a saying that there are as many types of kimchi as there are households in Korea. Many factors, including seasonality, regionality, and family recipes, make for the deep category. The common napa cabbage (Chinese leaf) kimchi is just one type; practically all vegetables can be made into kimchi. Beyond the familiar image of the red, spicy kimchi, there are other categories, such as white kimchi, with roots in the origins of kimchi.

The seasonality of the vegetables is integral, because kimchi preserves and highlights their flavors. And a key point in kimchi making is this: Each vegetable has an ideal seasoning and fermentation method that complements the nature of the ingredient. Once the main vegetable of the kimchi is decided, the seasoning and any supplemental ingredients can be selected accordingly.

The wide breadth of the kimchi category can be credited to Korea's seasons. Korea has four distinct seasons, each with clear characteristics and harvests. Spring vegetables tend to taste sweet, their textures very delicate, tender, and soft. Summer plants can become very tough due to excessive sunlight, often developing a bitter flavor. The most delicious vegetables are picked in fall, which provides the best weather for harvest. One of the ingredients harvested in fall is the Korean napa cabbage. This diversity of edible plants led to the Korean people developing deep skills on how to pair different ingredients in order to obtain the desired kimchi flavor. Thanks to the accumulation of thousands of years of knowledge, Korean kimchi can be made with any kind of plant imaginable.

*Mugeunji* refers to aged kimchi, which is made specifically to ferment for a long period of time. Because of the longer fermentation period, the kimchi mixture intended for *mugeunji* is made with a milder seasoning and stored at low temperatures to ferment for a minimum of six months up to years. Traditionally, *mugeunji* is prepared earlier than *kimjang*, which is the traditional process of communal preparation of kimchi in early winter. This way the taste of fermented kimchi can be enjoyed in the warmer seasons. *Mugeunji* is typically used as an ingredient in cooked dishes such as *jjigae* (stew) and *jjim* (steamed dishes), or washed to remove the seasoning and then used as a *ssam* (wrap) ingredient.

# Kimchi's History

Korea is a country where more than 70 percent of its land is mountainous terrain. Since ancient times, Korea's ancestors relied on this landscape and its vast variety of edible plants, along with fields of cultivated vegetables. Because vegetables were the most abundant source of food, they became significant to Korean meals, which naturally led to the development of ways in which they could be preserved and consumed. Kimchi is the most symbolic and representative of this culinary development, and it is undoubtedly Korea's most iconic vegetable-based food, and perhaps also its most singular.

Kimchi is a mix of vegetables, spices, and aromatics that develop a harmony of flavors through fermentation techniques and best practices developed over thousands of years. Today, there are more than two hundred different types of documented kimchi, each with its own unique combinations of ingredients and preparation methods. How did Koreans come to discover this magnificent dish and how did it develop through its history?

The history of kimchi dates back to approximately three thousand years ago. The first iteration of kimchi was made by simply salt-preserving native vegetables, such as *mu* (Korean radish), cucumber, and eggplant (aubergine). The addition of salt to raw vegetables softened the plant's fiber and that dehydrated it, transforming its texture. The salt also reduced the vegetal, grassy smell of raw plants, making it more delicious, naturally stimulating the salivary gland when eaten. The salt preservation prevented the growth of harmful bacteria and allowed the vegetables to be enjoyed over an extended period of time, a critical factor when food was scarce. However, the large amount of salt used in these first versions of kimchi was more akin to a salt-preserved vegetable than the enjoyable fermented *banchan* form of today.

**First to Ninth Centuries**

Between the first and ninth centuries, the preparation of kimchi evolved from dry-salting to brining in salt water. *Chimchae* was the name given to this method, loosely translating to "dipping vegetables in salt water." Through this change in method, the salt levels in the vegetables were reduced significantly. Importantly, this method also allowed an environment in which harmful bacteria growth was prevented but desirable microorganisms could thrive, introducing the method of fermentation to kimchi making. Fermentation opened the world to a new combination of sensations: sweetness, sourness, tanginess, and savory, all in one.

During the same period, ingredients began to be incorporated into the kimchi-making process, namely grains and *jang* (fermented soybean sauces). Grains accelerated the fermentation process, eliminated the unwanted bitter and vegetal taste of raw vegetables, and added natural sweetness. It further enhanced the clean, refreshing flavors of kimchi. The addition of *jang* to kimchi gave way to the production of amino acids in the vegetables, which enhanced its sweetness, depth, and freshness. It also further accelerated the fermentation process, ideal for the winter season's *kimjang* (the annual communal process of making kimchi).

**Ninth to Twelfth Centuries**

Between the ninth and twelfth centuries, through increased international trade, a great variety of foreign vegetables and spices were imported to Korea, marking yet another monumental moment in the evolution of kimchi. The introduction of vegetables such as watercress, chives, bamboo shoots, wax gourd, turnip, mustard green, scallion (spring onion), garlic, and ginger broadened the scope of kimchi greatly. New spices, such as pepper, *akane* (Sichuan pepper), and *chopi* (Japanese sanshō pepper), added complex aromas and flavors. The use of red flowers, like pasqueflower and cockscomb, visually enhanced kimchi with an appetizing red hue.

The introduction of aromatic plants and spices further extended the storage time of kimchi, and the incorporation of additional aromatic vegetables, such as garlic and ginger, began the tradition of creating a seasoning or stuffing for kimchi, instead of using only a simple brine and fermentation. This period is known as the beginning of the "seasoning culture" in kimchi.

**Thirteenth Century**

The thirteenth century marked when Chinese cabbage—which later evolved to be the Korean napa cabbage (Chinese leaf) of today—began to be imported to Korea. The earlier version of this cabbage was small, with thinner leaves that opened up widely, as opposed to the compact head of napa cabbage we are now accustomed to. It was also tough to chew, making it not ideal for consumption. Its initial use was mainly for medicinal purposes and was rarely used for kimchi or in cooking.

**Fifteenth Century**

In the fifteenth century, *jeotgal*, or fermented seafood, began to be used. Beginning with shrimp (prawn) *jeotgal*, it soon expanded to other *jeotgal*, such as croaker, anchovy, and more. Using fermented fish not only decreased the amount of salt used in kimchi, but also enriched its savory quality.

**Sixteenth to Nineteenth Centuries**

From the sixteenth to the nineteenth century, the evolution of kimchi continued, with the introduction of the chili pepper, further diversification of seasoning and fermentation ingredients. Red chili was first introduced in Korea in the sixteenth century, but it was only in the eighteenth century that it began to be used widely. The popularity of red chili made it the most popular kimchi ingredient, replacing other aromatic herbs and spices, such as black pepper and *akane*. Red chili enhanced the sweet and spicy flavor of kimchi and gave it its signature color.

**Twentieth Century**

By the twentieth century, the Chinese cabbage had been bred into a cabbage that was ideal in the Korean environment. It was named "full headed cabbage," paying homage to its large shape with full, compact layers of crunchy, sweet leaves. From that point on, the ideal qualities of the Korean napa cabbage made it the main ingredient used to make kimchi.

**Kimchi's "Seasoning Culture"**

From the start of kimchi's "seasoning culture" in the twelfth century to the height of its development in the nineteenth century, countless combinations of vegetables, chili, herbs, *jang*, and *jeotgal* led to the development of the recipes for modern kimchi. Seasoning recipes allowed for a wider variety of vegetables, such as the bitter dandelion, to be used as major kimchi ingredients. Today, the typical kimchi is red in color with a remarkable range of flavors: spicy, salty, sweet, fresh, and incredibly savory.

Kimchi became Korea's signature dish through more than three thousand years of constant changes and development. The diversification of ingredients, the development of fermentation techniques, and the evolution of seasoning skills enabled the customization of kimchi to suit anyone's taste.

Kimchi is a continuing case study in how generations of Koreans have sought the ideal way to enjoy delicious vegetables over a long period of time.

# Master Steps for Preparing Kimchi

There are a few guiding principles in making kimchi that will ensure the quality and taste. First is the main kimchi ingredient: Select an in-season vegetable for peak flavor, and adjust the method, the kimchi sauce, and the fermentation time according to the vegetable's characteristics. For example, there are many delicious vegetables available in the spring, including *bomdong* (spring napa cabbage), that have soft, fragrant leaves. These more tender spring vegetables should be made with just a little *jeotgal* (preserved seafood) and are suitable for short fermentation periods, or they can be made into *geotjeori* (Fresh Napa Cabbage Kimchi, page 62). Vegetables that are in season in fall and winter, including *mu* (Korean radish) and napa cabbage (Chinese leaf), have a firm texture that require it to be first brined. These vegetables are suitable for long-term fermentation, because they will not bruise or lose their texture over time. Below are the key steps to determine how to prepare any seasonal vegetable to make kimchi.

**Step 1: Select the Main Ingredient**

The first step in kimchi making is to choose the main ingredient, ideally a vegetable in season. Understanding the main ingredient, its texture, and its taste will determine the method and recipe.

The most common kimchi vegetables are napa cabbage (Chinese leaf), *mu* (Korean radish), and the Korean cucumber. Napa cabbage is the most well-known, its sweet and crunchy leaves setting the standard for kimchi. Korean radish is oval in shape and dense, with a sweet and spicy flavor that turns into a refreshing clean flavor after fermentation. The Korean cucumber has a very smooth texture and, compared to other countries' varieties, has thinner skin and fewer seeds.

**Step 2: Select the Fermentation Method**

Kimchi is unique in that recipes can be customized to suit personal taste. For example, tender vegetables can skip the fermentation process and be directly dressed with seasoning in the style of a salad. Tough, textured vegetables can be first salted or brined to transform texture and taste, to a state where the vegetables are susceptible to seasoning for a better-tasting kimchi, in which the flavors are married thoroughly.

**Step 3: Prepare the Condiment/Seasoning to Pair**

The seasoning of the kimchi will determine its final taste. Kimchi seasoning is made from a custom mix of aromatics, spices, herbs, fruits, *jeotgal*, *jang*, and grains. The seasoning mixture is customized to pair with the main vegetable.

The essential ingredients, which give kimchi its signature flavors, are:

**Gochugaru:** Korean red chilies are sun-dried whole and ground to this signature powder. Its dual sweet and spicy flavor profile is unique in the world and irreplaceable in the modern kimchi.

**Jang:** Made of fermented soybeans, *jang* has long been used for kimchi. The *jang* used to make kimchi is *cheongjang*, a clear soy sauce that is aged for less than one year, and has a light flavor and a translucent brown color. The amino acids in *cheongjang* gives kimchi a sweet, nutty taste.

**Jeotgal:** Korea is a country surrounded by ocean on three sides and has an abundance of seafood. The easy accessibility to seafood allowed Korean people to apply fermentation techniques to make *jeotgal*, the category of fermented seafood. *Jeotgal* is a great alternative to salt, because the proteins in the fish also adds to the umami quality of kimchi. The use of *jeotgal* also varies according to the region. In the south, where the temperatures are higher, more *jeotgal* is used, because its saltiness prevents the spoilage that may occur in warm weather; this results in a more savory kimchi.The north, on the other hand, tends to use minimal amounts of *jeotgal*, resulting in a smooth, clean, and refreshing kimchi. The two types of *jeotgal* that are most commonly used in Korea are *saeujeot* (salted shrimp) and *aekjeot* (Korean fish sauce, typically made with anchovies).

**Step 4: Fermentation**

Kimchi fermentation occurs without introducing any microorganisms to the process. It begins with the introduction of salt to the vegetable. This step allows slow salt absorption into the vegetable and brings out a deep and complex flavor, as well as a better texture.

After the seasoning is added, the kimchi is stored in a fermentation vessel. Traditionally, this was a lidded ceramic jar called an *onggi*, which was buried underground. Today, however, many people use large plastic purpose-built kimchi containers and specialized refrigerators instead. For proper fermentation, and the formation of the beneficial bacteria that help digestion, the kimchi needs to be stored between 65°–75°F (18°–24°C). This is followed by low-temperature fermentation, between 40°–55°F (5°–13°C), which is important when making kimchi for long-term storage.

# Napa Cabbage Kimchi
## Baechu Kimchi
## 배추김치

dF gF

The napa cabbage kimchi is one of the most iconic kimchis of Korea. It is typically made in fall or winter, when the napa cabbage is most delicious. When made in the winter, the brining time is 6–7 hours. In the summer, 3–4 hours is sufficient, however napa cabbage harvested in the summer is best prepared as the unfermented *baechu geotjeori* (Fresh Napa Cabbage Kimchi, page 62), because the softer texture is not ideal for fermented kimchi.

**Preparation time:** 1 hour, plus 7 hours brining time and 11–12 days fermentation
**Cooking time:** 10 minutes
**Makes:** 4½–5½ lb (2–2.5 kg)

**For the brined cabbage:**
1 large head napa cabbage/Chinese leaf (4½–5½ lb/2–2.5 kg)
1 cup (120 g) coarse sea salt

**For the rice slurry:**
1 tablespoon glutinous rice flour

**For the kimchi seasoning:**
½ cup (65 g) gochugaru (red chili flakes)
6 tablespoons minced garlic
1 tablespoon chopped fresh ginger
2 cups (16 fl oz/480 ml) Korean pear juice
1 tablespoon salted shrimp
3 tablespoons anchovy fish sauce
12 oz (350 g) mu (Korean radish), cut into 1½-inch (4 cm) matchsticks
3½ oz (100 g) onion, halved and thinly sliced
1¾ oz (50 g) scallions (spring onions), cut into 1½-inch (4 cm) lengths
1 oz (30 g) minari, cut into 1½-inch (4 cm) lengths

**Brine the cabbage:** Remove any damaged leaves from the cabbage. Make an incision 2 inches (5 cm) long at the base of the cabbage and pull the cabbage in half by tearing with your hands. With extra-large napa cabbage, cut into quarters.

In a bowl, stir to combine ½ cup (60 g) of the coarse salt with 4 cups (32 fl oz/950 ml) of water. Taking the halved cabbage, dip it into the salt water four times, making sure each leaf is evenly coated. Repeat for all. Sprinkle the remaining ½ cup (60 g) salt evenly over the cabbage, focusing on the thicker parts of the leaves and including the outer layers and the base.

Choose an airtight glass or ceramic container large enough to fit the kimchi with a small amount of breathing room at the top (to prevent overflow while fermentation occurs). Place the salted cabbage into the container cut-side up. Pour in the brine remaining in the bowl to cover. To prevent the cabbages from floating, set a heavier object, such as a water bottle, on the cabbage to keep it submerged.

Let the cabbage brine at room temperature for 6–7 hours. Check that the cabbage is sufficiently brined by gently bending the thickest part of the leaf; it should gently bend to the touch. Rinse the cabbage three times under cold running water, squeeze out excess water, and place the cabbage face down in a sieve to drain excess moisture. Discard the brine from the container.

**Make the rice slurry:** In a small saucepan, combine the glutinous rice flour and 1 cup (8 fl oz/240 ml) water and cook over medium heat, whisking constantly so that the flour does not clump. When bubbles begin to form, cook, while stirring, for another 3 minutes to form a slurry. Remove from the heat and let cool completely.

**Make the kimchi seasoning:** In a large bowl, combine the gochugaru, garlic, ginger, pear juice, salted shrimp, fish sauce, and cooled rice slurry and mix until evenly combined. Add the radish, onion, scallions, and minari and toss.

To assemble the kimchi, stuff each layer of the prepared cabbage with the kimchi seasoning mixture. After finishing each wedge, use the outermost leaf to enclose the cabbage and prevent the kimchi seasonings from escaping. Place the finished kimchi into the container with the cut-side facing up, pressing the cabbages down firmly so that there is no space left in the container. Pour any remaining kimchi seasoning over the pressed cabbages. Cover the surface of the kimchi with plastic wrap (cling film) to avoid contact with oxygen as much as possible and close the container. Let ferment at room temperature for 1–2 days and then move into the refrigerator for an additional 10 days.

The kimchi can be stored for more than 1 year if stored well in the refrigerator, as long as it prevented from coming into contact with oxygen as much as possible.

## Fresh Napa Cabbage Kimchi
### Baechu Geotjeori
### 배추겉절이

dF gF -30  [o]

*Baechu geotjeori* is a simple kimchi—made quickly and with a simple seasoning—for when napa cabbage (Chinese leaf) is out of season. It is usually made and enjoyed in the spring, when the soft spring cabbage is harvested, or in the summer heat, when this refreshing kimchi is best enjoyed. It goes well with noodles and is great as a salad along with meat dishes, such as pork ribs or *bulgogi*. In famous *kalguksu* (knife-cut noodles) restaurants in Korea, each restaurant has its signature *baechu geotjeori* to be enjoyed with noodles.

When making *geotjeori*, soft and not bitter vegetables—such as water parsley, oak leaf lettuce, and leek—are commonly used as the main ingredient. Sometimes fruits such as pears, apples, *yuja* (yuzu), and kumquat are added as well. Because this kimchi is not intended for long storage and should be enjoyed more like a salad, it's usually made in small quantities.

**Preparation time: 30 minutes**
**Makes: 14 oz (400 g)**

**For the vegetables:**
14 oz (400 g) napa cabbage (Chinese leaf)
2 scallions (spring onions)

**For the kimchi seasoning:**
4 teaspoons gochugaru (red chili flakes)
2½ teaspoons minced scallion (spring onion)
1 teaspoon minced garlic
¼ teaspoon ginger juice
1 teaspoon sugar
½ oz (12 g) salted shrimp

**For the garnish:**
½ teaspoon sesame seeds

**Prepare the vegetables:** Separate each napa cabbage leaf and cut into 1¼–1½-inch (3–4 cm) squares. Rinse the cut leaves in a sieve under cold running water and set aside. Trim the scallions and cut into 2½-inch (6 cm) lengths. Place the cabbage and scallion pieces in a large bowl.

**Make the kimchi seasoning:** In a small bowl, combine all the seasoning ingredients and mix until well incorporated.

Add the seasoning to the bowl of cabbage and mix well with your hands in a massaging motion, until the seasoning is well incorporated.

Plate and garnish with sesame seeds. Serve immediately, reserve at room temperature for about 1 day, or keep in the refrigerator for up to 1 week.

**Variation:** For a vegan version, substitute 2 teaspoons Yondu (Korean vegan seasoning sauce) or *cheongjang* (Korean light soy sauce) for the salted shrimp in the seasoning. Add 1 teaspoon of sesame oil when mixing with the vegetables.

## Cabbage Kimchi
### Yangbaechu Kimchi
### 양배추 김치

dF gF -30

Green cabbage kimchi can be made more quickly than the napa cabbage (Chinese leaf) kimchi. This cabbage kimchi is a great substitute when napa cabbage is hard to find or not in season.

**Preparation time: 15 minutes (plus optional 2–4 days fermentation)**
**Cooking time: 15 minutes**
**Makes: 14 oz (400 g)**

14 oz (400 g) green cabbage (about ¼ head)
1 oz (30 g) scallions (spring onions)
4 teaspoons gochugaru (red chili flakes)
½ oz (12 g) salted shrimp
1 teaspoon minced garlic
2½ teaspoons minced scallion (spring onion)
¼ teaspoon minced fresh ginger
1 teaspoon sugar

Remove any damaged outer leaves of the cabbage. Rinse the cabbage and cut into 1¼-inch (3 cm) chunks. Let drain in a sieve to remove any excess moisture. Cut the scallions into 2½-inch (6 cm) lengths.

In a large bowl, combine the gochugaru, salted shrimp, garlic, minced scallion, ginger, and sugar and mix until uniform. Add the cabbage and scallion pieces and toss until well incorporated.

Cabbage kimchi can be eaten as soon as it's made in the style of a side salad, or placed in an airtight container and fermented at room temperature for just 1 day, then moved to the refrigerator for 2–3 more days before enjoyed in its fermented form.

# White Kimchi
## Baek Kimchi
## 백김치

dF gF -3o

*Baek kimchi* translates to "white kimchi," and it's the perfect combination of the refreshing crunch of the napa cabbage (Chinese leaf) and the clear, acidic kimchi broth. The lack of spice in its refreshing broth makes it a universally beloved kimchi for all ages. The most important things in preparing this kimchi are making sure the brining process is thorough, and that there is enough liquid and to ensure that the cabbage is fully submerged.

Preparation time: 30 minutes, plus 7 hours brining and 5–7 days fermentation
Makes: 5½–6½ lb (2.5–3 kg)

**For the vegetables:**
4½–5½ lb (2–2.5 kg) napa cabbage (Chinese leaf)
1 lb (500 g) mu (Korean radish)
1¾ oz (50 g) scallions (spring onions)
1 oz (30 g) minari
3½ oz (100 g) onion

**For the brine:**
1 cup (120 g) coarse sea salt

**For the kimchi seasoning:**
7 oz (200 g) Asian pear, peeled and cut into chunks
3½ oz (100 g) onion, cut into chunks
5 tablespoons minced garlic
1 tablespoon chopped fresh ginger
1 tablespoon salted shrimp
2 tablespoons anchovy fish sauce

**Prepare the vegetables:** Create a 2-inch (5 cm) cut at the base of the napa cabbage and separate into two halves by tearing it apart with your hands. Cut the radish into 1½-inch (4 cm) matchsticks. Cut the scallions and minari into 1½-inch (4 cm) lengths. Halve and slice the onion.

**Make the brine:** In a bowl, combine ½ cup (60 g) of the salt and 4 cups (32 fl oz/950 ml) of water, dissolving fully. Take the halved napa cabbage and wash each layer with the salt water four times. Once washed, take the remaining ½ cup (60 g) salt and evenly salt the cabbage, sprinkling it over the thickest part of the cabbage leaves one by one. Place the salted cabbage into an airtight container, with the cut-sides up. Pour in the remaining salt water from the bowl. Place a weighted object, such as a water bottle, over the cabbage to submerge it fully as needed. Let brine at room temperature for 6–7 hours. Check that the cabbage is sufficiently brined by gently bending the thickest part of a leaf; it should gently bend to the touch. Rinse the brined cabbage three times under cold running water until the salt solution is rinsed off, squeeze out excess water, and place the cabbage face down in a sieve to drain. Discard the brine.

**Make the kimchi seasoning:** In a food processor, combine the pear, onion chunks, and 1 cup (8 fl oz/240 ml) water and blend until smooth. In a large bowl, combine the puree, garlic, ginger, salted shrimp, and fish sauce. Add the radish matchsticks, scallions, sliced onion, and minari to the mixture and toss to coat.

To make the kimchi, coat each napa cabbage leaf with the kimchi seasoning. Finish by wrapping with the outermost leaf around everything to prevent the kimchi seasonings from escaping. Repeat for all cabbage leaves. Choose an airtight glass or ceramic container large enough to fit the kimchi with a small amount of breathing room at the top (to prevent overflow while fermentation occurs). Place the stuffed cabbage with the cut-side facing up into the container. Cover with any remaining kimchi seasoning. Press to submerge the cabbage and to remove any air from the mixture. Cover the top with plastic wrap (cling film) to minimize air exposure, pressing out any space with your hands. Cover with lid.

Ferment at room temperature for 1–2 days. Move to the refrigerator for an additional 4–5 days before enjoying. The final kimchi will keep well for 2–3 months in the refrigerator.

**Variation:** For a vegan version, omit the salted shrimp and replace the anchovy fish sauce with Yondu (Korean vegan seasoning sauce).

# Water Kimchi
## Nabak Kimchi
## 나박김치

dF gF vg vE

*Nabak kimchi* is a broth-based kimchi made with napa cabbage and *mu* (Korean radish). While it is traditionally enjoyed in the springtime, it is a refreshing kimchi that can be enjoyed all year round.

**Preparation time:** 30 minutes, plus 5–6 days fermentation
**Makes:** 24 oz (680 g)

**For the vegetables:**
10 oz (300 g) mu (Korean radish)
1¾ oz (50 g) carrot
12 oz (350 g) napa cabbage (Chinese leaf)
1 oz (30 g) minari
½ oz (10 g) scallion (spring onion)
½ tablespoon coarse sea salt

**For the kimchi seasoning:**
2 oz (65 g) Asian pear, peeled
1¾ oz (50 g) fresh red chilies
2–3 cloves garlic, peeled
1 teaspoon minced fresh ginger
1 tablespoon gochugaru (red chili flakes)
2 tablespoons coarse sea salt

**Prepare the vegetables:** Peel the radish and carrot. Cut the radish, carrot, and cabbage into 1-inch (2.5 cm) squares that are 1/16 inch (2 mm) thick. Cut the minari and scallion into 1½-inch (4 cm) lengths. In a bowl, toss together the radish pieces and coarse salt and let brine for 10 minutes.

**Make the kimchi seasoning:** In a food processor, combine the pear, chilies, garlic, and ginger and blend until fine. Blend in the gochugaru, stirring until uniform. Place the mixture in either a muslin brew bag or square of fine cheesecloth, tying tightly so the ingredients don't spill out.

Choose an airtight glass or ceramic container large enough to fit the kimchi with a small amount of breathing room at the top (to prevent overflow while fermentation occurs). In the container, combine 7 cups (56 fl oz/1.7 liters) water and the salt and stir until dissolved. Add the bag of seasonings, the brined radish, and the rest of the vegetables. Close the container and let it ferment for 2 days at room temperature.

Remove the bag of seasonings, transfer to the refrigerator, and let ferment for an additional 3–4 days before it's ready to eat.

The nabak kimchi keeps well for about 2 weeks in the refrigerator.

# Young Summer Radish Kimchi
## Yeolmu Kimchi
## 열무김치

dF

*Yeolmu*, young radish, is only available in the summer, which is why this refreshing, crunchy *yeolmu* kimchi is symbolic of summer. The delicate, young radish breaks and bruises very easily during the kimchi-making process, which results in an unwanted grassy, vegetal flavor. Therefore, take care to minimize handling the ingredients during the process, tossing it more like a delicate salad instead of employing the more aggressive massaging technique used for kimchi made with sturdier vegetables, such as napa cabbage (Chinese leaf).

Instead of using all *gochugaru* (red chili flakes), *yeolmu kimchi* recipes use fresh red chili or whole dried red chilies to create a cleaner-tasting flavor to highlight the youthful *yeolmu* plant. While great as a side dish, this kimchi is more often used as part of a dish, often mixed directly into Spicy Bibimguksu (page 366) or *bibimbap* (mixed rice), especially Thick Doenjang Barley Bibimbap (page 107).

Preparation time: 30 minutes, plus 50 minutes brining and 2–3 days fermentation
Cooking time: 5 minutes
Makes: 2¼ lb (1 kg)

**For the brined yeolmu:**
2¼ lb (1 kg) yeolmu (young radish), cut into 2–2½-inch (5–6 cm) lengths
⅓ cup (40 g) coarse sea salt

**For the flour slurry:**
1 tablespoon all-purpose (plain) flour

**For the kimchi seasoning:**
12 fresh red chilies (about 10 oz/300 g total)
10 cloves garlic, peeled
1 teaspoon minced fresh ginger
14 oz (400 g) Asian pear, peeled, cored, and cut into chunks
1 tablespoon anchovy fish sauce
1 tablespoon coarse sea salt

**To assemble:**
3 oz (80 g) scallions (spring onions), cut into 2½-inch (6 cm) lengths
7 oz (200 g) onion, slivered
2 tablespoons gochugaru (red chili flakes)

**Brine the yeolmu:** In a large bowl, combine the yeolmu and coarse sea salt and mix gently. Brine for 20 minutes before mixing to reincorporate. Rinse gently under cold running water, repeating for three full washes. Transfer to a sieve to drain.

**Make the flour slurry:** In a small saucepan, combine 1 cup (8 fl oz/240 ml) water and the flour and whisk well to remove lumps. Set over medium-low heat and cook, stirring constantly. Once bubbling, cook for 3 minutes. Remove from the heat and let cool to room temperature.

**Make the kimchi seasoning:** In a food processor, combine the chilies, garlic, ginger, pear, fish sauce, and salt and blend until fine. If needed to get the mixture to blend, add 1 cup (8 fl oz/240 ml) water.

**Assemble the kimchi:** In a bowl large enough to hold the yeolmu and other ingredients, combine the brined yeolmu, flour slurry, blended kimchi seasoning, scallions, onion, gochugaru, and 2 cups (16 fl oz/480 ml) water (if no water was used to blend the seasonings, add another 1 cup/8 fl oz/240 ml) and toss gently until uniform.

Choose an airtight glass or ceramic container large enough to fit the kimchi with a small amount of breathing room at the top (to prevent overflow while fermentation occurs). Transfer the mixture to the container and cover the surface of the kimchi with plastic wrap (cling film), pressing out any excess air. Cover with a lid and ferment at room temperature for 2–3 days. Move to the refrigerator to keep cold. It is ready to eat and can be kept refrigerated for up to 2 months.

**Variation:** Versions of *yeolmu* kimchi include some napa cabbage. This combination of the fresh, crunchy young radish with the more savory, sweet flavors of napa can be a great balanced combination.

# Diced Radish Kimchi
## Kkakdugi
## 깍두기

dF gF

*Kkakdugi*, a kimchi made from diced *mu* (Korean radish), is most commonly and easily made in the winter when *mu* is in season and has an especially sweet flavor and crunchy texture.

Preparation time: 30 minutes, plus 6–8 days fermentation
Cooking time: 5 minutes
Makes: 2¼ lb (1 kg)

**For the vegetables:**
2¼ lb (1 kg) mu (Korean radish)
2 oz (60 g) scallions (spring onions)

**For the rice slurry:**
½ tablespoon glutinous rice flour

**For the kimchi seasoning:**
1¾ oz (50 g) onion, cut into chunks
2 tablespoons minced garlic
1 teaspoon minced fresh ginger
3 tablespoons salted shrimp
2 tablespoons anchovy fish sauce
4 tablespoons gochugaru (red chili flakes)
½ tablespoon coarse sea salt

**Prepare the vegetables:** Peel the radish and cut into ¾-inch (2 cm) cubes. Cut the scallions into 1½-inch (4 cm) lengths.

**Make the rice slurry:** In a small saucepan, combine ½ cup (4 fl oz/120 ml) water and the glutinous rice flour and cook over medium heat, whisking constantly so that the flour does not clump. Once bubbling, cook for another 3 minutes while stirring to form a slurry. Remove from the heat and let cool completely.

**Make the kimchi seasoning:** In a food processor, combine the onion, garlic, ginger, salted shrimp, and fish sauce and blend until uniform.

In a large bowl, combine the radish cubes, rice slurry, the pureed seasoning, gochugaru, and salt and toss until well combined. Add the scallions and mix well.

Transfer the mixture to a large airtight nonreactive container (it needs to be large enough to account for expansion during fermentation). Cover the top of the ingredients with plastic wrap (cling film) to reduce exposure to oxygen, and close the lid. Let ferment at room temperature for 2–3 days. Move to the refrigerator for another 4–5 days. It is ready to serve and can be stored for up to 2 months.

# Radish & Yellow Pepper Kimchi
## Mu & Yellow Pepper Seokbakji
## 무 & 노란 파프리카 섞박지

dF

*Seokbakji* is a type of radish kimchi, but unlike for the *kkakdugi* (Diced Radish Kimchi, page 68), the radish in *seokbakji* does not need to be cut in a uniform size. Strictly speaking, for a classic *seokbakji*, the radish would be cut freeform at an angle, similar to how one would sharpen a pencil with a knife. *Seokbakji* is often seen at restaurants that sell *seolleongtang* (Ox Bone Tang, page 335) and *gomtang* (Beef Bone Tang, page 334), because it usually has a slightly sweeter flavor than *kkakdugi*, with a more refreshing, watery base. It's typically made with *gochugaru*, but in this version pureed yellow bell pepper is used instead. The yellow in this kimchi will brighten up a table.

Preparation time: 30 minutes, plus 6–8 days fermentation
Cooking time: 5 minutes
Makes: 2¼ lb (1 kg)

For the vegetables:
2¼ lb (1 kg) mu (Korean radish)
2 oz (60 g) scallions (spring onions)
2½ oz (75 g) fresh green Cheongyang chilies

For the flour slurry:
1 tablespoon all-purpose (plain) flour

For the kimchi seasoning:
1¾ oz (50 g) garlic, peeled
3½ oz (100 g) onion, cut into chunks
7 oz (200 g) Asian pear, peeled and cut into chunks
2 tablespoons salted shrimp
2 teaspoons coarse sea salt
5½ oz (160 g) yellow bell pepper, seeded and cut into chunks

**Prepare the vegetables:** Peel the radish and cut either on a diagonal into slices 2½ inches (6 cm) long, or into disks ¾ inch (2 cm) thick and then each slice into 6 equal parts. Cut the scallions into 1½-inch (4 cm) lengths. Cut the chilies into ¾-inch (2 cm) lengths.

**Make the flour slurry:** In a small saucepan, combine 1 cup (8 fl oz/240 ml) water and the flour and whisk well to remove lumps. Set over medium-low heat and cook, stirring constantly. Once bubbling, cook for 3 more minutes. Remove from the heat and let cool to room temperature.

**Make the kimchi seasoning:** In a food processor, combine the garlic, onion, pear, salted shrimp, salt, and 1 cup (8 fl oz/240 ml) water and blend until fine. Transfer to a bowl and set aside. Add the yellow pepper to the blender with 1 cup (8 fl oz/240 ml) water and blend until fine. Add the pureed pepper to the bowl along with the cooled flour slurry, and mix until uniform.

Choose an airtight glass or ceramic container large enough to fit the kimchi with a small amount of breathing room at the top (to prevent overflow while fermentation occurs). Add the radish, scallions, and chilies along with the kimchi seasoning and mix until uniformly coated. Close the container and let ferment at room temperature for 2–3 days. Transfer to the refrigerator and ferment for 4–5 more days until ready to eat. It can be stored in the refrigerator for up to 2 months.

# Radish & Green Chili Kimchi
## Mu & Cheongyang Gochu Seokbakji
## 무 & 청양 고추 섞박지

dF

Although the use of *gochugaru*, the signature red chili powder, in kimchi is iconic (and Korea's history of using it dates back to the seventeenth century), kimchi does not have to be red. This recipe provides a modern recipe for green *mu* kimchi, using pureed fresh green Cheongyang chilies.

Preparation time: 20 minutes, plus 6–8 days fermentation
Cooking time: 5 minutes
Makes: 2¼ lb (1 kg)

For the vegetables:
2¼ lb (1 kg) mu (Korean radish)
2 oz (60 g) scallions (spring onions)

For the flour slurry:
1 tablespoon all-purpose (plain) flour

For the kimchi seasoning:
6 cloves garlic, peeled
3½ oz (100 g) onion, cut into chunks
7 oz (200 g) Asian pear, peeled and cut into chunks
2 tablespoons salted shrimp
1 teaspoon coarse sea salt
3½ oz (100 g) fresh green Cheongyang chilies

**Prepare the vegetables:** Peel the radish and cut either on a diagonal into slices 2½ inches (6 cm) long, or into disks ¾ inch (2 cm) thick and then each slice into 6 equal parts. Cut the scallions into 1½-inch (4 cm) lengths.

**Make the flour slurry:** In a small saucepan, combine 1 cup (8 fl oz/ 240 ml) water and the flour and whisk well to remove lumps. Set over medium-low heat and cook, stirring constantly. Once bubbling, cook for 3 more minutes. Remove from the heat and let cool to room temperature.

**Make the kimchi seasoning:** In a food processor, combine the garlic, onion, pear, salted shrimp, salt, and 1 cup (8 fl oz/240 ml) water and blend until fine. Transfer to a bowl and set aside. Add the chilies and 1 cup (8 fl oz/240 ml) water to the processor and coarsely blend. Add the pureed chilies to the bowl along with the cooled flour slurry and mix until uniform.

Choose an airtight glass or ceramic container large enough to fit the kimchi with a small amount of breathing room at the top (to prevent overflow while fermentation occurs). Add the radish, scallions, and kimchi seasoning and mix until uniformly coated. Close the container and let ferment at room temperature for 2–3 days. Move to the refrigerator to ferment for 4–5 more days until ready to eat. It can be stored in the refrigerator for up to 2 months.

# Radish Water Kimchi
## Dongchimi
## 동치미

dF gF vg vE

*Dongchimi* is a type of water kimchi made in the winter, when the Korean radish is at the height of its flavor and texture. Traditionally, *dongchimi* is made by first salt brining the whole *mu* radish, but many home cooks today skip this time-intensive process in favor of a modernized version, as showcased here. The distinctive broth of the kimchi is effervescent with a bright, acidic flavor that earns its nickname as Korea's "sprite" kimchi. The addictive broth is often used as a base broth for many cold noodle dishes, such as Pyongyang-Style Cold Buckwheat Guksu (page 373).

**Preparation time:** 30 minutes, plus 1 hour brining and 10–11 days fermentation
**Makes:** 4 lb (1.8 kg)

2¼ lb (1 kg) mu (Korean radish)
4 tablespoons coarse sea salt
9½ oz (270 g) onion, cut into 8 equal pieces
1 lb 5 oz (600 g) Asian pear, cut into 16 even pieces
1 oz (30 g) daepa (Korean scallion), halved
5 scallions (spring onions), cut into 2½-inch (6 cm) length
1 oz (30 g) garlic, thinly sliced
½ oz (10 g) fresh ginger, thinly sliced
2 fermented peppers (optional)

Cut the radish into thick sticks 2 inches (5 cm) long and 1 inch (2.5 cm) thick. Choose an airtight glass or ceramic container large enough to fit the kimchi with a small amount of breathing room at the top (to prevent overflow while fermentation occurs). Combine the radish and salt and brine for 1 hour.

Add 8½ cups (68 fl oz/2 liters) water, the onion, pear, daepa, scallions, garlic, ginger, and fermented peppers (if using) and seal. Ferment at room temperature for 3–4 days. Move to the refrigerator for an additional 7 days. Keep it refrigerated. It can be enjoyed for up to 6 months.

**Variations**

• In place of fermented peppers, you can any vinegar-pickled peppers.

• For a more savory flavor, use a cold light fish broth in place of the water.

# Vegan Jang Kimchi
## 장김치

df vg vE

*Jang kimchi* is a special type of kimchi seasoned with *ganjang* (Korean soy sauce) instead of *jeotgal* (salted seafood). In Korea's history of kimchi, *jeotgal* began to be used in kimchi making after the fifteenth century. Prior to that, kimchi was made using only salt and *ganjang*. The *ganjang* imparts a rich, savory flavor, distinct from the ones made from jeotgal. While it's less common than its counterpart, *jang* kimchi can be found at temples and at kimchi specialty restaurants or stores.

Preparation time: 1 hour, plus 1 hour brining time and 11–12 days fermentation
Cooking time: 20 minutes
Makes: 5½ lb (2.5 kg)

**For the vegetables:**
4½ lb (2 kg) napa cabbage (Chinese leaf)
12 oz (350 g) mu (Korean radish)
1¾ oz (50 g) scallions (spring onions)
1 oz (30 g) minari
3½ oz (100 g) onion

**For the brine:**
1 cup (120 g) coarse sea salt

**For the dasima rice slurry:**
¼ oz (5 g) dasima
1 tablespoon glutinous rice flour

**For the kimchi seasoning:**
½ cup (65 g) gochugaru (red chili flakes)
6 tablespoons minced garlic
1 tablespoon minced fresh ginger
2 cups (16 fl oz/480 ml) Korean pear juice
5 tablespoons Yondu (Korean vegan seasoning sauce) or cheongjang (Korean light soy sauce)
1 tablespoon coarse sea salt

**Prepare the vegetables:** Cut a 2-inch (5 cm) length incision at the base of the napa cabbage and tear the cabbage in half with your hands. With extra-large napa cabbage, cut into quarters. Cut the radish into 1½-inch (4 cm) matchsticks. Cut the scallions and minari into 1½-inch (4 cm) lengths. Halve and thinly slice the onion.

**Make the brine:** In a large bowl, combine 4 cups (32 fl oz/950 ml) water with ½ cup (60 g) of coarse salt. Taking the halved cabbage, dip it into the salt water four times, making sure each leaf is evenly coated. Repeat for all. Sprinkle the remaining ½ cup (60 g) salt evenly, focusing on the thicker parts of the leaves, including the outer layers and the base.

Choose an airtight glass or ceramic container large enough to fit the kimchi with a small amount of breathing room at the top (to prevent overflow while fermentation occurs). Place the salted cabbage into the container cut-side up. Pour in the remaining brine to cover. If the cabbage floats, place a heavy object, such as a water bottle, over the cabbage to keep it submerged. Let brine at room temperature for 6–7 hours. Check that the cabbage is sufficiently brined by gently bending the thickest part of the leaf; it should gently bend to the touch. Rinse the cabbage three times under cold running water, squeeze out excess water, and place the cabbage face down in a sieve to drain excess moisture. Discard the brine.

**Make the dasima rice slurry:** In a small saucepan, combine the dasima and 1 cup (8 fl oz/240 ml) and bring to a boil over high heat. Remove from the heat and let sit for 15 minutes. Discard the dasima and let the broth cool. Add the glutinous rice flour to the broth and cook over medium heat, whisking constantly to get rid of lumps. Once bubbling, cook for 3 minutes while stirring. Remove from the heat and let cool completely.

**Make the kimchi seasoning:** In a large bowl, combine the radish matchsticks, scallions, minari, onion, and gochugaru and toss to coat. Add the garlic, ginger, pear juice, Yondu, sea salt, and cooled dasima rice slurry and combine until uniform.

To assemble the kimchi, stuff each layer of the cabbage with the kimchi seasoning. Wrap the cabbage with the outermost leaf to prevent the kimchi seasonings from leaking. Place the finished kimchi in the airtight container with the cut-side up, pressing the cabbages down firmly so that there is no space left in the container. Pour any leftover kimchi seasoning on top. Cover the surface of the kimchi with plastic wrap (cling film) to avoid contact with oxygen and close the container. Let ferment at room temperature for 1–2 days. Move to the refrigerator for an additional 10 days. Kimchi can be stored for more than 1 year if stored well in the refrigerator.

# Stuffed Cucumber Kimchi
## Oi Sobagi
## 오이 소박이

dF

The cucumber is perhaps the quintessential summer vegetable of Korea. The crunchy, refreshing cucumber is perfect for quick kimchi that can be eaten more like a salad, without a long fermentation period. This kimchi is best made with small cucumbers with fewer seeds, because the soft, seedy portion of larger cucumbers is unfit for fermenting. If using larger cucumbers, remove the seeds and softer flesh.

**Preparation time:** 30 minutes, plus 20 minutes brining and 1–2 days fermentation
**Cooking time:** 5 minutes
**Makes:** 1 lb 5 oz (600 g)

1 lb 5 oz (600 g) small cucumbers, such as pickling cucumbers
1 tablespoon coarse sea salt

**For the flour slurry:**
1 tablespoon all-purpose (plain) flour

**For the kimchi seasoning:**
7 oz (200 g) Asian pear, peeled and cut into chunks
½ tablespoons salted shrimp
½ tablespoon anchovy fish sauce
1 tablespoon minced garlic
1 teaspoon minced fresh ginger

**For the kimchi stuffing:**
4 tablespoons gochugaru (red chili flakes)
1 oz (30 g) garlic chives, cut into ¾-inch (2 cm) lengths
1 scallion (spring onion), cut into ¾-inch (2 cm) lengths
1¾ oz (50 g) onion, slivered
1 tablespoon coarse sea salt

Stopping ⅜ inch (1 cm) short of the far end so the cucumber remains intact, slice the cucumbers lengthwise in half, then rotate the cucumber and make another lengthwise slice at right angles to the first slice. (Alternatively, quarter the cucumbers lengthwise, and trim to 2½-inch (6 cm) lengths.) In a bowl, combine the cucumbers with the salt and toss until well combined. Brine for 20 minutes. Wash the cucumbers under cold running water and set aside in a sieve to drain off excess moisture.

**Make the flour slurry:** In a small saucepan, combine ½ cup (4 fl oz/120 ml) water and the flour and whisk well to remove any lumps. Set over medium-low heat and cook, stirring constantly. Once bubbling, cook for 3 more minutes. Remove from the heat and let cool to room temperature.

**Make the kimchi seasoning:** In a food processor, combine the pear, salted shrimp, fish sauce, garlic, ginger, and ½ cup (4 fl oz/120 ml) water and blend until fine.

**Make the stuffing:** In a large bowl, combine the pureed seasonings, the gochugaru, chives, scallion, slivered onion, sea salt, and cooled flour slurry and mix well until uniform.

If the cucumbers have been cut into pieces, toss directly with the seasoning. If they have been kept intact, stuff the cross section with the seasoning until full. Choose an airtight glass or ceramic container large enough to fit the cucumbers with a small amount of breathing room at the top (to prevent overflow while fermentation occurs). Place the cucumbers in the container and cover with any remaining seasoning. Cover the surface directly with plastic wrap (cling film), pushing out any excess air. Cover the container and ferment at room temperature for 12 hours or store directly in the refrigerator. After 1–2 days, it's ready to eat and can be stored in the refrigerator for up to 2 weeks.

# Cucumber Water Kimchi
## Oi Mul-Kimchi
## 오이 물김치

dF

**Preparation time:** 30 minutes, plus 30 minutes brining and 3–4 days fermentation
**Cooking time:** 10 minutes
**Makes:** 1½–1¾ lb (700–800 g)

**For the brined cucumber:**
1½–1¾ lb (700–800 g) small cucumbers
Generous ½ cup (70 g) coarse sea salt

**For the flour slurry:**
2 teaspoons all-purpose (plain) flour

**For the kimchi stuffing:**
3½ oz (100 g) mu (Korean radish)
¼ teaspoon salt
1 oz (25 g) fresh red chilies
1 small thin scallion (spring onion), cut into 1½-inch (4 cm) lengths
½ oz (10 g) garlic chives, cut into 1½-inch (4 cm) lengths

**For the kimchi seasoning:**
14 oz (400 g) Asian pear, peeled, cored, and cut into chunks
3½ oz (100 g) onion, cut into chunks
1 tablespoon anchovy fish sauce
1 teaspoon minced garlic
½ teaspoon ginger juice
1 tablespoon coarse sea salt

*Oi mul-kimchi*, cucumber water kimchi, is a light summer kimchi with crispy cucumber and a refreshing broth.

**Brine the cucumbers:** Stopping ⅜ inch (1 cm) short of the far end so the cucumber remains intact, slice the cucumbers lengthwise in half, then rotate the cucumber and make another lengthwise slice at right angles to the first slice. (Alternatively, quarter the cucumbers lengthwise, and trim to 2½-inch/6 cm lengths.) Set aside in a heatproof container.

In a small pot, combine 3 cups (24 fl oz/710 ml) water and the salt and bring to a boil. Pour the boiling brine over the prepared cucumbers and let brine for 30 minutes. Wash the cucumbers under cold running water, then transfer to a sieve to drain.

**Make the flour slurry:** In a small saucepan, combine 3 cups (24 fl oz/710 ml) water and the flour and whisk well to remove lumps. Set over medium-low heat and cook, stirring constantly. Once bubbling, cook for 3 more minutes. Remove from the heat and let cool to room temperature.

**Prepare the kimchi stuffing:** Slice the radish into matchsticks 1½ inches (4 cm) long about ¹⁄₁₆ inch (2 mm) thick on a mandoline or using a knife. Toss in a bowl with the salt and lightly brine for 10 minutes.

Halve the chilies lengthwise and remove all seeds, then cut into thin diagonal slices of about ¹⁄₁₆ inch (2 mm) thick. Add the chilies, scallion, and chives to the brined radish and toss until well combined.

**Make the kimchi seasoning:** In a food processor, combine the pear, onion, fish sauce, garlic, ginger juice, and salt and blend until fine.

Add the pureed seasoning to the radish mixture along with the flour slurry and mix until uniform.

If the cucumbers have been cut into pieces, toss directly with the seasoning. If they have been kept intact, stuff the cross section with the seasoning until full.

Choose an airtight glass or ceramic container large enough to fit the cucumbers with a small amount of breathing room at the top (to prevent overflow while fermentation occurs). Place the cucumbers in the container and cover with any remaining seasoning. Cover the surface directly with plastic wrap (cling film), pushing out any excess air. Cover with a lid and ferment at room temperature for 1 day. Move into the refrigerator to ferment for 2–3 days. Finished kimchi keeps in the refrigerator for up to 1 month.

# Onion Kimchi
## Yangpa Kimchi
## 양파김치

dF gF

Onion kimchi is best when made with the first harvest of onions in the springtime, when the onions are less pungent and have a mild, sweet taste. Onion kimchi pairs particularly well with grilled pork belly.

**Preparation time:** 30 minutes, plus 30 minutes brining and 6 days fermentation
**Cooking time:** 5 minutes
**Makes:** 3 lb (1.4 kg)

**For the vegetables:**
2¼ lb (1 kg) onions
7 oz (200 g) mu (Korean radish)
¾ oz 20 g) garlic chives
¾ teaspoon salt

**For the brine:**
½ cup (60 g) coarse sea salt

**For the rice slurry:**
½ tablespoon glutinous rice flour

**For the kimchi seasoning:**
7 oz (200 g) Asian pear, peeled and cut into chunks
½ tablespoon salted shrimp
½ tablespoon anchovy fish sauce
1 tablespoon minced garlic
1 teaspoon minced fresh ginger
4 tablespoons gochugaru (red chili flakes)

**Prepare the vegetables:** Peel the onions and rinse under cold water. Set the root end of the onions down and cut down into the onions two-thirds of the way through, dividing them into 6–8 equal parts (like cutting a pie), keeping the onions intact. Cut the radish into 1½-inch (4 cm) matchsticks. Cut the chives into ¾-inch (2 cm) lengths.

In a small bowl, toss the radish with the salt and set aside.

**Make the brine:** In a large bowl, combine the coarse salt and 5 cups (40 fl oz/1.2 liters) water and stir until dissolved. Add the onions and brine for 30 minutes. Rinse under cold running water and let drain in a sieve.

**Make the rice slurry:** In a small saucepan, combine the glutinous rice flour and ½ cup (4 fl oz/120 ml) water and cook over medium heat, whisking constantly so that the flour does not clump. When bubbles begin to form, cook, stirring, for another 3 minutes to form a slurry. Remove from the heat and let cool completely.

**Make the kimchi seasoning:** In a food processor, combine the pear, salted shrimp, fish sauce, garlic, ginger, and ½ cup (4 fl oz/120 ml) water and blend until uniform. Pour into a large bowl, and combine with the rice slurry, gochugaru, chives, and salted radish and toss until uniform.

Stuff each onion with equal amounts of the kimchi seasoning mix. Choose an airtight glass or ceramic container large enough to fit the kimchi with a small amount of breathing room at the top (to prevent overflow while fermentation occurs). Place the onion in the container. Scrape any leftover kimchi seasoning over the onions and cover the surface with plastic wrap (cling film). Close the lid and let ferment at room temperature for 1 day. Move to the refrigerator to ferment for 5 more days. Onion kimchi will keep well for up to 6 months in the refrigerator.

# 장아찌 Jangajji Fermented Vegetables in Jang

*Jangajji* are one of Korea's most important fermentation and preservation foods, in which a whole host ingredients from both land and sea are preserved in *jang*. *Ganjang* (Korean soy sauce), *doenjang* (fermented soybean paste), and *gochujang* (red chili paste) are all used in varying combinations with *jeotgal* (preserved seafood), vinegars, and other special Korean products to create unique flavors. Like kimchi, *jangajji* is a great way to experience vegetables in a distinctly Korean way, its flavors and textures transformed by Korean *jang*. There are two categories of *jangajji*: salt-preserved or cooked.

Salt-preserved *jangajji* is prepared by salting the ingredients or drying them in the sun before combining them with the *jang*, *jeot* (preserved seafood), or vinegar.

Cooked *jangajji*, called *suk-jangajji*, is made by stir-frying pickled vegetables or simmering vegetables in soy sauce. Compared to salt-preserved *jangajji*, it has a shorter storage period. It is also called *"gapjang"-gwa* or *"gap"-jangajji,* borrowing the term *gap*, meaning "sudden," because it can be quickly made.

The biggest appeal of *jangajji* is its texture. Different from the crispy, snappy texture of raw or pickled vegetables, the unique crunch of *jangajji* comes from the osmotic process of the vegetables losing moisture while the *jang*-based liquid is absorbed. Especially in the case of cucumbers and radishes, the resulting texture is unique, and the savory *jang* flavors combined with the vegetables give birth to a whole new taste experience.

*Jangajji* are usually enjoyed as a *banchan* (side dish) for rice, but they also pair very well with Korean grilled meat dishes and oily dishes, such as fritters, to cut the richness and fat, while adding flavor and textural components.

The *jangajji* liquid remaining after a *jangajji* has been enjoyed can be boiled once and repurposed in many ways, including as a dipping sauce for deep-fried foods or used as a seasoning sauce for cold noodles.

# Onion Jangajji
## Yangpa Jangajji
## 양파 장아찌

dF vg vE -S

Onion *jangajji* is the most fundamental and popular *jangajji*, and it is also easy to make. It pairs well with all meat dishes and is a common basic *banchan* (side dish) in many restaurants.

**Preparation time: 20 minutes, plus 1–2 days marinating time**
**Cooking time: 15 minutes**
**Makes: 2¼ lb (1 kg)**

2¼ lb (1 kg) onions

**For the jangajji brine:**
2 cups (16 fl oz/480 ml) ganjang (Korean soy sauce)
1 cup (200 g) sugar
½ oz (15 g) dasima (optional)
2 dried shiitake mushrooms (optional)
1 cup (8 fl oz/240 ml) rice vinegar

Peel the onions, halve them, and cut each half into 6 equal wedges. Let dry completely.

**Meanwhile, make the jangajji brine:** In a small pot, combine the soy sauce, 2 cups (16 fl oz/480 ml) water, the sugar, dasima (if using), and shiitakes (if using) and bring to a boil. Add the vinegar and bring back to a boil. Remove from the heat, discard the dasima, and let cool completely. Once completely cool, remove and discard the shiitakes.

Place the onions and cooled brine in an airtight glass or ceramic container large enough to fit them with a small amount of headroom. Close the container and set in the refrigerator for 1–2 days before enjoying.

**Variation:** Add 2–3 sliced fresh chilies to the cooled *jangajji* brine to bring the chili fragrance to the dish.

# Garlic Jangajji
## Maneul Jangajji
## 마늘 장아찌

dF vg vE -S

Garlic *jangajji* is best when made in the springtime, when garlic bulbs are harvested. If intending to preserve for a long time, it is best to use whole garlic with the peel intact. For a quick version, peel and separate each clove. Poking two or three holes in each garlic with a toothpick (cocktail stick) will also speed up the ferment, making it ready to eat in 1 week.

**Preparation time: 20 minutes, plus 30 days fermentation**
**Cooking time: 15 minutes**
**Makes: 5½ oz (160g)**

8 heads garlic

**For the jangajji brine:**
2 cups (16 fl oz/480 ml) ganjang (Korean soy sauce)
1 cup (200 g) sugar
½ oz (15 g) dasima (optional)
2 dried shiitake mushrooms (optional)
1 cup (16 fl oz/480 ml) rice vinegar

Remove all outer skin of the garlic heads, leaving them intact, and run under cold water. Slice each head of garlic in half horizontally and dry off any excess water.

**Make the jangajji brine:** In a small pot, combine the soy sauce, 2 cups (16 fl oz/480 ml) water, the sugar, dasima (if using), and shiitakes (if using) and bring to a boil. Add the vinegar and bring back to a boil. Remove from the heat, discard the dasima, and let cool completely. Once cool, remove and discard the shiitakes.

Place the garlic and cooled brine in an airtight glass or ceramic container large enough to fit them with a small amount of headroom. Close the container and set in the refrigerator for 30 days.

# Radish Jangajji
## Mu Jangajji
## 무 장아찌

The thinly sliced *mu jangajji* can be used as a *ssam* (wrap), and it's commonly enjoyed with grilled pork belly. For a slight flavor twist, add some lemon zest for a brighter, citrus profile.

dF vg vE -S

**Preparation time:** 20 minutes, plus 1–4 days fermentation (depending on shape)
**Cooking time:** 15 minutes
**Makes:** 1½ lb (700 g)

1 mu (Korean radish; about 1½ lb/700 g)

**For the jangajji brine:**
2 cups (16 fl oz/480 ml) ganjang (Korean soy sauce)
1 cup (200 g) sugar
½ oz (15 g) dasima (optional)
2 dried shiitake mushrooms (optional)
1 cup (8 fl oz/240 ml) rice vinegar

Peel the radish and using a mandoline, slice either crosswise into ⅛-inch (3 mm) thick disks, or cut into sticks 2½ inches (6 cm) long and ½ inch (1.5 cm) thick.

**Make the jangajji brine:** In a small pot, combine the soy sauce, 2 cups (16 fl oz/480 ml) water, the sugar, dasima (if using), and shiitakes (if using) and bring to a boil. Add the vinegar and return to a boil. Remove from the heat, discard the dasima, and let cool completely. Once cool, remove and discard the shiitakes.

Place the radish and cooled brine in an airtight glass or ceramic container large enough to fit them with a small amount of headroom. Close the container and set in the refrigerator. The thinly sliced disk shapes will be ready to eat in 1–2 days; the stick shapes will require 3–4 days.

---

# Cucumber Jangajji
## Oi Jangajji
## 오이 장아찌

Cucumber *jangajji* is the iconic summer *jangajji*, and its crunchy texture makes it a delight to eat.

dF vg vE -S

**Preparation time:** 20 minutes, plus 1–2 days fermentation
**Cooking time:** 15 minutes
**Makes:** 1 lb 5 oz (600 g)

1 lb 5 oz (600 g) cucumbers

**For the jangajji brine:**
2 cups (16 fl oz/480 ml) ganjang (Korean soy sauce)
1 cup (200 g) sugar
½ oz (15 g) dasima (optional)
2 dried shiitake mushrooms (optional)
1 cup (8 fl oz/240 ml) rice vinegar

Halve the cucumbers lengthwise and scoop out the seedy core. For any cucumbers with small or very few seeds, this step can be omitted. Cut into 2½-inch (6 cm) lengths.

**Make the jangajji brine:** In a small pot, combine the soy sauce, 2 cups (16 fl oz/480 ml) water, the sugar, dasima (if using), and shiitakes (if using) and bring to a boil. Add the vinegar and return to a boil. Remove from the heat, discard the dasima, and let cool completely. Once cool, remove and discard the shiitakes.

Place the cucumber pieces and cooled brine in an airtight glass or ceramic container large enough to fit them with a small amount of headroom. Close the container and set in the refrigerator for 1–2 days before enjoying.

## Green Chili Pepper Jangajji
Put Gochu Jangajji
풋고추 장아찌

dF vg vE -S

When making fresh chili pepper *jangajji*, it's important to use taut, young green chilies with a pleasant crunchy texture. Ripe red chili peppers are too soft to be used to make *jangajji*.

**Preparation time:** 20 minutes, plus 2–7 days fermentation (depending on size)
**Cooking time:** 15 minutes
**Makes:** 7 oz (200 g)

7 oz (200 g) fresh green chili peppers

**For the jangajji brine:**
1 cup (8 fl oz/240 ml) ganjang (Korean soy sauce)
½ cup (100 g) sugar
¼ oz (5 g) dasima (optional)
1 dried shiitake mushroom (optional)
½ cup (4 fl oz/120 ml) rice vinegar

If using whole chilies, puncture each pepper two or three times with a fork. Otherwise, the pepper can be cut on a diagonal into slices ⅜ inch (1 cm) wide.

**Make the jangajji brine:** In a small pot, combine the soy sauce, 1 cup (8 fl oz/240 ml) water, the sugar, dasima (if using), and shiitake (if using) and bring to a boil. Add the vinegar and return to a boil. Remove from the heat, discard the dasima, and let cool completely. Once cool, remove and discard the shiitake.

Place the chilies and cooled brine in an airtight glass or ceramic container large enough to fit them with a small amount of headroom. Close the container and set in the refrigerator. If sliced, the chilies can be enjoyed in 2–3 days, and if left whole, they can be enjoyed in 7 days.

**Variation:** Adding 2 strips of lemon zest will impart a nice citrus flavor.

---

## Green Tomato Jangajji
그린토마토 장아찌

dF vg vE -S

You can use very firm cherry tomatoes (left whole) in place of the green tomatoes. Softer tomatoes will result in undesirable texture.

**Preparation time:** 20 minutes, plus 4 days fermentation
**Cooking time:** 15 minutes
**Makes:** 2¼ lb (1 kg)

4 green tomatoes

**For the jangajji brine:**
2 cups (16 fl oz/480 ml) ganjang (Korean soy sauce)
1 cup (200 g) sugar
½ oz (15 g) dasima (optional)
2 dried shiitake mushrooms (optional)
1 cup (8 fl oz/240 ml) rice vinegar

Cut each tomato into 6–8 wedges.

**Make the jangajji brine:** In a small pot, combine the soy sauce, 2 cups (16 fl oz/480 ml) water, the sugar, dasima (if using), and shiitakes (if using) and bring to a boil. Add the vinegar and return to a boil. Remove from the heat, discard the dasima, and let cool completely. Once cool, remove and discard the shiitakes.

Place the tomatoes and cooled brine in an airtight glass or ceramic container large enough to fit them with a small amount of headroom. Close the container and set in the refrigerator for 4 days.

## Cauliflower Jangajji
## 컬리 플라워 장아찌

dF vg vE -5

The firm texture of cauliflower makes it a great *jangajji* vegetable, because it retains a satisfying crunch.

**Preparation time:** 20 minutes, plus 5 days fermentation
**Cooking time:** 15 minutes
**Makes:** 1½ lb (700 g)

1 head cauliflower (about 1½ lb/ 700 g)

**For the jangajji brine:**
2 cups (16 fl oz/480 ml) ganjang (Korean soy sauce)
1 cup (200 g) sugar
½ oz (15 g) dasima (optional)
2 dried shiitake mushroom (optional)
1 cup (8 fl oz/240 ml) rice vinegar

Cut the cauliflower into bite-size pieces, removing any extra tough pieces of core or stem. Rinse under cold running water and set aside in a sieve to drain.

**Make the jangajji brine:** In a small pot, combine the soy sauce, 2 cups (16 fl oz/480 ml) water, the sugar, dasima (if using), and shiitakes (if using) and bring to a boil. Add the vinegar and return to a boil. Remove from the heat, discard the dasima, and let cool completely. Once cool, remove and discard the shiitakes.

Place the cauliflower pieces and cooled brine in an airtight glass or ceramic container large enough to fit them with a small amount of headroom. Close the container and set in the refrigerator for 5 days.

**Variation:** Adding lemon peels can add a citrus flavor to the *jangajji*.

---

## Asparagus Jangajji
## 아스파라거스 장아찌

dF vg vE -5

Applying the Korean *jangajji* technique to asparagus is a fun experience. The *jangajji* process reduces the often unwanted grassy, vegetal flavor of the asparagus without having to apply any heat, which retains its delicious, snappy crunch.

**Preparation time:** 20 minutes, plus 4 days fermentation
**Cooking time:** 15 minutes
**Makes:** 10 oz (300 g)

10 oz (300 g) asparagus

**For the jangajji brine:**
2 cups (16 fl oz/480 ml) ganjang (Korean soy sauce)
1 cup (200 g) sugar
½ oz (15 g) dasima (optional)
2 dried shiitake mushrooms (optional)
1 cup (8 fl oz/240 ml) rice vinegar

Trim off the tough base of the asparagus and peel the outer layer with a vegetable peeler. Cut the asparagus crosswise into halves or thirds, depending on preference, and let dry completely.

**Make the jangajji brine:** In a small pot, combine the soy sauce, 2 cups (16 fl oz/480 ml) water, the sugar, dasima (if using), and shiitakes (if using) and bring to a boil. Add the vinegar and return to a boil. Remove from the heat, discard the dasima, and let cool completely. Once cool, remove and discard the shiitakes.

Place the asparagus and cooled brine in an airtight glass or ceramic container large enough to fit them with a small amount of headroom. Close the container and set in the refrigerator for 4 days.

## Perilla Jangajji
## Kkaennip Jangajji
## 깻잎 장아찌

DF VG VE -S

Making perilla *jangajji* preserves the herbal fragrance of perilla so it can be enjoyed year-round. Even when there are no fresh *ssam* (wrap) vegetables available, the perilla *jangajji* can be used to make wraps and are delicious with grilled meats.

**Preparation time:** 20 minutes, plus 4 days fermentation
**Cooking time:** 15 minutes
**Makes:** 1¾ oz (50 g)

1¾ oz (50 g) perilla leaves

**For the jangajji brine:**
1 cup (8 fl oz/240 ml) ganjang (Korean soy sauce)
½ cup (100 g) sugar
¼ oz (5 g) dasima (optional)
1 dried shiitake mushroom (optional)
½ cup (4 fl oz/120 ml) rice vinegar

Rinse the perilla leaves individually under cold running water. Let any excess water drain in a sieve or wipe with a clean towel.

**Make the jangajji brine:** In a small pot, combine the soy sauce, 1 cup (8 fl oz/240 ml) water, the sugar, dasima (if using), and shiitake (if using) and bring to a boil. Add the vinegar and return to a boil. Remove from the heat, discard the dasima, and let cool completely. Once cool, remove and discard the shiitake.

Stack the perilla leaves in an airtight glass or ceramic container large enough to fit them with a small amount of headroom. Pour in the cooled brine. Close the container and set in the refrigerator for 4 days.

**Variation:** Add some sliced green chilies for a light, spicy flavor.

## Salt-Pickled Cucumbers
## Oiji
## 오이지

DF GF VG VE -S

Select small, hard-fleshed cucumbers with little seeds. Good choices are cucumbers sold specifically for pickling, such as the Kirby cucumber. To eat *oiji*, cut into very thin slices and rinse with cold water to desalt, then squeeze to drain excess liquid.

**Preparation time:** 30 minutes, plus 14 days fermentation
**Cooking time:** 20 minutes
**Makes:** 4½ lb (2 kg)

3 lb 5 oz (1.5 kg) small cucumbers, such as pickling cucumbers
½ cup (60 g) coarse sea salt

**For the brine:**
2 cups (240 g) coarse sea salt

In a large bowl, combine the cucumbers and coarse sea salt and rub together to remove any thorny exteriors and impurities. Rinse under cold running water and set aside to dry completely. The cucumbers must be as dry as possible.

**Make the brine:** In a large pot, combine 15 cups (120 fl oz/3.6 liters) water and the salt in a pot and bring to a gentle boil until the salt is completely dissolved. Remove from the heat.

Place the cleaned and dried cucumbers in an airtight glass or ceramic container large enough to fit them with a small amount of headroom. Pour in the brine. Keep the cucumbers entirely submerged in the brine by weighing them down with a heavy plate or bowl.

Close with the lid and keep in a cool environment at 68°–77°F (20°–25°C) with no direct light for 4 days to ferment.

After 4 days, pour the brine out into a large pot and bring to a boil. Remove from the heat and let the brine cool completely. Pour the brine back into the container and let ferment for 10 more days in the same cool environment before moving into the refrigerator. The oiji should have a yellow tone at this point and can be enjoyed for up to 6 months kept in the refrigerator.

**Variation:** For a sweeter, tangier recipe, replace the salt brine with a mixture of salt, sugar, and vinegar in one-to-one ratios, without any water.

# 젓갈 Jeotgal Fermented Seafood

*Jeotgal* is the category of traditional preserved food made by salting and fermenting animal protein, primarily seafood. The salt preservation and fermentation process break down the enzymes of the meat, which results in a deep, savory flavor profile.

Korea, as a nation surrounded on three sides by the ocean, developed *jeotgal* as a way to preserve its abundance of seafood for future consumption. Perishable seafood, including organs and eggs, needed to be preserved to keep them from spoiling and also to make them available over long periods of time. Since the types of seafood caught differs by region, the *jeotgal* culture of each region has developed in a unique way. Although on the face of it *jeotgal* may seem like a straightforward process, it actually treats each type or specific part of seafood in a precise and meticulous way to create unique *jeotgal*.

The most popular types of *jeotgal* are salted anchovies and shrimp (prawns); other popular *jeotgal* are made from various seafood, including oysters, squid, and octopus. There are more than a hundred types of unique *jeotgal* in existence. Of these *jeotgal*, *myeongran-jeot* (made from pollock roe), *changran-jeot* (made from fish innards), *ojingeo-jeot* (made with squid), and *jogae-jeot* (made from clams) are popular served as *banchan* (side dishes). *Saeu-jeot* (salted shrimp) and *myeolchi-jeot* (salted anchovy) are mostly used as ingredients in making kimchi.

*Jeotgal* plays a particularly important role in kimchi making, where the type of *jeotgal* used influences the final taste. The introduction of *jeotgal* and its complex, savory flavors to traditional kimchi making played a key role in diversifying the types of kimchi. The influence of *jeotgal* on kimchi flavors is especially noticeable in southern provinces of Korea, where strong-flavored *jeotgal* is used.

In addition to being one of the most important ingredients in kimchi, *jeotgal* is one of the most important ingredients in Korean cuisine. It is served as a *banchan* (side dish) to eat atop rice, used as a sauce in *ssam* (wraps), served as a sauce for grilled meats, and as a seasoning substitute for *ganjang* (Korean soy sauce) and salt to add savory depth to dishes. *Jeotgal* adds body and depth to dishes, creating layered savory flavor profiles in ways that can only be achieved through its unique ingredients and process.

## Salted Squid
### Ojingeo Jeotgal
### 오징어 젓갈

dF gF

The squid *jeotgal* is one of the most common *jeotgals* enjoyed as a *banchan* (side dish). It is typically made in the summertime, when the most squid are caught, and the *jeotgal* can be enjoyed year-round. Remove small amounts from the container just before serving as a *banchan* (side dish). It is often mixed with sesame seeds and minced scallions (spring onions) just before serving to taste.

**Preparation time: 30 minutes, plus 15 days salt-curing and 24 hours fermentation**
**Makes: 14 oz (400 g)**

Salt
1 lb 5 oz (600 g) fresh whole squid
½ cup (60 g) coarse sea salt
2 tablespoons gochugaru (red chili flakes)
1 teaspoon minced garlic
1 teaspoon jocheong (rice syrup)
¼ teaspoon ginger juice

Make a 3 percent salt solution: For every 1 cup (237 g) water, add 1 teaspoon (7 g) salt. Wash the squid in the salt solution. Cut the clean squid in half and remove all organs and cartilage. Slice the entire squid into slices 1⁄16 inch (2 mm) thick.

In a sterilized airtight glass container large enough to hold the jeotgal snugly, combine the sliced squid with the sea salt and combine until uniform. Cover with a lid and keep in the refrigerator for 15 days for the squid to cure in the salt.

When ready to season the squid, in a small bowl, combine the gochugaru, garlic, rice syrup, and ginger juice. Toss the seasoning mixture with the salt-cured squid and mix until uniform. Return to a sterilized airtight glass container, cover with a lid, transfer to the refrigerator and let ferment for a minimum of 24 hours. It can be kept for up to 1 year.

---

## Salted Anchovies
### Myeolchi Jeot
### 멸치젓

dF gF -S

There are three forms of preserved anchovy used in Korean cuisine: *aekjeot*, *yukjeot*, and *saengjeot*. All three forms of the salted anchovy are created in the course of a single process, much as *ganjang* (Korean soy sauce) and *doenjang* (fermented soybean paste) are created during the same process and separated.

*Aekjeot*, anchovy fish sauce, refers to the clear liquid remaining after filtering a cloudy layer of liquid resulting from the fermentation of salted anchovies. The *yukjeot* are the solids that are filtered out during the process, and the *saengjeot* refers to the ground remaining anchovies. Depending on the regional or familial recipe, all three are utilized in kimchi making. *Aekjeot* is also used in many other recipes across Korean cuisine, including when making soups or vegetable dishes.

**Preparation time: 30 minutes, plus 6 months fermentation**
**Cooking time: 45 minutes**
**Makes: 3 lb 5 oz (1.5 kg)**

¼ oz (5 g) dasima
3 tablespoons (40 g) glutinous rice
2¼ lb (1 kg) fresh anchovies, 4 inches (10 cm) long
2⅓ cups (300 g) coarse sea salt

In a small pot, combine 1½ cups (12 fl oz/360 ml) water and the dasima and bring to a boil over high heat. Reduce to medium heat and simmer for 10 more minutes. Strain the broth, discard the dasima, and return the broth to the pot.

Rinse the glutinous rice under cold running water until the water runs clear. Add the cleaned rice to the pot and cook over medium heat until it is as soft as porridge, about 30 minutes, stirring constantly to get rid of lumps. (Alternatively, you can cook the dasima broth and rice in a rice cooker.)

Clean the anchovies under cold running water to get rid of any impurities and set in a sieve to dry.

Measure out 7 ounces (200 g) of the dasima rice. In a large bowl, add the cleaned anchovies, the dasima rice, and 2 cups (250 g) of the salt, and combine well until uniform.

In a sterilized, airtight glass container large enough to hold the jeotgal snugly, add the anchovy mixture, pressing down each batch to ensure that any air bubbles are minimized. Sprinkle the remaining ⅓ cup (50 g) sea salt evenly over the surface and cover the surface with parchment (baking) paper, then cover once more with plastic wrap (cling film) to seal before closing the lid.

Let ferment in a cool, shaded area at 68°–77°F (20°–25°C) for 6 months before transferring to the refrigerator.

## Salted Shrimp
### Saeu-jeot
### 새우젓

dF gF ~S

*Saeu-jeot*, salted shrimp, is the most commonly used *jeotgal* (preserved seafood) in Korean cuisine. Salted shrimp are used as a seasoning when making kimchi, or as an ingredient in sauces, or as a popular condiment along with pork dishes.

The most important factor in the simple recipe is the freshness and quality of the shrimp and the taste of the salt used. The shrimp used to make *saeu-jeot* are tiny, measuring at about 1¼ inches (3 cm) in length. These type of shrimp are called *jeot-saeu* and are at their peak of flavor in June.

**Preparation time:** 30 minutes, plus 4 months fermentation
**Makes:** 1 lb 5 oz (600 g)

Salt
1 lb (500 g) small fresh shrimp
Generous ¾ cup (100 g) coarse sea salt

**Make a 3 percent salt solution:** For every 1 cup (237 g) water, add 1 teaspoon (7 g) salt. Rinse the shrimp in a bowl with the salt solution to wash away any impurities and set in a sieve to drain. In a large bowl, combine the cleaned shrimp and ⅔ cup (80 g) of the sea salt and toss until well combined.

In a sterilized airtight glass container large enough to hold the jeotgal snugly, add the salted shrimp and press each layer so that there are no air bubbles. Sprinkle the remaining 3 tablespoons (20 g) sea salt over the surface. Cover the top layer with plastic wrap (cling film) and close the lid. Place in the refrigerator to let ferment for 4 months before use.

---

## Ganjang-Marinated Crab
### Ganjang Gejang
### 간장게장

dF                                [◻]

The most important thing when making soy-preserved crab is to use fresh, live crab. To serve, first remove the whole crabs from the marinade. Separate the back shell from the body and set aside to plate, because the innards in the shell are a delicacy that can be eaten by mixing directly with 1 or 2 spoonfuls of rice. Using sharp scissors, cut the body in half down the middle and cut each side into halves.

**Preparation time:** 20 minutes, plus 3 days marination
**Cooking time:** 40 minutes
**Makes:** 5 lb 15 oz (2.7 kg)

2¼ lb (1 kg) fresh female blue crabs (about 4 crabs)

**For the broth:**
7 oz (200 g) onions, halved or quartered
1 oz (30 g) daepa (Korean scallion), cut into 2½-inch (6 cm) lengths
10 oz (300 g) apple, unpeeled and cut into 8 wedges
⅓-inch (8 mm) piece fresh ginger, thinly sliced
½ oz (15 g) dasima
2 dried red chilies
1½ oz (40 g) garlic, peeled

**For the jang marinade:**
2 cups (16 fl oz/480 ml) ganjang (Korean soy sauce)
1 cup (8 fl oz/240 ml) mirin
1 oz (25 g) fresh green Cheongyang chilies, thinly sliced on a diagonal

Rinse the blue crabs under cold running water, thoroughly scrubbing the shells, paying close attention to the belly area. Trim off the pointy, flesh-free ends of the crab leg with scissors. Once clean, place the crabs into a container stomach-side down and set in the refrigerator to drain any excess water.

**Make the broth:** In a large pot, combine the onion, daepa, apple, ginger, dasima, chilies, garlic, and 4 cups (32 fl oz/950 ml) water and bring to a boil over high heat. Reduce the heat to low and simmer for 30 minutes. Strain the liquid into another pot (discard the solids).

**Make the jang marinade:** To the broth in the pot, add the soy sauce and mirin and bring to a boil over high heat. Reduce heat to low and simmer for 5 more minutes. Add the sliced chilies before removing from heat and letting cool completely.

Remove the cleaned crabs from the refrigerator, discarding any released liquid and drying completely. Place the crabs stomach-side up in a sterilized airtight glass container large enough to hold them snugly and cover with the cooled marinade, making sure the crabs are submerged. Cover the container and transfer to the refrigerator to ferment for 3 days. After 3 days it is ready to eat and can be kept in the refrigerator for up to 7 days.

If the marinated crabs are to be kept beyond the 7-day mark, separate the crabs and the marinade. Freeze the marinated crabs in a freezer-safe airtight container or bag. The marinade should be strained and brought to boil once, cooled completely, and kept in the refrigerator. To eat, thaw the crab at room temperature and combine with the marinade before serving.

## Ganjang Marinated Shrimp
### Ganjang Saeu Jang
### 간장 새우장

dF

The inherent sweetness of the shrimp flesh goes well with the *ganjang* (Korean soy sauce) marinade, and the resulting bouncy texture is a great pairing served as a *banchan*.

**Preparation time: 20 minutes, plus 12 hours fermentation**
**Cooking time: 20 minutes**
**Makes: 1 lb 5 oz (600 g)**

10 heads-on jumbo shrimp (tiger prawns; 4 inches/10 cm long)
Salt

**For the marinade:**
¾ cup (6 fl oz/175 ml) ganjang (Korean soy sauce)
4 tablespoons rice wine
4 tablespoons mirin
4 tablespoons sugar
3½ oz (100 g) onion, thinly sliced
3–4 cloves garlic, halved
1¾ oz (50 g) fresh green chilies, cut into 1¼-inch (3 cm) diagonal slices

First trim the whiskers of the shrimp.

**Make a 3 percent salt solution:** For every 1 cup (237 g) water, add 1 teaspoon (7 g) salt. Wash the shrimp in the salt solution to remove any impurities and set aside in a sieve to let excess moisture dry.

**Make the marinade:** In a large pot, combining 1 cup (8 fl oz/240 ml) water, the soy sauce, wine, mirin, and sugar and bring to a boil over high heat. Remove from the heat and add the onion, garlic, and chilies and let cool completely until cold.

Place the cleaned and dried shrimp in a sterilized, airtight glass container large enough to hold them and pour over the cooled marinade, making sure that all the shrimp are submerged. Close the lid, transfer to the refrigerator, and let ferment for 12 hours. It can be kept up to 3 days in the refrigerator.

---

## Ganjang-Marinated Salmon
### Yeoneojang
### 연어장

dF

*Ganjang*-marinated salmon is a quick and easy *banchan* (side dish) to pair with rice.

**Preparation time: 20 minutes, plus 6 hours marinating time**
**Cooking time: 20 minutes**
**Makes: 2 lb 14 oz (1.3 kg)**

1 lb (500 g) salmon fillet

**For the marinade:**
3½ oz (100 g) onion, thinly sliced
⅓-inch (8 mm) piece fresh ginger, thinly sliced
3–4 cloves garlic, halved
1¾ oz (50 g) green Cheongyang chilies, cut into 1¼-inch (3 cm) diagonal slices
1 cup (8 fl oz/240 ml) ganjang (Korean soy sauce)
½ cup (4 fl oz/120 ml) rice cooking wine
1 tablespoon sugar

Skin the salmon, remove any pin bones, and cut into ¼-inch (5 mm) slices.

**Make the marinade:** In a pot, combine 1½ cups (12 fl oz/360 ml) water, the onion, ginger, garlic, chilies, soy sauce, wine, and sugar and bring to a boil over high heat. Remove from the heat as it begins to boil and let cool completely.

Place the salmon pieces in a sterilized airtight glass container large enough to hold the salmon snugly. Pour in the cold marinade, close the lid, and transfer to the refrigerator to marinate for at least 6 hours. It will keep in the refrigerator for up to 3 days.

# Fermented Flounder
## Gajami Sikhae
## 가자미 식해

*Sikhae* is a preserved food made by fermenting fish with *gochugaru* (red chili powder), salt, grain, and malt. It is mainly eaten in Gangwon-do and Hamgyeong-do, and various types of fish are used, but the most commonly used is flounder.

dF

**Preparation time:** 30 minutes, plus 5 days drying and 4 weeks fermentation
**Cooking time:** 20 minutes
**Makes:** 2¼ lb (1 kg)

Salt
2¼ lb (1 kg) whole flounder, cleaned and gutted, head removed
1 tablespoon sea salt
1 tablespoon barley malt powder

**For the dried mu:**
1 lb (500 g) mu (Korean radish)
½ tablespoon coarse sea salt

**For the millet:**
1 cup (200 g) millet, rinsed

**For the seasoning:**
2 tablespoons barley malt powder
3 tablespoons fine gochugaru (red chili powder)
1 tablespoon salted shrimp
1 tablespoon salted anchovy
2 tablespoons minced garlic
2 tablespoons minced fresh ginger
2 tablespoons jocheong (rice syrup)
2 tablespoons rice cooking wine
1 teaspoon coarse sea salt

**Make a 3 percent salt solution:** For every 1 cup (237 g) water, add 1 teaspoon (7 g) salt. Rinse the cleaned flounder in the salt solution and let dry for 2 days in a cool, well-ventilated location at around 59°F (15°C). After 2 days, cut the bone-in flounder into slices ⅜ inch (1 cm) thick. Sprinkle the 1 tablespoon sea salt and barley malt powder evenly over the flounder and cover. Let dry-age in the refrigerator for 3 days.

**Meanwhile, make the dried mu:** Cut the radish into ¼-inch (5 mm) matchsticks. In a bowl, toss with the coarse sea salt and let dry on a flat surface for 1 day with no sunlight at around 59°F (15°C).

**Cook the millet:** After the flounder is ready at the end of the 3 days, rinse the millet in a sieve at least two or three times under cold running water. In a saucepan on the stovetop (hob, or in a rice cooker), cook the millet with 1 cup (8 fl oz/240 ml) water until tender, about 20 minutes. Let cool completely.

**Prepare the seasoning:** Sift the barley powder through a sieve into a large bowl. Add the cooled cooked millet, aged flounder, dried mu, gochugaru, salted shrimp, salted anchovy, garlic, ginger, rice syrup, wine, and sea salt. Mix thoroughly until the mixture is uniform.

Place the mixture in a sterilized, airtight glass container large enough to hold the jeotgal snugly and close the lid. Transfer to the refrigerator to ferment for 4 weeks. The final sikhae can be kept for up to 6 months in the refrigerator.

밥 **Bap** Cooked Rice

In Korean, *bap* has two meanings. The first meaning is "cooked rice," the simple product of rice grains cooked in water. The second meaning of *bap* is "food" or "dining" in its entirety. The most common Korean greeting among friends and family is "have you had bap" instead of "have you eaten?" This interchangeability of *bap* with "meal" is rooted in the Korean psyche.

The importance of rice in Korean culture is naturally understood once one considers rice's origins. In Korea, rice was discovered between thirteen and fifteen thousand years ago; in fact, Korea has been cited as the place that rice originates from. Since ancient times, rice has provided the foundation of a meal, and the accompaniments—the *banchan* (side dishes)—provided additional nutrients and, more important, delicious flavors.

Why and how did this *banchan* culture come to be and evolve? Simple: It was to build a delicious meal around the foundation of rice. Central to Korean cuisine is this concept of *bap* and *banchan*. The Korean table consists of the basic rice along with a diverse array of *banchan* that fill up the table, composed of various flavors, textures, and temperatures. In addition to the spread of *banchan*, there are two often separate *banchan*: *guk* (soups) and *jjigae* (stews).

The way to properly eat *bap* and *banchan* is for each diner to choose how to match up the various components of the meal. This unique form of customization leads to the Korean adage that "cooking is finished in the mouth." There are three main ways to combine *bap* and *banchan*. The first way is to "fold" the rice into *guk*, or broth; the second is to wrap the rice in vegetables; and the third, and very popular, way is to mix the rice with various *banchan* in a bowl.

## Cooked Short-Grain White Rice
### Bap
### 흰밥

dF gF vg vE -5      [□]

In Korea, when one refers simply to "rice," it means polished short-grain white rice. It's without a doubt the most common staple food in Korea. However, short-grain rice does come in other forms besides polished; each type is categorized by how much of the rice's outer layers have been polished off. In ascending order of amount, the most common designations are: *hyun-mi* (brown rice), 5-*bundomi* (50 percent polished), 7-*bundomi* (70 percent polished), and finally white rice, which has 100 percent of the outer layers polished off. The more polished the rice is, the smoother and softer the rice's texture is and the sweeter its taste.

**Preparation time:** 5 minutes, plus 30 minutes soaking time
**Cooking time:** 25 minutes
**Makes:** 4 cups (800 g); 4 servings

2 cups (440 g) short-grain white rice

In a bowl, wash the rice in three or four changes of water until it is clear. Add fresh water to the bowl and let the rinsed rice soak for 30 minutes. Drain in a sieve to get rid of any excess water.

In a pot, combine the soaked rice and 2½ cups (20 fl oz/590 ml) water, cover with a lid, and bring to a boil over high heat. Reduce the heat to low and simmer for 15 minutes. Reduce the heat to the minimal heat level and let steam for 5 minutes. Fluff the rice with a spatula and serve immediately.

---

## Korean Scorched Bap
### Nurungji
### 누룽지

dF gF vg vE -5 -30

*Nurungji* is the crunchy rice crust that forms at the bottom of a cooking pot. Before the electric rice cooker was widely available, Korea's households used traditional cast-iron cauldrons called *gamasot* to prepare daily rice. Due to the nature of cast iron, each batch of rice would form the crunchy crust at the bottom, so naturally dishes were created to feature the *nurungji*.

One such example is *sungnyung*, a humble dish made by simply pouring hot water over this rice crust to form a simple yet aromatic rice broth, sometimes also simmering briefly so the broth gains the nutty flavor of the *nurungji*. *Sungnyung* is often enjoyed at the end of a meal as a comforting drink. The *nurungji* can be cooked in liquid for longer to create a *juk* (porridge). *Nurungji* can also be further dried and baked to create a snack, and it is often dried and used as a carb component of a dish such as *nurungji-tang* braised with a seafood-based *yuksu* (broth/stock). While the traditional, naturally formed *nurungji* from a cast-iron pot will have an inimitable savory flavor, today *nurungji* is often made by using leftover rice in a nonstick pan.

**Cooking time:** 20 minutes
**Serves:** 4

Generous 1 cup (210 g) Cooked Short-Grain White Rice (see above)

In a nonstick pan, spread the cooked white rice in a flat layer and drizzle 3 tablespoons of water over it. Set over medium heat and once the rice begins to crackle, reduce the heat to low and let slowly cook for 15 minutes to create nurungji.

**Variation:** To make sungnyung, combine the nurungji with 3 times the volume of water and boil for 5 minutes.

## Five-Grain Rice
### Ogokbap
### 오곡밥

dF gF vg vE -5

*Ogokbap*, literally meaning "five-grain rice," is a common rice dish format. The five different grains that are used can differ slightly based on the region or household. While it is enjoyed throughout the year, it was traditionally eaten on the first full moon of the year to wish for a bountiful year of good harvest, fortune, and health.

**Preparation time:** 10 minutes, plus 3 hours soaking time
**Cooking time:** 40 minutes
**Serves:** 4

- ½ cup (100 g) dried black beans
- 4 tablespoons millet
- 1½ cups (330 g) short-grain white rice
- ½ cup (110 g) glutinous rice
- 4 tablespoons glutinous millet, rinsed

Wash the dried black beans under cold running water. Place in a large bowl with water to generously cover and soak for 3 hours.

Meanwhile, soak the regular millet for 1 hour. Rinse both the short-grain rice and glutinous rice and let soak for 30 minutes. (The glutinous millet does not need to be soaked.)

In a pot, combine all the grains with 3 cups (24 fl oz/710 ml) water, stirring so that they are distributed evenly. Cover with a lid and bring to a boil over high heat. Reduce the heat to medium-low and cook for 20 minutes. After 20 minutes, reduce the heat to low and let steam for 10 more minutes. Remove the lid and stir well, releasing the steam. Cover again and let sit for 5 minutes. Serve immediately.

## Green Pea Bap
### Wandu Kong Bap
### 완두콩밥

dF gF vg vE -5

In late spring or early summer, the green pea is in season in Korea. Making rice with green peas results in a sweet-savory rice that welcomes the season. Because this is a two-ingredient rice, the quality of the peas is important for a delicious outcome. The peas should be hard to the touch and possess a strong, sweet flavor. While the peas can be cooked mixed into the rice from the beginning for ease, longer cooking time will discolor the peas.

**Preparation time:** 10 minutes, plus 30 minutes soaking time
**Cooking time:** 30 minutes
**Serves:** 4

- 2 cups (440 g) short-grain white rice
- ½ cup (80 g) fresh peas

In a bowl, wash the rice in three or four changes of water until it is clear. Add fresh water to the bowl and let the rinsed rice soak for 30 minutes. Drain in a sieve to get rid of any excess water.

In a pot, combine the rice and 2½ cups (20 fl oz/590 ml) water and cover with a lid. Bring to a boil over high heat. Reduce the heat to low and simmer for 15 minutes. Uncover, add the fresh peas, re-cover, reduce the heat to the minimum, and steam for 7 more minutes. Remove from the heat and stir the rice and peas together until well incorporated and serve immediately.

## Barley Bap
### Boribap
### 보리밥

dF vg vE -S

*Boribap* has an earthy, sweet flavor and a bouncy texture that is beloved in Korea, and it makes a perfect pairing mixed in with Thick Doenjang Barley Bibimbap (page 107), Young Summer Radish Kimchi (page 67), and all types of *namul* (vegetable side dishes). Barley is a grain with a chewy, toothsome texture and takes longer than rice to cook. So the barley needs to be partly cooked before cooking with the rice.

**Preparation time:** 10 minutes, plus 30 minutes soaking time
**Cooking time:** 40 minutes
**Serves:** 4

1 cup (220 g) short-grain white rice
1½ cups (300 g) pearl barley, rinsed

In a bowl, wash the rice in three or four changes of water until it is clear. Add fresh water to the bowl and let the rinsed rice soak for 30 minutes. Drain in a sieve to get rid of any excess water.

Meanwhile, in a pot, combine the barley with 6 cups (48 fl oz/1.4 liters) water and simmer over medium heat for 15 minutes. Drain in a sieve and rinse under cold running water. Set aside in the sieve to drain off any excess water.

In a pot, combine the cooked barley, soaked rice, and 2½ cups (20 fl oz/ 590 ml) water. Cover with a lid and bring to a boil over high heat. Reduce the heat to low and simmer for 15 minutes. Reduce to the lowest heat and steam for an additional 5 minutes. Open and stir with a spatula to mix and serve immediately.

**Variation:** For a faster version that does not require precooking the barley, use barley flakes and cook directly with the rice from the beginning. Because the barley flakes have been flattened and dried, they require a shorter cooking time and have a softer mouthfeel.

---

## Lotus Leaf Bap
### Yeonnip Bap
### 연잎밥

dF gF vg vE

The fragrant lotus leaf rice is a popular menu item in vegan restaurants. The filling of chewy glutinous rice mixed with grains and nuts makes for a savory, textured eating experience that pairs wonderfully with the floral fragrance of the lotus leaf. To shorten the cooking time, the beans and rices are precooked before wrapping in the lotus leaf, but even with the short steaming time, the aroma of the lotus leaf scents the filling.

**Preparation time:** 15 minutes, plus 3 hours soaking time
**Cooking time:** 40 minutes
**Serves:** 4

4 tablespoons dried black beans, rinsed
1½ cups (330 g) short-grain white rice
½ cup (110 g) glutinous rice
4 large lotus leaves
4 tablespoons hulled pumpkin seeds
16 ginkgo nuts
4 tablespoons pine nuts
4 tablespoons dried jujubes (Chinese red dates)

Place the beans in a small bowl with cold water to generously cover and soak for 3 hours.

Meanwhile, in a bowl, wash both rices in three or four changes of water until it is clear. Add fresh water to the bowl and let the rinsed rice soak for 30 minutes. Drain in a sieve to get rid of any excess water.

In a pot, combine both rices, the soaked beans, and 2¾ cups (22 fl oz/650 ml) water. Cover with a lid and bring to a boil over high heat. Reduce the heat to medium-low and cook for 20 more minutes. Remove from the heat, uncover, and mix well with a spatula.

Set up a steamer and bring the water to a boil.

Flatten out each leaf and add equal amounts of rice-and-bean filling to the center. Dividing evenly, top with pumpkin seeds, gingko nuts, pine nuts, and jujubes. Fold the lotus leaf tightly on all sides, securing the closure with a toothpick or a skewer. Add the wrapped packages to the steamer basket, set over the boiling water, and steam for 15 minutes. Serve hot on a plate, unwrapped.

## 비빔밥 Bibimbap Mixed Rice

*Bibimbap* can be said to be the most iconic rice dish of Korea. *Bibimbap* is a dish of cooked rice topped with a variety of prepared ingredients, such as *namul* (vegetable side dishes), meat, and *twigak* (deep-fried dishes) that the diner can then mix in. Its first documented form appears in the late 1800s, but it is estimated that it has a longer history.

From long ago, when Koreans held remote ancestral rites, such as mountain god rites, or rites honoring ancestors at home, the various ingredients and dishes prepared for the feast were eaten with rice. This original form of *jesatbap*, meaning "ancestral rite rice," seems to have evolved into the modern form of *bibimbap*.

The general archetype of *bibimbap* is made with various *namul*, meat, and *gochujang* (fermented soybean paste). There are traditional regional forms of *bibimbap* made with specific regional ingredients, and endless forms of *bibimbap* can be made by using *banchan* (side dishes) and seasonal ingredients.

Although *bibimbap* is a popular dish served at restaurants and *bibimbap*-specialized restaurants across the country, it is also commonly eaten at home, because it can be quickly prepared using simple ingredients and leftover *banchan*. A simple bowl of rice mixed with *gochujang* and sesame oil and topped with leftover *namul* and a fried egg makes for a hearty, nutritious meal. While *gochujang* is the main *jang* used in *bibimbap*, *ganjang* (Korean soy sauce) and *ssamjang* (dipping sauce for wraps) are also delicious substitutes.

During the Joseon dynasty, the Confucian philosophy of *obangsaek*—which means five universal colors: white, red, green, yellow, and black—was widely applied to the culinary arts, because it was believed to be the ideal aesthetic form. *Bibimbap* is a dish composed of rice (white), meat (red), *namul* (green), oil or fat (yellow), and fermented *jang* (black), making it an ideal *obangsaek* dish.

# Bibimbap
## 비빔밥

dF

*Bibimbap* is a rice-based dish made with well-cooked rice, a variety of colorful vegetables, and a meat-based ingredient. It's often made with sautéed beef and mixed with a seasoning sauce made from sesame, *ganjang* (Korean soy sauce), and *gochujang* (red chili paste). It was traditionally also called *hwa-ban*, which translates to "flower-rice," because it was said its beautifully arranged ingredients mimicked a well-groomed garden of flowers. Not only is it beautiful like a flower, but the harmony that each ingredient brings to the final mixed form makes it a delicious dish.

There are no set rules for which *namul* (vegetables dishes) to incorporate into a *bibimbap*, but it's best to use a colorful array for a delicious visual. For green vegetables, cucumber, zucchini (courgette), spinach, and *minari namul* are often used; for light-colored vegetables, mung bean sprouts, soybean sprouts, and Korean radish *namul* are often used; and for brown colors, fiddlehead fern or mushroom *namul* are often used. A quick pan-fried egg is a classic addition, but making clean, uniform *jidan* (traditional egg garnish) is a more classic plating technique.

**Preparation time: 35 minutes, plus 30 minutes rice soaking time**
**Cooking time: 1 hour**
**Serves: 4**

2 cups (440 g) short-grain white rice

**For the marinated beef:**
5 oz (150 g) ground (minced) beef
1 tablespoon ganjang (Korean soy sauce)
1 teaspoon sugar
1 teaspoon minced garlic
½ tablespoon sesame oil
Freshly ground black pepper

**For the bibimbap:**
2 tablespoons neutral cooking oil
5 oz (150 g) oyster mushrooms, shredded
Salt
3½ oz (100 g) carrots, cut into matchsticks 1½ inches (4 cm) long
5 oz (150 g) spinach
1 teaspoon ganjang (Korean soy sauce)
1 teaspoon ground sesame seeds
5 oz (150 g) soybean sprouts
1 teaspoon sesame oil
5 tablespoons Stir-Fried Gochujang (page 51)

Soak and cook the rice as directed on page 92 (see Cooked Short-Grain White Rice).

**Marinate the beef:** In a bowl, combine the beef, soy sauce, sugar, garlic, sesame oil, and black pepper to taste and mix until well incorporated. Set aside to marinate.

**Cook the bibimbap ingredients:** In a frying pan, heat 1 tablespoon of the cooking oil. Add the oyster mushrooms and salt to taste and stir-fry. Set aside. In the same pan, heat the remaining 1 tablespoon oil, add the carrots and salt to taste, and stir-fry. Set aside.

In a small pot, bring 3 cups (24 fl oz/710 ml) water to a boil. Add the spinach and blanch for 1 minute, then drain in a sieve and rinse immediately under cold running water. Gently squeeze the spinach to remove excess water and combine in a bowl with the soy sauce, ground sesame seeds, and salt to taste.

In the same pot, bring 3 cups (24 fl oz/710 ml) water to a boil. Add the soybean sprouts and blanch for 2 minutes. Drain. Combine in a bowl with the sesame oil and salt to taste.

In a frying pan, stir-fry the marinated ground beef until fully cooked, stirring to break up the lumps.

To serve, in each of four large individual bowls, place 1 cup (200 g) cooked rice. Plate each finished component in even amounts. Serve with the stir-fried gochujang on the side for people to add as they desire. To enjoy, add the stir-fried gochujang to taste and mix all the components and rice together.

**Variation:** Yak-gochujang (Stir-Fried Gochujang, page 51) adds a deeper flavor to the bibimbap, but you could make this instead with a mix of gochujang, sesame oil, maesil (fresh green plum) syrup, and sesame seeds to taste.

# Jeonju-Style Bibimbap
## Jeonju Bibimbap
## 전주 비빔밥

dF

This *bibimbap* recipe is a traditional recipe from the city of Jeonju. It's famous and beloved for its more formal, luxurious take on this classic dish. The rice in a proper Jeonju *bibimbap* is made with ox bone broth, and is finished with soybean sprouts. The final bean sprout rice is topped with a variety of ingredients such as *namul* (vegetable dishes), mung bean jelly, *yukhwe* (for example, a beef tartare), and finished with raw egg yolk and Stir-Fried Gochujang (page 51).

Preparation time: 25 minutes, plus 30 minutes soaking time
Cooking time: 25 minutes
Serves: 4

For the rice:
2 cups (440 g) short-grain white rice
2 cups (16 fl oz/500 ml) ox bone broth (available in Korean markets)
3½ oz (100 g) soybean sprouts

For the yukhwe:
1 tablespoon Korean pear juice
½ teaspoon sugar
1 teaspoon ganjang (Korean soy sauce)
1 teaspoon sesame oil
4½ oz (130 g) beef top round (topside) or eye of round, julienned

For the bibimbap:
1 tablespoon neutral cooking oil
3½ oz (100 g) carrots, julienned
Salt
2¾ oz (80 g) Spinach Namul (page 166)
2¾ oz (80 g) Dried Fiddlehead Namul (page 168)
2¾ oz (80 g) Korean Zucchini Namul (page 176)
2¾ oz (80 g) Korean Radish Saengchae (page 180)
4 oz (120 g) mung bean jelly
2¾ oz (80 g) Stir-Fried Gochujang (page 51)
4 raw egg yolks
32 pine nuts

**Prepare the rice:** In a bowl, wash the rice in three or four changes of water until it is clear. Add fresh water to the bowl and let the rinsed rice soak for 30 minutes. Drain in a sieve to get rid of any excess water.

In a pot, combine the soaked rice and bone broth, cover with a lid, and bring to a boil over high heat. Reduce the heat to low and simmer for 15 minutes. Add the bean sprouts, cover again, and steam for 7 minutes. Remove from the heat and stir, combining the rice and bean sprouts evenly.

**Make the yukhwe:** In a bowl, stir together the pear juice, sugar, soy sauce, and sesame oil. Add the beef and toss lightly to coat. Set aside.

**Assemble the bibimbap:** In a frying pan, heat the cooking oil over medium heat. Add the carrots, salt to taste, and stir-fry until softened. Set the carrot namul aside to cool.

To serve, in each of four large individual bowls, place 1 cup (200 g) cooked rice. Plate each namul and the mung bean jelly in even amounts around the rice. In the center, divide the yukhwe and stir-fried gochujang evenly, and top each with a raw egg yolk. Garnish with the pine nuts.

## Tongyeong-Style Bibimbap
## Tongyeong Bibimbap
## 통영 비빔밥

DF

The area around the coastal city of Tongyeong is famed for its abundance of quality seafood year-round and, of course, its seasonal specialty dishes. Some of its most famous dishes include Chungmu Gimbap (page 132), eel dishes, seafood soups, and more. But one of the most beloved staples is its namesake Tongyeong *bibimbap*, also nicknamed *neomulbap*.

This bibimbap is made with fresh seasonal sea vegetables and seaweed bursting with the essence of the sea. Depending on the season, the ingredients used vary. The fresh seaweed and sea vegetables are most delicious in the winter and spring. It is often served with a delicious soup made with tofu and clams or mussels to wash down the rice in between bites, and boiled octopus and gourd *namul* are other popular dishes to eat along with.

**Preparation time:** 35 minutes, plus 30 minutes rice soaking time
**Cooking time:** 1 hour
**Serves:** 4

- 4 cups (800 g) Cooked Short-Grain White Rice (page 92)
- 2¾ oz (80 g) Bean Sprout Namul (page 160)
- 2¾ oz (80 g) Spinach Namul (page 166)
- 2¾ oz (80 g) Tot Muchim (page 471)
- 3½ oz (100 g) fresh miyeok (wakame)
- 2¾ oz (80 g) Korean Radish Saengchae (page 180)
- 2¾ oz (80 g) Korean Zucchini Namul (page 176)
- 2 tablespoons sesame oil
- 2 tablespoons ground sesame seeds
- Gochuchjang (red pepper paste), optional

In each of four large individual bowls, place 1 cup (200 g) cooked rice. Plate each of the vegetable components in even amounts around the rice. Garnish with a drizzle of sesame oil and a sprinkling of ground sesame seeds.

While a tablespoon of gochujang can be added to taste, it's common to serve without to enjoy the flavors of the ingredients.

---

## Andong-Style Bibimbap
## Andong Heotjesatbap
## 안동 헛제삿밥

DF

The traditional *bibimbap* from Andong, a city in eastern Korea, uses soy sauce as its seasoning ingredient instead of the more common *gochujang* (red chili paste) or stir-fried *gochujang*. The *bibimbap* is often served as a part of a traditional spread including Beef & Radish Guk (page 324), *sanjuk* (traditional Korean meat and vegetable skewers), Napa Cabbage Jeon (page 232), steamed fish or tofu, and more. This combination of food is often eaten during *jesa*, which is any memorial ancestral ceremony.

**Preparation time:** 35 minutes, plus 30 minutes rice soaking time
**Cooking time:** 1 hour
**Serves:** 4

- 4 cups (800 g) Cooked Short-Grain White Rice (page 92)
- 2¾ oz (80) g soybean sprouts
- 2¾ oz (80 g) Spinach Namul (page 166)
- 2¾ oz (80 g) Fresh Fiddlehead Namul (page 168)
- 3½ oz (100 g) Bellflower Root Namul (page 170)
- 2¾ oz (80 g) Korean Radish Namul (page 180)
- 2 tablespoons sesame oil
- ½ cup (4 fl oz/120 ml) ganjang (Korean soy sauce)

In each of four large individual bowls, place 1 cup (200 g) cooked rice. Plate each vegetable component in even amounts around the rice. Finish with a drizzle of of sesame oil. Serve the ganjang on the side.

## Jeju Sea Urchin Bibimbap
### Jeju Seongge Bibimbap
### 성게 비빔밥

dF [ㅁ]

Although there are other traditional sea urchin dishes from Jeju, there's no better way to enjoy the full breadth of the sweet flavor of sea urchin than with a bowl of Jeju sea urchin *bibimbap*.

All the ingredients of a bibimbap are typically mixed before eating, but here the preferred approach is to eat in a more scooping fashion, getting some of each ingredient in every spoonful. Vegetables can be added to taste, such as thinly sliced cucumbers, onions, or *minari*.

**Preparation time:** 20 minutes, plus 30 minutes rice soaking time
**Cooking time:** 50 minutes
**Serves:** 4

- 2 cups (440 g) short-grain white rice
- 4 tablespoons ganjang (Korean soy sauce)
- 2 tablespoons sesame oil
- 3 tablespoons gim powder
- 13 oz (360 g) fresh sea urchins
- 2 tablespoons thinly sliced scallion (spring onion)
- 2 tablespoons sesame seeds

Soak and cook the rice as directed on page 92 (see Cooked Short-Grain White Rice).

In a large bowl, combine the cooked rice, soy sauce, sesame oil, and gim powder and mix until uniform.

In each of four large individual bowls, place 1 cup (200 g) cooked rice and top with sea urchin. Garnish with equal amounts of scallion and sesame seeds.

---

## Jinju-Style Bibimbap
### Jinju Bibimbap
### 진주 비빔밥

dF

*Jinju bibimbap* is a traditional local *bibimbap* known for its strong beef flavors, differentiating it from other regional specialties. It's topped with beef *yukhwe* (a raw beef dish) as a garnish, seasoned with Stir-Fried Gochujang (page 51). This *bibimbap* is often served with a beef blood soup in the style of Gyeongsang-do province, which is where the city of Jinju is.

**Preparation time:** 1 hour, plus 30 minutes rice soaking time
**Cooking time:** 1 hour 40 minutes
**Serves:** 4

- 2 cups (440 g) short-grain white rice

**For the yukhwe:**
- 5½ oz (160 g) beef top round (topside) or eye of round, julienned
- 1 tablespoon Korean pear juice
- ½ teaspoon sugar
- 1 teaspoon ganjang (Korean soy sauce)
- 1 teaspoon sesame oil

**For the bibimbap:**
- 2 oz (60 g) soybean sprouts
- 2 oz (60 g) Mung Bean Sprout Namul (variation, page 160)
- 2 oz (60 g) Korean Zucchini Namul (page 176)
- 2 oz (60 g) Korean Radish Saengchae (page 180)
- 2¾ oz (80 g) Spinach Namul (page 166)
- 2¾ oz (80 g) Fresh Fiddlehead Namul (page 168)
- 2 tablespoons sesame oil
- 4 tablespoons Stir-Fried Gochujang (page 51)

Soak and cook the rice as directed on page 92 (see Cooked Short-Grain White Rice).

**Make the yukhwe:** In a bowl, combine the beef, pear juice, sugar, soy sauce, and sesame oil and mix well until fully incorporated.

**Assemble the bibimbap:** In each of four large individual bowls, place 1 cup (200 g) cooked rice. Arrange the vegetable components in equal amounts around the rice. Dress the center of the bibimbap with a drizzle of of sesame oil and top with the yukhwe. Either top each bowl with 1 tablespoon of stir-fried gochujang or serve it on the side.

# Raw Fish Bibimbap
## Hwe Bibimbap
## 회 비빔밥

dF

Koreans love to eat raw fish dishes (*hwe*), as attested by the countless restaurants specializing in *hwe*. While *hwe* is typically enjoyed on its own, it has a special charm and a new flavor when eaten in the *bibimbap* form, topping freshly cooked rice and mixed with various vegetables. In addition to the suggestions here, you could use a variety of raw fish, including tuna, salmon, rockfish, or even sliced abalone or sea cucumber.

Preparation time: 30 minutes, plus 30 minutes rice soaking time
Cooking time: 40 minutes
Serves: 4

2 cups (440 g) short-grain white rice

**For the chojang sauce:**
4 tablespoons gochujang (red chili paste)
1 tablespoon ganjang (Korean soy sauce)
1 tablespoon sugar
1 tablespoon rice vinegar
1 teaspoon sesame seeds
½ teaspoon ginger juice

**For the bibimbap:**
7 oz (200 g) sushi-grade flounder fillet
1¾ oz (50 g) squid
2½ oz (70 g) lettuce, cut into ¼-inch (6 mm) shreds
4 perilla leaves, cut into ¼-inch (6 mm) shreds
5 oz (150 g) cucumber, finely julienned
3½ oz (100 g) onion, finely julienned
5 cloves garlic, thinly sliced

Soak and cook the rice as directed on page 92 (see Cooked Short-Grain White Rice).

**Make the chojang sauce:** In a small bowl, combine the gochujang, soy sauce, sugar, vinegar, sesame seeds, and ginger juice and mix until uniform.

**Prepare the bibimbap ingredients:** Cut the flounder into ¼-inch (4.5 mm) slices. Remove the skin from the squid and cut into slices of the same size.

In each of four large individual bowls, place 1 cup (200 g) cooked white rice. Top with the lettuce, perilla, cucumber, onion, and garlic. Top with equal parts flounder and squid. Either top each bowl with 2 tablespoons of the chojang sauce or serve it on the side.

# Raw Beef Bibimbap
## Yukhwe Bibimbap
## 육회 비빔밥

---

dF

*Yukhwe* is popular as a *banchan* (side dish), an appetizer, or as the main attraction, but it's also enjoyed as a *bibimbap* variation. Although the seasoning for the *yukhwe* is usually made with *gochujang* (red chili paste) or *ganjang* (Korean soy sauce), when served in the form of *bibimbap*, it's usually made with *yangnyeom*, a sweet and hot sauce made with soy sauce. *Yukhwe bibimbap* goes well with various vegetable dishes, such as bean sprouts, spinach, and mushroom. If you have any leftover vegetable dishes, add them to taste.

To make it easier to cut the meat into fine julienne, put it into the freezer for about 20 minutes beforehand. We recommend seasoning the *yukhwe* just before serving to further enhance the fragrance while eating.

**Preparation time:** 30 minutes, plus 30 minutes rice soaking time
**Cooking time:** 40 minutes
**Serves:** 4

2 cups (440 g) short-grain white rice

For the yukhwe seasoning:
1 teaspoon salt
½ teaspoon sugar
1 teaspoon ganjang (Korean soy sauce)
1 tablespoon sesame oil
1 teaspoon ground sesame seeds

For the sauce:
3 tablespoons gochujang (red chili paste)
1 tablespoon ganjang (Korean soy sauce)
1 tablespoon sesame oil
1 tablespoon honey
1 teaspoon fine gochugaru (red chili powder)
1 teaspoon ground sesame seeds

For the bibimbap:
220 g beef sirloin (rump) or strip loin, julienned
2½ oz (70 g) lettuce, cut into ¼-inch (6 mm) shreds
2 perilla leaves, cut into ¼-inch (6 mm) shreds
2 tablespoons crushed gim
7 oz (200 g) Asian pear, peeled and finely julienned
5 cloves garlic, thinly slivered
4 raw egg yolks

Soak and cook the rice as directed on page 92 (see Cooked Short-Grain White Rice).

**Make the yukhwe seasoning:** In a small bowl, combine all the ingredients and stir until uniform. Set aside.

**Make the sauce:** In a small bowl, combine all the ingredients and stir until uniform. Set aside.

**Assemble the bibimbap:** In a large bowl, combine the julienned beef and yukhwe seasoning and toss until well seasoned.

In each of four large individual bowls, place 1 cup (200 g) cooked rice. Top with equal amounts of lettuce and perilla. Garnish with the gim, pear, and garlic. Top with the seasoned yukhwe and garnish in the center with an egg yolk. Top each bowl with 2 tablespoons of the sauce or serve it on the side.

# Mushroom Bibimbap
## Beoseot Bibimbap
## 버섯 비빔밥

df vg

Thanks to Korea's development of mushroom cultivation techniques over the years, one can enjoy high-quality mushrooms year-round. Mushrooms are used in a variety of soups, hotpots, and *banchan* (side dishes) and are also great as a main ingredient in a *bibimbap*.

In fall, when in-season wild mushrooms become available in the markets, it is the ideal time to enjoy the full flavor of mushrooms. The mushrooms listed here are to preference and can be adjusted to either create a stronger or a lighter mushroom flavor.

Preparation time: 30 minutes, plus 30 minutes rice soaking time
Cooking time: 1 hour 5 minutes
Serves: 4

2 cups (440 g) short-grain white rice

**For the mushrooms:**
5 oz (150 g) oyster mushrooms
2¾ oz (80 g) king trumpet mushrooms
5½ oz (160 g) shiitake mushrooms
2¾ oz (80 g) beech mushrooms
4 tablespoons neutral cooking oil
Salt

**For the sauce:**
3 tablespoons ganjang (Korean soy sauce)
1 teaspoon sugar
1 teaspoon fine gochugaru (red chili powder)
2 tablespoons sesame oil
2 tablespoons minced scallion (spring onion)

**To finish:**
2 tablespoons neutral cooking oil
4 eggs

Soak and cook the rice as directed on page 92 (see Cooked Short-Grain White Rice).

**Prepare the mushrooms:** Trim away the base of the oyster mushrooms and shred using your hands. Cut the king trumpet mushrooms crosswise into ⅛-inch (3 mm) slices. Thinly slice the shiitake caps. Trim the base of the beech mushrooms. In a frying pan, stir-fry each mushroom type separately in some of the cooking oil, seasoning lightly with salt.

**Make the sauce:** In a small bowl, combine the soy sauce, 3 tablespoons water, the sugar, gochugaru, sesame oil, and scallion and mix until uniform.

**To finish:** In a nonstick frying pan, heat the cooking oil. Add the eggs (if they can all fit) and cook each egg to the desired level of doneness and set aside. (It's best to leave the yolk runny so it can be mixed into the bibimbap, adding moisture and richness.)

In each of four large individual bowls, place 1 cup (200 g) cooked rice. Arrange equal amounts of each of type of cooked mushroom around the rice. Garnish with a pan-fried egg in the center. Serve with the sauce on the side.

**Variation:** For a more refined version, instead of a fried egg, prepare a traditional egg garnish called *jidan* (see Egg Gimbap, page 134).

# Thick Doenjang Barley Bibimbap
## Gang Doenjang Bori Bibimbap
## 강된장 보리 비빔밥

dF

This *bibimbap*, with its deep, savory *doenjang* and the crisp vegetables and vegetable dishes with good acidity, delivers a very harmonious flavor profile. This *bibimbap* is popular to use in *ssam* (wraps), wrapping each bite with steamed pumpkin leaves or other steamed wrap leaf. The *gang doenjang* made here is also great to eat simply mixed with plain white rice.

**Preparation time:** 30 minutes, plus 30 minutes rice soaking time
**Cooking time:** 1 hour
**Serves:** 4

1 cup (220 g) short-grain white rice
1½ cups (300 g) pearl barley, rinsed

**For the gang doenjang:**
1 tablespoon sesame oil
4½ oz (125 g) aehobak (Korean zucchini), diced
5½ oz (160 g) shiitake mushrooms, diced
3½ oz (100 g) onion, cut into ⅓-inch (8 mm) dice
1 oz (30 g) daepa (Korean scallion), halved and cut into ¼-inch (6 mm) pieces
3½ oz (100 g) fresh green Cheongyang chilies, seeded and minced
4 tablespoons doenjang (fermented soybean paste)
1 tablespoon gochujang (red chili paste)
2 tablespoons anchovy powder
1¾ oz (50 g) fresh red chilies, seeded and minced

**For the bibimbap:**
4 lettuce leaves, cut into ¼-inch (6 mm) shreds
1¾ oz (50 g) chives, minced
2¾ oz (80 g) Young Summer Radish Kimchi (page 67), cut into 1-inch (2.5 cm) pieces
2¾ oz (80 g) Korean Radish Saengchae (page 180)

Soak and cook the rice and barley as directed on page 95 (see Barley Bap).

**Make the gang doenjang:** In a pot, heat the sesame oil over medium heat. Add the zucchini, shiitakes, onion, daepa, and green chilies and stir-fry for 3 minutes. Add the doenjang, gochujang, and anchovy powder and stir-fry for 3–4 more minutes. Add ½ cup (4 fl oz/120 ml) water and boil for 10 minutes over medium heat. Add the red chilies and remove from the heat.

**Assemble the bibimbap:** In each of four large individual bowls, place 1 cup (200 g) cooked barley rice. Arrange equal amounts of the lettuce, chives, radish kimchi, and radish saengchae around the rice. Top each bowl with 3 tablespoons gang doenjang.

**Variation:** Adding 1 teaspoon soybean powder or perilla seed powder to the gang doenjang or as a garnish to the bowl adds a more savory, nutty profile to the dish.

# Assorted Sea Vegetable Bibimbap
## Haecho Bibimbap
## 해초 비빔밥

dF

Few food cultures enjoy as many different types of sea vegetables as in Korea. In addition to the common *gim*, *dasima*, and *miyeok* (wakame) varieties, Koreans cook with many different types of sea vegetables. These days, assorted dried sea vegetables are sold through physical and online marketplaces, making it easy to access the fragrance and flavors of the sea even if you don't live near the coast.

The Vinegared Gochujang (page 51) pairs well with the flavors of the seaweed, but if you'd prefer, serve this with a soy sauce dressing instead. For the sea vegetables, if a prepacked assortment of sea vegetables is not available, choose a variety of different sea vegetables, such as *tot*, *miyeok*, *dasima*, glueweed, and agar-agar seaweed.

Preparation time: 25 minutes, plus 30 minutes rice soaking time
Cooking time: 45 minutes
Serves: 4

2 cups (440 g) short-grain white rice
¾ oz (20 g) assorted dried Korean seaweed (tot, miyeok, dasima, glueweed, agar-agar)
1 lb (500 g) green cabbage, finely sliced
2½ oz (75 g) cucumber, thinly julieneed
4 tablespoons flying fish roe
4 tablespoons sesame oil
4 tablespoons Vinegared Gochujang (page 51)

Soak and cook the rice as directed on page 92 (see Cooked Short-Grain White Rice).

Rehydrate the seaweed by soaking in cold water for 10 minutes.

In each of four large individual bowls, place 1 cup (200 g) cooked white rice and arrange the cabbage, cucumber, rehydrated seaweed, and a tablespoon of flying fish roe in each bowl. Add a tablespoon of sesame oil, top with a tablespoon of vinegared gochujang, and serve.

**Variation:** To make this dish vegan/vegetarian (or if you can't source the ingredient), you can omit the flying fish roe. Vegetable dishes, such as Bean Sprout Namul (page 160) or Mung Bean Sprout Namul (variation, page 160) are popular additions. For a stronger sea vegetable flavor, you can add crushed *gim* as garnish.

# Marinated Crab Bibimbap
## Gejang Bibimbap
## 게장 비빔밥

DF

One of the most sought-after dishes by both tourists and Korean expats is the Ganjang-Marinated Crab (page 86). Freshly cooked rice mixed in with the marinade made from the crabs full of roe is a dish that instantly makes one salivate even at the thought. This *bibimbap* is often enjoyed along with sliced seaweed to enjoy in each bite.

Preparation time: 1 hour 10 minutes, plus 3 days marination (for the crabs)
Cooking time: 1½ hours
Serves: 4

2 cups (440 g) short-grain white rice
4 Ganjang-Marinated Crabs (page 86)

**For the bibimbap:**
4 eggs
Neutral cooking oil
4 tablespoons marinade from the crabs
4 tablespoons sesame oil
2 tablespoons crushed gim
1¾ oz (50 g) fresh green Cheongyang chilies, minced

Soak and cook the rice as directed on page 92 (see Cooked Short-Grain White Rice).

To prepare the crabs for serving, remove the crab shell from each crab, scraping all the roe and organs into a large bowl. Cut the crabs into quarters using sharp scissors and carefully separate the meat from its body and legs into the bowl with gloved hands. Set aside.

**For the bibimbap:** Crack the eggs into a bowl and whisk until uniform. In a nonstick frying pan, add a small amount of cooking oil, add the egg mixture, and make a quick scrambled egg. Set aside.

In a large bowl, combine the cooked rice, marinade from the crabs, sesame oil, crushed gim, and chilies and mix until uniform.

To assemble, in each of four large individual bowls, place 1 cup (200 g) of the rice mixture. Top equal amounts of scrambled egg, then top with the crab meat and innards.

**Variation:** For a spicy version, increase the chopped fresh Cheongyang or add chopped pickled chilies. The scrambled eggs in this version can be replaced with pan-fried eggs, or even raw yolks.

# Cockle Bibimbap
## Kkomak Bibimap
## 꼬막 비빔밥

DF

The eastern part of Jeollanam-do in Korea is famous for its natural abundance of cockles. While the process of cleaning the cockles can be cumbersome, their unique taste and chewiness make it worth it, especially in *bibimbap*. The cockles' flesh is firm, so you can buy a lot of them when they are in season, boil them, and freeze to use throughout the year. A traditional cockle *bibimbap* is not typically served with *cho-gochujang* (vinegared *gochujang*), but we find the acidic profile balances well with the seasoned cockles. The vegetables can be adjusted to preference, and other popular additions include *gim* and assorted sea vegetables.

Preparation time: 30 minutes, plus 12 hours soaking time
Cooking time: 50 minutes
Serves: 4

2¼ lb (1 kg) cockles in the shell
2 cups (440 g) short-grain white rice

**For the cockle seasoning:**
4 tablespoons jinjang (Korean dark soy sauce)
2 tablespoons mirin
2 tablespoons sesame oil
1 tablespoon fine gochugaru (red chili powder)
1 tablespoon coarse gochugaru (red chili flakes)
1 tablespoon ground sesame seeds
1 teaspoon sugar
1 tablespoon minced daepa (Korean scallion)
1 teaspoon minced garlic

**For the bibimbap:**
2¾ oz (80 g) lettuce, cut into ¼-inch (6 mm) shreds
4 perilla leaves, cut into ¼-inch (6 mm) shreds
1¾ oz (50 g) chives, cut into ½-inch (1.5 cm) lengths
4 tablespoons Vinegared Gochujang (page 51)

Wash the cockles under cold running water. Set in a bowl of salted water to cover and soak for 12 hours or overnight to remove any impurities.

When ready to make the bibimbap, soak and cook the rice as directed on page 92 (see Cooked Short-Grain White Rice).

Drain the cockles. In a pot, combine the cockles with enough water to submerge them and bring to a boil. Add the cockles and stir until the shells open, about 3 minutes. Drain the cockles, pull out the meats, and set them in a bowl.

**Make the cockle seasoning:** In a large bowl, combine the soy sauce, mirin, sesame oil, both types of gochugaru, the sesame seeds, sugar, daepa, and garlic. Add the cockles and toss until well seasoned.

**Assemble the bibimbap:** In each of four large individual bowls, place 1 cup (200 g) cooked white rice. Arrange the lettuce, perilla, and chives around the rice. Top the rice with equal amounts of seasoned cockles. Top each with 1 tablespoon of the vinegared gochujang or serve on the side.

# Hot Stone Bibimbap
## Dolsot Bibimbap
## 돌솥 비빔밥

dF

This style of meat-topped *bibimbap* is served in a *dolsot*, which translates to "stone pot." The *dolsot* keeps the rice and vegetables warm during the meal, making it a popular serving style, and its signature sizzling sound is an additional appetite stimulant. There are no set rules for what the vegetables dishes should be, so choose from seasonal vegetables available. (Or use any leftover vegetables dishes you have on hand.)

**Preparation time:** 1 hour, plus 30 minutes rice soaking time
**Cooking time:** 2 hours
**Serves:** 4

2 cups (440 g) short-grain white rice

**For the beef:**
3½ oz (100 g) beef eye of round or top round (topside)
1 tablespoon ganjang (Korean soy sauce)
½ tablespoon sesame oil
1 teaspoon minced garlic
1 teaspoon sugar
Freshly ground black pepper
1 teaspoon neutral cooking oil

**For the bibimbap:**
Sesame oil, for drizzling
2¾ oz (80 g) Shiitake Namul (page 183)
2¾ oz (80 g) Korean Radish Saengchae (page 180)
2¾ oz (80 g) Spinach Namul (page 166)
2¾ oz (80 g) Bean Sprout Namul (page 160)
2¾ oz (80 g) Fresh Fiddlehead Namul (page 168)
4 pan-fried eggs
5 tablespoons Stir-Fried Gochujang (page 51)

Soak and cook the rice as directed on page 92 (see Cooked Short-Grain White Rice).

**Prepare the beef:** Cut the beef into julienne ⅛ inch (3 mm) thick. In a bowl, combine the soy sauce, sesame oil, garlic, sugar, and black pepper to taste. Add the beef and mix well until fully incorporated.

Heat a frying pan over medium heat and add the cooking oil. Add the seasoned beef and stir-fry until the meat is cooked, about 1 minute. Set aside on a plate.

**Assemble the bibimbap:** Into each of four dolsots, lightly drizzle some sesame oil. Add 1 cup (200 g) of cooked rice to each dolsot, garnish with the beef stir-fry and the vegetable dishes in equal amounts, and set a fried egg in the middle.

Set the prepared stone pots over medium-low heat until sizzling, 4–5 minutes. Serve with the stir-fried gochujang.

# 쌈밥 Ssambap Wrapped Rice

*Ssambap* refers to dishes in which rice is wrapped in a leafy vegetable. Many different vegetables can be used to make *ssam*, and while *ssamjang* is the most common condiment to use in *ssam*, many different combinations, including *doenjang* (fermented soybean paste) and *jeotgal* (preserved seafood), can be used. In general, at Korean barbecue restaurants, an array of *ssam* vegetables is served along with meats to create custom *ssam*.

Korea's *ssam* culture has a long history, and beyond the culinary significance, it also carries religious and ritualistic significance as well. When making offerings, the gift, whether loose rice or an object, was carefully wrapped in *hanji*, traditional Korean paper, or cloth to signify one's dedication and consideration in prayer for a good harvest and health. During the first full moon, there is a communal custom of eating *namul ssambap* to wish each other good fortune. In this sense, the unique *ssam* culture is one of great significance and pride to Korea, carrying on the Korean spirit of health and fortune.

This chapter presents recipes that are premade in the *ssam* form rather than exploring the cultural aspect of *ssam* cuisine (see page 209). The dishes presented here are commonly made for *dosirak*, Korean lunch boxes, or as a simple homemade meal.

# Miyeok or Dasima Ssambap
미역 쌈밥 (다시마 쌈밥)

Fresh *miyeok* (wakame) and *dasima* are inexpensive, common ingredients that are great for simple meals, especially when appetites run low in the summer. The seaweed can be enjoyed lightly blanched, dipped in *chojang* (vinegared soy sauce) along with vegetables, or, as here, made into a meal as a *ssambap* (rice wrap). If fresh seaweed is hard to source, substitute with salt-preserved seaweed, but make sure to rinse in cold water multiple times to completely remove the salt.

**Preparation time: 25 minutes, plus 30 minutes rice soaking time**
**Cooking time: 50 minutes**
**Serves: 4**

6½ oz (180 g) fresh miyeok (wakame) or dasima
Scant 2 cups (350 g) Cooked Short-Grain White Rice (page 92)
1 tablespoon sesame oil
1 teaspoon sesame seeds
2 pinches of salt
4 tablespoons Vinegared Gochujang (page 51)

Set up a large bowl of ice and water. Trim away any rough, thick ends from the seaweed and wash under cold running water until clean.

Bring a pot of water to a boil and blanch the seaweed for just 10 seconds. Transfer to the cold water to stop the cooking and rinse away any impurities. Squeeze dry and cut into pieces about the size of your hand (big enough to wrap around the rice).

In a bowl, combine the rice, sesame oil, sesame seeds, and salt and mix until uniform.

On each piece of seaweed, add 1 tablespoon of seasoned rice and roll into bite-size packages. Trim off any excess seaweed.

Set the ssambap on a plate. Serve with a saucer of vinegared gochujang for dipping.

**Variation:** While miyeok ssambap is most typically served with cho-gochujang, it's also often served with pieces of jeotgal (preserved seafood), such as octopus jeotgal or sea cucumber jeotgal to top each bite of ssambap. If you choose to serve with jeotgal, adjust the amount of salt used to season the rice as the jeotgal are salty.

## Squash Leaf & Cabbage Ssambap
### Hobakip & Yangbaechu Ssambap
### 호박잎 & 양배추 쌈밥

dF vg vE -5    [□]

The squash leaf *ssambap* is a popular dish that is reminiscent of summer days, because the squash leaf is in season starting in the early summer. The savory, sweet taste and the soft texture of steamed vegetables combined with the cooked rice seasoned with *ssamjang* creates a harmonious bite. It's an ideal menu for *dosirak* (lunch boxes) or picnics. The Young Summer Radish Kimchi (page 67), a sprightly summer kimchi, is a great pairing.

**Preparation time:** 25 minutes, plus 30 minutes rice soaking time
**Cooking time:** 50 minutes
**Serves:** 4

8 green cabbage leaves (outer layers)
8 squash leaves
Scant 2 cups (350 g) Cooked Short-Grain White Rice (page 92)
3 tablespoons ssamjang (dipping sauce for ssam)
1 tablespoon sesame oil

Set up a steamer and bring the water to a boil.

Add the cabbage and squash leaves to the steamer basket, set over the boiling water, and steam for 5 minutes. Remove from the heat and let cool to room temperature in a sieve.

In a bowl, combine the cooked rice, ssamjang, and sesame oil and mix well until uniform. Using hands, form into balls 1 inch (2.5 cm) in diameter and set aside.

To make the ssambap, spread out the squash and cabbage leaves on a flat surface. Place the seasoned rice balls in the center of each leaf and wrap carefully with the leaf to finish.

**Variation:** Play with the ssamjang by mixing in minced fresh Cheongyang chilies or pickled chilies for a spicier taste. Or pair with River Snail Doenjang (page 212) or gang doenjang (see Thick Doenjang Barley Bibimbap, page 107).

## Perilla Ssambap
### Kkaennip Ssambap
### 깻잎 쌈밥

dF -5    [□]

The perilla leaf might be considered the iconic herb of Korea, but its strong fragrance can be a challenge to those unfamiliar with it. Steaming the perilla leaves and wrapping them around rice tames the strong fragrance. Paired with the deep and savory flavor of the dipping sauce, this perilla *ssambap* can be enjoyed by all palates.

**Preparation time:** 30 minutes, plus 30 minutes rice soaking time
**Cooking time:** 40 minutes
**Serves:** 3–4

16 perilla leaves
Scant 2 cups (350 g) Cooked Short-Grain White Rice (page 92)
4 tablespoons Stir-Fried Gochujang (page 51)
1 tablespoon sesame oil
1 tablespoon sesame seeds

Set up a steamer and bring the water to a boil. Set up a large bowl of ice and water.

Add the perilla leaves to the steamer basket, set it over the boiling water, and lightly steam for 1 minute. Remove and transfer to the ice bath to cool down. Once completely cooled, remove from the water and squeeze gently to remove any excess water and let dry flat.

In a large bowl, combine the cooked rice with the stir-fried gochujang, sesame oil, and sesame seeds and mix well until uniform. Using hands, form into rice balls 1 inch (2.5 cm) in diameter.

Place a rice ball on top of the rough side (back side) of each perilla leaf and wrap well. Plate and serve.

## Ramp Namul Ssambap
Myeongi Namul Ssambap
명이 나물 쌈밥

dF -S

Ramps (wild garlic) are a fleeting (and often foraged) springtime treat, and the broad leaves are perfect for wrapping around rice to make a *ssambap*. So have this recipe ready to enjoy this delicious seasonal vegetable.

Preparation time: 20 minutes, plus 30 minutes rice soaking time
Cooking time: 40 minutes
Serves: 3–4

16 ramp (wild garlic) leaves
Scant 2 cups (350 g) Cooked Short-Grain White Rice (page 92)
2 tablespoons stir-fried anchovies (see Korean Rice Balls, page 135)
1 tablespoon minced almonds

Set up a steamer and bring the water to a boil.

Add the ramps to the steamer basket, set it over the boiling water, and steam for 30 seconds. Remove from the heat and let cool to room temperature on a flat surface, gently squeezing out any excess water.

In a bowl, combine the rice with the stir-fried anchovies and minced almonds and combine until uniform. Place a spoonful of seasoned rice on each ramp leaf and roll into bite-size packages. Plate and serve.

### Variations

• Use pickled ramp leaves instead of the plain steamed leaves (be sure to adjust the salt levels in the anchovy).

• Add some grilled pork jowl (pork cheek) or pork belly to the *ssambap*.

---

## Lettuce Ssambap
Sangchu Ssambap
상추 쌈밥

dF

Regular *ssamjang* (dipping sauce for wraps) or Stir-Fried Gochujang (page 51) can be used in place of the tuna *ssamjang*. This dish also can be made using Seoul-Style Bulgogi (page 274), Gwangyang-Style Bulgogi (page 272), or Spicy Pork Bokkeum (page 251).

Preparation time: 25 minutes, plus 30 minutes rice soaking time
Cooking time: 30 minutes
Serves: 4

For the tuna ssamjang:
1 tablespoon neutral cooking oil
6 tablespoons minced onion
3½ oz (100 g) drained canned tuna
3 tablespoons gochujang (red chili paste)
1 tablespoon doenjang (fermented soybean paste)
1 teaspoon fine gochugaru (red chili powder)
1 tablespoon sugar
1 teaspoon minced garlic

For the ssambap:
16 lettuce leaves (softer textured lettuce, such as butter lettuce is preferred)
3 cups (600 g) Cooked Short-Grain White Rice (page 92)
2 tablespoons sesame oil
1 teaspoon salt
2 tablespoons sesame seeds

**Make the tuna ssamjang:** In a large frying pan, heat the cooking oil over medium heat. Add the onion and stir-fry until it begins to turn translucent. Add the tuna, gochujang, doenjang, gochugaru, sugar, and garlic, stirring well until uniform. Reduce the heat to low and continue frying until all moisture has evaporated, 2–3 minutes. Set aside in a bowl.

**Assemble the ssambap:** Trim off any tough stems on the lettuce leaves that would make them hard to wrap. Cut out the harder stem area of the lettuce into a V shape with scissors and roll each leaf into a cone shape.

In a bowl, combine the cooked rice, sesame oil, and salt until uniform. Roll the rice into 1-inch (2.5 cm) balls. Place a rice ball in each cone-shaped lettuce wrap and plate on a large, flat plate. Add 1 teaspoon of tuna ssamjang to each rice ball, and sprinkle with sesame seeds to finish.

# Aged Kimchi Ssambap
## Mugeunji Ssambap
## 묵은지 쌈밥

dF gF

Perilla leaves or Cheongyang chilies are also popular ingredients in kimchi *ssambap*. Chop them and stir into the rice mixture. The tuna mixture can be replaced with other fillings, such as stir-fried anchovies (see Korean Rice Balls, page 135).

Preparation time: 20 minutes, plus 30 minutes rice soaking time
Cooking time: 15 minutes
Serves: 4

1 head store-bought cabbage mugeunji (kimchi that has been aged for at least 6 months; about 4½ lb/2 kg)

For the rice:
3 cups (600 g) Cooked Short-Grain White Rice (page 92)
3 tablespoons sesame oil
2 tablespoons sesame seeds
1 teaspoon salt

For the tuna:
8 oz (225 g) canned tuna, well drained
2 tablespoons mayonnaise
2 pinches of freshly ground black pepper

Discard any seasonings from the mugeunji and wash the entire head of cabbage under cold running water. Once any visible seasoning is off, submerge the mugeunji in cold water for 5 minutes to reduce the saltiness. Trim the thicker stem end of the mugeunji, dice, and set aside. Gently squeeze the remaining upper stem and leafy portion of the mugeunji to drain any excess liquid and set aside.

**Prepare the rice:** In a bowl, combine the cooked rice, sesame oil, sesame seeds, and salt. Add the diced mugeunji. Mix well until uniform.

**Prepare the tuna:** In a bowl, combine the tuna, mayonnaise, and black pepper and mix well until uniform.

Form the rice mixture into balls 1½ inches (4 cm) in diameter. Lay out each leaf of the washed and drained mugeunji on a flat surface and set a rice ball on top. Top with a tablespoon of the tuna mix and roll into a bite-size wrap. Plate and serve.

# 국밥 Gukbap Rice in Soup

*Gukbap* refers to a dish in which cooked rice is folded into *guk* (soup). It is both a Korean food culture as well as the category of soup served in this way. *Gukbap* is the classic everyman's food. The scope of the term is broad, because most *guk* or *tang* (long-simmered soup) can be made into a *gukbap* just by folding in cooked rice. *Seolleongtang* (Ox Bone Tang, page 335) or *gomtang* (Beef Bone Tang, page 334) are both examples of this, and they are often served with a bowl of rice for this purpose.

This chapter explores the most common *gukbap* that are both easily enjoyed at home and also served in *gukbap* restaurants. They can be served with the rice already added to the *guk* or served separately. When served separately, the format is called *ddaro-gukbap*, which translates to "separated *gukbap*."

Usually, a *gukbap* contains vegetables, such as *siraegi* (dried radish tops) or *ugeoji* (the outer leaves and stems of vegetables), bean sprouts, various types of meat, and tofu. From a nutrition perspective, with its good balance of carbohydrates, fat, protein, and minerals, a bowl of *gukbap* is a highly nutritious meal at an affordable price. As a result, it naturally took hold as a popular food enjoyed by the common citizen. In Korea, you can see people enjoying *gukbap* at all hours of the day, from people who begin their day with a breakfast of hearty *gukbap* to those who finish a late night of drinking with a warm *gukbap* to prevent a hangover.

# Bean Sprout Gukbap
## Kongnamul Gukbap
## 콩나물국밥

dF

The light bean sprout *gukbap* with an optional dash of *gochugaru* (red chili flakes) is one of the most popular, easy *haejang-guk* (hangover cure soups) of Korea. This soup is served in a single-serve flameproof earthenware pot called a *ttukbaegi*.

Preparation time: 25 minutes, plus 30 minutes rice soaking time
Cooking time: 1 hour
Serves: 4

10 oz (300 g) soybean sprouts
10 cups (80 fl oz/2.4 liters) Anchovy Broth (page 314)
1 tablespoon cheongjang (light Korean soy sauce)
1 teaspoon salt
4 cups (800 g) Cooked Short-Grain White Rice (page 92)
1 tablespoon minced garlic
5 oz (150 g) cleaned squid bodies, cut into ½-inch (1.5 cm) pieces
1½ oz (40 g) daepa (Korean scallion), sliced on a diagonal
1 oz (25 g) fresh red chilies, slivered
2 tablespoons fine gochugaru (red chili powder)
2 tablespoons salted shrimp
2 tablespoons crushed gim

Rinse the bean sprouts in a large colander under cold running water, sifting gently to shake off the skin or broken parts. Once clean, wash one or twice more in clear water and drain in a sieve to dry.

In a pot, bring the anchovy broth to a boil. Once boiling, add the soy sauce, salt, and bean sprouts. Cover and cook for 2 minutes. Scoop the bean sprouts out of the broth and set aside.

In each of four single-serve flameproof earthenware pots, combine 1 cup (200 g) cooked rice, the garlic, cooked bean sprouts, squid, daepa, chilies, gochugaru, and salted shrimp. Add 2½ cups (20 fl oz/590 ml) of broth and bring to a boil. Serve while hot, garnished with crushed gim.

**Variation:** For a heartier version of the *gukbap*, drizzle beaten eggs into the soup while cooking, or serve a soft-boiled egg on the side.

# Dried Pollock Gukbap
## Hwangtae Gukbap
## 황태국밥

dF

Dried pollock soup warms the body on a cold winter day and is especially popular for breakfast after a night out. The clean tastes from the pollock, radish, and bean sprouts combined with the comforting egg and rice makes this one of Korea's favorite comfort meals.

**Preparation time: 30 minutes, plus 40 minutes soaking and rehydrating time**
**Cooking time: 1 hour 15 minutes**
**Serves: 4**

2¾ oz (80 g) dried pollock
7 oz (200 g) mu (Korean radish)
2 tablespoons sesame oil
8 cups (64 fl oz/1.9 liters) Anchovy Broth (page 314)
1 teaspoon minced garlic
1 tablespoon cheongjang (light Korean soy sauce)
7 oz (200 g) bean sprouts
2 eggs, lightly beaten
1 oz (30 g) daepa (Korean scallion), sliced on a diagonal
Salt
4 cups (800 g) Cooked Short-Grain White Rice (page 92)

Rinse the pollock under cold running water. Cut into 1-inch (2.5 cm) pieces using sharp scissors, and soak in a bowl of cold water for 10 minutes to rehydrate.

Peel the radish and cut into 1-inch (2.5 cm) square pieces ¼-inch (6 mm) thick.

In a pot, heat the sesame oil over medium heat, add the rehydrated pollock and 2 tablespoons water, and stir-fry until the water begins to turn white. Add the anchovy broth, radish, garlic, and soy sauce and bring to a boil over medium heat. Cook for 15 minutes, then add the bean sprouts and boil for another 3 minutes. Add the egg mixture in a slow circular motion, then add the daepa. Once the soup reaches a boil again, remove from the heat and season with salt to taste.

In each of four Korean single-serve earthenware bowls or soup bowls, place 1 cup (200 g) cooked rice. Ladle in the soup and serve hot.

## Acorn Jelly Bap
### Dotori Mukbap
### 도토리 묵밥

dF          [ㅁ]

*Mukbap* is a type of *gukbap* made by pouring anchovy broth over *dotori-muk* (acorn jelly) and rice, along with kimchi and crushed gim. It is commonly eaten in Chungcheong-do, Gyeongsang-do, and Gangwon-do. While typically served warm, in the summer season it can be enjoyed with a refreshing cold broth version.

While acorn jelly can be made with store-bought powder, most Korean markets also sell the premade acorn jelly, which can be used in this recipe.

**Preparation time: 45 minutes, plus 30 minutes rice soaking time**
**Cooking time: 1 hour 25 minutes**
**Serves: 4**

- 1 lb 5 oz (600 g) acorn jelly
- 1 lb (450 g) Napa Cabbage Kimchi (page 60), cut into 1-inch (2.5 cm) pieces
- 1 tablespoon sugar
- 1 tablespoon sesame oil
- 6½ cups (52 fl oz/1.6 liters) Anchovy Broth (page 314)
- 2 tablespoons cheongjang (light Korean soy sauce)
- 1 tablespoon ganjang (Korean soy sauce)
- 1 tablespoon anchovy fish sauce
- 4 cups (800 g) Cooked Short-Grain White Rice (page 92)
- Crushed gim

Carefully cut the acorn jelly into matchsticks ¼ inch (6 mm) thick, taking care not to break them. (Do not cut the jelly any thinner, because the texture and flavor will suffer.) Set aside.

In a large bowl, combine the kimchi, sugar, and sesame oil and mix until well combined.

In a pot, combine the anchovy broth, both soy sauces, and fish sauce and stir until uniform. The broth can be served warmed or cold.

In each of four large individual bowls, place 1 cup (200 g) cooked rice. Top with the sliced acorn jelly, seasoned kimchi, and crushed gim to taste and pour in the broth until the rice is submerged. Serve.

**Variation:** A variety of vegetables, such as perilla and lettuce, can be added for flavor. Some variations include tofu as well.

---

## Hangover Gukbap
### Haejang Gukbap
### 해장국밥

dF

*Haejang gukbap* literally translates to "hangover rice soup." As the name suggests, this is a dish eaten the morning after drinking alcohol, but it is also loved as a hearty everyday meal, because it is both satisfying and nourishing. Each region has a different variation of the dish, and this popular recipe is from the central region of Korea in which a beef broth is boiled with cabbage, bean sprouts, *doenjang* (fermented soybean paste), and cow blood. (You can judge the freshness of cow blood by its bright red color.)

As a category, *haejang guk* also includes the beloved Bean Sprout Guk (page 320), Pollock Guk (page 326), and Clear Cod Tang (page 340).

**Preparation time: 40 minutes, plus 30 minutes rice soaking time**
**Cooking time: 1 hour 10 minutes (plus 8 hours if making homemade broth)**
**Serves: 4**

- 14 oz (400 g) cow blood
- 5½ oz (160 g) store-bought boiled ugeoji, cut into 2-inch (5 cm) pieces
- 3 tablespoons doenjang (fermented soybean paste)
- 2 tablespoons cheongjang (light Korean soy sauce)
- 2 tablespoons gochugaru (red chili flakes)
- 1 teaspoon minced garlic
- 8 cups (64 fl oz/1.9 liters) Beef Broth (page 315)
- 3½ oz (100 g) beef brisket, cut into 1 × ½-inch (2.5 × 1.3 cm) pieces
- 3½ oz (100 g) soybean sprouts
- 2 oz (60 g) daepa (Korean scallion), cut into 1-inch (2.5 cm) diagonal slices
- Salt
- 4 cups (800 g) Cooked Short-Grain White Rice (page 92)

Fill a pot with enough water to submerge the cow blood and bring the water to boil over high heat. Once boiling, add the cow blood and cook until the surface turns dark brown. Use a wooden spatula to break up the blood into 2-inch (5 cm) pieces. Boil until well cooked, for another 5 minutes. Transfer to a bowl of cold water to cool.

In a bowl, combine the ugeoji, doenjang, soy sauce, gochugaru, and garlic and toss to coat.

In a large pot, bring the broth to a boil over high heat. Add the brisket and seasoned ugeoji and return to a boil. Reduce the heat to medium and continue to boil for 15 minutes. Add the bean sprouts, daepa, and cow blood and boil until all vegetables are fully cooked, another 5 minutes. Taste and season with salt if needed.

Serve in individual soup bowls with individual bowls of cooked rice on the side.

# Korean Blood Sausage Gukbap
## Sundae Gukbap
## 순대국밥

dF

*Sundae gukbap* is a *gukbap* made from pig bone broth, with *sundae* (Korean blood sausage, page 222), along with other cuts of pork and pig organ meats (offal). The *sundae gukbap* is a really popular food, and restaurants that specialize in it can be found all over the country. It is usually served with Diced Radish Kimchi (page 68), perilla seed powder, and salted shrimp, so the diner can season the *gukbap* according to taste. Chives are also a common garnish.

Because it can be difficult to source the ingredients to make the pig bone broth, store-bought beef broth is often substituted. If you choose to use beef broth, consider adding more pork flavor to the soup by cooking thinly sliced pork shank directly with the soup. Also, boiled pork organs are often sold preboiled at markets in Korea; they typically include liver, pig ear, lung, stomach, and heart.

Preparation time: 25 minutes, plus 30 minutes rice soaking time
Cooking time: 50 minutes (plus 8 hours if making homemade broth)
Serves: 4

7 oz (200 g) sundae (Korean blood sausage), store-bought or homemade (page 222)
6½ oz (180 g) boiled pork organs

For the seasoning:
2 tablespoons coarse gochugaru (red chili flakes)
1 tablespoon fine gochugaru (red chili powder)
1 tablespoon minced garlic
1 tablespoon anchovy fish sauce
1 teaspoon cheongjang (light Korean soy sauce)

For the gukbap:
10 cups (80 fl oz/2.4 liters) Pork Bone Broth (page 314) or Beef Broth (page 315)
1 teaspoon salt
1 oz (30 g) daepa (Korean scallion), thinly sliced on a diagonal
4 cups (800 g) Cooked Short-Grain White Rice (page 92)
3½ oz (100 g) garlic chives, cut into 1-inch (2.5 cm) lengths
4 tablespoons perilla seed powder (optional)
4 tablespoons salted shrimp (optional)

Cut the blood sausage and boiled pork meat into large bite-size pieces.

**Make the seasoning:** In a bowl, combine both gochugarus, the garlic, fish sauce, and soy sauce until uniform. Set aside in a saucer to serve.

**Make the gukbap:** In a pot, bring the broth and salt to a boil over high heat. Add the blood sausage and pork meat and boil for 3 more minutes. Remove from the heat and add the daepa.

Into each of four individual bowls, evenly divide the soup and meat. Serve the cooked rice directly in the bowls or in separate individual bowls on the side. Garnish with the chives. In small bowls, serve the seasoning mixture, perilla seed powder (if using), and salted shrimp (if using) for diners to individually season to taste.

# Cabbage & Beef Gukbap
## Ugeoji Sogogi Gukbap
## 우거지 소고기 국밥

DF

In Korean cuisine, *ugeoji* refers to the tougher outer leaves of cabbage that are usually removed when trimming the vegetables. These outer layers are often sold dried, or boiled first and then dried, as a popular common *guk* (soup) ingredient. For this *gukbap*, you can use a beef broth in lieu of the water for a richer soup. Mushrooms or bean sprouts are common vegetables that are added into the soup to preference.

Preparation time: 30 minutes, plus 1 hour soaking time
Cooking time: 1 hour 25 minutes
Serves: 4

7 oz (200 g) beef brisket or shank, cut into 1-inch (2.5 cm) chunks
10 oz (300 g) ugeoji (outer leaves of napa cabbage/Chinese leaf)

For the ugeoji seasoning:
2 tablespoons doenjang (fermented soybean paste)
2 tablespoons cheongjang (Korean light soy sauce)
2 tablespoons gochugaru (red chili flakes)
2 tablespoons sesame oil
1 teaspoon salt

For the gukbap:
7 oz (200 g) mu (Korean radish)
2 tablespoons cheongjang (light Korean soy sauce)
1 oz (30 g) daepa (Korean scallion), thinly sliced on a diagonal
1 tablespoon minced garlic
Salt
4 cups (800 g) Cooked Short-Grain White Rice (page 92)

Place the beef chunks in a bowl of cold water and let soak in cold water for 30 minutes to remove the blood.

Set up a bowl of ice and water. In a pot of boiling water, cook the ugeoji until tender, about 10 minutes. Transfer to the ice bath to cool. Remove from the water and squeeze gently, removing all excess moisture. Cut into 1-inch (2.5 cm) pieces and set aside.

**Make the ugeoji seasoning:** In a large bowl, combine the doenjang, soy sauce, gochugaru, sesame oil, and salt, and mix until uniform. Add the cooked ugeoji and mix well until seasoned and set aside.

**For the gukbap:** Peel the radish and cut into 1-inch (2.5 cm) square pieces ½ inch (1.5 cm) thick.

In a pot, bring 8 cups (64 fl oz/ 1.9 liters) water to a boil. Add the meat and boil over high heat for 15 minutes. Reduce the heat to medium and skim away the foam and impurities. Add the soy sauce, radish, and seasoned ugeoji and cook for 15 minutes. Add the daepa and garlic and boil for 5 more minutes. Season to taste with salt.

In each of four single-serve Korean earthenware bowls or soup bowls, place 1 cup (200 g) cooked rice. Top with equal amounts of soup and serve hot. (Alternatively, the soup and rice can be served separately.)

## 볶음밥 Bokkeumbap Fried Rice

*Bokkeumbap* is a dish in which cooked rice is fried with various combinations of ingredients. In Asian countries where rice is the staple food, many different types of fried rice exist. In Korea, in addition to its simplest form, some *bokkeumbap* are made by stir-frying rice in leftover sauce from another main dish (as in Chuncheon-Style Chicken Stir-Fry, page 256) along with kimchi, *gim* powder, and other *banchan*, often directly on the grill.

*Bokkeumbap*, like *bibimbap* (mixed rice) or *deopbap* (rice bowls), can be customized depending on the ingredients used. Well-made *bokkeumbap* is when there are no clumps of rice and each grain is evenly coated in oil. To achieve this, many home cooks prefer using at least day-old rice, which tends to be drier, rather than freshly cooked rice, which tends to be stickier. Another useful tip is to use Korean precooked rice intended to be heated up in the microwave, but instead of microwaving the rice, simply break it apart in a bowl with a spatula and use it to make *bokkeumbap*.

# Kimchi Fried Rice
## Kimchi Bokkeumbap
## 김치 볶음밥

dF -30

Made with the two staples of any Korean home, rice and kimchi, the kimchi fried rice is beloved for its simplicity and ease of preparation. Depending on preference, popular additions include bacon, Spam, crushed *gim*, and sesame seeds, but it is just as delicious as a two-ingredient recipe. If the kimchi being used is aged and very acidic, add a tablespoon of sugar to balance the flavor.

**Preparation time: 15 minutes**
**Cooking time: 10 minutes**
**Serves: 4**

4 eggs
4 tablespoons neutral cooking oil, plus more for the eggs
2 oz (60 g) daepa (Korean scallion), cut into ⅛-inch (3 mm) dice
7 oz (200 g) Napa Cabbage Kimchi (page 60), cut into ¼-inch (6 mm) pieces
3½ oz (100 g) onion, cut into ⅛-inch (3 mm) dice
2 tablespoons ganjang (Korean soy sauce)
4 cups (800 g) Cooked Short-Grain White Rice (page 92), preferably day-old
Salt

In a frying pan, pan-fry the eggs in a little oil on only one side or over easy and set aside.

Heat a large frying pan over medium heat and add the 4 tablespoons cooking oil. Add the daepa and stir-fry until translucent. Add the kimchi and onion and stir-fry for 1 minute. Add the soy sauce and stir-fry for 30 seconds. Reduce the heat to low, add the cooked rice and stir-fry until well incorporated. Taste and season with salt as needed.

Top each serving of fried rice with a fried egg.

**Variation:** Adding some cured pork, such as bacon or ham, will give the dish a delicious savory flavor profile.

# Egg & Mushroom Fried Rice
## Gyeran Beoseot Bokkeumbap
## 계란 버섯 볶음밥

dF -30

**Preparation time:** 15 minutes
**Cooking time:** 10 minutes
**Serves:** 4

4 eggs
Salt
4 tablespoons neutral cooking oil, plus more for the eggs
2 oz (60 g) daepa (Korean scallion), cut into ⅛-inch (3 mm) pieces
7 cloves garlic, thinly sliced
9 oz (250 g) oyster mushrooms, trimmed and torn apart with your hands
1 tablespoon ganjang (Korean soy sauce)
2 tablespoon anchovy fish sauce
1 tablespoon sugar
4 cups (800 g) Cooked Short-Grain White Rice (page 92), preferably day-old
2 tablespoons sesame oil

Crack the eggs into a small bowl, season with 2 pinches of salt, and beat to combine.

Heat a frying pan over medium heat and lightly coat with cooking oil. Add the egg mixture and cook, mixing the eggs constantly with a large spatula, until they are cooked to desired doneness. Set aside in a bowl.

Heat a large frying pan over medium heat and add the 4 tablespoons of cooking oil. Add the daepa and cook until translucent. Add the garlic and stir-fry until golden. Add the oyster mushrooms and fry for 30 more minutes. Add the soy sauce, fish sauce, and sugar and simmer. Reduce the heat to low, add the cooked rice, and continue to stir-fry until the rice is well incorporated with the seasoning and vegetables. Add the scrambled eggs and mix well. Season to taste with salt.

Divide into individual bowls and finish with a light drizzle of the sesame oil. Serve hot.

### Variations

• A popular alternative seasoning for mushroom fried rice is oyster sauce.

• Because garlic goes well with butter, try this with 1 tablespoon of butter in place of the sesame oil at the end of the cooking process.

# Vegetable Fried Rice
## Chaeso Bokkeumbap
## 채소 볶음밥

dF vg –3o

Vegetable fried rice can be made easily using various vegetables at home. This is a recipe that's great even for children who do not like vegetables, because the finely diced vegetables in the well-seasoned fried rice makes for an easy, delicious meal. Oyster sauce or fish sauce can be used in place of the soy sauce, and throwing in some curry powder or turmeric adds both flavor and color.

**Preparation time:** 20 minutes
**Cooking time:** 10 minutes
**Serves:** 4

2 eggs
Salt
4 tablespoons neutral cooking oil, plus more for the eggs
1¾ oz (50 g) carrot, peeled and cut into ⅛-inch (3 mm) dice
1¾ oz (50 g) potatoes, peeled and cut into ⅛-inch (3 mm) dice
3½ oz (100 g) onion, cut into ⅛-inch (3 mm) slices
2 oz (60 g) daepa (Korean scallion), cut into ⅛-inch (3 mm) slices
2 tablespoons cheongjang (light Korean soy sauce) or Yondu (Korean vegan seasoning sauce)
1 tablespoon sugar
4 cups (800 g) Cooked Short-Grain White Rice (page 92), preferably day-old

Crack the eggs into a bowl with a pinch of salt and beat to combine.

Heat a frying pan over medium heat and lightly coat with cooking oil. Add the egg mixture and cook, mixing the eggs constantly with a large spatula until they are cooked to desired doneness. Set aside in a bowl.

Heat a large frying pan over medium heat and add the 4 tablespoons cooking oil. Add the carrot and potatoes and stir-fry until cooked and slightly translucent. Add the onion and daepa and stir-fry for 30 more seconds. Add the soy sauce and sugar and simmer. Reduce the heat to low, add the cooked rice, and stir-fry until well combined. Add the scrambled eggs, increase the heat to high, and stir-fry for 30 more seconds. Season to taste with salt.

Serve hot in individual bowls.

# 김밥
## Gimbap Gim Rice Rolls

*Gimbap* is a popular and common Korean dish made from cooked rice seasoned with salt and sesame oil and such ingredients as vegetables, fish, and meats rolled in *gim*, which are sheets of dried seaweed. It's easily transportable wrapped in foil or in containers as a boxed lunch, making it one of the most popular *dosirak* (packed meals) for picnics, excursions, or a simple lunch. While traditionally a humble meal, today there are many premium and creative shops that offer new modern combinations of *gimbap*.

Most Koreans become familiar with *gimbap* from an early age. It is a popular food for young children; even picky children will tend to eat rice wrapped in the savory, salty *gim*. *Gimbap* is ever present in all outings with family or friends, and for students in middle and high school, it is an affordable snack available at convenience stores. In adulthood, during busy mornings or late nights at work, a roll of *gimbap* is often a nutritious and delicious easy meal. In many ways, *gimbap* is one of the most important dishes of Korean cuisine, playing a ubiquitous role in the daily lives of Koreans.

# Gim-Wrapped Rice
## Gimbap
## 김밥

dF

This is the most common *gimbap* recipe, but the ingredients can be adjusted in many ways according to preference. Popular ingredients include cucumber, seasoned burdock, crabmeat, perilla leaf, and tofu.

**Preparation time: 30 minutes**
**Cooking time: 15 minutes**
**Serves: 4**

3 eggs
Salt
8 tablespoons neutral cooking oil
7 oz (200 g) carrots, peeled and julienned
9 oz (250 g) spinach, stemmed
2 sheets fish cake
1 tablespoon ganjang (Korean soy sauce)
1 tablespoon sugar

**For assembly:**
4 cups (800 g) Cooked Short-Grain White Rice (page 92)
1 tablespoon salt
2 tablespoons sesame oil, plus more for coating
8 sheets gim, labeled for use in gimbap
8 sticks ham, labeled for use in gimbap
8 sticks danmuji (yellow pickled radish), labeled for use in gimbap

Crack the eggs into a small bowl, add 2 pinches of salt, and beat until well combined.

In a nonstick frying pan, heat 1 tablespoon of the cooking oil over low heat. Add the egg mixture, folding to make a thick layer. Remove from the heat once cooked and set aside to cool. Slice the cooked eggs into sticks ½ inch (1.3 cm) thick and the length of the gim sheets.

In a nonstick frying pan, heat 3 tablespoons of the cooking oil over medium heat. Add the carrots with 2 pinches of salt and stir-fry for 3 minutes and set aside.

In another nonstick frying pan, heat 2 tablespoons of the cooking oil over medium heat. Add the spinach with 2 pinches of salt and stir-fry quickly. Add 4 tablespoons water and simmer until the spinach is cooked and wilted, about 3 minutes. Set aside.

Slice the fish cakes into ¼-inch (6 mm) slices. In a frying pan, heat the remaining 2 tablespoons cooking oil over medium heat. Add the soy sauce, sugar, and 4 tablespoons of water and fry until the water evaporates. Set aside.

**Assemble the gimbap:** In a large bowl, combine the cooked rice with the salt and sesame oil and mix until well combined. On a bamboo rolling mat, place a sheet of gim, rough side facing up, and flatten out ½ cup (100 g) of the seasoned rice evenly over the gim. From the bottom of the sheet, add the prepared carrot, spinach, fish cakes, ham, eggs, and pickled radish. Use both hands to tightly roll the mat, holding in the gimbap fillings, until completely rolled to the end. Repeat to make 7 more rolls.

Using a brush or the back of the spoon, lightly coat the outside of the rolls with sesame oil. Cut each roll with a sharp knife crosswise into ¾-inch (2 cm) slices. Plate on a flat dishware and serve immediately, or pack into a container.

# Chungmu Gimbap
## 충무 김밥

dF

The Chungmu *gimbap* is named after the city of Chungmu, the former name of today's Tongyeong, where it's still a popular local specialty. Chungmu *gimbap* is rolls of cooked rice wrapped in *gim*, served along with marinated squid and diced radish kimchi. It's eaten with toothpicks or similar utensils, pairing each bite of the plain rolls with the squid *seokbakji banchan*.

Preparation time: 30 minutes
Cooking time: 10 minutes
Serves: 4

**For the squid muchim:**
½ cup (30 g) mu-mallaengi (dried radish strips)
1 squid, cleaned
2 sheets fish cake
1 oz (30 g) daepa (Korean scallion), cut into ⅛-inch (3 mm) pieces
1 tablespoon sugar
1 tablespoon jinjang (Korean dark soy sauce)
1 tablespoon corn (golden) syrup
2 tablespoons fish sauce
2 tablespoons fine gochugaru (red chili powder)
1 tablespoon coarse gochugaru (red chili flakes)

**For the assembly:**
4 cups (800 g) Cooked Short-Grain White Rice (page 92)
1 tablespoon salt
2 tablespoons sesame oil, plus more for coating
8 sheets roasted gim, labeled for use in gimbap
7 oz (200 g) Diced Radish Kimchi (page 68)

**Make the squid muchim:** In a bowl of lukewarm water, rehydrate the dried radish strips for 10 minutes. Drain and squeeze to remove any excess water.

Meanwhile, in a pot of boiling water, blanch the squid for 2 minutes. Scoop out the squid (and keep the water boiling). Cut the body into 2 × ½-inch (5 × 1.3 cm) pieces. Cut the tentacles into 2-inch (5 cm) pieces and set aside. Slice the fish cakes into 2 × ½-inch (5 × 1.3 cm) pieces. Add them to the boiling water and blanch for 1 minute. Drain and set aside.

In a bowl, combine the prepared rehydrated radish strips, the squid, fish cakes, daepa, sugar, soy sauce, corn syrup, fish sauce, and both gochugarus and combine until evenly seasoned.

**Assemble the gimbap:** In a bowl, combine the cooked rice, salt, and sesame oil. Slice the roasted gim sheets into sixths. On the rough side of the gim, spread 1 tablespoon of the seasoned rice evenly and roll and repeat for all remaining gim sheets.

Using a brush or the back of a spoon, lightly coat the rolls in sesame oil. Plate the rolls along with the squid muchim and diced radish kimchi and serve immediately, or pack into a container.

# Tuna Gimbap
## Chamchi Gimbap
## 참치 김밥

dF

While there are endless variations of *gimbap*, the most popular menu item at *gimbap* restaurants is probably the tuna *gimbap*. The fillings can be made to preference, but it's highly recommended that perilla is included, because it's not only a great pairing but also protects the rest of the ingredients from the tuna or mayonnaise, preventing a potential mess.

**Preparation time:** 20 minutes
**Cooking time:** 15 minutes
**Serves:** 4

3 eggs
Salt
4 tablespoons neutral cooking oil
7 oz (200 g) carrots, peeled and julienned
5 oz (150 g) cucumber, julienned

For the tuna:
9 oz (250 g) canned tuna, well drained
2 tablespoons mayonnaise
1 tablespoon sugar
2 pinches of freshly ground black pepper

For assembly:
4 cups (800 g) Cooked Short-Grain White Rice (page 92)
1 tablespoon salt
2 tablespoons sesame oil, plus more for coating
8 sheets roasted gim, labeled for use in gimbap
16 perilla leaves
8 sticks danmuji (yellow pickled radish), labeled for use in gimbap

Crack the eggs into a small bowl, add 2 pinches of salt, and beat until well combined.

In a nonstick frying pan, heat 1 tablespoon of the cooking oil. Add the egg mixture, folding to make a thick layer. Remove from the heat once cooked and set aside to cool. Slice the cooked eggs into sticks ½ inch (1.3 cm) thick and the length of the gim sheet.

In a nonstick frying pan, heat the remaining 3 tablespoons of cooking oil over medium heat. Add the carrots with 2 pinches of salt, and stir-fry for 3 minutes. Set aside.

In a bowl, massage the cucumber with 2 pinches of salt and set aside. (You will need to squeeze the cucumber and discard any water that is released from it before incorporating into the gimbap.)

**Make the tuna mixture:** In a bowl, combine the tuna, mayonnaise, sugar, and black pepper and mix well until evenly incorporated.

**Assemble the gimbap:** In a large bowl, combine the cooked rice, salt, and sesame oil and mix until well combined. On a bamboo rolling mat, place a sheet of gim, rough side facing up, and flatten out ½ cup (100 g) of the seasoned rice evenly over the gim. Top the rice with 2 perilla leaves. From the bottom, add the prepared carrot, cucumber, tuna, eggs, and yellow pickled radish. Use both hands to tightly roll the mat, holding in the gimbap fillings, until completely rolled to the end. Repeat to make 7 more rolls.

Using a brush or the back of the spoon, lightly coat the outside of the rolls with sesame oil. Cut each roll with a sharp knife crosswise into ¾-inch (2 cm) slices. Plate on a flat dishware and serve immediately, or pack into a container.

# Egg Gimbap
## Gyeran Gimbap
## 계란 김밥

dF

The egg *gimbap* is a special type of *gimbap* that uses strips of eggs as the main ingredient. While it is a simple recipe, the harmony of the light eggs, savory fish cake, and sweet-and-sour yellow pickled radish is beloved by all.

**Preparation time: 20 minutes**
**Cooking time: 15 minutes**
**Serves: 4**

**For the egg jidan:**
8 eggs
1 teaspoon salt
1 tablespoon mirin
1 tablespoon neutral cooking oil

**For the stir-fried fish cake:**
4 sheets fish cake
3 tablespoon neutral cooking oil
2 tablespoons ganjang (Korean soy sauce)
1 tablespoon sugar

**For assembly:**
4 cups (800 g) Cooked Short-Grain White Rice (page 92)
1 tablespoon salt
2 tablespoons sesame oil, plus more for coating
8 sheets gim, labeled for use in gimbap
8 sticks danmuji (yellow pickled radish), labeled for use in gimbap

**Make the egg jidan:** Crack the eggs into a bowl, add the salt and mirin, and beat until well combined. In a nonstick frying pan, heat the cooking oil over low heat. Add a portion of the egg mixture to create a thin sheet. Remove from the heat once cooked and set aside to cool. Repeat until the egg mixture is finished. Thinly slice the cooked eggs and set aside.

**Make the stir-fried fish cake:** Slice the fish cake sheets into ⅛-inch (3 cm) slices. In a nonstick frying pan, heat the cooking oil over medium heat. Add the fish cake slices and cook for 1 minute. Add the soy sauce, sugar, and ½ cup (4 fl oz/120 ml) water and simmer until the water evaporates.

**Assemble the gimbap:** In a large bowl, combine the cooked rice, salt, and sesame oil and mix until well combined. On a bamboo rolling mat, place a sheet of gim, rough side facing up, and flatten out ½ cup (100 g) of the seasoned rice evenly over the gim. From the bottom of the sheet, add the yellow pickled radish, fish cakes, and eggs. Use both hands to tightly roll the mat, holding in the gimbap fillings, until completely rolled to the end. Repeat to make 7 more rolls.

Using a brush or the back of the spoon, lightly coat the outside of the rolls with sesame oil. Cut each roll with a sharp knife crosswise into ¾-inch (2 cm) slices. Plate on a flat dishware and serve immediately, or pack into a container.

# Korean Rice Balls
## Jumeok-bap
## 주먹밥

dF -3o

There are endless variations of rice balls that can be made, depending on the filling ingredients, shape, and the wrapping ingredient. *Jumeok-bap*, which translates to "fist-rice," can be made with cooked white rice filled in the center with strongly seasoned ingredients, such as *jeotgal* (preserved seafood), *bokkeum* (stir-fried ingredients), or modern ingredients, such as ham. It can also be made by mixing seasoned ingredients, such as meat stir-fry, anchovy stir-fry, and vegetable stir-fry, right into the rice and then shaped. This recipe showcases the simple and popular rice ball made with stir-fried baby anchovies.

While not as prominent as the *gimbap*, it's a popular item readily available in all convenience stores. The triangular rice ball is another popular form of rice balls.

Preparation time: 10 minutes
Cooking time: 10 minutes
Serves: 4

**For the anchovy stir-fry:**
3 tablespoons neutral cooking oil
4 oz (120 g) dried baby anchovies
1 teaspoon minced garlic
1 teaspoon sesame seeds
3 tablespoons cheongjang (light Korean soy sauce) or Yondu (Korean vegan seasoning sauce)
2 tablespoons mirin
4 tablespoons corn (golden) syrup

**For the rice balls:**
4 cups (800 g) Cooked Short-Grain White Rice (page 92)
1 tablespoons sesame oil
1¾ oz (50 g) seasoned gim powder

**Make the anchovy stir-fry:** In a nonstick skillet, heat the cooking oil over medium heat. Add the baby anchovies and stir-fry for 1 minute 30 seconds as if deep-frying. Add the garlic and stir well for 15 seconds. Add the sesame seeds, soy sauce, mirin, and corn syrup and continue to stir-fry for 1 minute. Set aside to cool on a plate.

**Make the rice balls:** In a large bowl, combine the cooked rice, sesame oil and the stir-fried anchovies and mix well until uniform. Shape into bite-size balls and coat with the seasoned gim powder. Plate on a flat dishware and serve.

## 솥밥 Sotbap Pot Rice

*Sotbap* refers to rice that has been cooked in a *sot*, which is a cauldron. In Korea, rice was traditionally cooked in either a *dolsot* (stone pot) or in a *gamasot* (iron pot). In modern Korea, rice is mostly cooked using electric rice cookers. The term *sotbap* also refers to the one-pot rice dishes that have been cooked together with various ingredients and are typically served in its pot. Korean *sotbap* are characterized by the use of a huge variety of vegetables.

*Sotbap* is especially popular as a dish to serve when entertaining, because it is a relatively simple yet highly satisfying dish that can easily feed a crowd. In addition, because it is typically prepared with in-season ingredients, it's a great showcase for the season's peak tastes. In spring, *namul* (greens) and bamboo shoots are popular ingredients; in summer, the seasonal delicacies, such as *euneo* (sweetfish), tomato, eggplant (aubergine), and corn, are used in many different ways to create delicious *sotbap*. In fall, mushrooms—ranging from the precious songyi mushroom to oyster and wood ear mushrooms—become the main ingredients. In winter, the abundance of seafood—king crab and oysters—as well as winter vegetables, such as *mu* (Korean radish), are the highlights. And the flavor combinations can be endlessly personalized to create unique, delicious *sotbap* all year long.

## Dried Namul Sotbap
### Gunnamul Sotbap
### 건나물솥밥

df vg vE

Using dried *namul* (wild greens) to make pot rice can make an excellent dish on its own. Rehydrated *namul* can be cooked directly with the rice without seasoning or precooking, but this method of seasoning and stir-frying before cooking with the rice results in a more savory, deep flavor. Dried *namul* is sold prepacked, and some types you might encounter are *gondeure* and *chwinamul*. Depending on the type of *namul*, the degree of dehydration, and storage conditions, the rehydration times may vary.

**Preparation time:** 1 hour, plus 4½ hours soaking time
**Cooking time:** 1 hour
**Serves:** 4

- 2¾ oz (80 g) dried namul (gondeure, chwinamul, etc.)
- 2 tablespoons cheongjang (light Korean soy sauce) or Yondu (Korean vegan seasoning sauce)
- 2 tablespoons perilla oil
- 1 teaspoon minced garlic
- 1 tablespoon neutral cooking oil
- 2 cups (440 g) short-grain white rice

Fill a large pot with 8½ cups (68 fl oz/2 liters) room temperature water, add the dried namul, and rehydrate for 4 hours.

In a pot of fresh water, cook the namul in simmering water until it has a soft natural texture, 30 minutes or longer as needed. Drain and rinse with cold water, then drain excess moisture; if not using on the day, set aside in the refrigerator in water.

Trim the fully rehydrated namul into 1-inch (2.5 cm) pieces. In a bowl, combine it with the soy sauce, perilla oil, and garlic and mix well.

In a frying pan, heat the cooking oil over medium heat. Add the seasoned namul and stir-fry until the seasoning is well incorporated.

In a bowl, wash the rice in three or four changes of water until it is clear. Add fresh water to the bowl and let the rinsed rice soak for 30 minutes. Drain in a sieve to get rid of any excess water.

In a cast-iron pot, combine the soaked rice, seasoned namul, and 2 cups (16 fl oz/480 ml) water. Cover with a lid and bring to a boil over high heat. Reduce the heat to medium-low and simmer for 15 minutes. Reduce the heat to the lowest setting and simmer for 15 more minutes. Remove from the heat and let steam for 5 more minutes before serving.

---

## Bean Sprout Sotbap
### Kong Namul Sotbap
### 콩나물 솥밥

df vg vE

This simple dish is made by cooking rice and soybean sprouts together in a pot. Mirin removes any potential dankness in the flavor of the bean sprouts and adds a slight sweetness to the rice. If you'd like, add a small piece of *dasima* to the pot to add to the savory taste of the rice.

**Preparation time:** 10 minutes, plus 30 minutes soaking time
**Cooking time:** 40 minutes
**Serves:** 4

- 2 cups (440 g) short-grain white rice
- 7 oz (200 g) soybean sprouts, rinsed and drained
- 1 tablespoon mirin

**For the seasoning sauce:**
- 4 tablespoons ganjang (Korean soy sauce)
- 2 tablespoons gochugaru (red chili flakes)
- 1 tablespoon sesame oil
- 1 teaspoon minced scallion (spring onion)
- 1 teaspoon minced garlic
- 1 teaspoon crushed sesame seeds

In a bowl, wash the rice in three or four changes of water until it is clear. Add fresh water to the bowl and let the rinsed rice soak for 30 minutes. Drain in a sieve to get rid of any excess water.

In a cast-iron pot, combine the soaked rice, bean sprouts, mirin, and 2 cups (16 fl oz/480 ml) water. Cover with a lid and bring to a boil over high heat. Reduce the heat to medium-low and simmer for 15 minutes. Reduce the heat to the lowest setting and simmer for 10 more minutes.

**Meanwhile, make the seasoning sauce:** In a small bowl, combine the soy sauce, 4 tablespoons water, the gochugaru, sesame oil, scallion, garlic, and sesame seeds. Set aside in a saucer or small bowl.

Serve the rice hot with the seasoning sauce on the side.

**Variation:** Instead of cooking the raw bean sprouts directly with the rice, to preserve the charming, crunchy texture of the bean sprouts, cook the sprouts separately and then use the cooking water to cook the rice. Add the bean sprouts during the final steaming process.

# Bamboo Shoot Sotbap
## Juksun Sotbap
## 죽순 솥밥

dF vg vE

Fresh bamboo shoots are only available for a small window in the late spring to early summer, but they are accessible year-round in the form of either canned or precooked. Even store-bought soy-marinated bamboo shoots can be used to make this *sotbap*. Of course, nothing will beat the subtle flavor of sweet, fresh bamboo shoots, which smell like sweet corn. Paired with the floral fragrance of *minari*, this dish is a delicacy to be enjoyed.

**Preparation time:** 10 minutes, plus 30 minutes soaking time
**Cooking time:** 40 minutes
**Serves:** 4

2 cups (440 g) short-grain white rice
7 oz (200 g) boiled bamboo shoots, cut into ⅛-inch (3 mm) matchsticks
2 tablespoons mirin
¼ oz (5 g) dasima
1¾ oz (50 g) minari, cut into ½-inch (1.3 cm) lengths

**For the seasoning sauce:**
4 tablespoons ganjang (Korean soy sauce)
2 tablespoons sesame oil
1 tablespoon sugar

In a bowl, wash the rice in three or four changes of water until it is clear. Add fresh water to the bowl and let the rinsed rice soak for 30 minutes. Drain in a sieve to get rid of any excess water.

In a pot, combine the soaked rice, bamboo shoots, mirin, dasima, and 2 cups (16 fl oz/480 ml) water. Cover with a lid and bring to a boil over high heat. Reduce the heat to low and simmer for 15 minutes. Reduce the heat to the lowest heat level and let steam for 10 minutes, then mix in the minari with a spatula.

**Meanwhile, make the seasoning sauce:** In a bowl, combine the soy sauce, sesame oil, and sugar. Set aside in a saucer or a small bowl.

Serve the rice hot with the seasoning sauce on the side.

**Variations**

• In addition to minari, cham namul, a fragrant wild green, is also a great pairing with the bamboo shoots.

• For more texture and flavor, add some burdock.

• Another way to make this is to stir the seasoning sauce in with the rice when cooking so it can absorb into the bamboo shoots.

# Pine Mushroom Sotbap
## Songyi Sotbap
## 송이 솥밥

df vg vE

The songyi mushroom (aka the pine mushroom or matsutake), which begins to appear around Chuseok (a major autumnal harvest festival and three-day holiday) in early September, is one of the most prized mushrooms in Korea, because its intense, floral aroma and precious texture cannot be replicated by any other mushroom. As such, it's often given as a luxurious gift. While there are many ways to enjoy this ingredient, one of the best ways to enjoy it while maximizing the flavor and texture is in the form of a *sotbap*.

**Preparation time:** 10 minutes, plus 30 minutes soaking time
**Cooking time:** 45 minutes
**Serves:** 4

9 oz (250 g) songyi mushrooms (pine mushrooms or matsutake)
¼ oz (5 g) dasima
2 cups (440 g) short-grain white rice
5 oz (150 g) oyster mushrooms
20 ginkgo nuts
1 tablespoon cheongjang (light Korean soy sauce)

**For the seasoning sauce:**
3 tablespoons ganjang (Korean soy sauce)
1 tablespoon sesame oil
1 tablespoon sugar
2 teaspoons minced scallion (spring onion)

Scrape off any dirt from the songyi mushrooms with a knife and clean them with a wet towel. Peel the skin and trim off any tough ends of the stems. Add the peel and scraps to a pot with 2 cups (16 fl oz/480 ml) water and the dasima and boil over medium heat for 15 minutes. Strain the broth and set aside to cool.

In a bowl, wash the rice in three or four changes of water until it is clear. Add fresh water to the bowl and let the rinsed rice soak for 30 minutes. Drain in a sieve to get rid of any excess water.

Slice the songyi mushrooms lengthwise into slices ¼ inch (6 mm) thick. Remove the roots of the oyster mushrooms and tear along the grain into thin strips with your hands.

In a small dry frying pan, pan-fry the gingko nuts for 2–3 minutes. Once cool enough to handle, rub or peel off the skins.

In a pot, combine the soaked rice, mushroom broth, light soy sauce, and oyster mushrooms. Cover with a lid and bring to a boil over high heat. Reduce the heat to low and simmer for 15 minutes. Reduce the heat to the lowest heat level, add the songyi mushrooms, cover, and let steam for 10 minutes.

**Meanwhile, make the seasoning sauce:** In a small bowl, combine the soy sauce, sesame oil, sugar, and scallion. Set aside in a saucer or a small bowl.

Serve the mushroom rice hot with the seasoning sauce on the side.

## Perilla & Mushroom Sotbap
### Deulkkae Beoseot Sotbap
### 들깨버섯솥밥

dF vg vE

Korea has a well-developed practice of mushroom cultivation, so a variety of fresh, high-quality mushrooms are available all year-round. Yet, when the weather cools in fall, delicious wild foraged mushrooms are in season and mushroom-based dishes come to mind more frequently. This recipe uses the readily available shiitake and oyster mushroom, but it can be modified using any mushroom.

**Preparation time:** 10 minutes, plus 30 minutes soaking time
**Cooking time:** 40 minutes
**Serves:** 4

2 cups (440 g) short-grain white rice
7 oz (200 g) fresh shiitake mushrooms
6½ oz (180 g) oyster mushrooms
1 tablespoon perilla seed powder

**For the seasoning sauce:**
4 tablespoons ganjang (Korean soy sauce)
1 tablespoon rice vinegar
1 tablespoon perilla oil
1 tablespoon minced chives
1 tablespoon roasted perilla seeds

In a bowl, wash the rice in three or four changes of water until it is clear. Add fresh water to the bowl and let the rinsed rice soak for 30 minutes. Drain in a sieve to get rid of any excess water.

Meanwhile, stem the shiitakes and slice the caps into ⅛-inch (3 mm) slices. Trim the bottoms of the oyster mushrooms and tear into small pieces following the grain.

In a dry nonstick frying pan, pan-fry the mushrooms over medium heat until lightly browned, about 1 minute. Set aside on a plate to cool.

In a pot, combine the soaked rice, perilla seed powder, and 2 cups (16 fl oz/480 ml) water. Cover with a lid and bring to a boil over high heat. Reduce the heat to low and simmer for 15 minutes. Reduce the heat to the lowest heat level, add the cooked mushrooms, cover, and let steam for 10 minutes.

**Meanwhile, make the seasoning sauce:** In a bowl, combine the soy sauce, vinegar, perilla oil, chives, and perilla seeds. Set aside in a saucer or a small bowl.

Serve the rice hot with the seasoning sauce along with.

**Variations**

• For a faster recipe, add the mushrooms directly to the rice from the beginning. The mushrooms will have a softer texture and will not smell as mushroom-y.

• For a spicier version, add some minced fresh Cheongyang chilies or any type of chili pepper.

---

## Oyster Sotbap
### Gul Sotbap
### 굴 솥밥

dF

In Korea, oysters are in season from October to January and are harvested in abundance along the southern coast. Shucked fresh oysters are easily accessible and affordable. Oyster and *mu* (Korean radish) make a great pairing due to the radish's refreshing, cool taste profile; cooking them together with rice creates a delicious meal.

The oysters only need to be cooked for a short amount of time, so they are added in the last 10 minutes of simmering.

**Preparation time:** 20 minutes, plus 30 minutes soaking time
**Cooking time:** 30 minutes
**Serves:** 4

2 cups (440 g) short-grain white rice
Salt
12 oz (350 g) shucked fresh oysters
5 oz (150 g) mu (Korean radish)

**For the seasoning sauce:**
4 tablespoons ganjang (Korean soy sauce)
1 tablespoon rice vinegar
1 tablespoon gochugaru (red chili flakes)
1 teaspoon minced scallion (spring onion)
1 teaspoon minced garlic
1 teaspoon crushed sesame seeds

In a bowl, wash the rice in three or four changes of water until it is clear. Add fresh water to the bowl and let the rinsed rice soak for 30 minutes. Drain in a sieve to get rid of any excess water.

Meanwhile, make a 3 percent salt solution. For every 1 cup (237 g) water, add 1 teaspoon (7 g) salt. Gently wash the fresh oysters in the salt solution to get rid of any impurities and drain in a sieve. Cut the radish into matchsticks 2 inches (5 cm) long and ⅛ inch (3 mm) thick.

**Make the seasoning sauce:** In a bowl, combine the soy sauce, vinegar, gochugaru, scallion, garlic, and sesame seeds. Set aside in a saucer or a small bowl.

In a pot, combine the soaked rice, radish, and 1¾ cups (14 fl oz/420 ml) water. Cover with a lid and bring to a boil over high heat. Reduce the heat to low and simmer for 15 minutes. Reduce the heat to the lowest heat level, add the oysters, and let steam for 10 minutes. Serve hot with the seasoning sauce on the side.

# Chicken Sotbap
## Gyeban
## 계반 (닭고기밥)

dF

*Samgyetang* (Herbal Chicken Tang, page 336) is the classic restorative summer dish in Korean cuisine. This chicken rice recipe is another great alternative. Made with chicken broth, it pairs well with a variety of nuts and vegetables as well.

Note that in Korea you can buy *samgyetang* herbal packages for seasoning the chicken broth, but they may be hard to source elsewhere. The packages include ginseng, astragalus root, and jujube, so add any of these if you can find them. Failing that, just add black peppercorns.

**Preparation time:** 1 hour
**Cooking time:** 40 minutes
**Serves:** 4

**For the chicken broth:**
1 lb 5 oz (600 g) bone-in, skin-on chicken thighs
1 package samgyetang (herbal chicken soup) mix
1 oz (25 g) garlic
½ oz (10 g) fresh ginger
1 oz (30 g) daepa (Korean scallion)

**For the sotbap:**
2 tablespoons neutral cooking oil
3 tablespoons ganjang (Korean soy sauce)
2 cups (440 g) short-grain white rice

**For the seasoning sauce:**
4 tablespoons ganjang (Korean soy sauce)
1 tablespoon mirin
1 tablespoon sesame oil
1 tablespoon gochugaru (red chili flakes)
1 teaspoon minced garlic
1 teaspoon minced scallion (spring onion)

**Make the chicken broth:** In a pot, combine the chicken, herbal package, garlic, ginger, daepa, and 5 cups (40 fl oz/1.2 liters) water. Bring to a boil over medium heat and cook for 30 minutes. Set aside the cooked chicken. Strain the broth and set aside. Remove any bones and skin from the cooked chicken and tear the meat into small strips by hand.

**Prepare the sotbap:** In a nonstick frying pan, heat the cooking oil over medium heat. Add the chicken strips and 2 tablespoons of the soy sauce and stir-fry until well seasoned.

In a pot, combine the rice, 2 cups (16 fl oz/480 ml) of chicken broth, and the remaining 1 tablespoon soy sauce. Cover with a lid and bring to a boil over high heat. Reduce the heat to low and simmer for 15 minutes. Reduce the heat to the lowest heat level, add the chicken, cover, and let steam for 10 minutes.

**Meanwhile, make the seasoning sauce:** In a bowl, combine the soy sauce, mirin, sesame oil, gochugaru, garlic, and scallion. Set aside in a saucer or a small bowl.

Serve the sotbap hot with the seasoning sauce on the side.

**Variation:** A popular variation adds ginkgo nuts, pine nuts, and sliced chestnuts while cooking the rice for a more robust dish.

## 덮밥 Deopbap Rice Bowls

*Deopbap* refers to a bowl of cooked rice that is served topped with a main *banchan* (side dish). The rice and *banchan* are prepared separately and combined in a single bowl. The most common *deopbap* include *gogi deopbap* (meat-based rice bowl), *ojingeo deopbap* (squid rice bowl), and kimchi *deopbap*.

The origin of the rice bowl format is unclear, but it is assumed to be an ancient and common practice throughout East Asia, where rice is the staple food. For one thing, because the entire meal is presented in a single bowl, it is easy and efficient, especially during a busy day. These days, as the average household size shrinks and there are many people who live alone, simple, convenient meal formats are becoming more popular. The *deopbap* has seen an increase in popularity and can be seen commonly in markets and convenience stores, even being sold in a simplified format called "cup rice."

# Bulgogi Deopbap
## 불고기 덮밥

dF

There are many regional *bulgogi* variations, but for the purposes of a *deopbap* (rice bowls), the Seoul style (with its brothiness and sweet marinade) is most apt. You can adjust the amount or thickness of the bulgogi broth to taste, and for a moist, brothy rice bowl, the starch thickener can be completely omitted. For convenience, the beef can be marinated a day in advance (or you could even use leftover *bulgogi*).

Preparation time: 10 minutes, plus 30 minutes marinating and soaking time
Cooking time: 40 minutes
Serves: 4

2 cups (440 g) short-grain white rice

**For the marinated beef:**
4 tablespoons jinjang (dark Korean soy sauce)
1 tablespoon light brown sugar
2 tablespoons Korean pear juice
1 tablespoon mirin
1 teaspoon minced scallion (spring onion)
1 teaspoon sesame oil
Pinch of freshly ground black pepper
1 lb (500 g) beef sirloin (rump), thinly cut into 1/16-inch (2 mm) slices

**For the bulgogi:**
1 oz (30 g) enoki mushrooms, torn into small pieces
1½ oz (40 g) fresh shiitake mushrooms, caps cut into 1/8-inch (3 mm) slices
2 oz (60 g) daepa (Korean scallion), thinly sliced on a diagonal
3½ oz (100 g) onion, cut into 1/8-inch (3 mm) slices
½ tablespoon potato starch or cornstarch (cornflour)

Soak and cook the rice as directed on page 92 (see Cooked Short-Grain White Rice).

**Meanwhile, marinate the beef:** In a large bowl, stir together the soy sauce, brown sugar, pear juice, mirin, scallion, sesame oil, and black pepper. Add the sliced beef, mix well, and let marinate for 30 minutes.

**Make the bulgogi:** Heat a nonstick frying pan over medium heat. Add the marinated beef, enoki mushrooms, shiitakes, daepa, and onion. Let the meat cook, without overstirring, until one side is brown. Add ½ cup (4 fl oz/120 ml) water and once the water begins to boil, add the potato starch and an additional 2 tablespoons water, then stir well to create a uniform consistency and fully cook the meat.

In each of four large individual bowls, place 1 cup (200 g) cooked rice. Top with equal amounts of bulgogi. Serve hot.

**Variation:** Omit the potato starch and instead pour in 1 egg at the end and simmer, covered, to create a softly cooked egg-*bulgogi* rice bowl.

# Spicy Pork Deopbap
## Jeyuk Deopbap
## 제육 덮밥

DF

In the same way that *bunsik* (casual street food) restaurants across the street from public schools provide popular simple dishes such as *tteokbokki* (stir-fried rice cakes), *sundae* (blood sausage), and *gimbap* (rice rolled in seaweed), there are many simple one-meal restaurants that provide easy lunch options around college campuses and business centers. Of these meals, the *jeyuk deopbap* is one of the most popular options as it's both delicious and filling.

**Preparation time:** 10 minutes, plus 30 minutes up to 12 hours marinating and soaking time
**Cooking time:** 30 minutes
**Serves:** 4

2 cups (440 g) short-grain white rice

**For the marinated pork:**
3 tablespoons gochujang (red chili paste)
3 tablespoons ganjang (Korean soy sauce)
1 tablespoon gochugaru (red chili flakes)
½ tablespoon sesame oil
1 tablespoon mirin
2 tablespoons light brown sugar
1 tablespoon minced garlic
¼ teaspoon freshly ground black pepper
1 lb (500 g) pork belly or picnic shoulder, sliced ⅛ inch (3 mm) thick

**For the stir-fried pork:**
1 tablespoon neutral cooking oil
7 oz (200 g) onion, cut into ⅛-inch (3 mm) slices
1 oz (30 g) daepa (Korean scallion), cut into ¼-inch (6 mm) diagonal slices

Soak and cook the rice as directed on page 92 (see Cooked Short-Grain White Rice).

**Meanwhile, marinate the pork:** In a large bowl, stir together the gochujang, soy sauce, gochugaru, sesame oil, mirin, brown sugar, garlic, black pepper, and 3 tablespoons water. Add the meat, mix well, and marinate for at least 30 minutes and up to 12 hours.

**Make the stir-fried pork:** In a nonstick frying pan, heat the cooking oil over medium heat. Add the onion and stir-fry for 30 seconds. Add the marinated pork and the daepa and cook, avoiding too much stirring. Once the meat is cooked on one side, add 4 tablespoons water and simmer until the meat is fully cooked.

In each of four individual bowls, place 1 cup (200 g) cooked rice. Top with equal amounts of pork. Serve hot.

# Doenjang Pork Belly Deopbap
## Doenjang Samgyup Deopbap
## 된장 삼겹 덮밥

DF

Thinly sliced pork belly is great as the popular *banchan* (side dish) Spicy Pork Bokkeum (page 251), but an alternative is to marinate it in *doenjang* (fermented soybean paste) before cooking. When cooking pork belly with *doenjang*, the mirin plays a key role, because the slight sweetness is great for balancing the overall taste. When purchasing pork belly, select either thinly sliced pork belly or ask the butcher to cut the pork belly into ¼-inch (6 mm) thick slices.

**Preparation time:** 40 minutes, plus 30 minutes marinating and soaking time
**Cooking time:** 30 minutes
**Serves:** 4

2 cups (440 g) short-grain white rice

**For the marinated pork belly:**
2 tablespoons doenjang (fermented soybean paste)
3 tablespoons mirin
2 tablespoons corn (golden) syrup
1 tablespoon ganjang (Korean soy sauce)
1 tablespoon sesame oil
1 tablespoon sugar
1 teaspoon salt
1 lb 5 oz (600 g) thinly sliced pork belly

**For the pork stir-fry:**
1 tablespoon neutral cooking oil
1 teaspoon minced garlic
7 oz (200 g) onion, cut into ⅛-inch (3 mm) slices
2 oz (60 g) daepa (Korean scallion), cut into ¼-inch (6 mm) diagonal slices
1 oz (25 g) fresh red chilies, halved and thinly sliced on a diagonal
Salt

Soak and cook the rice as directed on page 92 (see Cooked Short-Grain White Rice).

**Meanwhile, marinate the pork:** In a large bowl, stir together the doenjang, mirin, corn syrup, soy sauce, sesame oil, sugar, salt, and 4 tablespoons water. Add the pork belly slices and mix well. Let marinate for 30 minutes.

**Make the pork stir-fry:** In a nonstick frying pan, heat the cooking oil over medium heat. Add the garlic and stir-fry until translucent. Add the onion, daepa, and marinated pork belly and stir-fry for 3 minutes, adjusting the heat and stirring well as needed to avoid any burning. Add the chilies to finish, and season to taste with salt.

In each of four individual bowls, place 1 cup (200 g) cooked rice. Top with equal amounts of pork. Serve hot.

# Spicy Squid Deopbap
## Ojingeo Deopbap
## 오징어 덮밥

dF

The popular spicy squid *deopbap* can be time-consuming if you have to clean the squid, but today it's easy to buy already cleaned squid at the grocery store. Because the squid releases moisture during the cooking process, the marinade is best made with gochugaru, which will absorb some of the moisture.

**Preparation time:** 20 minutes, plus 30 minutes rice soaking time
**Cooking time:** 30 minutes
**Serves:** 4

2 cups (440 g) short-grain white rice

**For the marinated squid:**
14 oz (400 g) cleaned squid
2 tablespoons ganjang (Korean soy sauce)
1 tablespoon gochujang (red chili paste)
3 tablespoons gochugaru (red chili flakes)
1 tablespoon mirin
1 tablespoon light brown sugar
1 tablespoon minced garlic
½ tablespoon sesame oil
1 teaspoon salt
¼ teaspoon freshly ground black pepper
1 oz (30 g) daepa (Korean scallion), cut into ¼-inch (6 mm) diagonal slices
7 oz (200 g) onion, cut into ⅛-inch (3 mm) slices

**To finish:**
1 tablespoon neutral cooking oil

Soak and cook the rice as directed on page 92 (see Cooked Short-Grain White Rice).

**Meanwhile, marinate the squid:** Cut the squid into slices 1 inch (2.5 cm) long and ¼ inch (6 mm) wide. In a large bowl, stir together the soy sauce, gochujang, gochugaru, mirin, brown sugar, garlic, sesame oil, salt, and black pepper. Add the prepared squid, daepa, and onion and mix well. Let marinate for 10 minutes.

**To finish:** In a nonstick frying pan, heat the cooking oil over medium heat. Add the marinated squid and vegetables and stir-fry, adjusting the heat as necessary, because the gochujang marinade can easily burn. Cook until the squid is cooked through, about 5 minutes.

In each of four individual bowls, place 1 cup (200 g) cooked rice. Top with equal amounts of the squid mixture. Serve hot.

# Black Bean Sauce Deopbap
## Jjajangbap
## 짜장밥

dF

*Jjajang* (black bean sauce) is a beloved Chinese-style Korean recipe. While the most popular and common use is over noodles, it's also popular over rice. In the past, you had to start from scratch by stir-frying *chunjang* (black bean paste) in oil, but today premade stir-fried black bean paste is readily available. However, be careful, because some commercial sauces already have starch in them, so read the label before using.

Many home cooks add extra vegetables, such as carrots and potatoes, but this recipe replicates the style found in popular Chinese-Korean restaurants, which incorporate lots of onions and cabbage.

**Preparation time: 20 minutes, plus 30 minutes rice soaking time**
**Cooking time: 30 minutes**
**Serves: 4**

2 cups (440 g) short-grain white rice

**For the black bean sauce:**
3 tablespoons neutral cooking oil
7 oz (200 g) onions, cut into ¼-inch (6 mm) pieces
2 oz (60 g) daepa (Korean scallion), cut into thin (⅛-inch/3mm) slices
7 oz (200 g) ground (minced) pork
9 oz (250 g) green cabbage, finely diced
4 tablespoons store-bought stir-fried black bean paste
2 tablespoons jinjang (Korean dark soy sauce)
2 tablespoons sugar
1½ tablespoons potato starch or cornstarch (cornflour)
Salt

Soak and cook the rice as directed on page 92 (see Cooked Short-Grain White Rice).

**Meanwhile, make the black bean sauce:** In a nonstick frying pan, heat the cooking oil over medium heat. Add the onion and daepa and stir-fry until translucent. Add the ground pork, flattening and stirring well with a wooden spatula to avoid large clumps. Once the meat is browned, add the cabbage and cook for 3 minutes until well cooked. Add the stir-fried black bean paste, soy sauce, and sugar and mix well. Add 2 cups (16 fl oz/480 ml) water and bring to a boil. In a small bowl, stir together the starch and 3 tablespoons water. Once boiling, stir in the starch slurry and cook until it reaches a thick, uniform consistency. Season to taste with salt.

In each of four large individual bowls, place 1 cup (200 g) cooked rice. Top with equal amounts of black bean sauce. Serve hot.

# Korean-Style Curry Rice
카레라이스

dF

Curry was first introduced to Korea in the 1950s, and it began to gain popularity in the 1980s with the development of easy-to-make curry powders, and 3-minute curry meal kits. Today, it's still a common staple at home and is a taste that is liked by all ages. It's particularly popular in situations where it needs to serve a crowd, such as public schools and in the military.

This recipe highlights the most common vegetables used in homemade curry, but any variety of vegetables can be used. Popular vegetables include king trumpet mushrooms, tomatoes, bell peppers, broccoli, and more. The pork can be replaced with chicken or beef, and vegetarian versions are just as delicious. For a richer taste, add 1 tablespoon of butter at the end.

Preparation time: 20 minutes, plus 30 minutes rice soaking time
Cooking time: 30 minutes
Serves: 4

2 cups (440 g) short-grain white rice
4 tablespoons neutral cooking oil
5 oz (150 g) ground (minced) pork
10 oz (300 g) potatoes, peeled and cut into ½-inch (1.3 cm) cubes
3½ oz (100 g) carrots, peeled and cut into cubes
7 oz (200 g) onions, cut into ½-inch (1.3 cm) slices
3½ oz (100 g) Korean curry powder
Salt

Soak and cook the rice as directed on page 92 (see Cooked Short-Grain White Rice).

Meanwhile, in a nonstick frying pan, heat the cooking oil over high heat. Add the pork and stir-fry until the meat is browned. Add the potatoes and carrots and cook for 1 minute. Add the onions and cook until they are translucent, about 1 more minute.

Add 3 cups (24 fl oz/700 ml) water and boil until the vegetables are tender, about 3 minutes. Reduce the heat to medium and stir in the curry powder until it's well incorporated. Season to taste with salt.

In each of four large individual bowls, place 1 cup (200 g) cooked rice and top with equal amounts of curry. Serve hot.

# Mushroom & Mung Bean Sprout Deopbap
## Beoseot Sukju Deopbap
## 버섯 숙주 덮밥

dF

There are many mushroom *deopbap* recipes, and while mushrooms and beef are a classic pairing, mushrooms and mung bean sprouts are a great combination with a wonderful contrast in texture. If you like spice, add sliced Cheongyang chilies or serve topped with chili oil.

Preparation time: 30 minutes, plus 30 minutes rice soaking time
Cooking time: 25 minutes
Serves: 4

2 cups (440 g) short-grain white rice

**For the seasoning sauce:**
4 tablespoons ganjang (Korean soy sauce)
2 tablespoons oyster sauce
1 tablespoon sugar

**For the mushroom and mung bean stir-fry:**
2 tablespoons neutral cooking oil
1 oz (30 g) daepa (Korean scallion), cut into ¼-inch (6 mm) slices
5 cloves garlic, thinly sliced
3½ oz (100 g) onion, cut into ⅛-inch (3 mm) slices
7 oz (200 g) oyster mushrooms, hand torn into thin pieces
14 oz (400 g) white mushrooms, cut into ⅛-inch (3 mm) slices
1⅓ cups (5 oz/150 g) mung bean sprouts, rinsed
2 oz (60 g) chives, cut into 1-inch (2.5 cm) lengths
1 tablespoon potato starch or cornstarch (cornflour)
Salt

**For serving:**
1 tablespoon sesame seeds

Soak and cook the rice as directed on page 92 (see Cooked Short-Grain White Rice).

**Meanwhile, make the seasoning sauce:** In a bowl, combine 2 cups (16 fl oz/480 ml) water, the soy sauce, oyster sauce, and sugar until well combined. Set aside.

**Make the mushroom and mung bean stir-fry:** In a nonstick frying pan, heat the cooking oil over medium heat. Add the daepa and garlic and cook until translucent. Increase the heat to high, add the onion and both mushrooms, and stir-fry for 1 minute. Add the seasoning sauce, mung bean sprouts, and chives and bring to a boil. Once boiling, mix the starch with 2 tablespoons water and add, then stir well until uniform. Season to taste with salt as needed. Remove from the heat.

**To serve:** In each of four individual bowls, place 1 cup (200 g) cooked rice. Top with equal amounts of the mushroom stir-fry. Garnish with a pinch of sesame seeds. Serve hot.

반찬

Banchan Dishes to Accompany Rice

*Banchan* refers to all foods that accompany rice, and it also is used to collectively refer to everything other than rice in a Korean table setting. Even when rice is not served as the main dish, *banchan* are always served, and it can be said they are the key characteristic that makes up a Korean table setting. This can be seen when eating simple one-bowl meals, such as *guksu* (noodles), *mandu* (dumplings), *tteokguk* (rice cake soup), and *juk* (porridge), as *banchan* is served along with them. Even when eating Western food, such as pizza or fried chicken, some kind of pickle, such as cucumber or radish pickle, is used as a *banchan*, showing the importance of the *banchan* concept in the world of Korean food.

Although rice is considered the centerpiece of Korean cuisine, *banchan* is probably the most important aspect of Korean food culture. Without understanding *banchan*, one cannot begin to understand Korean cuisine's seasonal food, regional foods, cooking methods, ingredients, and seasonings.

Koreans often say that *banchan* is the real test of a restaurant's quality and skill. In a Korean restaurant, once the order for the main dishes has been placed, an array of *banchan* is served to complement the dishes ordered. Beyond the ever-present kimchi, the *banchan* are chosen and prepared to be in harmony with the main dishes. It's said that if the *banchan* served is delicious, it's foolproof that the main dishes will be delicious as well. Making delicious *banchan* requires a fundamental, thorough understanding of Korean cuisine. But to understand Korean cuisine and its food culture, you must start by understanding *banchan* culture.

# 나물 Namul Seasoned Vegetable Dishes

While famed for the tabletop barbecue that has quickly risen in global popularity, South Korea boasts one of the highest levels of per-capita vegetable consumption in the world. If you are curious as to how Koreans manage this feat, the answers are found on the plates on a typical Korean dining table. A study has found that a typical Korean meal is about 70 percent vegetables, much of it in the form of *banchan*. The vast majority of common banchan are vegetable-based. Rarely missing from a Korean meal are the staple *banchan*, kimchi and *namul* (seasoned vegetables). Although kimchi, arguably the most famous and iconic food of Korea, is familiar to many, what is *namul*?

*Namul* is a term with two meanings: It's both a category of dishes as well as a category of ingredients. As a botanical term, *namul* defines plants with edible leaves or stems. These edible plants can come from different environments—mountains, fields, or the sea. Two-thirds of South Korean land is mountainous, and, as a peninsula, three sides of Korea are bordered by sea. This presents an enormous diversity of indigenous sea and land vegetables. Without human design or effort, nature has framed the unique flavors and culture of *namul* cuisine.

As a culinary term, *namul* refers to the dishes created with these *namul* vegetables. There are countless *namul* preparation techniques that have evolved throughout Korean history. They range from techniques that can be applied to a wide range of *namul* vegetables to hyperspecific preparations that are designed to bring out the unique flavors or textures locked in a particular vegetable.

# The Importance of Namul Cuisine

For Koreans, *namul* is a food that invokes a mother's cooking and the flavors of home. The image of a mother figure preparing the family meal, preparing the day's *namul* with practiced movements, is a collective Korean memory. So are the childhood memories of returning home from school and sitting around the kitchen table to help prepare the *namul*: Adults remember the simple rhythms, such as snapping off the limp tails of bean sprouts. Simple, unpretentious meals of freshly made rice, warm and steaming, eaten with *namul banchan*—often ending all mixed in the rice bowl—are memories as important as any fancy, celebratory meal. *Namul* may seem a mundane vegetable side dish to both outsiders and Koreans alike, but it is a key part of Korean home meals, and it is emotion-rich, because its preparation is intertwined with warm memories of family and mothers.

Therefore, learning to cook Korean food begins with *namul*, a natural priority especially for those who grew up eating home-cooked Korean meals. Colloquial instructions from Korean mothers, echoed by all the homegrown recipes online, reflect the following philosophy: Use the freshest seasonal vegetables from the *sijang* (market in Korea); use tasty *jang*—*ganjang* (Korean soy sauce), *gochujang* (red chili paste), and *doenjang* (fermented soybean paste)—season with your hands; and you're bound to end up with a quick, delicious, and uncomplicated *namul*.

After many years and countless *namul* recipes, we have realized that this motherly advice contains the essence of *namul*: simplicity. Although *namul* cuisine might seem difficult to navigate because of the huge diversity, by mastering the following simple guiding principles, any cook can learn to enjoy vegetables both familiar and unfamiliar in many new ways—and maybe even better than the average Korean.

First, any and all vegetables you have on hand can become an ingredient for *namul*. There are no rules or limits about which vegetables you can or cannot use; in fact, the beauty of many Korean culinary techniques is that they can be applied widely. Regardless of whether they are a Korean vegetable or even an Asian vegetable, any vegetable has the potential to become a delicious *namul* with the application of the right *namul* techniques.

To know which technique to use for which vegetable, the first step is knowing that *namul* fall into the two broad categories: *saengchae*, which translates to "raw vegetables," and *sukchae*, which translates to "cooked vegetables."

For *saengchae*, uncooked vegetables are dressed or marinated. Choose vegetables that are pleasing to eat raw: those that do not have overtly bitter flavors and have a soft, delicate structure. For *sukchae*, vegetables are first blanched and then seasoned, stir-fried, or pan-braised. *Sukchae namul* is usually prepared with fibrous vegetables, or those vegetables with more bitter flavor profiles that benefit from being cooked.

A single vegetable can produce a wide variety of *namul* dishes by changing the preparation method. Moreover, a single plant can provide multiple distinct dishes, depending on which component of the plant—its leaf, fruit, root, or stem—is used.

Another key component of the Korean *namul* tradition is understanding how vegetables should be cut. Korean ancestors recognized that vegetables possess grain and direction (just as animal proteins, such as beef or fish, have) and developed preparation methods to enhance the inherent characteristics of vegetables. Thousands of years of culinary wisdom have dictated that the small details, such as the direction of a cut—going against or with the grain—create an important difference in not only the texture but the flavor of the final *namul* dish.

One of the most long-standing adages in the world of Korean cuisine is "the taste of food is the taste of *jang*." This brings us to the third and final *namul* principle to remember: The final flavor of a *namul* dish is determined by the *jang* (fermented soybean-based sauces), the foundational flavoring agent of Korean cuisine.

*Jang* acts in *namul* to enhance and complement the natural taste of the vegetables, adding depth of flavor while reducing or balancing bitter notes in many vegetables. All Korean *jang*—*ganjang, doenjang, gochujang*—are used in *namul* recipes in various combinations along with added seasonings to achieve a more balanced, complete flavored *jang*-based sauce called *yangnyeom-jang*.

With any vegetable, once the apt *namul* preparation method and *yangnyeom-jang* is applied to complement the vegetable's inherent texture and flavor, one can easily create a delicious and creative *namul*.

**Four Seasons of Namul**

If one had to guess the season based on a Korean meal, the surest way would be to look at the *namul* dishes. Preparations of *namul* follow a seasonal calendar, aligned to the natural rhythms of plants year-round.

In spring, the tender and fragrant vegetables sprout, having quietly endured the frozen earth and harsh snow throughout winter. These leafy greens are the main form of *namul* served during this ephemeral season. The lively flavors of spring *namul* are often top of mind when referring to *namul* as a whole.

In summer, plants that have grown in strong sun—namely, "fruiting vegetable plants" with lively, juicy, and crunchy textures—become the stars of the *namul* dishes. These include crispy and juicy cucumbers, peppers, eggplants (aubergines), and members of the squash family.

In fall, the focus turns to beneath the earth with root vegetables, such as *deodeok* (see Deodeok Pine Nut Saengchae, page 184) and bellflower roots (see Bellflower Root Namul, page 170), along with a diverse variety of mushrooms.

As the winter season approaches, the ocean's vegetables boast their flavors. Another charm of the winter season is the use of dried or preserved vegetables from the seasons prior. These preserved vegetables are often rehydrated and pan-fried to create a new *namul* that showcases a different flavor and texture from their fresh counterparts. Seasonal and fresh *namul* are always delicious, but these dried vegetables—*gosari* (fiddlehead fern), chwinamul (*Aster scaber*), squash—are reborn with a different taste, aroma, and texture that provide an entirely different eating experience and pleasure.

# Base Namul Sauces

There are countless recipes for *namul yangnyeom-jang* (base *namul* sauces), many variations arising from personal preferences, but the basic *yangnyeom-jang* ratios listed here will ensure a delicious *namul* dish. These sauces can be applied to both *saengchae* and *sukchae namul*. The *namul* sauces below make enough for 7 oz (200 g) vegetables.

### Nutty Yangnyeom

2 tablespoons cheongjang (light Korean soy sauce) or Yondu (Korean vegan seasoning sauce) or doenjang (fermented soybean paste): these add umami and saltiness; choose doenjang for deeper umami; choose soy sauce for a more straightforward flavor

1 tablespoon toasted sesame seeds: for nuttiness

1 tablespoon toasted sesame oil: for richness and a nutty aroma

In a small bowl, stir all the ingredients together until completely uniform.

### Sweet & Sour Yangnyeom

1 tablespoons ganjang (Korean soy sauce) or doenjang (fermented soybean paste): these add umami and saltiness; choose doenjang for deeper umami; choose soy sauce for a more straightforward flavor

1 tablespoon sugar: for sweetness

2 tablespoons rice vinegar: for tartness

In a small bowl, stir all the ingredients together until completely uniform.

### Spicy Yangnyeom (Nutty Profile)

2 tablespoons gochujang (red chili paste): for umami, salty, spicy, and sweet base flavor

1 tablespoon toasted sesame seeds: for nuttiness

1 tablespoon sesame oil: for richness and a nutty aroma

In a small bowl, stir all the ingredients together until completely uniform.

### Spicy Yangnyeom (Sweet & Sour Profile)

2 tablespoons gochujang (red chili paste): for umami, salty, spicy, and sweet base flavor

1 tablespoon sugar: for sweetness

2 tablespoon rice vinegar: for tartness

In a small bowl, stir all the ingredients together until completely uniform.

# Master Steps for Preparing Saengchae

Each vegetable of each season requires a specific preparation to best highlight its inherent characteristics. Before delving into individual recipes, we will first review the two major preparation methods: *saengchae* and *sukchae*.

*Saengchae* are made without cooking the vegetables or applying any heat. Because they're made with uncooked vegetables, *saengchae namul* retain a markedly fresh taste and texture. This is also a great preparation for fragrant or herbaceous vegetables.

Any vegetables without an overly fibrous body or that can be pleasantly eaten raw can be made into *saengchae*. Depending on the recipe, prior to seasoning with *yangnyeom-jang* (see Base Namul Sauces, page 155), the *namul* can be used fresh or first lightly salted to improve the texture. Most common vegetables used to make *saengchae* include *mu* (Korean radish), cucumbers, and lettuce, representing the preference to use vegetables with a pleasant crunch or bite with little to no bitterness. *Saengchae* is not unlike a dressed salad in Western cuisine.

For a *saengchae namul*, it is recommended that the *yangnyeom-jang* be as simple as possible, so it does not mask the natural texture and fragrance of the fresh *namul*.

*Saengchae* made using tender leaves should be eaten as soon as it's prepared. *Saengchae* made using sturdy *namul*, such as roots, can keep up to 2 days, and vinegar-based root *namul* can last up to 3 days with refrigeration.

### Step 1: Clean and Dry

*Saengchae namul* should be rinsed as gently as possible due to their delicate nature. Swish gently in a large bowl of water, not under running water, to avoid bruising.

Once the vegetables are clean, dry them thoroughly either by letting them sit in a sieve or gentle spinning in a salad spinner. Any excess moisture will negatively affect the texture and flavor of the final *namul* and interfere with an even incorporation of the *yangnyeom-jang*.

### Step 2: Trim

Trim the cleaned vegetables and cut into easy-to-eat sizes. This will ensure that the seasoning will coat each piece evenly.

### Step 3: Prepare the Seasoning

Choose the *yangnyeom-jang* base (see Base Namul Sauces, page 155) and add any other ingredients to change the taste and fragrance according to personal preference.

### Step 4: Dress the Namul

Keeping the integrity of the vegetables' textures intact is critical in *namul* making. Because *saengchae namul* is delicate and wilts easily, do not dress the prepared vegetables until just prior to serving.

For best results, when dressing the vegetables, use a bowl about three times the volume of the *namul*. Mix using only your fingertips or with chopsticks to avoid applying pressure.

### Step 5: Plate

The dressed raw vegetables may release additional liquid after being plated, so it is best to serve in shallow bowls or on plates with a slight depression.

Heap the *saengchae namul* in a mound, then "fluff" the dressed vegetables with chopsticks or utensils, as needed, to distribute the seasoning evenly.

# Master Steps for Preparing Sukchae

*Sukchae* are *namul* that are first cooked and then seasoned with *yangnyeom-jang* (see Base Namul Sauces, page 155). They can be prepared in three distinct ways: 1) simply blanched, 2) blanched or boiled and then pan-fried, or 3) pan-fried.

Vegetables that are exceptionally fragrant or inherently bitter are typically prepared in the *sukchae* method. Fibrous or tough vegetables are often first dehydrated prior to cooking in the *sukchae* method to soften the fibrous or woody texture. The most common of *sukchae namul* include bean sprouts, spinach, Korean fiddlehead fern (*gosari*), and Korean thistle (*gondeure*). Mountain vegetables, spring vegetables that are commonly dehydrated or are fibrous, mushrooms, and sea vegetables are often prepared as *sukchae namul*.

**Step 1: Clean**

Thoroughly clean the vegetables with cold water, making sure all dirt is removed. Discard any bruised or imperfect parts of the vegetable.

**Step 2: Blanch and Rinse**

A quick blanching in salted water can help preserve both the inherent color and the texture of the *sukchae* vegetables. The following amounts and times are for 7 oz (200 g) of vegetables:

In a large pot, combine 8½ cups (68 fl oz/2 liters) water (the water to vegetables ratio should be 10:1) and 1 tablespoon salt. Bring to a boil under high heat.

Add the vegetables to the boiling water and blanch for 2 minutes.

Remove and rinse under cold running water for at least 30 seconds to cool the vegetables quickly and stop further cooking.

**Step 3: Dry**

It is important that, after blanching, the vegetables are fully dried to ensure that the *yangnyeom-jang* will evenly incorporate into the *namul*. Use both hands to squeeze the vegetables gently, as if holding a ball, taking care not to bruise the vegetable to the point of it bleeding green.

**Step 4: Trim**

Trim the vegetables and cut into easy-to-eat sizes. This also ensures that the seasoning will coat each piece evenly. For leafy vegetables, we recommend cutting into 1½-inch (4 cm) lengths.

**Step 5: Prepare the Seasoning**

Choose the *yangnyeom-jang* base (see Base Namul Sauces, page 155) according to personal preference and add any other ingredients to achieve your desired taste and fragrance profile.

Note that many recipes for *namul* today call for minced garlic and scallions (spring onions). While they add body and fullness to the flavor, they also directly shorten the *namul* dish's storage time. If adding raw garlic or scallion, it should be eaten in a single sitting. Another method is to make garlic or scallion oil and to add it into the *yangnyeom-jang* instead of the raw garlic or scallion.

**Step 6: Dress the Namul**

For *sukchae namul*, it is critical that the *yangnyeom-jang* is absorbed into the vegetables themselves instead of simply coating the exterior. To ensure proper marriage, follow these steps.

For best results, use a bowl at least three times the volume of the *namul*.

The *namul* may be tightly clumped, because you squeezed them to remove any excess moisture. Prior to mixing with the *yangneyom-jang,* gently pull apart each individual vegetable to allow for even mixing.

When mixing the *namul* and *yangneyom-jang*, human hands are superior to any utensils. Using only your fingertips, delicately mix the vegetables with a repeated, tossing motion.

If the *namul* are delicate or young, avoid applying any pressure. If working with sturdy or tough vegetables, especially dried vegetables, apply more pressure to ensure that the *yangnyeom-jang* gets incorporated into the vegetable.

If the *yangneyom-jang* contains sesame oil or perilla oil, make sure the sauce itself is well emulsified before combining with the *namul* for a consistency of textures and flavors.

**Step 7: Pan-Frying**

If the *sukchae namul* are to be pan-fried, use medium heat and a short amount of time for delicate vegetables to ensure that the color and texture are preserved.

If cooking sturdier *sukchae namul,* including those made with dried vegetables, use lower heat, while slowly adding broth or water to simmer slowly until the *namul* texture turns into a soft, enjoyable mouthfeel.

**Step 8: Plating**

Plate the *sukchae namul* just prior to eating piled in a mound, "fluffing" the vegetables with chopsticks or utensils as needed.

# Bean Sprout Namul
## Kongnamul
## 콩나물

dF vg vE -5 -3o

Bean sprout *namul* can be easily found during any season in any corner store or food market in Korea. Soybean sprouts, with their somewhat fibrous stems and pungent vegetal smell when raw, are less common than the mung bean sprout in many other Asian countries. In Korea, however, they have long been the sprout of choice. The soybean sprout has a sturdier texture than the mung bean sprout, so it easily holds up in soups, stews, braises, or stir-fries. But the most popular way to consume these sprouts is in the form of this *namul*.

**Preparation time: 10 minutes**
**Cooking time: 10 minutes**
**Serves: 2–4**

9 oz (250 g) soybean sprouts
1 tablespoon salt

**For the sauce:**
1 tablespoon minced garlic
1 tablespoon minced scallion (spring onion)
1 teaspoon cheongjang (light Korean soy sauce)
1 teaspoon salt
2 tablespoons sesame oil

**For the garnish:**
Pinch of Korean red chili threads (optional)
Sesame seeds (optional)

Remove any bruised or dirty parts of the bean sprouts, including all the stringy roots, with your hands or scissors. Quickly rinse the sprouts in cold water and transfer to a sieve. The bean sprouts will easily start to go bad after washing, so it's best to use them as soon as possible.

In a large pot, combine 8½ cups (68 fl oz/2 liters) water and the salt and bring to a boil. Add the bean sprouts, return to a boil, and boil for 2 minutes. Scoop the bean sprouts out of the water with a sieve and let cool to room temperature.

**Make the sauce:** In a large bowl, mix together the garlic, scallion, soy sauce, salt, and sesame oil.

Fold the bean sprouts into the sauce and lightly toss until evenly coated. Mound the bean sprouts on a flat plate or shallow bowl and garnish with the chili threads and sesame seeds, if desired.

### Variations

• For a spicy version, add 1 tablespoon *gochugaru* (red chili flakes) to the sauce.

• For a more refreshing taste, add 1 tablespoon rice vinegar and 1 teaspoon sugar to the sauce.

• For Mung Bean Sprout Namul, make this with mung bean sprouts instead of soybean sprouts, reducing the blanching time and making up for the lack of texture by adding blanched minari and julienned mild red peppers.

# Korean Shepherd's Purse Namul
## Naeng-i Namul
## 냉이나물

Called *naeng-i* in Korean, shepherd's purse is a plant in the mustard family; it's beloved for its slightly bitter and spicy, yet earthy and fragrant taste. Both the leaves and roots are edible, each imparting a different flavor. The leaves and stems of the shepherd's purse balance sweetness and bitterness, as well as a spiciness akin to black pepper, wasabi, or Korean mustard. The roots, on the other hand, are sweeter and more earthy, in the way of corn silk and barley.

Shepherd's purse is widely available (both cultivated and foraged) and is most commonly used in *namul*. Its season starts in late winter and it is at its peak by the onset of spring. This is a traditional true spring *namul* that marks the beginning of the warmer seasons.

If you remove the roots before cleaning, it makes the process much easier, but the distinct earthy sweetness is found only in the roots. Even though this adds to the preparation time, we recommend that you clean and use the roots, with this caveat: If the *naeng-i* is overgrown or too tough and fibrous for it to be enjoyable, remove the roots.

If you have in-season shepherd's purse and want to use it later, blanch it and keep it frozen in a sealed plastic bag with about 2 added spoonfuls of water. To use, remove the amount desired and thaw. It's now good for use in soups or rice dishes.

**Preparation time:** 15 minutes
**Cooking time:** 10 minutes
**Serves:** 2–4

7 oz (200 g) Korean shepherd's purse
2 tablespoons salt

**For the sauce:**
1½ tablespoons doenjang (fermented soybean paste)
1 tablespoon gochujang (red chili paste)
1 tablespoon minced scallion (spring onion)
1 tablespoon sesame oil

Remove any discolored leaves and damaged roots from the shepherd's purse. For any larger leaves, cut in half. Rinse thoroughly under cold running water.

In a large pot, bring 8½ cups (68 fl oz/2 liters) water and the salt to a boil. Add the shepherd's purse and blanch for 45 seconds. Scoop out in a sieve and cool under cold running water. Let drain well and squeeze to remove excess moisture.

**Make the sauce:** In a bowl, stir together the doenjang, gochujang, scallion, and sesame oil.

Add the shepherd's purse leaves and gently massage until well seasoned. Plate in a shallow bowl and serve. It can be kept in an airtight container in the refrigerator for up to 2 days.

# Cham Namul
참나물

dF vg vE -5 -3o

Cham namul (*Pimpinella brachycarpa*) translates to "true *namul*." As its name suggests, it's a prized *namul*. with a unique fragrance and texture. The *namul*'s aroma has an impressive, refreshing quality—a combination of celery and mint. Sometimes it is mistakenly listed in markets as the vegetable mitsuba, but the way to tell is that the stems of *cham namul* will have a purplish color and the plant will smell strongly of celery.

A common way to prepare *cham namul* is to season it with *doenjang* (fermented soybean paste), but to highlight its unique fragrance and taste, it's best to lightly season with salt or light soy sauce.

**Preparation time: 10 minutes**
**Cooking time: 10 minutes**
**Serves: 2–4**

7 oz (200 g) cham namul
1 tablespoon salt

**For the sauce:**
1 tablespoon cheongjang
   (light Korean soy sauce)
1 teaspoon salt
1 tablespoon sesame oil
1 tablespoon ground sesame seeds

Remove any bruised leaves and trim off any parts of stem that are tough.

Set up a bowl of ice and water. In a large pot, bring 8½ cups (68 fl oz/ 2 liters) water and the salt to a boil. Add the cham namul and blanch for 20 seconds. Scoop out and transfer to the ice bath. Drain well in a sieve. Cut the cham namul into 2-inch (5 cm) lengths.

**Make the sauce:** In a bowl, stir together the soy sauce, salt, sesame oil, and sesame seeds.

Add the blanched cham namul and gently mix together until the namul is well seasoned. Plate and serve.

# Chrysanthemum Namul
## Ssukgat Namul
## 쑥갓나물

In selecting the prime chrysanthemum, look for bright, lively leaves and thinner stems with a natural sheen. Chrysanthemum is great as *namul*, but due to its unique herbal fragrance, which is both floral and pleasantly bitter, as well as its aesthetically beautiful leaves, Koreans most often will use it in *tang* (long-simmered soups), *guk* (soups), or *jjigae* (stews), either as a main or finishing ingredient to add a freshness to the dish. And it's also often seen as an herbal addition to a *ssam* (wrap) vegetable assortment. It's also enjoyed batter-fried as a crispy snack. Note that no matter how you decide to enjoy your chrysanthemum, you should cook it to just before it becomes too soft to enjoy its inherent fresh scent and flavor.

**Preparation time:** 10 minutes
**Cooking time:** 10 minutes
**Serves:** 2

7 oz (200 g) chrysanthemum greens
1 tablespoon salt

**For the sauce:**
1 tablespoon cheongjang
  (light Korean soy sauce)
1 teaspoon salt
1 teaspoon sugar
1 tablespoon sesame oil
1 tablespoon ground sesame seeds

Trim away any parts of the chrysanthemum stems that are too tough. Remove any discolored or bruised leaves. Wash in a bowl of cold water and rinse thoroughly two or three times, or until the chrysanthemum greens are free of dirt. Arrange all the chrysanthemum greens in a uniform direction and cut into 2-inch (5 cm) lengths. Keep the stems and leaves separate.

Set up a bowl of ice and water. In a large pot, bring 8½ cups (68 fl oz/ 2 liters) water and the salt to a boil. Add the chrysanthemum stems and blanch for 10 seconds. Drop in the chrysanthemum leaves and blanch for 10 seconds. Scoop out in a sieve and transfer to the ice bath to cool completely. Drain well in a sieve.

**Make the sauce:** In a bowl, stir together the soy sauce, salt sugar, sesame oil, and sesame seeds.

Add the chrysanthemums to the sauce and toss until well coated. Plate in a shallow bowl or plate to serve. It can be kept in an airtight container in the refrigerator for up to 2 days.

## Bamboo Shoot & Perilla Seed Namul
### Juksun Deulkkae Namul
### 죽순 들깨 나물

dF vg vE -3o

In a bamboo field, after a bout of spring rain, you can see all the bamboo shoots poking up above the ground seemingly out of nowhere. The Korean adage "post-rain bamboo shoots" is a common phrase to mean a situation where suddenly out of nowhere many things are happening.

Bamboo shoots have a long history in Asia. Originally from India and Malaysia, they have spread throughout China, Japan, and Korea, with five or six main varieties. The traditional types of Korean bamboo shoots are *bunjuk* and *wangjuk*. Compared to other bamboo types, the shape of these are thinner, the nodes are farther apart, and the outer shells a yellowish chestnut color. If storing the ephemeral bamboo shoots during its harvest season, it is best to boil and preserve as soon as possible, because the shoots will continue to ripen after harvest and, in so doing, lose flavor.

Preparation time: 10 minutes
Cooking time: 10 minutes
Serves: 2–4

**For the sauce:**
4 tablespoons perilla seed powder
2 tablespoons minced garlic
1 tablespoon sesame oil
1 tablespoon ganjang (Korean soy sauce)
1 teaspoon salt

**For the namul:**
10 oz (300 g) store-bought boiled bamboo shoots
1 oz (30 g) daepa (Korean scallion)
2 tablespoons neutral cooking oil

**Make the sauce:** In a small bowl, mix together the perilla seeds, garlic, sesame oil, soy sauce, and salt.

**Make the namul:** Slice the bamboo shoots into matchsticks 2 inches (5 cm) long and ¼ inch (6 mm) thick. Cut the daepa on a diagonal into ¼-inch (6 mm) slices.

In a frying pan, heat the cooking oil over medium heat. Add the bamboo shoots and stir-fry for 30 seconds. Add the sauce and ¾ cup (6 fl oz/200 ml) water and continue to stir-fry until the moisture has evaporated. Add the daepa, stir well, and remove from the heat. Serve on a plate.

---

## Spinach Namul
### Sigeumchi Namul
### 시금치 나물

dF vg vE -5 -3o    [ㅁ]

Native Korean spinach has characteristically wide and tough leaves, particularly thick stems, and purple-red hued roots. These are considered best for cooking. Compared to this indigenous Korean spinach, which takes about ninety days to mature for harvest, the readily available commercial spinach is more commonplace due to its shorter harvest time of only thirty days. In Korea, the most common and preferred method of cooking spinach is by a quick blanching and seasoning it with a *jang*-based sauce. This method highlights the spinach's inherent sweetness as well as its texture, which is more robust than its Western counterpart.

Preparation time: 10 minutes
Cooking time: 10 minutes
Serves: 2

7 oz (200 g) spinach
1 tablespoon sea salt

**For the sauce:**
1 teaspoon cheongjang (light Korean soy sauce)
1 tablespoon salt
2 tablespoon sesame oil
1 tablespoon ground sesame seeds

Remove any blemished spinach leaves (and trim off roots if the spinach is from the farmers' market). Separate the leaves and stems. Halve the bottoms of the stems lengthwise and rinse the cut leaves in cold water two or three times until clean, making sure all dirt at the root end of the stems is washed away.

Set up a bowl of ice and water. In a large pot, bring 8½ cups (68 fl oz/ 2 liters) water and the salt to a boil. Add the spinach and blanch for 20 seconds. Scoop out immediately and transfer to the ice bath to cool completely. (Note that the cooking time will vary depending on the type of spinach and its toughness, but spinach is easily overcooked and quickly loses its crunchy texture, which is important to this recipe.) Drain well and squeeze to remove excess moisture.

**Make the sauce:** In a bowl, stir together the soy sauce, salt, sesame oil, and sesame seeds.

Transfer the spinach to the bowl and toss well with the sauce until fully coated. Plate on a shallow bowl or a plate. Kept in an airtight container, this will keep up to 2 days in the refrigerator.

**Variation:** For a deeper and earthier taste, replace the soy sauce with 1 tablespoon *doenjang* (fermented soybean paste).

## Fresh Fiddlehead Namul
### Saeng Gosari Namul
### 생고사리 나물

dF vg vE

*Gosari*, similar to fiddlehead ferns, is one of Korea's most represented and beloved *san namul* (mountain vegetables). In spring, young shoots are harvested before they bear leaves and are then blanched and dehydrated for year-round usage.

Even in springtime, when it's in season, you are more likely to find trimmed and dried gosari namul in the markets. Even if home cooks are lucky enough to find fresh *gosari,* most are reluctant to cook with it, because the plant contains natural toxins that need to be removed by lengthy soaking.

**Preparation time:** 10 minutes, plus up to 24 hours soaking time
**Cooking time:** 10 minutes
**Serves:** 2

7 oz (200 g) gosari
2 tablespoons salt

**For the namul:**
2 tablespoons neutral cooking oil
1 tablespoon minced daepa (Korean scallion)
1 tablespoon minced garlic
2 tablespoons cheongjang (light Korean soy sauce)
1 tablespoon perilla seed powder
1 tablespoon perilla seed oil

Remove any ends of the gosari that are bruised or dried. Wash the plants thoroughly in clean water and drain to remove excess water.

In a large pot, bring 8½ cups (68 fl oz/2 liters) water and the salt to a boil. Add the gosari and boil until fully cooked, 5–7 minutes. Drain the gosari immediately and rinse thoroughly under cold running water. Transfer to a bowl of cold water and soak for at least 12 and up to 24 hours to get rid of any toxins and bitterness that may be present. Drain and cut the gosari into 1½-inch (4 cm) pieces.

**Make the namul:** In a frying pan, heat the cooking oil over low heat. Add the daepa and stir-fry for about 15 seconds. Add the garlic and stir-fry until the aromatics are released, about 20 seconds. Add the prepared gosari, increase the heat to medium, and stir-fry for about 30 seconds. Add the soy sauce and 4 tablespoons water and cook until the gosari is soft. Once all excess moisture has evaporated, add the perilla seeds and stir until well incorporated. Finish with the perilla oil and remove from the heat.

Plate the gosari on a large flat plate to let cool. Once cooled to room temperature, plate in a shallow bowl or plate. Eat immediately. It can be kept in an airtight container in the refrigerator for up to 2 days.

---

## Dried Fiddlehead Namul
### Geon Gosari Namul
### 건고사리 나물

dF vg vE [ㅁ]

*Gosari* has a warm and earthy taste, with a soft yet chewy and pleasantly fibrous texture that is often described as meaty. It is a main ingredient in some of the most common Korean dishes, such as *yukgaejang* (spicy shredded beef soup) or *bibimbap* (mixed rice), making it one of the most precious ingredients of Korean cuisine.

**Preparation time:** 1 hour, plus 3 hours soaking time
**Cooking time:** 10 minutes
**Serves:** 2

2¾ oz (80 g) dried gosari
2 tablespoons perilla seed oil
2 tablespoons cheongjang (light Korean soy sauce)
2 tablespoons neutral cooking oil
1 tablespoon minced daepa (Korean scallion)
1 tablespoon minced garlic
Salt
1 tablespoon sesame seeds

Place the dried gosari in a large pot, fill with about 8½ cups (68 fl oz/2 liters) room temperature water and rehydrate for about 3 hours.

In the same pot and soaking water, bring to a simmer and cook until tender-firm, about 30 minutes.

Let cool to room temperature in the cooking liquid. Rinse in cold water and then drain well. Any parts of the gosari at the end of this process that feel too rough to the hand should be trimmed off.

Transfer the trimmed gosari to a large bowl, add the perilla seed oil and soy sauce, and massage it into the gosari gently.

In a frying pan, heat the cooking oil over low heat. Add the daepa and stir-fry for about 15 seconds. Add the garlic and stir-fry until the aromatics are released, about 20 seconds. Add the prepared gosari, increase the heat to medium, and stir-fry together until the ingredients are combined. Once all excess moisture has evaporated, season with salt to taste. If the gosari namul is not tender yet, add a little water and stir-fry until the excess moisture has evaporated. Toward the end, add the sesame seeds and stir-fry until fully incorporated.

Remove from the heat and place the stir-fry on a large flat plate to cool to room temperature. Once cooled, plate in a shallow bowl or plate and serve. Cooked gosari namul can be kept in an airtight container in the refrigerator for up to 2 days.

## Daylily Namul
### Wonchuri Namul
### 원추리 나물

Known for the beauty of its orange and yellow blooms, the vibrant daylily is a wild plant that is native to the mountainous regions of Korea, although it is perhaps better known in many parts of the world as a decorative garden flower. In Korea, in early springtime, the *namul* made from the daylily's young shoots are a delicacy.

The young plant of the daylily has a sweet flavor profile and exhibits a delicate, soft texture that makes it a delightful *namul* ingredient. The entire plant, over its lifetime, can be utilized: Its roots are used to make an herbal broth base for soups and are also used in traditional Korean medicine. The young bulbs of the flower can be harvested and pan-fried or even made into *jangajji* (pickles), and the bloomed flowers can be dried and enjoyed as tea.

**Preparation time:** 10 minutes
**Cooking time:** 10 minutes
**Serves:** 2–4

10 oz (300 g) daylilies
2 tablespoons salt

**For the sauce:**
2 tablespoons gochujang (red chili paste)
1 tablespoon rice vinegar
1 teaspoon gochugaru (red chili flakes)
1 teaspoon ganjang (Korean soy sauce)
1 teaspoon minced scallion (spring onion)
½ teaspoon minced garlic

Peel the overlapping layers off the daylily stems. Thoroughly rinse with cold water to ensure that soil trapped in between layers is removed. Pat dry with a paper towels and then cut into 2-inch (5 cm) lengths.

Set up a bowl of cold water. In a large pot, bring 8½ cups (68 fl oz/2 liters) water and the salt to a boil. Add the daylily pieces and blanch for 45 seconds. Scoop out in a sieve and transfer to the cold water bath. Let cool to room temperature or cooler, then drain well and squeeze any excess water out without damaging the vegetables.

**Make the sauce:** In a bowl, combine the gochujang, vinegar, gochugaru, soy sauce, scallion, and garlic.

Add the daylilies to the bowl and mix lightly using you fingertips, until the daylilies are fully coated with the sauce. Plate and serve.

---

## Bellflower Root Namul
### Doraji Namul
### 도라지 나물

Bellflower root, *doraji*, grows throughout Korea and has long been enjoyed. Fragrant purple bellflower flowers grow in clusters in fields, and their edible roots are valued for both their nutrition and deliciousness. Dried bellflower root is used in Eastern medicine for its healing properties of the throat. While people believe that late summer and early fall are bellflower's peak season due to the large size the roots reach, the young roots harvested in spring have a better, sweeter flavor as well as a more tender texture.

**Preparation time:** 40 minutes
**Cooking time:** 5 minutes
**Serves:** 2–4

10 oz (300 g) bellflower roots
2 tablespoons salt
½ tablespoon minced garlic
½ tablespoon minced scallion (spring onion)
1 tablespoon neutral cooking oil
½ tablespoon sesame oil
½ tablespoon sesame seeds

Wash the bellflower roots until clean and remove any overly tough and fibrous ends with a knife. Peel the skin and cut each root lengthwise into 6–10 pieces. Combine in a bowl with 1 tablespoon of the salt and roughly massage to rid the roots of their bitter, tannic flavors. After massaging, wash off the salt and soak for 30 minutes in about 3 cups (24 fl oz/710 ml) water to get rid of the saltiness and bitter flavors. Drain and squeeze to get rid of any excess moisture.

In a bowl, combine the remaining 1 tablespoon salt, the garlic, and scallion and toss with the bellflower roots until well combined.

In a frying pan, heat the cooking oil over medium heat. Pan-fry the bellflower roots for 30 seconds and add 3 tablespoons water. Reduce the heat to low and simmer until most of the moisture is evaporated. Finish with sesame oil and seeds and mix until uniformly distributed. Remove from the heat. Plate and serve.

## Korean Thistle Namul
### Gondeure Namul
### 곤드레 나물

dF vg vE

Korean thistle (*Cirsium setidens*) is called *gondeure* colloquially (and also in most marketplaces), but this term is actually in regional dialect. The official name is *goryeo unggungkwee*. It is native to Korea and it especially grows in large quantities in the southern region of Gangwon-do. Most *gondeure* is sold in trimmed and dried forms.

Uncooked *gondeure* is bitter, but once cooked, its fragrance and flavor is earthy and sweet, akin to brewed dark-leafed tea, such as oolong. While *gondeure* can be prepared a number of different ways, the most common and beloved recipe is *gondeure bap*. The basic version of *gondeure bap* is to simply add a desired amount of preboiled *gondeure* to the rice when cooking it. But we particularly enjoy making *gondeure bap* with this *namul* recipe: Incorporate the *namul* into the rice just before cooking; it makes for a delicious *bap*.

**Preparation time:** 1 hour, plus 3 hours soaking time
**Cooking time:** 40 minutes
**Serves:** 2

2¾ oz (80 g) dried Korean thistle
2 tablespoons perilla seed oil
3 tablespoons ganjang (Korean soy sauce)
2 tablespoons neutral cooking oil
1 tablespoon minced daepa (Korean scallion)
1 tablespoon minced garlic
Salt

Fill a large pot with 8½ cups (68 fl oz/2 liters) room temperature water and soak the thistle for 3 hours.

In the same pot and soaking liquid, bring to a simmer and cook until firm-tender, about 30 minutes.

Let cool to room temperature in the cooking liquid. Transfer to a sieve and rinse under cold running water. Drain well.

In a large bowl, combine the thistle, perilla seed oil, and soy sauce and massage it into the thistle gently.

In a frying pan, heat the cooking oil over low heat. Add the daepa and stir-fry for about 15 seconds. Add the garlic and stir-fry until the aromatics are released, about 20 seconds. Add the prepared thistle, increase the heat to medium, and stir-fry together until the ingredients are combined. Once all excess moisture has evaporated, season with salt to taste. If the namul is not tender yet, add a little water and stir-fry until the excess moisture has evaporated.

Plate in a shallow bowl, making sure that the vegetable is plated loosely to allow ventilation, and serve. Eat immediately. It can be kept in an airtight container in the refrigerator for up to 2 days.

**Variation:** If you purchase fresh *gondeure*, trim off any parts that are indigestible. Although you can use them to make a *namul*, of course, they are particularly great for making into *jangajji* (pickles).

## Stonecrop Namul
### Dol Namul
### 돌나물

dF vg vE -3o

**Stonecrops** are a spring succulent vegetable noted for their small but thick and plentiful leaves, as well as a particular fragrance. The taste is refreshing and simple, but its singular fragrance can be polarizing to those who are sensitive to vegetal tastes. It has a robust and fast reproduction and easily adapts to various types of environments. It is more often prepared raw than cooked or made into a cold soup or water kimchi.

**Preparation time:** 5 minutes
**Serves:** 2–4

9 oz (250 g) stonecrop

**For the sauce:**
2 tablespoons ganjang (Korean soy sauce)
2 tablespoon rice vinegar
1 tablespoon gochugaru (red chili flakes)
1 tablespoon sugar
1 teaspoon sesame oil

Stonecrop is easily bruised while handling, and any bruises or tears will release an unwanted grassy, vegetal fragrance and flavor. Be as gentle as possible while washing with cold water to remove all dirt. Once clean, cut into 1-inch (2.5 cm) lengths for easy eating.

**Make the sauce:** In a large bowl, stir together the soy sauce, vinegar, gochugaru, sugar, and sesame oil.

Transfer the stonecrop to the bowl of sauce and gently mix by lifting the stonecrop with your fingertips repeatedly until well seasoned. Plate and serve.

## Cucumber Saengchae
### Oi-Saengchae
### 오이 생채

dF gF vg vE -30

Cucumbers in Korea are predominantly two categories: white cucumber and green cucumber. White cucumbers have a crisp, firm texture with a very fragrant, characteristically cucumber flavor, and these are best cooked or used in cold soups. The green cucumber has a melon-like flavor profile, with a more tender texture that absorbs marinades easily, and it is best suited for *saengchae* (raw vegetable dishes). Korean cucumbers are most similar to what is sold in the West as English or European cucumbers.

Cucumbers' high moisture content lends a refreshing sensation and unique flavor, and summer cucumbers have a slight savory aftertaste. Depending on the preparation, the pronounced flavors and textures change. It's most common to see cucumbers eaten raw or made into kimchi in Korea, but they are also enjoyed cooked. Heat elevates their umami and savory tastes, and while perhaps counterintuitive, quick-blanching cucumbers can result in an extra-crunchy texture.

**Preparation time: 20 minutes**
**Serves: 2–4**

7 oz (200 g) cucumber
2 tablespoons salt

**For the sauce:**
1 tablespoon fine gochugaru
    (red chili powder)
1 tablespoon rice vinegar
1 tablespoon sugar
1 teaspoon minced garlic
1 teaspoon minced scallion
    (spring onion)
1 tablespoon sesame seeds

In-season farmers' market cucumbers will probably have tiny stiff hairs; use coarse salt or a clean scrub to wipe down any spikes.

Halve the cucumber lengthwise and cut crosswise into ¼-inch (6 mm) half-moons.

In a bowl, combine the sliced cucumber with the salt and let brine for 10 minutes. After 10 minutes, thoroughly rinse off the salt in cold water. Drain and gently squeeze with your hands to get rid of any excess moisture and set aside.

**Make the sauce:** Combine all the sauce ingredients into a bowl and mix until well combined. Combine with the cucumbers and mix until evenly seasoned. Plate and serve.

---

## Overripe Cucumber Namul
### Nogak Namul
### 노각나물

dF vg vE -30

Overripe cucumbers are called *nogak* in Korea and are harvested in late summer. Summer cucumbers left on the plant to overripen will turn yellow. While fresh green summer cucumbers are more popular, there is a particular charm to the *nogak* cucumbers. Removing the tougher skin of the yellow and white cucumbers and their seeds results in a fragrant, crunchy flesh with a strong cucumber flavor. The fragrance and texture of the *nogak* lasts longer than those of the green cucumbers, which can easily wilt.

**Preparation time: 20 minutes**
**Serves: 2–4**

10 oz (300 g) overripe cucumber
1 tablespoon salt

**For the sauce:**
1 tablespoon gochujang
    (red chili paste)
1 tablespoon rice vinegar
½ tablespoon sugar
1 teaspoon minced garlic
1 teaspoon minced scallion
    (spring onion)
1 teaspoon sesame oil
1 teaspoon sesame seeds

Peel the cucumber and halve lengthwise. Using a spoon, remove the cucumber seeds. Slice crosswise into ¼-inch (6 mm) half-moons.

In a bowl, sprinkle the slices with the salt and let brine for 10 minutes. After 10 minutes, thoroughly rinse off the salt with cold water. Drain and gently squeeze with your hands to get rid of any excess moisture and set aside.

**Make the sauce:** In a separate bowl, combine the gochujang, vinegar, sugar, garlic, scallion, sesame oil, and sesame seeds and whisk until well combined.

Transfer the cucumbers to the bowl of sauce and mix until evenly seasoned. Plate and serve.

## Steamed Eggplant Namul
## Gaji Muchim Namul
## 가지 무침 나물

dF vg vE -S -3o  [ㅁ]

Eggplant (aubergine) has a unique texture that enables it to absorb various flavors well, so it is a great vegetable to make *namul* with. The eggplant's flavor pairs well with not only soy sauce but also with *doenjang* (fermented soybean paste), and even spicy chili oil. The delicate texture is better expressed when steamed rather than blanched. A shortcut for cooking eggplant *namul* is to slice it and steam it in a bowl, covered in plastic wrap (cling film), in the microwave.

**Preparation time:** 10 minutes
**Cooking time:** 10 minutes
**Serves:** 2–4

9 oz (250 g) Korean eggplants (aubergines), about 2

**For the sauce:**
1 tablespoon ganjang (Korean soy sauce)
1 tablespoon minced garlic
1 teaspoon salt
1 tablespoon sesame seeds
Sliced red chili (optional)

Cut off the stem ends of the eggplants and rinse under cold running water. Cut crosswise into 2-inch (5 cm)-long pieces. Cut each piece lengthwise into 8 to 12 thick matchsticks (the number you get will depend on the girth of the eggplant).

Set up a steamer and bring the water to a boil. Add the eggplants to the steamer basket, set it over the boiling water, and steam for about 2 minutes. Let cool to room temperature. Once cool, gently squeeze the eggplants with your hands to get rid of excess moisture, taking care not to exert too much force.

**Make the sauce:** In a bowl, stir together the soy sauce, garlic, salt, and sesame seeds.

Add the eggplants to the bowl and toss until lightly coated. Garnish with the sliced chili, if desired.

---

## Stir-Fried Eggplant Namul
## Gaji Bokkeum Namul
## 가지 볶음 나물

dF vg vE -3o

Eggplant (aubergine) pairs well with oil, which makes stir-fried eggplant *namul* an especially delicious preparation.

**Cooking time:** 10 minutes
**Preparation time:** 10 minutes
**Serves:** 2–4

5 Korean eggplants (aubergines)
2 tablespoons plus 1 teaspoon salt
1 tablespoon ganjang (Korean soy sauce)
1 tablespoon gochugaru (red chili flakes)
5 tablespoons neutral cooking oil
1 tablespoon minced scallion (spring onion)
1 tablespoon minced garlic
1 tablespoon sesame seeds

Cut off the stem ends of the eggplants and rinse under cold running water. Cut crosswise into 2-inch (5 cm)-long pieces. Cut each piece lengthwise into 8 to 12 thick matchsticks (the number you get will depend on the girth of the eggplant).

Evenly sprinkle 2 tablespoons of the salt over the eggplants and let sit for 30 minutes.

Meanwhile, in a small bowl, stir together the remaining 1 teaspoon salt, the soy sauce, and gochugaru. Set the seasoning aside.

Rinse the eggplants under cold running water two or three times to wash off the salt. Gently squeeze with your hands to get rid of any excess moisture.

In a frying pan, heat the cooking oil over low heat. Add the scallion and stir-fry for about 15 seconds. Add the garlic and stir-fry until the aromatics are released, about 20 seconds. Increase the heat to high, add the prepared eggplants and the reserved seasoning, and stir-fry until cooked, about 30 seconds. Add the sesame seeds toward the end and mix well.

Remove from the heat and plate.

## Korean Zucchini Namul
### Aehobak Namul
### 애호박 나물

DF GF -5 -3o [ㅁ]

There are many types of vegetables from the gourd family available in Korea, but the most commonly used is the *aehobak*, or Korean zucchini (courgette). While the *aehobak* is often mistaken as the same as the green zucchini commonly available in the West, the Korean zucchini is actually a different breed with different genes. The Korean zucchini is a little firmer and has a bit more sweetness, whereas common Western zucchini has a more umami to its flavor.

*Aehobak* is used in many different ways, such as stuffed with meat or in vegetable pancakes, but the best way to enjoy the inherent flavor of the Korean zucchini is in *namul* form. The *aehobak namul*, unlike most *namul*, often includes salted shrimp as a seasoning. A testament to the tradition behind this combination dates back to the 1800s, when the first known recipe to season zucchini with salted shrimp appeared in *Siuijeonseo*, a well-known cookbook of the era.

**Preparation time:** 15 minutes
**Cooking time:** 10 minutes
**Serves:** 2–4

7 oz (200 g) aehobak (Korean zucchini)
2 teaspoons salt
1 tablespoon sesame oil
½ tablespoon minced garlic
1 tablespoon salted shrimp
½ tablespoon ground sesame seeds

Halve the zucchini lengthwise and then cut crosswise into ⅛-inch (3 mm) half-moons. Sprinkle the salt evenly on the zucchini pieces and let sit for 10 minutes. This process will help harden the flesh enough so that when cooking, the zucchini retains its juices and shape. Wash off the salt with cold water and pat the zucchini dry with paper towels.

Heat a frying pan over medium heat. Add the sesame oil and then the zucchini and pan-fry until the zucchini become slightly translucent, about 1 minute. Add the garlic and salted shrimp and stir-fry quickly until fully incorporated.

Remove from the heat and transfer to a flat plate and spread out to cool.

Once the zucchini are sufficiently cooled, plate and finish with the ground sesame seeds.

---

## Dried Korean Zucchini Namul
### Aehobak Ogari
### 애호박 오가리

DF -5

*Ogari* refers to dried slices of Korean zucchini (courgette) or gourd. Originally, *ogari* was made by cutting the zucchini or gourd in a spiral ribbon along the axis. These long slices were used in many dishes, including a delicacy in which they were stirred with glutinous rice flour to make a rice cake. These days, store-bought products labeled "*ogari*" will be coin slices of the dried zucchini.

**Preparation time:** 15 minutes, plus 1 hour soaking time
**Cooking time:** 15 minutes
**Serves:** 2–4

2 oz (60 g) ogari (dried Korean zucchini)
2 tablespoons cheongjang (light Korean soy sauce)
1 tablespoon sesame oil
½ cup (4 fl oz/120 ml) Anchovy Broth (page 314)
½ tablespoon ground sesame seeds
Pinch of Korean red chili threads

In a bowl, cover the ogari with room temperature water and rehydrate for at least 1 hour. (It is important to ensure that it is fully rehydrated before cooking, because dried vegetables can retain a distinct bitterness otherwise.) Drain the ogari and squeeze out any excess water with your hands.

In a bowl, combine the rehydrated ogari, the soy sauce, and sesame oil and toss to fully incorporate.

Heat a frying pan over high heat. Add the seasoned ogari and anchovy broth and cook over high heat until most of the broth is absorbed into the zucchini.

Remove from the heat and evenly spread on a flat plate to cool.

Once the zucchini is sufficiently cooled to taste, plate and sprinkle with the ground sesame seeds. Garnish with the chili threads.

## Young Perilla Namul
### Kkaetsun Namul
### 깻순 나물

dF -30

Perilla leaves are mostly eaten when fully grown, but the young perilla leaves have a unique, sweet tenderness. The stems, which are soft and edible, can be blanched along with the leaves. The young perilla leaves dressed with seasoning is a delicacy that allows for a soft yet deep fragrance of the perilla plant.

**Preparation time:** 10 minutes
**Cooking time:** 10 minutes
**Serves:** 4

7 oz (200 g) young perilla leaves
1 tablespoon salt

**For the sauce:**
2 cups (16 fl oz/480 ml) Anchovy Broth (page 314)
2 tablespoons cheongjang (light Korean soy sauce)
2 tablespoons perilla oil
½ tablespoon minced garlic
1 teaspoon salt
1 teaspoon sugar

**For the namul:**
1 tablespoon neutral cooking oil
3 tablespoons perilla seed powder

Remove any damaged perilla leaves or any that are too tough, and cut out any tough stems with a small knife or scissors. Rinse the leaves thoroughly under cold running water and drain well.

Set up a bowl of ice and water. In a large pot, bring 8½ cups (68 fl oz/ 2 liters) water and the salt to a boil. Add the perilla leaves and blanch for 1½ minutes. Scoop out in a sieve and transfer to the ice bath to cool completely. Drain well and squeeze to remove excess moisture.

**Make the sauce:** In a bowl, stir together the broth, soy sauce, perilla oil, garlic, salt, and sugar.

Add the perilla leaves to the sauce and gently massage the sauce with the leaves.

**Make the namul:** In a frying pan, heat the cooking oil over high heat. Add the perilla leaves and when the sauce comes to a boil, reduce the heat to medium and add the perilla seed powder. Cook together until fully incorporated.

Remove from the heat and spread out on a large flat plate to cool before serving.

---

## Doenjang Napa Cabbage Namul
### Doenjang Baechu Namul
### 된장 배추 나물

dF vg vE -5 -30      [미]

The Korean napa cabbage (Chinese leaf) is originally from China but is now its own distinct variety developed over time. It is one of the main vegetables representing Korean cuisine along with *mu* (Korean radish), chilies, and garlic. Although napa cabbage may be best known as kimchi, an essential part of a meal spread, it makes an appearance in many other dishes, such as in soup, steamed, as fritters, and more. When eaten raw, it has a slight spiciness reminiscent of mustard and a slight sweetness and umami. When cooked, the sweetness is amplified.

**Preparation time:** 15 minutes
**Cooking time:** 10 minutes
**Serves:** 2–4

7 oz (200 g) napa cabbage (Chinese leaf)
1 tablespoon salt
1 tablespoon doenjang (fermented soybean paste)
1 teaspoon cheongjang (light Korean soy sauce)
1 teaspoon sesame oil
Sliced scallion (spring onion), (optional)

Remove any bruised or discolored leaves from the napa cabbage and cut out the tough root. Separate each leaf and rinse well with cold running water.

Set up a bowl of ice and water. In a large pot, combine 8½ cups (68 fl oz/2 liters) water and the salt and bring to a boil. Holding all the leaves together, dip the bottom (thicker) halves into the boiling water and blanch for 30 seconds. Drop the leaves in and blanch for another 30 seconds, a total of 1 minute. Immediately remove and transfer to the ice bath (or under cold running water) to stop further cooking.

Once fully cooled, remove the leaves and gently squeeze with your hands to remove all water. Cut the drained leaves into 2-inch (5 cm) lengths and tear with your hands along the grain of the cabbage into bite-size pieces.

In a bowl, combine the doenjang, soy sauce, and sesame oil and mix until fully combined. Add the shredded cabbage pieces and massage to marinate until well combined.

Serve garnished with the sliced scallion, if desired.

## Korean Radish Saengchae
### Mu Saengchae
### 무 생채

dF gF vg vE -s -3o

When preparing any *namul* made with *mu* (Korean radish), note that it is harder and crunchier near the stem part, with a stronger sweet flavor. Especially when making *namul* that requires cooking, it's best to use the top half of the *mu*. The vegetable's texture as well as its flavor change, depending on how it is cut. Cutting along the grain ensures that the texture remains crunchier. To heighten the crispy texture and the sour flavor of the *mu saengchae*, keep in the refrigerator and serve cold.

**Preparation time:** 10 minutes
**Serves:** 4

1 lb 5 oz (600 g) mu (Korean radish)
3 tablespoon rice vinegar
3 teaspoons fine gochugaru (red chili powder)
3 teaspoons sugar
2 teaspoons fine sea salt
4 teaspoons ground sesame seeds

Peel the radish and cut into matchsticks 2½ inches (6 cm) long and 1/16 inch thick.

In a bowl, combine the vinegar, gochugaru, sugar, salt, and ground sesame seeds and whisk until uniform. Add the radish and toss until well combined. Let marinate for a minimum of 5 minutes to ensure that the sauce is well incorporated into the radish pieces.

---

## Korean Radish Namul
### Mu Namul
### 무 나물

dF gF vg vE    [ㅁ]

*Mu* (Korean radish) is often eaten raw to enjoy its crunchy texture and refreshing flavor, but it is also delicious when stir-fried with oil and seasoned with perilla oil and seeds. If mishandled, the radish can easily break into small pieces. To prevent breakage, lightly brine the radish with salt before stir-frying, and add water to softly cook the radish after stir-frying for a short time.

**Preparation time:** 30 minutes
**Cooking time:** 5 minutes
**Serves:** 2–4

10 oz (300 g) mu (Korean radish)
2 tablespoons plus 1 teaspoon salt
3 tablespoons neutral cooking oil
1 tablespoon minced garlic
1 tablespoon minced scallion (spring onion)
1 tablespoon perilla seeds
1 teaspoon perilla oil

Peel the radish and cut into matchsticks 2 inches (5 cm) long and 1/8 inch (3 mm) wide, using a mandoline if you have one. Toss the radish with 2 tablespoons of the salt evenly and let sit for about 15 minutes. Once the radish reaches a state when it doesn't easily snap but instead bends to gentle pressure, rinse off to remove the salt and gently squeeze to remove excess moisture.

In a frying pan, heat the cooking oil over medium heat. Add the garlic and scallion and stir-fry for 30 seconds. Add the radish, perilla seeds, 2 tablespoons water, and the remaining 1 teaspoon salt and stir-fry until just soft or semi-translucent.

Remove from the heat and stir in the perilla oil. Plate and serve.

## Dried Radish Namul
### Mumallaengi Namul
### 무말랭이 무침

---
dF -3o

*Mumallaengi* refers to sliced and dried *mu* (Korean radish). Korean cuisine has a long history of preserving various seasonal vegetables during harvest time by dehydrating to store and use throughout the year. The *mumallaengi* is one of the most representative of this category.

Soaking the dried *mu* in water for too long will dissipate the sweet flavor of the *mu*, so only wash lightly with water. Rehydrating the dried *mu* with rice syrup results in a more pleasant chewy, crunchy texture.

**Preparation time:** 20 minutes
**Serves:** 2–4

3½ oz (100 g) dried Korean radish
2 tablespoons jocheong (rice syrup)
1½ oz (40 g) dried pepper leaves

**For the sauce:**
2 tablespoons gochugaru (red chili flakes)
1 tablespoon gochujang (red chili paste)
½ tablespoon anchovy fish sauce
1 tablespoon jocheong (rice syrup)
1 tablespoon minced garlic
1 tablespoon sesame oil
1 tablespoon sesame seeds

Wash the dried radish slices in a bowl with cold water and drain. Mix with the rice syrup and rehydrate for 10 minutes. Squeeze to remove excess water.

Meanwhile, wash the dried pepper leaves with cold water. In a bowl, combine the leaves with 90°–100°F (32°–38°C) water for 15 minutes until well rehydrated. Squeeze to remove excess water.

**Make the sauce:** In a large bowl, stir together the gochugaru, gochujang, fish sauce, rice syrup, garlic, sesame oil, and sesame seeds.

Add the rehydrated radish slices and pepper leaves to the sauce and mix well to combine.

## Radish Top Doenjang Namul
### Siraegi Doenjang Namul
### 시래기 된장 나물

---
dF

Korean radish is one of the most common and iconic vegetables of Korea. As such, all parts of it are used without waste, including the leafy green tops. Radish tops that have been softened and boiled prior to dehydrating are the best for cooking. While other radish tops can be used for this recipe, avoid using those that are too tough or bitter.

**Preparation time:** 30 minutes
**Cooking time:** 50 minutes
**Serves:** 4

1 oz (25 g) dried radish tops
1 teaspoon sugar
2 tablespoons doenjang (fermented soybean paste)
1 teaspoon cheongjang (light Korean soy sauce)
1 tablespoon perilla oil
1 teaspoon minced garlic
10 dried anchovies, heads and organs removed
1 oz (30 g) daepa (Korean scallion), thinly sliced on a diagonal
2 tablespoons perilla seed powder

In a pot, combine 8½ cups (68 fl oz/2 liters) water, the dried radish tops, and sugar. Bring to a boil and cook for 20 minutes. Let steep for 10 minutes off the heat. Drain and rinse with cold water. Squeeze well to remove all excess water.

In a pot, combine the cooked radish tops, doenjang, soy sauce, perilla oil, and garlic and mix well until well seasoned. Add 2 cups (16 fl oz/480 ml) water and the dried anchovies, cover with a lid, and bring to a boil. Once boiling, reduce the heat to medium-low and cook for 20 minutes.

Add the daepa and perilla seed powder and cook for 3 minutes.

**Variation:** The anchovies can be lightly pan-fried before using to reduce the fishy flavor.

## Enoki & Chive Namul
### Paengi Buchu Namul
### 팽이 부추 나물

dF vg vP -3o

Named after the *paeng* tree under which it likes to grow, the *paeng-i* mushroom, aka enoki mushroom, grows and germinates easily in many different environments and is suited for cultivation. While it's rarely consumed raw due to the often unpleasant, fungal scent, it's beloved for its mouthfeel. Its natural lifecycle peaks in late fall, but it can be easily found in markets year-around. It is not considered a high-quality mushroom, because it does not have a distinct fragrance or flavor, but this works to its advantage as an ingredient in many dishes, because it can be used to harmonize with flavors while adding a unique crunchy mouthfeel and a long, noodle-like shape. It is often used in stews, hotpots, and as a stuffing for grilled meat rolls.

**Preparation time:** 5 minutes
**Cooking time:** 10 minutes
**Serves:** 4

8 oz (220 g) enoki mushrooms
1 tablespoon ganjang
    (Korean soy sauce)
1 tablespoon sesame oil
½ tablespoon corn (golden) syrup
2¾ oz (80 g) chives, cut into 1-inch
    (2.5 cm) lengths
½ tablespoon ground black
    sesame seeds

Enoki mushrooms are often sold in individually wrapped packages that are marked with a cutting line for edible servings. From this line, cut ½ inch (1.3 cm) above—or where the mushrooms begin to separate. Wash the mushrooms under cold running water and separate the strands using your hands. Set aside to drain excess moisture.

Heat a dry nonstick frying pan over medium heat and dry-fry the enoki mushrooms until there is no moisture, 2–3 minutes. Transfer the mushrooms to a plate.

Add the soy sauce, sesame oil, and corn syrup and stir-fry over medium heat until it is cohesive and begins to boil. Add the chives and the cooked mushrooms and stir-fry for about 30 seconds. Add the ground sesame seeds and combine.

Remove from the heat and plate.

## Shiitake Namul
### Pyogo Beoseot Namul
### 표고 버섯 나물

dF vg vP -3o

Eastern Asian countries, including Korea, China, and Japan, all use the shiitake mushroom as a foundational ingredient. It grows in clusters at the base of trees in spring and fall, although it is also widely cultivated year-round. Compared to rare and luxurious mushrooms, such as the songyi mushroom, the readily available shiitake mushroom is thought of as the common mushroom. Yet its sweet taste, unique flavor, and texture make it not only the most beloved mushroom but also the most important.

The shiitake mushroom can be used in *namul*, as fritters, grilled, and in soups and hotpots with ease. When choosing especially fresh mushrooms, choose ones that have a lighter shade of brown with soft, white inner caps that aren't fully bloomed. The chubby ones are preferred to those that are skinny or flat, and the best-quality ones will have geometric crack marks that mimic the back of turtle shells.

**Preparation time:** 20 minutes
**Cooking time:** 15 minutes
**Serves:** 4

9 oz (250 g) fresh shiitake
    mushrooms
1 tablespoon cheongjang
    (light Korean soy sauce)
1 teaspoon salt
1 tablespoon perilla oil
1 tablespoon neutral cooking oil
1 tablespoon minced daepa
    (Korean scallion)
½ tablespoon ground sesame seeds

Trim the stems off the shiitake mushrooms and cut the caps into strips ⅛ inch (3 mm) wide.

Set up a steamer and bring a small amount of water to a boil. Add the mushrooms to the steamer basket, set it over the boiling water, and steam for about 1 minute. (Note that while it's possible to blanch or pan-fry instead, the fragrance and the texture is best highlighted when lightly steamed.)

In a bowl, add the soy sauce, salt, and perilla oil and combine until uniform. Add the steamed mushrooms and massage gently. Let marinate for about 10 minutes.

In a medium frying pan, heat the cooking oil over medium heat. Add the daepa and stir-fry for about 30 seconds. Add the seasoned mushrooms and stir-fry for 1 more minute.

Remove from the heat and plate. Garnish with ground sesame seeds.

**Variation:** If you have Nutty Yangnyeom (page 155) on hand, use 2 tablespoons of it in place of the soy-and-perilla oil mixture to season the shiitakes.

# Deodeok Pine Nut Saengchae
## Deodeok Jat Saengchae
## 더덕 잣 생채

dF gF vg vE −S

*Deodeok* is a plant that can be eaten in all its parts. Its young leaves are harvested and used in *namul*, and it can be dried to make tea. The form most commonly consumed is its root.

Its root contains both bitter and sweet flavors, with earthy, herbal tones that are similar to ginseng. It is exceptionally fibrous; when the skin is peeled, its flesh is almost cotton-like with visible strings. Larger roots will have a solid yellow core that should be removed before cooking. It's often marinated in *gochujang* (red chili paste) sauce and grilled, but in early spring, when the roots are more tender, it can be shredded by hand and made into a *namul*.

**Preparation time: 30 minutes**
**Serves: 2–4**

7 oz (200 g) deodeok
3 tablespoons pine nuts
2 tablespoons Korean pear juice
1 tablespoon rice vinegar
1 teaspoon sugar
½ teaspoon salt

In cold running water, with a clean metal scrub or brush, clean the surface of the deodeok to remove any dirt. Use a peeler to remove the skin, then soak in water for 15 minutes to remove the bitter taste.

After soaking, halve the deodeok lengthwise following the grain of the root. Using a wooden meat mallet or similar, pound lightly to flatten the deodok. Be gentle, as using too much force will break the root into pieces. Once flattened, gently use your hands to tear the deodeok into thin pieces along the fibers.

In a blender or food processor, combine the pine nuts, pear juice, vinegar, sugar, and salt and blend until fine. (Alternatively, make the sauce in a mortar and pestle for a coarser sauce. Start first with the pine nuts until finely ground, then add the rest of the ingredients.)

In a bowl, combine the shredded deodeok and the pine nut sauce and toss with your hands, massaging gently so that all combine evenly. Plate and serve.

# Seaweed & Squid Saengchae
## Miyeok Ojingeo Saengchae
## 미역 오징어 생채

dF

*Miyeok* (aka wakame) is a type of red-brown seaweed that grows to more than 3 feet (1 meter) long and is the most consumed type of seaweed in Korea. It's most often used in soup, both in hot and cold form, but is also used in *saengchae* (raw vegetable dishes). While it's possible to still find the fresh version in local markets (it's in season in winter), most households and markets will carry the dried form.

In Korea, the *miyeok* roots—the crunchy, knobby parts of the seaweed called *miyeok-gwi*—are sold separately from the softer, silky leaf parts, which are sold in many different forms, depending on their intended use. This showcases how rooted *miyeok* is to the daily cuisine and lives of Korea.

**Preparation time: 30 minutes**
**Cooking time: 15 minutes**
**Serves: 2–4**

½ oz/15 g dried miyeok
    (7 oz/200 g when rehydrated)
Salt
1 cucumber
½ cleaned squid body

**For the sauce:**
2 tablespoons gochujang
    (red chili paste)
1 tablespoon ganjang
    (Korean soy sauce)
2 tablespoons rice vinegar
1 tablespoon sugar
1 teaspoon minced garlic

In a large bowl or pot, combine water and salt (1 teaspoon salt for every 4 cups/32 fl oz/950 ml of water), stirred to dissolve. The salt helps maintain the flavor of the miyeok. Add the dried miyeok and let rehydrate at room temperature for about 20 minutes. Drain and gently squeezes out excess water.

In a large pot, bring enough water to fully submerge the miyeok to a boil. Add the miyeok and blanch for 2 minutes. Rinse under cold running water. Squeeze out excess water and cut into 2-inch (5 cm) lengths. (Alternatively, for a shortcut, microwave the rehydrated miyeok for 1 minute and let cool spread flat on a large plate.)

Meanwhile, halve the cucumber lengthwise and then cut crosswise on a diagonal into slices ⅛ inch (3 mm) thick. Weigh the cucumber and lightly brine with salt, about 2 percent of the weight of the cucumber and set aside.

Set up a bowl of ice and water. Score the squid body. In a pot, combine 4 cups (32 fl oz/950 ml) water and 1 teaspoon salt and bring to a boil. Add the scored squid to the boiling water and blanch for 1 minute. Place in the ice bath to stop the cooking process. Once completely cool, remove from water and cut into slices ¼ inch (6 mm) wide.

**Make the sauce:** In a bowl, mix together the gochujang, soy sauce, vinegar, sugar, and garlic. Add the prepared seaweed and toss until well combined. Add the cucumber and squid and toss.

Plate and serve cold.

# 무침 Muchim Seasoned

*Muchim* is a term that translates to "dish mixed with seasoning," or more simply "seasoned" or "mixed." In practice, it refers to a cold *banchan* (side dish) made with thoroughly seasoned raw or cooked ingredients.

While it may seem similar to the category of *namul*, the main ingredients in *namul* are vegetables or plant-based ingredients, but *muchim* can utilize any main ingredient, including vegetables, meat, and seafood. Because it's a dish enjoyed cold or at room temperature, including all of its ingredients, the seasoning sauce tends to be acidic and leans toward sweet. Vinegar is often added to sauces based on *jang*, such as soy sauce, *doenjang* (fermented soybean paste), and *gochujang* (red chili paste). Mustard, pine nuts, and sesame or black sesame are also often used as main ingredients for seasoning.

With the base *muchim* sauce prepared, many common ingredients found in home kitchens and refrigerators can be made into a *muchim*. The sauces below can be premade and kept in the refrigerator for up to 3 days.

---

**Vinegar Ganjang Muchim**

1 tablespoon ganjang (Korean soy sauce)

1 tablespoon sugar

2 tablespoons rice vinegar

In a small bowl, stir everything together until completely uniform.

**Savory Doenjang Muchim**

1 tablespoon doenjang (fermented soybean paste)

1 tablespoon sesame seeds

½ tablespoon sesame oil

In a small bowl, stir everything together until completely uniform.

**Vinegar Gochujang Muchim**

2 tablespoons gochujang (red chili paste)

1 tablespoon rice vinegar

1 tablespoon sugar

In a small bowl, stir everything together until completely uniform.

## Fried Lotus Root Doenjang Muchim
### Yeongeun Twigim Doenjang Muchim
### 연근 튀김 된장 무침

dF vg vE

Lotus root is a popular and accessible ingredient in Korea that's considered seasonless, but it's actually an ingredient that's difficult to harvest without damaging the root. Its peak is in fall, with the roots being the juiciest. Its skin is often tough and easily damaged, but a fresh, in-season lotus root can be enjoyed unpeeled for a more flavorful, fragrant dish.

This dish uses a commonly available ingredient called frying mix, which is preseasoned flour for making deep-fried foods. Actual ingredients in the mix will vary with the brand.

**Preparation time:** 25 minutes
**Cooking time:** 15 minutes
**Serves:** 2–4

10 oz (300 g) lotus root
1 tablespoon salt
1 tablespoon sugar
1 cup (120 g) Korean frying mix
Neutral cooking oil, for deep-frying

**For the sauce:**
1 tablespoon doenjang (fermented soybean paste)
2 tablespoons ground sesame seeds
1 teaspoon sesame oil

Peel the lotus root and cut into ½-inch (1.3 cm) slices. In a bowl, combine 3 cups (24 fl oz/710 ml) water, the salt, and sugar and mix until dissolved. Soak the cut lotus slices for about 20 minutes. Drain and pat dry with paper towels.

In a large bowl, combine the frying mix and 1 cup (8 fl oz/240 ml) water to make a batter. Add the lotus root slices.

Set a wire rack in a sheet pan. Pour 2 inches (5 cm) cooking oil into a large deep pot or deep-fryer and heat to 350°F (177°C). Fry each lotus root slice for about 2 minutes or until golden brown. Transfer the fried lotus roots to the wire rack and let cool to room temperature.

**Make the sauce:** In a large bowl, combine the doenjang, sesame seeds, and sesame oil until uniform.

Toss the fried lotus roots with the sauce until well dressed and plate to serve.

**Variation:** For those who prefer a lighter version of the dish, boil the lotus root instead and cool to room temperature before seasoning for a salad-like *muchim* version. If there is time, brining the lotus roots in the salt-sugar water solution overnight can enhance both the flavor and texture of the final product.

---

## Shishito Doenjang Muchim
### Kkwari Gochu Doenjang Muchim
### 꽈리고추 된장 무침

dF -3o

*Kkwari* peppers, aka shishito peppers, have a pleasant, tender texture when cooked and are great braised or pan-fried. Soy sauce is a well-known combination, but shishito braised with flour and seasoned with a *doenjang*-based sauce provides another delicacy, reminiscent of summer. In choosing shishito peppers, pick those that are elastic and firm to the touch, with no discoloration in the seeds.

**Preparation time:** 15 minutes
**Cooking time:** 10 minutes
**Serves:** 4

9 oz (250 g) shishito peppers, stemmed
1 teaspoon salt
3 tablespoons all-purpose (plain) flour

**For the sauce:**
1½ tablespoons doenjang (fermented soybean paste)
1 tablespoon sand lance fish sauce
1 tablespoon sesame oil
1 teaspoon gochugaru (red chili flakes)
1 tablespoon sesame seeds

Place the shishito peppers in a plastic bag with the salt and 1 tablespoon water. Add the flour, seal the bag, and shake until the peppers are well coated.

Set up a steamer and bring the water to a boil. Add the flour-coated shishito peppers to the steamer basket and sprinkle the flour remaining in the bag over the peppers. Cover and steam for 8 minutes. Remove from the heat and set aside to cool.

**Make the sauce:** In a bowl, combine the doenjang, fish sauce, sesame oil, gochugaru, and sesame seeds and mix until uniform.

Once the shishito peppers have cooled off, mix well with the sauce until evenly coated and plate.

**Variation:** For a gluten-free version, use glutinous rice flour to coat the peppers, which will have a chewier texture. This seasoning can be used with other mild peppers or vegetables for a savory snack as well.

## Green Laver & Radish Muchim
## Parae Mu Cho Muchim
## 파래 무 초무침

dF vg vE -3o

*Parae*, also known as green laver, is a seaweed that looks similar to the common *gim*, but it can be distinguished by its blue undertones and its silkier texture, as well as a unique citrus-like fragrance. It is often mixed with *gim* as a hybrid, or it's used to make *saengchae* (raw vegetable dishes), *jeon* (fritters), or even soup. Due to its soft texture, there is often dirt or impurities, so it requires a thorough cleaning process to prepare. Washing in warm water could reduce its fragrance, so we recommend using cool water at 40°–50°F (4°–10°C) with 5 to 7 percent salt (meaning 3–4 tablespoons/50–70 g salt for every 4 cups/ 32 fl oz/950 ml of water). Salt water is always recommended in washing sea vegetables, because it helps maintain their natural flavor and texture.

**Preparation time:** 25 minutes
**Serves:** 2–4

3¼ oz (90 g) fresh parae
1 tablespoon salt
1¾ oz (50 g) mu (Korean radish)
1¾ oz (50 g) Asian pear
1 tablespoon corn (golden) syrup

**For the sauce:**
1 tablespoon cheongjang (light Korean soy sauce)
1 teaspoon sugar
1 teaspoon sesame seeds
½ teaspoon sesame oil
½ teaspoon minced garlic

In a bowl, combine 8½ cups (68 fl oz/2 liters) cool water (45°–50°F/4°–10°C) with 2 teaspoons salt until dissolved. Add the parae and loosen and clean well, shaking thoroughly with fingertips. Remove from the water and cut the parae into 1-inch (2.5 cm) lengths.

Peel the radish and pear and cut both into matchsticks 1–2 inches (2.5–5 cm) long and ⅛ inch (3 mm) thick. In a bowl, combine the radish with 1 teaspoon salt and the corn syrup and let marinate for about 10 minutes to soften. Drain well.

**Make the sauce:** In a large bowl, combine the soy sauce, sugar, sesame seeds, sesame oil, and garlic and mix until uniform.

Add the parae, radish, and pear to the sauce and toss, taking care to not break up the pieces. Once evenly combined, plate onto a salad plate and serve.

**Variation:** Depending on preference, you can control how "wet" the *muchim* is by how much liquid you squeeze out of the *parae* after cleaning, as well as deciding to keep or retain the liquid released by the pear as it marinates. Some people prefer a wetter *muchim* while others prefer a much drier texture.

---

## Cockles & Wild Korean Chive Muchim
## Kkomak Dallae Muchim
## 꼬막 달래 무침

dF -3o    [ㅁ]

Cockles are a beloved mollusk that herald the onset of spring along the west coast of Korea. While small in size, the cockles' flesh is plump and savory, on the verge of sweet. While delicious to eat simply boiled, when eaten together with the spring *namul dallae* (wild Korean chives), the combination of sweet aromas evokes the essence of spring.

**Preparation time:** 15 minutes
**Cooking time:** 10 minutes
**Serves:** 2–4

10 oz (300 g) cockles
1 tablespoon coarse sea salt
½ tablespoon fine salt

**For the muchim:**
1 tablespoon ganjang (Korean soy sauce)
½ tablespoon gochugaru (red chili flakes)
1 teaspoon mirin
1 teaspoon sesame oil
½ teaspoon minced garlic
3/4 oz (20 g) wild Korean chives, trimmed and cut into 1½-inch (4 cm) lengths
½ teaspoon sesame seeds (optional)

In a large bowl, combine the cockles and coarse salt. Using the salt, scrub the cockles to remove dirt and impurities. Clean under cold running water thoroughly two to three times until the water runs clear.

In a pot, combine 4 cups (32 fl oz/ 950 ml) water and the fine salt and stir until the salt is dissolved. Add the cockles and stir over medium heat. Bring to a boi and cook until the cockle shells open, 2–3 minutes, and quickly transfer the cockles to a bowl. Separate the cooked meat from the shells and set aside to cool.

**Make the muchim:** In a bowl, stir together the soy sauce, gochugaru, mirin, sesame oil, and garlic. Add the cooked cockle meat and gently combine with the sauce, ensuring the tender meat is not damaged. Add the chives and gently toss together to evenly coat with the sauce.

Plate and garnish with sesame seeds, if desired.

## Clam, Bamboo Shoot, & Perilla Seed Muchim
### Bajirak Juksun Deulkkae Muchim
### 바지락 죽순 들깨 무침

dF

Spring in Korea feels as if it's getting shorter each year, and the appreciation for the spring's ephemeral bounty after the long winter feels more precious than ever. During the onset of spring, *namul* (wild greens) from the mountains and fields enrich everyday meals. From the end of April until May, bamboo shoots appear and Manila clams are in season, creating a delicious combination. Stir-fried together with perilla seeds the clams are a treat, but a *muchim* made with tofu and perilla seed sauce is also a unique experience to mark a spring day.

Preparation time: 15 minutes
Cooking time: 20 minutes
Serves: 4

2¾ oz (80 g) Manila clam meats
1 tablespoon salt
10 oz (300 g) cleaned bamboo shoots

For the sauce:
5 oz (135 g) soft tofu
3 tablespoons perilla seed powder
2 tablespoons honey
1 tablespoon perilla oil
1 tablespoon cheongjang (light Korean soy sauce)
½ teaspoon salt

Rinse the clam meat in 2 cups (16 fl oz/480 ml) water combined with the salt.

Bring a pot of water to a boil, add the clam meats, and blanch for 1½ minutes. Remove the meat and set aside to cool to room temperature.

Cut the bamboo shoots into slices about 1 inch (2.5 cm) thick. Bring another pot of water to a boil and blanch the bamboo shoot slices to rid it of its tannins. Remove the slices and set aside to cool to room temperature.

**Make the sauce:** In a blender, combine the tofu, perilla seed powder, honey, perilla oil, soy sauce, and salt and blend until smooth. (Alternatively, mix by hand with a whisk in a bowl.)

In a bowl, combine the clams, bamboo shoots, and the sauce and toss until fully seasoned. Plate on a shallow bowl or plate and serve.

## Gim & Clam Muchim
### Gim Jogaetsal Muchim
### 김 조갯살 무침

dF -30  [□]

*Gim* is a type of seaweed that grows like moss in the sea. Once harvested, it is laid out in sheet-like formations on a large flat surface to dry to make its basic culinary form. In Korea, *gim* begins to grow around October until spring. As the season warms in May, it disappears until the weather turn cool again.

There are many ways to cook and consume *gim*, but the most well-known and common form is brushed with oil, lightly salted, and grilled. This seasoned *gim* is a staple, basic *banchan* (side dish) that accompanies many everyday meals in Korea. Unseasoned *gim* is enjoyed grilled as well, often used as an ingredient in a dish or used as a garnish. Because of seasoned *gim*'s savory, delicious taste, moderate saltiness, and fragrant sesame oil, it's a national favorite "rice thief," a magic ingredient that can help children finish their rice even when low on appetite. No wonder it's one of the most beloved *banchan* in the country.

Preparation time: 15 minutes
Cooking time: 5 minutes
Serves: 2–4

For the sauce:
1½ tablespoons jinjang (Korean dark soy sauce)
1½ tablespoons rice vinegar
2 tablespoons sugar
1 tablespoon ground sesame seeds
1 teaspoon sesame oil
1 teaspoon minced garlic

For the muchim:
7 sheets unseasoned gim
3½ oz (100 g) clam meats, fresh or cooked
1¾ oz (50 g) onion, cut into ⅛-inch (3 mm) slices

**Make the sauce:** In a bowl, combine the soy sauce, vinegar, sugar, sesame seeds, sesame oil, and garlic. Set aside.

**Prepare the muchim:** Place the sheets of gim on a large flat microwave-safe plate and microwave for 30 seconds. Repeat with the other side. After cooling to room temperature, tear by hand into 1-inch (2.5 cm) squares.

If using raw clams, bring a pot of water to a boil and blanch the clams for 30 seconds. Transfer to a bowl of cold water to cool to room temperature. Drain and pat dry. If the clam meat is preboiled, rinse lightly and pat dry.

Add the gim, clam meat, and sliced onions to the sauce and toss until evenly coated. Plate to serve.

## Whelk & Minari Muchim
## Golbaengi Minari Muchim
## 골뱅이 미나리 무침

dF –30

*Golbaengi*, or whelk, is commonly available in canned form. Because of its strong savory flavor, it is a popular drinking snack in Korea. It is typically served seasoned with a spicy sauce along with *somyeon* (thin wheat noodles). When mixed with in-season *minari*, the combination of the bitter minari and the savory whelk is a delicacy to be savored. Note that in some parts of the Western world the canned whelk may be labeled as scungilli.

**Preparation time:** 20 minutes
**Serves:** 2–4

**For the sauce:**
1½ tablespoons rice vinegar
½ tablespoon ganjang (Korean soy sauce)
1 tablespoon mirin
½ tablespoon sugar
2 tablespoons gochujang (red chili paste)
1 tablespoon gochugaru (red chili flakes)
½ tablespoon minced garlic
½ tablespoon sesame oil

**For the muchim:**
1 can (8.25 oz/235 g) water-packed whelks, drained and halved
¾ oz (20 g) minari, cut into 2½-inch (6 cm) lengths
1¾ oz (50 g) onion, thinly sliced
1 tablespoon sesame seeds

**Make the sauce:** In a bowl large enough to comfortably mix the whelks and vegetables, combine the vinegar, soy sauce, mirin, and sugar and stir until the sugar is completely dissolved. Add the gochujang, gochugaru, garlic, and sesame oil and combine until uniform consistency.

**Assemble the muchim:** Add the whelk, minari, and onion to the bowl of sauce and mix well until all the ingredients are coated with the sauce. Plate and garnish with the sesame seeds.

---

## Vinegared Seaweed & Squid Muchim
## Miyeok Ojingeo Cho Muchim
## 미역 오징어 초무침

dF                                          [ㅁ]

The combination of squid, at the height of its flavors in summer, and the pleasant texture of fresh, almost crunchy seaweed, tossed together in the sweet-sour vinegar sauce is a great appetizer plate.

It is important that all the ingredients and plates are cold. Accompanying the sauce with crushed ice or lightly freezing the sauce and making a granita to top the *muchim* are also popular methods that increase the refreshing nature of the dish.

**Preparation time:** 20 minutes
**Cooking time:** 30 minutes
**Serves:** 2–4

2 teaspoons salt
½ cleaned squid body, cut crosswise into matchsticks as thin as possible, 1⁄16 inch (2 mm) thick
½ oz (10 g) dried seaweed

**For the sauce:**
4 tablespoons rice vinegar
3 tablespoons ganjang (Korean soy sauce)
2 tablespoons sugar
1 teaspoon minced garlic

**For the muchim:**
3½ oz (100 g) onion, thinly sliced
1 teaspoon sesame seeds
1 scallion (spring onion), cut into thin matchsticks

Set up a bowl of ice and water. In a pot, combine 3 cups (24 fl oz/710 ml) water and 1 teaspoon of the salt and bring to a boil over high heat. Add the squid slices and blanch for 30 seconds, then immediately place into the ice bath to completely cool.

In a large bowl, combine 3 cups (24 fl oz/710 ml) water and the remaining 1 teaspoon salt and stir until dissolved. Add the dried seaweed and let hydrate for 15 minutes.

Meanwhile, in a pot, bring 3 cups (24 fl oz/710 ml) water to a boil.

Once the seaweed is fully hydrated, blanch it in the boiling water for 1 minute. Remove from the heat and cool under cold running water until completely cool. Gently squeeze the excess water from the seaweed. Cut into 2½-inch (6 cm) lengths and set aside.

**Make the sauce:** In a microwave-safe bowl, combine the vinegar, soy sauce, and sugar. Microwave for 30 seconds or until the sugar is fully dissolved. Stir in the garlic. Let cool in the refrigerator.

**Make the muchim:** Set the sliced onion aside in a bowl of cold water for 15 minutes to remove its pungency. Drain or pat dry.

In a shallow bowl or large plate, neatly arrange the blanched seaweed, onions, and squid. Pour the sauce over everything. Garnish with sesame seeds and scallion and serve.

## Dried Shredded Squid Muchim
### Jinmichae Muchim
### 진미채 무침

dF -30  [ㅁ]

This is one of the most popular *banchan* (side dish) staples in Korea. Made with shredded dried squid, easily found in Korean grocery stores, it keeps well for a long time. It has a pleasant, addictive chew and its sweet-spicy flavor is easily beloved. Pan-frying the squid enhances the savory flavors of the squid and the sauce, but for a softer texture in the squid, it is fine to skip the last step.

**Preparation time:** 10 minutes
**Cooking time:** 10 minutes
**Serves:** 2–4

3½ oz (100 g) dried shredded squid

**For the sauce:**
1 tablespoon gochujang (red chili paste)
1 tablespoon rice wine or cooking wine
½ tablespoon mayonnaise
½ tablespoon sesame oil
2 teaspoons corn (golden) syrup
½ teaspoon yangjo ganjang (naturally brewed soy sauce)
1 teaspoon gochugaru (red chili flakes)

**For the muchim:**
½ tablespoon neutral cooking oil
1 teaspoon sesame seeds

Trim the dried squid, which typically comes packaged in long shredded lengths, into pieces 1½–2 inches (4–5 cm) long. In a bowl, massage the trimmed squid with 3 tablespoons room temperature water until the water is absorbed.

**Make the sauce:** In a bowl, combine the gochujang, wine, ½ tablespoon water, the mayonnaise, sesame oil, corn syrup, soy sauce, and gochugaru and mix until well combined.

**For the muchim:** Add the rehydrated squid to the sauce and massage together until well combined.

In a large frying pan, heat the neutral oil over medium-low heat and stir-fry the squid for 2–3 minutes. Sprinkle the sesame seeds evenly over the squid and remove from the heat.

While the taste is best when eaten freshly prepared, it is delicious refrigerated for up to 1 week.

---

## Pollock Hwe Muchim
### Myungtae Hwe Muchim
### 명태회 무침

dF gF

Pollock was abundant in Korea throughout its history, so there are many dishes that have developed to enjoy this fish. Even within Korea, each region boasts its own unique recipes and even nicknames. While it's most commonly seen in its dehydrated form as an ingredient, a fresh-caught pollock is delicious as a *hwe* (raw sliced seafood or meat).

**Preparation time:** 30 minutes, plus 6 hours fermentation
**Serves:** 4

10 oz (300 g) fresh sushi-grade pollock
5 oz (150 g) mu (Korean radish)
4 tablespoons rice vinegar
3 tablespoons sugar
2 tablespoons salt

**For the sauce:**
4 tablespoons gochugaru (red chili flakes)
2 tablespoons rice vinegar
2 tablespoons sesame oil
2 tablespoons corn (golden) syrup
1 tablespoon minced garlic
1 tablespoon ground sesame seeds
½ tablespoon salt

Cut the pollock into thin slices and then julienne further into bite-size pieces. Cut the radish into matchsticks 2 × ⅛ inch (5 cm × 3 mm).

In a bowl, combine the vinegar, sugar, and salt, stirring until the salt and sugar are dissolved. Add the pollock and radish slices and marinate for about 20 minutes, or until bouncy to the touch. Gently squeeze the pollock and radish to drain any excess moisture.

**Make the sauce:** In a large bowl, combine the gochugaru, vinegar, sesame oil, corn syrup, garlic, ground sesame seeds, and salt and mix until uniform.

Add the pollock and radish and toss until well combined. Transfer to an airtight container and let ferment for 6 hours to overnight in the refrigerator. Plate and serve.

**Variations**

- If desired, add young scallion and minari slices just before serving.

- This can also be made using dried pollock. Depending on the quality of the dried pollock, it can still remain tough when rehydrated. In that case, add 1 tablespoon of mayonnaise to the sauce.

# Long-Arm Octopus & Zucchini Chomuchim
## Nakji Aehobak Chomuchim
## 낙지 애호박 초무침

dF -3o

*Nakji*, the Korean long-arm octopus, which is a smaller species than the large octopus, is often enjoyed raw or stir-fried in sauce, but it is also delicious when lightly blanched and seasoned with a vinegar-based sauce. It goes well with a variety of vegetables, but is particularly harmonious with the savory, sweet *aehobak* (Korean zucchini).

**Preparation time:** 20 minutes
**Cooking time:** 10 minutes
**Serves:** 4

7 oz (200 g) long-arm octopus
2 tablespoons all-purpose (plain) flour
3½ oz (100 g) aehobak (Korean zucchini)

**For the sauce:**
4 tablespoons rice vinegar
2 tablespoons anchovy fish sauce
2 tablespoons sugar
1 tablespoon gochugaru (red chili flakes)
1 teaspoon sesame oil
1 teaspoon sesame seeds
½ teaspoon minced garlic

**For the muchim:**
1 teaspoon salt
1 young scallion (spring onion), thinly sliced
Sesame seeds

In a bowl, combine the octopus with the flour and massage thoroughly to clear impurities. Rinse off the flour under cold running water. Once clean, cut the octopus into 3-inch (8 cm) lengths and set aside.

Cut the zucchini into matchsticks about 2½ inches (6 cm) long and 1/16 inch (2 mm) wide and set aside.

**Make the sauce:** In a large bowl, combine the vinegar, fish sauce, sugar, gochugaru, sesame oil, sesame seeds, and garlic and mix until uniform.

**Make the muchim:** In a large pot, combine 4 cups (32 fl oz/950 ml) water and salt and bring to a boil. Add the prepared octopus and cook for 30 seconds. Add the zucchini and boil for 30 more seconds. Use a sieve to scoop everything out and drain off excess water; do not rinse with cold water.

While still warm, add the octopus and zucchini to the large bowl with the sauce and mix well until fully combined. Plate the muchim and garnish with the sliced scallion and additional sesame seeds to taste.

# Brisket & Chive Muchim
## Chadolbagi Buchu Muchim
## 차돌박이 부추 무침

dF gF -3o

*Chadolbagi* is a very popular cut of brisket in Korea. Almost paper-thin slices of brisket boast a deeply savory, nutty taste due to the layer of fat. Easily accessible at the market, it's a great meat to have in the refrigerator or the freezer, perfect for a quick party dish or for making a special *banchan* (side dish). The thinly sliced brisket is particularly delicious with chives seasoned with vinegar and *aekjeot* (fish sauce), the bittersweet chive harmonizing with the savory, fatty meat.

**Preparation time: 10 minutes**
**Cooking time: 5 minutes**
**Serves: 4**

3½ oz (100 g) onion
14 oz (400 g) thinly sliced beef brisket
Salt
1 tablespoon neutral cooking oil

**For the sauce:**
2 tablespoons rice vinegar
2 tablespoons anchovy fish sauce
2 tablespoons gochugaru (red chili flakes)
1 tablespoon sugar
1 teaspoon sesame oil
1 teaspoon minced garlic

**For the muchim:**
5 oz (150 g) chives, cut crosswise into 5 pieces
2½ oz (75 g) fresh red chilies, halved and thinly sliced on a diagonal

Thinly slice the onion and place in a cold water bath for about 5 minutes to reduce its pungency. Drain and dry off in a sieve or on paper towels. Set aside.

Lightly salt the thinly sliced brisket. In a frying pan, heat the cooking oil over high heat. Quickly stir-fry the brisket slices until just cooked and remove from the heat.

**Make the sauce:** In a bowl, combine the vinegar, fish sauce, gochugaru, sugar, sesame oil, and garlic and mix until uniform.

**Assemble the muchim:** Add the onion, chives, and chilies to the sauce and toss until coated evenly. Plate the resulting sauce into a shallow bowl or deep plate. Plate the cooked brisket on top of or adjacent to the chive sauce and eat together.

**Variation:** Although pan-frying the brisket results in a more pronounced meaty, oily flavor that many enjoy, if you'd prefer a lighter dish, blanch the brisket in boiling water. For the blanched version, it's recommended to lightly season the cooked meat with sesame oil after blanching (this adds back some richness). Serve the sesame-dressed brisket cold, tossed with the chive sauce.

# Raw Beef Muchim
## Yukhwe Muchim
## 육회 무침

dF -3o

The culture of eating fresh, raw beef as a delicacy exists in many countries. In Korea, raw beef is eaten in julienned form. Each region has a different recipe for the seasoning, but the most common and basic seasoning is made with ganjang (Korean soy sauce), sesame oil, and sugar.

Raw beef is delicious with Asian pear, raw egg yolk, and pine nuts, so these ingredients are often served together.

**Preparation time: 25 minutes**
**Serves: 2**

5 oz (150 g) lean beef tenderloin (fillet) or top round (topside)

For the sauce:
½ tablespoon ganjang (Korean soy sauce)
½ tablespoon gochujang (red chili paste)
1 teaspoon minced garlic
1 teaspoon light brown sugar
1 teaspoon honey
1 teaspoon rice cooking wine

For the muchim:
3½ oz (100 g) Asian pear, cut into 2-inch (5 cm) matchsticks
1 egg yolk
1 small scallion (spring onion), thinly sliced
1 teaspoon sesame seeds

Place the beef in the freezer for 10 minutes for easy slicing. Cut into long sticks about 2¾ inches (7 cm) long and ⅛-inch (3 mm) thick. Set aside.

**Make the sauce:** In a large bowl, combine the soy sauce, gochujang, garlic, brown sugar, honey, and wine and stir well. Add the beef and mix until the sauce is evenly incorporated.

**For the muchim:** Plate the julienned pears and the seasoned beef. Place the egg yolk on top of the beef muchim and garnish with the scallion and sesame seeds before serving.

# Chicken Mustard Muchim
## Dakgogi Gyeoja Muchim
## 닭고기 겨자 무침

dF

Preparation time: 15 minutes
Cooking time: 40 minutes
Serves: 3–4

**For the chicken:**
2 boneless, skinless chicken breasts
2–3 cloves garlic, peeled
1 oz (30 g) daepa (Korean scallion)
2 tablespoon rice wine
½ tablespoon salt

**For the sauce:**
4 tablespoons rice vinegar
1½ tablespoons Korean mustard
2 tablespoons sugar
1 tablespoon ganjang (Korean soy sauce)

**For the muchim:**
2½ oz (75 g) cucumber
1¾ oz (50 g) red onion, julienned
3½ oz (100 g) Asian pear, julienned
Black sesame seeds

This dish is made by seasoning shredded cooked chicken with a mustard-based sauce. If the chicken and vegetables sit together for too long, they will leak liquid and make the sauce watery. So, either combine with the sauce just before serving or plate separately to be combined at the table, like a salad. The vegetables that complement the dish include julienned carrots, bell pepper, tomato, and more; bitter or spicy greens, such as radish sprouts, are also delicious.

**Cook the chicken:** Score the chicken breasts so that they will cook evenly and faster. In a pot, combine about 4 cups (32 fl oz/950 ml) water (or enough to fully cover the chicken), the garlic, daepa, and wine and bring to a boil. Add the chicken and boil for 30 minutes. Remove the chicken and cool to room temperature.

Once the chicken is brought to room temperature, shred with your hands along its natural fibers into a bowl. Evenly season the shredded chicken with the salt.

**Make the sauce:** In a large bowl, combine the vinegar, mustard, sugar, and soy sauce and mix until evenly combined.

**Prepare the muchim:** Quarter the cucumber lengthwise and scrape out the seeds. Cut the cucumber on a diagonal into slices. Add the shredded chicken, cucumber, onion, and pear to the sauce and mix until well seasoned. Plate and garnish with black sesame seeds.

# 회 Hwe Raw

*Hwe* was first recorded in Korea in the early seventeenth century in a recipe calling for raw, thinly sliced fish eaten with ginger, scallion (spring onion), and mustard paste. It has long been enjoyed in Korea and has evolved into a beloved culinary category.

Depending on the season, a wide range of fish or seafood is enjoyed raw. In Korea, it is perfectly common to see large aquariums filled with fresh, live seafood of all kinds in restaurants and markets. With the consistent, high demand for live seafood, there are even trucks that are equipped specifically to deliver live seafood, including shellfish. Sea cucumbers, sea pineapple, abalone, and even squid are transported live and butchered fresh to order, enjoyed as *hwe*.

The most popular fish for *hwe* include various flatfish, sea bream, sea bass, trout, and salmon; seasonal fish favorites include kingfish and yellowtail. Premium fish that are considered a delicacy, such as flounder, stone bream, and saw-edged perch, are consumed in all their parts, including their intestines and cheeks.

Each fish has its own inherent flavor, aroma, and texture, so it's important to pair the *yangnyeom-jang* (seasoning sauce) accordingly. As a general rule, white-fleshed fish are great with lighter seasoning, such as soy sauce, and fatty fish, such as mackerel, go well with sauces made with *chojang* (vinegared *gochujang*) or *doenjang* (fermented soybean paste). Rich, red-fleshed fish, such as salmon, harmonize with wasabi or mustard paired with soy sauce, and shellfish are most often paired with *chojang*.

While fresh *hwe* is great eaten on its own, it is also great to eat along with vegetables and in *ssam* (wraps). *Hwe* is also often used as a part of a rice bowl or noodles.

# Seasoned Skate Hwe
## Hongeo Hwe Muchim
## 홍어회 무침

dF

In Korea, skate *hwe* typically refers to fermented skate. However, it is a very polarizing food, because the powerful aroma and flavor is reminiscent of ammonia. A more popular and less challenging skate *hwe* is this *muchim* (seasoned dish) in which refreshing vegetables, such as minari, and raw skate are tossed in a *chojang* (vinegared gochujang)-based sauce. This skate *hwe* highlights the textural difference between its skin, which has a pleasant chew, and the soft, sweet flesh.

Raw skate is difficult to source commercially, because it's in high demand. Although skate was once a common fish enjoyed with *makgeolli* (Korean rice wine), in recent years, because of its increased popularity, its population has dramatically decreased due to overfishing, and its status has become more precious.

Preparation time: 35 minutes
Serves: 2–4

For the sauce:
2 tablespoons sugar
2 tablespoons rice vinegar
1½ tablespoons gochujang (red chili paste)
1½ tablespoons fine gochugaru (red chili powder)
1 tablespoon soy sauce
1 tablespoon corn (golden) syrup
1 tablespoon ginger juice
1 tablespoon sesame oil
1 teaspoon minced garlic

For the muchim:
14 oz (400 g) skate
2 cups (16 fl oz/480 ml) makgeolli (Korean rice wine)
2¾ oz (80 g) mu (Korean radish)
7 oz (200 g) Asian pear
1 tablespoon salt
1 tablespoon rice vinegar
1 tablespoon sugar
2½ oz (75 g) cucumber, cut into ⅛-inch (3 mm) diagonal slices
3½ oz (100 g) onion, thinly sliced
3½ oz (100 g) minari, cut into 2-inch (5 cm) lengths

**Make the sauce:** In a large bowl, combine the sugar, vinegar, gochujang, gochugaru, soy sauce, corn syrup, ginger juice, sesame oil, and garlic and mix until well incorporated.

**Prepare the muchim:** Remove the intestines and fins from the skate and peel away the skin. Cut the skate across the grain into ¼-inch (6 mm) pieces. In a bowl, soak the sliced skate in the makgeolli for 15 minutes. Drain the skate, squeezing to remove any excess moisture, and set aside.

Meanwhile, slice the radish and pear into slices 2 × ½ × ⅛ inch (5 × 1.3 × 0.3 cm). Combine in a bowl with the salt, vinegar, and sugar and let brine for 10 minutes. Drain and squeeze out excess water.

Add the skate, radish, pear, cucumber, onion, and minari to the bowl of sauce and toss well. Plate on a large plate to serve.

## Assorted Hwe
### Saengseon Hwe
### 생선회

dF -30   [□]

To give the fish plate eye-appeal, decorate with edible leaves and vegetables, such as perilla, lettuce, julienned radish, and more. And to serve the *hwe* as part of a *ssam* (wraps) platter, be sure to include green Cheongyang chilies, sliced garlic, *ssamjang* (dipping sauce for *ssam*), *cho-gochujang* (vinegared *gochujang*), along with any fresh vegetables.

**Preparation time: 20 minutes**
**Serves: 4**

10 oz (300 g) halibut
10 oz (300 g) sea bream
5 oz (150 g) tuna
5 oz (150 g) striped horse mackerel
½ oz (15 g) radish sprouts
2 tablespoons grated fresh wasabi
4 tablespoons ganjang (Korean soy sauce)

For any whole fish, remove the scales, intestines, and head. For all the fish, divide the flesh into two clean, even slices and pat dry.

Slice the prepared fish into the preferred thickness.

Arrange the *hwe* slices on a large plate. On a small side plate, plate the radish sprouts and grated wasabi. Serve with a side saucer of ganjang.

---

## Raw Fish in Cold Broth
### Mul Hwe
### 물회

dF

Another Korean method that showcases the many facets of the *hwe* culture in Korean cuisine is *mul hwe*, raw fish in cold broth. The chilled broth is seasoned with *gochujang* (red chili paste), vinegar, or even *doenjang* (fermented soybean paste) and is served iced. A variety of raw fish and seafood can be used in the recipes, along with sea vegetables and kimchi.

**Preparation time: 35 minutes**
**Serves: 4**

14 oz (400 g) raw fish, preferably white fish, such as those in the flounder and squid family

**For the broth:**
5 cups (40 fl oz/1.2 liters) Anchovy Broth (page 314)
8 tablespoons Vinegared Gochujang (page 51)
2 tablespoons rice vinegar
4 tablespoons sesame seeds

**For the mul hwe:**
4½ oz (125 g) green cabbage, thinly sliced
5 lettuce leaves, thinly sliced
2½ oz (75 g) cucumber, halved lengthwise and thinly sliced on a diagonal
3½ oz (100 g) onion, thinly sliced
5 perilla leaves, thinly sliced
1 oz (30 g) minari, cut into 1-inch (2.5 cm) lengths
1 oz (30 g) thin scallions (spring onions), cut into 1-inch (2.5 cm) lengths

For whole fish, scale the fish and then remove the organs and head. Cut the flesh into two fillets. Pat the fillets dry.

Slice the prepared fillets into thin bite-size slices to taste.

**Make the broth:** In a bowl, combine the anchovy broth, vinegared gochujang, vinegar, and sesame seeds and refrigerate until serving.

**Make the mul hwe:** In large bowls, first plate the cabbage and lettuce. Place the raw fish in the center. Arrange the cucumber, onion, perilla, minari, and scallions around the fish. Pour in the cold broth gently.

Serve cold.

## Seasoned Hwe
## Hwe Muchim
## 회무침

dF –3o

While *hwe* is most commonly enjoyed on its own and simply dipped in preferred sauces, it's also enjoyed as a *muchim* dish in which it is tossed in seasoning with vegetables. Especially when eating along with rice as a *banchan* (side dish), the combination of rice and seasoned *hwe muchim* charms even the palates of those who are not fans of the texture or taste of regular *hwe*.

For *muchim*, a wide variety of fish can be enjoyed. White fish, such as flounder, are a staple; however, oilier fish, such as tuna or trout, can be a rich, complex addition, while fresh, fatty fish, such as mackerel or sardines, are a delicacy in the *muchim* form.

**Preparation time: 30 minutes**
**Serves: 2–4**

14 oz (400 g) raw fish (according to preference)
8 tablespoons Vinegared Gochujang (page 51)
2½ oz (75 g) cucumber, halved and thinly sliced on a diagonal
3½ oz (100 g) onion, julienned
5 perilla leaves, slivered
1 oz (30 g) minari, cut into 1-inch (2.5 cm) lengths
1 oz (30 g) scallions (spring onions), cut into 1-inch (2.5 cm) lengths
2 tablespoons sesame seeds

For any whole fish, remove the scales, intestines, and head. Divide the flesh into 2 clean, even slices and pat dry.

Once the fish is prepared, slice the fish into the preferred thickness.

In a large bowl, add the vinegared gochujang and fish and combine gently. Add the vegetables and toss until coated evenly with the sauce and well distributed.

Arrange on a large flat plate and garnish with the sesame seeds.

### Variations

• Change up the vegetables to taste. Common choices include Asian pears, napa cabbage (Chinese leaf), lettuce, chilies, and more.

• Fatty fish can be tossed in heftier sauces, such as those based on *ssamjang* (dipping sauce for *ssam*) or *doenjang* (fermented soybean paste).

---

## Squid Hwe
## Ojingeo Hwe
## 오징어 회

dF –5 –3o

The texture of squid changes rapidly once killed, and Korea is one of the few places where it can be enjoyed as fresh as possible, when its texture is bouncy and chewy and the taste is sweet. The final taste and mouthfeel is determined by the size of the cut, and it's worth exploring the range of thickness to find your favorite.

Squid has a naturally savory, umami flavor. It can be enjoyed by itself, but for those who prefer an additional pop of savory flavors, sprinkle some sesame seeds on top. Although less common, for the freshest of squid, its organs can be steamed or blanched and enjoyed along with the hwe for a savory snack.

**Preparation time: 20 minutes**
**Serves: 4**

3–4 whole squid

**For the seasoning:**
4 tablespoons ganjang (Korean soy sauce)
2 tablespoons wasabi, freshly grated if possible
AND/OR
4 tablespoons Vinegared Gochujang (page 51)

Cut the squid in half with the fins facing downward. Hold the body down with one hand while pulling the tentacles firmly with the other to remove the organs. Remove the long cartilage from the body and peel off the top layer of skin.

Scrape out any remaining innards from the space right above where the tentacles attach to the head and below the eye. Under the tentacles is the beak, which can be squeezed and gently pulled to remove. Trim the two long arms to the length of the other tentacles.

Wash the clean squids under cold running water until fully clean and pat dry with paper towels.

If the squid are small, cut the body crosswise into the desired width. For larger squid, cut it in half lengthwise and then slice it crosswise. Typically, only the body of the squid is used for hwe, because it's the sweeter part with better texture. The tentacles can be kept for use in another dish; if desired, they can be cut into smaller bite-size pieces and served along with the body.

In a saucer, serve the ganjang and wasabi without stirring, and/or a saucer of vinegared gochujang to dip the squid hwe.

## Webfoot Octopus & Minari Hwe
Jjukkumi Minari Ganghwe
쭈꾸미 미나리 강회

dF -S

*Ganghwe* refers to the type of dish in which blanched vegetables, such as *minari* and scallions (spring onions), are rolled or tied around another ingredient. This dish is often made with beef and *jidan* (traditional egg garnish), but it's also delicious with lightly blanched seafood. In particular, seafood of the cephalopod family, such as squid or webfoot octopus, make a great pairing with the fragrance and texture of blanched *minari* and the acidic, sweet-spicy vinegared *gochujang* (red chili paste).

**Preparation time:** 25 minutes
**Cooking time:** 15 minutes
**Serves:** 4

16 webfoot octopus
2 tablespoons salt
32 stalks minari
8 tablespoons Vinegared Gochujang (page 51)

Rinse the octopus under cold running water and trim away the eyes with scissors. From the fold at the base of the head, cut upward using scissors to remove any roe and organs. The roe can be kept for another use. Remove the beak in the underside, where the legs meet the body, by squeezing with two fingers.

Transfer the trimmed octopus to a bowl with the salt and massage gently to remove any impurities. Wash with cold water two times.

Trim and discard the ends of the minari stalks and remove any bruised stems. Separate the leaves and any thin stalks, keeping just the thick stalks for use.

Set up a bowl of ice and water. In a pot, bring 8 cups (64 fl oz /1.9 liters) water to a boil over high heat. Once boiling, add the minari to the boiling water, putting the thick stalk ends in first and blanch for 20 seconds. Transfer immediately to the ice bath to cool. Drain in a sieve. Blanch the octopus in the same boiling water for 40 seconds and transfer to a sieve to cool.

Once cool enough to handle, halve the octopus lengthwise, and wrap each half with a stalk of the blanched minari, tying at the end to secure. Plate the minari-wrapped octopus on a flat plate, and serve along with a saucer of vinegared gochujang for dipping.

---

## Parboiled Octopus Hwe
Muneo Sukhwe
문어 숙회

dF -S

Octopus caught off Korea's east coast has always been a precious ingredient reserved for ceremonies, such as ancestral rites and weddings. Because of this, recipes for octopus are usually simple without much seasoning or cooking in order to honor the prized ingredient. It's often simply parboiled and thinly sliced to enjoy as a *sukhwe*. In Korea, the light chewy texture of parboiled octopus is preferred over fully cooked octopus.

**Preparation time:** 30 minutes
**Cooking time:** 45 minutes
**Serves:** 4–5

7 oz (200 g) mu (Korean radish), cut into 2-inch (5 cm) pieces
½ oz (15 g) dasima
2 tablespoons rice cooking wine
2¼ lb (1 kg) octopus (1 whole octopus)
3 tablespoons coarse sea salt
8 tablespoons Vinegared Gochujang (page 51)

In a large pot, combine 8 cups (64 fl oz/1.9 liters) water, the radish, and dasima. Bring to a boil over high heat. Once boiling, reduce the heat to medium and cook for 10 minutes. Discard the dasima, add the wine, and cook for 15 more minutes.

Meanwhile, wash the octopus under cold running water. Flip the head inside out at the fold, and using scissors, remove and discard the organs and the ink sac. In a large bowl, combine with the coarse sea salt and massage the octopus, including the tentacles, thoroughly to remove any impurities. Wash with clean water two or three times until clean, and set in a sieve to drain.

Dip the octopus into the boiling broth three or four times to firm it up. Add it to the boiling broth and cook for 6 minutes. Remove from the heat and let stand for 10 minutes in the hot broth. Transfer to a bowl to cool at room temperature.

Once the octopus is cool, separate the octopus head and the individual tentacles, removing the beak. Cut the tentacles on a diagonal into ¼-inch (6 mm) slices. The head is less flavorful than the tentacles, so save it for another recipe to use with sauce, or slice and serve along with the tentacles.

Arrange the sliced octopus on a large plate. Serve with the vinegared gochujang for dipping.

# Ssam Wrapped
## 쌈

Of the many ways that Koreans enjoy vegetables, a method that cannot be overlooked is the unique eating method of *ssam*. *Ssam* are wraps made by topping a large vegetable leaf with rice or grains along with meat, seafood, or vegetable, and finishing with *ssamjang* (a sauce for *ssam*). The large leaf-wrapped bundle represents an abundance of good fortune, so *ssam* is not only an enjoyable way for Koreans to eat vegetables, it is also a meal that bids good fortune among its company.

Korea's barbecue restaurants' tables are never without *ssam*. But even when there's no meat present, *ssam* is a style of eating that can easily be enjoyed with any *banchan* (side dish) spread. In traditional Korean houses, adjacent to the house or estate was a sustenance vegetable garden. Even without a special main dish or *banchan*, a substantial and happy meal could be put together with fresh vegetables from the garden and staples, such as *ssamjang*, kimchi, *and doenjang jjigae* (a stew made with fermented soybean paste).

# Korea's Ssam Culture

A "wrap" culture exists in most cuisines. But there are a few differences in the Korean *ssam* cuisine that make it unique:

First, while most countries' wraps are made from some type of carbohydrate with meat or vegetables as the filling, for Korean *ssam* the vegetable are the wrappers, and the filling base is often a carbohydrate—rice—along with other proteins, sauces, or *banchan*. The name of the *ssam* comes from whatever vegetable is being used as the wrapper.

The most common wrapper to this day is lettuce, and the earliest written records show that the lettuce *ssam* has been eaten since the Three Kingdoms era (AD 220 to 280). Of the many leafy vegetables that are harvested from spring to fall, large and crispy leaves—lettuce, napa cabbage (Chinese leaf), perilla leaves—are eaten raw to keep their fresh texture and taste alive. Cabbage, squash leaves, butterbur leaves, and *gomchwi* (Fischer's ragwort) are blanched and then used as wrapping. When eating *ssam* with meat or fish *hwe* (raw seafood), other fragrant vegetables, such as *minari* and mugwort, are added for enhanced flavors. In winter, when there are no fresh vegetables available, *ssam* is made using rehydrated vegetables leaves or by using roasted seaweed, raw or blanched seaweed, or sea vegetables, and even using kimchi or pickled radish.

The second difference is *ssamjang*, the sauce that's used in *ssam*. The *ssamjang* used in each *ssam* depends on the ingredients that are used. The basic *ssamjang* used for vegetable wrapping is based on *doenjang* (fermented soybean paste) and *gochujang* (red chili paste). Typically, various vegetables are added to the base *ssamjang*, as well as ingredients that range from dried nuts and fruits to river snails and clams, depending on the preference and regional cuisine. When eating *ssam* made from sea vegetables, the *ssamjang* can be replaced with Vinegared Gochujang (page 51) or even *jeotgal* (preserved seafood). For raw meat and fish *ssam*, fresh garlic or chili is often added to the *ssam* along with the *ssamjang*.

Aside from being used in *ssam* as the sauce, *ssamjang* is often on the dining tables of Korea as an all-purpose sauce for dipping vegetables—cucumbers, carrots, peppers—as is done with Western crudites, or as a seasoning dip for meat or fish. *Ssamjang*, in short, is a sauce that allows harmonious pairings of ingredients. Vegetables, proteins, and even rice can be enhanced with a little *ssamjang*.

The third differentiating factor for the *ssam* cuisine of Korea is the temperature of the ingredients. *Ssam* vegetables are typically cold and crunchy, and the fillings, including both the rice and the protein, are served warm. It's a unique way to enjoy two different, contrasting textures and temperatures in one dish. The first bite of *ssam* begins cold, crunchy, and filled with the pleasantly bittersweet flavors of vegetables. Within a few bites, the warm, sweet, and nutty aroma of the cooked rice and the fatty, delicious flavors of the meat begin to fill the mouth harmoniously. The fresh *ssamjang* filled with layers of spice and earthiness cuts the oiliness, culminating in a festival of flavors in the mouth. After finishing that first bite of *ssam*, a spoonful from the array of flavors decorating the table—a warm spoonful of Doenjang Jjigae (page 347) or a sip of the refreshing broth from Radish Water Kimchi (page 72)—reveals itself to be a fantastic pairing no less than any wine.

# Stir-Fried Gochujang & Lettuce Ssam
## Yak-Gochujang & Sangchu Ssam
## 약고추장, 상추쌈

DF

*Yak-gochujang* has two definitions. It can refer to a type of *gochujang* (red pepper paste) that is made with glutinous rice as the base and more *gochugaru* (red chili flakes) than the common gochujang, making it a coarser and more dense paste. But most often *yak-gochujang* refers to *gochujang* stir-fried with ground (minced) beef and honey. *Yak-gochujang* is often used in *ssam* or *bibimbap* (mixed rice).

As a child, when too lazy to prepare a proper meal after school, the *yak-gochujang* in the refrigerator is the perfect food for making a simple meal, topped on warm rice. Commercially available *yak-gochujang* in a tube is also an easy solution to bring on trips for quick meals, especially on international trips for when one misses the taste of Korea.

Preparation time: 15 minutes, plus 30 minutes rice soaking time
Cooking time: 1 hour
Serves: 4

**For the stir-fried gochujang:**
3 tablespoons neutral cooking oil
7 oz (200 g) ground (minced) beef
3½ oz (100 g) onion, minced
2 tablespoons minced daepa (or scallion), minced
2 tablespoons minced garlic
1 tablespoon ganjang (Korean soy sauce)
1 tablespoon doenjang (fermented soybean paste)
2 tablespoons mirin
½ cup (120 g) corn (golden) syrup
2 cups (450 g) gochujang (red chili paste)

**For the ssam:**
2 cups (400 g) Cooked Short-Grain White Rice (page 92)
20 lettuce leaves

**Make the stir-fried gochujang:** In a nonstick frying pan, heat the cooking oil over medium heat, Add the ground beef and stir-fry, breaking up the beef evenly to get rid of clumps. Fry until all the excess moisture released from the beef has evaporated, because undercooking could spoil the yak-gochujang.

Add the onion and daepa and stir-fry until translucent. Add the garlic and stir-fry for another 3 minutes to cook the garlic, but taking care that it does not brown.

Add the soy sauce, doenjang, mirin, corn syrup, and gochujang in that order and stir-fry until evenly combined. Once it starts to boil, reduce the heat to low and cook for 15 minutes, stirring occasionally to avoid any burning or overcooking.

**For the ssam:** Serve individual bowls of rice, with the lettuce and stir-fried gochujang served communally.

# River Snail Doenjang & Squash Leaf Ssam
## Urung Doenjang & Hobakip Ssam
## 우렁된장, 호박잎쌈

dF

River snails inhabit clean rivers, ponds, and other freshwater bodies. In Korea, where rice is a staple crop and a large part of its agriculture, river snails are easily found in the rice paddies and irrigation channels all over the country. After the monsoon season at the end of the exhausting summer heat, it's a natural phenomenon to experience a loss of appetite. During these times, this recipe is a popular seasonal delicacy.

River snails, fresh vegetables, and doenjang are brought to a bubbling boil, the salty-sweet-umami flavors revitalizing the droopiest of appetites. Although this is great wrapped in crunchy, sweet lettuce, steamed cabbage, or perilla leaves to draw out its fragrance, the best combination may be with blanched pumpkin leaves at the peak of their season. It is good to note that *doenjang* can vary in levels of saltiness, so always taste while cooking to achieve preferred levels of salt.

Preparation time: 20 minutes, plus 30 minutes rice soaking time
Cooking time: 40 minutes
Serves: 4

For the sauce:
4 tablespoons doenjang (fermented soybean paste)
2 tablespoons perilla seed powder
1 tablespoon sesame oil
1 teaspoon minced garlic
1 teaspoon honey

For the snail doenjang:
4 oz (120 g) prepared river snail meat
1 tablespoon all-purpose (plain) flour (optional)
2½ oz (75 g) firm tofu
2 tablespoons neutral cooking oil
3½ oz (100 g) onion, cut into medium dice
4½ oz (125 g) aehobak (Korean zucchini), cut into medium dice
2¾ oz (80 g) fresh shiitake mushrooms (or rehydrated from dried), stemmed

For the ssam:
20 pumpkin leaves
2 cups (400 g) Cooked Short-Grain White Rice (page 92)

**Make the sauce:** In a bowl, combine the doenjang, perilla seed powder, sesame oil, garlic, and honey and mix well until fully incorporated. Set aside.

**Assemble the snail doenjang:** The river snail meat, which is typically sold cleaned and cooked in Korean or Asian supermarkets, should be rinsed after removing it from the package. If there is any noticeable residue or smell, place the meat in a bowl, sprinkle with the flour, and massage into the meat for about 30 seconds or until incorporated, then rinsed under cold running water until fully clean.

Using either the flat of a knife and a cutting board, or in a large bowl with your hands, break apart the tofu until it's a coarse texture.

In a frying pan, heat the cooking oil over medium heat. Add the onion, zucchini, and shiitakes and cook until the onions are translucent and the shiitakes and zucchini begin releasing liquid. Add the sauce and boil for 5 minutes. Add the river snail meat and the broken tofu and boil for 3 minutes more. The snail doenjang can be served hot or chilled.

**For the ssam:** In a pot of boiling water, blanch the pumpkin leaves for 2 minutes to tenderize. Drain and let cool.

Serve individual bowls of rice, with the pumpkin leaves and snail doenjang served communally.

### Variations

• To add spice to the river snail doenjang, you can either add 1 tablespoon gochugaru (red chili flakes) to the sauce or top the final dish with sliced fresh Cheongyang chilies.

• If one prefers a thinner texture, stir ½ cup Anchovy Broth (page 314) into the mixture.

## Cho-gochujang & Fresh Miyeok Ssam
### Cho-gochujang & Saeng Miyeok Ssam
### 초고추장, 생미역쌈

dF vg vE

*Cho-gochujang* is literally the combination of *cho* (vinegar) and *gochujang*. It's casually referred to as *chojang* for short, but because this could also refer to the combination of vinegar and *ganjang*, it's more proper to call it *cho-gochujang*. It is made with mainly *gochujang* and *cho* along with other ingredients, such as garlic and ginger, and it embodies the preferred Korean flavors of spicy, sweet, and bright acidity. The simplicity of the ingredients in making the sauce means that the quality of the gochujang and the rice vinegar matter greatly, so seek out the best.

This mainstay sauce is extremely versatile, but is especially good with *hwe* (raw fish). Another way that it is commonly enjoyed is with blanched fresh greens. There are also regional dishes in which to enjoy this condiment, such as in Jeolla-do, where *sundae* (Korean blood sausage) is often dipped in *cho-gochujang*.

Preparation time: 20 minutes, plus 30 minutes rice soaking time
Cooking time: 25 minutes
Serves: 4

**For the cho-gochujang:**
3 tablespoons sugar
2 tablespoons corn (golden) syrup
1 tablespoon finely minced garlic
⅔ cup rice vinegar
1⅔ cups (14 oz/400 g) gochujang (red chili paste)

**For the ssam:**
2 cups (400 g) Cooked Short-Grain White Rice (page 92)
20 squares (2 inches/5 cm) fresh miyeok (wakame)

**Make the cho-gochujang:** In a bowl, combine the sugar, corn syrup, garlic, and vinegar until well incorporated and the sugar has dissolved. Add the gochujang and mix until evenly mixed. The sauce can be used immediately, but letting it sit in an airtight container in the refrigerator overnight results in a more integrated flavor profile.

**For the ssam:** Serve individual bowls of rice, with the miyeok and cho-gochujang served communally.

**Variation:** Some like to add sesame seeds or oil to the sauce. If you do, be sure to add only the desired amount just before plating for use, because the nutty fragrance dissipates fairly quickly if left to sit with the sauce.

# Aged Kimchi Ssam
## Mugeunji Ssam & Suyuk
## 묵은지쌈 & 수육

DF -S

*Ssam* can be made with Fresh Napa Cabbage Kimchi (page 62), which is unfermented, or even with unseasoned napa cabbage (Chinese leaf). Another choice is to use *mugeunji*, or aged kimchi, which has a deep, strong, acidic taste imparted by its long fermentation. Aged kimchi is easily accessible in Korean markets, or if you make your own Napa Cabbage Kimchi (page 60), fermenting it for 3 to 4 weeks to develop its acidity.

Because the *mugeunji* is so strongly flavored, instead of eating it on its own, it achieves a great balance as an ingredient in dishes. It can be used to wrap around freshly cooked white rice, but it's also a great pairing with rice simply seasoned with sesame oil, sesame seeds, and a touch of salt. It's also a common *ssam* accompaniment to *hwe* (raw fish), especially fatty fish, such as salmon and amberjack, or to the pork included here.

Preparation time: 25 minutes, plus 30 minutes rice soaking time
Cooking time: 1 hour 25 minutes (less if you have pork suyuk on hand)
Serves: 4

½ head store-bought cabbage mugeunji (kimchi that has been aged at least 6 months; about 2¼ lb/1 kg)
2 tablespoons perilla oil

For the ssam:
1 lb 5 oz (600 g) Pork Suyuk (page 218)
2 cups (400 g) Cooked Short-Grain White Rice (page 92)

Wash the mugeunji under cold running water, making sure that the excess kimchi ingredients, such as gochugaru, are well rinsed. Squeeze the cleaned cabbage lightly with your hands to get rid of any excess water.

Place the cabbage in a bowl and drizzle the perilla oil evenly over it. Gently massage the cabbage with your hands to incorporate the fragrance into the cabbage.

Trim off the root end to separate the leaves. Cut the leaves 2 inches (5 cm) lengthwise and plate. Some people choose to only trim the root part off and use whole leaves to wrap.

**For the ssam:** Serve individual bowls of rice, with the mugeunji and pork suyuk served communally.

## 편육 & 수육
## Pyunyuk & Suyuk Pressed & Boiled Meats

*Pyunyuk* translates to "pressed meat" (the name comes from the thin, small cuts made to the meat) and can be considered Korean charcuterie. *Pyunyuk* is made by boiling meat, separating it from the bones, and pressing it into a shape. It is eaten cold and thinly sliced. When made of beef, brisket, shank, tongue, and head meat are often used. When made of pork, pork belly, head meat, pig's feet (trotters), and skin are used for high levels of collagen.

To make *pyunyuk*, first the meat is soaked in cold water to remove the blood, because if not properly drained, the color of the *pyunyuk* will be red. Once cleaned, the meat is cooked in a large pot of boiling water. Once cooked, salt is added to the boiling water to season the meat. For beef, whole scallions (spring onions) and garlic are added to the boiling water for flavoring, and when boiling pork, ginger is added to the boiling water to remove any unwanted smells.

Typical sauces or condiments for beef *pyunyuk* are *cho-ganjang* (vinegar and soy sauce) or mustard-based sauces. Pork *pyunyuk* is often accompanied with salted shrimp and kimchi. *Suyuk*, which means "boiled meat," is often served at big gatherings and feasts, such as during *kimjang* (traditional communal kimchi making) or ancestral ceremonies. Depending on the type of meat—often pork, but also beef—and the specific cuts, different *suyuks* are named accordingly, such as pork feet *suyuk* and beef brisket *suyuk*. Regional specialties exist, such as *dombe suyuk* from Jeju, a black pig *suyuk* that is served on a cutting board—the word *dombe* means "cutting board" in Jeju regional dialect.

Because *suyuk* is a dish made up of a single main ingredient, meat, it is most important to remove any impurities or unwanted smells from the meat during the cooking process. The meat should be soaked in cold water for at least half a day to remove the blood. The soaked meat is then boiled by itself to remove all impurities. The water is then discarded and clean water is used to reboil the meat with aromatic ingredients, such as onions, scallions, peppercorns, garlic, and ginger. Rice wine and *soju* (Korean clear spirits) are often added.

Pork *suyuk* is usually served with salted shrimp or with radish kimchi, *ssamjang* (dipping sauce for *ssam*), and leafy vegetables, such as lettuce. Served together with the *ssam* ingredients, the pork *suyuk* can easily transform into a *bossam* (a boiled pork main dish). Beef *suyuk* is often served with onion *muchim* (seasoned raw onions) or garlic chive *muchim* (seasoned raw garlic chives).

# Pork Head Pyunyuk
## Dwaeji Meori Pyunyuk
## 돼지머리고기 편육

dF gF

The pork head *pyunyuk* is a dish that's rarely missed at a festive gathering or a banquet.

Preparation time: 30 minutes, plus 2 hours soaking and 6 hours 20 minutes setting time
Cooking time: 1 hour 15 minutes
Serves: 4–6

2¼ lb (1 kg) pork head meat
2 oz (60 g) daepa (Korean scallion), cut into several pieces
7 oz (200 g) onions, peeled
1¾ oz (50 g) garlic, peeled
¾ oz (20 g) fresh ginger
½ cup (4 fl oz/120 ml) rice wine or soju (Korean clear sprits)
2 tablespoon doenjang (fermented soybean paste)
10 black peppercorns
2 bay leaves

Remove any hairs or impurities from the surface of the pig's head. Butcher the head into pieces of about 4 inches (10 cm) and soak the meat in about 8½ cups (68 fl oz/2 liters) cold water for 2 hours, changing the water every 20 minutes, to drain the blood.

In a large stockpot, combine 12¾ cups (102 fl oz/3 liters) water, the cleaned meat, daepa, onions, garlic, ginger, wine, doenjang, peppercorns, and bay leaves. Bring to a boil over high heat. Once boiling, reduce the heat to medium and cook until the meat is fully cooked and soft, about 1 hour.

Once fully cooked, remove the meat from the broth. While still hot (but OK to handle), remove all the meat from the bones. It doesn't matter if the meat breaks down into small pieces during this process.

To mold the pyunyuk, enclose the separated meat while still warm either in a large cloth bag, such as a cheesecloth or muslin bag, or into a rectangular mold, such as a terrine, baking dish, loaf pan, or similar. Place a heavy object on top to ensure that the meat is pressed down for a minimum of 20 minutes.

After the shape is formed from the pressure, either move the meat into an airtight container or seal completely with plastic wrap (cling film). Move into the refrigerator for a minimum of 6 hours to cool completely to solid. Once prepared, peyonyuk can be refrigerated for up to 3 days.

Slice the resulting pork head pyunyuk into thin slices and plate.

## Pork Suyuk
### Dwaeji Suyuk
### 돼지 수육

dF gF  [ㅁ]

**Preparation time:** 10 minutes
**Cooking time:** 1 hour
**Serves:** 3

1 lb 5 oz (600 g) pork belly, cut into pieces 2½–3 inches (6–8 cm) wide
1 oz (30 g) daepa (Korean scallion), cut crosswise into 3 pieces
3½ oz (100 g) onion, peeled and left whole
½ oz (10 g) fresh ginger
7 cloves garlic, peeled
½ cup (4 fl oz/120 ml) rice wine or soju (Korean clear spirits)
1 tablespoon doenjang (fermented soybean paste)
Kimchi, for serving (optional)

The most popular form of *suyuk* is the pork *suyuk*. Made with whole strips of fatty cuts, most commonly the pork belly, the resulting meat is tender and pleasantly chewy.

In a large pot, combine 3 cups (24 fl oz/710 ml) water, the pork belly, daepa, onion, ginger, garlic, wine, and doenjang. Cover with a lid and bring to a boil over high heat. Once boiling, reduce the heat to medium and boil for 50 minutes.

Remove the pork belly and thinly slice into scant ¼-inch (5 mm) slices. Plate and serve with kimchi, if desired.

## Beef Suyuk
### Sogogi Suyuk
### 소고기 수육

dF

**Preparation time:** 15 minutes, plus 1 hour soaking time
**Cooking time:** 1 hour 45 minutes, plus cooling time
**Serves:** 2–4

1½ lb (700 g) beef banana heel, beef head, or beef brisket
2 oz (60 g) daepa (Korean scallion), cut into pieces
½ cup (4 fl oz/120 ml) soju (Korean clear spirits)

**For the sauce:**
3 tablespoons ganjang (Korean soy sauce)
2 tablespoons rice vinegar
1 tablespoon sugar
1 teaspoon Korean mustard
1 teaspoon minced garlic

**For serving:**
3½ oz (100 g) onion, cut into slices ⅛ inch (3 mm) thick
1¾ oz (50 g) garlic chives, cut into 1-inch (2.5 cm) lengths

The banana heel is a little known cut of beef with both a good meat flavor and a good, lean texture that makes it ideal for making *suyuk*. Brisket can be used as well to make beef *suyuk*. After boiling the meat, the beef broth can be cooled and used in other recipes. Save the broth and simmer any leftover beef *suyuk* in the reserved beef broth and serve warm.

Cut the beef into slices 3 inches (7.5 cm) thick and soak in cold water for 1 hour to remove the blood.

In a large pot, bring 12 cups (96 fl oz/2.8 liters) water to a boil over high heat. Once boiling, add the daepa and soju. Add the beef, reduce the heat to medium-low, and cook for 1 hour 30 minutes, skimming the foam. Remove from the heat and let steam for 15 minutes.

Transfer just the meat to a dish and let cool. Strain the broth and set aside separately to use as beef broth.

**Make the sauce:** In a small bowl, combine the soy sauce, 3 tablespoons water, the vinegar, sugar, mustard, and garlic and mix well until uniform.

**To serve:** Once the meat is cool enough to handle, slice the beef into ¼-inch (6 mm) slices. Arrange the beef on a large plate and moisten with 2 tablespoons of the reserved beef broth. Plate the onion and chives in the center of the plate on top of the beef slices, and dress with the sauce.

# Oxtail Suyuk
## Sokkori Suyuk
## 소꼬리 수육

dF

While oxtail is commonly used to make a rich beef broth, it's also eaten in Korean cuisine in the form of *suyuk*. To make the *suyuk*, oxtail is boiled for 2–3 hours until the meat falls easily off the bones. It's best eaten warmed in the broth to enjoy the softened collagen. If eaten cold, the collagen turns pleasantly chewy, which is another delicacy.

**Preparation time: 30 minutes, plus 1 hour soaking time**
**Cooking time: 4 hours**
**Serves: 4**

- 4½ lb (2 kg) oxtail, cut crosswise into 1-inch (2.5 cm) pieces
- 6 garlic cloves, peeled
- 3½ oz (100 g) onion, peeled and left whole
- 2 oz (60 g) daepa (Korean scallion), cut into a few pieces

**For the dipping sauce:**
- 3 tablespoons ganjang (Korean soy sauce)
- 3 tablespoons pureed Asian pear
- 1 tablespoon sugar
- 1 teaspoon Korean mustard

**For serving:**
- 4 tablespoons ganjang (Korean soy sauce)
- 3½ oz (100 g) garlic chives, cut into 2-inch (5 cm) lengths
- 1 oz (30 g) daepa (Korean scallion), thinly sliced
- 2 tablespoons gochugaru (red chili flakes)
- 2 tablespoons sugar

Soak the sliced oxtails in cold water for 1 hour to remove the blood.

In a large pot, combine 10 cups (80 fl oz/2.4 liters) water and the oxtail, bring to a boil, and boil for 10 minutes to remove impurities. Discard the water and wash the oxtail under cold running water. Fill the pot with 10 cups (80 fl oz/2.4 liters) water and add the oxtail, garlic, onion, and daepa. Bring to a boil over high heat. Once boiling, reduce the heat to medium and cook for 3 hours, skimming foam throughout, until the meat is falling-off-the-bone tender. During the cooking process, add small amounts of water as needed to keep the meat submerged. Transfer the fully cooked meat to a tray or plate. Strain the broth and set aside.

**Make the dipping sauce:** In a small bowl, stir together the soy sauce, pear puree, sugar, and mustard.

**To serve:** In a wide, shallow pot, combine the cooked oxtail, ½ cup (4 fl oz/120 ml) of the reserved oxtail broth, the soy sauce, garlic chives, sliced daepa, gochugaru, and sugar. Simmer over low heat to warm through. Serve as a communal hotpot format along with individual saucers of the dipping sauce.

# Goat Suyuk
## Yeomso Suyuk
## 염소 수육

DF

Goat meat is consumed in small amounts in Korea, especially in comparison to beef, pork, and chicken. It is usually prepared as *tang* (long-simmered soup) or *suyuk*. Goat is considered a restorative food and is often cooked with many different medicinal ingredients. Its strong gamey flavor is great when paired with a sauce based on *doenjang* (fermented soy bean paste).

**Preparation time: 15 minutes, plus 1 hour soaking time**
**Cooking time: 1 hour 30 minutes**
**Serves: 4**

1¾ lb (800 g) goat neck meat
3 cups (865 g) doenjang (fermented soybean paste)
1 cup (8 fl oz/240 ml) soju (Korean clear spirits)
1¾ oz (50 g) fresh ginger

**For the goat suyuk:**
½ cup (4 fl oz/120 ml) mirin
2 tablespoons doenjang (fermented soybean paste)
2 oz (60 g) daepa (Korean scallion), cut into pieces
1¾ oz (50 g) fresh ginger

**For the sauce:**
6 tablespoons Vinegared Gochujang (page 51)
3 tablespoons perilla seed powder
1 tablespoon minced garlic
1 tablespoon perilla oil

**For serving:**
3½ oz (100 g) garlic chives

Soak the goat meat in cold water for 1 hour to remove the blood.

In a large pot, combine 8 cups (64 fl oz/1.9 liters) water, the doenjang, soju, and ginger and bring to a boil over high heat. Once boiling, add the goat meat, reduce the heat to medium low, and boil for 30 minutes, skimming the foam. Discard the water and rinse the goat meat under cold running water.

**Make the suyuk:** In a large pot, combine 8½ cups (68 fl oz/2 liters) water, the goat meat, mirin, doenjang, daepa, and ginger and bring to a boil over high heat. Boil for 15 more minutes, then reduce the heat to medium and cook for another 45 minutes. Skim the foam during the cooking process. If the liquid reduces too much, add more water as needed to keep the meat submerged.

Remove from the heat and transfer the meat to a plate to cool. Once cool enough to handle, cut into slices 2 inches (5 cm) long and ¼ inch (6 mm) thick. The broth can be strained and saved to use as a base for a soup.

**Make the sauce:** In a small bowl, stir together the vinegared gochujang, perilla seed powder, garlic, and perilla oil. Set aside in a saucer.

**To serve:** Set up a steamer and bring the water to a boil. Add the chives to the steamer basket and arrange the goat suyuk on top. Set the basket over the boiling water and steam for 2 minutes. Serve in the steamer with the saucer of sauce alongside.

# Korean Blood Sausage
## Sundae
## 순대

dF

*Sundae*, Korean blood sausage, was traditionally a precious food prepared only for festive meals. Not only did traditional *sundae* require the freshest of meat and ingredients, it was also a demanding multistep process. Today, with the rise of mass production, simplified ingredients, and easy substitutions, *sundae* has become one of the most popular, economic, and common street foods.

Preparation time: 25 minutes, plus 3 hours soaking time
Cooking time: 1 hour
Serves: 4

10 oz (300 g) sausage casings
2 tablespoons coarse sea salt
6 tablespoons all-purpose (plain) flour
1½ cups (330 g) glutinous rice
3½ oz (100 g) napa cabbage (Chinese leaf)
2 cups (450 g) seonji (pig's blood)
3 tablespoons minced daepa (Korean scallion)
5 oz (150 g) ground (minced) pork
1¾ oz (50 g) pork fat, minced
1 tablespoon doenjang (fermented soybean paste)
1 tablespoon ganjang (Korean soy sauce)
1 tablespoon salt
1 teaspoon sugar
1 teaspoon hyssop powder
½ teaspoon freshly ground black pepper

For serving:
4 teaspoons salt
2 teaspoons gochugaru (red chili pepper)
1 teaspoon freshly ground black pepper

Massage the sausage casings thoroughly with the coarse salt and then rinse under cold running water. Massage the casings with the flour thoroughly and rinse well in cold water again. Soak the casings for 3 hours in cold water.

Meanwhile, wash the glutinous rice and soak in water for a minimum of 1 hour. Drain in a sieve.

Set up a steamer and bring the water to a boil.

Line the steamer basket with a wet cloth, spread the glutinous rice in the basket, and steam for 20 minutes; the rice should not be cooked to softness. Remove from the heat and spread evenly over a flat surface to let cool.

In a pot of boiling water, cook the cabbage until softened, about 7 minutes. Drain and finely chop.

In a large bowl, combine the cooled rice and the pig's blood and mix until well combined. Add the chopped cabbage, daepa, ground (minced) pork, pork fat, doenjang, soy sauce, salt, sugar, hyssop powder, and black pepper and combine until evenly incorporated.

Remove the sausages casings from the water, drain well, and tie one end closed with a thread. Using a sausage funnel or sausage stuffer, push the prepared filling into the casing until stuffed. Complete the encasing by tying the other end with a string.

Fill a pot with enough water to cover the sundae and bring to a boil. Once boiling, drop in the sundae and boil for 30 minutes over medium heat. Reduce the heat to low. Use a skewer to make a few punctures along the sundae to ensure that the sausage is fully cooked, and continue cooking for 10 more minutes. Remove the sundae from the pot and let cool at room temperature.

**To serve:** Once the sundae has cooled, cut into slices ⅜ inch (1 cm) thick. Transfer to a plate. Serve along with a salt seasoning by combining the salt, gochugaru, and black pepper.

# Muk Starch Jelly

묵

*Muk* refers to a gelatinous food made from the starch of various grains or nuts. The most common starches used include mung bean, buckwheat, acorn, and corn. Each has its own distinct characteristics: Mung bean *muk* is known for a soft pleasant texture, and buckwheat *muk* boasts a deep, savory flavor profile. Acorn *muk* has a distinct nutty flavor beloved in Korea, and the *muk* made from corn has a silky, bouncy texture similar to some noodles. Mung bean *muk* is best enjoyed in spring, corn in summer, acorn in fall, and buckwheat in winter.

*Muk* can be used to make a variety of dishes. It is often made into a *muchim* (seasoned dish), the jelly tossed with seasonal vegetables and a soy-based sauce. The soft mung bean *muk* is most popular with spring vegetables, such as minari and mung bean sprouts, and dressed in *cho-ganjang* (vinegared soy sauce) or sesame oil and salt. The nuttiness of acorn *muk* pairs well with raw cucumbers or mugwort dressed in a strong seasoning of *gochugaru* (red chili flakes) and ganjang (Korean soy sauce). The savory buckwheat *muk*, enjoyed in wintertime, is best mixed with sliced and seasoned napa cabbage (Chinese leaf) kimchi.

The quality of *muk* is judged by its elasticity and clarity and evenness in its coloration. *Muk* should be eaten as soon as it is made, because if left in the refrigerator for a long time, the starch will age and harden. When using premade *muk*, it is best first to blanch it in boiling water and let cool before using it in a dish.

# Acorn Jelly Muchim
## Dotori Muk Muchim
## 도토리묵 무침

dF vg vE -30

Acorn jelly *muchim* (seasoned dish) is great as a *banchan* (side dish) along with rice and an array of dishes, but it's a very popular standalone dish, especially as a drinking snack. It's a delicious and common pairing for *makgeolli* (Koean rice wine). While acorn jelly can be made with store-bought powder, most Korean markets will also sell premade acorn jelly.

**Preparation time:** 10 minutes
**Serves:** 4

**For the sauce:**
3 tablespoons ganjang (Korean soy sauce)
1½ tablespoons gochugaru (red chili flakes)
1 tablespoon rice vinegar
1 tablespoon sesame oil
1 tablespoon sugar
1 tablespoon minced scallion (spring onion)
1 tablespoon ground sesame seeds
1 teaspoon minced garlic

**For the muchim:**
14 oz (400 g) acorn jelly
5 oz (150 g) cucumber
1¾ oz (50 g) onion, thinly sliced
3 perilla leaves, cut into ribbons ¾ inch (2 cm) wide
8 sprigs mugwort, thick stems removed, cut into 1½-inch (4 cm) lengths

**Make the sauce:** In a large bowl, combine the soy sauce, gochugaru, vinegar, sesame oil, sugar, scallion, ground sesame seeds, and garlic.

**Prepare the muchim:** Cut the acorn jelly block into 2½ × 1½ × ½-inch (6 × 4 × 1.3 cm) rectangular slices. Halve the cucumber lengthwise and cut on a diagonal into slices 2½ inches (6 cm) long and 1/16 inch (2 mm) thick.

Add the sliced acorn jelly, cucumber, onion, perilla leaves, and mugwort to the sauce and mix gently, avoiding crushing the jelly. Plate and serve.

**Variation:** Any vegetables that you enjoy eating raw, such as carrots, can be added along with the cucumber and onion.

---

# Chilled Kimchi & Acorn Jelly Soup
## Kimchi Muksabal
## 김치 묵사발

dF gF -30

One of the ways to enjoy *muk* is in the form of a chilled soup called *muksabal*. The broth is made with cold beef broth or anchovy broth seasoned with soy sauce or kimchi. The kimchi *muksabal* is an easy recipe, and the harmony of kimchi, *muk*, and the cold broth makes for a refreshing, craveable dish.

While acorn jelly can be made with store-bought powder, most Korean markets also sell the premade acorn jelly, which can be used in this recipe.

**Preparation time:** 15 minutes
**Serves:** 4

**For the kimchi broth:**
2 cups (16 fl oz/480 ml) kimchi juice
6 cups (48 fl oz/1.4 liters) Anchovy Broth (page 314)
5 tablespoons rice vinegar
3 tablespoons sugar
2 tablespoons sand lance fish sauce

**For the soup:**
10 oz (300 g) Napa Cabbage Kimchi (page 60)
2 tablespoons sesame oil
1 lb 5 oz (600 g) acorn jelly
3½ oz (100 g) onion, cut into ⅛-inch (3 mm) slices
5 oz (150 g) cucumber, cut into ⅛-inch (3 mm) matchsticks

**Make the kimchi broth:** In a bowl, combine the kimchi juice, anchovy broth, vinegar, sugar, and fish sauce and mix well until uniform and the sugar is dissolved. Transfer to the refrigerator and keep cold.

**Prepare the soup:** Cut the kimchi into slices ¼ inch (6 mm) thick and transfer to a bowl, Season with the sesame oil, mixing well.

Cut the acorn jelly into batons 2 inches (5 cm) long and ¼ inch (6 mm) thick. Divide the acorn jelly among 4 individual bowls. Top with the seasoned kimchi, onion, and cucumber. Gently pour in the kimchi broth. Serve cold.

## Buckwheat Jelly Muchim
### Memil Muk Gim Muchim
### 메밀묵 김무침

dF gF vg vE -S -30   [ㅁ]

*Memil muk*, buckwheat jelly, with *gim*, Korean seaweed, is a *muchim* (seasoned dish) that highlights the savory, nutty flavors inherent to buckwheat. It can be prepared with sesame oil and seeds or perilla oil and seeds. While buckwheat jelly can be made with store-bought powder, most Korean markets will also sell the premade buckwheat jelly.

**Preparation time:** 5 minutes
**Cooking time:** 5 minutes
**Serves:** 2

10 oz (300 g) memil-muk (buckwheat jelly)
2 tablespoons sesame oil or perilla oil
1 sheet gim
1 teaspoon sesame seeds or perilla seeds
½ teaspoon salt

Cut the buckwheat jelly into slices 2½–3 inches (6–8 cm) long and ½ inch (1.3 cm) wide.

In a medium pot, bring lightly salted water to a boil over high heat. Carefully drop in the cut buckwheat jelly, taking care not to break the delicate jelly into pieces. Blanch for only 30–40 seconds and either drain or scoop out with a sieve. Drain all excess water.

In a bowl, toss the jelly with 1 tablespoon of the sesame oil until all the pieces are evenly coated. Set aside.

Heat a frying pan over low heat and toast the sheet of gim until crispy. Remove from the heat and break or cut into small pieces.

In a large bowl, combine the prepared jelly, the roasted seaweed pieces, sesame seeds, ½ teaspoon salt, and the remaining 1 tablespoon sesame oil and mix gently with a gloved hand so that the jelly does not break. Once evenly incorporated, plate and serve.

**Variation:** The recipe is open for many tweaks. Blanched spring herbs, such as mugwort or *minari*, are a fragrant, pleasurable addition. *Memil muk* also pairs very well with kimchi, so it's often tossed with chopped kimchi as well.

---

## Agar Jelly
### Umutgasari Muk
### 우뭇가사리 묵

dF gF vg vE -S

Agar, or agar-agar, is a jelly-like substance made from algae. The *muk* made from agar has a different texture than the *muk* made from gelatin or starch, separating easily into smaller pieces. It's considered a popular diet food, because it has little to no calories and a high fiber content.

**Preparation time:** 15 minutes, plus 1½ hours soaking and 4 hours setting time
**Cooking time:** 50 minutes
**Serves:** 4–8

2¾ oz (80 g) agar seaweed

Wash the seaweed in a large bowl with water, swishing well with your hands. Repeat the process three times with fresh water. In a pot, soak the seaweed in 12 cups (96 fl oz/ 2.8 liters) water for 30 minutes.

Bring to a boil in the soaking water over high heat. Once boiling, reduce the heat to low and cook for 40 minutes, stirring constantly.

Line a colander with cheesecloth or fine muslin (with enough overlap to fold over the seaweed). Set a colander over a small stainless steel pan that will serve as a mold for the jelly (if necessary, use long chopsticks or wooden spoons to support the colander). Pour the boiled agar mixture into the lined colander, fold the cloth into the center, and press firmly to press the liquid down into the waiting mold. The remaining seaweed can be used once or twice more for future recipes.

Let the agar jelly cool for 4 hours at room temperature to set before use.

## Agar Jelly in Cold Soybean Broth
## Umutgasari Kongguk
## 우뭇가사리 콩국

dF vg vE -5 -3o

Agar jelly is best eaten in a broth instead of on its own, because it has no inherent flavor. It makes a great pairing with bean broth or pine nut broth. On a hot summer day, a bowl of agar jelly in soybean broth makes for a refreshing, quick meal.

**Preparation time:** 10 minutes
**Serves:** 4

1 lb 5 oz (600 g) agar jelly, store-bought or homemade (page 226), cut into matchsticks ⅛ inch (3 mm) thick
2½ oz (75 g) cucumber, cut into matchsticks ⅛ inch (3 mm) thick
8½ cups (68 fl oz/2 liters) Soybean Cold Broth (page 315), well chilled
2 tablespoons black sesame seeds
Salt

Divide the julienned agar jelly among individual bowls and top with the cucumber. Gently pour in the soybean broth, and garnish with black sesame seeds. Serve salt on the side for seasoning.

## Mung Bean Jelly Muchim
## Cheongpo Muk & Minari Muchim
## 청포묵 미나리 무침

dF gF vg vE -5 -3o    [ㅁ]

*Cheongpo muk* is made from the starch of mung beans. It is most often served seasoned with crushed *gim* (seaweed) or a chili-spiced soy sauce. It is also a popular ingredient in *bibimbap* (mixed rice). When paired with the fragrant *minari*, it is best to minimize the seasoning to enjoy the texture of the *muk* and the fragrance of *minari*.

**Preparation time:** 5 minutes
**Cooking time:** 10 minutes
**Serves:** 2

10 oz (300 g) mung bean jelly
1½ teaspoons salt
1 teaspoon plus 1 tablespoon sesame oil
2 oz (60 g) minari, cut into 2–2½-inch (5–6 cm) lengths
1 teaspoon ground sesame seeds

Cut the mung bean jelly block into matchsticks 2½–3 inches (6–8 cm) long and ¼ inch (5 mm) thick.

In a large pot, bring 5 cups (40 fl oz/1.2 liters) water to a boil and add 1 teaspoon salt. Gently add the mung bean jelly, being careful not to break into pieces. Boil for 30–40 seconds or until the jelly is translucent. Scoop out the mung bean jelly in a sieve to drain. Keep the pot of water boiling.

In a large bowl, mix the mung bean jelly with 1 teaspoon sesame oil and toss gently.

Add the minari to the boiling water and blanch for 30 seconds. Drain and quickly run the minari under cold running water to stop the cooking. Squeeze off any excess water and set aside.

Add the blanched minari to the bowl of jelly along with the remaining ½ teaspoon salt and the remaining 1 tablespoon sesame oil and the ground sesame seeds and gently toss with your fingertips to avoid breaking the jelly.

# 전 & 부침개 Jeon & Buchimgae Savory Pancakes

*Jeon*, also called *jeon-yu*, is made from thinly sliced or shredded fish, meat, or vegetables that are battered and pan-fried in oil. Oyster, shrimp (prawns), mushroom, chili, and squash *jeon* are the most common. *Jeon* dates back to the Korean royal court cuisine of the Joseon dynasty (1392–1910).

Another style of Korean pancake are *buchimgae*, in which minced ingredients are stirred into a thick batter that gets cooked in a large thin round. *Buchimgae* are also called *buchim, jijim, jimjimgae,* or *jeonbyung*. Two of the most typical examples are *buchimgae* made with shredded zucchini (courgette) or kimchi.

The main difference between the two styles of pancakes is that *jeon* is made by battering the individual ingredients, whereas *buchimgae* actually stirs the ingredients into the batter. Together, *jeon* and *buchimgae* represent one of the most important foods of Korean cuisine. They are always included in any traditional *janchi-sang* (a celebratory feast) or *jaesa-sang* (ceremony to honor ancestors). For Koreans, perhaps because the sound of cooking *jeon* in oil is reminiscent of the sound of rain, *jeon* and *buchimgae* are the foods that rank highest for cravings on a rainy day in Korea.

There are a few key pieces of advice that will contribute to a great *jeon* or *buchimgae*: 1) enliven the natural colors in its ingredients, 2) make the surface crispy, 3) cook in the right amount of oil to avoid greasiness or excessive richness, 4) if serving with a sauce, make sure it does not overpower the natural flavors of the ingredients, and 5) cook just until the insides are soft and well cooked, without any runny batter, lumps, or undercooked textures. And perhaps most important: *Jeon* and *buchimgae* are always best eaten freshly cooked. So it's okay to prepare the ingredients and batter ahead, but do not cook until just before serving.

## Garlic Chive & Buckwheat Jeon
### Buchu Memil Jeon
### 부추 메밀전

DF VG VE

A popular *jeon* in Gangwon-do, in northeastern South Korea where buckwheat is produced, the combination of the sweet fragrance of cooked chives and a savory buckwheat batter is a charming one. The chives in this recipe can be easily swapped out for cabbage or kimchi. Although this is made with a vegan seasoning, a typical Korean version might use a little *jeotgal* (preserved seafood) in addition to the salt. Pancakes made with buckwheat flour are easier to tear than wheat flour pancakes, so it's best to keep the size small. Using a large spatula or two spatulas while flipping will help maintain the shape.

**Preparation time:** 15 minutes
**Cooking time:** 20 minutes
**Serves:** 4

1 cup (120 g) buckwheat flour
1 teaspoon Yondu (Korean vegan seasoning sauce)
½ teaspoon salt
2 tablespoons neutral cooking oil
3½ oz (100 g) garlic chives, left whole
1 fresh red chili, seeded and thinly sliced on a diagonal

In a bowl, stir together the buckwheat flour, 1 cup (8 fl oz/240 ml) room temperature water, Yondu, and salt until uniform.

In the frying pan, heat 1 tablespoon of the cooking oil over low heat. Place about 20 chives and 4–5 slices of chili in the pan, setting all the chives in the same direction and not overlapping. Using a ladle, gently pour a little of the buckwheat batter over the chives (just enough to hold the chives together), tilt the pan in a circular motion to coat as evenly and thinly as possible to form a round shape. Cook until the pancake is two-thirds cooked through, then flip with a spatula and pan-fry until golden brown on the second side. Repeat with the remaining ingredients.

---

## Garlic Chive & Korean Radish Jeon
### Buchu Mu Jeon
### 부추 무전

DF VG VE -30

*Mu* (Korean radish) is particularly delicious during fall and winter, when it is sweet and without bitterness. It is delicious in a variety of dishes and also inexpensive, making it a common ingredient. The crunchy texture of the mu, along with its clean sweetness, harmonizes beautifully with the fragrance of the chives.

The *mu* pieces are boiled here, but they could easily be prepared in the microwave instead. In the microwave, place the *mu* pieces in a microwave-safe bowl or a deep plate with 2 tablespoons water, seal with plastic wrap (cling film), and microwave for 4 minutes.

**Preparation time:** 5 minutes
**Cooking time:** 20 minutes
**Serves:** 2

**For the batter:**
1 oz (25 g) fresh green Cheongyang chilies, stemmed and seeded
1 oz (30 g) garlic chives
⅔ cup (85 g) Korean pancake mix

**For the radish:**
14 oz (400 g) mu (Korean radish)
1 teaspoon salt

**For the jeon:**
5 tablespoons neutral cooking oil

**Make the batter:** In a blender, combine ⅔ cup (85 g) water, the chilies, and chives and blend until fine. In a bowl, combine the puree with the Korean pancake mix and stir to blend. Set aside.

**Prepare the radish:** Cut crosswise into ⅜-inch (1 cm) rounds, trimming the tough skin. If the radish is particularly large, trim the rounds to about a 2½-inch (6 cm) diameter.

In a pot, combine 3 cups (24 fl oz/710 ml) water, the trimmed radish rounds, and the salt and bring to a boil. Once boiling, reduce the heat to medium and boil for 5 more minutes. Transfer the radish to a plate to cool.

**Make the jeon:** In a frying pan, heat 1 tablespoon of the cooking oil over medium heat. Working in batches so as not to crowd the pan, dip each piece of radish into the chive batter and fry for 1½–2 minutes on each side. Repeat with the remaining ingredients, adding more oil as needed.

# Napa Cabbage Jeon
## Baechu Jeon
## 배추전

df vg vE -5 -30

The napa cabbage (Chinese leaf) *jeon* is particularly delicious in late fall and winter, when the cabbage is at the peak of its flavors. While the dish is extremely simple, it succeeds in highlighting the often overlooked complexity of napa cabbage, ranging from savory to sweet.

**Preparation time: 5 minutes**
**Cooking time: 15 minutes**
**Serves: 2**

10 oz (300 g) napa cabbage (Chinese leaf)
1 cup (125 g) Korean pancake mix
½ teaspoon perilla oil
3 tablespoons neutral cooking oil
2 tablespoons ganjang (Korean soy sauce)

Separate the cabbage leaves individually and flatten any stubborn or thick leaves by lightly rapping them with the back of a knife or making a thin slice in them. Set aside.

In a bowl, combine the pancake mix, ⅔ cup (5 fl oz/160 ml) water, and the perilla oil and mix until uniform.

Set a wire rack in a sheet pan. In a frying pan, heat 1 tablespoon of the cooking oil over medium-low heat. Reduce the heat to low before frying. Working in batches, dip each leaf in the batter, coating the whole leaf evenly, place in the pan, and fry for 2–3 minutes on each side, or until golden. Note that each jeon should be flipped only once. Transfer the leaves to the wire rack to drain. Repeat for all napa cabbage leaves.

Serve the jeon with a side saucer of soy sauce.

**Variation:**

**Spring Napa Cabbage Jeon (Bomdong Jeon):** This recipe can also be made with bomdong, which is young napa cabbage that is only available in the spring. Bomdong has a more savory profile than regular baechu, and many prefer its unique crisp texture in jeon. If you want to try it, just use the same weight of spring napa cabbage. The rest of the ingredients and method remain the same.

## Potato Jeon
## Gamja Jeon
## 감자전

dF gF vg vE -S -3o   [□]

**Preparation time:** 15 minutes
**Cooking time:** 15 minutes
**Serves:** 1–2

7 oz (200 g) potatoes
1 teaspoon Yondu
  (Korean vegan seasoning sauce)
3 tablespoons neutral cooking oil

Potato *jeon* is one of the most commonly made *jeon* in Korea, and is a classic summer dish. Gangwon-do is famous for its potatoes, so the potato *jeon* is one of its signature local foods.

Peel the potatoes and finely grate them on a box grater. (Because grated potatoes become quickly discolored, it's important to grate just before cooking.) In a bowl, combine the potatoes with the Yondu, tossing to coat.

In a large frying pan, heat 1 tablespoon of the cooking oil. Over medium-low heat. Using a large spoon or ladle, create a 1½–2-inch (4–5 cm) round with the potato mixture. Add as many more jeon as will fit in the pan. Increase the heat to medium and fry on each side for 1 minute 30 seconds. Repeat with the remaining ingredients.

---

## Julienned Potato Jeon
## Gamja-chae Jeon
## 감자채전

dF vg vE -S -3o

**Preparation time:** 10 minutes
**Cooking time:** 10 minutes
**Serves:** 1–2

**For the dipping sauce:**
1 tablespoon ganjang
  (Korean soy sauce)
1 tablespoon rice vinegar
1 teaspoon sugar

**For the jeon:**
7 oz (200 g) potatoes
1 teaspoon salt
1 tablespoon potato starch
2 tablespoons neutral cooking oil

The julienned potato *jeon* is a popular variation of the Potato Jeon (see above). The shredded format of the potato highlights its charming texture and is a pleasure to eat.

**Make the dipping sauce:** In a bowl, stir together the soy sauce, vinegar, 1 tablespoon water, and the sugar.

**Make the jeon:** Peel the potatoes and cut them into very thin matchsticks, 1/16 inch (2 mm) thick. In a bowl, combine the julienned potatoes, salt, potato starch, and 1 tablespoon water. Using chopsticks, toss together until well combined.

In a frying pan, heat the cooking oil over medium heat. Using a standard spoon, scoop a spoonful of potato mixture into the pan, creating a round. Press down to create as flat a jeon as possible. Fry until golden brown on the first side, about 2 minutes. Flip and fry on the second side for 1 minute 30 seconds–2 minutes. Repeat for all remaining potatoes.

Serve hot with the dipping sauce on the side.

## Korean Zucchini Jeon
### Aehobak Jeon
### 애호박전

dF vg -5 -3o

*Aehobak* is a Korean native summer vegetables during the season. It's used most commonly in *jeon*, because this preparation brings out the savory, sweet profile of the zucchini (courgette). Note that when making *jeon* with wet ingredients such as zucchini, it's key to salt them lightly to rid them of some of their moisture so the batter will adhere better.

**Preparation time:** 15 minutes
**Cooking time:** 15 minutes
**Serves:** 4

- 5 oz (150 g) aehobak (Korean zucchini)
- 1 egg
- ½ teaspoon salt
- 2 tablespoons all-purpose (plain) flour
- 2 tablespoons neutral cooking oil

Cut the zucchini crosswise into rounds about ⅜ inch (1 cm) thick. Spread out evenly on a large sheet pan, avoiding any overlap, and salt lightly and evenly. Let sit for 2 minutes. Pat off the moisture with paper towels.

Meanwhile, in a bowl, gently beat the egg (avoiding foaming). On a large plate, evenly spread the flour.

Set a wire rack in a sheet pan. In a frying pan, heat 1 tablespoon of the cooking oil over medium heat. Dredge both sides of the zucchini in the flour and then shake off any excess. Dip in the beaten egg. Add the zucchini to the frying pan in a single layer, fitting 4–5 pieces to avoid crowding the pan. Pan-fry until cooked on the first side, about 3 minutes. Flip and pan-fry the other side for about 2 minutes. Transfer to the rack to drain. Repeat with the remaining ingredients.

## Pine Nut & King Trumpet Mushroom Jeon
### Jat Saesongyi Beoseot Jeon
### 잣 새송이버섯전

dF vg -5 -3o

This *jeon* highlights the subtle savory notes of the king trumpet mushroom, along with the savory nuttiness of the pine nuts. For any *jeon* with a wet ingredient, such as mushrooms, it's important to salt them to draw out some of the moisture before batter-frying. Using a rotary cheese grater is an easy way to produce a fine pine nut powder.

**Preparation time:** 5 minutes
**Cooking time:** 15 minutes
**Serves:** 3

- 3 king trumpet mushrooms
- 1 teaspoon salt
- 1 tablespoon pine nuts
- 2 eggs
- 4 tablespoons Korean pancake mix
- 5 tablespoons neutral cooking oil

Cut the king trumpet mushroom lengthwise into slices ¼ inch (5 mm) thick. Lay out the slices on a flat surface and salt lightly. Let sit for 5 minutes to remove excess moisture. Pat dry.

Meanwhile, in a spice grinder (or using a rotary cheese grater), grind the pine nuts to a fine powder. (Alternatively, mince finely with a knife.) Set aside.

Set up a dredging station by beating the eggs well and then straining through a sieve into a shallow bowl. Spread the pancake mix on a plate. Spread the pine nut powder on a second plate.

Heat a frying pan over low heat and add 1 tablespoon of the cooking oil. Working in batches to avoid crowding the pan, dredge the mushroom slices first in the pancake mix, then dip into the beaten egg, letting the excess drip off. Place in the frying pan and fry for 1 minute on each side. Finish by dipping one side of the cooked mushroom into the pine nut powder and plate (alternatively, dust the cooked mushrooms with the pine nut after cooking). Repeat with the remaining ingredients.

# Perilla Jeon
## Kkaennip Jeon
## 깻잎전

dF -3o

Perilla *jeon* is made by filling the fragrant perilla leaf with a seasoned ground (minced) meat stuffing. This *jeon* is both delicious and beautiful, making it a common dish for the holidays. In addition to beef-based stuffings, there are many other ingredients that can be used, such as pork, seafood, and mushrooms—or ground and seasoned tofu for a "meaty" vegetarian or vegan version.

Preparation time: 10 minutes
Cooking time: 20 minutes
Serves: 3–4

### For the filling:
1¾ oz (50 g) medium or firm tofu
7 oz (200 g) ground (minced) beef
1¾ oz (50 g) onion, finely diced
¾ oz (20 g) garlic chives, minced
¾ oz (20 g) carrot, finely diced
1 tablespoon minced garlic
1 tablespoon minced scallion (spring onion)
1 tablespoon yangjo ganjang (naturally brewed soy sauce)
½ tablespoon sugar
1 teaspoon Korean pancake mix
Freshly ground black pepper

### For the jeon:
12 perilla leaves, rinsed and patted dry
2 tablespoons Korean pancake mix
1 egg
1 egg yolk
2 tablespoons neutral cooking oil

**Make the filling:** Using a knife or your hands, coarsely break up the tofu (to resemble meat crumbles). In a large bowl, combine the tofu, beef, onion, chives, carrot, garlic, scallion, soy sauce, sugar, pancake mix, and black pepper to taste and mix until well combined.

**Make the jeon:** Dip the back of each perilla leaf in the pancake mix and lay out the leaves on a large plate or tray with the coated-side up. Cover half of each leaf lengthwise with a thin layer of the filling and fold in half. Using a sieve, lightly dust each side with the Korean pancake mix.

In a bowl, combine the whole egg and egg yolk and mix until uniform. Strain the egg mixture through a fine sieve into another bowl.

In a frying pan, heat the cooking oil over low heat. Working in batches of 3–4 at a time, take each perilla jeon and dip into the beaten egg and place onto the pan, frying on each side for 2½–3 minutes. Repeat with the remaining jeon, adding more oil as necessary.

**Variation:** For a more sweet and savory filling, stir-fry the onions prior to adding to the filling.

# Beef Jeon
## Yukjeon
## 육전

dF

*Yukjeon* is made by pan-frying thinly sliced beef coated in flour and egg. The deep savory flavor of the meat, presented in a clean simple way, is the highlight of this dish. Jeollanam-do is particularly famous for its *yukjeon*, which is usually served with thinly sliced scallions (spring onions) seasoned with gochugaru (red pepper powder) and sesame oil.

Preparation time: 15 minutes
Cooking time: 20 minutes
Serves: 4

**For the marinated beef:**
10 oz (300 g) beef strip loin, flat iron steak, chuck tender, inside round
2 teaspoons sugar
1 teaspoon sesame oil
½ teaspoon salt
¼ teaspoon freshly ground black pepper

**For the jeon:**
3 eggs
½ teaspoon salt
3 tablespoons neutral cooking oil
1 cup (130 g) all-purpose (plain) flour

**Marinate the beef:** Cut the beef in slices 1/16 inch (2 mm) thick. In a large bowl, stir together 1 tablespoon water, the sugar, sesame oil, salt, and black pepper until uniform. Add the sliced beef and marinate for about 2 minutes. Set the meat in a sieve to drain the excess marinade. Remove any excess moisture by dabbing with paper towels and spread out each individual piece on a sheet pan, avoiding overlap.

**Make the jeon:** In a shallow bowl, gently whisk the eggs and salt until a uniform texture (avoiding foaming).

Heat the cooking oil in a frying pan over low heat, coating the pan evenly. Using a fine-mesh sieve, sift the flour evenly over the beef slices, flip, and coat the second side. Working in batches, dip the individual slices of meat in the beaten egg to coat thinly, letting the excess drip off. Pan-fry the beef without turning until the egg coat is fully cooked, and flip just once to the other side and cook evenly. It is important to maintain a low, even heat throughout the pan-fry process for a tender, evenly cooked yukjeon. Repeat with the remaining beef, adding more oil as needed.

Transfer the cooked jeon to a plate and serve hot.

# Beef-Stuffed Pepper Jeon
## Sogogi Gochu Jeon
## 소고기 고추전

dF -3o

This *jeon* is made by first stuffing a mild green chili pepper with a beef filling before batter-frying. The spice and crunch of the pepper paired with the savory beef filling makes for a balanced, delicious *jeon* that has long been beloved in Korea. If there is additional preparation time, lightly pan-fry the diced onions before adding to the meat filing, because this increases the savory sweetness of the mix.

Preparation time: 15 minutes
Cooking time: 10 minutes
Serves: 2

**For the meat filling:**
7 oz (200 g) ground (minced) beef
1¾ oz (50 g) onion, finely diced
¾ oz (20 g) chives, minced
¾ oz (20 g) carrot, finely diced
1 tablespoon minced garlic
1 tablespoon minced scallion (spring onion)
1 tablespoon ganjang (Korean soy sauce)
½ tablespoon sugar
1 teaspoon Korean pancake mix
Pinch of freshly ground black pepper

**For the jeon:**
10 long mild green chili peppers
3 tablespoons Korean pancake mix
1 egg
1 egg yolk
2 tablespoons neutral cooking oil

**Make the meat filling:** In a large bowl, combine the beef, onion, chives, carrot, garlic, scallion, soy sauce, sugar, pancake mix, and black pepper and mix until even.

**Prepare the jeon:** Stem the green peppers. Halve them lengthwise and remove any seeds. Lightly dust the inside of the peppers with some of the pancake mix. Fully fill with the prepared meat filling and set aside.

In a bowl, beat together the whole egg and egg yolk. Strain the egg mixture through a fine sieve into another bowl and set aside.

With a sieve, lightly sift the remaining pancake mix over the filled peppers (with the meat filling-side up).

Heat a large frying pan over low heat and add 1 tablespoon of the cooking oil. Working in batches of 4–5 peppers, dip each pepper into the egg mixture to coat all sides and place in the pan, meat-side down. Fry for 2–3 minutes. Flip to fry for an additional 1 minute. Repeat with the remaining oil and peppers.

Serve hot.

# Korean Batter-Fried Meat Patties
## Yuk Won Jeon
## 육원전

dF

*Yuk won jeon* are a mainstay *jeon* of Korea's holidays. They are made from seasoned ground (minced) beef and tofu, formed into patties, and then dredged in flour and egg before being pan-fried.

Preparation time: 15 minutes
Cooking time: 20 minutes
Serves: 2

For the meat patties:
3½ oz (100 g) firm tofu
1½ teaspoons salt
2 teaspoons sesame oil
10 oz (300 g) ground (minced) beef
2 tablespoons minced scallion (spring onion)
2 teaspoon minced garlic
1 teaspoon ground sesame seeds
1 teaspoon sugar
Pinch of freshly ground black pepper
1¾ oz (50 g) minced toasted peanuts
2 tablespoons minced toasted pine nuts

For the jeon:
2 eggs
1 egg yolk
2 tablespoons all-purpose (plain) flour
4 tablespoons neutral cooking oil

**Make the meat patties:** Squeeze the water out of the tofu in a tea towel and mince (or push it through a coarse sieve). In a bowl, combine the crumbled tofu, ½ teaspoon of the salt, and 1 teaspoon of the sesame oil and mix until even.

In a separate bowl, combine the beef, scallion, garlic, ground sesame seeds, sugar, black pepper, and remaining 1 teaspoon each salt and sesame oil and mix until uniform.

In a large bowl, combine the tofu mixture, beef mixture, peanuts, and pine nuts. Using your hands, form 6–7 patties 2 inches (5 cm) in diameter and ⅜ inch (1 cm) thick.

**Make the jeon:** In a bowl, add the whole eggs and egg yolk and beat until even. Strain the egg mixture through a fine sieve into another bowl and set aside.

Place the patties on a large flat surface. Using a sieve or your hands, lightly dust both sides of the patties with the flour.

Heat a large frying pan over low heat and add the cooking oil. Working in batches of 5–6 at a time, dip each patty into the beaten eggs and place in the frying pan, being careful not to overcrowd. Fry for 4 minutes on each side over low heat.

Plate and serve while hot.

**Variation:** While frying, garnish one side of the patties with thinly sliced red and green chili peppers for a traditional garnish.

# Seafood & Scallion Jeon
## Haemul Pajeon
## 해물파전

dF

Preparation time: 20 minutes
Cooking time: 20 minutes
Serves: 4

**For the seafood:**
4 oz (120 g) cleaned squid (about ½ squid)
8 shrimp (prawns), peeled, deveined, and minced
7 oz (200 g) shucked oysters, minced
½ teaspoon minced garlic

**For the batter:**
2 eggs, separated
1 cup (125 g) Korean pancake mix
1 teaspoon salt
1 teaspoon sesame oil

**For the jeon:**
3½ oz (100 g) scallions (spring onions), cut into 3-inch (8 cm) lengths
1¾ oz (50 g) minari, cut into 3-inch (8 cm) lengths
4 tablespoons neutral cooking oil
½ oz (12 g) fresh red chilies, seeded and finely julienned

*Haemul pajeon*, seafood and scallion (spring onion) *jeon*, is one of the most beloved *jeon* of Korea, and this can be seen in the sheer number of restaurants that specialize in this particular dish. The fresh seasonal seafood and scallions make a delicious pairing. The Dongnae region of Busan is particularly famous for its *haemul pajeon*.

**Prepare the seafood:** Cut the cleaned squid into thin strips $\frac{1}{16}$ inch (2 mm) wide and 1¼ inches (3 cm) long. In a bowl, combine the squid, shrimp, oysters, and garlic and mix until uniform.

**Make the batter:** In a bowl, beat the eggs whites with the pancake mix, 1 cup (8 fl oz/240 ml) water, the salt, and sesame oil and combine until uniform. In a small bowl, beat the egg yolks and set aside.

**Make the jeon:** You will be making five small pancakes, one at a time.

In a frying pan, heat 1 tablespoon of the cooking oil over medium heat. Stir one-fifth of the scallions and minari into the batter to coat. Using chopsticks or tongs, pull out the coated scallions and minari and spread evenly in the frying pan (leaving the batter in the bowl). Evenly distribute one-fifth of the chopped seafood mixture over it and drizzle with one-fifth of the batter and one-fifth of the egg yolk mix on top. Garnish with one-fifth of the sliced red chilies. After 2 minutes, flip the jeon and let cook for 2 more minutes.

Repeat to make the remaining jeon with the remaining ingredients, adding more oil as needed.

## Garlic Chive & Oyster Jeon
## Buchu Gul Jeon
## 부추굴전

dF -3o

Oysters are delicious on their own, but when cooked with eggs, their savory flavors and soft texture are highlighted. Another method of making garlic chive and oyster *jeon* is to place a spoonful of the mix of the egg and chive first in the pan, placing an oyster, and folding in half like a dumpling. This is the regional style of Tongyeong. It is also possible to substitute scallions (spring onions) in place of the chives.

**Preparation time: 10 minutes**
**Cooking time: 15 minutes**
**Serves: 2**

3½ oz (100 g) shucked oysters
1 egg
1 egg yolk
½ oz (10 g) garlic chives, finely minced
4 tablespoons all-purpose (plain) flour
2 tablespoons neutral cooking oil

Make a 3 percent salt solution: For every 1 cup (8 fl oz/240 ml) water, add 1 teaspoon (7 g) salt. Wash the oysters in the salt solution to rid them of any impurities. Drain to get rid of any excess water.

In a bowl, combine the whole egg and egg yolk and mix until well combined. Strain the egg mixture through a fine sieve into another bowl. Stir in the chives. Spread the flour on a wide plate.

Dredge the oysters in the flour, shaking off any excess.

In a frying pan, heat the cooking oil over low heat. Frying only 5–6 oysters at a time, dip each oyster into the egg mixture, place in the heated pan, and fry for about 1½ minutes on each side. Repeat for all oysters.

---

## Fish Jeon
## Jeonyueo
## 전유어

dF -3o

Fish-based *jeon* usually uses white fish with mild-flavored flesh, such as pollock, cod, and sea bass. When cooked in the *jeon* method, the savory taste of the plump flesh is elevated and is a truly delicious dish.

**Preparation time: 10 minutes**
**Cooking time: 15 minutes**
**Serves: 2**

7 oz (200 g) skinless white fish fillets, such as cod or pollock
½ teaspoon salt
½ teaspoon ground white pepper
1 tablespoon rice cooking wine
2 eggs
1 egg yolk
2 tablespoons all-purpose (plain) flour
2 tablespoons neutral cooking oil, plus more if needed

With a knife held at an angle to the cutting board, slice the fish fillet into 2–2½-inch (5–6 cm)-wide pieces. Spread the cut fish on a cutting board without overlapping and evenly sprinkle them with the salt, white pepper, and wine evenly. Let sit for 5–7 minutes.

In a bowl, beat together the whole eggs and egg yolk. Strain the egg mixture through a fine-mesh sieve into another bowl. Spread the flour evenly on a large flat plate.

In a large frying pan, heat the cooking oil over low heat. Working in batches to avoid crowding the pan, dredge both sides of the fish slices in the flour, shaking off any excess. Dip the coated fish into the egg mixture. Set in the frying pan to evenly cook on each side for 2 minutes. Pan-fry the remaining fish in the same way, adding more oil as needed.

## Tips for Making Buchimgae

The consistency of the batter is the most important part of the cooking process. For 5–7 ounces (150–200 g) of base ingredients, here are the proper proportions for the batter:

**Basic batter**
1 cup (8 fl oz/240 ml) water + 1 cup (125 g) Korean pancake mix (buchimgaru)

**Crispy batter**
1 cup (8 fl oz/240 ml) water + ½ cup (125 g) Korean pancake mix + ½ cup (60 g) Korean frying mix

When using wet ingredients, such as kimchi, reduce the water content of the batter.

Using a consistent medium heat is very important in achieving the right results.

Unlike *jeon*, which uses a minimal amount of oil, much more cooking oil is required to get a properly crispy *buchimgae*, almost in the style of deep-frying in the pan.

## Kimchi Buchimgae
### 김치 부침개

dF -5 -3o

Kimchi *buchimgae* is one of Korea's favorite *jeon* and *buchimgae*. Combining two staples in a household—well-fermented kimchi and flour—is a recipe that comes to mind on a rainy day. While just kimchi is delicious, it goes well with many ingredients that can easily be found in the refrigerator, such as cheese, pork, ham, bacon, and all kinds of seafood.

**Preparation time:** 10 minutes
**Cooking time:** 20 minutes
**Serves:** 4

- 1 cup (150 g) Napa Cabbage Kimchi (page 60)
- 1 cup (125 g) Korean pancake mix
- ½ teaspoon salt
- 3 tablespoons neutral cooking oil

Trim the kimchi into easy-to-eat julienne or minced pieces and set aside. Save any of the kimchi juice to incorporate into the batter.

In a bowl, combine the kimchi, pancake mix, ½ cup (4 fl oz/120 ml) water (and any kimchi juice), and salt and mix until uniform.

In a frying pan, heat 1 tablespoon of the cooking oil over medium-low heat. Take a spoonful of the mixture and create a thin round. Add as many buchimgae as you can without crowding the pan. Cook on each side for 2 minutes. Repeat for the remaining mix.

---

## Shrimp & Chive Buchimgae
### Saeu Buchu Buchimgae
### 새우부추부침개

dF -5 -3o  [ㅁ]

The sweet and savory taste of shrimp (prawns) goes well with the fragrance of chives. Depending on the texture and shape desired, the shrimp can be finely chopped and formed into a round shape or can be fried whole. Even when left whole, the other ingredients incorporated will make it technically a *buchimgae*.

**Preparation time:** 10 minutes
**Cooking time:** 15 minutes
**Serves:** 2

- 4 tablespoons Korean pancake mix
- 7 oz (200 g) shrimp (prawns), peeled, deveined, and coarsely chopped
- 1¾ oz (50 g) chives, minced
- 1 oz (25 g) fresh green Cheongyang chili, cut into thing rings
- 4 tablespoons neutral cooking oil
- 2 tablespoons ganjang (Korean soy sauce)

In a bowl, combine the pancake mix, 4 tablespoons water, the shrimp meat, chives, and chili and mix until uniform. Set aside.

In the frying pan, heat the cooking oil over medium heat. Spoon the mixture in the pan, creating rounds of 1½–2½ inches (4–6 cm) diameter. Fry for about 1½ minutes on each side. Repeat for the remaining mix.

Serve the buchimgae with a side saucer of soy sauce.

# Mung Bean Buchimgae
## Nokdu Buchimgae
## 녹두 부침개

dF gF

The mung bean *buchimgae* is a quintessential food of North Korea. The mung bean is native to North Korea and is one of its biggest agricultural crops. Many North Korean restaurants—such as places that specialize in *pyongyang naengmyeon* (Pyongyang-Style Cold Buckwheat Guksu, page 373)— will feature this as a main dish. Called "the king of *buchimgae*," because it is a traditional dish that requires the a lot of time and ingredients (compared with other *buchimgae*), mung bean *buchimgae* is never missing from a holiday feast or family gatherings.

Of all the Korean *buchimgae*, this recipe is the most delicious when it's golden and crispy, so to get the ideal crispy exterior, it's best to pan-fry with a generous amount of cooking oil.

Preparation time: 15 minutes, plus 5 hours soaking time
Cooking time: 30 minutes
Serves: 3–4

5 oz (150 g) dried mung beans
1 tablespoon short-grain white rice
1 teaspoon salt

**For the seasoned pork:**
3½ oz (100 g) ground (minced) pork
1 teaspoon sesame oil
½ teaspoon minced garlic
½ teaspoon ginger juice
½ teaspoon rice wine
½ teaspoon salt
Pinch of freshly ground black pepper
1 tablespoon neutral cooking oil

**For the buchimgae:**
1¾ oz (50 g) store-bought cooked gosari or rehydrated from dried (see page 168), well drained
1¾ oz (50 g) Napa Cabbage Kimchi, store-bought or homemade (page 60)
1 oz (30 g) daepa (Korean scallion)
1 tablespoon Yondu (Korean vegan seasoning sauce)
½ tablespoon sesame oil
8 tablespoons neutral cooking oil
1 oz (25 g) fresh red chilies, finely sliced crosswise on a diagonal
2 tablespoons ganjang (Korean soy sauce)

In a large bowl, combine the mung beans, rice, and 5 cups (40 fl oz/1.2 liters) water and let soak for 5 hours.

Discard all the separated skins and drain. In a sieve, rinse the mung beans under cold running water.

In a blender, combine the mung beans and rice, 1 cup (8 fl oz/240 ml) water, and the salt and blend until fine and smooth.

**Season the pork:** In a large bowl, combine the pork, sesame oil, garlic, ginger juice, wine, salt, and black pepper and mix until well incorporated.

In a frying pan, heat the cooking oil over medium heat. Add the seasoned pork and stir-fry for 3 minutes, stirring to break up the meat. Remove from the heat and set aside.

**Prepare the buchimgae:** Cut the blanched gosari into ¾–1¼-inch (2–3 cm) lengths. Rinse the kimchi under cold running water to remove any visible seasoning, and squeeze gently to remove any excess water. Finely julienne the kimchi. Quarter the daepa lengthwise and cut into crosswise 1½-inch (4 cm) lengths.

In a large bowl, combine the mung bean-rice puree, the stir-fried pork, gosari, kimchi, and daepa. Add the Yondu and sesame oil and combine well until fully incorporated.

In a large frying pan, heat 3 tablespoons of the cooking oil over medium-low heat. Once heated, pour the mixture into the pan in rounds 4¾ inches (12 cm) in diameter and ⅜ inch (1 cm) thick, placing a thin ring of red chili in the center. Fry each side until golden and crispy, about 4 minutes each.

Repeat with the remaining mixture and red chili rings, adding more cooking oil as needed.

Serve the buchimgae with a side saucer of soy sauce.

# Bokkeum Stir-Fried

볶음

Bokkeum are dishes of meat, seafood, and vegetables that are preseasoned and stir-fried in a pan. They are a category of banchan (side dishes) that is often prepared just prior to serving, and meat- or seafood-based bokkeum will be the main banchan of a meal. At Korean restaurants that operate an à la carte menu, a main bokkeum banchan will be accompanied by a set of standard mit-banchans (pickled or preserved sides), such as kimchi.

Most Korean bokkeum dishes start by stir-frying aromatics, such as scallions (spring onions) and garlic, in oil. The main ingredient will have been seasoned with a sauce based on ganjang (Korean soy sauce), doenjang (fermented soybean paste), or gochujang (red chili paste). Pork and chicken are often marinated in a gochujang-based sauce, and beef is often marinated in a ganjang-based sauce. Because jang-based marinades or sauces can easily burn over high heat, it is important to maintain the heat at medium while stir-frying.

While there are many bokkeum sauce variations and even premade sauces available commercially, there are two simple base recipes that can be utilized with any ingredients. The following sauces make enough for 3 oz (100 g) of ingredients to be stir-fried.

---

**Ganjang Bokkeum Base**

1 tablespoon ganjang (Korean soy sauce)

½ tablespoon sugar

1 teaspoon minced scallion (spring onion)

1 teaspoon minced garlic

½ teaspoon sesame oil

Freshly ground black pepper, to taste

In a small bowl, stir everything together until completely uniform.

**Gochujang Bokkeum Base**

1 tablespoon gochujang (red chili paste)

1 tablespoon ganjang (Korean soy sauce)

1 tablespoon rice cooking wine (optional)

1 tablespoon sugar

1 tablespoon gochugaru (red chili flakes)

1 teaspoon minced scallion (spring onion)

1 teaspoon minced garlic

½ teaspoon sesame oil

Freshly ground black pepper, to taste

In a small bowl, stir everything together until completely uniform.

# Spicy Pork Bokkeum
## Jeyuk Bokkeum
## 제육 볶음

dF

The most common grilled pork cuts in Korea are pork belly and neck. As a result, other parts that are less consumed are available at an affordable price. Among these cuts, pork shoulder and pork butt have been popularized as *jeyuk bokkeum*, a popular dish made with thinly sliced leg meat seasoned with *gochujang*-based seasoning. *Jeyuk bokkeum* is delicious simply pan-fried, especially when grilled over charcoal. It is also popular as a rice bowl ingredient.

**Preparation time:** 10 minutes, plus 30 minutes up to 12 hours marinating time
**Cooking time:** 15 minutes
**Serves:** 4

**For the marinated pork:**
3 tablespoons ganjang (Korean soy sauce)
2 tablespoons gochugaru (red chili flakes)
2 tablespoons light brown sugar
1 tablespoon gochujang (red chili paste)
1 tablespoon rice cooking wine
1 tablespoon minced garlic
½ tablespoon sesame oil
½ teaspoon freshly ground black pepper
1 lb (500 g) pork belly or pork shoulder, cut into slices ⅛ inch (3 mm) thick

**For the bokkeum:**
1 tablespoon neutral cooking oil
7 oz (200 g) onion, sliced ⅛ inch (3 mm) thick
2 oz (60 g) daepa (Korean scallion), cut into ¼-inch (6 mm) diagonal slices

**Marinate the pork:** In a large bowl, combine the soy sauce, gochugaru, brown sugar, gochujang, wine, garlic, sesame oil, and black pepper and mix until uniform. Add the pork and mix well. Let marinate for 30 minutes at room temperature or up to 12 hours in the refrigerator.

**Make the bokkeum:** In a nonstick frying pan, heat the cooking oil over medium heat. Add half of the onion and daepa and cook until the vegetables begin to turn translucent, about 30 seconds. Add the marinated pork and cook, avoiding stirring too much. Once the first side begins to turn brown, add 4 tablespoons water and stir-fry for 4–5 minutes. Add the remaining scallion and onion and briefly stir-fry before removing from the heat. Transfer to a large plate and serve hot.

# Garlic Scape & Dried Shrimp Bokkeum
## Maneuljong Geon Saeu Bokkeum
## 마늘종 건새우 볶음

dF -3o

**Preparation time:** 10 minutes
**Cooking time:** 15 minutes
**Serves:** 2

5 oz (150 g) garlic scapes
Salt

**For the sauce:**
2 tablespoons gochujang (red chili paste)
1 tablespoon yangjo ganjang (naturally brewed soy sauce)
1 tablespoon mirin
1 teaspoon sesame oil
½ teaspoon sesame seeds

**For the stir-fry:**
2 tablespoons neutral cooking oil
2 teaspoons minced garlic
2 oz (60 g) small dried shrimp

Garlic scapes are the flower stems of the garlic plant. While it retains the same pungent flavor and fragrance as garlic when raw, once cooked it releases a savory, delicious flavor with a wonderful snappy texture. Its balanced, nuanced garlic flavors are great in stir-fries with all types of meat and seafood, and its crunch makes it a favored pickle ingredient.

Trim off any very thick (or very thin) parts of the garlic scapes and cut crosswise into 1½-inch (4 cm) lengths.

Set up a bowl of ice and water. In a small pot of salted boiling water, blanch the garlic scapes for 30 seconds. Drain and transfer to the ice bath to stop cooking. Drain and set in a sieve to drain excess water.

**Make the sauce:** In a bowl, combine the gochujang, 1 tablespoon water, the soy sauce, mirin, sesame oil, and sesame seeds and mix until well combined.

**Make the stir-fry:** In a frying pan, heat the cooking oil over medium-low heat. Add the minced garlic and cook for 30 seconds. Increase the heat to medium, add the dried shrimp, and cook for 1 minute. Add the garlic scapes and the sauce and stir-fry for an additional 2 minutes before removing from the heat. Plate and serve.

## Shishito & Anchovy Bokkeum
Kkwari-gochu & Myeolchi Bokkeum
꽈리고추 멸치 볶음

dF -30

The pleasant, mild fragrance of the *kkwari gochu*, also known as the shishito pepper, is popular in *banchan* (side dish) cuisine in Korea. The *kkwari gochu*'s flavors are a great pairing for dried anchovy and it's often a staple in Korean households. Because it's made with the dried anchovy, it can be stored for a long time.

**Preparation time: 5 minutes**
**Cooking time: 10 minutes**
**Serves: 2–4**

7 kkwari (shishito) peppers
2 tablespoons neutral cooking oil
2 oz (60 g) dried baby anchovies
½ teaspoon minced garlic
½ teaspoon yangjo ganjang (naturally brewed soy sauce)
2 tablespoons rice cooking wine
2 tablespoons light corn syrup (honey)
1 teaspoon sesame oil
¼ teaspoon sesame seeds

Stem the shishitos and cut into thirds (or easy-to-eat pieces, depending on their size).

In a frying pan, heat 1 tablespoon of the cooking oil over medium heat. Add the small anchovies and stir-fry until well-fried, about 1½ minutes. Remove from the heat and set aside on a plate.

In a clean frying pan, add the remaining 1 tablespoon cooking oil and heat over medium heat. Add the garlic and stir-fry for 20–30 seconds. Add the cooked anchovies, shishitos, soy sauce, wine, and corn syrup and stir-fry for 1 minute. Stir in the sesame oil and remove from the heat.

Just before serving, sprinkle with the sesame seeds and mix until well combined. In an airtight container, it will last up to 6 days.

**Variation:** It is popular to add nuts, such as pine nuts, almonds, or walnuts, to taste, or to just simply stir-fry the anchovies without any other accompaniments.

---

## Roasted Seaweed Flakes
Gim Jaban
김자반

dF gF vg vE -5 -30

Roasted seaweed flakes makes a typical and supereasy *banchan* (side dish). They also are a great, light drinking snack.

**Preparation time: 5 minutes**
**Cooking time: 5 minutes**
**Serves: 2**

1½ tablespoons sesame oil
1 teaspoon sugar
½ teaspoon salt
1 teaspoon sesame seeds
5 sheets unseasoned, unroasted gim

In a small bowl, stir together the sesame oil, sugar, salt, and sesame seeds until the sugar and salt are dissolved.

Place the sheets of seaweed in a large zip-seal plastic bag and crumble into small pieces. Once the seaweed is in flake-like pieces, add the sauce to the bag and shake vigorously until well mixed.

Heat a frying pan over medium heat. Add the seasoned seaweed flakes and stir-fry until crisp, 2–3 minutes. Plate and serve.

# Stir-Fried Vegetables & Glass Noodles
## Japchae
## 잡채

----

DF

**Preparation time:** 35 minutes
**Cooking time:** 15 minutes
**Serves:** 2–4

8½ oz (240 g) glass noodles

**For the seasoned pork:**
5 oz (150 g) pork sirloin, cut into matchsticks 1½ × ¼ inch (4 cm × 6 mm)
2 tablespoons ganjang (Korean soy sauce)
1 tablespoon rice cooking wine
1 teaspoon sugar

**For the bokkeum:**
3½ oz (100 g) dried wood ear mushrooms
4 oz (120 g) young or baby spinach
2 tablespoons neutral cooking oil
2¾ oz (80 g) fresh shiitake mushrooms, stemmed, caps thinly sliced
7 oz (200 g) onions, thinly slivered
3½ oz (100 g) carrots, cut into ⅛-inch (4 mm) matchsticks
3½ oz (100 g) chives, cut into 1-inch (2.5 cm) lengths

**For the japchae sauce:**
5 tablespoons ganjang (Korean soy sauce)
2 tablespoons sesame oil
2 tablespoons light brown sugar
1 tablespoon mirin
1 tablespoon corn (golden) syrup
1 tablespoon minced garlic
1 teaspoon salt, plus more to taste

*Japchae* is made by stir-frying a diverse set of ingredients, including meat, mushrooms, and vegetables and mixing with boiled glass noodles (aka cellophane noodles). It can serve as a main meal or can be served as a communal *banchan* (side dish), or even eaten over rice in a rice bowl. The original *japchae* was actually made without any noodles but was made with ingredients that were julienned and stir-fried to create a noodle-like aesthetic. The glass noodles were added to the dish in the 1930s, when the noodles had begun to be imported to Korea and were quickly gaining popularity. While traditionally each component is stir-fried separately, these days it's often stir-fried all together for ease and then mixed with the glass noodles.

Soak the glass noodles in water for 30 minutes.

**Meanwhile, season the pork:** In a bowl, combine the pork, soy sauce, wine, and sugar and marinate for 10 minutes.

**Make the bokkeum:** In a bowl of water, soak the wood ear mushrooms until fully rehydrated. Drain and cut into 1-inch (2.5 cm) pieces. Cut the spinach into 1-inch (2.5 cm) pieces.

In a nonstick frying pan, heat the cooking oil over medium heat. Add the marinated pork and stir-fry for 30 seconds. Add the shiitake and wood ear mushrooms and briefly stir-fry. Add the onions and carrots and stir-fry for 1 more minute. Add the spinach and chives and mix well and remove from the heat. Transfer to a large plate to cool.

**Make the japchae sauce:** In a small bowl, stir together the soy sauce, 4 tablespoons water, the sesame oil, brown sugar, mirin, corn syrup, garlic, and salt.

Bring a pot of water to a boil. Add the soaked glass noodles and cook for 7 minutes. Drain and shake to remove excess water.

In a large nonstick skillet, add the cooked noodles and the japchae sauce and stir-fry over medium heat until the excess moisture has evaporated. Add the cooked vegetables and stir-fry for 30 seconds until uniform. Season to taste with salt as needed. Plate and serve.

# Chuncheon-Style Chicken Stir-Fry
## Chuncheon Dak Galbi
## 춘천 닭갈비

dF

*Chuncheon dak galbi*, or Chuncheon-style chicken stir-fry, is a famous regional specialty of the Chuncheon region of Gangwon-do. The chicken is marinated in a spicy-sweet *gochujang* (red chili paste)-based sauce, and stir-fried with vegetables and rice cakes. This is typically done on a purpose-built round, cast-iron, unridged griddle (grill) pan.

In restaurants, after the *dak galbi* is finished cooking, it is customary to stir-fry rice with the remaining sauce along with minced kimchi and seaweed. Home cooks in Korea will traditionally finish this dish by stir-frying rice, letting no sauce go to waste.

Preparation time: 20 minutes
Cooking time: 20 minutes
Serves: 2

For the marinated chicken:
4 tablespoons gochujang (red chili paste)
2 tablespoons gochugaru (red chili flakes)
2 tablespoons mirin
2 tablespoons corn (golden) syrup
2 tablespoons minced garlic
2 tablespoons minced scallion (spring onion)
1 tablespoon ganjang (Korean soy sauce)
1 tablespoon sesame oil
½ teaspoon minced fresh ginger
¼ teaspoon freshly ground black pepper
½ teaspoon sesame seeds
14 oz (400 g) boneless, skinless chicken thighs

For the stir-fry:
1 cup (100 g) fresh tteok (Korean rice cakes)
9 oz (250 g) green cabbage
3½ oz (100 g) onion
1 oz (30 g) daepa (Korean scallion)
2½ oz (75 g) Korean sweet potato
3 perilla leaves
1 tablespoon neutral cooking oil

**Marinate the chicken:** In a large bowl, combine the gochujang, gochugaru, mirin, corn syrup, garlic, scallion, soy sauce, sesame oil, ginger, black pepper, and sesame seeds. Cut the chicken into 1½-inch (4 cm) pieces. Add to the sauce and let marinate for 10–20 minutes.

**Meanwhile, prepare the stir-fry ingredients:** Rinse any excess starch off the rice cakes under cold running water and set aside in a sieve to drain off any excess water. Cut the cabbage into 1½-inch (4 cm) chunks. Cut the onion into ⅜-inch (1 cm) slices. Halve the daepa lengthwise and cut crosswise into 2½-inch (6 cm) lengths. Halve the Korean sweet potato lengthwise and then crosswise into slices ¼ inch (5 mm) thick. Cut the perilla leaves into quarters.

In a large frying pan, heat the cooking oil over medium heat. Add the marinated chicken along with all the vegetables and the rice cakes and stir-fry for 10 minutes. Plate and serve hot.

## Stir-Fried Beef & Cucumber
Sogogi Oi Baetduri
소고기오이뱃두리

dF -3o

*Baetduri* is an old Korean word that comes from *hangari*, an earthenware vessel for storing sauces or honey. As a culinary term, *baetduri* is a dish of cucumbers braised or stir-fried with soy sauce and honey. This dish is made by stir-frying cucumber with seasoned beef, and the texture of the crunchy cooked cucumber makes it a delight to eat.

**Preparation time: 10 minutes**
**Cooking time: 10 minutes**
**Serves: 2**

10 oz (300 g) cucumber
2 teaspoons salt

**For the marinated beef:**
1 tablespoon jinjang (dark Korean soy sauce)
1 tablespoon sugar
½ teaspoon minced garlic
1 teaspoon sesame oil
Freshly ground black pepper
3½ oz (100 g) beef tenderloin or sirloin (rump), thinly sliced

**For the stir-fry:**
1 tablespoon neutral cooking oil
1 teaspoon sesame seeds
½ teaspoon sesame oil

Cut the cucumber lengthwise into eighths. Cut off the seeds and cut the cucumber crosswise into 1½–2-inch (4–5 cm) pieces. In a bowl, toss the cucumber with the salt and let brine for 5 minutes. Rinse under cold running water. Gently squeeze the cucumber with a clean tea towel to remove any excess water and set aside.

**Marinate the beef:** In a bowl, combine the soy sauce, sugar, garlic, sesame oil, and black pepper to taste and mix until uniform. Cut the beef into matchsticks 2½ inches (6 cm) long against the grain of the beef. Add the beef to the bowl with the marinade and gently massage to incorporate the marinade.

**Make the stir-fry:** In a frying pan, heat the cooking oil over medium heat. Add the cucumber and stir-fry for 1 minute, then scoop out onto a plate. Add the seasoned beef to the pan and stir-fry over medium heat for 1 minute. Return the cucumber to the pan and stir-fry together for 30 seconds. Add the sesame seeds and sesame oil to finish and remove from the heat. Plate and serve.

---

## Korean Zucchini Bokkeum
Aehobak Saeujeot Bokkeum
애호박 새우젓 볶음

dF gF -3o

*Aehobak*, or Korean green zucchini (courgette), is often seasoned with salted shrimp, because the two ingredients harmonize well. This recipe can be replicated using a variety of other vegetables, and the resulting stir-fry can be used as a topping for a rice bowl. Replace the salted shrimp with soy sauce for a vegan version.

**Preparation time: 15 minutes**
**Cooking time: 5 minutes**
**Serves: 2–4**

9 oz (250 g) aehobak (Korean zucchini)
2 teaspoons salt
2 tablespoons sesame oil
3½ oz (100 g) onion, sliced ⅛ inch (3 mm) thick
1 tablespoon minced garlic
1 oz (30 g) daepa (Korean scallion), sliced ⅛ inch (3 mm) thick
2 tablespoons salted shrimp
1 teaspoon ground sesame seeds

Halve the zucchini lengthwise and cut crosswise into ⅛-inch (3 mm) half-moons. Sprinkle with the salt and let brine for 10 minutes. Rinse under cold running water and drain excess water or use paper towels to pat dry.

In a nonstick frying pan, heat the sesame oil over medium heat. Add the onion and garlic and stir-fry for 15 seconds. Add the zucchini and cook for about 1 minute or until the zucchini begins to turn translucent. Add the daepa and salted shrimp and mix well.

Transfer to a plate and garnish with the sesame seeds.

# 구이 Gui Grilled

*Gui* refers to dishes that are cooked by grilling various vegetables, seafood, and meats over a direct or indirect heat source. In Korean food, *gui* dishes have classically been grilled over charcoal. Other characteristics specific to Korean grilling are the well-developed art of hyperspecific cuts of meat, the various knife techniques for tenderizing or trimming the meat into thin slices, and the culture of marinating.

While many of the dishes in this section are delicious grilled over charcoal, plancha, or other forms of traditional fire grills, the recipes in the book are the home cook's version of *gui*, which are made on the stovetop (hob) in a frying pan, which is much more easily accessible to everyone.

There are two basic ways to season a *gui* dish: simply grilled with oil and salt or in a marinade—made with *ganjang* (Korean soy sauce), *doenjang* (fermented soybean paste), or *gochujang* (red chili paste) combined with oil, scallion (spring onion), and garlic. Depending on the type of fish or meat, other seasonings may be added to the basic recipe. Meat tastes better when cooked briefly over a strong fire, so it is best to first marinate the meat to be sure that it is well seasoned throughout before it is cooked. However, when using a *gochujang*-based marinade, it is best to first grill the meat with just oil and salt prior to adding the *gochujang* sauce, because the sauce, which has sugar in it, can burn before the meat is fully cooked. When cooking vegetables, *doenjang*-based sauces are best, because they complement the earthy taste of the vegetables and pair beautifully with charcoal aromas. Beef is typically cooked medium-rare for a better taste and texture, but pork is cooked until well done.

The classic Korean *gui* dishes are the famous *bulgogi* and *galbi*. Each region of Korea has a distinct way of preparing *bulgogi*, not only in its seasoning but even in the types of grills and grilling methods used. *Galbi*, meaning ribs, typically refers to beef short ribs. *Galbi gui* is usually prepared simply with salt and oil, although *ganjang*-based marinated *galbi gui* is also popular.

# Characteristics of Korea's Grilled Meat Culture

### Distinct, Hyperspecific Cut

The first most distinct characteristic of Korea's popular grilled meat cuisine is that of the butchering technique. Animals are divided into various distinct cuts, and each is enjoyed for its unique flavor and texture. Korea's Ministry of Agriculture, Food and Rural Affairs has 39 official recognized cuts for beef, and commercially there are about 120 distinct subcategories of cuts that are sold and eaten.

### Vegetable Banchan

The second defining characteristic of grilled meat cuisine is that it's always accompanied by a variety of vegetables. More than 50 percent of a Korean barbecue meal spread is composed of vegetable *banchan* (side dishes). Using these vegetables, Koreans enjoy their grilled meats in many different ways in one meal.

Grilled meats are enjoyed dipped in *gochujang*, *ssamjang* (dipping sauce for *ssam*), sesame oil and salt, salted shrimp, and more. Depending on the cut, some grilled meats are first marinated in sauces made from these ingredients. Each bite of the grilled meat can be eaten paired with kimchi, *jangajji* (pickles), *namul* (vegetable dishes), *muchim* (seasoned dishes), and any *banchan* in the meal spread. *Ssam* (wrap) vegetables are used to wrap the meat and any desired combination of these *banchan* and sauces into a unique bite. Vegetable *banchan* and *ssam* vegetables are often grilled along with the meat, cooked in the rendered fat, and meals are often finished by creating a fried rice using the remaining ingredients. Grilled meats are always enjoyed in these various ways in one meal, adding to the pleasure of the eating experience.

### Communal Tabletop Grilling

The third defining characteristic of grilled meat cuisine is the communal cooking method of a Korean barbecue. In Korean cuisine, the meat is grilled at the table on a tabletop grill, cooked during the meal. This is to enjoy the meats at their prime, optimal temperature just after cooking.

### Specialized Grills

The fourth defining characteristic is the various grill types that are commonly used in Korean grill culture. They can be made of diverse materials, including cast iron, copper, metal grates, stone, and more. Various heat sources, such as charcoal, gas, firewood, and hay, are used depending on the cut of the meat. Koreans have developed many grill shapes specific to popular cuts of meat. For fatty cuts, such as pork belly, there is style of slanted plate grill that allows the pork fat to render and drip out into a container. For *bulgogi*, which is often enjoyed with broth, there is a specially shaped grill with a concave dip in the center of the grill so that the broth and the sauce can collect during the cooking process.

### Meticulous Knife Work

The knife work applied to meat for Korean grilling is also unique. These are methods that have been developed over the long history of Korean cuisine to highlight the hyperspecific cuts of meats, including the direction and thickness of the cuts. Compared to many other cuisines, where thicker cuts such as steak is the main style, in Korean cuisine, depending on the specific part of the animal, different knife cuts are applied. Depending on the type of meat and the desired outcome, the slice thickness is determined as well as the direction of the cut (against or with the grain) and at what angle. Often, different cuts for the same meat can be combined to highlight the texture of the meat.

Because of these well-developed knife techniques, many tough cuts of meat can be grilled and end up both delicious and tender. Moreover, it's possible for diners to enjoy one part of the animal in tens of different ways, each expressing a different texture and ultimately flavor. For example, in Western grilling, a steak can be grilled on six sides, but in the Korean methodology, it would be divided up into ten different cuts and grilled on thirty to sixty sides.

## Doenjang-Marinated Pork Gui
## Doenjang Yangnyeom Dwaeji Gui
## 된장양념돼지구이

dF -30 [ㅁ]

Coating the pork in *doenjang* (fermented soybean paste) imparts a balanced, but deeper, more savory, nutty taste to the cooked pork.

**Preparation time:** 10 minutes
**Cooking time:** 10 minutes
**Serves:** 2

4 tablespoons doenjang (fermented soybean paste)
4 tablespoons rice cooking wine
14 oz (400 g) pork belly, thinly sliced to 1/16 inch (2 mm) thick
½ teaspoon sesame seeds
½ oz (10 g) garlic chives, slivered
1 small scallion (spring onion), slivered

In a bowl, stir together the doenjang and wine and have the baster ready.

Heat a frying pan over medium heat. Add the slices of pork to the pan, avoiding overlap. Flip the meat when the first side is cooked. After flipping, brush the meat with the baster. Repeat until all the meat is cooked. Transfer the cooked meat to a plate once cooked.

Serve garnished with sesame seeds, chives, and scallion and serve immediately.

**Variation:** This option is for if you have slices of pork belly thicker than ⅜ inch (1 cm). Mix the doenjang and wine in a small bowl. Score the slices of pork belly and cut into 2½-inch (6 cm) lengths if needed. In a large bowl or container, coat the pork with the marinade and cover. Let marinate for a minimum of 1 hour, up to 1 day. Heat a frying pan over medium heat and cook until fully cooked on both sides. Serve garnished with sesame seeds, chives, and scallion.

---

## Pork Rib Gui
## Dwaeji Galbi
## 돼지갈비

dF

Pork ribs marinated in soy sauce have long been a favorite restaurant item in Korea. Of Korea's countless pork barbecue restaurants, the most common are pork belly barbecue restaurants and pork rib restaurants.

The proper way to cut the meat is to carve it away from the bone (the way you would butterfly meat), resulting in a tender and long strip that is left attached at one end to the bone. The long piece of meat itself is often scored for the marinade.

**Preparation time:** 20 minutes, plus 12 hours marinating time
**Cooking time:** 10–15 minutes
**Serves:** 2–3

2¼ lb (1 kg) bone-in pork ribs, cut into 1½-inch (4 cm) lengths

**For the marinade:**
7 oz (200 g) Asian pear, peeled and cut into chunks
1¾ oz (50 g) onion, peeled and cut into chunks
4 tablespoons jinjang (dark Korean soy sauce)
2 tablespoons rice cooking wine
2 tablespoons mirin
2 tablespoons light brown sugar
1 tablespoon Yondu (Korean vegan seasoning sauce)
1 tablespoon corn (golden) syrup
1 tablespoon minced garlic
1 teaspoon minced fresh ginger
1 teaspoon sesame oil
¼ teaspoon freshly ground black pepper

To cut the pork rib, make a lateral cut directly above the bone and slice almost through the meat, leaving it attached to the bone at one end by a ¼ inch (5 mm). Open and flatten the meat and repeat as you would to butterfly meat, cutting it into thinner sections and opening it up like a book as you go, leaving the end of each cut hinged to the previous cut by a ¼ inch (5 mm). Continue slicing through and unfolding until the pork rib is a singular strip of thin meat attached to the bone at one end.

**Make the marinade:** In a blender, combine ½ cup (4 fl oz/120 ml) water, the pear, onion, soy sauce, wine, mirin, brown sugar, Yondu, corn syrup, garlic, ginger, sesame oil, and black pepper and blend until finely incorporated.

In an airtight container, combine the pork rib and the marinade, making sure all parts of the meat are covered. Let marinate for at least 12 hours in the refrigerator. Note that marinated pork ribs will keep in the refrigerator for up to 3 days.

Heat a frying pan over medium heat. Add the pork ribs and cook for 2 minutes on each side or until fully cooked. Serve hot.

# Gochujang-Marinated Pork Gui
## Gochujang Jeyuk Gui
## 고추장 제육구이

dF

*Gochujang* (red chili paste) seasoning goes well with pork, which has an inherently strong flavor and aroma. It is common to stir-fry *gochujang jeyuk* with an assortment of vegetables in a pan, but cooking the marinated meat by itself gives a deeper taste to the meat and seasoning. If available, cook over a charcoal grill for extra smoked flavor.

**Preparation time:** 10 minutes, plus 30 minutes up to 12 hours marinating time
**Cooking time:** 20 minutes
**Serves:** 2

**For the marinated pork:**
3 tablespoons gochujang (red chili paste)
1 tablespoon yangjo ganjang (naturally brewed soy sauce)
1 tablespoon mirin
1 tablespoon gochugaru (red chili flakes)
1 tablespoon light brown sugar
1 tablespoon minced garlic
½ tablespoon sesame oil
½ tablespoon sesame seeds
¼ teaspoon freshly ground black pepper
14 oz (400 g) pork belly or picnic shoulder, thinly sliced to ⅛ inch (3 mm) thick

**To finish:**
1 tablespoon neutral cooking oil

**Marinate the pork:** In a small bowl, stir together the gochujang, 2 tablespoons water, the soy sauce, mirin, gochugaru, brown sugar, garlic, sesame oil, sesame seeds, and black pepper.

In an airtight container, combine the thinly sliced pork and the marinade and gently massage until fully and evenly seasoned. Seal and marinate for at least 30 minutes at room temperature, but ideally for at least 12 hours in the refrigerator.

**To finish:** Remove from the refrigerator when ready to cook. Heat a frying pan over medium heat and drizzle in the cooking oil. Arrange the pork slices and cook until all sides are evenly cooked. Reduce the heat as needed while cooking, because gochujang-based marinades are susceptible to burning.

## Gochujang-Marinated Chicken Gui
### Gochujang Dak Gui
### 고추장 닭구이

dF [□]

This spicy version of chicken *gui* is made by marinating chicken in a *gochujang* (red chili paste)-based sauce before grilling. *Gochujang*-based seasonings become more savory when cooked, and develop a smoky flavor if grilled over a wood or charcoal fire, elevating the chicken's flavors. Make these on an outdoor grill (barbecue) if you have access to one.

Preparation time: 10 minutes, plus 1 hour up to 12 hours marinating time
Cooking time: 20 minutes
Serves: 2

**For the marinated chicken:**
3 tablespoons gochujang (red chili paste)
2 tablespoons mirin
1 tablespoon yangjo ganjang (naturally brewed soy sauce)
1 tablespoon rice cooking wine
1 tablespoon light brown sugar
½ tablespoon minced garlic
½ teaspoon minced fresh ginger
14 oz (400 g) boneless, skin-on chicken thighs

**To finish:**
1 tablespoon neutral cooking oil
½ teaspoon sesame seeds (optional)
1 scallion (spring onion), thinly sliced (optional)

**Marinate the chicken:** In a small bowl, stir together the gochujang, mirin, soy sauce, wine, brown sugar, garlic, and ginger.

In a large airtight container or bowl, combine the chicken thighs and the marinade, making sure all chicken pieces are well coated in the marinade. Let marinate in the refrigerator for a minimum of 1 hour, but ideally at least 12 hours.

**To finish:** In a large frying pan, heat the cooking oil over medium heat. Add the marinated chicken thighs skin-side down and pan-fry for 1 minute. Flip and cook the other side for 1 minute, before flipping again to the skin side. Cover the pan, reduce the heat to low, and cook for an additional 3 minutes.

Plate the cooked chicken and garnish with the sesame seeds and scallion, if desired.

---

## Ganjang-Marinated Chicken Gui
### Ganjang Dak Gui
### 간장 닭구이

dF

For a quick version of the dish, thinly slice the chicken meat to marinate. For a more fragrant version of the dish, grill over charcoal.

Preparation time: 10 minutes, plus 1 hour up to 12 hours marinating time
Cooking time: 20 minutes
Serves: 2

**For the marinated chicken:**
4 tablespoons aged jinjang (dark Korean soy sauce)
2 tablespoons mirin
1 tablespoon rice cooking wine
1 tablespoon light brown sugar
½ tablespoon minced garlic
½ teaspoon minced fresh ginger
14 oz (400 g) boneless, skin-on chicken thighs

**To finish:**
1 tablespoon neutral cooking oil
½ teaspoon sesame seeds (optional)
1 scallion (spring onion), thinly sliced (optional)

**Marinate the chicken:** In a small bowl, stir together the soy sauce, mirin, wine, brown sugar, garlic, and ginger.

In a large airtight container or bowl, combine the chicken thighs and the marinade, making sure all the chicken pieces are well coated in the marinade. Let marinate in the refrigerator for a minimum of 1 hour, but ideally at least 12 hours.

**To finish:** In a large frying pan, heat the cooking oil over medium heat. Add the marinated chicken thighs skin-side down and pan-fry for 1½ minutes. Flip and cook the other side for a minute, before flipping again to the skin side. Cover the pan, reduce the heat to low, and cook for an additional 3 minutes.

Plate the cooked chicken and garnish with the sesame seeds and scallion, if desired.

# Gochujang-Marinated Duck Gui
## Ori Gochujang Gui
## 고추장 오리구이

dF

Duck is more delicious when paired with *gochujang* (red chili paste)-based sauces, rather than soy sauce-based or *doenjang* (fermented soybean paste)-based sauces, because the spicy, sweet flavors of the *gochujang* harmonize with the savory duck fat.

**Preparation time:** 15 minutes, plus 30 minutes up to 12 hours marinating time
**Cooking time:** 20 minutes
**Serves:** 2

**For the marinated duck:**
3 tablespoons gochujang (red chili paste)
1 tablespoon yangjo ganjang (naturally brewed soy sauce)
1 tablespoon mirin
1 tablespoon gochugaru (red chili flakes)
1 tablespoon light brown sugar
1 tablespoon minced garlic
½ tablespoon sesame oil
¼ teaspoon freshly ground black pepper
14 oz (400 g) skin-on, boneless duck leg or breast, sliced ⅛ inch (3 mm) thick

**To finish:**
3½ oz (100 g) onion, cut into ⅛-inch (3 mm) slices
1 tablespoon neutral cooking oil
¾ oz (20 g) chives, cut into 3-inch (8 cm) lengths
½ tablespoon sesame seeds

**Marinate the duck:** In a small bowl, combine the gochujang, 2 tablespoons water, the soy sauce, mirin, gochugaru, brown sugar, garlic, sesame oil, and black pepper.

In an airtight container, combine the marinade and the sliced duck, making sure any bones are removed, and marinate for at least 30 minutes and up to 12 hours in the refrigerator.

**To finish:** When ready to cook, add the onion slices to the marinated duck and mix evenly.

Preheat an outdoor grill (barbecue) or a stovetop (hob) grill pan (griddle pan) to medium heat.

If cooking indoors, add the oil to the grill pan. Add the duck and onion to the grill grates or pan and cook over medium heat until the duck is cooked to medium to well done.

On a large plate, evenly spread out the prepared chives. Plate the cooked duck on top, sprinkling the sesame seeds evenly as garnish.

---

# Mackerel Gui
## Godeungeo Gui
## 고등어 구이

dF  gF  -5  -3o

*Godeungeo gui*, salt-grilled mackerel, also called *go-galbi* in the city of Busan and Gyeongnam province, is a popular dish as a meal or when drinking. While it can impart a strong fish smell when pan-fried at home, it can also be simply prepared in an air fryer.

**Preparation time:** 15 minutes
**Cooking time:** 5 minutes
**Serves:** 4

4 mackerel fillets (5 oz/150 g each)
Salt
4 tablespoons neutral cooking oil

Pat the mackerel dry with paper towels. Season the flesh side of each fillet with a pinch of salt and let brine for 10 minutes.

Pour the cooking oil into a nonstick frying pan and place the mackerel skin-side down. Set over high heat and cook for 2 minutes. Reduce the heat to medium-low, flip the fillets to the flesh side, and cook for 1½ minutes. Serve hot.

## Gochujang Whitebait Gui
### Baengeopo Gochujang Gui
### 고추장 뱅어포 구이

dF -3o

*Baengeo-po* are sheets of pressed dried small whitefish or icefish. Readily available in Korean supermarkets, it makes a really easy *banchan* (side dish) when brushed with seasoning and grilled.

Preparation time: 10 minutes
Cooking time: 15 minutes
Serves: 2

For the sauce:
2 tablespoons gochujang (red chili paste)
1 tablespoon minced garlic
½ tablespoon minced scallion (spring onion)
2 teaspoons sugar
1 teaspoon ground sesame seeds
1 teaspoon sesame oil

To assemble:
2 sheets baengeo-po (whitebait sheet)
½ tablespoon neutral cooking oil
½ tablespoon sesame oil
½ teaspoon sesame seeds

**Make the sauce:** In a bowl, stir together the gochujang, 1 tablespoon water, the garlic, scallion, sugar, ground sesame seeds, and sesame oil. Set the sauce aside.

**To assemble:** Cut the baengeo-po sheets in half. In a small saucer, combine the cooking oil and sesame oil until well incorporated. Brush each side of the sheets with the mixture.

Heat a large frying pan over low heat. Add the baengeo-po and fry on both sides until golden, avoiding any charring. Remove from the heat.

Lay one cooked baengeo-po sheet on a cutting board and brush with the reserved sauce. Place another sheet on top and brush on more sauce and set aside. Repeat for the remaining pieces.

Heat a frying pan over low heat and cook the seasoned baengeo-po on both sides for 2 minutes each. Remove from the heat and cut the finished sheets into easy-to-eat, 1½ × 2½-inch (4 × 6 cm) pieces. Sprinkle the sesame seeds as a garnish to finish. In an airtight container, this will keep for up to 5 days.

## Bonnet Bellflower Root Gui
### Deodeok Gui
### 더덕 구이

dF vg vE

*Deodeok*, bonnet bellflower root, has a pleasantly subtle bitter flavor and has health benefits similar to ginseng. When pounding the *deodeok* at home, the natural fragrance is so strong that it can perfume the house. It used to be foraged in the mountains of Korea, but now it is field cultivated as well and is much more commonly available.

Preparation time: 20 minutes
Cooking time: 20 minutes
Serves: 4

14 oz (400 g) deodeok

For the gochujang sauce:
1 tablespoon gochujang (red chili paste)
1 tablespoon corn (golden) syrup
1 tablespoon sesame oil
1 tablespoon gochugaru (red chili flakes)
½ tablespoon ganjang (Korean soy sauce)
½ tablespoon sugar
1 teaspoon minced garlic

For cooking:
4 tablespoons sesame oil
1 tablespoon ganjang (Korean soy sauce)
1 tablespoon sesame seeds

Wash the deodeok in a large bowl with cold water to get rid of all dirt. Trim away any hardened parts and peel the skin. Slice the deodeok lengthwise in half. Cover a cutting board with plastic wrap (cling film), place the deodeok on top, cover it with another sheet of plastic, wrap, and pound out using a tenderizer until flattened.

**Make the gochujang sauce:** In a small bowl, stir together the gochujang, 1 tablespoon water, the corn syrup, sesame oil, gochugaru, soy sauce, sugar, and garlic.

**Cook the deodeok:** In a small bowl, stir together the sesame oil and soy sauce. Brush the sesame oil mixture evenly onto both sides of the deodeok. Heat a nonstick pan over medium heat, add the deodeok, and cook for 30 seconds on each side. Reduce the heat to low. Using a spoon, begin to evenly brush the gochujang sauce over both sides of the deodeok, staying over low heat to avoid burning. Serve hot garnished with sesame seeds.

Banchan

# Galbi

*Galbi* translates to "ribs" or "short ribs." Beef ribs and pork ribs are both popular in Korean cuisine.

When referring simply to *galbi*, Koreans will probably think of beef short ribs. Grilled beef short ribs are considered the best cut of all grilled meats, and this dish embodies the Korean grilled meat culture in its essence.

Short ribs have a great taste due to the optimal balance of the rich beef meat and marbling. The cow has thirteen rib bones in total. The first five ribs are designated as *bon-galbi,* the sixth through eighth ribs are designated as *ggot-galbi*, and the ninth through thirteenth as *cham-galbi*. *Bon-galbi* is the toughest of the rib cuts and is used for long-cooking dishes, such as soups. *Cham-galbi* is often sliced bone-in and used for LA *galbi*, or its meat is trimmed to make different meat grill cuts. The most prized and delicious cut of these is the *ggot-galbi,* translating to "flower short ribs."

These "flower ribs" contain the most tender meat of all the ribs, and they have the highest quality of marbling of all parts of the entire cow. They also boast a thick size compared to the other ribs, adding to their status. Because the short rib meat is attached to the bone, the muscle fibers are thicker than the sirloin or tenderloin and the connective tissue is well developed. While these features add to the deep flavors of the ribs, if incorrectly handled the meat can be tough to chew. In Korea, applying different knife cuts and scoring the meat has been used for centuries to solve these problems. The traditional butchering method of cutting the ribs into long sheets while keeping the meat intact to the bone, or scoring one short rib more than one hundred times, are long-standing methods. The two common ways to prepare these short ribs are to simply grill them unseasoned to enjoy the flavor of the meat on its own or to marinate them in *jang* (fermented soybean sauces)-based seasonings.

# LA Short Rib Gui
## LA Galbi
## LA갈비

dF

The LA *galbi* is a dish that was created and popularized by Korean immigrants in the United States and then became a hit in the motherland as well. LA *galbi* created a new style of butchering short ribs, where the ribs are left connected but cut across all of the rib bones to make smaller strips.

While most origin stories for LA *galbi* are probably urban myths, the most plausible one is that the name is derived from the English word "lateral," because the ribs are cut laterally, cutting across all the ribs. The theory is that Koreans who immigrated to the United States began to butcher the rib meat in this way to make it easier to grill in the smaller format of Korea's signature tabletop grill. Today, many restaurants specialize in LA *galbi* even in Korea, and ribs cut this way are also easily available in many supermarkets, making it not only a favorite during holidays, but also accessible for everyday home-cooked meals.

Preparation time: 20 minutes, plus 12 hours up to 1 day marinating time
Cooking time: 10–15 minutes
Serves: 2

1 lb 5 oz (600 g) LA-style Korean short ribs

**For the marinade:**
7 oz (200 g) Asian pear, peeled
3 tablespoons jinjang (dark Korean soy sauce)
3 tablespoons rice cooking wine
1 tablespoon mirin
1 tablespoon corn (golden) syrup
1 tablespoon light brown sugar
2 tablespoons minced garlic
2 tablespoons minced scallion (spring onion)
1 teaspoon sesame oil
½ teaspoon minced fresh ginger
¼ teaspoon freshly ground black pepper

**To finish:**
1 scallion (spring onion), slivered

Because the short ribs were cut across a lot of bones, there may be impurities or bone fragments that remain attached to the flesh. Rinse the ribs under cold running water, then set them in a sieve to drain well. Pat dry with paper towels.

**Make the marinade:** Grate the pear into a bowl. Add 6 tablespoons water, the soy sauce, wine, mirin, corn syrup, brown sugar, garlic, scallion, sesame oil, ginger, and black pepper and stir until well incorporated.

In a large airtight container, combine the short ribs and the marinade and mix until well incorporated. Let marinate for at least 12 hours and up to 1 day in the refrigerator.

**To finish:** When ready to cook, remove the container from the refrigerator. Place the marinated short ribs in a large, cold frying pan and set the frying pan over medium-low heat (higher heat will caramelize or burn the marinade). Cook for 2 minutes on each side, or until both sides are well cooked.

Serve the cooked short ribs garnishes with the scallion.

# Korean Short Rib Patties Gui
## Tteok Galbi
## 떡갈비

DF

*Tteok galbi* is a dish that's made of seasoned ground (minced) short rib meat shaped into a tube around the rib bone and grilled. The name literally translates to "rice cake short ribs," a reference to the tube shape of the meat mixture. It is a dish that Koreans of all ages enjoy due to its tender, seasoned meat.

Traditional *tteok galbi* is cooked over a medium-heat charcoal fire, but these days it is more often cooked on the stovetop (hob), or even in the oven. Also, instead of wrapping the meat mixture around a bone, these are simply cooked as patties. If beef short rib is unavailable, any lean beef cut can be used in its place, including ground (minced) beef.

Preparation time: 30 minutes, plus 30 minutes marinating time
Cooking time: 10 minutes
Serves: 2

14 oz (400 g) beef short ribs
3½ oz (100 g) Asian pear, peeled
2 tablespoons ganjang (Korean soy sauce)
2 tablespoons minced scallion (spring onion)
1 tablespoon light brown sugar
1 tablespoon minced garlic
1 teaspoon sesame oil
1 teaspoon freshly ground black pepper
1 tablespoon glutinous rice flour
1 tablespoon neutral cooking oil

Remove any tough tendons from the short ribs. Using a knife, coarsely grind (mince) the meat, avoiding using a processor or making too fine of a mixture for the mouthfeel.

Grate the pear into a bowl. Add the soy sauce, scallion, brown sugar, garlic, sesame oil, and black pepper. Add the ground meat, sprinkle with the rice flour, and mix until well combined. Let marinate in the refrigerator for 30 minutes.

Remove from the refrigerator. Divide the mixture into 4 equal portions and shape into round patties 1 inch (2.5 cm) thick.

In a frying pan, heat the cooking oil over medium heat. Add the patties and cook for 2 minutes on the first side. Reduce the heat to low and cook the other side for 2–3 minutes to finish. Plate and serve.

**Variation:** Many variations include ingredients added either to the beef mixture or as garnish, including the addition of chopped nuts, such as pine nuts, almonds, or walnuts.

# Bulgogi

*Bulgogi* refers to dishes in which thinly sliced meat is marinated in various seasonings and traditionally grilled over an open fire. Different types of meat, including chicken, duck, beef, and pork, can be used to make *bulgogi*, but when referred to simply as *bulgogi*, it refers to beef *bulgogi*. When made with another type of meat, another word is added before *bulgogi*, such as duck *bulgogi* or pork *bulgogi*.

There are two distinct types of *bulgogi*: those traditionally grilled over charcoal and those made with meat broth. In addition, there are many other regional methods of cooking, such as stir-fried in a pan or simmered in an earthenware pot.

Each region in Korea has a signature style of cooking bulgogi, and there are three famous regional *bulgogi* recipes. The Seoul *bulgogi* pours beef broth onto the grilled meat for a simmered effect and has a sweet flavor. Gwangyang-style *bulgogi* highlights the inherent flavor of the beef by minimizing the seasoning used, marinating the meat just prior to grilling. And finally, the Eonyang *bulgogi* grills the sliced marinated beef in chunkier clumps over charcoal.

# Gwangyang-Style Bulgogi
## Gwangyang Bulgogi
## 광양 불고기

dF -3o

This style of *bulgogi* originates from Gwangyang, Jeollanam-do, in the southern tip of Korea. It is distinct from other styles of *bulgogi* in that instead of marinating the thinly sliced beef, it's seasoned just before grilling over charcoal.

Gwangyang has long been known for its production of charcoal and charcoal grilling in its regional cuisine. Grilled over the best charcoal, the meat's inherent flavors are heightened, and the minimal, light seasoning was developed to highlight the harmonization of the charcoal and beef.

**Preparation time: 10 minutes**
**Cooking time: 10 minutes**
**Serves: 2**

2 tablespoons jinjang (dark Korean soy sauce)
½ tablespoon light brown sugar
1 tablespoon rice cooking wine
1 tablespoon minced garlic
1 teaspoon sesame oil
¼ teaspoon freshly ground black pepper
14 oz (400 g) beef sirloin, thinly sliced to ⅛ inch (4 mm) thick
Scallion, thinly sliced, or pine nut powder (optional)

In a large bowl, stir together the soy sauce, brown sugar, wine, garlic, sesame oil, and black pepper. Set aside.

Prepare an outdoor grill (barbecue), preferably charcoal.

Just before grilling, fold the beef into the soy mixture. Add the slices to the grill and cook evenly on both sides. If desired, garnish the plated meat with thinly sliced scallion or pine nut powder to finish.

# Seoul-Style Bulgogi
## Seoul Bulgogi
## 서울식 불고기

dF

The Seoul style of *bulgogi* is distinct in its use of broth and the sweetness of the marinade. It begins by grilling the meat and vegetables (such as onions and mushrooms) and then finishes by pouring a seasoned broth and simmering together. In the home kitchen, many people typically cook with the broth from the beginning in the style of hotpots (see pages 356–363). The traditional method is to cook over a specialized hill-shaped hot plate, with a concave outer ring to hold in the broth. The *bulgogi* is first grilled in the center, with the broth being poured in later, boiling with the meat to be enjoyed in two different forms. In specialized Seoul-style *bulgogi* restaurants, glass noodles or *naengmyun* (North Korean noodles) are often added into the broth to round out the meal.

Preparation time: 15 minutes, plus 30 minutes up to 12 hours marinating time
Cooking time: 15 minutes
Serves: 2

For the marinated beef:
4 tablespoons jinjang (dark Korean soy sauce)
1 tablespoon light brown sugar
2 tablespoons Korean pear juice
1 tablespoon mirin
1 tablespoon rice cooking wine
1 tablespoon minced garlic
1 tablespoon minced scallion (spring onion)
1 teaspoon sesame oil
¼ teaspoon freshly ground black pepper
14 oz (400 g) beef sirloin (topside), thinly sliced to 1/16 inch (2 mm) thick

For the vegetables:
1 oz (30 g) enoki mushrooms
1½ oz (40 g) fresh shiitake mushrooms
1 oz (30 g) daepa (Korean scallion)
3½ oz (100 g) onion

For the broth:
½ large sheet (10 g) dasima
1 dried shiitake mushroom
1 teaspoon cheongjang (light Korean soy sauce)
3 mugwort leaves

**Marinate the beef:** In a small bowl, combine the soy sauce, brown sugar, pear juice, mirin, wine, garlic, scallion, sesame oil, and black pepper and mix until uniform. In an airtight container, combine the marinade and the beef and let marinade for at least 30 minutes and up to 12 hours in the refrigerator.

**Prepare the vegetables:** Remove the roots from the enoki mushrooms. Remove the stems from the shiitake mushrooms and cut the caps into ⅛-inch (3 mm) slices. Slice the daepa on a diagonal into ⅛-inch (3 mm) thick 2½-inch (6 cm) long slices. Cut the onion into ⅛-inch (3 mm) slices. Set all the vegetables aside.

**Make the broth:** In a pot, combine 2 cups (16 fl oz/480 ml) water, the dasima, dried shiitake, and soy sauce and bring to a boil over high heat. Reduce the heat to medium and boil for 10 minutes before removing from the heat.

When ready to cook, in a bowl, combine the marinated beef slices, fresh mushrooms, daepa, and onion and mix together.

**If using a traditional Korean grill:** Heat the grill over medium heat. Once heated, grill the bulgogi mix in the center, enjoying the meat as it is cooked. When one-third of the meat remains in the pan, pour the prepared broth into the side of the grill and combine with the remaining beef. Add the mugwort. Eat it as you would a hotpot.

**If cooking on the stovetop (hob):** Heat a deep frying pan or a shallow pot over medium heat. Add the bulgogi mix and pan-fry. When it's about halfway cooked, pour in the broth and let simmer for 2–3 minutes, adding in the mugwort to garnish at the end. Plate in a deep plate or shallow bowl to serve. If using a tabletop burner, reduce the heat to the lowest setting while enjoying.

# Eonyang-Style Bulgogi
## Eonyang Bulgogi
## 언양 불고기

dF

A local specialty of Eonyang, Ulsan, a city in southeastern Korea, this version of *bulgogi*, marinated thin-sliced beef, is unique in that it's pounded and massaged into a loose patty-like thickness and grilled over charcoal. Eonyang was famous for its slaughterhouses during the Japanese colonial period, and its cuisine gained national fame through word of mouth among highway construction workers during the 1960s.

Preparation time: 10 minutes, plus 30 minutes marinating time
Cooking time: 10 minutes
Serves: 2

14 oz (400 g) beef sirloin (rump), cut into thin 1/16-inch (2 mm) thick slices

**For the marinade:**
3 tablespoons jinjang (dark Korean soy sauce)
1 tablespoon light brown sugar
1 tablespoon honey
1 tablespoon minced garlic
1 tablespoon minced scallion (spring onion)
1 teaspoon sesame oil
¼ teaspoon freshly ground black pepper

Place the beef slices on a cutting board. Tenderize by gently tapping with the spine of the knife in both directions.

**Make the marinade:** In a large bowl, combine the soy sauce, brown sugar, honey, garlic, scallion, sesame oil, and black pepper. Add the beef and combine with the sauce, gently massaging in the marinade. Let marinate for 30 minutes. (The bulgogi can be marinated in the refrigerator for days in advance of grilling.)

Preheat a charcoal grill (barbecue) or a stovetop (hob) grill (griddle) pan to medium heat.

Using your hands, assemble the meat slices into 2 loose thin patties about 4 inches (10 cm) in diameter and ⅜ inch (1 cm) thick. Place the patties on the grill grates or in the pan and grill until the patties are cooked on both sides.

**Variation:** Grilling sliced shiitake mushrooms or chives along with the beef is a popular way to add additional flavor and aroma.

# 조림 Jorim Braised

*Jorim* refers to meat, fish, or vegetables seasoned and simmered in a sauce over a low flame until the sauce is reduced to a glaze. The most important part of making *jorim* dishes is that the sauce is well absorbed into the ingredient, and that the flavor and nutrition of the ingredients are well incorporated into the sauce, while maintaining the integrity of the ingredients. As such, *jorim* should be cooked at low temperatures for a long time and requires that the seasoning be light at first.

Radishes and potatoes are popular ingredients in *jorim* dishes due to their firm structures. When cooking with these types of vegetables, too little water can cause the ingredients to stick to the bottom of the pan or pot, so it is advisable to increase the volume of water when incorporating these vegetables. The pan or pot used to make *jorim* dishes should have a heavy bottom to distribute the heat evenly over the long cooking time, and it is important to have a lid to control the moisture and heat.

*Jorim* made with beef and vegetables are usually made with a soy sauce-based seasoning, and pork and chicken *jorim* are most popular paired with either a soy sauce or *gochujang* (red chili paste)- based seasoning. Fish-based *jorim* can be paired with various seasonings made from soy sauce, *doenjang* (fermented soybean paste), and *gochugaru* (red chili flakes) for a clean, spicy finish.

The base sauces below can be used to make a simple, satisfying *jorim* using the protein of one's choice and vegetables. The following sauces make enough for 1 pound (500 g) of protein, such as fish, pork, or chicken.

---

**Ganjang-Based Sauce**

4 tablespoons ganjang (Korean soy sauce)

1 tablespoon minced garlic

1 tablespoon minced scallion (spring onion)

2 teaspoons corn (golden) syrup or rice syrup

½ teaspoon minced fresh ginger

**Optional:** 2 tablespoons gochugaru (red chili flakes)

In a small bowl, stir everything together with ⅔ cup (5 fl oz/160 ml) water until completely uniform.

**Doenjang-Based Sauce**

3 tablespoons doenjang (fermented soybean paste)

½ tablespoon ganjang (Korean soy sauce)

½ tablespoon sugar

½ teaspoon minced fresh ginger

**Optional:** 1 teaspoon gochugaru (red chili flakes

In a small bowl, stir everything together with 1 cup (8 fl oz/ 240 ml) water until completely uniform.

# Tofu Jorim
Dubu Jorim
두부 조림

Tofu *jorim* is one of the most common *banchan* (side dishes) in a home setting. The *jorim* sauce is delicious, and a bite of tofu *jorim*, its sauce, and freshly made rice is one of the most beloved in Korean cuisine. We highly recommend trying this easy-to-enjoy bite.

**Preparation time: 10 minutes**
**Cooking time: 15 minutes**
**Serves: 2**

10 oz (300 g) firm tofu
½ teaspoon salt
1 tablespoon sesame oil

**For the sauce:**
2 tablespoons jinjang (dark Korean soy sauce)
1 tablespoon mirin
1 tablespoon minced garlic
1 tablespoon gochugaru (red chili flakes), optional
½ tablespoon sesame oil
1 teaspoon sugar

**For the jorim:**
7 oz (200 g) onions, halved and thinly sliced
1 oz (30 g) daepa (Korean scallion), cut into 1½–2½-inch (4–6 cm) julienne
½ teaspoon sesame seeds

Halve the block of tofu and cut each half into slices ½ inch (1.3 cm) wide. Spread the cut pieces on a flat surface, lightly salt all the pieces, and let sit for 5 minutes. Remove all excess moisture from the tofu after 5 minutes with paper towels.

Heat a frying pan over medium heat and add the sesame oil. Pan-fry the tofu slices on each side for 2 minutes. Place the cooked tofu pieces on a large plate.

**Make the sauce:** In a bowl, stir together ⅔ cup (5 fl oz/160 ml) water, the soy sauce, mirin, garlic, gochugaru (if using), sesame oil, and sugar.

**Make the jorim:** In a deep frying pan or a pot, layer in half of the onion. Place the fried tofu pieces on top, avoiding overlapping, and cover with the rest of the onions. Cover with the sauce and set the pan over high heat. Once the sauce comes to a boil, cover with a lid, reduce the heat to medium-low, and simmer for 5 minutes. Uncover and spoon the sauce evenly over the tofu. Add the daepa and simmer for 5 minutes over medium heat.

Serve on a large plate or in a bowl. Garnish with sesame seeds.

**Variation:** To add depth to the flavor, add 5–7 Korean dried anchovies to the sauce.

## Soft-Boiled Egg Jangjorim

Dalgyal Bansuk Jangjorim

달걀반숙 장조림

dF vE -5 [o]

**Soft-boiled egg *jangjorim* is the perfect pairing for rice, and the sauce from this dish can be a great base for additional dishes, such as Spicy Bibimguksu (page 366) or *bibimbap* (mixed rice).**

**Preparation time: 10 minutes, plus 3–4 hours marinating time**
**Cooking time: 20 minutes**
**Serves: 2–3**

1 cup (8 fl oz/240 ml) yangjo ganjang (naturally brewed soy sauce)
½ cup (4 fl oz/120 ml) mirin
5 tablespoons light brown sugar
3½ oz (100 g) onion, cut into chunks
6 eggs

**For garnish (optional):**
1 oz (25 g) fresh green chili, diced
1 oz (25 g) fresh red chili, diced
½ tablespoon sesame seeds

In a small saucepan, combine the soy sauce, ½ cup (4 fl oz/120 ml) water, the mirin, brown sugar, and onion and boil just until all the sugar is dissolved. Remove from the heat and set the sauce aside.

Set up a bowl of ice and water. In a pot, place the eggs with water to cover. Bring to a boil over high heat and boil for 6½ minutes. Transfer the eggs to the ice bath to quickly cool. Peel the eggs.

Remove the onion from the sauce and discard. In an airtight container, place the peeled soft-boiled eggs and pour in the sauce until the eggs are fully submerged. If using the garnish, add them now.

Let sit at room temperature for 3–4 hours or until fully cooled. The eggs can be stored in the refrigerator for up to 3 days.

---

## Dasima Konjac Jorim

다시마 곤약 조림

dF vg vE

**This recipe is a simple *banchan* (side dish) made with *dasima* seaweed and konjac root, but the savory flavor of the *dasima* and the bouncy texture of the konjac is a great combination. Various ingredients can be added, including quail eggs and *mu* (Korean radish), or for a spicy kick, some fresh Cheongyang chilies.**

**Preparation time: 10 minutes, plus 30 minutes soaking time**
**Cooking time: 20 minutes**
**Serves: 2–4**

2 large sheets dasima (1½ oz/40 g)
7 oz (200 g) konjac root, cut into 1-inch (2.5 cm) bite-size pieces
3 tablespoons ganjang (Korean soy sauce)
2 tablespoons rice cooking wine
2 tablespoons sugar
1 tablespoon sesame oil

In a bowl, soak the dasima in 3 cups (24 fl oz/710 ml) warm water for 30 minutes to rehydrate fully. Reserving 1 cup (8 fl oz/240 ml) of the soaking water, drain the dasima. Cut into 1-inch (2.5 cm) bite-size pieces.

In a small pot of boiling water, blanch the konjac for 1 minute. Drain and set aside to cool.

In a pot, combine the soy sauce, wine, and sugar with the reserved dasima soaking water and bring to a boil over medium heat. Once boiling, add the dasima and konjac pieces and cook until most of the moisture has evaporated, about 13 minutes. Stir in the sesame oil and serve.

# Young Cabbage & Anchovy Doenjang Jorim
## Eolgari Myeolchi Doenjang Jorim
## 얼갈이 멸치 된장조림

dF

**Preparation time:** 20 minutes
**Cooking time:** 30 minutes
**Serves:** 2

1 head young napa cabbage (Chinese leaf; about 1 lb 5 oz/600 g)
½ teaspoon salt
4 tablespoons doenjang (fermented soybean paste)
1 tablespoon cheongjang (light Korean soy sauce)
1 tablespoon minced garlic

**For the jorim:**
1 tablespoon perilla oil
3 cups (24 fl oz/710 ml) Vegetable Broth (page 313), Beef Broth (page 315), or water
15 dried anchovies
½ oz (15 g) daepa (Korean scallion), cut into scant ¼-inch (5 mm) lengths
1¾ oz (50 g) fresh red chilies, cut on a diagonal into thin rings
1¾ oz (50 g) fresh green chilies, cut on a diagonal into thin rings

Young cabbages have a delicious savory flavor profile. Cooked with the equally savory *doenjang* (fermented soybean paste) and dried anchovies, this *jorim banchan* is delicious when mixed with rice or used as a substitution for *ssamjang* (dipping sauce for *ssam*) when eating *ssam* (wraps).

Remove the root from the napa cabbage and separate into individual leaves. Rinse each leaf under cold running water.

Set up a large bowl of ice and water. In a pot, bring 4¼ cups (34 fl oz/1 liter) water and the salt to a boil. Add the cabbage and blanch for 2–3 minutes. Immediately transfer the cabbage to the ice bath to completely cool. Gently squeeze the cooled cabbage with your hands to remove excess water and cut into 2½-inch (6 cm) pieces.

In a large bowl, combine the doenjang, soy sauce, and garlic. Add the cabbage and toss until fully mixed. Let marinate for about 10 minutes.

**Make the jorim:** In a pot, heat the perilla oil over medium heat. Add the seasoned cabbage and stir-fry for 2–3 minutes. Add the broth or water, the anchovies, and daepa and bring to a boil over high heat. Once it reaches a boil, reduce the heat to medium and simmer for 20 minutes. Stir in the chilies and remove from the heat.

Serve in deep bowls.

**Variation:** To make a vegetarian or vegan version, omit the anchovies.

## Peanuts & Beans Jorim
### Kongjaban Ttangkong Jorim
### 콩자반 땅콩 조림

dF vg vE

Braised beans, *kongjorim*, is a common *banchan* (side dish) that was often included in lunch boxes. It's easy to make and keeps well, and the sweet salty beans are great eaten with rice. While it's usually made with black beans, it can also be made with kidney beans.

**Preparation time:** 10 minutes, plus 2 hours soaking time and chilling time
**Cooking time:** 30 minutes
**Serves:** 2–4

1 cup (180 g) dried black beans
6 tablespoons ganjang (Korean soy sauce)
3 tablespoons rice cooking wine
3 tablespoons corn (golden) syrup
1 tablespoon sugar
½ cup (80 g) roasted peanuts
1 tablespoon sesame oil
1 teaspoon sesame seeds

Rinse the black beans under cold running water. Set in a bowl with water to cover and soak for 2 hours.

In a pot, bring 5 cups (40 fl oz/1.2 liters) water to a boil. Once boiling, add the soaked beans, reduce the heat to medium, and cook for 15 minutes. Add the soy sauce, wine, corn syrup, and sugar and braise until the liquid has reduced by half, about 10 minutes.

Add the roasted peanuts and cook until the moisture has almost fully evaporated, about 5 minutes. Stir in the sesame oil and sesame seeds. Transfer the braised beans and peanuts to a bowl and let cool completely. Serve chilled.

## Potato & Shishito Jorim
### Gamja Kkwarigochu Jorim
### 감자 꽈리고추 조림

dF vg vE -30

The best of the potato crops are harvested beginning in late spring, and this is one of the most representative of the early summer *banchan* (side dishes). The fragrance that fills the kitchen when boiling fresh, sweet potatoes and shishitos with the soy marinade is enough to make one immediately hungry. It's great with wine, and can also be a great side to rice and meat.

**Preparation time:** 10 minutes
**Cooking time:** 15 minutes
**Serves:** 2

**For the sauce:**
3 tablespoons yangjo ganjang (naturally brewed soy sauce)
1½ tablespoons light brown sugar
1 tablespoon minced scallion (spring onion)
2 teaspoons minced garlic

**For the jorim:**
1 tablespoon neutral cooking oil
10 oz (300 g) potatoes, peeled and cut into ⅜–¾-inch (1–2 cm) cubes
3½ oz (100 g) onion, slivered
5–6 shishito peppers, stemmed but whole
½ teaspoon sesame oil
¼ teaspoon sesame seeds

**Make the sauce:** In a bowl, stir together ½ cup (4 fl oz/120 ml) water, the soy sauce, brown sugar, scallion, and garlic. Set aside.

**Make the jorim:** In a deep frying pan or wok, heat the cooking oil over medium heat. Add the potato cubes and stir-fry evenly for about 2 minutes. Add the sauce and onion, cover with a lid, and let simmer over medium heat for 6–7 minutes. Uncover, add the shishitos and simmer for 2–3 minutes. Remove from the heat, add the sesame oil and the sesame seeds, and stir well.

## Lotus Root Jorim
### Yeongeun Jorim
### 연근 조림

dF vg vE -30

The lotus root, the tuber of the lotus flower, is in season in fall, but it is available year-round. It is one of the favorite ingredients in Korea, because of its unique crunchy texture. This braised lotus root dish, simmered with soy sauce and sugar, is particularly popular and can be often seen on home tables and restaurants alike. Some cooks like to peel the lotus root and soak it in vinegar water to remove the astringent taste before cooking.

**Preparation time:** 10 minutes
**Cooking time:** 20 minutes
**Serves:** 2–4

9½ oz (275 g) lotus roots
3 tablespoons ganjang (Korean soy sauce)
1 tablespoon sugar
1 tablespoon rice cooking wine
1 tablespoon corn (golden) syrup
1 teaspoon sesame oil

First prepare the lotus roots. Wash the lotus roots well until cold running water and peel. Cut into thin ⅛-inch (3 mm) slices.

In a saucepan, combine the lotus roots and ¾ cup (6 fl oz/175 ml) water and bring to a boil over medium heat. Once boiling, cook for 5 minutes. Add the soy sauce, sugar, and wine and continue to cook until the moisture has almost fully evaporated, about 10 more minutes. Add the corn syrup and sesame oil and stir well until uniform. Serve hot.

---

## Beef Jangjorim
### Sogogi Jangjorim
### 소고기 장조림

dF                                        [ㅁ]

One of the most popular dishes of *jorim* cuisine, the beef *jangjorim* is without a doubt one of the best pairings for a warm bowl of rice. Even without any other *banchan* (side dishes), a good *jangjorim* provides a hearty, delicious meal in one. For an added touch of richness, drizzling sesame oil (or in modern times, a little butter) and mixing together with rice creates a singular dish fit for any diner.

It's important to select a lean cut of beef. And if you can only find presliced meat, skip the blanching step and simply marinate with the sauce.

**Preparation time:** 10 minutes
**Cooking time:** 1 hour 20 minutes
**Serves:** 4

10 oz (300 g) beef brisket or shank meat, cut into 2-inch (5 cm) cubes
3½ oz (100 g) onion, peeled
1 oz (30 g) daepa (Korean scallion), cut into several pieces
⅓-inch (8 mm) piece fresh ginger
8 black peppercorns
7 cloves garlic, peeled

For the jorim:
¾ cup (6 fl oz/175 ml) yangjo ganjang (naturally brewed soy sauce)
4 tablespoons light brown sugar
2 tablespoons rice cooking wine
1 dried red chili pepper
4 kkwari (shishito) peppers

Bring a small pot of water to a boil. Add the beef cubes and blanch for 4–5 minutes. Drain and cool the beef under cold running water to wash off any excess fat and impurities from the meat.

In a pot, combine the blanched meat, 3 cups (24 fl oz/710 ml) water, the onion, daepa, ginger, peppercorns, and garlic and bring to a boil over high heat. Reduce the heat to medium-low and boil for 30 minutes. Remove the meat from the pot and let cool at room temperature for 5 minutes (discard the cooking liquid and solids). Either shred the meat using your hands, or cut the meat against the grain as thin as possible with a knife.

**Make the jorim:** In a pot, combine the soy sauce, 3 cups (24 fl oz/710 ml) water, the brown sugar, wine, chili, and peppers. Add the beef and bring to a boil over high heat. Once it reaches a boil, reduce to medium heat and simmer for 25 minutes. Discard the dried chili.

When serving, first plate the appropriate amount of meat per serving and pour over 2–3 tablespoons of the cooking liquid or enough to make sure that the meat stays moist. Any remaining jangjorim can be kept in an airtight container in the refrigerator for up to 5 days.

**Variation:** It's popular to add boiled eggs in the last step.

# Beef Short Ribs Jorim
## Sogalbijjim
## 소갈비찜

---

dF

This short rib dish makes an appearance during any important holiday feast or celebration, including being a favorite birthday dish. The short rib is one of the most popular cuts of beef in Korea, and this dish highlights the tender rib meat and bone-in flavors with the soy sauce–based *jorim*. The resulting sauce of this dish is especially flavorful and should not be wasted, so make sure to enjoy the braising sauce by serving it over rice.

Preparation time: 15 minutes, plus 1½ hours soaking, standing, and marinating time
Cooking time: 1 hour
Serves: 3

2¼ lb (1 kg) bone-in beef short rib, cut into 1½-inch (4 cm) chunks

**For the sauce:**
5 tablespoons yangjo ganjang (naturally brewed soy sauce)
2 tablespoons light brown sugar
2 tablespoons mirin
7 oz (200 g) Asian pear, peeled and cut into chunks
3½ oz (100 g) onion, peeled and cut into chunks
3 tablespoons minced scallions (spring onions)
2 tablespoons minced garlic
2 tablespoons sesame oil
1 tablespoon ground sesame seeds
½ teaspoon freshly ground black pepper

**For the broth:**
3–4 cloves garlic, peeled
½ oz (10 g) fresh ginger
½ oz (15 g) daepa (Korean scallion)
3½ oz (100 g) onion, peeled
½ teaspoon black peppercorns

**For the jorim:**
7 oz (200 g) mu (Korean radish), cut into 1¼-inch (3 cm) cubes
3½ oz (100 g) carrots, cut into 1¼-inch (3 cm) cubes
1½ oz (40 g) fresh shiitake mushrooms, stemmed, caps quartered
7 oz (200 g) onions, cut into 1¼-inch (3 cm) cubes
1 oz (30 g) daepa (Korean scallion), cut into 1½-inch (4 cm) lengths

Soak the short ribs in cold water for 30 minutes to remove the blood and impurities. Drain and rinse them.

**Meanwhile, make the sauce:** In a blender, combine the soy sauce, brown sugar, mirin, pear, onion, scallions, garlic, sesame oil, ground sesame seeds, and black pepper and blend until smooth.

**Make the broth:** In a pot, bring 7 cups (56 fl oz/1.7 liters) water to a boil. Once boiling, add the short ribs. When the water comes back to a boil, remove the ribs and rinse under running water. Keep the pot of cooking liquid on the stove (hob).

Return the ribs to the pot. Add the garlic, ginger, daepa, onion, and peppercorns. Bring to a boil over medium heat and cook for 20 minutes. Remove from the heat and let sit for 20 minutes. Remove the short ribs from the broth, but reserve the broth.

**Make the jorim:** Add the short ribs to another large pot. Add the blended sauce and mix well, ensuring that all pieces are covered. Let marinate for 30 minutes.

Add the radish, carrots, and shiitakes to the short ribs. Pour the reserved broth through a sieve into the pot (discard the solids). Cover the pot with a lid and bring to a boil over high heat. Reduce to medium heat and boil for 30 minutes. Add the onions and daepa and boil for another 10 minutes.

Serve the hot dish in a large bowl.

**Variation:** Adding dried red chili peppers or fresh shishito peppers when adding the onion and daepa at the end will give a nice pepper fragrance to the dish.

# Chicken Wing Jorim
## Dak-nalgae Jorim
## 닭날개 조림

dF

This is a dish made by first pan-grilling chicken wings, then braising them in a savory soy sauce–based sauce. Compared to the popular seasoned deep-fried chicken wings, this dish boasts a clean, savory flavor. *Yuja* (yuzu) syrup is added to incorporate a fragrant citrus fragrance. It's good as a *ban-chan* (side dish) but also great as a snack or as a drinking food. The sugar content can be adjusted to taste, and to incorporate spiciness, add some Cheongyang chilies.

**Preparation time:** 20 minutes
**Cooking time:** 15 minutes
**Serves:** 2–4

**For the sauce:**
6 tablespoons ganjang (Korean soy sauce)
4 tablespoons rice cooking wine
2 tablespoons sugar
2 tablespoons corn (golden) syrup
2 tablespoons yuja (yuzu) syrup

**For the jorim:**
4 tablespoons neutral cooking oil
24 chicken wings
2 teaspoons sesame seeds

**Make the sauce:** In a bowl, combine the soy sauce, 5 tablespoons water, the wine, sugar, corn syrup, and yuja syrup and mix well until uniform.

**Make the jorm:** In a nonstick frying pan, heat the cooking oil over medium heat. Add the chicken wings and brown on both sides, about 5 minutes total. Add the sauce and braise over medium heat until the liquid has fully reduced and the chicken wings are well coated with the shiny sauce, 10–15 minutes.

Serve the braised chicken wings garnished with the sesame seeds.

# Gochujang Chicken Jorim
## Dakbokkeumtang
## 닭볶음탕

DF

While it's commonly referred to as chicken *bokkeum tang*, combining the words *bokkeum* (stir-fry) and *tang* (soup or broth), this chicken dish is actually a *gochujang* (red chili paste)-based *jorim* dish. It's one of the most commonly prepared home dishes using chicken and is a widely popular dish.

**Preparation time:** 15 minutes
**Cooking time:** 25 minutes
**Serves:** 2–4

1 whole poussin or spring chicken (about 1 lb/500 g)

For the sauce:
3 tablespoons gochujang (red chili paste)
2 tablespoons yangjo ganjang (naturally brewed soy sauce)
2 tablespoons gochugaru (red chili flakes)
2 tablespoons minced garlic
1 tablespoon sugar
1 tablespoon mirin
1 tablespoon corn (golden) syrup
¼ teaspoon freshly ground black pepper

For the jorim:
2½ oz (75 g) potato, peeled and cut into 1¼-inch (3 cm) cubes
3½ oz (100 g) carrots, peeled and cut into 1¼-inch (3 cm) cubes
3½ oz (100 g) onion, cut into 1¼-inch (3 cm) cubes
1½ oz (40 g) fresh shiitake mushroom, stemmed, caps thinly sliced
1 oz (30 g) daepa (Korean scallion), cut into ⅜-inch (1 cm) diagonal slices
1 tablespoon neutral cooking oil
1 teaspoon sesame oil
½ teaspoon sesame seeds

Clean the chicken, making sure all the organs have been removed. Leaving it bone-in, cut the chicken into 1¼–1½-inch (3–4 cm) pieces. Rinse the pieces under cold running water to remove any blood. Pat dry with paper towels and set aside.

**Make the sauce:** In a bowl, combine the gochujang, soy sauce, gochugaru, garlic, sugar, mirin, corn syrup, and black pepper and mix until uniform.

**Make the jorim:** In a large bowl, combine the chicken, potato, carrots, onion, shiitakes, daepa, and the sauce and mix well. Let marinate for 5 minutes.

In a saucepan, heat the cooking oil over medium heat. Add the seasoned chicken mixture and stir-fry for 3–4 minutes. Add 3 cups (24 fl oz/710 ml) water. Increase the heat to high, cover with a lid, and bring to a boil. Reduce the heat to medium and boil for another 20 minutes. Remove from the heat and let stand for 5 minutes.

Stir in the sesame oil just before plating. Serve in bowls or deep plates. Garnish with sesame seeds.

Variations

• Omit the carrots if desired.

• Shredded perilla leaves are also a popular garnish along with the sesame seeds.

• To make a one-pot meal, add ½ cup (50 g) tteok (rice cakes) 5 minutes before removing from the heat.

# Andong Chicken Jorim
## Andong Jjim-dak
## 안동찜닭

dF

Originating from the city of Andong, in the central part of South Korea, Andong chicken is a famed *jorim* recipe based on soy sauce. It has become such a national staple that there are thousands of "Andong Chicken" specific restaurants throughout the country.

Preparation time: 15 minutes
Cooking time: 40 minutes
Serves: 2

1 whole poussin or spring chicken (about 1 lb/500 g)

For the sauce:
3 tablespoons jinjang (dark Korean soy sauce)
2 tablespoons yangjo ganjang (naturally brewed soy sauce)
2 tablespoons mirin
2 tablespoons light brown sugar
2 tablespoons rice syrup (or corn/ golden syrup)
1 tablespoon rice cooking wine
½ teaspoon freshly ground black pepper

For the jorim:
1 tablespoon neutral cooking oil
5 oz (150 g) potato, peeled, halved, and sliced ½ inch (1.3 cm) thick
3½ oz (100 g) carrots, peeled and cut into ½-inch (1.3 cm) rounds
3½ oz (100 g) onion, cut into slices ¾ inch (2 cm) thick
2½ oz (75 g) cucumber, unpeeled, cut into rounds ½ inch (1.3 cm) thick
1 oz (30 g) daepa (Korean scallion), cut into 1½-inch (4 cm) length
2 tablespoons minced Cheongyang chili
2 tablespoons minced garlic

Make sure all the organs have been removed from the chicken. Still with the bone-in and skin-on, cut the chicken into 1¼–1½-inch (3–4 cm) pieces. Rinse the chicken pieces under cold running water to get rid of any blood. Pat dry with paper towels and set aside.

**Make the sauce:** In a large bowl, combine both soy sauces, the mirin, brown sugar, rice syrup, wine, and black pepper and mix until uniform.

**Make the jorim:** Add the chicken and 1½ cups (12 fl oz/360 ml) water to the bowl of sauce and toss to coat. Set aside to marinate for 5 minutes.

Heat a pot or cast-iron skillet over medium heat and drizzle in the cooking oil. Reserving the marinade in the bowl, place the chicken pieces, skin-side down, into the pot and cook for 2 minutes. Stir in the potato and carrots. Add the sauce remaining in the bowl along with 1½ cups (12 fl oz/360 ml) water and boil for 20 minutes over medium heat.

Add the cucumber, daepa, chili, and garlic and boil over high heat for 2–3 minutes.

**Variation:** In many restaurants and at home, tteok (rice cakes) or glass noodles are added to the dish to make a full meal.

## Pig's Feet Jorim
### Jokbal
### 족발

dF

*Jokbal* is pig's feet (trotters) long braised in a soy sauce–based broth. The meat is served off the bone and thinly sliced. It's one of the most popular delivery foods in Korea. Instead of the lean hind legs, the front legs are mostly used for cooking *jokbal*. Depending on preference, it's eaten dipped with salted shrimp or simple salt.

**Preparation time:** 15 minutes, plus 2½ hours soaking and chilling time
**Cooking time:** 2 hours
**Serves:** 4

- 2¼ lb (1 kg) pig's feet (trotters)
- 7 oz (200 g) onions, halved
- 3¼ oz (90 g) daepa (Korean scallion), cut into 3-inch (7.5 cm) pieces
- 10 oz (300 g) apples, halved
- 10 cloves garlic
- 1½ cups (12 fl oz/360 ml) ganjang (Korean soy sauce)
- 1 cup (240 g) corn (golden) syrup
- ½ cup (100 g) granulated sugar
- 4 tablespoons light brown sugar
- 1 tablespoon black peppercorns
- 2 fresh green Cheongyang chilies, halved

Soak the pig's feet in water for 2 hours to remove any blood. Rinse the soaked pig's feet under cold running water and place in a pot. Add water to cover and bring to a boil for 10 minutes to remove any impurities. Drain and rinse the pig's feet under cold running water.

In a large pot, combine the pig's feet with twice the volume of water (about 10½ cups/88 fl oz/2.5 liters). Add the onions, daepa, apples, garlic, soy sauce, corn syrup, granulated sugar, brown sugar, peppercorns, and chilies. Boil over high heat, uncovered, for 1 hour. The pig's feet should take on the dark color of the seasoning while the liquid reduces. Remove from the heat and let steam for 10 minutes, then remove the pig's feet and let cool for 10 minutes at room temperature. (Discard the cooking liquid.)

Transfer to the refrigerator and cool for 30 minutes. Slice to serve.

---

## Kimchi Pork Belly Jorim
### Kimchi Samgyupsal Jjim
### 김치 돼지삼겹살찜

dF [◻]

Kimchi and pork belly is one of the most famous and beloved combinations in Korean cuisine, and the kimchi pork belly *jorim* is one of the most popular preparations of pork belly. The pork belly should be sufficiently braised until it is tender and the kimchi's flavors are well absorbed into the meat.

**Preparation time:** 20 minutes
**Cooking time:** 40 minutes
**Serves:** 2

- 1 tablespoon neutral cooking oil
- 14 oz (400 g) pork belly, unsliced
- 10 oz (300 g) Napa Cabbage Kimchi, store-bought or homemade (page 60)
- 3½ oz (100 g) onion, cut into slices ¾ inch (2 cm) thick
- 1 oz (30 g) daepa (Korean scallion), cut on a diagonal into 1½-inch (4 cm) lengths
- 1 tablespoon minced garlic
- 3 cups (24 fl oz/710 ml) Beef Broth (page 315), Vegetable Broth (page 313), or water
- 2 tablespoons cheongjang (light soy sauce)
- 2 tablespoons gochugaru (red chili flakes)
- 1 tablespoon sugar

Drizzle the cooking oil into a large pot. Add in this order: the whole pork belly, kimchi, onion, daepa, and garlic. Add the broth or water, soy sauce, gochugaru, and sugar. Cover with a lid and bring to a boil over high heat. Once boiling, reduce the heat to medium and boil until the sauce reduces and the pork belly is fully cooked, about 40 minutes.

Remove from the heat and let stand covered for 10–20 minutes to tenderize the meat.

To serve, cut the pork belly into ¼-inch (5 mm) slices and arrange in a deep plate. Plate the kimchi alongside the pork.

# Mackerel Jorim
## Godeungeo Jorim
## 고등어 조림

dF -3o

Mackerel is the most commonly used fish in Korea's *jorim* cuisine. Historically, mackerel was abundant in the Korean seas, which made it very accessible. The savory flavors of its meat has always been beloved by Koreans and is enjoyed cooked in many ways. In summer, mackerel *jorim* dishes are enjoyed with potatoes, and in winter, with *mu* (Korean radish). It serves both as a great *anju* (a snack to have with drinks) as well as a main *banchan* (side dish) to complete a meal.

**Preparation time:** 10 minutes
**Cooking time:** 20 minutes
**Serves:** 2

1 whole mackerel (about 14 oz/400 g)
2 tablespoons rice cooking wine

**For the sauce:**
4 tablespoons yangjo ganjang (naturally brewed soy sauce)
3 tablespoons mirin
1 tablespoon sugar
1 tablespoon gochugaru (red chili flakes)
1 tablespoon minced garlic
½ teaspoon minced fresh ginger

**For the jorim:**
5 oz (150 g) potato, cut into ½-inch (1.3 cm) slices
3½ oz (100 g) onion, halved and cut into slices ¾ inch (2 cm) thick
1 oz (30 g) daepa (Korean scallion), cut on a diagonal into ½-inch (1.3 cm) slices.
1 oz (25 g) green Cheongyang chili, cut on a diagonal into ½-inch (1.3 cm) slices.
1 oz (25 g) fresh red chili
Sesame seeds (optional)

Gut and clean the mackerel and remove the head. Cut the mackerel crosswise, through the backbone, into sections 1½ inches (4 cm) wide. Place the mackerel in a bowl, toss with the wine, and let sit for 5 minutes. Drain and pat dry with paper towels. Set aside.

**Make the sauce:** In a bowl, combine ¾ cup (6 fl oz/175 ml) water, the soy sauce, mirin, sugar, gochugaru, garlic, and ginger and mix until uniform.

**Make the jorim:** In a pot, layer all the potato pieces. Layer the mackerel pieces on top, followed by the sliced onion. Pour in the sauce, cover the pot, and bring to a boil over high heat. Once boiling, uncover, reduce the heat to medium, and simmer for 10 minutes. Add the daepa and the chilies and simmer for 1–2 more minutes. Remove from the heat.

In a deep plate or bowl, evenly plate the mackerel and potato and finish with the sauce to make sure that the dish remains moist. Garnish with sesame seeds, if desired.

**Variations**

• In winter when *mu* (Korean radish) is in season, use it in place of the potato, in the same amount.

• For those who love kimchi, reduce the soy sauce by one-third and replace with ripe kimchi to taste.

# Pomfret & Korean Zucchini Jorim
## Aehobak Byeongeo Jorim
## 애호박 병어조림

dF -3o

In Korea, from late spring in May through the summer months of August, pomfret is in season. Pomfret's meat remains tender and savory even after long simmering, and its texture and flavor is great with in-season produce, such as *aehobak* (Korean zucchini) and potatoes.

The flavor-soaked, tender pomfret meat on top of white rice is a seasonal treat. The long-simmered zucchini (courgette) and potatoes are equally flavorful and shouldn't be missed.

Preparation time: 10 minutes
Cooking time: 20 minutes
Serves: 2

For the sauce:
4 tablespoons jinjang (dark Korean soy sauce)
2 tablespoons mirin
1 tablespoon rice cooking wine
1 tablespoon gochugaru (red chili flakes)
½ tablespoon light brown sugar
½ teaspoon minced fresh ginger

For the jorim:
5 oz (150 g) potato, cut into ¾-inch (2 cm) slices
3½ oz (100 g) onion, thinly sliced
4½ oz (125 g) aehobak (Korean zucchini), cut into rounds ¾ inch (2 cm) thick
1 whole pomfret (about 14 oz/400 g), gutted and cleaned
1 oz (30 g) daepa (Korean scallion), cut on a diagonal into 1½-inch (4 cm) slices
2 tablespoons minced garlic
½ oz (12 g) fresh red chili, thinly sliced on a diagonal
½ oz (12 g) fresh green Cheongyang chili, thinly sliced on a diagonal
½ teaspoon sesame seeds

**Make the sauce:** In a bowl, combine the soy sauce, mirin, wine, gochugaru, brown sugar, and ginger and mix until uniform. Set aside.

**Make the jorim:** In a large pot, layer the potatoes, avoiding overlapping. Next, layer with the onion, add ½ cup (4 fl oz/120 ml) water, and bring to a boil over high heat. Once boiling, reduce the heat to medium and add, in this order: the zucchini, pomfret, and sauce. Cover with a lid and boil for 5 minutes.

Uncover and gently stir to make sure that fish is evenly covered in the sauce. Reduce the heat to low and simmer for 5 minutes. Add the daepa, garlic, and chilies and stir in so that the sauce is covering the fish. Let simmer for 5 more minutes and remove from the heat.

On a communal platter, arrange a layer of potato and zucchini. Top the vegetables with the fish, and finish by pouring over sauce from the pot. Garnish with sesame seeds and serve.

**Variations**

• In the warmer months, garnish with mugwort for the fragrance.

• In the winter season, replace the potato with mu (Korean radish) because it is in season.

• This recipe is also great with flounder as well.

# Spicy Monkfish Jorim
## Agwi-jjim
## 아귀찜

DF

While known widely as *agwi-jjim*, which translated is "steamed monkfish," it is actually a long-simmered *jorim* dish rather than steamed. It's often cooked with sea squirt, but because sea squirt is hard to source overseas, it's fine to cook without it. It is served seasoned with a stimulating spicy *gochugaru* (red chili flakes)-based sauce and is often paired with milder dishes, such as Korean Rice Balls (page 135). It's a popular drinking food but is also great enjoyed as a meal.

Preparation time: 20 minutes
Cooking time: 40 minutes
Serves: 2–4

For the sauce:
5 tablespoons gochugaru (red chili flakes)
3 tablespoons ganjang (Korean soy sauce)
3 tablespoons corn (golden) syrup
2 tablespoons rice cooking wine
1 tablespoon gochujang (red chili paste)
1 tablespoon anchovy fish sauce
1 tablespoon minced garlic
1 teaspoon freshly ground black pepper

For the jorim:
2¼ lb (1 kg) monkfish, preferably the whole monkfish if possible
3½ oz (100 g) mu (Korean radish), cut into 2-inch (5 cm) square pieces ¼ inch (6 mm) thick
7 oz (200 g) soybean sprouts
2 oz (60 g) daepa (Korean scallion), cut into ¼-inch (6 mm) diagonal slices
1¾ oz (50 g) fresh green Cheongyang chili, cut on a diagonal into thin rings
2 tablespoons potato starch
2½ oz (70 g) minari, cut into 2-inch (5 cm) lengths

**Make the sauce:** In a bowl, combine the gochugaru, soy sauce, corn syrup, wine, gochujang, fish sauce, garlic, and black pepper and mix well until uniform. Set aside.

**Make the jorim:** Cut the monkfish into 2-inch (5 cm) pieces. In a small pot of boiling water, blanch the monkfish for 2 minutes to get rid of any unwanted fishy flavors. Drain and set aside to cool.

In a pot, combine 2 cups (16 fl oz/480 ml) water, the radish, and the reserved sauce and cook over medium heat for 5 minutes. Add the monkfish and bean sprouts and mix well. Braise until the liquid reduces by half, about 7 minutes. Add the daepa and chili and cook for 2 more minutes.

In a small bowl, stir the potato starch with 2 tablespoons water until smooth. Stir the starch slurry into the soup and cook to thicken. Add the minari and mix well. Serve hot in a shallow bowl.

# 찜 Jjim Steamed

*Jjim* means to steam, and dishes called *jjim* can be translated to "steamed dish." But there are two interpretations of this idea in Korea: The first is the literal form in which ingredients are cooked by steaming over boiling water. But the second refers to a category of dishes in which seasoned meat, fish, or vegetables are simmered gently in a broth. This second category of dishes, such as the popular *galbi jjim* and *jjim dak*, are actually braises or stews (see Andong Chicken Jorim, page 288 for an example). This chapter, however, deals only with the first category of dishes in which the ingredients are truly steamed.

In steamed dishes, since the ingredients do not come into direct contact with a cooking liquid or other ingredients, the flavors and the shape of the main ingredient remains unchanged. Delicate dishes, such as *mandu* (dumplings), tofu, and fish, are often cooked as *jjim*, so that their shapes and inherent flavors can be preserved and enjoyed. In addition, since oil is rarely used in *jjim* dishes, this method lets the inherent flavors of an ingredient shine.

The ideal amount of water to use in a steamer is half the volume of the steamer. Ingredients should not be placed in the steamer until the water begins to boil, and the underside of the lid should be wrapped with a cotton cloth to prevent water droplets from falling onto the food.

The most popular ingredients in Korean's *jjim* cuisine are fish, shellfish, vegetables, and eggs. These ingredients are often steamed as is or topped with a sauce before steaming. When steaming fish, *namul* (wild greens) and vegetables are often added. A popular form of fish *jjim* includes vegetables, such as bean sprouts and chives, which are enjoyed together in a single bite with the fish.

## 5-Minute Egg Jjim
### Gyeran Jjim
### 5분 계란찜

dF vE -5 -3o

*Gyeran jjim*, steamed egg, is arguably the most common *banchan* (side dish) on a Korean dinner table. There are two ways to make this dish: an "instant" version using the microwave, as well as the proper steamed method. One can easily add depth to the flavor by swapping out the water in the recipe with an anchovy broth, as well as incorporating salted shrimp instead of the Yondu.

**Preparation time:** 2 minutes
**Cooking time:** 3–10 minutes
**Serves:** 2

2 eggs
½ teaspoon sesame oil
2 teaspoons Yondu
 (Korean vegan seasoning sauce)
1 scallion (spring onion), minced

**"Instant" Version**
In a microwave-safe bowl, crack in the eggs, add the sesame oil, and mix well together. Add the Yondu and ⅔ cup (5 fl oz/160 ml) water and stir until well combined.

Cover the bowl with plastic wrap (cling film) and microwave for 1 minute 30 seconds. Remove the bowl from the microwave and stir the scallion into the egg mixture until evenly combined. Re-cover and microwave for 1 minute 30 seconds. Remove wrap and serve.

**Steamer Version**
Set up a steamer and bring the water to a boil.

In a bowl, crack in the eggs. Add the sesame oil, ⅔ cup (5 fl oz/160 ml) water, and the Yondu and combine well. Strain through a fine-mesh sieve into a bowl to remove any texture. Add the minced scallion and cover the bowl with plastic wrap (cling film).

Add the bowl to the steamer basket, set it over the boiling water, and steam for 10 minutes. Remove from the heat, uncover, and serve.

---

## Pork Belly & Mung Bean Sprout Jjim
### Samgyupsal Sukju Jjim
### 삼겹살 숙주찜

dF -3o

Because pork belly is high in fat content, cooking it by steaming with mung bean sprouts provides a clean, light way to enjoy the delicious savory flavor of the popular cut. Other vegetables, including tender mushrooms, or fragrant herbs, such as *minari* and chives, can be included in the steamer to add flavor and texture.

**Preparation time:** 5 minutes
**Cooking time:** 10 minutes
**Serves:** 2

7 oz (200 g) mung bean sprouts
14 oz (400 g) pork belly, thinly sliced
½ teaspoon freshly ground
 black pepper

**For the dipping sauce:**
2 tablespoons ganjang
 (Korean soy sauce)
1 tablespoon rice vinegar
1 tablespoon sugar
1 teaspoon gochugaru
 (red chili flakes)
1 teaspoon fresh lemon juice
1 teaspoon sesame seeds

**To serve:**
2 scallions (spring onions), slivered

Set up a steamer and bring the water to a boil.

On the bottom of the steamer basket, layer the mung bean sprouts. Top with a layer of pork belly slices, avoiding bunching or overlapping. Season the pork belly slices evenly with the black pepper.

Set the basket over the boiling water, cover, and steam for 10 minutes.

**Meanwhile, make the dipping sauce:**
In a small bowl, combine the soy sauce, vinegar, sugar, gochugaru, lemon juice, and sesame seeds. Pour into a saucer and set aside.

**To serve:** Remove the steamer from heat, uncover, and garnish with the scallions. Either plate as is onto a flat wide plate or serve from the steamer. Serve with the dipping sauce on the side.

## Doenjang Eggplant Jjim
### Doenjang Gaji Jjim
### 된장 가지찜

dF

*Doenjang gaji jjim* is a popular dish in North Korea, where the unique cuisine of *doenjang* (fermented soybean paste)-based dishes are well developed. The *doenjang's* heavy body and deep savory flavor make for a great sauce when steamed with eggplant (aubergine), which absorbs the rich flavors well. This dish is mainly made in summer, when eggplant is most delicious.

Preparation time: 15 minutes
Cooking time: 20 minutes
Serves: 2

For the stuffing:
5 oz (150 g) ground (minced) beef
4 tablespoons doenjang (fermented soybean paste)
1 tablespoon sesame oil
1 tablespoon gochugaru (red chili flakes)
1 tablespoon ganjang (Korean soy sauce)
2 teaspoons honey
1 teaspoon minced garlic
½ teaspoon freshly ground black pepper

For the eggplant:
4 Korean eggplants (aubergines)
1 tablespoon all-purpose (plain) flour

**Make the stuffing:** In a bowl, combine the beef, doenjang, sesame oil, gochugaru, soy sauce, honey, garlic, and black pepper and mix well until fully combined.

**Stuff the eggplant:** Leaving about ¾ inch (2 cm) of the stem end intact, cut the eggplants lengthwise into quarters.

Dust all the cut sides of the eggplants with the flour, shaking off any excess or any clumps. Dividing evenly, stuff the opening of the eggplants with the beef stuffing (this is messy; use your hands). Arrange them on a plate that will fit in the steamer as you work.

Set up a steamer and bring the water to a boil.

Add the plate of eggplants to the steamer basket, set it over the boiling water, cover with a lid, and steam for 20 minutes. Remove from the steamer and serve hot.

---

## Napa Cabbage with Chilies Jjim
### Cheongyang Gochu Baechu Jjim
### 청양고추 배추찜

dF gF vg vE -30    [ㅁ]

Napa cabbage (Chinese leaf) is sweetest and most crispy after the fall season. At that time of year, the cabbage is enjoyed with a simple seasoning and is easily steamed in the microwave. You can enjoy this cabbage *jjim* as a snack along with white wine, perhaps with a side of egg yolks for dipping. It also makes a great side dish for heavier mains.

Preparation time: 5 minutes
Cooking time: 5 minutes
Serves: 1

10 oz (300 g) napa cabbage (Chinese leaf), about ¼ head

For the sauce:
½ oz (12 g) fresh green Cheongyang chili, seeded and minced
½ oz (12 g) fresh red chili, seeded and minced
½ scallion (spring onion), thinly sliced
1 tablespoon Yondu (Korean vegan seasoning sauce)
1 teaspoon sugar
1 teaspoon rice vinegar
½ teaspoon sesame oil
½ teaspoon sesame seeds

Separate the napa cabbage leaves and rinse under cold running water. Shake off any excess water and lay flat on a microwave-safe plate large enough to hold them. Cover with plastic wrap (cling film) and microwave for 3 minutes 30 seconds.

**Meanwhile, make the sauce:** In a small bowl, combine the chilies, scallion, Yondu, sugar, vinegar, sesame oil, and sesame seeds and mix until uniform.

Remove the steamed cabbage from the microwave and plate. Evenly dress with the sauce before serving.

## Anchovy Doenjang Perilla Jjim
## Myeolchi Doenjang Kkaennip Jjim
## 멸치 된장 깻잎찜

dF  −3o

In summer, making *jjim* using in-season leafy vegetables, such as perilla or pumpkin leaf, and *doenjang* (fermented soybean paste) is a savory and seasonal delicacy. While the ingredients here are a simple, harmonious combination of the savory and earthy *doenjang*, the deep sea flavors of the anchovies and the herbal, minty perilla make a delicious balance.

**Preparation time:** 5 minutes
**Cooking time:** 10 minutes
**Serves:** 4

20 perilla leaves

**For the sauce:**
4 Korean dried anchovies
1 oz (25 g) fresh green Cheongyang chili, minced
1 tablespoon doenjang (fermented soybean paste)
½ tablespoon minced garlic
1 teaspoon sesame oil

Rinse the perilla leaves one at a time under cold running water. Set aside to dry off completely.

**Make the sauce:** Remove the head and any visible intestines from the dried anchovies. Mince the anchovies and add to a bowl. Add the chili, 5 tablespoons water, the doenjang, garlic, and sesame oil and mix well until uniform.

Set up a steamer and bring the water to a boil.

In a shallow bowl, lay 2 perilla leaves side by side. Spoon a small amount of the sauce evenly over both leaves and stack 2 perilla leaves on top. Repeat the layering process for the remaining ingredients.

Add the bowl to the steamer basket, set it over the boiling water, cover, and steam for 5 minutes. Remove from the steamer. Either serve warm (as a banchan) or store in an airtight container for up 4 days refrigerated.

---

## Ray with Bean Sprout Jjim
## Kongnamul Gaorijjim
## 콩나물 가오리찜

dF                                    [ㅁ]

The ray with bean sprout *jjim* is an easily made dish, because bean sprouts and ray are both readily available in Korea. The nutty flavors of cooked bean sprouts and the savory flavor of ray pair beautifully together.

**Preparation time:** 15 minutes
**Cooking time:** 20 minutes
**Serves:** 3–4

1 whole ray, cleaned (1½ lb/700 g), cleaned
2 tablespoons rice cooking wine
3½ oz (100 g) soybean sprouts

**For the sauce:**
1 oz (30 g) garlic chives, cut into ½-inch (1.3 cm) length
1 tablespoon minced garlic
½ tablespoon minced daepa (Korean scallion)
1 tablespoon mirin
1 tablespoon ganjang (Korean soy sauce)
1 teaspoon gochugaru (red chili flakes)
1 teaspoon sesame oil
½ teaspoon sesame seeds

Make a 3 percent salt solution: For every 1 cup (237 g) water, add 1 teaspoon (7 g) salt. Wash any impurities off the cleaned, gutted ray with the salt solution. Pat dry with paper towels. Place on a large plate, sprinkle with the wine, and let sit for 5 minutes.

Set up a steamer and bring the water to a boil.

Layer the bean sprouts evenly in the steamer basket. Place the ray over the sprouts. Set the basket over the boiling water, cover, and steam for 20 minutes. Remove from the heat and let stand covered for 5 minutes.

**Meanwhile, make the sauce:** In a bowl, stir together the chives, garlic, daepa, mirin, soy sauce, gochugaru, sesame oil, and sesame seeds.

To serve, plate the bean sprouts. Then add the cooked ray fish. Evenly season the ray with the sauce.

# 튀김 Twigim Deep-Fried

*Twigim* is both the method of cooking an ingredient by deep-frying, as well as the category of deep-fried dishes. Ingredients, such as vegetables, fish, and meat, are cooked in high-temperature oil for a short amount of time. The ingredient can be deep-fried as is, coated in a batter or bread crumbs, or wrapped in dumpling skin.

Traditionally, the main ingredient in *twigim* cuisine is vegetables. *Bugak* is a style of *twigim* in which dehydrated vegetables or seaweed are coated with a glutinous rice flour paste, dehydrated again, and then deep-fried to create a crispy chip. *Twigak*, on the other hand, are dried vegetables or seaweed that are simply deep-fried as is. By using dehydrated vegetables, these two traditional categories of *twigim* allowed people to enjoy seasonal vegetables throughout the four seasons. For a long time, traditional *twigim* were pretty restricted to these two types, but the influence of global cuisines and the development of industrial soybean manufacturing in Korea have helped evolve the category to include a variety of ingredients and dishes.

Modern *twigim* typically belong to the broader category of *bunsik*, or street foods. Popular vegetables for *twigim* include potatoes, *goguma* (Korean sweet potato), and chili peppers. Squid and shrimp are popular seafood *twigim* found commonly in restaurants and street stalls. *Twigim* made from *tteok* (rice cakes) and *gim-mari* (seasoned glass noodles rolled in *gim*) are popular, and, of course, the Korean fried chicken is one of the most commonly eaten foods. Korean fried chicken is known for its crispy texture and unique sauces made from *gochujang* (red chili paste) and soy sauce, and it has gained popularity on a global scale.

When making *twigim*, preseasoning the ingredients is important for flavor. It is critical that the ingredients are well prepared to remove any excess moisture, because water content causes oil to splutter as well as causes separation between the ingredient and the batter. It is also recommended to sift the flour when making the *twigim* batter. Using ice to drop the batter temperature is a great tip to produce a crispier skin, and, finally, it is important to deep-fry the *twigim* just before serving for freshness.

# Korean Fried Chicken
## Dak Twigim
## 닭튀김

dF

In Korea today, when referring to simply "chicken," one automatically thinks of Korean fried chicken. The deep-fried chicken is a ubiquitous, popular chicken dish in modern Korean cuisine. Many forms exist, including Korea's market-style, deep-fried whole chicken, the American style of thick-battered fried chicken, and more. This recipe represents the most common Korean fried chicken. The coating is made with a commercially available seasoned flour mixture sold specifically for Korean fried chicken.

**Preparation time: 20 minutes**
**Cooking time: 20 minutes**
**Serves: 2**

1¾ lb (800 g) bone-in, skin-on chicken pieces
1 tablespoon MSG/salt blend (mat-sogeum; available in Korean markets)
1 teaspoon sugar
1 teaspoon freshly ground black pepper
Neutral cooking oil for deep-frying (about 8½ cups/68 fl oz/2 liters)
1½ cups (180 g) Korean seasoned fried chicken mix

Pat the chicken pieces dry with paper towels. In a bowl, sprinkle the chicken with the MSG/salt blend, sugar, and black pepper and mix well. Let sit for 15 minutes.

Pour 3–4 inches (7.5–10 cm) oil into a large deep pot or deep fryer and heat to 355°F (180°C).

In a small bowl, stir together 6½ tablespoons of the fried chicken mix and 4–5 tablespoons water to make a batter and mix well until uniform. Place the remaining generous 1 cup (130 g) fried chicken mix in a large plastic bag.

Working with one piece at a time, place the seasoned chicken in the plastic bag and shake well until the chicken is well coated. Let settle for 30 seconds before removing from the bag, shaking off any excess mix.

Set a wire rack in a sheet pan. Once the oil is up to temperature, reduce the heat to medium-low. Add the chicken pieces, starting with any larger pieces, such as a thigh or drumstick. Deep-fry for 12 minutes, or until cooked through. Remove and set on the rack to cool for 3 minutes. Plate and serve.

# Sweet and Spicy Korean Fried Chicken
## Yangnyeom Dak Twigim
## 양념 닭튀김

dF

Korean fried chicken seasoned with a sauce made with soy sauce, *gochujang* (red chili paste), *gochugaru* (red chili flakes), and corn (golden) syrup is as popular and common as the Korean Fried Chicken (page 303). This recipe is an easy way to enjoy fried chicken with different flavors, by eating half as simply fried and the other half tossed in this sauce. The coating is made with a packaged fried chicken mix commonly sold in Korea.

Preparation time: 10 minutes
Cooking time: 20 minutes
Serves: 2

For the sauce:
3 tablespoons corn (golden) syrup
2 tablespoons ketchup
2 tablespoons gochujang (red chili paste)
2 tablespoons ganjang (Korean soy sauce)
1 tablespoon minced garlic
½ tablespoon fine gochugaru (red chili powder)
1 tablespoon sugar

For the chicken:
1¾ lb (800 g) bone-in, skin-on chicken pieces
1 tablespoon mat-gogeum (MSG/salt blend)
1 teaspoon sugar
1 teaspoon freshly ground black pepper
Neutral cooking oil for deep-frying (about 8½ cups/68 fl oz/2 liters)
1½ cups (180 g) Korean seasoned fried chicken mix

**Make the sauce:** In a small saucepan, combine the corn syrup, ketchup, gochujang, soy sauce, garlic, gochugaru, and sugar and bring to a boil over medium heat, stirring well. Once boiling, reduce the heat to low and simmer for 3 minutes before removing from the heat.

**For the chicken:** Pat the chicken dry with paper towels. In a bowl, sprinkle the chicken with the MSG/salt blend, sugar, and black pepper and mix well. Let sit for 15 minutes.

Pour 3–4 inches (7.5–10 cm) neutral oil into a large deep pot or deep fryer and heat to 355°F (180°C).

In a small bowl, stir together 6½ tablespoons of the fried chicken mix and 4 tablespoons water to make a batter and mix well until uniform. Place the remaining generous 1 cup (130 g) fried chicken mix in a large plastic bag.

Working with one piece at a time, place the seasoned chicken in the plastic bag and shake well until the chicken is well coated. Let settle for 30 seconds before removing from the bag, shaking off any excess mix.

Set a wire rack in a sheet pan. Once the oil is up to temperature, reduce the heat to medium-low. Add the chicken pieces, starting with any larger pieces, such as a thigh or drumstick. Deep-fry for 12 minutes, or until cooked through. Remove and set on the rack to cool for 3 minutes.

Sauce the chicken by combining the fried chicken with the desired amount of sauce and tossing well in the bowl. Plate and serve immediately.

# Stuffed Peppers Twigim
## Gochu Twigim
## 고추 튀김

dF

The peppers used in this recipe can be chosen according to spice preference: Cheongyang are spicy and Korean cucumbers are mild. Use all of one or both. Because the filling takes a longer time to cook thoroughly, the stuffed peppers are fried at a lower temperature for a longer time than the typical *twigim*. The moisture from the stuffing can make the fry batter moist, so some cooks like to double-fry for a crispy result.

**Preparation time:** 15 minutes
**Cooking time:** 20 minutes
**Serves:** 4

**For the pork stuffing:**
5 oz (150 g) firm tofu
14 oz (400 g) ground (minced) pork
1 tablespoon ganjang (Korean soy sauce)
1 teaspoon minced garlic
1 teaspoon salt
2 pinches of freshly ground black pepper

**For the twigim:**
Neutral cooking oil for deep-frying (about 3 cups/24 fl oz/700 ml)
8 Korean cucumber peppers (long thin mild peppers)
8 green Cheongyang chili peppers
2 tablespoons plus 1⅔ cups (200 g) Korean frying mix
Ganjang (Korean soy sauce), for dipping (optional)

**Make the pork stuffing:** In a bowl, mash the firm tofu until fine with your hands. Add the pork, soy sauce, garlic, salt, and black pepper and thoroughly combine.

**For the twigim:** Pour 3–4 inches (7.5–10 cm) cooking oil into a large deep pot or deep fryer and heat to 320°F (160°C).

Slice all the peppers lengthwise and remove the seeds. In a large plastic bag, add 2 tablespoons of the frying mix, add the peppers, and shake well until the peppers are well coated. Take out the peppers and stuff each pepper half with the pork stuffing. Dust any frying mix left in the plastic bag over the filling.

In a bowl, combine the remaining 1⅔ cups (200 g) frying mix and 1 cup (8 fl oz/240 ml) water and mix well to make a uniform batter.

Line a tray with paper towels. Working in batches, use chopsticks to dip each stuffed pepper into the batter and drop into the heated oil. Deep-fry until the outside is golden brown, 4–5 minutes. Transfer to the tray. Plate and serve as is or with ganjang for dipping.

## Crispy Pork Twigim
### Dwaeji Chapsal Twigim
### 돼지고기 찹쌀 튀김

dF

This dish marries the savory flavor of pork with the subtle sweetness of glutinous rice. The use of the glutinous rice flour instead of the wheat flour commonly used for frying provides a crispy yet chewy texture that is beloved. This deep-fried pork goes well with a sweet-and-sour sauce, but it's also great served with a simple cabbage or scallion (spring onion) and garlic chive salad.

**Preparation time:** 20 minutes
**Cooking time:** 20 minutes
**Serves:** 2–4

**For the marinated pork:**
1 tablespoon rice cooking wine
1 tablespoon ganjang (Korean soy sauce)
1 teaspoon minced Cheongyang chili
1 teaspoon sugar
1 teaspoon sesame oil
1 teaspoon freshly ground black pepper
12 oz (350 g) boneless pork shoulder, cut into slices a generous ⅛ inch (4 mm) thick

**For the twigim:**
Neutral oil for deep-frying (about 8½ cups/68 fl oz/2 liters)
1 cup (110 g) glutinous rice flour

**Marinate the pork:** In a bowl, combine the wine, soy sauce, chili, sugar, sesame oil, and black pepper. Add the pork and toss to coat well. Let marinate for 10 minutes.

**For the twigim:** Pour 3–4 inches (7.5–10 cm) neutral oil into a large deep pot or deep fryer and heat to 355°F (180°C).

Spread the glutinous rice flour on a large flat plate. Take the individual slices of the marinated pork and dredge in the flour on both sides to coat and set aside for 30 seconds so that the pork can absorb the starch.

Set a wire rack in a sheet pan. Working in batches, deep-fry the pork slices until the pork is crispy and golden, 7–9 minutes. Transfer to the wire rack to drain.

Serve while crispy.

---

## Spring Vegetable Twigim
### Namul Twigim
### 나물 튀김

dF vg vE -30     [ㅁ]

*Namul twigim* is a dish mainly eaten in spring, when wild spring vegetables are abundant. Due to the ephemeral nature and fragrance of the springtime *namul*, this *twigim* dish is always a delicacy to have.

**Preparation time:** 10 minutes
**Cooking time:** 20 minutes
**Serves:** 4

**For the cho-ganjang:**
3 tablespoons ganjang (Korean soy sauce)
2 tablespoons rice vinegar
1 teaspoon sugar

**For the twigim:**
Neutral cooking oil for deep-frying (about 3 cups/24 fl oz/700 ml)
3½ oz (100 g) shepherd's purse
3½ oz (100 g) cham namul
3½ oz (100 g) Korean chrysanthemum
3 tablespoons potato starch
1⅔ cups (200 g) Korean frying mix

**Make the cho-ganjang:** In a bowl, stir together ½ cup (4 fl oz/120 ml) water, the soy sauce, vinegar, and sugar until the sugar dissolves.

**For the twigim:** Pour 3–4 inches (7.5–10 cm) neutral oil into a large deep pot or deep fryer and heat to 355°F (180°C).

Rinse all the vegetables under cold running water and set in a sieve to dry. In individual plastic bags, add the well-dried vegetables and 1 tablespoon of potato starch to each bag and shake vigorously until the vegetables are evenly coated with potato starch.

In a bowl, combine the frying mix and 1 cup (8 fl oz/240 ml) cold water and mix well until uniform.

Line a tray with paper towels. Working in batches of one vegetable at a time, use chopsticks to dip each of the starch-coated vegetables into the batter and drop into the heated oil. Cook for about 2 minutes and transfer to the paper towels to drain.

Serve hot with the cho-ganjang.

# Seasoned Semi-Dried Pollock Twigim
## Kodari Gangjeong
## 코다리 강정

dF

*Kodari*, which is semidried pollock, is popular braised in sauces, such as a *jorim*. This crispy version, seasoned, deep-fried, and coated in a sweet, savory syrup, is a delicacy.

Preparation time: 25 minutes
Cooking time: 40 minutes
Serves: 4

1 lb 5 oz (600 g) semidried pollock (3 whole)
2 tablespoons rice cooking wine
2 tablespoons ganjang (Korean soy sauce)
1 teaspoon sugar

For the sauce:
3 tablespoons corn (golden) syrup
2 tablespoons ganjang (Korean soy sauce)
1 tablespoon rice cooking wine
1 tablespoon gochujang (red chili paste)
1 tablespoon fine gochugaru (red chili powder)
1 tablespoon sugar
½ tablespoon minced garlic

For the twigim:
Neutral cooking oil for deep-frying (about 8½ cups/68 fl oz/2 liters)
1 cup (190 g) potato or sweet potato starch

Wash the whole pollock under cold running water and remove the heads. Using scissors, trim off any gills and fins. Cut into 2-inch (5 cm) pieces. In a bowl, combine the pollock with the wine, soy sauce, and sugar and mix well. Let marinate for 15 minutes.

**Meanwhile, make the sauce:** In a small saucepan, combine the corn syrup, soy sauce, wine, gochujang, gochugaru, sugar, and garlic and bring to a boil over medium heat, stirring well. Once boiling, reduce the heat to low and continue to simmer for 3 minutes. Remove from the heat.

**For the twigim:** Pour 3–4 inches (7.5–10 cm) of cooking oil into a large deep pot or deep fryer and heat to 355°F (180°C).

Place the potato starch in a large plastic bag. Add the pollock pieces and shake vigorously to coat. Set aside for 30 seconds so that the pollock can absorb the starch.

Set a wire rack in a sheet pan. Working in batches, deep-fry the pollock until the skin is crispy and golden, about 6 minutes. Transfer to the wire rack to cool for 30 seconds.

Transfer to a large bowl, add the prepared sauce, and toss well until fully coated. Serve on a large plate.

# Seaweed Roll Twigim
## Gimmari Twigim
## 김말이 튀김

dF vg vE

*Gimmari*, deep-fried seaweed rolls, are a popular street snack, a staple in *bunsik* restaurants (casual street food restaurants). Its filling is made with boiled glass noodles (aka cellophane noodles) seasoned with freshly ground black pepper, with a small amount of vegetables. A Korean favorite, this snack is usually eaten with *tteokbokki* (rice cakes in sauce), dipped in the *tteokbokki* sauce.

Preparation time: 35 minutes
Cooking time: 35 minutes
Serves: 4

**For the glass noodles:**
9 oz (250 g) glass noodles
2 tablespoons ganjang (Korean soy sauce)
1 tablespoon sugar
1 tablespoon sesame oil
1 teaspoon salt
½ tablespoon freshly ground black pepper

**For the twigim:**
7 sheets gim (labeled for use in gimbap)
Neutral cooking oil for deep-frying (about 8½ cups/68 fl oz/2 liters)
¾ cup (90 g) Korean frying mix

**Prepare the glass noodles:** Soak the noodles in water for 20 minutes.

Bring a pot of water to a boil over high heat. Add the soaked noodles and cook for 7 minutes. Drain and rinse under cold water to cool. Let sit in the sieve to drain excess water.

In a nonstick frying pan, combine the drained noodles, soy sauce, sugar, sesame oil, salt, and black pepper. Set over medium heat and and pan-fry for 1 minute. Transfer to a plate to cool.

**For the twigim:** Pour 3–4 inches (7.5–10 cm) into a large deep pot or deep fryer and heat to 355°F (180°C).

Lay out a sheet of gim and lay about 2 tablespoons of seasoned glass noodles across it. Roll the gim up tightly. Seal the ends by applying a small amount of water to them. Repeat for the remaining ingredients. Cut the finished gimmari crosswise into thirds.

In a bowl, combine ½ cup (60 g) of the Korean frying mix and ½ cup (4 fl oz/120 ml) cold water and mix to make a uniform batter. Set the remaining 4 tablespoons Korean frying mix on a flat plate. Working in batches, roll the gimmari in the dry frying mix, dip into the batter, and deep-fry for 3 minutes. Transfer to a plate to cool for 2 minutes. Deep-fry again for 3 minutes for a crispy roll. Serve hot.

## 육수 Yuksu Broths

The broths used in Korean cooking can be made with animal meat, such as pork, chicken, or beef, as well as from dehydrated seafood (including anchovy, pollock, and shrimp/prawns) and from vegetables that are more prominent and unique.

Scallion (spring onion) roots, Korean radish and radish peel, onion peel, *dasima*, dried mushrooms, and dried chilies are key ingredients in Korean broth. Soybeans and sesame seeds are also used often in both broths and broth-based dishes.

Another idiosyncratic Korean "broth" is the liquid (brine) from kimchi. The fermented liquid, especially in the case of *dongchimi* (Radish Water Kimchi, page 72), imparts a distinctive flavor to the broth. This style of broth is excellent in cold dishes. *Dongchimi guksu* is a popular noodle dish that uses *dongchimi* "broth," and in *naengmyeon*, a cold noodle dish, beef broth and *dongchimi* broth are combined to create a balanced broth.

There is another uniquely Korean ingredient used as broth: rice water. Rice water is the cloudy white water that is the by-product of washing rice. When washing rice, the first wash is discarded, but the second or third wash is often kept and used as the base of a broth or as a substitute for water or broth in soups or stews. Rice water adds a subtle earthy, savory flavor to dishes and is a common home-cooking practice.

## Vegetable Broth
### Chaesu
### 채수

dF gF vg vE -S

Many common vegetables will release a deep, savory flavor when long-boiled and can be used as a broth base. In particular, dried mushrooms are full of rich, complex flavors and are great as broth ingredients; onion and *daepa* (Korean scallion) are also traditionally used to add a savory sweetness. *Dasima* is a great sea vegetable used in many broths to create complexity, and *mu* (Korean radish) brings a refreshing, gentle sweetness when added to broths. Any vegetable scraps (such as the trimmings from onions or scallions) that would make good broth should be collected and frozen for whenever needed.

**Preparation time:** 10 minutes
**Cooking time:** 40 minutes
**Makes:** 10 cups (80 fl oz/2.4 liters)

1 large sheet (20 g) dasima
1 oz (30 g) dried shiitake mushrooms
14 oz (400 g) onions, cut into 2-inch (5 cm) chunks
7 oz (200 g) mu (Korean radish), cut into 2-inch (5 cm) chunks
2 oz (60 g) daepa (Korean scallion), cut into 2-inch (5 cm) lengths
Dried red chilies or chili flakes (optional)

In a large pot, combine 12 cups (96 fl oz/2.8 liters) water, the dasima, and dried shiitake mushrooms and bring to a boil over high heat. Once boiling, add the vegetables (and chilies if using), reduce heat to medium, and boil for 30 minutes. Strain and discard the solids

---

## Chicken Stock
### Dak Yuksu
### 닭 육수

dF gF -S

While chicken stock is one of the most common bases in Western cuisine, it's not widely used in Korea. It is still a useful ingredient to have on hand and keep frozen to use not only in broth-based dishes but as a base seasoning in many different dishes.

Chicken meat that has been boiled for more than 1 hour usually has no flavor and is not worth using in other dishes. If you'd like, you can take the chicken meat off the bone after the first 30 minutes of cooking and return the bones to the pot. Then shred the meat by hand and save for use in other dishes, such as salads and noodle dishes. For a stronger chicken flavor, first roast the chicken in the oven or in a frying pan prior to making the stock.

**Preparation time:** 30 minutes
**Cooking time:** 1 hour
**Makes:** 10 cups (80 fl oz/2.4 liters)

1 whole chicken, cut into 6–8 pieces
6–7 cloves (25 g) garlic, peeled
7 oz (200 g) onions, cut into chunks
2 oz (60 g) daepa (Korean scallion), cut into several pieces
10 black peppercorns

If possible, buy the chicken already cut up, because they are easily available. Make sure all of the innards have been cleaned out and rinse off any blood.

In a large pot, combine the chicken pieces and 12 cups (96 fl oz/2.8 liters) water and bring to a boil over medium heat. Cook for 30 minutes, skimming any impurities or foam that rise to the surface.

Add the garlic, onion, daepa, and peppercorns and boil for 30 more minutes. Strain the stock.

## Anchovy Broth
## Myeolchi Yuksu
## 멸치 육수

dF gF -S

Anchovy broth is the most widely used ingredient in broth-based Korean cuisine. Anchovies used for broth should have a healthy shine and smooth scales. Because anchovy broth is used so commonly by Korean home cooks, there are widely available prebatched soup packages, complete with anchovies, *dasima*, and dried vegetables, sold in markets.

**Preparation time:** 10 minutes
**Cooking time:** 35 minutes
**Makes:** 10 cups (80 fl oz/2.4 liters)

2 oz (60 g) dried anchovies
1 large sheet (20 g) dasima
2 oz (60 g) daepa (Korean scallion), cut into several pieces

Clean the dried anchovies by slitting the stomach and removing the black organs. If the anchovies are not fully dried, microwave for 30 seconds to dehydrate fully and to dissipate any unwanted fishy fragrance.

In a pot, combine 12 cups (96 fl oz/2.8 liters) water, the dasima, and dried anchovies and bring to a boil over medium heat. Remove and discard the dasima when the water begins to boil. Boil for 10 minutes. Add the daepa and boil for 20 more minutes. Strain and discard solids.

**Variation:** There are many ways to vary this simple anchovy-based broth, such as adding dried shrimp or dipori, a type of dried herring.

---

## Pork Bone Broth
## Dwaeji Sagol Yuksu
## 돼지 사골 육수

dF gF -S

Pork bone broth is made from pork back bones or leg bones, and is the base for popular Korean dishes such as Korean Blood Sausage Gukbap (page 124), Pork Back Bone Tang (page 339), and many other pork-based *gukbap* (soups with rice). It's a labor-intensive broth to make at home, so often beef broth, which is commonly available store-bought, is used in its place. However, the clean yet deep, savory flavor of the pork bone broth is distinct from its counterpart.

If using pork bones with a significant amount of meat on them, pull the meat off the bones after 1 hour of cooking and save to use in another dish. Return the bones to the pot and continue making the bone broth. While some people like to add aromatics, such as peppercorns, bay leaf, and ginger, to get rid of any "porky" smell, if the bones are fresh, preboiling them (see below) should be sufficient.

**Preparation time:** 20 minutes, plus 1 hour soaking and 12 hours chilling time
**Cooking time:** 8-12 hours
**Makes:** 10 cups (80 fl oz/2.4 liters)

6 lb 10 oz (3 kg) pork bones (back bones or leg bones)

Soak the pork bones in cold water for 1 hour to remove the blood. Rinse under cold water and add to a large pot along with enough water to submerge the bones. Bring to a boil over high heat and boil for 5 minutes. Drain and rinse the pork bones under cold water.

Add the rinsed bones to the pot, add 15 cups (120 fl oz/3.6 liters) water, and bring to a boil over high heat, skimming any impurities and foam that rise. Reduce the heat to medium and continue to cook until the broth is white and milky with some viscosity, an additional 8-12 hours (depending on the strength of your heat source), making sure that the water is at a boil at all times (versus simmering). Add more water as needed.

Strain the broth and discard the bones. Transfer to a large container and let chill in the refrigerator for 12 hours. Discard the layer of solid fat that forms on top. The broth can be frozen in single-serving portions for ease.

## Beef Broth
### So Yuksu
### 소 육수

dF gF -S

Having a well-made, clear beef broth on hand makes creating delicious Korean dishes—such as dumpling soup, bean sprout soup, seaweed soup, or *naengmyun* (North Korean noodles) to name a few—both easy and delicious. A simple version of this broth requires just beef, but the addition of *dasima* achieves more umami.

Brisket is a fattier piece of beef that contains a deep, satisfying savory flavor; the shank is a leaner cut of meat that has a full beef flavor and is ideal for creating broths.

Preparation time: 30 minutes, plus 1 hour soaking and 12 hours chilling time
Cooking time: 2 hours
Makes: 10 cups (80 fl oz/2.4 liters)

14 oz (400 g) boneless beef shank
10 oz (300 g) beef brisket, cut into thirds
1 large sheet (20 g) dasima, broken in half

Soak the beef in cold water for 1 hour, draining off and changing the water several times. At the same time, combine the dasima and 4 cups (32 fl oz/950 ml) cold water to rehydrate for 1 hour.

In a large pot, combine the cleaned meat with 12 cups (96 fl oz/2.8 liters) water and bring to a boil over high heat. Once the water is boiling, reduce the heat to medium, skimming any foam or impurities that rise. Add the rehydrated dasima and its soaking water to the pot. The viscous dasima will catch more impurities in the broth; continue to skim. Discard the dasima.

Continue to boil the beef and broth for 1 more hour over medium heat. Let the meat sit in the broth for 30 minutes before removing it. Strain the broth into a container. Let cool in the refrigerator for 12 hours. Remove the layer of fat that forms. Strain the broth again before using.

## Soybean Cold Broth
### Kong Gukmul
### 콩 국물

dF gF vg vE -S

In Korea, there's a category of cuisine that uses finely ground soybean or nuts as a base ingredient. In summer, the broth can be made in a large batch and frozen for later, which is perfect for making the summer delicacy Cold Soybean Guksu (page 374).

Adding ground nuts, such as pine nuts or peanuts, can add a natural sweetness. Instead of soybeans, use a equal amount of dried black beans or sesame seeds to make a broth.

Preparation time: 30 minutes, plus 3 hours soaking time
Cooking time: 30 minutes
Makes: 6 cups (48 fl oz/1.4 liters)

Generous 1 cup (200 g) dried soybeans, rinsed
2 tablespoons sesame seeds

In a large bowl, combine the soybeans with twice its volume of water and soak for 3 hours. Rinse the soybeans with cold water and drain.

In a pot, combine the soybeans with 3 cups (24 fl oz/710 ml) water and bring to a boil over high heat. Once boiling, reduce the heat to medium and boil for 10 minutes. Remove from the heat and let sit for 5 minutes before draining.

Combine the cooked soybeans with cold water in a large bowl and gently rub off any skins. Discard the skins and drain the soybeans in a sieve.

In a blender or food processor, combine the cooked soybeans, 6 cups (48 fl oz/1.4 liters) water, and the sesame seeds and blend until fine. Strain through a fine-mesh sieve into a container. It should be the consistency of nut milk. Let cool completely in the refrigerator.

# Guk & Tang Soups
## 국 & 탕

In a proper Korean table spread, it's rare that a broth-based dish, such as *guk* or *tang*, is missing. Both of these dishes, *guk* and *tang*, are soups. They are made from long-brewed broths and stocks and both focus on bringing out the inherent flavors of its ingredients. The major differences are that *guk* is served in individual servings and *tang* (an honorific word for "soup") is generally cooked for a longer amount of time and is often served as a communal dish.

Korean cuisine pairs these dishes with cooked rice, combining the cooked rice directly into the broth to eat. After the rice is finished, the broth is savored until the last drop, often drunk straight from the bowl. The combination of rice, the solid soup ingredients, and broth are what makes up the Korean broth culture, or *guk-mul*. The importance of broth in this scenario is represented by the Korean word for food itself: *eum-sik*; *eum* is the verb "to drink" and *sik* is the word for "chew." In Korea, food is always thought of as a combination of solid food and liquid food; drinking and eating are in the same line of thought.

In Korean cuisine, *mul* (water) and, by extension, broths are a focal point of not only cooking equipment (such as the traditional *sot*, or cauldron, used to daily cook rice and soups) but also table settings. For example, it is because of the *guk* culture of meals that are so broth-focused that Korea developed the pairing of spoon and chopsticks for eating. Other tableware created includes large individual bowls, deep plates, saucers, and *ttukbaegi* (earthenware bowls) to hold the broth and sauces of dishes. Even many *banchan* (side dishes) will come with broth or marinades, which naturally led to the development of shallow bowls or deep plates.

## Egg & Potato Guk
### Dalgyal Gamja Guk
### 달걀 감자국

dF vE -S -3o

**Preparation time:** 15 minutes
**Cooking time:** 15 minutes
**Serves:** 4

10 oz (300 g) potatoes
9 cups (72 fl oz/2.1 liters) Vegetable Broth (page 313)
2 tablespoons cheongjang (light Korean soy sauce) or anchovy fish sauce
Salt
2 eggs, beaten
¾ oz (20 g) daepa (Korean scallion), cut into ¼-inch (6 mm) diagonal slices

Eggs and potatoes are two of the most commonly found ingredients in any Korean kitchen. In Korea, where a traditional morning meal doesn't differ too much from a simple evening meal, *guk* is a staple for many for breakfast as well. This recipe is a favorite home-cooking recipe that provides a hearty meal to start the day, especially welcome by those who prefer to have *guk* for their meals. If potatoes are unavailable, this simple dish can be made with just the eggs.

Peel the potatoes and cut them lengthwise into quarters. Cut each quarter crosswise into slices ¼ inch (6 mm) thick. Set aside in water.

In a soup pot, bring the vegetable broth to a boil over high heat. Once boiling, add the sliced potatoes, reduce the heat to medium heat, and cook until the potatoes are firm-tender, about 8 minutes.

Stir in the soy sauce and salt to taste. Pour the beaten eggs into the soup in a gentle, circular motion. Once it starts to boil, add the daepa and remove from the heat. Taste and add more seasoning if needed.

Serve hot in individual bowls.

---

## Seaweed & Tofu Doenjang Guk
### Miyeok Dubu Doenjang Guk
### 미역 두부 된장국

dF vg vE

**Preparation time:** 20 minutes
**Cooking time:** 25 minutes
**Serves:** 4

8 g dried miyeok (wakame)
7 cups (56 fl oz/1.7 liters) Vegetable Broth (page 313)
2 tablespoons doenjang (fermented soybean paste)
½ tablespoon coarse gochugaru (red chili flakes)
1 tablespoon cheongjang (light Korean soy sauce)
10 oz (300 g) firm tofu, cut into ½-inch (1.3 cm) cubes
2 scallions (spring onions), thinly sliced

The deep, savory earthy flavor of doenjang, the fragrance of the sea from the seaweed, and the heartiness of the tofu makes this soup extremely comforting and satisfying, without using many ingredients. It's also great for if you're on a diet, because it's deeply satisfying and nutritious but not high in calories.

Soak the miyeok in warm water for 10 minutes to rehydrate. Drain in a sieve, then cut into 1-inch (2.5 cm) pieces and set aside.

Meanwhile, in a soup pot, bring the broth to a boil.

Once boiling, add the rehydrated miyeok and boil for 15 minutes. Add the doenjang to the soup by pushing it through a small sieve (this results in a clearer broth; if you add the doenjang directly, the broth will be cloudier). Add the gochugaru, soy sauce, and tofu and boil for 5 more minutes. Adjust the seasoning as needed before removing from the heat and adding the scallions.

Serve hot in individual bowls.

### Variations

• For a spicier broth and a deeper flavor in the soup, add ½ tablespoon gochujang (red chili paste).

• For a more savory broth, replace the vegetable broth with anchovy broth and season with fish sauce.

Banchan

## Gim Guk
김국

dF vE -3o

*Gim* (seaweed) is most commonly available in its dried form in large sheets, or prepacked into smaller bite-size pieces suitable for *banchan* (side dishes). In Korea, one can also find *gim* in more diverse forms, including its fresh version, or dried in balls instead of as sheets. *Gim guk* can be made with the most common dried version, but it can be substituted with fresh *gim* as well. Adding an egg is a quick way to add some protein, but the soup is delicious and nutritious made just with *gim*.

**Preparation time:** 10 minutes
**Cooking time:** 10 minutes
**Serves:** 4

4 sheets gim
7 cups (56 fl oz/1.7 liters) Vegetable Broth (page 313)
2 tablespoons cheongjang (light Korean soy sauce)
1 teaspoon sesame oil
2 eggs, lightly beaten
¾ oz (20 g) daepa (Korean scallion), thinly sliced on a diagonal
Salt and freshly ground black pepper

In a dry frying pan, roast each sheet of gim on each side until crisp. Place the sheets in a zip-seal plastic bag and crush with your hands until finely crushed. (Alternatively, shred the gim with your hands or cut with scissors or a knife, but the bag method prevents mess.)

In a soup pot, combine the broth, soy sauce, and sesame oil and bring to a boil. Once boiling, add the crushed gim. After 1 minute, pour in the beaten eggs in a slow, circular motion around the pot. When it returns to a boil, add the daepa and remove from the heat. Season to taste with salt and black pepper.

Serve hot in individual bowls.

---

## Spinach Doenjang Guk
Sigeumchi Doenjang Guk
시금치 된장국

dF vg vE                      [m]

The spinach *doenjang guk* is a quick and easy dish to prepare when you want to begin the day with a warming bowl of soup with rice. This light and delicious *guk* gets a depth of flavor from the *doenjang*, which harmonizes beautifully with the sweetness of the spinach. The rice water (which is the cloudy water that comes from washing rice) is a great base for many soups and stews.

**Preparation time:** 20 minutes
**Cooking time:** 30 minutes
**Serves:** 4

**For the broth:**
8 cups (64 fl oz/1.9 liters) rice water
1 sheet dasima
6 oz (175 g) mu (Korean radish)
1½ oz (40 g) daepa (Korean scallion)

**For the soup:**
9 oz (250 g) spinach, well rinsed
3 tablespoons doenjang (fermented soybean paste)
1 tablespoon rice cooking wine
1 tablespoon cheongjang (light Korean soy sauce)
1 oz (25 g) fresh green Cheongyang chili (optional), thinly sliced on a diagonal
Salt

**Make the broth:** In a soup pot, combine the rice water, dasima, radish, and daepa and bring to a boil over medium heat. Boil for 15 minutes. Strain the broth (discard the solids).

**Make the soup:** Cut the spinach into 2-inch (5 cm) pieces and set aside.

In a soup pot, combine the broth, doenjang, wine, and soy sauce and bring to a boil. Add the spinach and chili (if using) and boil for 3 minutes. Season to taste with salt and remove from the heat.

Serve hot in individual bowls.

**Variations**

• For a milder version, omit the chili. Or to go in the other direction, add gochugaru (red chili flakes) to taste.

• Substitute chard or cluster mallow for the spinach, but blanch the chard before adding it to get rid of the strong vegetal flavor. And for the mallow, it's important to remove any tough stems.

• Adding dried shrimp or fresh Korean cyclina clam is another common variation. Dried shrimp are an especially good choice if you make this with mallow.

## Korean Zucchini Jeot Guk
### Aehobak Jeot Guk
### 애호박 젓국

dF gF

In Seoul and Gyeonggi province, clear soup seasoned with *jeotgal* (preserved seafood) was traditionally enjoyed. In the *aehobak jeot guk*, beef is a common addition. Variations made with clam meat or oysters are also delicious. Korean zucchini (courgette) is in season in the summertime, but this warm soup is a dish that comes to mind even more in fall, when the cool winds begin to mark the end of summer.

**Preparation time:** 20 minutes
**Cooking time:** 25 minutes
**Serves:** 4

- 9 oz (260 g) aehobak (Korean zucchini)
- 5 oz (145 g) firm tofu
- 6 cups (48 fl oz/1.4 liters) Anchovy Broth (page 314)
- 2 tablespoons salted shrimp
- 2 tablespoons rice cooking wine
- ½ tablespoon minced garlic
- 1½ oz (40 g) daepa (Korean scallion), thinly sliced on a diagonal
- 1 oz (25 g) fresh green Cheongyang chili, thinly sliced on a diagonal
- Salt

Quarter the zucchini lengthwise and slice crosswise into slices ¼ inch (6 mm) thick. Cut the tofu into bite-size rectangles ½ inch (1.3 cm) thick.

In a soup pot, bring the anchovy broth to a boil. Add the zucchini and tofu and cook until the zucchini is cooked to semitranslucent. Add the salted shrimp, wine, garlic, daepa, and chili and boil for 5 minutes. Season to taste with salt. and remove from the heat.

Serve hot in individual bowls.

**Variations**

• For a clearer soup, wash the tofu under cold running water before boiling and use just the brine of the salted shrimp.

• To easily turn this soup into a jjigae (stew), reduce the amount of water and add more vegetables.

---

## Bean Sprout Guk
### Kongnamul Guk
### 콩나물국

dF vg vE -30    [ㅁ]

*Kongnamul guk* is a type of *guk* where it's best if the broth used is made with only scallion (spring onion) and garlic and a light seasoning. Each household has a different preference for how to season the soup, with common choices being fish sauce, shrimp sauce, salt, or soy sauce.

Even just a few decades ago, many households would grow their own soybean sprouts at home. Today, however, because fresh soybean sprouts are readily available in the market year-round, they are a ubiquitous staple in Korean households.

**Preparation time:** 15 minutes
**Cooking time:** 10 minutes
**Serves:** 4

- 10 oz (300 g) soybean spouts
- 8 cups (64 fl oz /1.9 liters) Vegetable Broth (page 313)
- 1 teaspoon minced garlic
- 1 teaspoon salt
- 1 teaspoon cheongjang (light Korean soy sauce)
- 1 oz (30 g) daepa (Korean scallion), cut on a diagonal into thick pieces
- 1 oz (25 g) fresh red chilies, slivered

Wash the bean sprouts in a large bowl of cold water, shaking them gently to shake off the skins. Wash again under cold running water one or two times until clean. Drain and set aside to dry.

In a soup pot, bring the vegetable broth to a boil. Once boiling, add the bean sprouts, garlic, salt, and soy sauce and stir well. Cover with a lid and boil until the bean sprouts are fully cooked, about 5 minutes. Add the daepa and red chilies and bring to a boil. Remove from the heat. Adjust the seasoning to taste.

Serve hot in individual bowls.

**Variation:** To make the soup more refreshing, add julienned Korean radish to the soup along with the bean sprouts.

## Kimchi & Bean Sprout Guk
## Kimchi Kongnamul Guk
## 김치 콩나물국

dF  [ㅁ]

Rich meat-based *haejang-guk* (hangover soup) can be great, but this lightly simmered kimchi and bean sprout *guk* is one of the easiest cures to make the morning after. Served with warm, fresh rice, it makes a favorite and comforting combination.

If the kimchi is made with *jeotgal* (preserved seafood), the savory levels may already be sufficient. Otherwise, you can augment the umami here by adding fish sauce or salted shrimp as a part of the seasoning. Adding the liquid from kimchi can also add a nice tartness to the soup.

**Preparation time:** 20 minutes
**Cooking time:** 20 minutes
**Serves:** 4

7 oz (200 g) soybean sprouts
3½ oz (100 g) Napa Cabbage Kimchi, store-bought or homemade (page 60)
8 cups (64 fl oz/1.9 liters) Anchovy Broth (page 314)
1 teaspoon minced garlic
1 oz (30 g) daepa (Korean scallion), thinly sliced on a diagonal
Salt

In a large bowl, rinse the bean sprouts in cold water. Gently shake handfuls of bean sprouts, removing any skin or broken parts. Rinse with cold water one or two more times until clean and set aside to drain.

Brush any excess seasoning off the kimchi, cut into 1-inch (2.5 cm) pieces, and add to a soup pot. Add the anchovy broth and garlic and bring to a boil. Boil for 5 minutes until the kimchi is cooked. Add the bean sprouts and boil for another 5 minutes. Once the bean sprouts are well cooked, add the daepa and season to taste with salt.

Serve hot in individual bowls.

---

## Beef & Seaweed Guk
## Sogogi Miyeok Guk
## 소고기 미역국

dF

*Miyeok guk* is an important dish in Korean culture. Mothers traditionally eat this dish after giving birth, because the nutritional value is said to be perfect for building strength postbirth. It's also usually eaten on one's birthday as a celebration of this tradition. But more than just a celebratory food, it's one of the most beloved everyday Korean dishes. The version of *miyeok guk* made with beef (as here) is perhaps the most common, but in coastal areas, seaweed soup is made with various seafood, such as white fish, abalone, clams, yellow pollock, and sea urchin.

Stir-frying the seaweed in oil before boiling brings out the savoriness of the seaweed to create a deeper, richer broth. There's no set rule for which cut of beef to use, but typically a leaner cut is chosen, because it makes the soup taste "beefier."

**Preparation time:** 45 minutes
**Cooking time:** 35 minutes
**Serves:** 4

¾ oz (20 g) dried miyeok (wakame)
Salt
5 oz (150 g) boneless beef shank or tenderloin, preferably grass-fed
2 tablespoons neutral cooking oil
2 tablespoons sesame oil
2 tablespoons cheongjang (light Korean soy sauce)
2 tablespoons sand lance fish sauce

In a large bowl, soak the seaweed in water for 40 minutes to rehydrate. Drain. If using natural dried miyeok that hasn't been commercially processed, rub the rehydrated seaweed with a spoonful of salt to remove any impurities and rinse several times in water. Cut the seaweed into 1-inch (2.5 cm) pieces.

Meanwhile, thinly slice the beef and cut into ½-inch (1.3 cm) squares.

In a large soup pot, heat the cooking oil over medium heat. Add the beef and stir-fry until browned. Add the sesame oil, rehydrated seaweed, and soy sauce and continue to stir-fry until well incorporated. Add 9 cups (72 fl oz/2.1 liters) water and boil over medium heat for 20 minutes.

Add the fish sauce and salt to taste (the reason for using both is that seasoning with just salt can result in a mild flavor and seasoning with just the fish sauce can lead to an overly fishy flavor).

Serve hot in individual bowls.

### Variations

• Some cooks like to add rehydrated seaweed at the very end of the cooking process for a clean texture.

• Another common variation is to add 1 tablespoon minced garlic when boiling.

## Beef & Radish Guk
Sogogi Mu Guk
소고기 무국

dF [o]

The beef *mu guk* is easy to make and is a widely beloved soup, making it a common household staple. It is consumed nationwide, but there are some regional style variations: A spicy version is made with *gochugaru* (red chili flakes) and a more refreshing version is made with bean sprouts. Some recipes will call for stir-frying the beef in sesame oil before adding the broth, and some will stir-fry the radish. Here, we present a simple, standard recipe in a clean style.

Preparation time: 20 minutes
Cooking time: 45 minutes
Serves: 4

5 oz (150 g) boneless beef shank or brisket, cut into 1-inch (2.5 cm) chunks
2 tablespoons cheongjang (light Korean soy sauce)
12 oz (350 g) mu (Korean radish), peeled and cut into 1-inch (2.5 cm) square pieces ½ inch (1.3 cm) thick
1 tablespoon minced garlic
1 tablespoon sesame oil
Freshly ground black pepper
1 oz (30 g) daepa (Korean scallion), thinly sliced on a diagonal
Salt

In a soup pot, bring 8 cups (64 fl oz/1.9 liters) water to a boil. Add the beef and skim any impurities and foam. Reduce the heat to medium and boil for 20 minutes.

Add the soy sauce and radish and boil for another 10 minutes. Add the garlic, sesame oil, and black pepper to taste and boil for another 5 minutes. Stir in the daepa, remove from the heat, and season with salt to taste.

Serve hot in individual bowls.

## Horsehead Tilefish & Radish Guk
Okdom Mu Guk
옥돔 무국

dF -S

The horsehead tilefish, called *ok-dom* in Korean, is a treasured fish that's caught off Jeju Island, and the *mu guk* made with it is a signature delicacy of Jeju. This fish is also used there to make seaweed soup, but this tilefish *mu guk* better showcases the inherent prized flavors of the fish.

The soup is lightly seasoned (no garlic, no fish sauce) to enjoy the flavors of the tilefish. When this guk is served at *jaesa* (ancestor-honoring) ceremonies, even the scallions (spring onions) and soy sauce are not used, seasoning only with salt.

Preparation time: 20 minutes
Cooking time: 30 minutes
Serves: 4

1 whole horsehead tilefish (8–9 oz/230–250 g), cleaned and gutted
12 oz (350 g) mu (Korean radish)
1 tablespoon cheongjang (light Korean soy sauce)
Salt
2 scallions (spring onions), thinly sliced

Remove any remaining scales from the horsehead tilefish and rinse off under cold running water. Remove the fins using sharp scissors. Cut the fish crosswise through the spine and ribs (bones and all) into sections 2 inches (5 cm) wide. Rinse the pieces again under running water. Reserve the head.

Peel the radish and cut into 2-inch (5 cm) lengths. Cut each piece lengthwise into slices ⅛ inch (3 mm) thick and cut those slices into matchsticks ⅛ inch (3 mm) thick.

In a soup pot, bring 8 cups (64 fl oz/1.9 liters) water to a boil over high heat. Once boiling, add all of the fish including the head, and reduce the heat to medium. Boil for 15 minutes. Once the broth turns white, add the radish and boil for another 5 minutes. Season with soy sauce and salt to taste and stir in the scallions.

Serve hot in individual bowls.

## Pollock Guk
### Hwangtae Mu Guk
### 황태 무국

dF

Pollock soup is one of the most famous *haejang* ("hangover") soups of Korea. Its refreshing taste makes it a favored *guk* for when under the weather (or hungover). It is made with dried pollock, which has less fat content than other common fish. The most prized version of this dried fish is called *deodeok bukeo* (a reference to the *deodeok* root), because of the yellowish color of the fish's flesh from repeating a freezing and thawing process during the winter drying.

If you don't have beef broth, use Anchovy Broth (page 314), Vegetable Broth (page 313), or rice water (page 312). If using rice water, adding 1 teaspoon of rice flour will add body to the broth.

Preparation time: 20 minutes
Cooking time: 25 minutes
Serves: 4

2½ oz (70 g) dried shredded pollock
2 tablespoons sesame oil
6 cups (48 fl oz/1.4 liters) Beef Broth (page 315)
7 oz (200 g) mu (Korean radish), cut into 1-inch (2.5 cm) square pieces ¼ inch (6 mm) thick
1 teaspoon minced garlic
1 tablespoon cheongjang (light Korean soy sauce)
10 oz (300 g) firm tofu, cut into slices 1 inch (2.5 cm) thick
2 eggs, lightly beaten
1 oz (30 g) daepa (Korean scallion), sliced on a diagonal
Salt
Gochugaru (red chili flakes; optional)

Rinse the shredded pollock under cold running water. Cut into 1-inch (2.5 cm) lengths and set aside.

In a soup pot, heat the sesame oil over medium heat, add the pollock, and stir-fry for 30 seconds. Add a small amount of the beef broth and continue to stir-fry until the broth starts to turn white. Add the remaining broth, the radish, garlic, and soy sauce and cook over medium heat until the radish is tender, 15–20 minutes.

Add the tofu, beaten eggs, and daepa. Once boiling, remove from the heat and season to taste with salt. If desired, add some gochugaru.

Serve hot in individual bowls.

---

## Squid & Radish Guk
### Ojingeo Mu Guk
### 오징어 무국

dF

Made with in-season fall squid and Korean radish, the *ojingeo mu guk* has a uniquely savory flavor profile. The squid itself imparts a deep, savory flavor to the broth, even if made simply with water instead of the anchovy broth. Adding the heat of chilies makes this a popular hangover cure.

Preparation time: 20 minutes
Cooking time: 25 minutes
Serves: 2–3

7 oz (200 g) squid, cleaned
2 tablespoons neutral cooking oil
7 oz (200 g) mu (Korean radish), peeled and cut into slices ¼ inch (6 mm) thick
5 cups (40 fl oz/1.2 liters) Anchovy Broth (page 314)
1 teaspoon minced garlic
2 tablespoons anchovy fish sauce
1 tablespoon cheongjang (light Korean soy sauce)
1 tablespoon gochugaru (red chili flakes)
1 oz (30 g) daepa (Korean scallion), thinly sliced on a diagonal
1¾ oz (50 g) fresh red chilies, thinly sliced on a diagonal

Rinse the squid body and tentacles well under cold water. Trim the squid body into 2 × ½-inch (5 × 1.3 cm) strips. Cut the tentacles into 2-inch (5 cm) lengths.

In a pot, heat the cooking oil over high heat. Add the sliced radish and stir-fry until the radish begins to turn translucent. Add the squid and continue to stir-fry for 1 minute. Add half of the anchovy broth, the garlic, fish sauce, and soy sauce. Boil for 5 minutes, then add the remainder of the anchovy broth and the gochugaru. Boil for 5 more minutes. Stir in the daepa and chilies and let boil briefly before removing from the heat.

Serve hot in individual bowls.

# Baby Jumbo Shrimp & Napa Cabbage Doenjang Guk
## Bori Saeu Ugeoji Doenjang Guk
## 보리새우 우거지 된장국

dF

There are many Korean dishes that incorporate the autumnal napa cabbage (Chinese leaf), but the most used application is, of course, for kimchi. When making kimchi, the first few green outer layers of the cabbage are discarded, because they're too tough for kimchi. But these scraps do not go to waste: They are boiled until tender and used as an ingredient, called *ugeoji*, in many different soups and even vegetable sides. In this dish, the sweet and earthy flavors of the *ugeoji* and the savory sea fragrance of the jumbo shrimp (tiger prawns) is perfect for cold winter days.

*Ugeoji* is a good thing to make ahead in batches to be used later. Cook as directed, then squeeze tightly to remove excess moisture. Form into balls the size of baseballs about 7 ounces (200 g) each. This amount is good for three to four people in soup, simmered dishes, or vegetables sides. It's a great staple to have on hand and can be stored in the freezer for use year-round.

Preparation time: 25 minutes
Cooking time: 20 minutes
Serves: 4

For the ugeoji:
14 oz (400 g) ugeoji (outer leaves of napa cabbage/Chinese leaf)
½ teaspoon salt
3 tablespoons doenjang (fermented soybean paste)
1 teaspoon minced garlic

For the soup:
8 cups (64 fl oz/1.9 liters) Anchovy Broth (page 314)
2 oz (60 g) daepa (Korean scallions), cut into ½-inch (1.3 cm) diagonal slices
3½ oz (100 g) baby jumbo shrimp (tiger prawns)
2 fresh green Cheongyang chilies, finely diced
Salt

**Make the ugeoji:** Thoroughly wash the outer green leaves of the napa cabbage. In a large pot, bring at least 8½ cups (68 fl oz/2 liters) water to a boil. Once boiling, add the napa cabbage leaves and cook until the thick white stem ends turn translucent and soft, about 7 minutes. Drain and let cool in a bowl of cold water for 5 minutes. Drain and gently squeeze to remove excess water. Cut into 1-inch (2.5 cm) squares.

In a bowl, toss together the ugeoji, salt, doenjang, and garlic and massage thoroughly until well seasoned.

**Make the soup:** In a pot, combine the seasoned ugeoji with the anchovy broth and boil over high heat for 10 minutes. Add the daepa and jumbo shrimp and boil for 5 more minutes. Season to taste with salt as needed.

## Maesaengi Oyster Guk
### Maesaengi Gul Guk
### 매생이 굴국

dF -S -3o  [□]

*Maesaengi* is a winter seaweed delicacy, mainly harvested off the Korean southern coast and in season from November to February. It grows in the form of dark green bundles of silky, thin threads, thinner than hair. It contains a strong aroma of the sea and flavors to match. Similar to other seaweeds, it contains high levels of iron, iodine, and calcium and is noted for its health benefits. With just two main ingredients in this soup, the *maesaengi* and oyster, one can truly enjoy the taste of the deep sea.

**Preparation time:** 10 minutes
**Cooking time:** 10 minutes
**Serves:** 4

10 oz (300 g) fresh maesaengi
7 oz (200 g) shucked oysters
8 cups (64 fl oz/1.9 liters) Anchovy Broth (page 314)
2 tablespoons cheongjang (light Korean soy sauce)
Salt

Fill a large bowl with cold water, add the seaweed, massaging and shaking it thoroughly to remove any impurities. Repeat the process with clean water. Drain off excess water in a sieve.

If you shucked the oysters yourself, clean the oyster meats gently in a bowl of cold salted water.

In a soup pot, combine the anchovy broth and soy sauce and bring to a boil. Add the seaweed and oysters and boil for just 3 minutes. Remove from the heat and season to taste with salt as needed.

Serve hot in individual bowls.

---

## Cold Eggplant Guk
### Gaji Naeng-guk
### 가지 냉국

dF vg vE -3o

Eggplants (aubergines) are a great vegetable to use in a *naeng-guk* (cold soup), because they absorb flavors very well. Precooking eggplants in the microwave instead of in a steamer allows them to steam by using their own moisture content without diluting their flavor. The eggplants are seasoned separately before adding them to the soup, so they can absorb the flavors directly in their more concentrated form.

**Preparation time:** 10 minutes
**Cooking time:** 5 minutes
**Serves:** 4

3 Korean eggplants (aubergines)
1 tablespoon ganjang (Korean soy sauce)
1 teaspoon minced garlic
5 tablespoons rice vinegar
2 tablespoons sugar
1 tablespoon cheongjang (light Korean soy sauce)
1 teaspoon salt
2 scallions (spring onions), thinly sliced
1 oz (25 g) green Cheongyang chilies, thinly sliced on a diagonal
Ice cubes

Quarter the eggplants lengthwise and then cut crosswise into 1-inch (2.5 cm) lengths. Set in a microwave-safe bowl and cover with plastic wrap (cling film). Microwave for 2 minutes. Let cool to room temperature. Remove the eggplant skin and tear by hand to ¼-inch (6 mm) pieces. Place the eggplants in a bowl, add the soy sauce and garlic, and mix until well incorporated.

In a large bowl, combine 3 cups (24 fl oz/700 ml) water, the vinegar, sugar, light soy sauce, and salt and mix until uniform. Add the seasoned eggplants, scallions, and chilies and mix. Add ice to make the broth extra cold, and adjust seasoning to taste.

Serve in individual bowls.

# Cold Cucumber & Seaweed Guk
## Oi Miyeok Naeng-guk
## 오이 미역 냉국

dF vg

The cold cucumber *miyeok guk* is perfect for the summer season, when appetites run low. Featuring cucumbers, seasoned with light soy sauce and vinegar, it is one of the most popular *naeng-guk* (cold soups) of Korea. While the fish sauce adds body and savory flavor profile to the dish, simply replace it with soy sauce for a vegan version.

**Preparation time: 40 minutes**
**Cooking time: 5 minutes**
**Serves: 4**

15 g dried miyeok (wakame)
1¾ oz (50 g) onion, thinly sliced
5 tablespoons rice vinegar
1 tablespoon fresh lemon juice
2 tablespoons sugar
1 tablespoon cheongjang (light Korean soy sauce)
1 tablespoon Yondu (Korean vegan seasoning sauce)
1 teaspoon salt
5 oz (150 g) cucumber, cut into long matchsticks
2–3 cloves garlic, thinly sliced
1 oz (25 g) fresh green Cheongyang chili, thinly sliced
Ice cubes
Sesame seeds (optional)

Soak the dried seaweed in water for 30 minutes. Drain and cut into 1-inch pieces. For a softer texture, after rehydrating, blanch in a small pot of boiling water for 30 seconds and shock in cold water.

Meanwhile, soak the onion slices in cold water for 10 minutes to reduce the pungency.

In a large bowl, combine 3 cups (24 fl oz/700 ml) water, the vinegar, lemon juice, sugar, soy sauce, Yondu, salt and mix well. Add the seaweed, cucumber, garlic, and chili. Add ice and adjust seasoning to taste.

Serve in individual bowls. Garnish with sesame seeds if desired.

# Cold Chicken Guk
## Chogye Naeng-guk
## 초계 냉국

dF

**Preparation time:** 1 hour, plus overnight chilling
**Cooking time:** 15 minutes
**Serves:** 3–4

**For the stock:**
1 extra-small whole chicken (2 lb/910 g), such as a Cornish hen or poussin, cut in half
5 cloves garlic, peeled but whole
1 oz (30 g) daepa (Korean scallion), cut into 2 pieces

**For the mustard chicken:**
3 tablespoons rice vinegar
2 tablespoons sugar
1 tablespoon hot mustard
1 tablespoon ganjang (Korean soy sauce)
1 teaspoon minced garlic

**For the soup:**
3½ oz (100 g) onion, thinly sliced
5 oz (150 g) cucumber, cut into thin matchsticks
7 oz (200 g) mu (Korean radish), cut into thin matchsticks
2½ teaspoons salt
2 teaspoons sugar
4 tablespoons rice vinegar
1 tablespoon cheongjang (light Korean soy sauce)
1¾ oz (50 g) carrot, cut into thin matchsticks

The vegetables used in this chilled chicken soup can change depending on seasonality. Sweet bell peppers, cabbage, and perilla are all popular, and sliced cherry tomatoes are also a summer staple. To make a more complete meal, serve this with buckwheat noodles or medium-thick wheat noodles.

**Make the stock:** In a large pot, combine the chicken, 6⅓ cups (48 fl oz/1.5 liters) water, the garlic, and daepa and boil for 20 minutes. Remove the fully cooked chicken and set aside to cool. Strain the stock through a fine-mesh sieve (discard the solids). Refrigerate the cooked chicken and stock separately. Let the stock rest overnight to allow any fat to solidify. Discard the layer of fat and strain the stock again before using.

**Make the mustard chicken:** In a medium bowl, combine the vinegar, sugar, mustard, soy sauce, and garlic and mix until uniform. Shred the chicken meat, add to the seasoning ingredients in the bowl, and combine until seasoned uniformly. Set aside in the refrigerator.

**Prepare the soup:** Soak the onion slices in water for 15 minutes to remove the pungency and then drain. At the same time, place the cucumber and radish in each of two bowls. Add 1 teaspoon of salt and 1 teaspoon of sugar to each and toss well. Let sit for 15 minutes, then rinse in cold water. Gently squeeze out any excess water.

In a large bowl, combine 4 cups (32 fl oz/950 ml) of the cooled chicken stock, the vinegar, light soy sauce, and ½ teaspoon salt and mix until the seasoned broth is uniform.

Divide the mustard-seasoned chicken among individual soup bowls. Dividing evenly, top with each of the vegetables. Pour in the cold seasoned broth. Serve chilled.

# Beef Bone Tang
## Gomtang
## 곰탕

DF

*Gomtang*, one of Korea's most iconic soups, is synonymous with restorative foods eaten to provide nourishment for the body. *Gomtang* and *seolleongtang* (Ox Bone Tang, page 335), both soups made from a base bone broth, are sometimes referred to interchangeably. Yet there are key differences: *Gomtang*'s broth incorporates cuts of meat to the broth for a clearer and savory taste, while *seolleongtang*'s broth is made with primarily bones. This *gomtang* recipe showcases one in which a light bone broth is fortified by boiling with various meats.

Preparation time: 15 minutes,
    plus 3 hours soaking time
Cooking time: 4 hours
Serves: 6

**For the broth:**
1 lb (500 g) beef leg bones
7 oz (200 g) beef brisket
7 oz (200 g) boneless beef shank
7 oz (200 g) beef stomach
7 oz (200 g) beef small intestines
1 oz (30 g) mu (Korean radish)
2 oz (60 g) daepa (Korean scallion)
1 oz (30 g) garlic, peeled

**For the meat:**
1 tablespoon cheongjang
    (light Korean soy sauce)
1 teaspoon minced garlic
1 teaspoon sesame oil
1 teaspoon salt

**For the soup:**
4 tablespoons cheongjang
    (light Korean soy sauce)
1 tablespoon salt

**For serving:**
Salt
Freshly ground black pepper
Thinly sliced daepa (Korean scallion)

**Make the broth:** Soak the beef leg bones in cold water for 3 hours to remove any blood and impurities. In a large pot, combine the beef leg bones with water to cover. Boil over high heat for 5 minutes. Discard the water and rinse the bones under cold running water. In the same pot, with fresh water to cover, cook the bones over medium heat for 3 hours. Discard the bones.

Meanwhile, soak the brisket and shank in cold water for 30 minutes to remove any blood and impurities. (The stomach and intestines should be purchased already cleaned.)

To the pot of bone broth, add the brisket, shank, stomach, and intestines and boil over medium heat for 40 minutes. Skim the foam and oil that forms throughout the boiling period.

Add the radish, daepa, and garlic and boil for 20 minutes. Remove from the heat and set aside the meat and radish (discard the daepa and garlic). Strain the broth. Cut the radish into 1-inch (2.5 cm) square pieces ¼ inch (6 mm) thick and set aside.

**Season the meat:** Slice the brisket and shank to the same size as the radish. Slice the stomach and intestines into 1-inch (2.5 cm) pieces. In a large bowl, combine the soy sauce, garlic, sesame oil, and salt. Add the meat pieces and toss together.

**For the soup:** Season the strained broth with the soy sauce and salt.

**To serve:** Add each meat and radish to individual bowls and ladle the hot lightly seasoned broth over the ingredients. Serve along with saucers of salt, black pepper, and sliced daepa to season to taste individually at the table.

## Beef Short Rib Tang
### Galbi Tang
### 갈비탕

dF

If desired, for a more highly seasoned meat, lightly marinate the ribs with soy sauce, sesame oil, and freshly ground black pepper when scoring the ribs. For the most flavor, it is best to boil the ribs with the fat still on, then skim the rendered fat while boiling.

**Preparation time: 15 minutes, plus 3 hours soaking time**
**Cooking time: 1 hour 45 minutes**
**Serves: 4**

**For the beef broth:**
2¼ lb (1 kg) beef short ribs, cut into pieces 2 inches (5 cm) wide
2 oz (60 g) daepa (Korean scallion)
3½ oz (100 g) onion
1 oz (30 g) garlic

**For the soup:**
1 egg
Salt
Neutral cooking oil
10 oz (300 g) mu (Korean radish), cut into 1-inch (2.5 cm) square pieces ¼-inch (6 mm) thick
4 tablespoons cheongjang (light Korean soy sauce)
1 oz (30 g) daepa (Korean scallion), sliced

**Make the beef broth:** Soak the beef ribs in a large bowl of cold water for 3 hours, changing the water twice.

In a large pot, combine the beef with water to cover, bring to a boil, and boil for 10 minutes. Drain and rinse the ribs under cold running water.

In a large pot, combine the beef, 8 cups (64 fl oz/1.9 liters) cold water, daepa, onion, and garlic and boil over medium heat for 1 hour, skimming the oil and impurities that rise. Strain the broth into a clean large pot. Remove the meat and discard the other solids. Remove any tough tendons or fat on the meat.

**Make the soup:** Crack the egg and separate the white and yolk into separate bowls. Loosen, seasoning each lightly with salt. Wet a paper towel with some cooking oil and wipe a thin film on the bottom of a frying pan. Heat over low heat, add the yolk, and cook in a thin sheet. Repeat to cook the egg white in a thin sheet. Cut the egg sheets into thin strips 2 inches (5 cm) long.

Add the radish and beef to the beef broth and simmer over low heat for 20 minutes. Add the soy sauce and sliced daepa and simmer for 3 more minutes. Season to taste with salt.

Serve in individual bowls garnished with the egg white and yolk strips.

---

## Ox Bone Tang
### Seolleongtang
### 설렁탕

dF gF

*Seolleongtang* is made by simmering beef bones for a long period of time. The milky white soup is famous for its richness and depth of flavor, yet it is soft and gentle from the long braise. Because it is rich in collagen, it has a distinct rich texture, but it maintains a lightness that makes one feel rejuvenated. At home, the prized beef bones are brewed not only once, but two or three times, to extend the broth, which is considered to be one of the most restorative foods in Korean cuisine. Many Koreans share the memories of eating *seolleongtang* for several days at home when beef bones were acquired or gifted.

**Preparation time: 15 minutes, plus 3 hours soaking time**
**Cooking time: 8 hours**
**Serves: 6**

1 lb (500 g) cow's feet (trotters)
2¼ lb (1 kg) beef leg bones
7 oz (200 g) beef brisket
7 oz (200 g) boneless beef shank
2 oz (60 g) daepa (Korean scallion)
1 oz (30 g) garlic

**For serving:**
Salt
Freshly ground black pepper
Thinly sliced daepa (Korean scallion)

Soak the feet and leg bones in cold water for 3 hours to remove any blood and impurities. Drain.

In a large pot, combine the feet, bones, and cold water to cover, bring to a boil over high heat and boil for 5 minutes. Discard the water and rinse the trotters and bones under cold running water.

Refill the pot with the feet and bones and cold water to cover. Bring to a boil over medium heat and cook for 5 hours, skimming off any impurities. When the broth is a milky white color, remove the bones and set aside. Strain the broth.

Refill the large pot again with the feet and bones and cold water to cover. Bring to a boil over medium heat and cook for 3 hours.

Meanwhile, soak the brisket and shank in cold water for 30 minutes to remove any blood and impurities.

Add the first batch of strained broth to the pot with the feet and bones, along with the brisket, shank, daepa, and garlic and boil for 1 hour. Remove all the meat, bones, and feet and strain the broth. Set the broth aside to settle, then remove any excess oil that rises to the top.

**To serve:** Thinly slice the meat. In individual bowls, plate the cuts of brisket and shank and ladle over the hot broth. Serve along with saucers of salt, black pepper, and sliced daepa to season to taste individually at the table.

# Herbal Chicken Tang
## Samgyetang
## 삼계탕

dF gF

*Samgyetang* is the classic restorative food of the summertime. In Korea, small young chickens are bred and sold specifically for making this soup. These smaller chickens have a tender meat perfect for the dish, and the size is best for the traditional plating, which is to serve a whole chicken in individual bowls. Eating the soup, with its ginseng and other medicinal herbs, paired with the chicken stock, provides a lasting healthy energy.

**Preparation time: 15 minutes, plus 1 hour soaking time**
**Cooking time: 1 hour**
**Serves: 4**

1½ cups (330 g) glutinous rice
4 whole Cornish hens or poussins (1¼ lb/500–600 g each)
8 cloves garlic, peeled
8 dried jujubes (Chinese red dates)
8 chestnuts, peeled
4 ginseng roots (about 1½ oz/40 g total), peeled
Salt and freshly ground black pepper
1 oz (30 g) scallions (spring onions), minced

Rinse the glutinous rice in a sieve under cold running water, then let it soak in a bowl of cold water for 1 hour. Drain well.

Trim off the tails and the fatty area of the necks of the chickens. Rinse out any blood or remaining scraps of innards.

Dividing evenly, stuff the chickens with the glutinous rice. Add to each 2 garlic cloves, 2 jujubes, 2 chestnuts, and 1 ginseng. Cross the legs and tie with kitchen string to keep the stuffing in.

In a large pot, combine the stuffed chickens with 15 cups (120 fl oz/3.6 liters) water. Bring to a boil over high heat. Once boiling, reduce the heat to medium-low and boil for 50 minutes, skimming any foam or impurities that rise.

Set a whole chicken into each of four large bowls or small individual earthenware pots and remove the string. Ladle the hot broth over each chicken and serve hot. Set out saucers of salt, pepper, and scallions to add to taste.

# Korean Chicken Tang
## Dak Gomtang
## 닭곰탕

dF

*Dak gomtang*, Korean chicken soup, is lighter and simpler to make than *samgyetang* (Herbal Chicken Tang, page 336), which requires ginseng and herbs. It is typically served with a side of *dadaegi* (Korean spicy paste), which each diner can use to adjust the spice level of the soup. The classic *dak gomtang* is great with rice folded directly in as a *gukbap*, and it's common to add noodles instead as well.

Preparation time: 25 minutes
Cooking time: 1 hour
Serves: 4

**For the stock:**
2 Cornish hens, poussins or extra-small chickens (1¾–2¼ lb/800 g–1 kg each), halved
3½ oz (100 g) onion, in chunks
2 oz (60 g) daepa (Korean scallion), in pieces
1½ oz (40 g) garlic, peeled

**For the spicy paste:**
4 tablespoons gochugaru (red chili flakes)
2 tablespoons cheongjang (Korean light soy sauce)
1 tablespoon minced garlic
1¾ oz (50 g) scallions (spring onions), thinly sliced

**For the soup:**
1 tablespoon salt
2 oz (60 g) sliced daepa (Korean scallion)
1 teaspoon freshly ground black pepper

**Make the stock:** Rinse any blood or remaining organs from the insides of the chickens. In a large pot, combine the chickens, 4 quarts (4 liters) water, the onion, daepa, and garlic and bring to a boil over high heat. Once boiling, reduce the heat to medium and boil for 25 minutes, skimming off any foam that rises.

Remove the chicken to cool slightly until cool enough to handle. Pull the meat off the bones and tear by hand to bite-size pieces and set aside. (To keep the shredded chicken meat from drying out while finishing the soup, you can lightly season it with soy sauce or gochugaru.)

Return the bones to the pot and continue to boil for 20 minutes. Strain the stock and discard the solids.

**Make the spicy paste:** In a bowl, combine 3 tablespoons of the strained chicken stock with the gochugaru, soy sauce, garlic, and scallions and mix until uniform. Set aside in a saucer.

**To finish the soup:** Return the strained stock to the pot. Add the shredded chicken and the salt. Serve in individual bowls, garnish with sliced daepa and a dash of black pepper, and serve hot along with the spicy paste.

# Pork Back Bone Tang
## Dwaeji Gamja Tang
## 돼지 감자탕

dF

This pork soup, which is made with a bone broth from long-braised pork bones, has been one of the most popular working man's foods in Korea throughout its history. This is not just because it's delicious, but because it is extremely filling, inexpensive, and easily shared as a meal or a dish to eat while drinking. Although the Korean word *gamja* in this recipe title literally translates to "potato," it actually refers to the back bones of the pork. (This is not commonly known in Korea either, but important to note.)

If boiled *ugeoji* is hard to source, use 1½ ounces (40 g) of dried *ugeoji* or *siraegi* (dried radish top greens) and soak in water to rehydrate and boil in water for 30 minutes before adding to the soup.

**Preparation time: 15 minutes, plus 3 hours soaking time**
**Cooking time: 1½ hours**
**Serves: 4**

**For the bone broth:**
2¼ lb (1 kg) pork back bones
3 tablespoons rice cooking wine

**For the seasoning:**
5 tablespoons cheongjang (light Korean soy sauce)
3 tablespoons gochugaru (red chili flakes)
2 tablespoons anchovy fish sauce
1 tablespoon doenjang (fermented soybean paste)
1 tablespoon gochujang (red chili paste)
1 tablespoon minced garlic

**For the soup:**
1 lb 5 oz (600 g) potatoes, quartered
10 oz (300 g) store-bought boiled ugeoji (outer leaves of napa cabbage/Chinese leaf), cut into 2-inch (5 cm) pieces
2 oz (60 g) daepa (Korean scallion), cut into 2-inch (5 cm) lengths
10 perilla leaves, cut crosswise into 2-inch (5 cm) strips
3 tablespoons perilla seed powder

**Make the bone broth:** Soak the pork back bones in a large bowl of cold water for 3 hours, changing the water twice.

Drain again and place in a pot with water to cover. Bring to a boil and cook for 10 minutes. Drain and rinse the bones with cold water.

In a large pot, combine the bones, about 8 cups (64 fl oz/1.9 liters) water (or enough to submerge the bones), and the wine and boil over medium heat for 30 minutes.

**Meanwhile, make the seasoning:** In a bowl, stir together the soy sauce, gochugaru, fish sauce, doenjang, gochujang, and garlic until uniform.

**Make the soup:** Add the seasoning sauce to the boiling pot of pork broth and stir to loosen the sauce and incorporate into the broth. Add the potatoes and ugeoji and cook until tender, about 30 minutes.

Add the daepa and perilla leaves and cook for 5 more minutes. Finish with the perilla seed powder.

Serve hot in a large bowl.

# Clear Cod Tang
## Malgeun Daegu Tang
## 맑은 대구탕

dF

Adding rice cooking wine or mirin at the end of the cooking will reduce any unwanted fishiness and create a refreshing tasting soup. Some cooks like to add a splash of rice vinegar to further enhance this refreshing flavor. Often, a dipping condiment of soy sauce and vinegar is served alongside to eat with the fish.

**Preparation time:** 25 minutes
**Cooking time:** 25 minutes
**Serves:** 4

6 cups (48 fl oz/1.4 liters) Anchovy Broth (page 314)
2¼ lb (1 kg) cod, cut into 2-inch (5 cm) chunks
7 oz (200 g) mu (Korean radish), cut into 1-inch (2.5 cm) square pieces ¼ inch (6 mm) thick
3½ oz (100 g) soybean sprouts
5 oz (150 g) firm tofu, cut into 1-inch (2.5 cm) square pieces ¼ inch (6 mm) thick
1 oz (30 g) daepa (Korean scallion), thinly sliced on a diagonal
1 oz (25 g) fresh green Cheongyang chili, thinly sliced on a diagonal
2¾ oz (80 g) minari, cut into 1-inch (2.5 cm) lengths
3 tablespoons rice cooking wine
1 teaspoon ginger juice
Salt

In a large pot, bring the anchovy broth to a boil over medium heat. Once boiling, add the cod and radish and cook for 10 minutes.

Add the bean sprouts and tofu and continue to boil for 5 more minutes.

Add the daepa, chili, and minari and boil for 3 more minutes. Add the wine and ginger juice and adjust the seasoning as needed with salt.

Serve hot.

# Spicy Cod Tang
## Daegu Maeuntang
## 대구 매운탕

dF

Using just *gochugaru* (red chili flakes) will result in a cleaner spicier soup, but adding the *gochujang* (red chili paste) will result in an earthier, more deeply flavored tang. Some cooks also add soy sauce. You can substitute soy sauce for the fish sauce, but the fish sauce will create a more strongly flavored, savory soup.

Preparation time: 25 minutes
Cooking time: 20 minutes
Serves: 4

**For the seasoning:**
4 tablespoons gochugaru (red chili flakes)
2 tablespoons mirin
1 tablespoon gochujang (red chili paste)
1 tablespoon cheongjang (light Korean soy sauce)
1 tablespoon anchovy fish sauce
1 tablespoon minced garlic
½ teaspoon minced fresh ginger

**For the soup:**
6 cups (48 fl oz/1.4 liters) Anchovy Broth (page 314)
2¼ lb (1 kg) cod, cut into 2-inch (5 cm) chunks
7 oz (200 g) mu (Korean radish), cut into 1-inch (2.5 cm) square pieces ¼ inch (6 mm) thick
3½ oz (100 g) soybean sprouts
5 oz (150 g) firm tofu, cut into 1-inch (2.5 cm) square pieces ¼ inch (6 mm) thick
2¾ oz (80 g) minari, cut into 1-inch (2.5 cm) lengths
1 oz (30 g) daepa (Korean scallion), thinly sliced on a diagonal
1 oz (25 g) fresh green Cheongyang chili, thinly sliced on a diagonal
Salt
1¾ oz (50 g) Korean chrysanthemum greens, cut into 1-inch (2.5 cm) pieces

**Make the seasoning:** In a bowl, stir together the gochugaru, mirin, gochujang, soy sauce, fish sauce, garlic, and ginger until uniform.

**Make the soup:** In a large pot, combine the anchovy broth and the seasoning and bring to a boil over medium heat. Once boiling, add the cod and radish and cook for 10 minutes. Add the bean sprouts and tofu and continue to boil for 5 more minutes. Add the minari, daepa, and chili and boil for 3 more minutes. Adjust the seasoning as needed with salt.

Remove from the heat, garnish with chrysanthemum greens, and serve.

# Seafood Tang
## Haemul Tang
## 해물탕

dF

The seafood in the soup can be changed according to preference or depending on what's in season, including squid, mussels, and more. The vegetables can also include napa cabbage (Chinese leaf), zucchini (courgette), mushrooms, and more. Some recipes will incorporate doenjang (fermented soybean paste) to taste in the seasoning for a deeper, more savory taste.

Preparation time: 30 minutes
Cooking time: 20 minutes
Serves: 4

For the seafood:
4 oz (120 g) Korean long-arm octopus
1 tablespoon flour or coarse salt
1 blue crab
8 short-necked clams
3¼ oz (90 g) sea squirts
6 shrimp (prawns)

For the seasoning:
3 tablespoons gochugaru (red chili flakes)
2 tablespoons rice cooking wine
1 tablespoon gochujang (red chili paste)
1 tablespoon doenjang (fermented soybean paste)
1 tablespoon cheongjang (light Korean soy sauce)
1 tablespoon fish sauce
1 tablespoon minced garlic
1 teaspoon minced fresh ginger

For the soup:
6 cups (48 fl oz/1.4 liters) Anchovy Broth (page 314)
3½ oz (100 g) mu (Korean radish), cut into 1-inch (2.5 cm) square pieces ¼ inch (6 mm) thick
2¾ oz (80 g) soybean sprouts
1 oz (30 g) daepa (Korean scallion), thinly sliced on a diagonal
1 oz (25 g) green Cheongyang chili, thinly sliced on a diagonal
2¾ oz (80 g) minari, cut into 1-inch (2.5 cm) lengths
Salt
1¾ oz (50 g) Korean chrysanthemum greens, cut into 1-inch (2.5 cm) lengths

**Prepare the seafood:** In a large bowl, combine the octopus with the flour or coarse salt, and massage well into the octopus, especially the tentacles. Rinse well under cold running water. Remove the beak by hand before chopping the octopus into 2-inch (5 cm) pieces. Clean the blue crab thoroughly with cold water and a small brush. Remove its back shell and gills and cut into 4 pieces. Wash the clams, sea squirt, and shrimp under cold running water and set aside.

**Make the seasoning:** In a small bowl, stir together the gochugaru, wine, gochujang, doenjang, soy sauce, fish sauce, garlic, and ginger until uniform.

**Make the soup:** In a large pot, combine the anchovy broth and the seasoning and bring to a boil over medium heat, loosening the seasoning well so that it's well mixed in. Once boiling, add the octopus, radish, blue crab, clams, and sea squirt and cook until the radish is translucent, about 10 minutes.

Add the shrimp and bean sprouts and boil for 5 more minutes. Add the daepa, chili, and minari. Once boiling again, season to taste with salt as needed and remove from the heat.

Garnish with the chrysanthemum greens and serve hot.

# Spicy Blue Crab Tang
## Kkotge Tang
## 꽃게탕

dF

When Koreans refer to crab, most think of the Korean blue crab, which is the most common and representative type in Korea. The Korean blue crab is at the peak of its season in fall. The female and male crabs can be distinguished by their stomachs. For the purposes of making soup, the male is more desirable, because it's filled with sweet meat.

Various vegetables can be used, but the zucchini (courgette) and *mu* (Korean radish) should not be omitted, because the sweet taste of the zucchini and the refreshing taste of the radish pairs deliciously with the crab. Mugwort is a popular garnish for a fragrant flavor.

**Preparation time:** 25 minutes
**Cooking time:** 20 minutes
**Serves:** 4

4 male blue crabs (2 lb 10 oz/1.2 kg total)

**For the seasoning:**
3 tablespoons gochugaru (red chili flakes)
2 tablespoons mirin
1 tablespoon cheongjang (light Korean soy sauce)
1 tablespoon gochujang (red chili paste)
1 tablespoon doenjang (fermented soybean paste)
1 tablespoon anchovy fish sauce
1 tablespoon minced garlic
1 teaspoon salt

**For the soup:**
8 cups (64 fl oz/1.9 liters) Anchovy Broth (page 314)
7 oz (200 g) mu (Korean radish), cut into 1-inch (2.5 cm) square pieces ¼ inch (6 mm) thick
3½ oz (100 g) onion, cut into ¼-inch (6 mm) pieces
4½ oz (125 g) aehobak (Korean zucchini), cut into 1-inch (2.5 cm) square pieces ¼ inch (6 mm) thick
1 oz (30 g) daepa (Korean scallion), thinly sliced on a diagonal
1 oz (25 g) fresh green Cheongyang chili, thinly sliced on a diagonal
6 oz (175 g) enoki mushrooms, trimmed and quartered

Clean the blue crabs thoroughly with a brush. Cut the pointy edges of the legs where there is no meat. Insert a finger between the stomach and back shell and remove the back shell. Cut the gills off with scissors. Pat dry with a tea towel and cut the body into quarters.

**Make the seasoning:** In a bowl, stir together the gochugaru, mirin, soy sauce, gochujang, doenjang, fish sauce, garlic, and salt and mix well.

**Make the soup:** In a large pot, combine the anchovy broth and the seasoning and stir to loosen the seasoning. Bring to a boil over high heat. Once boiling, reduce the heat, add the crab and radish, and cook for 5 minutes, skimming the foam. Add the onion and zucchini and cook for 5 more minutes. Add the daepa, chili, and enoki mushrooms. Once boiling again, remove from the heat.

Serve hot in individual bowls.

# Fresh Loach Tang
## Namdo Chueo Tang
## 남도 추어탕

dF

Each region has a particular way of preparing freshwater loach, whether it's boiling the fish whole or mashed, using a bay leaf in the broth, or incorporating beef broth.

**Preparation time:** 20 minutes
**Cooking time:** 1½ hours
**Serves:** 4

1 lb 5 oz (600 g) live freshwater loaches
Coarse salt

**For the seasoning:**
3 tablespoons ganjang (Korean soy sauce)
2 tablespoons doenjang (fermented soybean paste)
1 tablespoon gochugaru (red chili flakes)
1 tablespoon glutinous rice
1 teaspoon minced garlic

**For the soup:**
10 oz (300 g) store-bought boiled ugeoji (outer leaves of napa cabbage/Chinese leaf), cut into 1-inch (2.5 cm) pieces
3½ oz (100 g) store-bought boiled taro stem, cut into 1-inch (2.5 cm) pieces
1 tablespoon perilla seed powder
3½ oz (100 g) garlic chives, cut into 2-inch (5 cm) lengths
1 oz (25 g) fresh green Cheongyang chili, thinly sliced on the diagonal
1 tablespoon ground chopi (sanshō pepper)

In a large pot, salt the fish generously with coarse salt and let sit covered for 5 minutes, which will kill the fish. Rinse well under cold running water, rubbing well with rubber-gloved hands to remove the slippery texture of the fish. Repeat until clean.

In a large pot, combine the cleaned loaches and 8½ cups (68 fl oz/ 2 liters) water, bring to a simmer over low heat, and simmer for 1 hour.

**Meanwhile, make the seasoning:** In a bowl, stir together the soy sauce, doenjang, gochugaru, rice, and garlic.

Remove the fish and set the pot of broth aside. Set a coarse-mesh sieve or colander over a bowl. Mash the fish with a wooden spatula through the sieve, catching the mashed meat in the bowl. Discard the bones. (Alternatively, pick the meat off the bones and pulse in a blender or food processor to mash.)

**Make the soup:** In a large bowl, combine the ugeoji, taro stems, and the seasoning and toss to coat. Add to the broth along with the mashed fish and boil over medium heat for 20 minutes.

Add the perilla powder, chives, and chili and let boil once more before removing from the heat.

Serve in individual bowls, with a saucer of ground chopi to add to taste.

# 찌개 Jjigae Stews

*Jjigae* is a dish in which the ratio of solid ingredients to broth is equal. These stews are also characterized by strong seasoning and, depending on the seasoning ingredient, *jjigae* can be roughly categorized into *doenjang jjigae* (seasoned with fermented soybean paste), *gochujang jjigae* (seasoned with red chili paste), and clear *jjigae*.

*Doenjang jjigae*, one of the most popular stews eaten by Koreans, has different tastes, depending on the type of *doenjang* used. Many ingredients are used along with the staple tofu, zucchini (courgette), and anchovies. *Gochujang jjigae* can be made with tofu and vegetables, while clear *jjigae* are seasoned with salt and salted shrimp and tofu, zucchini, Korean radish, and clams are staple ingredients.

Traditionally, the proper way to serve *jjigae* was in individual servings as a *banchan* (side dish). Depending on the total number of *banchan* per person, the type of table setting would be named appropriately, such as *3 chup sang* or *5 chup sang*. Although similar dishes, such as soups, are not counted as a *banchan*, *jjigae* and *jeongol* (hot-pots) are. These days, soups are still served in individual servings, but *jjigae* and *jeongol* are usually a communal dish to be shared. The typical way of eating *jjigae* is to ladle yourself some *jjigae* broth and ingredients out of the communical bowl and into your own rice bowl.

# Doenjang Jjigae
# 된장 찌개

dF -3o

*Doenjang jjigae* is one of the most common *jjigaes* to make at home. It's one of Korea's soul foods, reminiscent of the memories of a warm home-cooked meal. While the signature fragrance may be unfamiliar at first, the savory, earthiness of the *doenjang* paired with the sweetness of the cooked vegetables can create a delicious and deep flavor in a short amount of time.

**Preparation time:** 10 minutes
**Cooking time:** 20 minutes
**Serves:** 2

- 2½ tablespoons doenjang (fermented soybean paste)
- 2 cups (16 fl oz/480 ml) Anchovy Broth (page 314) or water
- 1¾ oz (50 g) onion, cut into ¾-inch (2 cm) cubes
- 1¾ oz (50 g) potato, halved and cut into 1/16-inch (2 mm) slices
- 1½ oz (40 g) fresh shiitake mushrooms, cut into ¾-inch (2 cm) cubes
- 1¾ oz (50 g) aehobak (Korean zucchini), halved lengthwise and cut crosswise into ¼-inch (5 mm) slices
- 3¼ oz (90 g) firm tofu, halved lengthwise and cut crosswise into ¼-inch (5 mm) pieces
- ½ tablespoon minced garlic
- ½ oz (15 g) daepa (Korean scallion), thinly sliced on a diagonal
- 1 oz (25 g) fresh green Cheongyang chili, thinly sliced on a diagonal

In a pot, heat the doenjang over medium low heat for 2–3 minutes, stirring to avoid burning. Add the anchovy broth and bring to a boil over medium heat. Add the onion, potato, and shiitakes and boil for 10 more minutes. Add the zucchini, tofu, and garlic and boil for 2 more minutes. Add the daepa and chili and remove from the heat.

Serve hot in the pot.

# Thick Doenjang Jjigae
## Gang Doenjang Jjigae
## 강된장 찌개

dF

*Gang doenjang jjigae* is a variation of *doenjang jjigae* (page 347), where the ingredients are diced into smaller sizes and the broth is minimal to none. It's usually used to mix directly with rice or eaten with *ssam* (wraps) instead of ssamjang (dipping sauce for *ssam*). It's a style of *doenjang jjigae* where the deep, savory flavor of the *doenjang* is the star. If you are using homemade *doenjang*, the salt levels may be much higher than store-bought *doenjang*. In that case, increase the amount of vegetables and reduce the amount of *doenjang* used to taste.

Preparation time: 15 minutes
Cooking time: 20 minutes
Serves: 4

- 1 teaspoon sesame oil
- 3½ oz (100 g) aehobak (Korean zucchini), cut into ⅓-inch (8 mm) dice
- 3½ oz (100 g) onion, cut into ⅓-inch (8 mm) dice
- 5½ oz (160 g) shiitake mushrooms, cut into ⅓-inch (8 mm) dice
- 2 oz (60 g) daepa (Korean scallion), halved lengthwise and cut crosswise into ¼-inch (6 mm) slices
- 4 tablespoons doenjang (fermented soybean paste)
- 1 tablespoon gochujang (red chili paste)
- 2 tablespoons anchovy powder
- 3½ oz (100 g) fresh green Cheongyang chilies, seeded and minced
- 2 fresh red chili peppers, seeded and minced

In a pot, heat the sesame oil over medium heat. Add the zucchini, onion, shiitakes, and daepa and stir-fry for 3 minutes. Add the doenjang, gochujang, and anchovy powder and stir-fry for 3–4 more minutes. Add ½ cup (4 fl oz/120 ml) water and boil for 10 minutes. Stir in both chilies and remove from the heat.

Serve hot.

---

# Kimchi Jjigae
## 김치 찌개

dF -3o   [ㅁ]

The smell of boiling kimchi *jjigae* will trigger hunger in Koreans as much as that of meat being grilled. Because most Koreans will have kimchi readily available in the refrigerator at all times, it makes for a quick everyday dish. It's a great solution for kimchi that's become too fermented to enjoy on its own, because it is delicious stir-fried with oil and made into this stew.

Beef broth can be used instead of water (or anchovy broth) for a deeper, savory kimchi *jjigae*. The *jjigae* is often better the next day for a more infused flavor. This base recipe can be combined with all kinds of fatty meats, such as pork belly, or easily accessible canned fish, such as tuna.

Preparation time: 5 minutes
Cooking time: 30–35 minutes
Serves: 2

- 1 tablespoon cooking oil or sesame oil
- 10 oz (300 g) Napa Cabbage Kimchi (page 60), cut into ¾–1¼-inch (2–3 cm) slices
- 1¾ oz (50 g) onion, thinly sliced
- 2 cups (16 fl oz/480 ml) water or Anchovy Broth (page 314)
- ½ tablespoon minced garlic
- 1 tablespoon Yondu (Korean vegan seasoning sauce)
- 1½ oz (40 g) firm tofu, cut into 1½-inch (4 cm) slices ¼ inch (6 mm) thick
- 1 oz (30 g) daepa (Korean scallion), thinly sliced on a diagonal

In a pot, heat the cooking oil over medium heat. Add the kimchi and onion and stir-fry for 2–3 minutes. Add the water and increase the heat to high. Once boiling, reduce to medium heat, cover with a lid, and boil for 15–20 minutes.

Stir in the garlic and Yondu and add the tofu on top. Boil for 3 minutes. Garnish with the daepa and remove from the heat.

Serve hot.

## Kimchi & Ground Soybean Jjigae
### Kimchi Kongbiji Jjigae
### 김치 콩비지 찌개

dF gF  [□]

Tofu and kimchi are a well-known pairing. In the same way, *kong biji* (ground soaked soybeans) paired with well-fermented kimchi come together in the balanced savory-tart flavors in this *jjigae*. Adding pork gives the stew a richer flavor, but a vegan version using vegan kimchi and *kong biji* is just as delicious. If store-bought *kong biji* is unavailable, make your own by soaking 9 ounces (250 g) dried soybeans in water for 6 hours minimum and finely grinding in a blender with 2 cups (16 fl oz/480 ml) water.

**Preparation time:** 20 minutes
**Cooking time:** 35 minutes
**Serves:** 2

- 7 oz (200 g) Napa Cabbage Kimchi (page 60)
- 7 oz (200 g) boneless pork shoulder
- 2 tablespoon minced garlic
- 1 tablespoon sesame oil
- 1 teaspoon Yondu (Korean vegan seasoning sauce)

**For the jjigae:**
- 3 cups (24 fl oz/710 ml) water or Anchovy Broth (page 314)
- 2 cups (400 g) kong biji (ground soaked soybeans)
- 1 tablespoon Yondu (Korean vegan seasoning sauce) or anchovy fish sauce

Cut the kimchi into ½-inch (1.3 cm) pieces and set aside with its juices.

Cut the pork shoulder into ½-inch (1.3 cm) squares. In a bowl, combine the pork with the garlic, sesame oil, and Yondu and toss to coat well. Let sit for 5 minutes.

**Make the jjigae:** In a large pot, dry-fry the marinated pork and kimchi over medium heat for 3–4 minutes. Add the water or broth and bring to a boil over high heat. Once boiling, reduce the heat to medium and boil for 10 minutes. Add the ground soybeans on top and do not stir in (stirring it will cause it to sink and stick to the bottom). Reduce the heat to medium-low, cover with a lid, and simmer for 10 minutes. Stir in the Yondu and and boil for 1–2 more minutes over medium heat. Remove from the heat and let steam for 2–3 more minutes before serving.

---

## Cod Roe & Tofu Jjigae
### Myeongran Dubu Jjigae
### 명란 두부 찌개

dF gF -3o

*Jjigae* or *guk* (soup) that use *jeotgal* (fermented seafood) as a flavoring pair well with tofu. The strong, savory flavors from the *jeotgal* are balanced out by the gentle, soft flavors and textures of the tofu.

**Preparation time:** 10 minutes
**Cooking time:** 15 minutes
**Serves:** 2

- 3½ oz (100 g) firm tofu, cut into ¾-inch (2 cm) cubes
- 1½ oz (40 g) myeongran (cod roe), cut into ¾-inch (2 cm) pieces
- 2 oz (60 g) aehobak (Korean zucchini), halved lengthwise and cut crosswise into ¼-inch (5 mm) half-moons
- 1 teaspoon minced garlic
- ½ tablespoon salted shrimp
- 3 stalks minari, cut into 1½-inch (4 cm) lengths
- ¼ oz (7.5 g) daepa (Korean scallion), cut into 1½-inch (4 cm) lengths on a diagonal
- 1 oz (25 g) red chili pepper, seeded and thinly sliced on a diagonal
- Salt

In a pot, bring 3 cups (24 fl oz/710 ml) water to a boil over high heat. Once boiling, add the tofu, cod roe, zucchini, and garlic and boil for 5 minutes. Reduce the heat to medium and season with the salted shrimp. Add the minari and daepa and boil for 1–2 minutes. Garnish with red chili, remove from the heat, and adjust seasoning to taste with salt.

Serve hot.

# Seafood & Soft Tofu Jjigae
## Haemul Sundubu Jjigae
## 해물 순두부 찌개

dF

After adding the *gochugaru* (red chili flakes), it's important to reduce the heat to low so that it doesn't burn. For a richer *jjigae*, you can fry about 2 ounces (60 g) of ground (minced) pork just before you cook the onions.

**Preparation time:** 20 minutes, plus 30 minutes soaking time
**Cooking time:** 20 minutes
**Serves:** 2

- 10 Manila clams
- 2 tablespoons neutral cooking oil
- 2 tablespoons sesame oil
- 3 tablespoons minced onion
- 2 tablespoons gochugaru (red chili flakes)
- ⅓ teaspoon minced fresh ginger
- 1 tablespoon cheongjang (light Korean soy sauce)
- 3½ oz (100 g) squid, cut into 2½ × ½-inch (6 × 1.3 cm) strips
- 1⅓ cups (10.5 fl oz/315 ml) water or Beef Broth (page 315)
- 12 oz (330 g) soft tofu
- 4 shrimp (prawns)
- 1 tablespoon minced garlic
- 1 egg
- 1 teaspoon salt
- ¼ teaspoon freshly ground black pepper
- ½ oz (15 g) daepa (Korean scallion), sliced on the diagonal

Soak the clams in salt water for at least 30 minutes (and ideally overnight) to get rid of any impurities.

In a pot, heat the cooking oil and sesame oil over medium heat. Add the onion and stir-fry until translucent, 2–3 minutes. Reduce the heat to low, add the gochugaru and ginger, and stir-fry for 1–2 minutes. Add the soy sauce and increase the heat to medium. Add the squid and clams and stir-fry for 1–2 more minutes.

Add the water or broth, increase the heat to high, and bring to a boil. Add the soft tofu by spooning into 7–8 pieces, along with the shrimp and garlic. Boil for 3–4 more minutes.

Crack the egg directly into the soup and poach (don't stir). Season with the salt and black pepper, add the daepa, and boil for 2 more minutes over high heat.

Remove from the heat and serve.

# White Soft Tofu & Oyster Jjigae
Gul Baek Sundubu Jjigae
굴 백순두부 찌개

dF gF -30

Salting the soft tofu lightly before adding it into the jjigae will not only season the tofu but also prevent it from breaking into pieces as easily.

**Preparation time:** 10 minutes
**Cooking time:** 25 minutes
**Serves:** 2

6 live oysters or 6 shucked oysters
1 sheet dasima (2-inch/5 cm square)
5 oz (150 g) mu (Korean radish), peeled and cut into 1½-inch (4 cm) square pieces ⅒ inch (0.2 cm) thick
12 oz (330 g) soft tofu
1 tablespoon salted shrimp
1 teaspoon minced garlic
¼ oz (7.5 g) daepa (Korean scallion), very thinly sliced on a diagonal
6 garlic chives or Korean chrysanthemum greens, cut into 1½-inch (4 cm) lengths
½ oz (12 g) fresh green Cheongyang chili, very thinly sliced on a diagonal
½ oz (12 g) fresh red chili pepper, very thinly sliced on a diagonal (optional)
¼ teaspoon freshly ground black pepper

Shuck the oysters if purchased whole. Cut the dasima as thinly as possible with sharp scissors.

In a pot, combine 4 cups (32 fl oz/950 ml) water, the dasima, and radish and boil over high heat. Once boiling, reduce the heat to medium and boil for 10 minutes.

Add the soft tofu and boil for 5 minutes over high heat. Add the oysters, salted shrimp, garlic, and daepa and boil for 1 more minute. Add the chives, chilies, and black pepper and remove from the heat.

Serve hot.

# 전골 Jeongol Hotpot

*Jeongol* are Korean hotpots, a pot of broth served with meat and vegetables on the side to add to the broth. They are most often cooked at the table on a tabletop burner. Unlike other brothy dishes, such as *guk* (soups) and *jjigae* (stews), *jeongol* are typically served at restaurants with an array of raw ingredients to be added to the prepared broth by individual diners at the communal table. The diners then eat from the hotpot as the ingredients are cooked. This style of serving is great if you are entertaining, because the communal style of eating is convivial—and the hotpot can be stretched by adding more ingredients and broth in order to spend more time at the table sharing conversation. However, for an everyday home-cooked meal, the ingredients are added to the broth ahead of time.

There is a record of this tradition of sharing a communal meal—called *jeon-rip-tu*—dating from the Joseon era (1392–1897). The meal was served in a pot in the shape of an upside-down *beonggeogi*—a traditional Korean style of hat worn by certain aristocrats in the Joseon era. On the flat rim of the hat, meat was grilled, and in the hollow part, broth and vegetables were boiled, eaten communally. In this way, it seems that sharing a slow-cooked meal and conversation has been a centerpiece of communal gatherings since ancient times.

# Pyeongyang-Style Beef Jeongol
## Eobok Jaengban
## 어복쟁반

dF

**Preparation time:** 25 minutes
**Cooking time:** 15 minutes
**Serves:** 4

**For the sauce:**
1 oz (30 g) daepa (Korean scallion), minced
3 tablespoons ganjang (Korean soy sauce)
1 tablespoon minced garlic
1 tablespoon sesame oil
1 teaspoon ground sesame seeds

**For the broth:**
4 cups (32 fl oz/950 ml) Beef Broth (page 315)
2 tablespoons cheongjang (light Korean soy sauce)
1 teaspoon salt

**For the hotpot:**
2¾ oz (80 g) Beef Suyuk (page 218) made with beef head
8 oz (220 g) Beef Suyuk (page 218) made with beef brisket
4 oz (120 g) boiled beef tongue
2 oz (60 g) minari, cut into 1-inch (2.5 cm) lengths
¾ oz (20 g) napa cabbage (Chinese leaf), cut crosswise into 1-inch (2.5 cm) slices
11 oz (320 g) fresh shiitake mushrooms, stemmed, caps quartered
5½ oz (160 g) oyster mushrooms, trimmed and hand-torn into bite-size pieces
2 boiled eggs, peeled and halved
3½ oz (100 g) Asian pear, cut into slices ¼ inch (6 mm) thick
2 oz (60 g) daepa (Korean scallion), slivered
2 pinches of Korean red chili threads

This beef hotpot recipe is one of the representative traditional dishes of Pyeongyang, North Korea. It's made by thinly slicing beef brisket, head meat, and other cuts and arranging in a brass hotpot, topped with cooked eggs, daepa (Korean scallion), and more as garnish and cooked in broth.

**Make the sauce:** In a bowl, stir together the daepa, soy sauce, 2 tablespoons water, the garlic, sesame oil, and sesame seeds until uniform. Set aside in individual saucers.

**Make the broth:** In bowl, stir together the beef broth, soy sauce, and salt.

**Make the hotpot:** Slice both suyuks and the beef tongue into generous ⅛-inch (4 mm) slices. In a wide, shallow pot, neatly arrange the meat slices, vegetables, mushrooms, eggs, and pear and garnish with the slivered daepa and red chili threads. Gently pour in the seasoned beef broth and bring to a boil over high heat. Cook for 5 minutes.

Serve hot in the communal hotpot.

**Variation:** At the end of the meal, add naengmyeon (buckwheat noodles) to the remaining broth.

# Small Intestines Jeongol
## Gopchang Jeongol
## 곱창 전골

dF

In Korean cuisine, dishes made with intestines are well developed. Intestines are popular to eat grilled or even steamed, but they are also a popular type of *jeongol*. In this hotpot format, where the intestines are braised along with various vegetables and stock, their unique flavor is less pronounced, making them approachable even by those unfamiliar with the culture of eating intestines.

Preparation time: 30 minutes
Cooking time: 20 minutes
Serves: 4

For the seasoned meat:
3 tablespoons gochugaru (red chili flakes)
3 tablespoons ganjang (Korean soy sauce)
1 tablespoon gochujang (red chili paste)
1 tablespoon rice cooking wine
1 tablespoon sugar
1 tablespoon minced garlic
½ tablespoon doenjang (fermented soybean paste)
1 teaspoon minced fresh ginger
9 oz (250 g) beef small intestines
7 oz (200 g) beef stomach

For the broth:
2 cups (16 fl oz/500 ml) Beef Broth (page 315)

For the hotpot:
3½ oz (100 g) green cabbage, cut into 2-inch (5 cm) pieces
3½ oz (100 g) garlic chives, cut into 2-inch (5 cm) lengths
3½ oz (100 g) mu (Korean radish), cut into 2-inch (5 cm) square pieces ½ inch (1.3 cm) thick
3½ oz (100 g) onion, slivered
2 oz (60 g) daepa (Korean scallion), cut into 2-inch (5 cm) lengths
2¾ oz (80 g) oyster mushrooms, trimmed and hand-torn into bite-size pieces
1¾ oz (50 g) fresh green Cheongyang chilies, slivered
5 oz (150 g) firm tofu, cut into 2-inch (5 cm) square pieces ½ inch (1.3 cm) thick
Freshly ground black pepper

**Season the meat:** In a bowl, combine the gochugaru, soy sauce, gochujang, wine, sugar, garlic, doenjang, and ginger and mix until uniform. Add the intestines and stomach, and massage until well incorporated.

**Make the broth:** In a pot, combine the broth and 2 cups (16 fl oz/500 ml) water and bring to a low simmer.

**Make the hotpot:** In a wide, shallow pot, add the seasoned meat, the vegetables, mushrooms, chilies, and tofu and pour in the broth. Bring to a boil over high heat. Once boiling, reduce the heat to medium and boil for 10 minutes or until sufficiently cooked. Using scissors, cut both the intestines and stomach into bite-size pieces. Add black pepper to taste.

Serve hot.

# Tofu Jeongol
## Dubu Jeongol
## 두부 전골

dF

The *dubu jeongol* is made just with tofu and vegetables. While mild, it's best to enjoy without excess seasoning so that the inherent flavor of each vegetable and the savory flavor of tofu can be enjoyed.

Preparation time: 25 minutes
Cooking time: 10 minutes
Serves: 4

For the broth:
4 cups (32 fl oz/950 ml) Anchovy Broth (page 314)
2 tablespoons cheongjang (light Korean soy sauce)
2 tablespoons mirin
1 teaspoon minced garlic

For the hotpot:
1 lb 5 oz (600 g) firm tofu
Cooking oil
7 oz (200 g) mu (Korean radish), cut into 1-inch (2.5 cm) square pieces ½ inch (1.3 cm) thick
4½ oz (125 g) aehobak (Korean zucchini), cut into 1-inch (2.5 cm) square pieces ½ inch (1.3 cm) thick
4 oz (120 g) king trumpet mushroom, sliced ¼ inch (6 mm) thick
3½ oz (100 g) fresh shiitake mushrooms, sliced ¼ inch (6 mm) thick
2¾ oz (80 g) mung bean sprouts
2 oz (60 g) daepa (Korean scallion), cut on the diagonal into ¼-inch (6 mm) slices
1 oz (25 g) fresh green Cheongyang chilies
1 oz (25 g) fresh red chilies

**Make the broth:** In a bowl or pot, stir together the anchovy broth, soy sauce, mirin, and garlic.

**Make the hotpot:** Halve the block of tofu lengthwise, then cut each piece crosswise into slices ½ inch (1.3 cm) thick. In a frying pan, heat a drizzle of cooking oil, lightly pan-fry the tofu on both sides until lightly golden, and set aside.

In a wide, shallow pot, neatly arrange the radish, zucchini, mushrooms, bean sprouts, daepa, chilies, and tofu and pour in the broth. Bring to a boil over high heat. Once boiling, reduce the heat to medium and cook for 5 minutes.

Serve hot as a communal dish.

# Mushroom & Cabbage Jeongol
## Beoseot Baechu Jeongol
## 버섯 배추 전골

dF vg vE

This hotpot is often made with sliced beef sirloin (rump) for a savory flavor profile, but this vegetarian version made with just mushrooms is savory on its own. The types of mushrooms used in the dish can be customized. A popular seasonal fall variation includes the shingled hedgehog mushroom and *matsutake* (songyi mushroom). While the *cho-ganjang* (vinegar and soy sauce mixture) is the typical sauce to serve along with, it can be eaten without any seasoning or with a mustard-based sauce as well.

**Preparation time:** 25 minutes
**Cooking time:** 10 minutes
**Serves:** 4

**For the cho-ganjang:**
3 tablespoons ganjang (Korean soy sauce)
2 tablespoons rice vinegar
1 tablespoon sugar

**For the broth:**
1 tablespoon cheongjang (light Korean soy sauce)
1 tablespoon Yondu (Korean vegan seasoning sauce)
1 tablespoon sugar
½ tablespoon minced garlic

**For the hotpot:**
3½ oz (100 g) fresh shiitake mushrooms, cut into ¼-inch (6 mm) slices
4 oz (120 g) king trumpet mushroom, cut into ¼-inch (6 mm) slices
4 oz (120 g) oyster mushrooms, trimmed and hand-torn
2¾ oz (80 g) enoki mushrooms, trimmed and hand-torn
7 oz (200 g) napa cabbage (Chinese leaf), cut into 1-inch (2.5 cm) slices
3½ oz (100 g) onion, cut into 1-inch (2.5 cm) slices
2 oz (60 g) daepa (Korean scallion), cut into 1-inch (2.5 cm) slices
1 oz (25 g) fresh green Cheongyang chili, minced

**Make the cho-ganjang:** In a small bowl, stir together the soy sauce, vinegar, sugar, and 3 tablespoons water. Stir until the sugar is fully dissolved.

**Make the broth:** In a pot, combine 4 cups (32 fl oz/950 ml) water, the soy sauce, Yondu, sugar, and garlic and bring to a simmer.

**Make the hotpot:** In a wide, shallow pot, neatly arrange the mushrooms, cabbage, onion, daepa, and chili. Gently pour in the hot broth. Bring to a boil over high heat. Once boiling, reduce the heat to medium and cook for 5 minutes.

Serve as a communal dish with the cho-ganjang in individual saucers for dipping the cooked vegetables.

# Dumpling Jeongol
## Mandu Jeongol
## 만두 전골

dF

This hotpot is made by simmering *mandu* (dumplings) as the main ingredient along with mushrooms and other vegetables. While dumplings are also great in vegetable- or anchovy-based broths, they go best with beef broth along with meat. The hotpot can be made using a spicy seasoning, as in this recipe, but it can also be prepared as a clear hotpot, served along with vinegared soy sauce for dipping.

Preparation time: 25 minutes
Cooking time: 50 minutes
Serves: 4

For the broth:
5 oz (150 g) beef, cut into chunks
2 tablespoons cheongjang (light Korean soy sauce)

For the seasoning:
2 tablespoons gochugaru (red chili flakes)
1 tablespoon anchovy fish sauce
1 tablespoon rice cooking wine
1 tablespoon minced garlic

For the hotpot:
7 oz (200 g) napa cabbage (Chinese leaf), cut into 1-inch (2.5 cm) pieces
16 dumplings, such as Meat & Tofu Mandu (page 387)
3½ oz (100 g) fresh shiitake mushrooms, cut into ¼-inch (6 mm) slices
3½ oz (100 g) onion, thinly sliced
2 oz (60 g) daepa (Korean scallion), thinly sliced

**Make the broth:** In a pot, combine the beef, 4¼ cups (34 fl oz/1 liter) water, and the soy sauce and bring to a boil over medium heat. Cook for 40 minutes. Strain the broth and set aside. Reserve the meat for this hotpot or save for another recipe.

**Make the seasoning:** In a bowl, combine the gochugaru, fish sauce, wine, and garlic and mix until uniform.

**Make the hotpot:** In a wide, shallow pot, first lay down the cabbage slices. Neatly arrange the dumplings, mushrooms, onion, and daepa on top. Gently pour in the beef broth until it almost covers the ingredients. Add the seasoning mixture, bring to a boil over medium heat, and cook until the mandu and vegetables are cooked through, about 5 minutes.

Serve hot and continue to boil at the table, serving into individual bowls throughout to enjoy.

# Guksu Noodles

국수

*Guksu*, or noodles, are popular for serving at feasts or when entertaining guests. Long noodles traditionally represent a long life, which is why they are served at celebrations, such as birthdays, weddings, and other ceremonies, to wish a long life and good fortune. They're also often eaten as a simple one-bowl lunch.

*Guksu* are classified according to the grain or starch used to make the noodles. They can be further divided into hot noodles eaten in warm broth, cold noodles eaten in cold broth or *dongchimi* (radish kimchi) broth, and *bibim* noodles, which are mixed together with other ingredients. They can be made of flour, such as wheat flour, rice flour, or buckwheat flour. They're made in a variety of ways, including hand-rolled and cut, and extruded through a mold. They are also cooked in various methods: boiling, pan-frying, deep-frying, and more.

In Korea, the history of *guksu* is estimated to have begun during the Three Kingdoms era (57 BCE–668 CE), although there is no documented evidence. The first documentation is in the Goryeo dynasty (918–1392), when noodles were recorded as dishes served at ancestral rites and ceremonies, as well as made and sold at temples. In the past, *guksu* were primarily made of buckwheat and other starchs, but today the most popular are made with wheat flour.

These days, with the long shelf life and accessibility of dried store-bought noodles, they have become a pantry staple. The speed and ease with which thin *guksu* can be cooked have definitely contributed to their popularity as an everyday convenience food.

# Anchovy Broth Guksu
## Myeolchi Janchi Guksu
## 멸치 잔치국수

dF

The common anchovy-broth based *janchi guksu*, or "banquet noodles," can look humble, but it is one of the most important dishes in Korean noodle cuisine. While simple, it is a dish that can showcase the tastes of Korea, such as anchovy broth, Napa Cabbage Kimchi (page 60), egg *jidan* (garnish), and *jang* (fermented soy-based sauces).

The noodles are typically served at weddings, birthdays, and other festive occasions, but they are also a popular meal made at home, in simple restaurants, and in markets. Although the kimchi is not a necessary ingredient here, its tart and savory flavors make it a popular addition.

**Preparation time:** 20 minutes
**Cooking time:** 25 minutes
**Serves:** 4

**For the broth:**
6 cups (48 fl oz/1.4 liters) Anchovy Broth (page 314)
2 tablespoons cheongjang (light Korean soy sauce)
½ tablespoon salt
1 tablespoon rice cooking wine

**For the garnishes:**
4½ oz (125 g) aehobak (Korean zucchini)
Cooking oil
Salt
1¾ oz (50 g) carrot
2¾ oz (80 g) Napa Cabbage Kimchi (page 60; optional)
Sesame oil (optional)
2 eggs

**For the noodles:**
14 oz (400 g) somyeon (thin wheat flour noodles)
Gim, crushed (optional)

**Make the broth:** In a large pot, combine the anchovy broth, soy sauce, salt and wine and bring to a boil to combine. Set aside.

**Make the garnishes:** Cut the zucchini into 2 × ⅛-inch (5 cm × 4 mm) matchsticks. In a frying pan, heat a small amount of cooking oil, add the zucchini, season lightly with salt, and stir-fry for 1 minute. Set aside to cool on a plate. Cut the carrots into similar matchsticks. In the same frying pan, add the carrot (more oil if needed) and season lightly with salt. Stir-fry for 1 minute and set aside.

If using kimchi, use only the white stem parts of the fermented kimchi and cut them into matchsticks or small dice (to your preference). In a frying pan, heat a drizzle of sesame oil over medium heat. Add the kimchi and stir-fry for 30 seconds and set aside.

Separate the egg whites and yolks into separate bowls. Beat each with a small pinch of salt. In a nonstick frying pan, heat a drizzle of cooking oil over low heat. Add the egg yolks and cook into a thin "pancake." Remove from the pan and repeat with the egg whites. When cool enough to handle, cut the egg pancakes into strips 2 inches (5 cm) long and ⅛ inch (3 mm) wide. Set aside.

**Cook the noodles:** Bring a large pot of water to a boil. Add the noodles and cook for 3 minutes. If the water begins to foam or boil, add a splash of cold water or ice to calm it down. Drain the noodles and rinse well under cold running water until cool.

Divide the noodles evenly among four large bowls. Top with zucchini, carrot, kimchi (if using), and egg strips. Pour in the hot seasoned anchovy broth and serve. If desired, garnish with crushed gim.

# Spicy Bibimguksu
## Bibimguksu
## 비빔국수

dF -30

This is a very customizable bowl of noodles. Use whatever vegetables you prefer, or serve the seasoned noodles on their own for a simple dish. You can also swap out the cabbage kimchi for Young Summer Radish Kimchi (page 67) for a more refreshing taste.

Preparation time: 15 minutes
Cooking time: 10 minutes
Serves: 4

**For the vegetables:**
14 oz (400 g) Napa Cabbage Kimchi (page 60)
2½ oz (75 g) cucumbers
4 lettuce leaves

**For the seasoning:**
4 tablespoons rice vinegar
3 tablespoons gochujang (red chili paste)
2 tablespoons ganjang (Korean soy sauce)
2 tablespoons maesil syrup (Korean green plum syrup)
1 tablespoon sesame oil
1 tablespoon gochugaru (red chili flakes)
1 tablespoon light brown sugar

**For the noodles:**
1 lb (500 g) dried somyeon (thin wheat flour noodles)
4 tablespoons ground sesame seeds
2 boiled eggs, halved lengthwise

**Prepare the vegetables:** Remove the root of the kimchi and cut lengthwise into four sections. Cut crosswise into matchsticks ¼ inch (6 mm) thick. Cut the cucumber into matchsticks ⅛ inch (3 mm) thick. Cut the lettuce into ¼-inch (6 mm) shreds.

**Make the seasoning:** In a bowl, stir together the vinegar, gochujang, soy sauce, maesil syrup, sesame oil, gochugaru, and brown sugar and mix well until uniform.

**Make the noodles:** Bring a large pot of water to a boil. Add the noodles, stirring well to avoid clumping, and cook for 3 minutes. If the water begins to foam or boil, add a splash of cold water or ice to calm it down. Drain the noodles and rinse well under cold running water until cool.

In a large bowl, combine the cooked noodles with the kimchi and seasoning mixture and mix until uniform.

Divide the noodles among bowls. Top each bowl with cucumber, lettuce, 1 tablespoon ground sesame seeds, and a halved boiled egg.

# Hamheung-Style Spicy Bibimguksu
## Hamheung Bibim Naengmyeon
## 함흥 비빔냉면

DF

Unlike Pyongyang-style *naengmyeon* (a cold noodle dish), which is made with buckwheat noodles, Hamheung-style *naengmyeon* is made with extremely thin noodles made from potato or sweet potato starch. The chewy texture of the thin noodles works better tossed with a strongly seasoned sauce than in a mild cold broth, so it's better known as *bibim naengmyeon*, or mixed cold noodles. It is sometimes served with a splash of cold broth just to make it easy to mix with the sauce.

Preparation time: 15 minutes, plus 40 minutes fermentation up to overnight and 30 minutes marinating time
Cooking time: 1 hour 15 minutes
Serves: 4

**For the spicy sauce:**
3½ oz (100 g) onion
3½ oz (100 g) Asian pear
1 oz (30 g) daepa (Korean scallion)
6 tablespoons apple cider vinegar
2 tablespoons cheongjang (light Korean soy sauce)
4 tablespoons gochugaru (red chili flakes)
2 tablespoons gochujang (red chili paste)
2 tablespoons corn (golden) syrup
2 tablespoons sugar
1 tablespoon minced garlic
1 teaspoon ginger juice

**For the beef:**
6½ oz (180 g) beef brisket
1 oz (30 g) daepa (Korean scallion)
2–3 cloves garlic
½ oz (10 g) fresh ginger

**For the quick-pickled vegetables:**
4 oz (120 g) mu (Korean radish)
2½ oz (75 g) cucumbers
½ cup (4 fl oz/120 ml) rice vinegar
½ cup (100 g) sugar

**For the noodles:**
7 oz (200 g) Asian pear
2 boiled eggs
1 lb (480 g) Hamheung naengmyeon noodles

**Make the spicy sauce:** Ideally it should be made the day before, if possible. In a blender or food processor, combine the onion, pear, daepa, vinegar, and soy sauce and blend until fine. Scrape into a bowl. Add the gochugaru, gochujang, corn syrup, sugar, garlic, and ginger juice and mix well until uniform. Refrigerate to ferment, but if making on the day, ferment in the refrigerator for at least 40 minutes.

**Prepare the beef:** Soak the brisket in a bowl of cold water for 20 minutes to remove the blood. In a large pot, combine the beef with 8 cups (64 fl oz/1.9 liters) water, the daepa, garlic, and ginger, Bring to a boil over high heat. Once boiling, reduce the heat to medium and boil for 1 hour. Remove the brisket and once cooled enough, cut into slices ¼ inch (6 mm) thick. Strain the broth and reserve for another use.

**Meanwhile, quick-pickle the vegetables:** Cut the radish into 2 × ½-inch (5 × 1.3 cm) rectangles ⅛ inch (3 mm) thick. Halve the cucumbers lengthwise and cut on a diagonal into slices ⅛ inch (3 mm) thick. In a large bowl, combine ½ cup (4 fl oz/120 ml) water, the vinegar, and sugar, and stir to dissolve the sugar. Add the radish and cucumber slices, toss to coat, and let marinate for 30 minutes. After it has been well seasoned, remove and squeeze the vegetables tightly to remove excess moisture and set aside.

**Make the noodles:** Bring a large pot of water to a boil.

Meanwhile, peel the Asian pear, cut it into 2 × ½-inch (5 × 1.3 cm) rectangles ⅛ inch (3 mm) thick, and set aside.

Add the noodles to the boiling water and cook until tender, according to the package directions. If the water begins to foam or boil, add a splash of cold water or ice to calm it down. Drain the noodles and rinse well three or four times under cold running water until cool.

Divide the noodles among four individual bowls. Top each with 3 tablespoons of the spicy sauce. Garnish with slices of brisket, pickled vegetables, pear slices, and halved boiled eggs. Serve with any remaining sauce at the table (or refrigerate the leftover sauce; it will keep in the refrigerator for 3–4 days).

## Ganjang & Perilla Oil Bibimguksu
## Ganjang Deulgireum Bibimguksu
## 간장 들기름 비빔국수

Although a simple dish with just a few ingredients, the combination of buckwheat noodles, perilla oil, and sesame seeds creates a fragrant combination that makes this a popular mixed noodle dish. Because it's such a simple recipe, using quality ingredients is key.

**Preparation time:** 15 minutes
**Cooking time:** 10 minutes
**Serves:** 4

- 5 tablespoons ganjang (Korean soy sauce)
- 2 tablespoons rice vinegar
- 2 tablespoons sugar
- 1 lb (500 g) memil guksu (Korean buckwheat noodles)

**For serving:**
- 12 tablespoons perilla oil
- 4 tablespoons ground sesame seeds
- 4 sheets roasted gim, thinly snipped or crushed
- 2 scallions (spring onions), thinly sliced

In a small bowl, combine the soy sauce, vinegar, sugar, and 4 tablespoons water and mix until the sugar is completely dissolved. Set the sauce aside.

Bring a large pot of water to a boil. Add the noodles and cook until tender according to the package directions. If the water begins to foam or boil, add a splash of cold water or ice to calm it down. Drain the noodles and rinse well three or four times under cold running water until cool.

In a large bowl, combine the noodles and the sauce and mix until uniform.

**To serve:** Divide the noodles among four bowls. Top with 3 tablespoons perilla oil, 1 tablespoon ground sesame seeds, and 1 tablespoon gim. Garnish with the scallions.

---

## Zucchini Bibimguksu
## Aehobak Bibimguksu
## 애호박 비빔국수

Even when there are no other vegetables at home, stir-frying *aehobak* (Korean green zucchini) is enough to make a delicious, quick noodle dish. The seasoning of the zucchini should be strong enough, because it's the sole seasoning for the noodles. If you'd like, you can use leftover Korean Zucchini Namul (page 176) instead of the zucchini here. Simply season the cooked noodles with soy sauce and perilla oil and top with the zucchini.

**Preparation time:** 15 minutes
**Cooking time:** 10 minutes
**Serves:** 4

**For the zucchini:**
- 3 tablespoons ganjang (Korean soy sauce)
- 2 tablespoons gochugaru (red chili flakes)
- 1 tablespoon gochujang (red chili paste)
- 1 tablespoon minced garlic
- 3 tablespoons perilla oil
- 2 oz (60 g) daepa (Korean scallion), cut into ¼-inch (6 mm) diagonal slices
- 1 lb (500 g) aehobak (Korean zucchini), cut into matchsticks ¼-inch (6 mm) thick

**For the noodles:**
- 1 lb (500 g) somyeon (thin wheat flour noodles)
- 2 tablespoons ground sesame seeds

**Make the zucchini:** In a small bowl, stir together the soy sauce, gochugaru, gochujang, and garlic.

In a nonstick frying pan, heat the perilla oil over medium heat. Add the daepa and zucchini and stir-fry for 30 seconds. Add the sauce and stir-fry for 1 more minute until the zucchini is well cooked.

**Make the noodles:** Bring a large pot of water to a boil. Add the noodles and cook for 4 minutes. If the water begins to foam or boil, add a splash of cold water or ice to calm it down. Drain the noodles and rinse well under cold running water until cool.

Divide the noodles among four individual bowls. Top with the zucchini stir-fry and garnish with sesame seeds. Serve hot.

# Cold Buckwheat Guksu with Hwe
## Hwe Naengmyeon
## 회 냉면

dF

While similar to Hamheung-Style Spicy Bibimguksu (page 368), *hwe naengmyeon* is topped with fermented seasoned raw fish. This recipe is the traditional version that uses fermented pollock, although these days fermented seasoned skate is more popular and common. The chewy noodles combined with the spicy seasoned raw fish, with the tart flavors that comes from the fermentation, is a refreshing combination.

For those who prefer a "slurpier" noodle dish, add 3–4 tablespoons of Beef Broth (page 315) when serving.

Preparation time: 30 minutes, plus 40 minutes chilling time up to overnight and 30 minutes marinating time
Cooking time: 15 minutes
Serves: 4

For the spicy sauce:
3½ oz (100 g) Asian pear
¼ oz (15 g) daepa (Korean scallion)
3 tablespoons apple cider vinegar
2 tablespoons cheongjang (light Korean soy sauce)
2 tablespoons gochugaru (red chili flakes)
2 tablespoons sugar
1 tablespoon corn (golden) syrup
1 tablespoon gochujang (red chili paste)
1 teaspoon ginger juice

For the quick-pickled vegetables:
4 oz (120 g) mu (Korean radish)
2½ oz (75 g) cucumber
½ cup (4 fl oz/120 ml) rice vinegar
½ cup (100 g) sugar

For the noodles:
7 oz (200 g) Asian pear
14 oz (400 g) Hamheung naengmyeon buckwheat noodles
7 oz (200 g) Pollock Hwe Muchim (page 194)
2 boiled eggs, halved

**Make the spicy sauce:** If possible, make this the day before. In a blender, combine the Asian pear, daepa, vinegar, and soy sauce and blend until fine. Scrape into a bowl, add the gochugaru, sugar, corn syrup, gochujang, and ginger juice, and mix well until uniform. Refrigerate overnight, if possible, but if making on the day, refrigerate for at least 40 minutes for the flavors to come together.

**Make the quick-pickled vegetables:** Cut the radish into 2 × ½-inch (5 × 1.3 cm) rectangles ⅛ inch (3 mm) thick. Halve the cucumber lengthwise and cut on a diagonal into slices ⅛ inch (3 mm) thick. In a large bowl, stir together ½ cup (4 fl oz/120 ml) water, the vinegar, and sugar, and stir to dissolve the sugar. Add the radish and cucumber slices, toss to coat, and let marinate for 30 minutes. After it has been well seasoned, remove and squeeze the vegetables tightly to remove excess moisture and set aside.

**Make the noodles:** Bring a large pot of water to a boil.

Meanwhile, peel the Asian pear and cut into 2 × ½-inch (5 × 1.3 cm) rectangles ⅛ inch (3 mm) thick and set aside.

Add the noodles to the boiling water and cook until tender according to the package directions. If the water begins to foam or boil, add a splash of cold water or ice to calm it down. Drain the noodles and rinse well 3–4 times under cold running water until cool.

In a large bowl, combine the noodles with the sauce and mix until uniform.

Plate the seasoned noodles into individual bowls. Garnish with the pollock muchim, quick-pickled vegetables, pear slices, and halved boiled eggs and serve.

# Pyongyang-Style Cold Buckwheat Guksu

Pyongyang Naengmyeon

평양냉면

dF

Pyongyang-style noodles are a type of *mulnaengmyeon*, which means buckwheat noodles served in a cold broth. The noodles are made of buckwheat flour and the broth is a mixture of broth from Korean radish kimchi and beef broth. While it has long been a popular dish, it has seen a spike in popularity in recent years. It can be enjoyed without any seasoning, or with mustard sauce or vinegar as well. Restaurants that serve this dish all have different broths, ranging from fish broth to pork broth, quail broth, and more. If *naengmyeon* noodles are hard to source, you can use soba noodles.

**Preparation time:** 15 minutes, plus 50 minutes soaking and pickling time
**Cooking time:** 1 hour 15 minutes
**Serves:** 4

**For the beef:**
6½ oz (180 g) beef brisket
1 oz (30 g) daepa (Korean scallion)
2–3 cloves garlic
½ oz (10 g) fresh ginger

**For the quick-pickled vegetables:**
4 oz (120 g) mu (Korean radish)
2½ oz (75 g) cucumber
½ cup (4 fl oz/120 ml) rice vinegar
½ cup (100 g) sugar

**For the broth:**
2 cups (16 fl oz/480 ml) liquid from Radish Water Kimchi (page 72)
2 tablespoons sugar
1 tablespoon rice vinegar
1 teaspoon salt

**For the noodles:**
7 oz (200 g) Asian pear
14 oz (400 g) Pyongyang naengmyeon buckwheat noodles
2 boiled eggs, halved lengthwise

**Prepare the beef:** In a bowl of cold water, soak the brisket for 20 minutes to remove the blood. In a large pot, combine the brisket with 8½ cups (68 fl oz/2 liters) water, the daepa, garlic, and ginger. Bring to a boil over high heat. Once boiling, reduce the heat to medium and boil for 1 hour. Remove the brisket and once cooled enough, slice into slices ¼ inch (6 mm) thick. Strain the broth.

**Meanwhile, quick-pickle the vegetables:** Cut the radish into 2 × ½-inch (5 × 1.3 cm) rectangles ⅛ inch (3 mm) thick. Halve the cucumber lengthwise and cut on a diagonal into slices ⅛ inch (3 mm) thick. In a large bowl, combine together ½ cup (4 fl oz/120 ml) water, the vinegar, and sugar, and stir to dissolve the sugar. Add the radish and cucumber slices, toss to coat, and let marinate for 30 minutes. After it has been well seasoned, remove and squeeze the vegetables tightly to remove excess moisture and set aside.

**Make the broth:** Measure out 6 cups (48 fl oz/1.4 liters) of the beef broth and combine in a bowl with the kimchi liquid, sugar, vinegar, and salt. Refrigerate to chill.

**Make the noodles:** Bring a large pot of water to a boil.

Meanwhile, peel the Asian pear and cut it into 2 × ½-inch (5 × 1.3 cm) rectangles ⅛ inch (3 mm) thick. Set aside.

Add the noodles to the boiling water and cook for 4 minutes. If the water begins to foam or boil, add a splash of cold water or ice to calm it down. Drain the noodles and rinse well 3–4 times under cold running water until cool.

Plate the noodles into individual bowls. Garnish with slices of brisket, pickled vegetables, pear slices, and halved boiled eggs. Ladle in the cold broth and serve cold.

## Cold Kimchi Guksu
### Kimchi Guksu
### 김치 국수

dF -30

This dish of refreshing kimchi noodles is a popular alternative to *naengmyeon* (cold noodles) or *bibimguksu* (mixed noodles) in the summertime. The cold kimchi broth can also be eaten with rice folded into it, or eaten as a chilled soup.

Preparation time: 15 minutes
Cooking time: 10 minutes
Serves: 4

For the broth:
2 cups (16 fl oz/480 ml) kimchi juice
8 cups (64 fl oz/1.9 liters) Anchovy Broth (page 314)
5 tablespoons rice vinegar
2 tablespoons fish sauce

For the noodles:
10 oz (300 g) Napa Cabbage Kimchi, store-bought or homemade (page 60)
2 tablespoons sesame oil
14 oz (400 g) somyeon (thin wheat flour noodles)
2½ oz (75 g) cucumber, cut into long matchsticks
2 boiled eggs, halved lengthwise

**Make the broth:** In a bowl, combine the kimchi juice, anchovy broth, vinegar, and fish sauce and mix well. Refrigerate to chill.

**Make the noodles:** Bring a large pot of water to a boil.

Meanwhile, cut the napa cabbage kimchi into thin matchsticks or dice (according to your preference). In a bowl, toss with the sesame oil and set aside.

Add the noodles to the boiling water and cook for 4 minutes. If the water begins to foam or boil, add a splash of cold water or ice to calm it down. Drain the noodles and rinse well under cold running water until cool.

Divide the noodles among four individual bowls. Top each bowl with kimchi, cucumber, and a halved boiled egg. Ladle in the broth and serve cold.

---

## Cold Soybean Guksu
### Kong Guksu
### 콩 국수

dF vE -S -30       [ㅁ]

*Kong guksu* is a popular delicacy, especially in summer. By making a batch of the soybean broth ahead, one can enjoy the dish throughout the summer without heating up the kitchen—except to quickly cook the noodles. Cucumbers and eggs are mainly used as garnish, but tomatoes and radish sprouts are also popular.

Because the soybean broth changes texture over time if preseasoned, it's usually seasoned at the table or just before serving.

Preparation time: 10 minutes
Cooking time: 15 minutes
Serves: 4

1 lb (450 g) somyeon (thin wheat flour noodles)
2½ oz (75 g) cucumber, cut into matchsticks 2 inches (5 cm) long
2 boiled eggs, halved lengthwise
6 cups (48 fl oz/1.4 liters) Soybean Cold Broth (page 315), well chilled
Fine salt

Bring a large pot of water to a boil. Add the noodles and cook for 4 minutes. If the water begins to foam or boil, add a splash of cold water or ice to calm it down. Drain the noodles and rinse well under cold running water until cool.

Divide the noodles among individual bowls. Top each with cucumber and a halved boiled egg. Ladle in the soybean broth and serve cold, with a side of salt to season to taste.

# Busan-Style Cold Wheat Guksu
## Busan Milmyeon
## 부산 밀면

dF

*Milmyeon*, a thin wheat noodle, originated in Busan during the Korean War, when displaced people used the wheat flour that was available to them as relief food to mimic the traditional *naengmyeon* buckwheat noodles. The noodles are often served in a meat broth made from pork and beef, garnished with a large dollop of spicy sauce. Compared to the acidic, refreshing taste of *naengmyeon* broth, *milmyeon* boasts a deep, savory flavor of the meat and the spicy taste of the gochugaru sauce. If you have trouble sourcing *milmyeon*, which is a fresh noodle, replace it with *somyeon*, a dried noodle, and use the package directions for cooking times.

Preparation time: 15 minutes, plus 40 minutes chilling time up to overnight
Cooking time: 15 minutes
Serves: 4

**For the spicy sauce:**
3½ oz (100 g) Asian pear
2 tablespoons cheongjang (light Korean soy sauce)
1 tablespoon apple cider vinegar
2 tablespoons corn (golden) syrup
2 tablespoons fine gochugaru (red chili powder)
1 tablespoon minced garlic
2 teaspoons sugar
1 teaspoon gochujang (red chili paste)
1 teaspoon ginger juice

**For the broth:**
6 cups (48 fl oz/1.4 liters) Beef Broth (page 315)
2 cups (16 fl oz/480 ml) Pork Bone Broth (page 314)
4 tablespoons ganjang (Korean soy sauce)
1 teaspoon salt

**For the noodles:**
2½ oz (75 g) cucumber
4 slices Pork Suyuk (page 218; optional)
14 oz (400 g) fresh milmyeon noodles
2 boiled eggs, halved

**Make the spicy sauce:** Ideally this should be made a day ahead if possible. In a blender, combine the pear, soy sauce, and vinegar and blend until fine. Scrape into a bowl, add the corn syrup, gochugaru, garlic, sugar, gochujang, and ginger juice and mix well until uniform. Refrigerate overnight, or if making on the day, refrigerate for at least 40 minutes for the flavors to come together.

**Make the broth:** In a large bowl, combine the broths, soy sauce, and salt and mix well until uniform.

**Make the noodles:** Bring a large pot of water to a boil.

Meanwhile, halve the cucumber lengthwise and then cut on a diagonal into slices ⅛ inch (3 mm) thick. Slice the pork suyuk (if using) into thin slices.

Add the noodles to the boiling water and cook until tender according to the package directions, usually only about 1½ minutes. If the water begins to foam or boil, add a splash of cold water or ice to calm it down. Drain the noodles and rinse well three or four times under cold running water until cool.

Divide the noodles among individual bowls. Garnish with pork slices (if using), cucumber, and halved boiled eggs. Top each bowl with 2 tablespoons of the spicy sauce and ladle in the broth. Serve.

# Mushroom Kalguksu
## Beoseot Kalguksu
버섯 칼국수

DF VG VE -30

*Kalguksu* noodle dishes are commonly made with a meat- or seafood-based broths, but using a vegetable broth base with spicy seasoning is also delicious. For vegetable *kalguksu* dishes, incorporating a variety of mushrooms is a great way to add depth and texture.

Preparation time: 20 minutes
Cooking time: 10 minutes
Serves: 4

**For the vegetables:**
3½ oz (100 g) oyster mushrooms
2½ oz (75 g) enoki mushrooms
2½ oz (75 g) king trumpet mushroom
2¾ oz (80 g) fresh shiitake mushrooms
2½ oz (75 g) potato
2 oz (60 g) aehobak (Korean zucchini)

**For the noodle soup:**
2 tablespoons cheongjang (light Korean soy sauce)
2 tablespoons gochujang (red chili paste)
2 tablespoons gochugaru (red chili flakes)
1 tablespoon mirin
1 teaspoon doenjang (fermented soybean paste)
1 teaspoon minced garlic
8 cups (64 fl oz/1.9 liters) Vegetable Broth (page 313)
1 lb (450 g) dried kalguksu noodles or 1 lb 7 oz (650 g) fresh kalguksu noodles

**Prepare the vegetables:** Remove the roots of the oyster and enoki mushrooms and tear by hand into bite-size slices. Halve the king trumpet mushroom lengthwise and slice each half lengthwise into strips ¼ inch (6 mm) thick. Remove the stems from the shiitakes and slice the caps into strips ¼ inch (6 mm) wide. Peel the potato and cut into matchsticks 1 inch (2.5 cm) long and ¼ inch (6 mm) thick. Halve the zucchini lengthwise and cut crosswise into slices ¼ inch (6 mm) thick.

**Make the noodle soup:** In a small bowl, stir together the soy sauce, gochujang, gochugaru, mirin, doenjang, and garlic. Stir some of the vegetable broth into the mixture to loosen it. In a large pot, combine the rest of the vegetable broth and the seasoning mixture and bring to a boil over high heat. Once boiling, reduce the heat to medium, add the potato, and cook for 1 minute. Add the noodles, stirring well to avoid clumping, and cook until the noodles are tender according to the package directions. Once the broth begins to boil again, add all the mushrooms and the zucchini and boil for 4–5 minutes. Remove from the heat.

Serve hot in individual bowls.

# Littleneck Clam Kalguksu
## Bajirak Kalguksu
## 바지락 칼국수

dF -3o

*Kalguksu*, which translates to "knife-cut noodles," were originally made by rolling out a flour dough and slicing it into thin noodles to be cooked in soup. There are many types of *kalguksu* dishes based on the ingredients used. Anchovies, clams, chicken, *jang* (fermented soy sauces), and even red beans (adzuki) can be used to make the broth. This popular recipe uses *bajirak* clams, or littleneck clams, which are harvested in abundance off the southern coast. This clam-and-noodle dish was originally from Gyeonggi-do, but it is now commonplace nationwide and is one of the most popular *kalguksu* recipes.

**Preparation time:** 20 minutes
**Cooking time:** 10 minutes
**Serves:** 4

**For the clam broth:**
8 cups (64 fl oz/1.9 liters) Anchovy Broth (page 314)
14 oz (400 g) littleneck clams
2 tablespoons cheongjang (light Korean soy sauce)
1 teaspoon salt

**For the noodle soup:**
1 lb (450 g) dried kalguksu noodles or 1 lb 7 oz (650 g) fresh kalguksu noodles
1¾ oz (50 g) fresh green Cheongyang chilies, seeded and thinly sliced on a diagonal
1 oz (25 g) fresh red chilies, seeded and thinly sliced on a diagonal
3½ oz (100 g) onion, cut into slices ⅛ inch (3 mm) thick
4½ oz (125 g) aehobak (Korean zucchini), cut into slices ⅛ inch (3 mm) thick
1 tablespoon minced garlic

**Make the clam broth:** In a large pot, bring the anchovy broth to a boil over high heat. Add the littleneck clams. Once the clams begin to open, boil for 2 minutes before removing the clams and setting them aside in their shells. Season the broth with the soy sauce and salt.

**Make the noodle soup:** Bring the seasoned broth to a boil. Add the noodles, stirring well to avoid clumping. Once it reaches boil, add the chilies, onion, zucchini, and garlic and cook until the noodles are tender according to the package directions. Add the cooked littleneck clams and cook for 30 more seconds.

Serve in individual bowls.

# Gangwondo-Style Tadpole-Shaped Guksu
## Gangwondo Olchaengi Guksu
## 올챙이 국수

dF

*Olchaengi guksu* translates to "tadpole noodles," which are so-named because of their unique tadpole-like shape. The noodles are made from dried corn or fresh corn, and the procedure for making them resembles the process for making *muk* (starch jelly). Originating from the mountainous region of Gangwon-do, where the main crops include corn, the corn-based noodles were a natural development. Because of their short shape, the noodles are eaten with a spoon rather than chopsticks.

You can also make these noodles from dried corn kernels: Soak 10 ounces (300 g) dried corn in boiling water, then boil the soaked corn in 2¾ cups (22 fl oz/600 ml) water to fully rehydrate. Grind the cooked corn, then let the ground corn settle to separate the solids from the liquid. Pour off and discard the liquid and use the solids to cook into noodles over low heat.

Preparation time: 30 minutes
Cooking time: 15–25 minutes
Serves: 4

For the olchaengi noodles:
5 cups (800 g) fresh corn kernels
4 tablespoons cornstarch (cornflour)

For the sauce:
3 tablespoons ganjang (Korean soy sauce)
1 tablespoon minced green Cheongyang chili
1 tablespoon gochugaru (red chili flakes)
1 teaspoon minced garlic
1 teaspoon ground sesame seeds
1 tablespoon sesame oil

For serving:
7 oz (200 g) Young Summer Radish Kimchi (page 67) or kimchi of preference

**Make the olchaengi noodles:** In a blender, combine the corn kernels with 1¼ cups (9½ fl oz/ 295 ml) of water and blend until fine. Press through a fine-mesh sieve into a pot. Add the cornstarch. Bring to a boil over low heat, stirring constantly with a silicone spatula, until the moisture evaporates and the starch is cooked and thickened to a jelly-like consistency, 15–25 minutes.

Fill a large bowl with ice and water. Suspend a colander or perforated metal steam insert over the bowl (but not touching the water) and pour in the corn mixture slowly, pressing gently with a flexible spatula, creating drops that look like tadpoles. Let the noodles cool completely in the ice water, then drain.

**Make the sauce:** In a bowl, combine the soy sauce, chili, gochugaru, garlic, ground sesame seeds, and sesame oil and mix well until uniform.

**To serve:** Divide the noodles among four individual bowls. Top with 1 tablespoon of the sauce. Garnish with 2 large spoonfuls of kimchi and serve cold.

# Freshwater Fish Stew Guksu
## Eotangguksu
## 어탕 국수

dF

*Eotangguksu* is a dish of noodles cooked in a stew made from finely ground freshwater fish. There are any number of freshwater fish that can be used, including freshwater sprats, catfish, crucian carp, and more. Freshwater fish commonly have an especially fishy or earthy flavor, so to compensate for that, they are cooked with a lot of cabbage, taro stems, and other earthy vegetables and seasoned heavily with *doenjang* (fermented soybean paste) and the aromatic ground *chopi* (sanshō pepper). If you'd like a stronger, more savory flavor, replace the napa cabbage (Chinese leaf) with kimchi.

A similar dish named *mori guksu* exists in the Pohang region that is made with saltwater fish, such as cod, in a seafood stock. Depending on the season, the type of seafood and vegetables used varies.

Preparation time: 1 hour 15 minutes
Cooking time: 15 minutes
Serves: 4

**For the fish stew:**
1½ lb (700 g) freshwater fish, cleaned and gutted

**For the seasoned napa cabbage:**
7 oz (200 g) napa cabbage (Chinese leaf)
3 tablespoons gochugaru (red chili flakes)
2 tablespoons doenjang (fermented soybean paste)
2 tablespoons minced garlic
1 tablespoon gochujang (red chili paste)
1 tablespoon cheongjang (light Korean soy sauce)
1 teaspoon salt

**For the noodles:**
3½ oz (100 g) store-bought boiled taro stems, cut into 2-inch (5 cm) lengths
14 oz (400 g) medium-thick flour noodles or dried kalguksu noodles
3½ oz (100 g) garlic chives, cut into 2-inch (5 cm) lengths
2 oz (60 g) daepa (Korean scallions), halved lengthwise and cut into 1-inch (2.5 cm) diagonal slices
1¾ oz (50 g) fresh Cheongyang green chilies, cut into slices ¼ inch (6 mm) thick
1 tablespoon ground chopi (sanshō pepper)

**Make the fish stew:** Remove the fish's head and gills. In a large pot, combine the fish and 12 cups (96 fl oz/2.8 liters) water. Cook for 1 hour over medium heat. Strain into a large pot through a large coarse-mesh sieve. Use a wooden spatula to press the cooked fish through the sieve (discard the skin and bones).

**Season the napa cabbage:** Set up a bowl of ice and water. In a pot of boiling water, blanch the napa cabbage for about 3 minutes. Transfer to the ice water to cool.

Meanwhile, in a large bowl, combine the gochugaru, doenjang, garlic, gochujang, soy sauce, and salt.

When the napa cabbage is cooled, squeeze with your hands to remove excess water. Cut into 1-inch (2.5 cm) pieces. Add to the seasoning sauce and combine well.

**Cook the noodles:** Bring the fish stew to a boil over high heat. Add the taro stems and the seasoned cabbage. Once boiling and foam begins to form, skim off the foam and reduce the heat to medium. Add the noodles, chives, scallion, and chilies and cook for 3 minutes. Once the noodles are sufficiently cooked, remove from the heat and season to taste.

Serve in individual bowls, garnished with chopi powder.

# Spicy Chewy Cold Guksu
## Bibim Jjolmyeon
## 비빔 쫄면

*Jjolmyeon* are thick flour noodles characterized by their chewiness, and this dish is on the menus of many *bunsik* restaurants (casual street food restaurants). The dish is topped with a variety of common vegetables, but a staple ingredient is the crunchy, sweet shredded green cabbage. Instead of using sesame oil, just the sesame seeds can be used.

Preparation time: 15 minutes
Cooking time: 15 minutes
Serves: 4

**For the sauce:**
5 tablespoons rice vinegar
4 tablespoons sugar
2 tablespoons gochugaru (red chili flakes)
2 tablespoons gochujang (red chili paste)
2 tablespoons cheongjang (light Korean soy sauce)
1 tablespoon minced garlic
1 teaspoon ginger juice

**For the noodles and serving:**
1 lb 6 oz (640 g) jjolmyeon noodles
9 oz (250 g) green cabbage, cut into ⅛-inch (3 mm) shreds
3½ oz (100 g) carrots, cut into ⅛-inch (3 mm) matchsticks
2½ oz (75 g) cucumber, cut into ⅛-inch (3 mm) matchsticks
4 perilla leaves, cut into thin shreds
2 boiled eggs, halved lengthwise
4 tablespoons sesame oil

**Make the sauce:** In a bowl, combine the vinegar, sugar, gochugaru, gochujang, soy sauce, garlic, and ginger juice and mix until uniform.

**Cook the noodles:** Set up a large bowl of ice and water. Bring a large pot of water to a boil. Separate the dried noodles loosely by pressing them with your hands so that they fall apart. Add the noodles to the boiling water and cook for 4–5 minutes, stirring well with chopsticks to prevent sticking to each other or the pot. Drain the noodles and cool them in the ice water, stirring with your hands. Once completely cool, drain.

**To serve:** In a bowl, combine the noodles with the sauce and toss to coat well. Divide the noodles among four bowls. Top each bowl with the cabbage, carrots, cucumber, and perilla leaves. Add a halved boiled egg, and drizzle each with 1 tablespoon sesame oil.

# Gangwondo-Style Buckwheat Guksu
## Gangwondo Makguksu
## 막국수

dF gF vg vE

A local specialty of Gangwon-do, *makguksu* is a dish of buckwheat noodles in broth or *dongchimi* (radish kimchi) broth, topped with a sauce and vegetable garnish to be mixed in. While original recipes call for chicken broth, today, *dongchimi* broth is the more popular broth used.

Preparation time: 20 minutes, plus 40 minutes chilling time up to overnight
Cooking time: 10 minutes
Serves: 4

**For the sauce:**
5 oz (150 g) apple
3½ oz (100 g) Asian pear
4 tablespoons cheongjang (light Korean soy sauce)
4 tablespoons rice vinegar
scant ½ cup (3½ fl oz/100 ml) lemon-lime soda (fizzy drink)
4 tablespoons gochugaru (red chili flakes)
3 tablespoons sugar
1 tablespoon Korean mustard
1 tablespoon gochujang (red chili paste)
1 tablespoon minced garlic
1 teaspoon ginger juice

**For the noodles:**
14 oz (400 g) buckwheat noodles
4½ oz (125 g) green cabbage, cut into ⅛-inch (3 mm) slices
3½ oz (100 g) onion, cut into ⅛-inch (3 mm) slices
1¾ oz (50 g) carrot, cut into ⅛-inch (3 mm) matchsticks
2½ oz (75 g) cucumber, cut into ⅛-inch (3 mm) matchsticks
6 lettuce leaves, cut into thin ribbons
4 perilla leaves, cut into thin ribbons
2 tablespoons sesame oil
3 tablespoons sesame seeds
3 tablespoons gim powder
1 cup (8 fl oz/240 ml) dongchimi broth (juice from Radish Water Kimchi, page 72)

**Make the sauce:** Ideally, it should be the made day before. In a food processor, combine the apple, pear, soy sauce, and vinegar and blend until fine. In a bowl, combine the puree with the lemon-lime soda, gochugaru, sugar, mustard, gochujang, garlic, and ginger juice and mix until well combined. The sauce is best when made a day ahead and refrigerated to develop flavors, but if making on the day, refrigerate for at least 40 minutes.

**Make the noodles:** Bring a large pot of water to a boil. Add the noodles and cook for 4–5 minutes. If the water begins to foam or boil, add a splash of cold water or ice to calm it down. Drain the noodles and rinse well under cold running water until cool.

Plate the noodles in the center of a large serving plate and pour the sauce around the noodles. Top the noodles with the vegetables and garnish with the sesame oil, sesame seeds, and gim powder. Pour the dongchimi broth over the noodles to finish and serve.

# Hand-Torn Guksu
## Sujebi
## 수제비

dF

*Sujebi* is one of the most beloved noodle dishes, along with *kalguksu* (knife-cut noodles), and are usually cooked in the same broth as *kalguksu* dishes. Broths made with anchovies, chicken, and clams are mainly used, but *sujebi* are also added to a variety soup bases. This recipe showcases the most basic and popular version, the anchovy broth *sujebi*.

Preparation time: 15 minutes, plus 1 hour resting time
Cooking time: 15 minutes
Serves: 4

**For the sujebi dough:**
2½ cups (300 g) all-purpose (plain) flour

**For the anchovy jang broth:**
8 cups (64 fl oz/1.9 liters) Anchovy Broth (page 314)
3 tablespoons cheongjang (light Korean soy sauce)
1 tablespoon rice cooking wine
1 tablespoon salt

**For the noodles:**
5 oz (150 g) potato, quartered lengthwise and cut into ¼-inch (6 mm) slices
9 oz (250 g) aehobak (Korean zucchini), halved lengthwise and cut crosswise into slices ¼ inch (6 mm) thick
1 oz (30 g) daepa (Korean scallion), cut into ½-inch (1.3 cm) diagonal slices
Salt

**Make the sujebi dough:** In a bowl, combine the flour and a scant ½ cup (3½ fl oz/100 ml) water and knead for 5 minutes or until the dough is uniform. Place into a zip-lock plastic bag and let rest for at least 1 hour.

**Make the anchovy jang broth:** In a pot, combine the broth, soy sauce, wine, and salt and bring to a boil.

**Cook the noodles:** Add the potato to the boiling broth and cook for 5 minutes. Add the zucchini. Flatten the sujebi dough with your hands and begin tearing off thin, bite-size pieces and dropping them directly into the boiling broth until all the dough is used. Add the daepa slices. Taste and add salt if needed.

Serve in individual bowls.

# 만두 Mandu Dumplings

*Mandu*, Korean dumplings, is a broad category with variations based on the ingredients used to make the wrapper, as well as the ingredients used in the filling. Typically, the wrapper is made with flour, but substitutes, such as buckwheat, can be used, and some dumpling doughs are flavored (and colored) with vegetable juices. There are various different shapes of *mandu*, such as the *beyongsi mandu*, the royal court's traditional half-moon shape made without any folds, *kyu-a-sang mandu*, a dumpling shaped like a sea cucumber, and the *pyeonsu mandu*, a square summer dumpling.

Dumplings are enjoyed in many cultures around the world, but what sets Korea's dumplings apart is that the traditional *mandu* almost always uses ground tofu and kimchi as a filling ingredient. The more traditional flavor profile of *mandu* intentionally leans mild, so that it can be eaten with soy sauce. The modern *mandu* typically includes glass noodles as a filling.

*Mandu* can be made in large amounts and frozen for use later, although because assembling dumplings is so labor-intensive, many home cooks—as well as restaurants—purchase pre-made frozen dumplings. To fill that need, many large Korean food companies offer a wide and diverse array of *mandu*, many of which are exported to the global market.

# Meat & Tofu Mandu
## Gogi Dubu Mandu
## 고기 두부 만두

dF

Depending on the region, season, and family, the fillings of a *mandu* vary. But the most popular and common dumpling is made with the two main ingredients; pork and tofu. Although *mandu* wrappers can be made from scratch, it's a labor of love, and store-bought wrappers are readily available.

**Preparation time:** 1 hour
**Cooking time:** 15 minutes
**Serves:** 4

**For the filling:**
1 lb (500 g) ground (minced) pork
2 tablespoons ganjang (Korean soy sauce)
1 tablespoon minced garlic
1 lb (450 g) firm tofu
10 oz (300 g) mung bean sprouts
3 tablespoons neutral cooking oil
3½ oz (100 g) garlic chives, cut into ⅛-inch (3 mm) pieces
1 egg
1 tablespoon salt

**For the cho-ganjang:**
3 tablespoons ganjang (Korean soy sauce)
2 tablespoons rice vinegar
1 teaspoon gochugaru (red chili flakes)

**For the dumplings:**
48 large mandu wrappers

**Make the filling:** In a bowl, season the pork with the soy sauce and garlic and mix well. Set aside to develop flavors.

In a separate bowl, mash the firm tofu with your hands until fine and uniform. Wrap in a cheesecloth (muslin) or similar and squeeze to drain excess moisture.

In a small pot of boiling water, blanch the mung bean sprouts for 2 minutes. Drain well and let cool. Once cool, chop into ⅛-inch (3 mm) pieces.

In a frying pan, heat the cooking oil over high heat. Add the seasoned pork and stir-fry, breaking it up as it cooks, until cooked through. Transfer to a bowl to cool to room temperature.

Add the tofu, mung bean sprouts, chives, egg, and salt to the cooked pork and mix well until uniform.

**Make the cho-ganjang:** In a small bowl, stir together the soy sauce, vinegar, 3 tablespoons water, and the gochugaru until uniform. Set aside in a saucer.

**Make the dumplings:** Place a mandu wrapper in the palm of your non-dominant hand and lightly apply water to the outer edge. Place 1 tablespoon of filling in the center. Fold the mandu wrapper into a half-moon shape and press the center of the edge to fix, then press the outer edges firmly together to seal, leaving no air bubbles. Repeat for all the remaining ingredients.

Set up a steamer and bring the water to a boil. Add the mandu to the steamer basket, set it over the boiling water, cover, and steam for about 10 minutes.

Plate the steamed dumplings on a large flat plate and serve with cho-ganjang on the side for dipping.

# Kimchi Mandu
# 김치 만두

dF

Kimchi dumplings are one of the most iconic foods of Korea. As with other *mandu*, the type of kimchi used and the method for these dumplings have regional differences. In the south, kimchi is used without washing off any seasoning. In the north and middle of the country, the kimchi seasonings are rinsed off before adding. In the north, additional ingredients, such as tofu, are added for a milder flavor profile.

**Preparation time: 1 hour**
**Cooking time: 15 minutes**
**Serves: 4**

For the filling:
1 lb (500 g) ground (minced) pork
2 tablespoons ganjang (Korean soy sauce)
1 tablespoon minced garlic
1¾ lb (800 g) Napa Cabbage Kimchi, store-bought or homemade (page 60)
10 oz (300 g) firm tofu
10 oz (300 g) mung bean sprouts
3 tablespoons neutral cooking oil
7 oz (200 g) onions, finely diced
1 egg
2 tablespoons minced scallion (spring onion)
1 tablespoon salt

For the cho-ganjang:
3 tablespoons ganjang (Korean soy sauce)
2 tablespoons rice vinegar
1 teaspoon gochugaru (red chili flakes)

For the dumplings:
60 large mandu wrappers

**Make the filling:** In a bowl, season the pork with the soy sauce and garlic and mix well. Set aside to develop flavors while you prep the other filling ingredients.

Wipe off any solid seasonings from the kimchi and finely dice.

In a separate bowl, mash the firm tofu with your hands until fine and uniform and wrap in a cheesecloth (muslin) or similar and squeeze to drain excess moisture.

In a small pot of boiling water, blanch the mung bean sprouts for 2 minutes. Drain and let cool in a sieve. Once cooled, cut into ⅛-inch (3 mm) pieces.

In a frying pan, heat the cooking oil over high heat. Add the seasoned pork and onions and stir-fry, breaking up the meat. While the meat is cooking, add the diced kimchi and stir-fry for 3 minutes. Scrape into a bowl to cool. Add the tofu, mung bean sprouts, egg, scallion, and salt and mix well until uniform.

**Make the cho-ganjang:** In a small bowl, stir together the soy sauce, 3 tablespoons water, the vinegar, and gochugaru and mix until uniform. Set aside in a saucer.

**Assemble the dumplings:** Place a mandu wrapper in the palm of your nondominant hand and lightly apply water to the outer edges. Place 1 tablespoon of filling in the center. Fold the mandu wrapper into a half-moon shape and press the center of the edge to fix, then press the outer edges firmly together to seal, leaving no air bubbles. Repeat for all remaining ingredients.

Set up a steamer and bring the water to a boil. Add the mandu to the steamer basket, set it over the boiling water, cover, and steam for about 10 minutes.

Plate the steamed dumplings on a large flat plate and serve with cho-ganjang on the side for dipping.

# Fish Mandu
## Eo-mandu
## 어만두

dF

With origins in royal Korean cuisine, *eo-mandu* are made with thin slices of croaker or pollock for the wrapper instead of the typical flour wrappers. Here, the fish "wrapper" is stuffed with a beef-and-mushroom filling. Another well-known example of this style of dumpling stuffs slices of mullet with tofu.

**Preparation time:** 30 minutes
**Cooking time:** 30 minutes
**Serves:** 2–4

**For the filling:**
3½ oz (100 g) ground (minced) beef
2¾ oz (80 g) fresh shiitake mushrooms, finely diced
1¾ oz (50 g) rehydrated wood ear mushrooms, minced
2 tablespoons ganjang (Korean soy sauce)
1 teaspoon sugar
½ teaspoon minced garlic
3½ oz (100 g) mung bean sprouts
1 teaspoon plus 1 tablespoon neutral cooking oil
2½ oz (75 g) cucumber, cut into matchsticks
Pinch of salt

**For the mustard jang:**
2 tablespoons Korean mustard
2 tablespoons rice vinegar
1 tablespoon sugar
1 teaspoon ganjang (Korean soy sauce)

**For the dumplings:**
1 lb 5 oz (600 g) croaker fillet
Salt
4 tablespoons mung bean powder

**Make the filling:** In a bowl, combine the beef, shiitakes, wood ears, soy sauce, sugar, and garlic and mix until uniform. Set aside to develop flavors while you prepare the other filling ingredients.

In a small pot of boiling water, blanch the mung bean sprouts for 2 minutes. Drain and let cool in a sieve. Once cool, chop into ⅛-inch (3 mm) pieces.

In a small nonstick frying pan, heat 1 teaspoon of the oil and stir-fry the cucumber with the salt for 30 seconds and set aside to cool.

In a nonstick frying pan, heat the remaining 1 tablespoon cooking oil over medium heat. Add the beef-and-mushroom mixture and stir-fry for 2 minutes, breaking up the meat as it cooks. Set aside to cool.

Once the meat mixture is cooled, in a large bowl, mix together the meat mixture, bean sprouts, and cucumber until uniform.

**Make the mustard jang:** In a small bowl, stir together the mustard, vinegar, 1 tablespoon water, the sugar and soy sauce. Set aside in a saucer.

**Assemble the dumplings:** Slice the fish fillet into 3 × 2-inch (7.5 × 5 cm) pieces ⅛ inch (3 mm) thick. Lightly season with a pinch of salt.

Set one piece of the fillet on a cutting board and dust the flesh side with mung bean powder. Place about ½ tablespoon of the filling in the center of the fish, fold it in half, and press the edges to seal. Lightly coat the edges with the mung bean powder to make sure that the fish "wrapper" does not open. Repeat for all the remaining ingredients.

Set up a steamer and bring the water to a boil. Add the dumplings to the steamer basket, set it over the boiling water, cover, and steam for about 4 minutes.

Plate the steamed dumplings on a large flat plate and serve with the mustard jang on the side for dipping.

# Pyeonsu Mandu
편수

dF

The *pyeonsu mandu* is a local dish of Kaesong at the southern end of the peninsula. The dumplings are made with mostly vegetables and are mainly enjoyed in the summer, paired with brisket soup. Unlike most dumplings, these are usually enjoyed cold instead of hot. The store-bought mandu wrappers are trimmed to a square shape, and the edges of the dumpling are gathered in the center for a unique shape.

Preparation time: 1 hour
Cooking time: 15 minutes
Serves: 4

### For the filling:
- 9 oz (250 g) ground (minced) beef
- 5½ oz (160 g) fresh shiitake mushrooms, cut into ⅛-inch (3 mm) matchsticks (caps halved first if large)
- 2 tablespoons ganjang (Korean soy sauce)
- ½ tablespoon minced garlic
- 1 teaspoon sesame oil
- 2 teaspoons salt
- 1 lb (500 g) aehobak (Korean zucchini), cut into ⅛-inch (3 mm) matchsticks
- 5 oz (150 g) mung bean sprouts
- 4 tablespoons neutral cooking oil
- 2½ oz (75 g) cucumber, cut into ⅛-inch (3 mm) matchsticks

### For the dumplings:
- 32 large mandu wrappers
- 64 pine nuts
- 2 cups (16 fl oz/480 ml) Beef Broth (page 315)
- 2 tablespoons cheongjang (light Korean soy sauce)

**Make the filling:** In a bowl, combine the beef, shiitakes, soy sauce, garlic, sesame oil, and 1 teaspoon of the salt. Set aside for the flavors to develop while you prepare the other filling ingredients.

In a bowl, toss the zucchini and the remaining 1 teaspoon salt and brine for 15 minutes. Squeeze to remove excess moisture.

Meanwhile, in a small pot of boiling water, blanch the mung bean sprouts for 2 minutes. Drain and let cool in a sieve. Once cool, cut into pieces ¼ inch (6 mm) long.

In a nonstick frying pan, heat 1 tablespoon of the cooking oil over medium heat. Add the seasoned ground beef and stir-fry for 3 minutes, breaking up the meat. Transfer to a bowl to cool. Add 2 tablespoons of the cooking oil to the pan and stir-fry the zucchini until just before it changes color. Set aside on a plate to cool. Stir-fry the cucumber with the remaining 1 tablespoon cooking oil and set aside to cool.

When all the components have cooled, combine them in a bowl and toss until uniform.

**Assemble and cook the dumplings:** Trim the mandu wrappers to make them square. Place ½ tablespoon of filling in the center of a wrapper and top with 2 pine nuts. Pull the four corners into the center to make a cross pattern and press with the fingertips to seal all the edges. Repeat for all the remaining ingredients.

Set up a steamer and bring the water to a boil. Add the dumplings to the steamer basket, set it over the boiling water, cover, and steam for about 5 minutes. Set the dumplings aside to cool.

When ready to serve, season the beef broth with the soy sauce. Serve the dumplings in the lightly seasoned beef broth and eat with a spoon.

# Rolled Mandu
## Gullim Mandu
## 굴림만두

dF

If there are no *mandu* wrappers available or there is no time to make dumplings, *gullim mandu* ("rolled dumplings") are a convenient substitute. They are made by rolling the filling ingredients into balls and rolling them in flour to create a thin outer layer that substitutes for the traditional wrapper. The rolled mandu is often used in *jeongol* (hotpots) for a neater dish, because there is no dumpling dough to come undone.

Preparation time: 1 hour
Cooking time: 15 minutes
Serves: 4

For the cho-ganjang:
3 tablespoons ganjang (Korean soy sauce)
2 tablespoons rice vinegar
1 teaspoon gochugaru (red chili flakes)

For the "filling":
1 lb (500 g) ground (minced) pork
2 tablespoons ganjang (Korean soy sauce)
1 tablespoon minced garlic
10 oz (300 g) mung bean sprouts
10 oz (300 g) firm tofu
3½ oz (100 g) garlic chives, finely sliced
2 egg yolks
1 tablespoon salt

For the "dumplings":
1½ cups (195 g) all-purpose (plain) flour
6 egg whites

**Make the cho-ganjang:** In a small bowl, stir together the soy sauce, 3 tablespoons water, the vinegar, and gochugaru. Set aside in a saucer.

**Make the "filling":** In a large bowl, combine the pork, soy sauce, and garlic and set aside to develop flavors while you prepare the other filling ingredients.

In a small pot of boiling water, blanch the mung bean sprouts for 2 minutes. Drain and let cool in a sieve. Once cool, cut into ⅛-inch (3 mm) pieces.

In a bowl, mash the firm tofu with your hands until fine and uniform. Wrap the tofu in a cheesecloth (muslin) or similar and squeeze to drain excess moisture.

Add the mung bean sprouts, tofu, chives, egg yolks, and salt to the pork and mix until uniform. Roll the mixture into 1-inch (2.5 cm) balls.

**Make the "dumplings":** Set the flour on a large plate. In a shallow bowl, beat the egg whites. Roll the balls in the flour until well coated, then dip into the egg whites. Roll again in the flour to coat fully and set aside.

Set up a steamer and bring the water to a boil. Add the balls to the steamer basket, set it over the boiling water, cover, and steam for about 12 minutes.

Plate the steamed dumplings on a large flat plate and serve with cho-ganjang on the side for dipping.

# Flat Mandu
## Napjak Mandu
## 납작만두

*Napjak mandu*, or flat dumplings, originated in the southeastern city of Daegu. It's a simple *mandu* stuffed mainly with chives and vermicelli noodles that is steamed and then pan-fried. It is typically served with onions and cabbage, and it's a popular side to *tteokbokki* (stir-fried rice cakes). This recipe showcases the version that's served with cabbage salad.

Preparation time: 30 minutes, plus 20 minutes soaking time
Cooking time: 30 minutes
Serves: 4

For the mandu:
9 oz (250 g) glass noodles
1 tablespoon sesame oil
2 tablespoons ganjang (Korean soy sauce)
1 tablespoon sugar
1 teaspoon salt
3½ oz (100 g) chives, cut into ⅛-inch (3 mm) pieces
20 large mandu wrappers

For the cabbage salad:
2 tablespoons rice vinegar
2 tablespoons sesame oil
1 tablespoon cheongjang (light Korean soy sauce)
1 tablespoon sugar
1 tablespoon gochugaru (red chili flakes)
1 teaspoon gochujang (red chili paste)
4½ oz (125 g) green cabbage, cut into ⅛-inch (3 mm) shreds
1¾ oz (50 g) carrot, cut into ⅛-inch (3 mm) matchsticks
1¾ oz (50 g) onion, thinly sliced
1 oz (30 g) thin chives, cut into 2-inch (5 cm) lengths

To finish:
5 tablespoons neutral cooking oil

**Prepare the mandu:** Soak the glass noodles in water for 20 minutes to rehydrate.

In a small of boiling pot, cook the noodles for 5 minutes. Drain and rinse under cold running water. Set aside to drain. Cut the cooled glass noodles into ⅛-inch (3 mm) pieces.

In a nonstick frying pan, combine the noodles, sesame oil, soy sauce, sugar, and salt and stir-fry over medium heat for 1 minute. Add the chives and stir-fry for 10 more seconds. Set aside on a plate to cool.

Place a mandu wrapper in the palm of your nondominant hand and lightly apply water to the outer edges. Place 1 tablespoon of filling in the center. Fold the mandu wrapper into a half-moon shape and press the center of the edge to fix, then press the outer edges firmly to seal tightly, leaving no air bubbles. Repeat for all the remaining ingredients.

Set up a steamer and bring the water to a boil. Add the mandu to the steamer basket, set it over the boiling water, cover, and steam for about 5 minutes.

**Meanwhile, make the cabbage salad:** In a small bowl, stir together the vinegar, sesame oil, soy sauce, sugar, gochugaru, and gochujang. Set the salad dressing aside. In a large bowl, toss together the cabbage, carrot, onion, and chives.

**To finish:** In a nonstick frying pan, heat the cooking oil over medium heat. Add the steamed mandu and fry on both sides until crispy and golden brown.

Add the dressing to the cabbage salad and toss well to coat.

Plate the pan-fried dumplings on a large plate. Top with the cabbage salad. Serve hot.

# 죽 Juk Porridge

*Juk*, or porridge, is a dish with the longest history in Korea, predating both steamed rice and *tteok* (rice cakes). As Korea was developing into an agricultural society, grains, such as rice, were boiled in earthenware pots with a lot of water. The object was to break down the grains and release their starch to make a soft, thick, easily digestible mixture.

*Juk* is has long been considered a healthy dish to start one's day. Even in the Royal Court, where five meals were served during the day, *juk* was the first dish that the King ate daily to prepare his stomach. *Juk's* health benefits have been recorded in many historic texts, including the *Dongui Bogam*, a sevententh-century treatise on Eastern medicine.

To this day, *juk* is a humble yet soul-satisfying food that requires love and attention to make well.

# Types of Juk

*Juk* is first categorized by the grain, seed, or nut used. Basic *juk* is made with rice, and the additional ingredients determine the dish:

**Rice combined with other grains:** Nonglutinous rice creates the base for the *juk*, supplemented with additional starches or seeds. The added ingredient is then used for the name of the dish, for example red bean juk, sesame juk, or mung bean juk.

**Nuts:** The most commonly used are pine nuts, peanuts, and walnuts. All nuts can be used with rice to make *juk*.

**Vegetables:** Popular vegetables are chrysanthemum and siragi. All spring vegetables and kimchi can be used in juk. Seaweed is also added.

**Protein:** Poultry, meat, fish, seafood.

**Medicinal and herbal ingredients:** These are important in the culture of *juk*, because *juk* is often used as a restorative, healthy dish. Jujubes (Chinese red dates), ginseng, and mushrooms are often used and any herbal medicinal ingredients can be added.

**Miscellaneous ingredients:** These include milk.

Basic *juk* is made by first soaking short-grain rice (glutinous rice) in water to soften and then cooking with six times its volume in water over low heat while stirring constantly for 40–50 minutes. Plain white rice *juk* is the most basic version made with whole or ground rice. The ideal ratio is about 1:6 rice to water for a basic *juk*. When cooking with whole grains of rice, they are sometimes stir-fried with sesame oil before boiling to impart a toasted taste. There are three subcategories of *juk* distinguished by the shape of the grain used, and there are conventions around which recipe uses which version:

**Ongeun-juk:** This is *juk* made from whole soaked grains.

**Wonmi-juk:** This is *juk* made from coarsely ground grains.

**Bidan-juk:** This is *juk* made from finely ground rice, where there's no solid form of the grain used. An example of *bidan-juk* is the classically prepared Pine Nut Juk (page 397), which has a very smooth consistency.

There are other *juk*-related dishes, including *mieum*, where the fully cooked *juk* is strained through a fine sieve and served in liquid form. For a dish called *eungi*, grains are ground and soaked in water to separate the pure starch. This starch is then cooked with water to make a fine, loose porridge. Both of these dishes require more water than the standard *juk* ratio, with *mieum* at a ratio of 1:7 or 1:8 rice to water and *eungi* at 10:1.

# Cooking Juk

Cooking rice and *juk* involve the same process of breaking down starch, but the amount of water and heat levels are different. While seemingly simple, it is difficult to make a proper juk. Here are some guides to help with your success.

## Cooking Tools

Using a pot with a heavy bottom is important. Ideally, it should be stainless steel, because aluminum and cast-iron pots can impart unwanted flavors, and rice easily sticks in a thin aluminum pan. You need a sturdy tool for stirring. A wooden spatula is the most common tool used; silicone spatulas also can work, but they often lack the power to stir and scrape.

## Stir-Frying

For *juk*, the rice can be stir-fried before boiling or it can simply be boiled. Stir-frying whole grains prior to boiling is the traditional method. If stir-frying ground or powdered grains, they must be fully dried, because using wet ingredients will cook the powder.

## Stirring

When cooking *juk*, many people make the mistake of stirring constantly while cooking to prevent sticking and clumping. Unfortunately, this causes an overly starchy texture and can release the distinct and unwanted smell of starch. Moreover, stirring constantly causes an artificial breakdown of ingredients instead of the natural breakdown of ingredients that's desired. It's important to stir slowly and gently before the *juk* begins to boil to properly cook the ingredients, and only occasionally once the *juk* begins to boil.

## Seasoning

*Juk* is seasoned at the very end, when all ingredients are fully cooked and broken down, or just before serving. It's important to season at the end, because the ingredients absorb the seasoning differently over time, changing the taste. Especially for *juk* made with whole grains, once seasoned it should be tasted again and adjusted before serving. Typically, seasoning is salt and soy sauce (and honey for sweet versions) and can be adjusted to preference.

## Heat Levels

Cooking grains for *juk* begins over medium heat and increases to high to boil. The heat goes back down to medium to simmer, then is finally allowed to gently cook and steam over low heat. Depending on the final texture and consistency of the *juk*, it may finish with high heat for the last few seconds. The reason for using medium heat at the beginning is the porridge may burn if using higher heat. If at any point the *juk* begins to burn, do not scrape up the burned part. Carefully pour the unburned *juk* into a new pot and keep cooking.

## Pine Nut Juk
### Jat Juk
### 잣죽

dF gF vg vE -S

Korea is the top producer of fine pine nuts in the world. If you have access to Korean pine nuts, there's no better way to showcase them than in this delicious, fragrant pine nut *juk*. *Gapyeong* (yellow pine nuts), which are harvested in the mountains of Gapyeong once every three years, are the best in class. The high mountains have the best growing conditions for these large, hard pine nuts with a soft, savory butter-like fragrance.

Preparation time: 15 minutes, plus 1 hour soaking time
Cooking time: 40 minutes
Serves: 2

½ cup (68 g) pine nuts
⅓ cup (73 g) short-grain white rice
Salt

In a blender, combine the pine nuts and ½ cup (4 fl oz/120 ml) water and blend until fine. Set a fine-mesh sieve over a bowl and strain the pine milk into it.

Wash the rice in a bowl of cold water three or four times. Drain the rice and return it to the bowl. Add fresh water twice the volume of the rice and let soak for 1 hour.

Drain the soaked rice and add it to a blender with ½ cup (4 fl oz/120 ml) water and blend until fine. Set a fine-mesh sieve over a bowl and strain the rice milk into it.

In a heavy pot, bring 1⅓ cups (10.5 fl oz/315 ml) water to a boil over high heat. Reduce the heat to low and add the pine nut milk and boil for 5 minutes, stirring so that the pine nut residue doesn't stick to the bottom. Add the rice milk and boil for 30 minutes, stirring constantly. Remove from the heat, cover, and let steam for 5 minutes.

Season with salt to taste before serving. Serve in individual bowls.

## Kimchi & Bean Sprout Juk
### Kimchi Kongnamul Juk
### 김치 콩나물죽

dF -3o

This is a really quick recipe, especially if you keep kimchi, bean sprouts, and cooked rice on hand. If anchovy broth is available, use it in place of the water for a more savory *juk*. The sesame oil can be replaced with perilla oil to preference. For a spicier *juk*, add *gochugaru* (red chili flakes) or minced Cheongyang chilies to taste. For a deeper spice, add a small amount of *gochujang* (red chili paste) to the broth.

Preparation time: 10 minutes
Cooking time: 10 minutes
Serves: 2

1 tablespoon sesame oil
1¾ oz (50 g) Napa Cabbage Kimchi (page 60), thinly sliced
1 cup (200 g) Cooked Short-Grain White Rice (page 92)
1 oz (30 g) soybean sprouts
1 tablespoon Yondu (Korean vegan seasoning sauce)
2 scallions (spring onions), slivered
Sesame seeds
Crushed gim

In a heavy pot, heat the sesame oil over medium heat. Add the kimchi and stir-fry for 1–2 minutes. Add 4 cups (32 fl oz/950 ml) water and bring to a boil over high heat. Once boiling, add the cooked rice and boil for 5 more minutes. Add the bean sprouts, cover with a lid, reduce the heat to medium, and cook for 3–4 minutes. Remove from the heat and stir in the Yondu.

Serve in individual bowls garnished with the scallions, and sesame seeds and gim to taste.

# Sweet Pumpkin Juk
## Danhobak Juk
## 단호박죽

dF gF vg vE -S

In fall, when winter squash are ripe for harvest, the sweet pumpkin *juk* is made with winter squash, such as kabocha (Japanese pumpkin) or *neulgeun hobak* (Korean "old pumpkin"). It's beloved by all ages for its lovely, sweet flavor. This sweet *juk* is made with glutinous rice flour instead of short-grain rice. If you can't source glutinous rice flour, substitute with 3 tablespoons cooked rice. If you have access to canned Korean red beans (adzuki beans), stir in a tablespoon of the beans at the end.

**Preparation time:** 20 minutes
**Cooking time:** 25 minutes
**Serves:** 2

1 kabocha squash (14–16 oz/400–500 g)
2 tablespoons glutinous rice flour
1 teaspoon salt
3 tablespoons sugar

Halve and seed the squash. Peel and cut the squash into 12 pieces. Place the pieces in a large microwave-safe bowl or container and cover with a lid or plastic wrap (cling film). Microwave for 6 minutes. In a blender, combine the cooked squash and 1 cup (8 fl oz/240 nl) water and blend until fine and uniform.

In a small bowl, combine the glutinous rice flour and ½ cup (4 fl oz/120 ml) water and stir until uniform. Set aside.

In a heavy pot, combine 2 cups (16 fl oz/480 ml) water and the squash puree and boil over high heat. Once boiling, add the glutinous rice mixture, reduce the heat to low, and simmer for 10 minutes, stirring constantly to avoid clumping or burning. Remove from the heat, cover with a lid, and let steam for 5 minutes.

Before serving, season with the salt and sugar. Serve in individual bowls.

---

# Doenjang Spinach Juk
## Doenjang Sigeumchi Juk
## 된장 시금치죽

dF gF

This porridge is light on the stomach and restorative, but it still makes a delicious and filling meal. The savory flavor of *doenjang* and the sweetness of the spinach harmonize well.

**Preparation time:** 15 minutes, plus 1 hour soaking time
**Cooking time:** 45 minutes
**Serves:** 2

⅔ cup (145 g) short-grain white rice
5 oz (150 g) spinach
1 tablespoon doenjang (fermented soybean paste)
8 dried shrimp, minced
1 tablespoon gochujang (red chili paste)
1 tablespoon minced scallion (spring onion)
½ tablespoons minced garlic
Sesame oil
¼ teaspoon ground sesame seeds

Wash the rice in cold water three or four times. In a bowl, combine the rice with three times its volume of water and soak for 1 hour. Drain the soaked rice in a sieve.

Set up a bowl of ice and water. In a small pot of boiling water, blanch the spinach for just 30 seconds. Transfer to the bowl of cold water to cool completely. Gently squeeze out all excess water with your hands and cut into ¾–1¼-inch (2–3 cm) pieces.

In a heavy pot, stir-fry the doenjang over low heat for 1 minute. Add 5 cups (40 fl oz/1.2 liters) water and the shrimp and bring to a boil over high heat. Once boiling, add the rice and boil for 25 minutes over medium heat, until the rice has turned into a starchy consistency.

Add the gochujang, scallion, and garlic and boil for 5 more minutes. Remove from the heat, cover with lid, and steam for 5 minutes.

Serve in individual bowls and garnish with 2–3 drops of sesame oil and ground sesame seeds.

## Mung Bean Juk
### Nokdu Juk
### 녹두죽

dF gF vg vE -S

Mung bean *juk* is a simple savory porridge made with mung beans and rice. It is easy to digest and known for its health benefits. If you soak the mung beans the night before, it will shorten the cooking time.

Preparation time: 30 minutes, plus 1 hour soaking time
Cooking time: 1 hour
Serves: 2

7 oz (200 g) peeled mung beans
⅔ cup (145 g) short-grain white rice
¼ teaspoon salt
¼ teaspoon sugar

In a pot, combine the mung beans and 6⅓ cups (48 fl oz/1.5 liters) water and bring to a boil over high heat. Once boiling, reduce the heat to medium and boil for 30 minutes. Reserving the cooking liquid, drain the mung beans. Combine the mung beans and 2 cups (16 fl oz/480 ml) of the reserved cooking liquid and push through the sieve into a bowl. Let settle into starch on the bottom and a clear liquid on top.

Wash the rice three or four times with cold water. In a bowl, combine the rice with three times its volume in water and let soak for 1 hour. Drain the soaked rice in a sieve.

In a heavy pot, add only the clear top portion of the boiled mung bean water (reserve the bottom portion). Add the soaked rice and bring to a boil over high heat. Once boiling, add the remaining cooked mung beans, reduce the heat to medium, and boil for 30 minutes. Stir occasionally to make sure that no lumps form. Remove from the heat, cover with a lid, and let steam for 5 minutes.

Before serving, season with the salt and sugar. Serve in individual bowls.

## Red Bean Juk
### Pat Juk
### 팥죽

dF gF vg vE -S

The red bean *juk* is a sentimental dish of the wintertime, its warmth and sweetness a savored memory. There is an old Korean tradition of eating red bean *juk* during the winter solstice to thwart off evil spirits and bad luck.

Preparation time: 15 minutes, plus 2 hours soaking time
Cooking time: 3 hours
Serves: 4

1 cup (220 g) short-grain white rice
2 cups (390 g) dried red beans (adzuki beans), well rinsed
3 tablespoons boiling water
¼ teaspoon salt
1 cup (110 g) glutinous rice flour
Salt and sugar, for serving

Wash the rice twice with cold water. In a bowl, combine the rice with three times its volume in water and soak for 2 hours. Strain the rice with a sieve and set aside.

Meanwhile, in a pot, combine the red beans and 8 cups (64 fl oz/1.9 liters) water and bring to a boil over high heat. Once boiling, drain the beans and discard the water. In the same pot, add the once-cooked beans and 8 cups (64 fl oz/1.9 liters) fresh water and bring to a boil over high heat. Cook for 10 minutes, then reduce the heat to medium and cook until the red beans have softened enough to easily crush, about 1½ hours. Strain through a sieve into a bowl, reserving 8 cups (64 fl oz/1.9 liters) of the cooking liquid. Let the red bean water settle into starch on the bottom and clear liquid on the top.

Meanwhile, in a small bowl, stir together the 3 tablespoons boiling water and the salt. In a bowl, slowly pour the hot salted water into the glutinous rice flour, massaging to create a uniform dough. Form into balls ½ inch (1.5 cm) in diameter. Set aside covered with wet paper towels or plastic wrap (cling film) to keep them from drying out.

In a heavy pot, add the clear portion of the red bean water. Bring to a boil over high heat. Once boiling, add the soaked rice, reduce to medium heat, and boil for 30 minutes. Once the rice is of a starchy consistency, add the crushed red beans and boil over medium heat for 10 minutes, stirring occasionally. Add the glutinous rice balls and continue boiling until the glutinous rice balls float to the top. Remove from the heat, cover with a lid, and steam for 5 minutes.

Serve in individual bowls. Serve with salt and sugar to season to taste.

# Chicken Juk
## Dak Juk
## 닭죽

dF

The chicken *juk* is one of the most restorative dishes in Korean cuisine, often made with ginseng, jujube (Chinese red date), ginkgo nuts, and more. The short-grain rice can be replaced with glutinous rice, but regardless it's a delicacy enjoyed most often in the summertime. If high-quality chicken stock is readily available, use it instead of the stock here and cook the rice with diced vegetables, such as carrots, onions, mushrooms, and more.

**Preparation time: 1 hour**
**Cooking time: 1 hour 45 minutes**
**Serves: 2**

⅔ cup (145 g) short-grain white rice
1 Cornish hen, poussin or other small chicken (1½–1¾ lb/700–800g)
1 oz (30 g) daepa (Korean scallion)
7 oz (200 g) onions, cut into chunks
1 oz (25 g) garlic, peeled
5 black peppercorns
Salt or cheongjang (light Korean soy sauce)
Sliced scallion (spring onion)
¼ teaspoon ground sesame seeds

Wash the rice with cold water three or four times. In a bowl, combine the rice with three times its volume of water and soak for 1 hour. Drain well.

Meanwhile, rinse the blood and any scraps of innards from inside the chicken. In a large pot, combine the chicken, 10 cups (80 fl oz/2.4 liters) water, the daepa, onions, garlic, and peppercorns and bring to a boil over high heat. Once boiling, reduce the heat to medium and simmer for 40 minutes.

Transfer the chicken to a large bowl and separate the meat from the bones. Shred the meat along the grain by hand into large bite-size piece and set aside. Strain the stock and discard the solids. Pour the stock into a large heavy pot.

Add the soaked rice to the pot of chicken stock and bring to a boil over high heat. Once boiling, reduce the heat to medium and boil, stirring occasionally to prevent the rice from sticking to the pot, until it reaches a starchy consistency, about 30 minutes. Add the chicken meat and cook for another 5 minutes. Remove from the heat, cover with a lid, and let sit for 5 minutes.

Just before serving, season with salt or soy sauce to taste. Serve in individual bowls and garnish with the sliced scallion and ground sesame seeds.

# Abalone Juk
## Jeonbok Juk
## 전복죽

dF

Abalone *juk* is one of the most prized dishes for restoring an ailing body, because abalone is highly nutritious. Although traditionally an expensive delicacy, abalone is more accessible today. This warm *juk* is a great way to enjoy both the savory flavors of the abalone innards and the plump, delicious flesh of its meat, which releases its deep aromas with every chew.

**Preparation time: 40 minutes, plus 1 hour soaking time**
**Cooking time: 40 minutes**
**Serves: 4**

1 cup (220 g) short-grain white rice
4 live abalones (1 lb/440 g)
2 tablespoons sesame oil
6 cups (48 fl oz/1.4 liters) hot water
1 teaspoon cheongjang (light Korean soy sauce)
1 teaspoon salt

Wash the rice in three or four changes of cold water. In a bowl, combine the rice with three times its volume of cold water and let soak for 1 hour. Drain in a sieve.

Using a brush, thoroughly clean the abalone while they are still in the shell, and then remove the meat from the shell using your hands. Separate the innards and the meat. Finely dice the innards and set aside. Thinly slice the abalone meat.

In a heavy pot, heat the sesame oil over medium heat. Add half of the sliced abalone meat and stir-fry quickly. Add the soaked rice and the abalone innards and continue to stir-fry for 3–4 minutes, stirring constantly with a wooden spatula to incorporate the sesame oil into the rice evenly. Add the hot water gradually in three to four additions, stirring well after each. Once the juk is boiling, reduce the heat to low and simmer, stirring occasionally, for 20 minutes. Once it reaches a starchy, thick consistency, remove from the heat and add the remaining abalone meat on top in an even layer. Cover with a lid and let sit for 5 minutes.

Before serving, season with the salt and soy sauce to taste. Serve in individual bowls.

# Tteok Rice Cakes

In Korean cuisine, in addition to rice and noodles, *tteok* (rice cakes) are a traditional staple food that are incorporated into many different dishes. *Tteokguk* (Rice Cake Soup, page 408), a dish traditionally eaten on the first day of the new year, and *tteokbokki* (stir-fried *tteok*) are the most common and popular *tteok* dishes.

*Tteok* are made with grain flour, most typically rice flour. The cakes can be made by simply steaming the flour, or steaming it and then pounding or kneading it into shape. Although some dishes made with *tteok*, such as *tteokbokki* and *tteokguk*, are eaten as a full meal, these compact little cakes are more commonly consumed as snacks and desserts.

*Tteok* are especially popular served with traditional tea or coffee and, as a result, different ways of pairing them with new flavors and textures are constantly evolving. *Tteok* are also a popular treat to offer guests as a gift at any ceremony or celebration in Korea. This *tteok*-gifting tradition has its roots in times when rice was scarce, meaning that a dense cake made of rice signified luxury, and thus celebrated a special moment or expressed gratitude.

# Gochujang Stir-Fried Tteok
## Gochujang Tteokbokki
## 고추장 떡볶이

dF -30

*Gochujang tteokbokki* is the most common form of *tteokbokki*, found in street stalls, casual restaurants, and in the home kitchens of Korea. The *gochujang* (red chili paste) sauce is made with a balance of sweet and spicy ingredients. A number of different vegetables can be added, but the most basic ingredients are daepa (Korean scallion) and fish cake, which adds umami to the dish.

**Preparation time:** 15 minutes
**Cooking time:** 10 minutes
**Serves:** 4

1 lb (440 g) tteokbokki rice cakes

**For the sauce:**
5 tablespoons ganjang (Korean soy sauce)
4 tablespoons sugar
3 tablespoons gochujang (red chili paste)
3 tablespoons fine gochugaru (red chili powder)
2 tablespoons corn (golden) syrup
1 teaspoon freshly ground black pepper

**For the tteokbokki:**
4 sheets fish cakes, cut into 2 × ½-inch (5 × 1.3 cm) strips
2 oz (60 g) daepa (Korean scallion), cut into ½-inch (1.3 cm) diagonal slices

If the rice cakes are dried (shelf stable), soak them in lukewarm water for about 10 minutes, then drain. Fresh or thawed frozen rice cakes do not need to be rehydrated.

**Make the sauce:** In a saucepan, combine 3 cups (24 fl oz/710 ml) water, the soy sauce, sugar, gochujang, gochugaru, corn syrup, and black pepper and stir until well combined.

**Make the tteokbokki:** Add the rice cakes to the sauce and bring to a boil. Once boiling, add the fish cakes and cook for 5 minutes. Add the daepa and remove from the heat once it reaches a boil.

Plate and serve hot.

# Ganjang Stir-Fried Tteok
## Ganjang Tteokbokki
## 간장 떡볶이

dF

To add a little spice to this *tteokbokki*, omit the bell pepper and use a couple of tablespoons of minced fresh Cheongyang chili or other green chili. Another way to add spice would be to use chili oil for stir-frying the rice cakes and beef.

**Preparation time:** 20 minutes
**Cooking time:** 15 minutes
**Serves:** 4

1 lb (440 g) tteokbokki rice cakes

**For the sauce:**
4 tablespoons ganjang (Korean soy sauce)
3 tablespoons sugar
2 tablespoons sesame oil
1 tablespoon mirin
1 tablespoon minced garlic
1 teaspoon freshly ground black pepper

**For the tteokbokki:**
5 oz (150 g) beef, top round (topside) or foreshank
1 king oyster mushroom
2 tablespoons neutral cooking oil
3½ oz (100 g) onion, cut into ¼-inch (6 mm) slices
2¾ oz (80 g) green bell pepper, cut into 2 × ¼-inch (5 cm × 6 mm) slices
2 oz (60 g) daepa (Korean scallion), cut into ½-inch (1.3 cm) diagonal slices

If the rice cakes are dried (shelf stable), soak them in lukewarm water for about 10 minutes, then drain. Fresh or thawed frozen rice cakes do not need to be rehydrated.

**Make the sauce:** In a small bowl, combine the soy sauce, sugar, sesame oil, mirin, garlic, and black pepper and mix well until uniform. Set aside.

**Prepare the tteokbokki:** Cut the beef into 2 × ¼-inch (5 × 0.6 cm) matchsticks and set in a bowl. Add 1 tablespoon of the sauce and massage to coat. Halve the mushroom lengthwise and cut crosswise into slices ¼ inch (6 mm) thick.

In a large frying pan, heat the cooking oil over high heat. Add the rice cakes and beef and stir-fry for 30 seconds. Add the sauce and 4 tablespoons water and cook until the water evaporates. Add the mushroom, onion, bell pepper, and daepa and stir-fry for 1 more minute. Check that the rice cakes are cooked through before removing from the heat.

Serve hot on a large plate.

# Shallow-Fried Tteok
## Gireum Tteokbokki
## 기름 떡볶이

For a crispier texture, add a tablespoon of sugar at the end of the cooking process, when most of the moisture has evaporated, and stir well. This will result in a caramelized flavor and a crispier texture.

**Preparation time:** 15 minutes
**Cooking time:** 15 minutes
**Serves:** 4

1 lb (440 g) tteokbokki rice cakes

**For the sauce:**
3 tablespoons ganjang
    (Korean soy sauce)
2 tablespoons sesame oil
2 tablespoons sugar
1 tablespoon corn (golden) syrup
1 tablespoon gochugaru
    (red chili flakes)
1 tablespoon fine gochugaru
    (red chili powder)

**To shallow-fry the tteok:**
3 tablespoons neutral cooking oil

If the rice cakes are dried (shelf stable), soak them in lukewarm water for about 10 minutes, then drain. Fresh or thawed frozen rice cakes do not need to be rehydrated.

In a medium saucepan of boiling water, boil the rice cakes for 4 minutes. Drain in a sieve.

**Make the sauce:** In a small bowl, combine the soy sauce, sesame oil, sugar, corn syrup, and gochugaru and mix well until uniform. In a large bowl, combine the sauce with the cooked rice cakes and mix well.

**Shallow-fry the tteok:** In a large nonstick frying pan, heat the cooking oil over over high heat. Add the seasoned rice cakes, reduce the heat to low, and cook, stirring to avoid burning the gochugaru, as if deep-frying the rice cakes, until the outer surface is crispy.

Serve on a large plate.

---

# Rice Cake Soup
## Tteokguk
## 떡국

*Tteokguk* is a soup made by using *tteok* that have been sliced into thin oval shapes and cooking them to tender in broth. It is one of the most significant dishes in Korean tradition. On the first day of the new year, *tteokguk* was eaten as the first meal in tribute to ancestors.

**Preparation time:** 25 minutes
**Cooking time:** 20 minutes
**Serves:** 4

4 oz (120 g) beef brisket, cut into
    bite-size pieces
2 tablespoons cheongjang (light
    Korean soy sauce)
1 tablespoon sesame oil
6 cups (48 fl oz/1.4 liters) Beef Broth
    (page 315), Anchovy Broth (page
    314), Vegetable Broth (page 313),
    or water
2 eggs
14 oz (400 g) sliced tteok
    (coin-shaped rice cakes)
1 tablespoon minced garlic
3 scallions (spring onions),
    thinly sliced on a diagonal
Salt

In a bowl, toss the beef with the soy sauce and set aside to marinate for 10 minutes.

In a pot, heat the sesame oil over medium heat. Add the beef and stir-fry for 2 minutes. Pour in the broth and bring to a boil, skimming the foam.

Meanwhile, crack the eggs into a small bowl and beat with chopsticks until uniform.

Add the rice cakes and garlic to the soup and boil for 5 minutes. Once the rice cakes are soft, gently pour in the egg in a circular motion. Once the soup comes back to a boil, add the scallions and season to taste with salt.

Remove from the heat and serve hot in individual bowls.

# Husik Desserts

후식

*Husik*, which translates to "after-meal," refers to a category of sweets that are enjoyed not only after a meal but also along with a cup of tea. The three broad categories of *husik* are *tteok* (rice cakes), various confections (such as cookies), and *eumcheongryu*, which are traditional beverages.

Dessert rice *cakes* (*tteok*) are made by steaming or cooking grain flour and forming the dough into shapes. There is a Korean proverb that translates to "rice cake instead of rice," which signifies that *tteok* are so delicious that the average person would rather eat *tteok* than a meal. Another proverb translates to "there are separate stomachs for rice and rice cakes." *Tteok* were especially important for holidays and feast days, but our ancestors made and enjoyed various rice cakes all year-round, using different seasonal ingredients for each season.

*Gwajul*, the traditional name for Korean cookies, have their origins in fruit-shaped cookies that were baked when fruits were not available. There are a variety of *gwajul*, such as *yumil-gwa*, which are made by pan-frying or deep-frying dough in oil; *jeong-gwa*, made by stewing cooked fruit or roots in rice syrup or honey; *gwa-pyeon*, made by boiling and straining fruit; *suksil-gwa*, made by mixing or stewing fruits with other ingredients; and *yeot-gangjeong*, a candy bar–like type of confection made with grains, seeds, or nuts mixed with grain syrup. Just like *tteok*, these types of confections are always present at celebrations.

*Eumcheongryu* is a generic term for nonalcoholic beverages. Most representative of this category are traditional beverages, such as *sujeonggwa* (sweet cinnamon tea), *sikhye* (sweet rice punch), and *hwachae* (azalea punch). Beverages, such as *sungnyung,* made from rice, and *jehotang*, a tea made from medicinal ingredients and honey, are representative of the Korean beverage tradition in which grains, medicinal ingredients, flowers, herbs, and fruits are made into drinks.

# Sweet Korean Pancakes
## Hotteok
## 호떡

*Hotteok*, sweet Korean pancakes, are one of the most popular and common *husik* dishes found in markets and street stalls throughout Korea. It is one of the most nostalgic childhood memories for Koreans as well. The filling can be as simple as cinnamon sugar, but adding various nuts to the filling make it richer and more delicious.

Preparation time: 30 minutes, plus 30 minutes rising time
Cooking time: 20 minutes
Serves: 4

**For the dough:**
1 cup (8 fl oz/240 ml) warm water (82°–86°F/28°–30°C)
2 teaspoons active dry (fast-action dried) yeast
¼ cup (60 g) milk, at room temperature
¼ cup (50 g) granulated sugar
1 teaspoon salt
4 tablespoons neutral cooking oil
1½ cups (195 g) white bread (strong white) flour
⅓ cup (40 g) glutinous rice flour

**For the filling:**
¾ cup (143 g) packed light brown sugar
½ teaspoon ground cinnamon
½ cup (60 g) minced peanuts and walnuts

**For cooking:**
2 tablespoons neutral cooking oil

**Make the dough:** In a bowl, combine the warm water and yeast and stir until uniform. Cover with plastic wrap (cling film) and let sit for 15 minutes. Add the milk, sugar, salt, and oil and stir until uniform.

In a separate bowl, combine the bread flour and glutinous rice flour and mix until uniform. Add the yeast-milk mixture, stir until it forms a dough, and then mix for 10 minutes with your hands. Set the dough in a bowl, cover with plastic wrap (cling film), and let stand in a warm place (about 86°F/30°C) until the dough is doubled in size, about 30 minutes. The oven is a great place for this: Preheat the oven to 200°F (90°C/Gas Mark ¼) for 1–2 minutes. Then turn it off and use the residual heat of the oven to proof the dough.

**Meanwhile, make the filling:** In a small bowl, combine the brown sugar and cinnamon. Add the minced nuts and toss until uniform.

**Cook the pancakes:** In a frying pan, heat the cooking oil over low heat. Rub a small amount of cooking oil directly on your hands to prevent the dough from sticking. Tear the dough into small egg-size pieces. Flatten each piece into a round with both hands and add 1 tablespoon of the filling in the center. Fold the four sides of the dough into the center and seal. Place the dough seam-side down into the pan and flatten with a spatula. Pan-fry for 30 seconds, flip, and cook until golden brown and fully cooked.

Repeat for all pancakes. Serve hot.

# Poached Asian Pear
## Baesuk
## 배숙

*Baesuk* is one of the most typical and traditional *husik* beverages and is made by poaching Asian pear with black peppercorns in honey water or sugar water. The gentle sweetness of the Asian pear and the mild aroma of the black peppercorn harmonize beautifully.

Preparation time: 20 minutes, plus 6 hours chilling time
Cooking time: 40 minutes
Serves: 4

1¾ oz (50 g) fresh ginger, peeled and thinly sliced
½ Asian pear
12 black peppercorns
4 tablespoons brown sugar
4 tablespoons granulated sugar
8–12 pine nuts

In a pot, combine the sliced ginger and 9 cups (72 fl oz/2.1 liters) water and bring to a boil over high heat. As soon as it reaches a boil, reduce the heat to low and simmer for 30 minutes. Strain the broth and discard the ginger slices.

Peel and halve the Asian pear and remove the seeds and core. Cut into quarters. On the outer round side of each pear slice, insert 3 peppercorns at equal intervals, pressing in with your hands.

In a pot, heat the ginger broth over high heat. Add the brown and granulated sugars and stir until dissolved. Reduce the heat to medium, add the pear quarters, and simmer for 5 minutes. Remove from the heat and let the broth and pear cool to room temperature. Set in a container and refrigerate until completely chilled, about 6 hours. (The cooked pear will last in the refrigerator for up to 1 week.)

To serve, set each pear in a bowl and submerge with the broth. Garnish with 2–3 pine nuts.

## Red Bean Shaved Ice
### Patbingsu
### 팥빙수

*Bingsu*, shaved ice, is Korea's summer dessert. *Patbingsu* is one of the most traditional and representative of the *bingsu* category, and many varieties exist, including those made with different seasonal fruits. *Injeolmi*, a rice cake coated in soybean powder, is a common topping to add.

**Preparation time:** 20 minutes, plus 20 minutes chilling
**Cooking time:** 5 minutes
**Serves:** 2

5 tablespoons milk
2¼ lb (1 kg) ice block
2 tablespoons condensed milk
5 tablespoons canned sweetened red beans (adzuki beans)
1 tablespoon misutgaru (Korean multigrain powder)

Prepare a glass bowl by placing in the refrigerator until cold. (In Korea, this dish is served communally; however, if you'd prefer, you can chill two bowls.)

Just before serving, pour the milk into the chilled bowl(s). Shave the ice as finely as possible in an ice shaving machine (aka snow cone machine) into the bowl(s). Drizzle the condensed milk over the shaved ice, top with the sweet red beans, and sprinkle the misutgaru over the beans.

Serve immediately.

---

## Kaesong Honey Cookie
### Kaesong Yakgwa
### 개성약과

*Yakgwa* is a type of deep-fried cookie; its name comes from the word *yak* meaning "medicine" and *gwa* meaning "cookie." It is considered one of the most luxurious cookies of the noble sweets, and it's an important part of Korean holidays, ancestral rites, and festivals. While most *yakgwa* are round, the Kaesong *yakgwa* is distinct in its square shape and multiple layers that give it a brittle texture.

**Preparation time:** 30 minutes, plus 1–12 hours draining time and 2 hours soaking time
**Cooking time:** 1 hour
**Serves:** 4

1½ cups all-purpose (plain) flour
1 teaspoon salt
¼ teaspoon freshly ground black pepper
3½ tablespoons sesame oil

**For the honey syrup:**
4 tablespoons sugar
½ tablespoon honey
3 tablespoons soju (Korean distilled liquor)

**For the ginger syrup:**
2 cups jocheong (rice syrup)
4 teaspoons minced fresh ginger

**To finish:**
Neutral cooking oil, for deep-frying (about 6 cups/48 fl oz/1.4 liters)
Pine nut powder

In a large bowl, combine the all-purpose flour, salt, black pepper, and sesame oil and mix until uniform. Press through a sieve into a bowl and set aside.

**Make the honey syrup:** In a small pot, combine 4 tablespoons water, the sugar, and honey and cook over low heat for 5–7 minutes. Let cool to room temperature. Once cool, add the soju and mix well.

**Make the ginger syrup:** In a separate small pot, combine the rice syrup, ½ cup (4 fl oz/120 ml) water, and the ginger and bring to a boil. Remove from the heat and let cool to room temperature.

In a large bowl, combine the flour mixture and the honey syrup and mix well until a solid uniform dough forms. Roll out the dough with a rolling pin to a thickness of ¼ inch (6mm) and fold it in half, then roll it out again with a rolling pin and fold it in half. Repeat this three times. Roll out the final dough to a ⅓-inch (8 mm) thickness. Cut into 1⅓-inch (3.5 cm) squares. Pierce the center of each square twice with a toothpick or skewer.

**To finish:** Set a wire rack in a sheet pan. Pour 2 inches (5 cm) cooking oil into a large deep pot or deep fryer and heat to 194°F (90°C). Add the yakgwa squares and fry for 15 minutes. Set aside on the rack. Increase the temperature of the oil to 320°F (160°C), and refry the yakgwa squares for 3–5 minutes or until browned. Transfer the yakgwa squares to the wire rack to drain for a minimum of 1 hour and up to 12 hours.

Soak the finished yakgwa in the ginger syrup for 2 hours, then remove from the syrup and store in an airtight container. (The finished yakgwa can be kept for up to 5 days, and can be kept for up to 1 month in the refrigerator.)

Just before serving, garnish with pine nut powder.

# Raised Rice Cake
## Jeungpyeon
## 증편

dF gF vg vE

*Jeungpyeon* is a steamed rice cake that is fluffy and pleasantly chewy, with a sweet flavor and a subtle acidity from the fermented alcohol and is traditionally enjoyed during the summertime. Although most freshly made foods will spoil quickly in the heat of the summer, the *jeungpyeon* is protected by the live cultures in the unpasteurized *makgeolli* (Korean rice wine). Those cultures are also important for giving the rice cake its rise.

Preparation time: 30 minutes,
    plus 7 hours fermentation
Cooking time: 35 minutes
Serves: 4

For the dough:
4 cups (440 g) nonglutinous rice flour
1 cup (8 fl oz/240 ml) unpasteurized makgeolli (Korean rice wine)
1 cup (8 fl oz/240 ml) water, warmed to 104°F (40°C)
½ cup (100 g) sugar

For the garnish:
2 dried jujubes (Chinese red dates)
20 yellow pine nuts

To finish:
1 teaspoon neutral cooking oil
¼ teaspoon black sesame seeds

**Make the dough:** Sift the rice flour through a fine-mesh sieve into a large bowl. Add the makgeolli, warm water, and sugar and mix well, forming into a dough. Cover with plastic wrap (cling film) and let ferment for 4 hours.

Remove the air bubbles by lightly kneading, cover again with plastic wrap, and let the dough ferment for 2 hours.

Again, remove the air bubbles by lightly kneading, cover again with plastic wrap, and let the dough ferment for 1 hours.

**Meanwhile, prepare the garnish:** Seed and finely slice the jujubes. Pinch off the hard end from the pine nuts. Set aside.

**To finish:** Choose a square cake pan that is at least 2¾ inches (7 cm) deep and can fit in your steamer. Grease it with 1 teaspoon cooking oil. Pour the dough into the pan (it should come up two-thirds of the way. Top evenly with the jujubes, pine nuts, and sesame seeds.

Set up a steamer and bring the water to a boil.

Add the cake pan to the steamer basket, set it over the boiling water, cover, and steam over low heat for 10 minutes. Boost the heat to high and steam for 20 minutes. Then reduce the heat to low and steam for 5 minutes to finish.

Cut into small squares and serve.

---

# Sweet Rice with Nuts & Jujubes
## Yaksik
## 약식

dF vg vE    [ㅁ]

*Yaksik* is a sweet dish made of steamed glutinous rice with dried fruits and nuts, such as jujubes (Chinese red dates), chestnuts, and pine nuts, mixed with honey, oil, and soy sauce. Also called *yakbap*, which translates to "honey rice," from the word *yak*, the traditional word for honey, and *bap*, meaning "rice." It is a traditional sweet that is always served during holiday feasts, weddings, and other festivities.

Preparation time: 30 minutes,
    plus 5 hour soaking time
Cooking time: 1 hour 40 minutes
Serves: 4

2 cups (440 g) glutinous rice

For the jujube paste:
10 oz (300 g) dried jujubes (Chinese red dates), rinsed

For the yaksik:
6 chestnuts
10 dried jujubes (Chinese red dates)
1 tablespoon pine nuts
1 tablespoon jinjang (dark Korean soy sauce)
3 tablespoons light brown sugar
3 tablespoons sesame oil

For serving:
¾ teaspoon ground cinnamon
10 pine nuts

Rinse the glutinous rice twice in a sieve under cold water. Soak the glutinous rice in a large bowl of cold water for 5 hours.

**Meanwhile, make the jujube paste:** In a small pot, combine the jujubes and 2 cups (16 fl oz/480 ml) water and bring to a boil over high heat. Once boiling, reduce the heat to medium and boil until the water reduces to 4 tablespoons, stirring as needed. Push the jujubes through a sieve into a bowl, crushing the jujubes and removing the seeds. Set aside.

Set up a steamer and bring the water to a boil.

Line a steamer basket with a fine cloth, spread the soaked rice in the basket, and then set it over the boiling water. Cover and steam for 40 minutes.

**Prepare the yaksik:** Peel the chestnuts and cut each chestnut into 6 pieces. Remove the seeds from the jujubes and quarter them.

In a large bowl, combine the steamed rice with 4 tablespoons of the jujube paste, the soy sauce, brown sugar, and sesame oil and mix with a wooden spoon or spatula until uniform, taking care to not clump or crush the rice grains. Once well incorporated, gently fold in the chestnuts and jujubes and mix until uniform.

Set up the steamer again. Spread the rice mixture in an 8-inch (20 cm) square baking dish and set in the steamer basket. Cover and steam over high heat for 1 hour.

**To serve:** Sprinkle the dessert evenly with cinnamon and pine nuts. Cut into 2-inch (5 cm) squares to serve.

# Traditional Korean Donuts
## Kaeseong Juak
## 개성주악

dF vg vE          [ㅁ]

*Kaesong juak* are deep-fried cakes made of a glutinous rice and wheat flour dough stirred with *makgeolli* (Korean rice wine). This form of dessert originates and is most popular in the Kaesong region, where it was traditionally served to special guests, at weddings, or as gifts.

Preparation time: 20 minutes
Cooking time: 40 minutes
Serves: 4

For the juak dough:
3 cups (330 g) glutinous rice flour
1 cup (130 g) all-purpose (plain) flour
6 tablespoons sugar
½ cup (4 fl oz/120 ml) unpasteurized makgeolli (Korean rice wine)
2 tablespoons boiling water

For the syrup:
2 cups (700 g) jocheong (rice syrup)
1 cup (335 g) honey
¾ oz (20 g) fresh ginger, sliced
½ teaspoon salt
1 teaspoon ground cinnamon

To finish:
Neutral cooking oil, for deep-frying
Sliced jujubes (Chinese red dates), seeds (such as sunflower), or minced nuts

**Make the juak dough:** In a large bowl, sift in the glutinous rice flour and all-purpose flour through a fine sieve. Mix in the sugar well before adding the makgeolli and forming the dough. Stir in the boiling water and knead until uniform.

Tear off a piece of dough about 1 inch (2.5 cm) in diameter and press it into a flat round 1½ inches (4 cm) in diameter and ½ inch (1.3 cm) thick. Make a hole in the center with a thumb and index finger to make a donut shape.

**Make the syrup:** In a pot, combine the rice syrup, 1 cup (8 fl oz/240 ml) water, the honey, ginger, and salt and bring to a boil over high heat. Once boiling, reduce the heat to medium and boil until the mixture is syrupy, about 7 more minutes. Stir in the cinnamon, mix well, and remove from the heat.

**To finish:** Set a wire rack in a sheet pan. Pour 3 inches (7.5 cm) cooking oil into a large deep pot or deep fryer and heat to 248°F (120°C).

Drop in the formed donuts. Once they float, increase the temperature of the oil to 320°F (160°C) and fry until the donuts are browned, 3–4 minutes. Set the fried donuts on the rack to drain.

Dip each donut into the syrup to coat and return to the wire rack.

Garnish as desired with jujubes, seeds, or nuts. The donuts can be kept in a cool temperature for up to 3 days.

---

# Yuja Punch
## Yuja-hwachae
## 유자화채

dF gF vg vE -S

*Yuja-hwachae* is made with finely cut yuja (yuzu) peel and the juice of both the yuja and Asian pear. The unique fragrance of yuja and the sweet, cooling flavor of Asian pear go well together, and the juicy flavor of the pomegranate seed garnish as well as its jewel-like color adds to both the flavor and aesthetic. Because yuja is harvested in winter in Korea, this is a typical winter *husik* beverage. Yuja is mainly grown in the southern regions of Korea, and the fruit from Goheung is especially famous.

Preparation time: 20 minutes
Cooking time: 20 minutes plus 2–3 hours chilling time
Serves: 4

3 yuja (yuzu)
1½ cups (300 g) plus 6 teaspoons sugar
½ Asian pear
10 pine nuts
30 pomegranate seeds

Rinse the yuja under cold running water and cut each fruit into 6 pieces. Separate the peel and flesh. Peel the yuja zest (the thin colored layer) off the white pith with a vegetable peeler. Keeping the zest and the white pith separate, cut into very thin slivers (a scant ¹⁄₁₆ inch/1 mm) about 1½ inches (4 cm) long. Place in two separate bowls, cover each with 1 teaspoon sugar each, toss well, and set aside.

Remove the seeds from the yuja flesh and cut into 6 pieces. Add to a bowl with 3 teaspoons sugar, toss well, and set aside to macerate for 10 minutes.

Peel the pear and cut into matchsticks 1½ inches (4 cm) long and a scant ¹⁄₁₆ inch (1 mm) thick. Place in a bowl, cover with 1 teaspoon sugar, toss well, and set aside to macerate.

In a pot, combine 1½ cups (300 g) sugar and 4 cups (32 fl oz/950 ml) water. Bring to a boil over high heat. Once boiling, remove from the heat and let the syrup cool completely in a container in the refrigerator.

To serve, place the sugared yuja fruit in the center of a punch bowl. In a clockwise pattern, place the pear slices, yuja zest, and yuja pith in an alternating pattern. Garnish in the center with pine nuts and pomegranate seeds. Gently pour the cold sugar syrup into the center, allowing each ingredient to float naturally in place. Ladle the punch into small bowls. (Any leftover punch can be kept in the refrigerator for up to 4 days.)

## Sweet Rice Punch
### Sikhye
### 식혜

dF vg vE -S

*Sikhye* is one of the most popular sweet beverages of Korea and is always served during the holidays. It is a grain-based drink made by steeping rice with malt for a sweet taste. It is best enjoyed when extremely cold, lightly frozen so that a small amount of ice forms on top.

**Preparation time:** 20 minutes plus 3 hours soaking and 2–3 hours chilling time
**Cooking time:** 6½ hours
**Makes:** 10–12 cups (2.4–2.8 liters)

2 cups (350 g) malted barley powder
15 cups (120 fl oz/3.6 liters) warm water (86°F/30°C)
2 cups (440 g) short-grain white rice
¾ oz (20 g) fresh ginger
2 cups (400 g) sugar
Pine nuts

In a large bowl, combine the malt powder and warm water, stirring well to incorporate. Let soak for 1 hour. Massage the soaked malted barley with your hands, and strain through a fine-mesh sieve. Let the malted barley liquid sit for 2 hours until the liquid separates from the solids.

Meanwhile, rinse the rice with cold water and let it soak in water for 30 minutes. In a rice cooker, combine the rice and 2 cups (16 fl oz/480 ml) water and set to cook.

Carefully pour off the clarified liquid at the top of the malt mixture (discard the solids). Transfer the liquid to a small pot and warm to 104°F (40°C).

In a large bowl, combine the cooked rice with the warmed liquid and mix well. Pour the mixture into a rice cooker or Instant Pot and set to keep warm for 6 hours.

Set a sieve over a pot and pour the rice-barley mixture into the sieve. Rinse the rice in the sieve under cold water and set aside in a bowl of cold water to soak. Add the ginger and sugar to the liquid and bring to a boil over high heat. Once boiling, reduce the heat to medium and simmer for 5 minutes. Strain the boiled punch through a fine cloth or sieve and let cool completely in the refrigerator.

Ladle the chilled punch into individual bowls or cups and add 1 tablespoon of soaked rice (discard the remainder) to each bowl. Garnish with 2 or 3 pine nuts.

The punch can be kept in the freezer for up to 3 months and in the refrigerator for up to 4 days. When storing, the rice can be kept together with the liquid.

## Sweet Cinnamon Tea
### Sujeonggwa
### 수정과

dF gF vg vE                              [o]

Along with *sikhye* (sweet rice punch, above), *sujeonggwa* is one of the most prominent dessert drinks of Korea. The combination of ginger, cinnamon, and persimmon create a harmonious sweetness that's been a national favorite for centuries.

**Preparation time:** 20 minutes, plus at least 4 hours chilling time
**Cooking time:** 1 hour
**Serves:** 3

1¾ oz (50 g) cinnamon sticks
1½ oz (40 g) fresh ginger
1 cup (190 g) packed light brown sugar

**For serving:**
3 dried persimmons
9 pine nuts

Rinse the cinnamon sticks under cold running water quickly and cut into 1½-inch (4 cm) lengths. In another pot, combine the cinnamon sticks and 5 cups (40 fl oz/1.2 liters) water. Bring to a boil over high heat. Once boiling, reduce the heat to medium and boil for 40 minutes. Strain through a sieve and discard the cinnamon.

Meanwhile, peel the ginger and very thinly slice (a scant 1/16 inch/1 mm). In a pot, combine the ginger and 5 cups (40 fl oz/1.2 liters) water. Bring to a boil over high heat. Once boiling, reduce the heat to medium and boil for 30 minutes. Strain through a sieve and discard the ginger slices.

In a large pot, combine the ginger water and the cinnamon water and add the brown sugar. Bring to a boil over high heat. Once boiling, reduce the heat to medium and boil for 15 minutes. Let cool, then transfer to a container to store in the refrigerator until cold. The sujeonggwa is best served as cold as possible, or even slightly iced by placing it in the freezer 30 minutes prior to serving.

At least 3–4 hours prior to serving, remove the leaves of the dried persimmon and remove the seeds. Add the dried persimmons to the cold sujeonggwak to soak.

To serve, set each persimmon in a bowl and pour in the cooled sujeonggwa. Garnish with 3 pine nuts. It can be kept in the refrigerator for up to 5 days with the persimmons removed, and can be kept longer in the freezer.

명인

Master Artisans

The term "master" refers to people who have devoted their lives to pursuing perfection in one expertise. In this chapter are recipes and stories from the current masters of each important category of food that makes up the Korean table.

Master Hee Sook Cho shares recipes for *bugak* (battered dishes) and *twigak*. Master Mal Soon Lee represents the *banga* cuisine (traditional Korean home cooking).

Master Soon Do Ki showcases *jang*, the basic sauce of Korean food. Master Kwang Hee Park presents kimchi, the epitome of Korean vegetable fermentation.

Master Yeong Geun Park shares his expertise on *galbi* and *bulgogi* to represent Korea's meat culture. Master Myeong Hwan Seo showcases the desserts that punctuate the *hansik* meal.

Master Jung Yoo Huh presents dishes that showcase the commonality of North Korean and South Korean cuisine through the cuisine of Kaesong in North Korea. Master Ji Soon Kim shares the traditional heritage of Jeju Island and its cuisine.

Monk Jeong Kwan represents Korean temple food, which has its foundations in the *namul* (vegetable side dish) culture of Korea. Finally, Master ceramist Gyung Kyun Shin shares his philosophy of Korean ceramics—considered the "clothing" of cuisine—and his unique recipes.

Korea's food culture continues to evolve every day, thanks to these masters who have devoted each of their lives to *hansik*, working tirelessly to pass on timeless wisdom of *hansik* history and to create its future. There is a deep sense of emotion present in the food of those who do not simply cook with their body and mind, but also with their soul. Each recipe presented here in this chapter contains a lifetime's worth of contemplation, and the work of each master is present in the selection of each ingredient and each step of the recipe. Through their stories, we hope to convey the identity of *hansik* and its beauty.

# Hee Sook Cho

Chef Hee Sook Cho has over forty years of experience and is recognized as the best female chef of Korea and the godmother of Korea's chefs. In 2020, she was recognized as the Best Female Chef in Asia's 50 Best Restaurants list and she was included in the *Forbes* female 50 over 50 Asia 2022 list.

In 2019, she established the beautiful Michelin-star restaurant Hansik Gongbang, specializing in the traditional Korean royal court and family cuisine. While using traditional Korean cooking techniques, Chef Cho incorporates modern ingredients along with world-class techniques and modern plating, imparting the influence of her creative vision in evolving the *hansik* cuisine to the next generation of Korean chefs and to the world.

Hansik Gongbang restaurant
32, Dasan-ro, Jung-gu, Seoul, South Korea

## Korea's Bugak & Twigak Culture

*Bugak* is a dish in which seaweeds, such as gim, as well as vegetables, such as perilla leaves, red chili peppers, and potatoes, are cut into appropriate sizes, coated with glutinous rice batter, dried, and then fried in oil. Food that is deep-fried without being battered is called *twigak*.

The most distinct characteristics of Korea's *bugak* and *twigak* are that the ingredients are dried before being fried. Because of this, seasonal vegetables can be preserved and enjoyed all year-round. The most important factor in cooking *bugak* is the primary step of cooking the dried ingredients, such as steaming or blanching, as well as the consistency of the glutinous rice paste, and, finally, the temperature of the oil.

## Deep Fried Dasima
### Dasima Twigak
### 다시마 튀각

dF gF vg vE –S

*Dasima twigak* is a dish made by deep-frying *dasima* in quality oil and seasoning with sugar and optional sesame seeds.

**Preparation time:** 30 minutes
**Cooking time:** 15 minutes
**Serves:** 4

8-inch (20 cm) square dried dasima
2 cups (16 fl oz/480 ml) neutral cooking oil, for deep-frying
2 teaspoons sugar

Wipe both sides of the dried dasima with clean, wet paper towels to lightly rehydrate. Once softened, cut into 2-inch (5 cm) squares with scissors and set aside to completely dry, about 20 minutes.

In a deep pot or deep fryer, heat the cooking oil to 374°F (190°C). Using tongs, deep-fry each piece of dasima for 10 seconds. Remove the cooked dasima to a tray and lighty sprinkle the sugar on the dasima while hot.

---

## Gim Bugak
### 김 부각

dF vg vE –S

*Gim bugak* is a *banchan* (side dish) made by deep-frying dried *gim* that has been brushed with glutinous rice paste. It is a great drinking snack and is often enjoyed with beer, in the same manner as potato chips.

**Preparation time:** 1 hour 40 minutes, plus 1 hour rehydrating and 1–2 days drying time
**Cooking time:** 20 minutes
**Serves:** 4

⅔ cup (100 g) glutinous rice flour
1 teaspoon ganjang (Korean soy sauce)
1 teaspoon neutral cooking oil, plus 2 cups (16 fl oz/480 ml) for deep-frying
½ teaspoon salt
5 sheets unseasoned gim

In a small bowl, soak the rice flour in 1⅔ cups (13.5 fl oz/400 g) water for 1 hour until well rehydrated.

Heat a pot over medium-low heat and add the glutinous rice-and-water mixture. Mix well with a wooden spatula with a flat edge in a scraping motion. Once the water begins to boil, reduce to the lowest heat and stir vigorously to keep the rice paste from sticking. Once the rice paste becomes clear, stir for 5 more minutes and then add the soy sauce, 1 teaspoon neutral cooking oil, and the salt and mix well until uniform. Remove from the heat, cover with a lid, and let steam for 5 minutes. Let cool to room temperature.

Lay a sheet of the gim on a cutting board or tray and using a silicone spatula, carefully cover one side of the gim with the glutinous rice paste. Because gim can easily tear, take care to slowly and gently apply the paste. Repeat with the remaining gim and glutinous rice paste.

Set the prepared gim in a perforated tray or large sieve and let dry in a cool spot with good air circulation for 1–2 days until fully dried. When the glutinous rice paste is no longer sticky, cut each sheet of gim into 6–8 rectangular pieces with scissors.

In a deep pot or deep-fryer, heat the cooking oil to 356°–374°F (180°–190°C).

Line a tray with paper towels. Flash-fry the gim for 2–3 seconds and set on the paper towels. Serve as is or with any desired dipping sauce.

# Perilla Bugak
## Kkaennip Bugak
## 깻잎 부각

*Perilla bugak* is the most common vegetable *bugak*, because its large flat sturdy leaves makes it great for brushing with glutinous rice paste and frying. This recipe can be applied to any edible green leaf vegetable.

Preparation time: 40 minutes, plus 1 hour rehydrating and 2–3 days drying time
Cooking time: 15 minutes
Serves: 5

- ⅔ cup (100 g) glutinous rice flour
- 1 teaspoon ganjang (Korean soy sauce)
- 1 teaspoon neutral cooking oil, plus 2 cups (16 fl oz/480 ml) for deep-frying
- ½ teaspoon salt
- 1½ teaspoons sea salt
- 2 oz (60 g) perilla leaves (40–50 leaves)

In a small bowl, soak the rice flour in 1⅔ cups (13.5 fl oz/400 g) water for 1 hour until well rehydrated.

Heat a pot over medium-low heat and add the glutinous rice-and-water mixture. Mix well with a wooden spatula with a flat edge in a scraping motion. Once the water begins to boil, reduce to the lowest heat and stir vigorously to keep the rice paste from sticking. Once the rice paste becomes clear, stir for 5 more minutes and then add the soy sauce, 1 teaspoon neutral cooking oil, and the salt and mix well until uniform. Remove from the heat, cover with a lid, and let steam for 5 minutes. Let the glutinous rice paste cool to room temperature.

Set up a large bowl of ice and water. In a pot, bring 8 cups (2 liters) water to a boil. Add the sea salt and perilla leaves and blanch for 1½ minutes. Scoop out and cold-shock in the ice water. Once cool, stack the perilla leaves and squeeze gently to remove excess moisture.

Lay out each of the perilla leaves on a large flat tray and brush well with the glutinous rice paste.

Set the prepared perilla leaves on a perforated tray or large sieve and let dry in a cool spot with good air circulation for 2–3 days until fully dry. Once fully dried (when the glutinous rice paste has no moisture to the touch), transfer the perilla leaves to a plastic bag and keep in an airtight container for storage.

Line a tray with paper towels. In a deep pot, heat the cooking oil to 356°–374°F (180°–190°C). Flash-fry the perilla leaves as if dipping into the oil and set on the paper towels to drain.

# Potato Bugak
## Gamja Bugak
## 감자 부각

dF gF vg vE -5

The inherent starch in the potato allows it to be made into a *bugak* without the typical glutinous rice paste application. The potato is blanched and air-dried before deep-frying.

**Preparation time: 30 minutes, plus 2–3 hours soaking and 2 days drying time**
**Cooking time: 15 minutes**
**Serves: 4**

2 potatoes (about 1 lb/450 g total)
1 tablespoon salt
2 cups (16 fl oz/480 ml) neutral cooking oil, for deep-frying

Using a knife or a mandoline, cut the potatoes into 1/16-inch (2 mm) slices. Soak in cold water for 2–3 hours to remove the starch, changing the water three times throughout. Drain the soaked potatoes in a sieve to remove excess water.

In a pot, bring 2 cups (16 fl oz/480 ml) water and the salt to a boil. Working in 3–4 batches, blanch the potatoes until they become translucent in the center. Set the blanched potato slices in a single layer on a wide perforated tray.

Set the tray of potatoes in a cool spot with good air circulation to dry for 2 days, or until fully dried.

In a large pot, heat the cooking oil to 374°F (190°C).

Line a tray with paper towels. Flash-fry the potatoes for 2–3 seconds and set on the paper towels to drain.

# Mal Soon Lee

Master Mal Soon Lee is considered to be an authority of *banga* cuisine, which originated from the Joseon dynasty. *Banga* cuisine culture is especially important in understanding the roots of *hansik*, as it framed the cultural practice of ingredient sourcing, seasonality, distinct familial traditions and generational recipes, the development of regional cuisines, and more.

Master Lee is one of the most important figures in the development and transmission of this Korean food culture. She is a successor to In-hee Kang, a master of *banga* food and traditional food whose unique recipes and ingredients in her literature are known in detail from her long-standing experience, including those wisdoms seldomly documented in modern recipes. Master Lee established the Korean Traditional Food Research Association to pass on this knowledge and research to future generations and is revered in the culinary community.

Korean Traditional Food Research Association
17, Tongil-ro 26-gil, Seodaemun-gu, Seoul, South Korea

## Korea's Namul Culture

The psyche of Korean cuisine is focused on elevating everyday ingredients rather than hard-to-source, luxury ingredients. Korean cuisine highlights the innate flavors of common and simple ingredients, carefully prepared and meticulously cooked without waste or carelessness. The most important spirit of Korean food is to cook with the intention of taking care of the diner, preserving the beauty of the ingredients in modesty, recognizing that even fancy, luxury ingredients lose their value with overhandling.

The food culture of *namul* is the most representative of this spirit. *Namul* vegetables are considered a humble ingredient, available in abundance year-round. Yet, it takes careful consideration and handling of vegetables to highlight their inherent taste, fragrance, and texture in both cooking method and seasoning. The development of *namul* cuisine is rooted in the belief that each vegetable should be handled with respect, its abundance valued, and that there should be endless research to elevate its taste through technique and cuisine.

Koreans enjoy raw vegetables through a robust *ssam* (wraps) culture. Yet, cooked vegetable *ssam* showcase the methods in which the savory taste of vegetables is highlighted, through the gentle cooking process of steaming the seasonal vegetables to provide a soft, enjoyable texture. This is one of the many ways in which Koreans have discovered a new way to enjoy vegetables, always taking the potential of a humble vegetable into consideration.

# Cooked Vegetable Ssam
## Sukchae Ssam
## 숙채소쌈

dF -3o

*Sukchae ssam* translates to "cooked vegetable wraps." It's a dish that's eaten widely in the early summertime. By blanching or steaming *ssam* vegetables, it reduces any toxicity in the young plants and softens the texture of the tough young vegetables. There are many versions of this *ssam* depending on the ingredients or the main ingredients served along with.

Even when eaten simply with just rice and *ssamjang* (dipping sauce for *ssam*) as the filling, the fragrance of the vegetables makes for a delicious, varied bite. The savory and soft texture of cooked vegetables offer a different charm from the refreshing bite of raw vegetable *ssam*. Any leafy vegetables can be used in this recipe year-round, using whatever is in season.

Preparation time: 15 minutes
Cooking time: 15 minutes
Serves: 4

For the ssam vegetables:
10 chard leaves
10 fuki (butterbur) leaves
10 gomchwi leaves
10 perilla leaves

For the beef:
7 oz (200 g) beef sirloin (rump)
2 teaspoons sesame oil
2 teaspoons minced scallion (spring onion)
2 teaspoons ground sesame seeds
1 teaspoon ganjang (Korean soy sauce)
1 teaspoon ginger juice
1 teaspoon minced garlic
¼ teaspoon sugar
¼ teaspoon freshly ground black pepper

For serving:
Ssamjang (dipping sauce for ssam)
Yak-gochujang (Stir-Fried Gochujang, page 51)

**Prepare the ssam leaves:** Trim off the stems of the chard, fuki, and gomchwi. Wash the prepared leaves under cold running water and set aside to dry.

**Prepare the beef:** Finely chop the beef. In a large bowl, combine the sesame oil, scallion, sesame seeds, soy sauce, ginger juice, sugar, and black pepper and mix well until uniform. Add the prepared beef and mix well until well seasoned.

To assemble the ssam, top each of the ssam leaves with 1 teaspoon of the seasoned beef and spread thinly. In a large flat plate that fits into your steamer basket, add the prepared ssam leaves in stacks of 10.

Add the plate to the steamer basket, set it in the steam, and bring to a boil over high heat. Once the water is boiling, steam for 5 minutes. Remove from the heat.

**To serve:** Plate the sukchae ssam on a flat plate. Serve along with desired sauces, including ssamjang and yak-gochujang.

# Soon Do Ki

Master Soon Do Ki is the tenth descendant of the Yangjin-jae clan and Jangheung-go clan of Damyang, Jeollanam-do, and has been selected by the Korean government as the nation's thirty-fifth Food Master Artisan. Her family has more than three hundred years of tradition in making traditional *jang* (fermented soybean-based sauces) and Master Ki has been making traditional *jang* for fifty years. Master Ki's *jang* is recognized as the best in Korea for her demanding standards in ingredients, traditional methods, and preservation.

**Kisoondo Traditional Jang**
154-15, Yucheon-gil, Changpyeong-myeon, Damyang-gun, Jeollanam-do, South Korea

## Korea's Jang: The Most Important Factors of Jang

A Korean adage states that a family with sweet *jang* has great fortune. This showcases the mindset of home cooks that making good *jang* for the family is the basis of the happiness of the daily lives of her family. The taste and health of the family lies in the sincerity in making *jang*, which is the foundation for all meals. I always do my best as if I were performing a sacred ritual while making my *jang*, refraining from any wrongdoing or carelessness, even in my gestures and thoughts, believing that all intent will show in the final product.

The beginning of *jang* making starts with sincerity and devotion. While perhaps an outdated notion, the intentions rooted in the heart are important in the preparation of any cuisine. In the *jang* culture, even the smallest mistake or shortcut becomes visible in the final product over time. Starting from the raw materials of soybeans, water, and salt, if any mistake is involved in the process, a good *jang* cannot be created. Making *jang* was the most precious family event of our ancestors during the year, because it affected the health and well-being of the family for years to come. Each process affects the next, so any mistakes result in a discarding of the entire *jang*.

Made from just three ingredients—soybeans, bamboo-roasted salt, and water—the selection of the raw ingredients first determines the quality.

Soybeans that are neither too large nor small are carefully selected from fresh soybeans harvested that year. *Meju* (dried fermented soybeans) is made on the last day of November in the lunar calendar. The fermentation of the *meju* determines the flavor and quality of the *jang*, and it is considered one of the most important steps along with the fermentation in the *hangari* (fermentation vessel). The soybeans are first cooked until tender, formed into the *meju* blocks, and then carefully dehydrated. We then use organic hay made from wheat and use it to tie and

then air-dry and ferment the *meju* blocks, carefully maintaining the humidity and temperature. Overfermentation will result in a foul odor and rot; well-fermented *meju* blocks will exude a deep, savory fragrance.

The fermented *meju* blocks are then washed well and dried before the brining process. The salinity levels and the quality of the salt used is important. When using sea salt, it is important that the salt has had the bitterns removed. The salt should be dry without any moisture and break easily at the fingertips. Starting in the 1980s, we have used salt roasted in bamboo, made in-house. Bamboo-roasted salt is preferred, because the sweet fragrance of the bamboo is imparted to the salt, and the roasting process removes any excess moisture and unwanted taste. This is perfect for making *jang*.

The ideal salinity varies from region to region. Because Damyang is located in the south, where the weather is warm, our ideal salinity is maintained at 21 baud. The amount of *meju* and brine is about 1:2 or 1:1.5. After sixty to ninety days of brining the *meju* blocks, it is separated into liquid and solid *jang*. *Ganjang*, the liquid, is separated into that intended for the clear, light *cheong-jang* and the deeper colored and fragranced *jung-ganjang* (also called *jungjang*). In addition, *ganjang* intended for *jinjang* (the darkest of the soy sauces) is kept with the *meju* inside the *hangari* for one more year with the added bamboo water. At the end of the year, when filtering, a small amount of the "seed *ganjang*," which is passed down the generations, is added and fermented for four more years to make the *jinjang*.

*Doenjang*, which is the solid soybean paste, is aged in the *hangari* covered with traditional cloths to prevent any impurities from entering, including any insects. At one point, we even sealed the entrances of the *hangari* with *hanji* (traditional Korean paper) to prevent any external influences from entering.

A well-made *jang* is first determined by its flavor and fragrance. There is no mustiness or odor, but instead a deep sweetness. Which *jang* is used depends on its depth of color and flavor, and Korean recipes will specify which type of soy sauce to use: *cheongjang, jung-ganjang,* or *jinjang*. The older the *ganjang*, the deeper the flavor and fragrance. In cooking, *doenjang* is best when it's just finished; as *doenjang* is aged, it will become milder flavored and deeper in color.

# Fermented Soybeans
## Cheonggukjang
## 청국장

dF gF vg vE −5

*Cheonggukjang* is made by boiling soybeans until they are fully cooked and then fermenting them in straw, rice, or wheat for two or three days. It is made much more quickly than *doenjang* and is famed for its deep, earthy flavor and distinct smell.

**Preparation time:** 30 minutes, plus 6 hours soaking time and at least 1 month fermentation
**Cooking time:** 2½ hours
**Serves:** 4

7 oz (200 g) dried soybeans
Salt

Soak the soybeans in a large bowl of cold water for 6 hours.

In a pot, combine the soaked soybeans and 4 cups (32 fl oz/950 ml) water. Cover and bring to a boil over high heat. Once boiling, reduce the heat to medium and cook for 2 hours, adding more water as the water evaporates to prevent burning. At the end of 2 hours, there should be little water remaining and the soybeans should be soft to the touch and easily crushable by hand. Remove from the heat, cover, and let steam for 30 minutes. Drain the soybeans in a colander.

Cover the entire colander with a large plastic bag and ferment at 122°F (50°C) for 42 hours. In a Korean home setting, this temperature is achieved by setting the soybeans on a heating pad and covering with a blanket.

In a large bowl, combine the fermented soybeans with salt 3 percent the volume of the soybeans and mash together in a mortar into a coarse paste. Divide into portions of about 6 tablespoons (100 g) and seal in plastic wrap (cling film) or a zip-seal plastic bag and store in the refrigerator for up to 1 month.

---

# Bamboo Shoot & Fermented Soybean Stew
## Juksun Cheonggukjang Jjigae
## 죽순 청국장 찌개

dF vg vE −30

The most representative dish made using *cheonggukjang* (fermented soybeans) is the *cheonggukjang jjigae*, which is one of the "soul foods" of Korea that reminds the eater of their mother's cuisine. Using rice water or *myeolchi yuksu* (anchovy broth) as the base of this *jjigae* is the best way to achieve the inherent depth of flavor in cheonggukjang. This family recipe of Soon Do Ki is very special as it incorporates the ephemeral bamboo shoots that mark the springtime; the bamboo shoots elevating the deep, earthy flavor of *cheonggukjang*.

**Preparation time:** 10 minutes
**Cooking time:** 10 minutes
**Serves:** 2–3

3 cups (24 fl oz/710 ml) rice water
8 oz (220 g) cheonggukjang (Fermented Soybeans, see above), store-bought or homemade
3½ oz (100g) bamboo shoots, cut into 1-inch (2.5 cm) bite-size pieces
14 oz (400 g) tofu, cut into 1-inch (2.5 cm) bite-size pieces
½ aehobak (Korean zucchini), cut into 1-inch (2.5 cm) bite-size pieces
½ onion, cut into 1-inch (2.5 cm) bite-size pieces
½ enoki mushroom
1 fresh green Cheongyang chili, stemmed and seeded
1 fresh red chili, stemmed and seeded
½ daepa (Korean scallion), cut into 1-inch (2.5 cm) bite-size pieces
2 teaspoons ganjang (Korean soy sauce)

In a pot, combine the rice water and fermented soybeans and bring to a boil over high heat, stirring to make sure that the paste loosens thoroughly.

Once boiling, add the bamboo shoots, tofu, zucchini, onion, mushroom, and chilies and boil until the vegetables are cooked through, about 10 minutes. Add in the daepa and soy sauce to season. Serve hot.

# Napa Cabbage & Fermented Soybean Muchim
## Baechu Cheonggukjang Muchim
## 배추 청국장 무침

dF vg vE -3o

The sweet, savory flavors inherent in the napa cabbage (Chinese leaf) is heightened when seasoned with the depth of flavor of *cheonggukjang* (Fermented Soybeans, page 437). This vegetable dish is one of the signature *banchan* (side dishes) of Master Ki.

**Preparation time: 15 minutes**
**Cooking time: 10 minutes**
**Serves: 4–6**

1 teaspoon salt
2¼ lb (1 kg) napa cabbage (Chinese leaf), halved lenghthwise
1 tablespoon ganjang (Korean soy sauce)
7 oz (200 g) cheonggukjang (Fermented Soybeans, page 437), store-bought or homemade
2 teaspoons sesame oil
½ tablespoon minced garlic
3 tablespoons minced scallion (spring onion)
1 teaspoon ground sesame seeds

In a pot, combine 3 cups (24 fl oz/710 ml) water and the salt and bring to a boil. Once boiling, add the cabbage, root end first, and cook for 3 minutes. Drain the cabbage and let cool. Once cool enough to handle, cut into 1¼–1½-inch (3–4 cm) squares and squeeze to remove excess water.

In a bowl, combine the cooked cabbage and soy sauce and mix well until the cabbage is well seasoned. Squeeze the cabbage again to remove excess moisture.

In a bowl, combine the seasoned cabbage with the fermented soybeans, sesame oil, garlic, and scallion and massage well to combine. Mix in the ground sesame seeds.

# Kwang Hee Park

As the best kimchi master in Korea, Kwang Hee Park not only cultivates her kimchi ingredients directly in Pyeongchang, Gangwon-do, but also spends her life making various kimchi and *jangajji* (pickles) with the freshest seasonal ingredients. Korea's best chefs visit Master Park to learn kimchi methods and often source kimchi for their restaurants from her.

Her research primarily focuses on how to highlight the inherent flavors of the vegetables in kimchi making, and she continues to research ways to use new vegetables or lesser known ingredients in kimchi. One example of her research and famously unique kimchi recipes is one made with dandelions.

**Park Kwanghee Kimchi**
69-3, Oksuam-gil, Mitan-myeon, Pyeongchang-gun, Gangwon-do, South Korea

## Selecting Kimchi Ingredients

**Napa Cabbage**

Napa cabbage (Chinese leaf) from the high altitudes of Gangwon-do from the end of May to December, and in fall and winter from Pyeongchang, is the most delicious. From January to April, cabbage from Haenam in Jeolla-do is best. The best napa cabbage for kimchi usually weighs about 6 pounds 10 ounces (3 kg) at 80 percent density. There should be no black spots at the base of the root, and it should not be too hard to the touch where it bends slightly to pressure. It should not have curly leaves, and the outer leaves should be fresh and green.

**Red Chili Peppers**

Gangwon-do, which has a large temperature variation, uses chilies grown in Pyeongchang for their good color and sugar content. While even the first harvest provides good fruit, its color is dark due to the strong sun, the second and third harvest is best, because the chili changes to bright red, perfect for kimchi usage. The chilies are first sun-dried and then used as the base for gochugaru, providing a vibrant color and sweet taste to the kimchi.

**Salt**

Sea salt from the Shinan region (Imjado, Bigeumdo) that has had bitterns removed and been stored for more than five years is the best.

**Jeotgal**

Salted shrimp made with shrimp caught in May and June off the southern coast provide the best flavor. Salted anchovies are made from fish caught in the South Sea or off Jeju Island. Those that have been aged for more than five years are best. It is important to select salted anchovies without any pungent, fishy flavors.

**Yuksu (Broth/Stock)**

Using broth made from shiitake, *dasima*, *dipori* (Korean sardine), anchovy, pollock, dried shrimp, onion, *daepa* (Korean scallion), and more in kimchi can help kill off any unwanted bacteria and imparts a balanced, deep flavoring to the kimchi. It can help feed good organisms during the fermentation process and results in a more flavorful kimchi.

**Starch and Flour Slurry**

This is the slurry used to feed the organisms during the fermentation process. Rice is a common slurry ingredient, but starchy vegetables, such as potato, sweet potatoes, and corn, have been used in mountainous regions where rice was scarce. The root vegetables were cooked and mashed and the corn was used by boiling and using the boiled water. In fall, sweet potatoes were fermented and dehydrated to create a powder to make the base of the paste. In coastal cities, short-grain rice, glutinous rice, soybeans, or flours were used to make the slurry.

# Napa Cabbage Kimchi
## Baechu Kimchi
## 배추김치

dF

Brining is the most important first step in making kimchi, because it sets the foundation for the fermentation. The brining period is affected by the size of the napa cabbage (Chinese leaf) and the thickness of its leaves, as well as the salinity of the salt used. In the standards of Korean products, when using Korean sea salt that has gone through five-plus years of bittern removal, the ideal brining period for summer napa cabbage is 8 hours, and winter cabbage is 14 hours. Using sea salt that has not gone through the bittern removal process will result in overly salty kimchi with a bitter aftertaste. France's Le Guerandais salt and Halen Môn salt from Wales is best for a 6-hour brine.

A starchy slurry is used in kimchi making as food for the microorganism, and only a small amount is needed. All-purpose (plain) flour, potato, or sweet potato powders can all be used instead of the glutinous rice flour, but the raw soybean flour is critical, because it acts to delay the fermentation process, thus preventing the kimchi from aging too quickly. If it is difficult to obtain raw (unroasted) soybean flour, it can be substituted by gently boiling unsoaked dried soybeans, grinding them, and filtering through a sieve. If glutinous rice flour is hard to source, cooked glutinous rice can be blended in a mixer to substitute.

Unused kimchi seasoning can be kept in an airtight container in the refrigerator. It can be used to make a quick cucumber or *mu* kimchi.

Preparation time: 30 minutes, plus 12½ hours brining time and 16–30 days fermentation
Cooking time: 50 minutes
Serves: 10

**For the brined cabbage:**
22 lb (10 kg) napa cabbage (Chinese leaf; about 3 large heads)
3½ cups (1 kg) sea salt

**For the vegetable broth:**
5 quarts (5 liters) spring water
1¾ oz (50 g) dried anchovies
¾ oz (20 g) dried shiitake mushrooms
¾ oz (20 g) dasima
1 onion, cut into chunks
5 daepa (Korean scallions), cut into pieces

**For the rice flour slurry:**
3 tablespoons glutinous rice flour
1 tablespoon unroasted soybean flour

**For the kimchi seasoning:**
3½ oz (100 g) salted shrimp
2¾ oz (80 g) freshly shucked oyster meat
4 cups (480 g) fine gochugaru (red chili powder)
½ cup (4 fl oz/120 ml) anchovy fish sauce (aged 5 years)
10 tablespoons minced garlic
1 tablespoon ginger juice
1 tablespoon sugar
2 lb 10 oz (1.2 kg) mu (Korean radish), cut into 2¾ × 1/16-inch (7 cm × 2 mm) matchsticks
6 oz (170 g) mustard greens or chives, cut into ¾-inch (2 cm) lengths
6 oz (170 g) scallions (spring onions), cut into ¾-inch (2 cm) lengths

**Brine the napa cabbage:** In a large bowl, combine 7½ quarts (7 liters) water and 1¾ cups (500 g) sea salt and stir until the salt is fully dissolved. Clean the napa cabbage by removing any loose outer leaves and cut lengthwise in half. Soak the napa cabbage in the salt water brine for 30 minutes.

Remove the brined napa cabbage (reserve the liquid). Evenly distribute the remaining 1¾ cups (500 g) sea salt between the layers of each half head of napa cabbage. Arrange the salted cabbage in a separate large bowl. Pour the brine over the napa cabbages. To be sure that all the cabbages are submerged, fill a large bowl with water and set atop the cabbages to weigh them down. Brine the cabbages for 8 hours. After the brining period, rinse the cabbages under cold running water and squeeze to remove any excess moisture. Let sit in a sieve for 4 hours to drain.

**Make the vegetable broth:** In a large pot, combine the spring water, anchovies, shiitakes, dasima, onion, and daepa and bring to a boil. Once boiling, reduce the heat to low and boil for 30 minutes. Remove from the heat and let cool. Once cool, strain the broth (discard the solids) and set aside.

**Make the rice flour slurry:** In a small pot, combine 2 cups (16 fl oz/480 ml) of the cooled vegetable broth, the glutinous rice flour, and soybean flour and use a hand-held blender to mix until uniform. Let sit for 10 minutes. Bring to a boil over medium heat while stirring. Once boiling, reduce to low heat and simmer for 10 minutes. Remove from the heat and let cool.

**Make the kimchi seasoning:** In a blender or food processor, combine the salted shrimp and oyster meat and blend until fine. In a large bowl, combine 14 cups (115 fl oz/3.3 liters) of the cooled vegetable broth with the rice flour slurry and mix until uniform. Add the blended shrimp and oysters, gochugaru, fish sauce, garlic, ginger juice, and sugar and mix until uniform. Stir in the radish, mustard greens, and scallions and let sit for 30 minutes.

To stuff the napa cabbage, add the seasoning between the leaves of each brined cabbage, one leaf at a time, and then place each cabbage in a 16 × 12 inch (40 × 30 cm) airtight fermentation container. When stacking the cabbages, press to make sure that there are no air bubbles in between the layers. Cover the top with 2 or 3 loose cabbage leaves and close the lid.

Ferment at 59°–77°F (15°–25°C) for 12 hours or at 59°–65°F (15°–18°C) for 20 hours. Move to a kimchi refrigerator and ferment for 15 days, at which point it is ready to eat. (Alternatively, you can use a regular refrigerator, placing the kimchi in the lowest-temperature area.) However, the prime kimchi flavor takes 1 month in the refrigerator.

# White Kimchi
## Baek Kimchi
## 백김치

dF

Because white kimchi can turn to a darker color if the kimchi is exposed to air during the fermentation process, make sure to make enough broth to submerge the cabbages.

**Preparation time:** 1 hour, plus 3½ hours brining time and 16–30 days fermentation
**Cooking time:** 1 hour
**Serves:** 10

**For the brined cabbage:**
6 lb 10 oz (3 kg) small heads napa cabbage (Chinese leaf)
1 cup (300 g) sea salt

**For the broth and flour slurry:**
Vegetable broth (see Napa Cabbage Kimchi, page 444)
Rice flour paste (see Napa Cabbage Kimchi, page 444)

**For garnish:**
7 dried jujubes (Chinese red dates)
7 chestnuts, peeled
7 pine nuts
1 teaspoon Korean red chili threads

**For the kimchi seasoning:**
3½ oz (100 g) salted shrimp
1.2 kg mu (Korean radish), cut into 2¾ × ¹⁄₁₆-inch (7 cm × 2 mm) matchsticks
9 tablespoons anchovy fish sauce (aged 5 years)
7 tablespoons (100 g) minced garlic
2 teaspoons ginger juice
1 tablespoon sugar
6 oz (170 g) mustard greens or chives, cut into ¾-inch (2 cm) lengths
6 oz (170 g) scallions (spring onions), cut into ¾-inch (2 cm) lengths

**Brine the napa cabbage:** In a large bowl, combine 12¾ cups (102 fl oz/ 3 liters) water with ½ cup (150 g) sea salt and stir until the salt is fully dissolved. Clean the napa cabbages by removing any loose outer leaves and cut lengthwise in half. Soak the napa cabbages in the salt water brine for 30 minutes.

Remove the brined napa cabbages (reserve the brine). Evenly distribute the remaining ½ cup (150 g) sea salt between the layers of each half head of napa cabbage. Arrange the salted cabbages in a separate large bowl. Pour the brine over the napa cabbages. To be sure that all cabbages are submerged, fill a large bowl with water and set atop the cabbages to weigh them down. Brine the cabbages for 1 hour. After the brining period, rinse the cabbages under cold running water and squeeze to remove any excess moisture. Let sit in a sieve for 2 hours to drain.

**Make the broth and flour slurry:** First make the vegetable broth as directed in Napa Cabbage Kimchi on page 444. Then make the rice flour slurry as directed (you need the broth to make the slurry).

**Prepare the garnish:** Seed and sliver the jujubes. Cut the chestnuts into thin matchsticks. Pinch off the hard tip of the pine nuts. Measure out the chili threads.

**Make the kimchi seasoning:** In a blender or small food processor, process the salted shrimp until fine. In a large bowl, combine the radish, blended salted shrimp, 7 tablespoons of the anchovy fish sauce, and half of the rice flour slurry and mix well until uniform. Let sit for 5 minutes to develop flavors and soften the radish. Once the radish is softened, add the garlic, ginger juice, and sugar. Add the mustard greens and scallions and mix until well combined. The garnishes can be added directly to this mixture or added as garnish at the end.

In a bowl, combine 3 cups (24 fl oz/710 ml) of the cooled vegetable broth, the remaining rice flour paste, and the remaining 2 tablespoons anchovy fish sauce. Set the kimchi broth aside.

To stuff the napa cabbages, add the seasoning between the leaves of each brined cabbage, one leaf at a time, and then place each cabbage in a 16 × 12 inch (40 × 30 cm) airtight fermentation container. When stacking the cabbages, press to be sure that there are no air bubbles in between the layers. Cover the top with two or three loose cabbage leaves, pour in the kimchi broth, and close the lid.

Ferment at 59°–77°F (15°–25°C) for 12 hours or at 59°–65°F (15°–18°C) for 20 hours. Move to a kimchi refrigerator and ferment for 15 more days, at which point it is ready to eat. (Alternatively, you can use a regular refrigerator, placing the kimchi in the lowest-temperature area.) However, the prime kimchi flavor takes 1 month in the refrigerator.

# Yeong Geun Park

Park Yeong Geun is the chef of the most prominent Korean beef restaurant, with over 35 years of research resulting in a wealth of knowledge around Korean beef culture. He developed the famed "Diamond Cutting Technique," a procedure that cuts both the front and back of Korean ribs without breaking them. This technique makes for an easy eating experience by tenderizing the tough part of the bone in a diamond shape. Not only does the Diamond Cutting Technique improve the aging process of the meat, but it creates a better canvas for marinades and produces delicious charring when the meat is grilled.

Chef Park has also researched the best pairings of cuts of beef to different dishes, including *bulgogi*, grilled dishes, and cold noodles dishes to name a few, and even has developed specialized refrigeration technologies for aging beef.

Byeok-je Galbi restaurant
1-4 Yangjae-daero 71-gil, Bangi 1(il)-dong, Songpa-gu, Seoul, South Korea

## Korean Hanwoo

**Diamond Cutting Technique**

*Galbi* (beef short rib) is the most prized beef cut in Korean cuisine. This cut is particularly delicious, because it has both the tender meat as well as the tougher, chewier meat that is packed with flavor. Because Koreans prize a tender cut of beef, I began to research cutting methods that would maximize the tenderness of the short rib. The signature Diamond Cutting Technique of Byeok-je Galbi was so-named because the sheath between the meat looks like a diamond when the meat is spread out. The purpose of this cutting technique is manyfold: First, it tenderizes the rib meat. Second, it lets the fragrance of the charcoal permeate the slits in the meat, seasoning it thoroughly with the fragrance. Third, it allows a deep permeation of the marinade. Fourth, it looks beautiful.

When working with beef ribs, they can become flabby regardless of the season, especially in summer. It takes about 100 knife cuts to work one rib. After going through the process of butchering the ribs, they are sliced apart and the meat is cooled in a refrigerator at 35°–37°F (2°–3°C) to reach a prime texture to make the diamond cuts.

The fat and tendons are removed from the beef ribs and each rib is separated from the carcass. The rib bones are then machine-cut across into 3-inch (8 cm) lengths. For each short rib, first, the fat and tendon from the inside of the rib is removed, and then the rib is flipped to the side where the majority of the tender meat is. The meat is "butterflied" into one long strip of meat that stays connected to the bone. This is done by slicing the meat thinly without going all the way through and constantly flipping the meat and cutting until you end up with one long strip of meat about ¼ inch (6–7 mm) thick. Once the long filets are created, the meat is sliced (but not all the way through) at a 13–15-degree angle at ⅛–¼-inch (4–6 mm) intervals. We flip the strip of meat and rotate 180 degrees and repeat the process up to the part where the rib bone and the meat connect. We then roll the strip of meat around the bone and this is how it is taken to table for cooking. When a strip of meat is pulled out, the holes look like diamond pieces, giving it its name.

**Korean Beef**

The best Korean beef (*hanwoo*) has a beef marbling score (BMS) of 9. Even after choosing the best quality meat, it is necessary to handle it properly, including butchering, aging, and cooking techniques. For example, at our restaurant, after the initial slaughter, the beef carcass is refrigerated for a full day and butchered further before it's evaluated for its grade. It's delivered to our restaurant in four whole animal pieces and then butchered to specifications. There are 10 different distinct cuts that are made, and from these 10 parts it's further specialized to 39 distinct sub-cuts. The 39 cuts are then broken down into service-quality cuts that result in 120 distinct parts that are intended to highlight their individual quality, flavor, and texture.

In seasoning Korean beef, Korean *ganjang* (soy sauce) is the best ingredient. The flavor and the balance of a well-made *ganjang* makes perfect harmony with the beef's fat and meat, elevating its savory flavor without covering the inherent taste. In pursuing the true taste of Korean barbecue, the meat must be flavored with Korean *ganjang*.

# Snowflake Marinated Short Rib

## Seolhwa Yangnyeom Galbi
## 설화 양념갈비

DF

*Seolhwa* translates to "snowflake," and this short rib is so-named because the marbling on the best-in-class short ribs of Byeok-je Galbi restaurant mimics the shapes of pristine snowflakes. The marinade in this recipe was developed to highlight the savory taste of the short ribs while tenderizing the meat. Cooked over charcoal, the marinade caramelizes and enhances the sweet, savory flavors of the short ribs; it is a flavor that's beloved by all Koreans. The marinated short rib is traditionally eaten on the most important celebrations. When cooking the meat, it's best to grill over the indirect heat of a gentle charcoal fire, or in a frying pan over low heat without any additional cooking oil.

The short ribs should not be marinated any longer than 24 hours ahead, because the juices from the meat will begin to seep out after 24 hours, the short ribs will begin to become too salty and sweet, and the meat will become overly tenderized, giving it an unpleasant texture. Any marinade made ahead must be kept in the refrigerator.

Preparation time: 30 minutes, plus 18–24 hours marinating time
Cooking time: 10 minutes
Serves: 2

- 3 tablespoons ganjang (Korean soy sauce)
- 3 tablespoons corn (golden) syrup
- 2 tablespoons brown sugar
- 1 teaspoon granulated sugar
- 1 oz (30 g) daepa (Korean scallion), green tops only
- 2 tablespoons pureed or grated Asian pear
- 1 tablespoon pureed or pasted garlic
- 1 teaspoon pureed onion
- 1 teaspoon mirin
- 1 teaspoon cooking sake
- Pinch of freshly ground black pepper
- 2 rolls of diamond-cut short ribs

In a saucepan, combine ⅔ cup (5 fl oz/160 ml) water, the soy sauce, corn syrup, brown sugar, granulated sugar, and daepa greens and bring to a boil over high heat. Once boiling, reduce the heat to medium-low and cook for 20 minutes.

Discard the daepa greens, add the pear, garlic, onion, mirin, sake, and black pepper, and bring just to a boil. Remove from the heat and let cool.

To marinate the short ribs, in an airtight container, combine the short ribs and cooled marinade. Let marinate in the refrigerator for at least 18 hours but not longer than 24 hours.

**If charcoal grilling:** Set up a two-zone charcoal fire in an outdoor grill (barbecue) to low heat. Add the short ribs to the cooler side of the grill to avoid burning the marinade. Cook the meat on both sides, flipping often.

**If cooking on the stovetop (hob):** Heat a large dry frying pan over low heat. Place just the marinated short ribs in the pan (no oil). Cook on each side over low heat for 1–2 minutes (this will ensure that it's cooked well throughout). Then increase the heat to high and cook on each side for 30 seconds. Remove from the heat.

Cut the short ribs into bite-size pieces and serve hot on a plate.

# Snowflake Bulgogi
## Seolhwa Hanwoo Bulgogi
## 설화 한우 불고기

dF

Byeok-je Galbi's *bulgogi* is famed for the soy sauce marinade that has been perfected to complement the beef without overpowering the inherent flavors of beef. Take care not to marinate the beef for longer than 30 minutes, because that will result in the meat being too salty and tough. If you'd like, add vegetables, such as sliced onions, scallions (spring onions), or enoki mushrooms, to the pan when the meat is halfway cooked.

**Preparation time: 25 minutes, plus 1 hour marinating time**
**Cooking time: 5 minutes**
**Serves: 2–3**

1 cup (8 fl oz/240 ml) spring water
5 tablespoons jinjang (Korean dark soy sauce)
3 tablespoons corn (golden) syrup
2 tablespoons light brown sugar
1 tablespoon granulated sugar
1 oz (30 g) daepa (Korean scallion), green tops only
3 tablespoons pureed or grated Asian pear
2 tablespoons pureed onion
1 tablespoon mirin
1 teaspoon sesame oil
1 teaspoon cooking sake
¼ teaspoon freshly ground black pepper
1 lb (500 g) beef sirloin (rump), cut into slices ⅛ inch (3 mm) thick

In a saucepan, combine the spring water, soy sauce, corn syrup, brown sugar, granulated sugar, and daepa greens and bring to a boil over high heat. Remove from the heat, discard the daepa greens, and let the marinade cool.

Once cool, add the pear puree, onion, mirin, sesame oil, sake, and black pepper to the marinade and stir well. Let sit for 30 minutes.

In a large bowl, combine the beef with the cooled marinade and mix well. Let marinate for 30 minutes.

Heat a dry frying pan (no oil) over medium heat. Add the meat, spreading it out to avoiding clumping, and cook, stirring, until the meat is cooked through, about 5 minutes.

Serve hot.

# Myeong Hwan Seo

Chef Myeong Hwan Seo is the best authority in Korea on *tteok* (rice cakes) and Korean sweets. Based on his study of traditional recipes, he established Mijuckgamgak, which translates to "aesthetic sense," an institute devoted to researching, cultivating, and evolving the identity of Korean rice cakes and *hangwa* (confections). The most important aspect of *hansik* (traditional Korean cuisine) in his definition revolves around seasonality.

**Mijuckgamgak**
329-32, Seongsan-ro, Seodaemun-gu, Seoul, South Korea

## Korean Husik Culture

The most important factor in Korean *husik* (desserts) is learning from tradition while making progress using modern techniques and knowledge. Learning the foundational recipes and wisdom of our ancestors while adapting to new cooking techniques is a part of preserving and evolving our cuisine's culture.

Korea's *husik* culture is firmly rooted in seasonality. *Tteok* are made from seasonal ingredients; in spring, the *namul* (wild greens), herbs, and flowers foraged and harvested in the mountains and fields define the rice cake recipes. In summer, fruits are used to make *hwachae* (punch) and grains are processed and steamed to make *jeungpyeon* (steamed rice cake). In fall, fruits or roots are used to make fragrant *tteok* or *jeonggwa* (candied confections). In winter, rice cakes and *jeonggwa* are made with dried fruits and nuts, and *gwajul* (honey cakes) are also made by fermenting rice and soybean water. There is a different taste of each season captured in a variety of ways and recipes, passed down through the generations.

# Fried Twists
## Maejak-gwa
## 매작과

*Maejak-gwa* is so-named because it looks like a sparrow sitting on a plum tree: *mae* translates to "plum" and *jak* to "sparrow" in *hanja* (Chinese characters). Deep-fried in oil, the fried twists are savory and satisfyingly crunchy. The ginger and cinnamon harmonize to a delicious fragrance. This particular recipe from Master Seo also highlights the pine nut's fragrance. Pair with warm tea, such as pu-erh or green tea.

Make the dough shortly before deep-frying, because if it sits too long, the fried twists will be tough.

Preparation time: 30 minutes
Cooking time: 1 hour
Serves: 4

**For the syrup:**
5½ tablespoons sugar
5 tablespoons ginger juice
4 tablespoons honey
1 teaspoon salt

**For the dough:**
¾ cup (97 g) all-purpose (plain) flour
1 tablespoon sesame oil
1 tablespoon sugar
1 tablespoon makgeolli (Korean rice wine)

**For the maejap-gwa:**
Flour, for rolling out
Neutral cooking oil, for deep-frying
¼ teaspoon ground cinnamon
1 cup (90 g) pine nut powder

**Make the syrup:** In a small pot, combine ½ cup (4 fl oz/120 ml) water, the sugar, ginger juice, honey, and salt and bring to a boil over medium-low heat. Once boiling, reduce the heat to low and cook until it reaches a thick consistency, 10–15 minutes. Let cool completely.

**Make the dough:** Sift the flour into a bowl. Add the sesame oil and mix well, then run through the sieve again. In a separate bowl, combine 2½ tablespoons water, the sugar, and makgeolli and mix until the sugar is fully dissolved. Combine with the flour and mix well until uniform.

**Shape and cook the maejap-gwa:** Dust a work surface with about 1 tablespoon flour. Set the dough on the surface and use a rolling pin to roll out to a 1/16-inch (2 mm) thickness. Cut into 1 × 2½-inch (2.5 cm × 6 cm) rectangles. In the center of each rectangle, cutting the long way, make a 1½-inch (4 cm) slit. Put one short side of the dough through the slit and turn it over to create a twisted ribbon-like shape.

Set a wire rack in a sheet pan. Pour 2 inches (5 cm) cooking oil into a large deep pot or deep fryer and heat to 212°F (100°C). Drop in the twisted dough and once they begin to float to the top, increase the oil temperature to reach 302°F (150°C) and fry until golden brown, 2–3 more minutes. Let sit for 1–2 minutes on the wire rack. Deep-fry a second time at 302°F (150°C) for a more savory flavor. Drain on the wire rack.

Dip each deep-fried twist into the cold syrup to coat and let the excess syrup run off. Lightly sprinkle the cinnamon evenly over the twists and garnish with the pine nut powder to finish with a savory, fragrant note.

## Pan-Fried Flower Rice Cakes
### Hwa Jeon
### 화전

dF gF vE

*Azalea hwa jeon* is a rice cake that can only be made in spring, when azalea is in bloom. It is a round, flat rice cake made with glutinous rice flour dough and cooked in oil. In other seasons, the azalea blossom can be substituted with other edible flowers as garnish.

Preparation time: 20 minutes
Cooking time: 20 minutes
Serves: 2

13 azalea flowers
1 cup (160 g) glutinous rice flour
2 tablespoons hot water
2 teaspoons sugar
4 teaspoons perilla oil
1 tablespoon pine nut powder
¼ teaspoon ground cinnamon
1 tablespoon honey

Remove the stamens from the azalea flowers and gently rinse the petals in water. Arrange them on a tea towel to dry.

In a bowl, place the glutinous rice flour. Gently pour in the hot water and knead into a dough for 10 minutes. Divide the kneaded dough into about 13 portions of ½ ounce (12 g each) and form each into flat disk about 2 inches (5 cm) in diameter.

Sprinkle the sugar in a sheet pan and have at the ready. In a nonstick frying pan, heat the perilla oil over medium-low heat. Add the rice cakes and fry on both sides until cooked through. Gently press the flower petals into the dough. Lightly pan-fry the flower side so that the petals stick. Set the rice cakes onto the sugar in the sheet pan.

Dip the bottom of each rice cake into the pine nut powder to coat and lightly sprinkle the flower side with the cinnamon. Lightly drizzle with honey and plate to serve.

---

## Azalea Punch
### Jindallae Hwachae
### 진달래 화채

dF gF vE

This drink can only be made when azaleas are in bloom in spring, and it is a beautiful drink to enjoy, both with one's eyes and mouth.

Preparation time: 10 minutes, plus 10 hours steeping time
Cooking time: 20 minutes
Serves: 4

⅔ cup (1¾ oz/50 g) omija (red magnolia) berries
¾ cup (150 g) plus 1 tablespoon sugar
3 tablespoons plus 1 teaspoon honey
30 azalea flowers
1 tablespoon mung bean starch
1½ teaspoons pine nuts

Place the omija berries in a large heatproof bowl. In a pot, bring 4¼ cups (34 fl oz/1 liter) water to a boil. Remove from the heat and let cool for 10 minutes. Pour the just-boiled water over the omija berries and let steep at room temperature for 10 hours.

In a pot, combine 1¼ cups (10 fl oz/300 ml) water and the sugar and simmer while stirring to avoid any burning. Once boiling, remove the sugar syrup from the heat and stir in the honey. Let cool completely.

Strain the omija tea into a large container. Add the sugar-honey syrup and mix well until the liquid is uniform. Transfer the punch base to the refrigerator to chill.

Remove the stamens of the azalea flowers and gently wash the petals in water. Arrange on a tea towel to dry.

Set up a bowl of ice water. Bring a small pot of water to a boil. Lightly coat the flowers in mung bean starch and drop in the coated flowers for just 3 seconds. Cold-shock in the cold water to cool. Remove the azalea flowers from the water and gently squeeze to remove excess moisture.

In a large glass bowl, add the azalea flowers and gently pour in the chilled omija punch base. Garnish with pine nuts and serve cold.

# Steamed Pine Nut Cake
## Jat Seolgi
## 잣설기

df gf ve

The *seolgi-tteok,* which is made from nonglutinous rice flour and is pure white in color, represents purity and health in Korean tradition. It has been the traditional gift that parents give to their friends and acquaintances to celebrate the one hundredth day after their child has been born to wish that the child grow up to be pure and healthy. The texture of the rice cake is soft and pillowy, and Master Seo's signature *tteok* recipe adds pine nuts for their elegant fragrance.

Skin-off dried red beans (adzuki beans) are ivory-yellow in color. They are widely available in Korea and may be found, sold as *geopi-pat*, in Korean grocery stores.

**Preparation time:** 1 hour, plus 10 hours soaking time
**Cooking time:** 3 hours
**Serves:** 4

**For the red bean paste:**
5 oz (150 g) skin-off dried red beans (adzuki beans)
1 tablespoon honey
1 teaspoon ganjang (Korean soy sauce)
Neutral cooking oil

**For the rice flour dough:**
3⅔ cups (580 g) fine nonglutinous rice flour
3⅓ tablespoons honey
2 tablespoons sugar
4 tablespoons pine nut powder

**Make the red bean paste:** Soak the dried red beans in 4 cups (32 fl oz/950 ml) cold water for 10 hours, or until rehydrated. Strain the water into a large bowl or container, place the soaked red beans in a separate large bowl with irregularities such as a colander, and rinse roughly with the soaking water.

In a pot of boiling water, cook the red beans until softened, 1 hour. Rinse the red beans thoroughly with cold water. Return to a pot of boiling water and cook until the beans will crush easily when pressed; they should be soft to the touch and crumbly but not mushy. Drain the beans in a colander.

Set up a steamer and bring the water to a boil. Line a steamer basket with cloth and add the beans. Set the basket over the boiling water, cover, and steam for 1 hour over medium heat, stirring the beans halfway through. Let steam for 20 more minutes over low heat.

Transfer the beans to a coarse-mesh sieve set over a bowl and use a wooden spatula to mash through the sieve while the beans are still hot. Stir in the honey and soy sauce and set aside to develop flavors.

Lightly coat a heavy pot with cooking oil and heat over high heat. Add the red bean mixture and stir gently, to avoid the beans sticking or becoming a uniform mash, until there is no liquid remaining.

**Make the rice flour dough:** In a large bowl, combine the rice flour with ¾ cup (2 oz/60 g) of the red bean paste and stir until uniform. Add the honey and sugar and stir until uniform. Add ⅓ cup plus 1 tablespoon (3½ fl oz/100 ml) water and stir until uniform. Filter the mixture through a sieve into a large bowl. Add the pine nut powder to the filtered rice flour dough powder and gently mix together until the dough has a soft, flaky texture.

Set up the steamer again.

Line the steamer basket with a fine cloth. Spread the remaining red bean paste in an even layer in the basket, then top with an even layer of the rice flour dough. Cover and steam for 25 minutes. Remove from the heat and let steam away from the heat for 5 minutes. (Alternatively, assemble and steam the cake in a traditional *siru*, a Korean earthenware steamer.)

Cut into 4 slices and serve.

# Jung Yoo Huh

Jung Yoo Huh is the third-generation owner-chef of Yongsusan restaurant, established in 1980 by her grandmother, which specializes in the regional food of Kaesong in North Korea. Yongsusan proudly serves traditional foods passed down from generation to generation, and it's the first restaurant in Seoul to offer a multicourse menu. Master Huh continues to preserve Kaesong cuisine while developing new recipes created with all the traditional techniques and ingredients.

**Yongsusan restaurant**
2 Changdeokgung 1-gil, Jongno-gu, Seoul, South Korea

## Kaesong Cuisine

Because Kaesong is a geographical region that includes plains, seas, and mountains, it has an abundance of foods from land, sea, and air. This abundance led Kaesong to become a cuisine capital, with royal food traditions developing as early as the Goryeo dynasty (918–1392). Its cuisine, which uses seasonings that are never overly salty or saucy, highlights the inherent flavors of ingredients. In addition, its liquor culture and tea culture are well developed, as well as drinking foods and sweets to pair.

# Kaesong Bossam Kimchi
## 개성식 보쌈김치

dF gF

In making the traditional Kaesong *bossam* kimchi, the brining step is the most important. The quality of the fresh seafood and salted shrimp is another key factor. The flavor of the broths used and the harmonious combination of brisket broth and seafood broth is a signature flavoring of this regional royal kimchi recipe.

Preparation time: 1 hour, plus 8 hours brining time and 7–9 days fermentation
Cooking time: 1 hour
Serves: 5

**For the brined cabbage:**
2 heads napa cabbage (Chinese leaf)
1⅓ cups (5½ oz/160 g) coarse sea salt

**For the shrimp broth:**
10 fresh head-on shrimp (prawns)

**For the kimchi filling:**
9½ oz (265 g) mu (Korean radish), cut into 1 × ¼-inch (2.5 cm × 5 mm) matchsticks
1 tablespoon salt
5 oz (150 g) fresh octopus
14 oz (400 g) Asian pear
5 scallions (spring onions), cut into 1¼-inch (3 cm) lengths
10 stalks minari, cut into 1¼-inch (3 cm) lengths
5 chestnuts, shelled and very thinly sliced
5 dried jujubes (Chinese red dates), seeded and slivered
10 pine nuts
Pinch of Korean red chili threads

**For the kimchi seasoning:**
4 tablespoons fine gochugaru (red chili powder)
3 tablespoons minced garlic
2 tablespoons anchovy fish sauce
2 tablespoons sugar
¼ teaspoon ginger juice

**For the kimchi broth:**
2 tablespoons salted shrimp
2 cups (16 fl oz/480 ml) Beef Broth (page 315)

**Brine the napa cabbage:** Halve the napa cabbage heads lengthwise and create a slight slit in each half head of cabbage. In a large bowl, combine 8½ quarts (8 liters) water and the coarse sea salt to make a 2 percent salt solution. Wet each leaf of the cabbages with the salt water, and salt generously with the remaining salt. Let brine for 8 hours.

**Meanwhile, make the shrimp broth:** Remove the shrimp heads and shells and add to a small pot with 2½ cups (20 fl oz/590 ml) cold water. (Refrigerate the shrimp.) Bring to a boil over high heat. Once boiling, reduce the heat to medium-low and cook for 20 minutes. Remove from the heat. Discard the shrimp heads and shells and cool the broth in the refrigerator.

After the cabbages have finished brining, wash each half head under cold running water two times, and squeeze to remove any excess moisture. Drain in a sieve.

Remove the first 20 layers of the cabbage and set aside. Julienne the remaining inner cabbage into 1½-inch (4 cm) lengths.

**Make the kimchi filling:** In a bowl, toss the radish with the salt and set aside. Cut the shrimp into small dice. Clean the octopus and cut into 1½-inch (4 cm) lengths. Peel the pear, remove the core and seeds, and cut into 8 flat slices, from top to bottom.

In a large bowl, combine the julienned brined napa cabbage, the radish, shrimp, octopus, pear, scallions, minari, chestnuts, jujubes, pine nuts, and chili threads and mix well until uniform.

**Make the kimchi seasoning:** In a small bowl, combine the gochugaru, garlic, fish sauce, sugar, and ginger juice. Add the seasonings to the kimchi filling and toss to coat.

To assemble the bossam kimchi, in a bowl of about 5 inches (12 cm) in diameter and 4 inches (10 cm) deep, layer in 4 brined napa cabbage leaves, placing the thickest stem part in the center of the bowl and each of the leaves facing outward in four different directions. If the leaves are not large enough to fully cover the bowl, add more leaves as needed. Add one-fifth of the kimchi filling and wrap the cabbage leaves inward to cover fully. Place the wrapped kimchi into a 10 × 12 × 10-inch (25 × 30 × 25 cm) fermentation container. Repeat to make 5 bundles. When stacking the cabbages, press to be sure that there are no air bubbles in between the layers.

**Make the kimchi broth:** Press the salted shrimp through a fine sieve into a pot, pressing with a wooden spatula. Add the cold shrimp broth and beef broth and mix well. Pour the combined broths over the bossam kimchi in the container, and press the kimchi gently down to be sure that it's submerged. Place a heavy dish or a lid on top to make sure that it's submerged. Close the lid and let ferment at room temperature for 2 hours in the summer and 2 days in the winter. Transfer to the refrigerator and ferment for a minimum of 1 week before ready to eat. The kimchi keeps up to 1 month in the refrigerator, and when serving serve a whole bundle.

# Pyongyang-Style Cold Buckwheat Noodles
## Pyongyang Naengmyeon
## 평양냉면

dF

When enjoying Pyongyang *naengmyeon*, a North Korean delicacy, it's best to first taste the dish without adding the common accompaniments of vinegar and mustard to appreciate the deep flavor of the beef broth and to enjoy the inherent refreshing taste of the noodles. Vinegar and mustard can be added to preference in moderation after this initial flavor has been experienced. *Naengmyeon* is also best enjoyed with its classic pairing dishes, such as *bulgogi* or *galbi*, and it's best paired with a glass of soju (Korean clear spirits).

Preparation time: 30 minutes, plus 6 hours soaking time
Cooking time: 2½ hours
Serves: 2

For the naengmyeon broth:
2 lb 10 oz (1.2 kg) beef brisket
1 tablespoon salt
2 oz (60 g) daepa (Korean scallion)
1¾ oz (50 g) onion
1 oz (25 g) garlic
½ oz (10 g) fresh ginger
5 black peppercorns
½ oz (15 g) Chinese licorice
2 tablespoons cheongjang (light Korean soy sauce)

For the garnishes:
1¾ oz (50 g) mu (Korean radish)
¾ teaspoon salt
½ teaspoon corn (golden) syrup
1 teaspoon minced garlic
1 teaspoon sugar
1¾ oz (50 g) cucumber
¼ teaspoon salt

For the buckwheat noodles:
4 cups (480 g) buckwheat flour
7½ tablespoons (60 g) goguma (Korean sweet potato) starch
7½ tablespoons (60 g) all-purpose (plain) flour
1¼ cups (10 fl oz/300 ml) boiling water

**Make the naengmyeon broth:** Place the beef brisket in a large bowl and cover with water. Let soak for 6 hours, changing the water every 2 hours, to remove the blood.

Fill a large pot with 8½ cups (68 fl oz/2 liters) water and bring to a boil over high heat. Once boiling, add the brisket and boil for 2–3 minutes. Remove the brisket and discard the water. Fill the pot with 4½ quarts (4.5 liters) fresh water and the salt and bring to a boil over high heat. Once boiling, add the brisket, daepa, onion, garlic, ginger, peppercorns, and licorice and cook over high heat for 30 minutes. Reduce the heat to medium and cook for 40 minutes. Reduce the heat to low heat and cook for 50 more minutes.

Strain the broth, reserving the brisket but discarding the other solids. Stir the soy sauce into the broth. Let the broth cool completely, then strain again through a fine-mesh sieve and transfer to the refrigerator.

**Make the garnishes:** Cut the radish into ¾ × 2½-inch (2 × 6 cm) thin slices. In a bowl, combine the radish slices with ½ teaspoon salt and corn syrup and brine for 5 minutes. Once the radish begins to release its moisture, add the garlic and sugar and mix well. Transfer to the refrigerator.

Cut the cucumber into very thin slices a scant ¹⁄₁₆ inch (1 mm) thick. In a bowl, combine the cucumber with the remaining ¼ teaspoon salt and brine for 5 minutes. Squeeze to remove any excess moisture and keep the cucumbers in the refrigerator.

Cut away any fat from the boiled brisket and cut against the grain into 2 × 1¼-inch (5 × 3 cm) slices ¹⁄₁₆ inch (2 mm) thick. Transfer the sliced brisket to an airtight container and store in the refrigerator.

**Make the buckwheat noodles:** In a large bowl, combine the buckwheat flour, sweet potato starch, and all-purpose flour and mix well until uniform. Add the boiling water slowly in four or five additions, kneading constantly. Knead for 10 minutes until well combined. Wrap tightly in plastic wrap (cling film) and set aside.

In a naengmyeon noodle machine, add water and once the water is boiling, add the buckwheat dough and make the noodles. Cook for 1 minute 20 seconds, then drain and rinse well under cold water until the starch is washed away.

Squeeze the noodles with both hands to remove any excess water. Place each individual serving into a large bowl, in a neat ball. Garnish the noodles with the radish, cucumber, and brisket slices. Pour in the cold broth and serve.

# Kaesong-Style Square Mandu
## Kaesong Pyeonsu
## 개성편수

dF

*Kaesong pyeonsu* is a *mandu* (dumpling) unique to the Kaesong region. It is characterized by its square shape. It is made by making a dough, cutting it into squares, adding the filling, and folding in its corners to attach at the center to form a pyramid-like shape. It is a common variation to pour brisket broth over the cooked *pyeonsu mandu* when serving.

Preparation time: 30 minutes, plus 3 hours resting time
Cooking time: 30 minutes
Serves: 4

**For the mandu wrappers:**
3 cups (390 g) all-purpose (plain) flour, plus more for dusting
1 teaspoon salt
½ egg white
½ tablespoon neutral cooking oil
¾ cup (6 fl oz/175 ml) boiling water

**For the beef and shiitake:**
3½ oz (100 g) beef sirloin (rump) or brisket, cut into 1 × 1/16-inch (2.5 cm × 2 mm) matchsticks
1¾ oz (50 g) fresh shiitake mushroom, stemmed, caps julienned
½ tablespoon minced garlic
½ tablespoon ganjang (Korean soy sauce)
½ tablespoon mirin
½ tablespoon sugar
½ tablespoon sesame oil
½ tablespoon neutral cooking oil
½ teaspoon freshly ground black pepper

**For the mandu filling seasoning:**
1 tablespoon ganjang (Korean soy sauce)
½ tablespoon sugar
½ tablespoon minced garlic
½ tablespoon sesame oil
½ tablespoon perilla oil
½ teaspoon neutral cooking oil
½ teaspoon sesame seeds
½ teaspoon salt
½ teaspoon freshly ground black pepper

**For the mandu filling:**
½ aehoboak (Korean zucchini)
1 teaspoon salt
½ onion, finely diced
½ stalk daepa (Korean scallion), finely diced
1 egg

**For the mandu:**
30 pine nuts

**Make the mandu wrappers:** In a bowl, combine the flour, salt, egg white, and cooking oil and combine well until uniform. Slowing add the boiling water in two or three additions while kneading the dough. Knead for 10 more minutes. Once uniform, cover the bowl with plastic wrap (cling film) and transfer to the refrigerator to rest for 2–3 hours.

Dust a work surface with flour and place the dough on the work surface. Shape into a long cylinder 1½ inches (4 cm) in diameter. Cut crosswise into ¾-inch (2 cm) pieces. Using a rolling pin, roll out each piece to a thin sheet and cut into 3-inch (8 cm) squares. Dust each wrapper with flour so it does not stick, and store the wrappers in a plastic bag at room temperature.

**Make the beef and shiitake:** In a bowl, combine the beef, shiitake, garlic, soy sauce, mirin, sugar, sesame oil, cooking oil, and black pepper and mix well. Let marinate for 5 minutes. Heat a dry frying pan over medium heat. Add the beef-shiitake mixture and stir-fry until cooked. Set aside on a large plate to cool.

**Make the mandu filling seasoning:** In a small bowl, stir together the soy sauce, sugar, garlic, sesame oil, perilla oil, cooking oil, sesame seeds, salt, and black pepper. Set aside.

**Make the mandu filling:** Scrape out the seedy core of the zucchini and cut it into 1 × 1/16-inch (2.5 cm × 2 mm) matchsticks. In a small bowl, combine the zucchini and salt and brine for 5 minutes. Squeeze out the excess water in a cloth. In a dry frying pan, stir-fry the zucchini for 2–3 minutes over low heat. Set aside to cool.

Repeat the same steps for the finely diced onion.

In a large bowl, combine the zucchini, onion, daepa, beef-shiitake mixture, egg, and the mandu filling seasoning and mix well until uniform.

**Form and cook the mandu:** Place a mandu wrapper on a cutting board and wet the edges with water using your fingertips. Place 1 tablespoon of the mandu filling in the center of the mandu wrapper and garnish with one pint nut. Fold the four corners in toward the center and seal the edges to make a cross pattern. Repeat for all remaining ingredients.

Set up a steamer and bring the water to a boil.

Add the mandu to the steamer basket, set it over the boiling water, cover, and steam for about 3 minutes.

Plate the cooked pyeonsu mandu and serve.

# Ji Soon Kim

Ji Soon Kim is the master of Jeju cuisine and has devoted her life to researching and disseminating the island's traditional cuisine in order to preserve its unique food culture. Together with her son Yong-jin Yang, she established the Jeju Local Food Conservation Research Institute. In 2012, in cooperation with Jeju Island, the institute published *The Wisdom and Taste of Jeju People: Traditional Local Food*, a formal encyclopedia of traditional Jeju food. In 2016, Master Kim opened Nangpoon Bapsang, a restaurant specializing in Jeju's traditional food, contributing directly to promoting the value of Jeju's food culture to locals and visitors alike.

**Nangpoon Bapsang restaurant**
28 Yeondong 6-gil, Jeju-si, Jeju-do, South Korea

## Jeju Cuisine

The chief characteristic of Jeju food is the simplicity of the cooking methods. However, the simplicity does not imply ease, but instead strict foundational rules; the most important being the freshness of the ingredients. The simplicity in the cuisine's seasonings is intended to highlight the inherent flavors of the fresh ingredients.

On Jeju Island, seafood is the daily source of protein. Because fish and shellfish omit a palpable odor and texture when its quality fails, these simple preparations helped the people of Jeju detect when ingredients were subpar.

**Local Doenjang**

When talking about the simplicity of the cooking methods, there is a controversy over the definition of simplicity in seasoning. In particular, the use of *doenjang* (fermented soybean paste) as the main ingredient in seasoning is unmatched by any other Korean region.

In most regions, *doenjang* is used in cooking hot foods, such as *jjigae* (stews). *Doenjang* in Jeju can be treated as a cooked food on its own, because Jeju *doenjang* does not produce the unidentifiable smell, which is often referred to as funky (*gunnae*), that many other region's *doenjang* produces. This is due to the short aging process of Jeju's *doenjang*, which still produces a uniform and stable flavor. Jeju's short-aged *doenjang* is often used directly as a *ssamjang* (dipping sauce of wraps), mixed with vinegar, and eaten as a dip in dishes, such as *hwe* (raw seafood or meat) and boiled pork. It is even stirred into cold water and eaten as a cold soup. The ways that it's utilized are countless and its ease of use and deliciousness showcases why additional seasoning was unnecessary.

In addition, the by-product of *doenjang*, *ganjang* (Korean soy sauce), was also used to season many foods simply. Additional preserves, such as vinegars made from fermenting foraged herbs (such as shindari and ash leaf) from the base of Mount Halla, were also used as simple dressings, and crops, such as garlic and sesame seeds, were used as simple seasonings as well.

**Variety of Grains**

The volcanic island of Jeju does not have soil that retains water well, so unlike the mainland, it was not good grounds for rice farming. Only a little over 1 percent of its lands were used for rice farming, and due to its scarcity, commoners rarely ate or even were in contact with the rice crop. This, however, became the reason the island developed dishes using a variety of alternative grains.

The most popular grain was barley, followed by glutinous millet and buckwheat. These grains in combination with beans, sorghum, and more were used to make *bap*. Root vegetables, such as sweet potato and potato, were incorporated into the mixed-grain dish, and even a variety of land vegetables (radish, *naengi* (shepherd's purse), chrysanthemum, and sea vegetables (*tot*, *parae*) became a part of the mixed-grain *bap*. While rooted in the efforts to stretch the prized main grains, it became a cuisine of its own, developing delicious recipes that are enjoyed to this day. The use of buckwheat is also highly developed on Jeju. Not only does it exist in forms of *bap* recipes but is also made into noodles, cakes, fritters, and more.

**Preserved Foods and Fresh Vegetables**

Compared to the rest of Korea, Jeju does not have a well-developed history of preserved foods. This is because of its high humidity and temperature, which accelerated the process of fermentation and prevented the lifespan of fermented foods. On the other hand, its climate allowed fresh vegetables to be harvested even in the winter season, lending to Jeju's inclusion of fresh vegetables in every meal. The influence of the climate on its use of vegetables extended to the kimchi culture. While Jeju cuisine still incorporates kimchi recipes in every season, it's made in small amounts and eaten fresh. The same applied to pickled and preserved foods, which appeared in daily meals but were made in small amounts and were relatively young compared to the mainland. There was little imperative for Jeju to make *jeotgal* (preserved seafood), because fresh seafood was available year-round, not counting those that were caught in such large amounts that they would go to waste.

**Development of Guk**

As Jeju's main dish was mixed-grain rice, which was tougher to digest on its own compared to cooked rice, *guk* (soup) was always served along with it to make the digestion easier. It's common to see multiple types of simple *guk* on a Jeju table spread, and while lighter, clear *guk* is very common, the richer *jjigae* is not traditional to Jeju.

The highlight of Jeju's *guk* recipes is the variety of fish *guk*. Even deep-water oily fish, such as the mackerel, which are not used in *guk* recipes on the mainland due to their fishiness, are used to make clear soups in Jeju. This is a testament to the extreme freshness of the fish available in Jeju, where it's possible to prepare and cook with fish that has been caught on the same day.

# Napa Cabbage & Doenjang Guk
## Baechu Doenjang Guk
## 배추된장국

DF GF DF VG –5

In Jeju, the napa cabbage (Chinese leaf) was by far the most consumed vegetable all year-round, excluding the one-month period in the beginning of summer, when the napa cabbage is just sprouting. It was such a ubiquitous vegetable that when one refers to *namul* (vegetable dishes), it implies napa cabbage. Most of the native cabbages of Jeju were of a varietal that had sparse leaves, but fuller-leaved cabbages similar to the modern varietal were found, including those that looked like mustard greens. In the past, the native cabbage had a slight bitter flavor, so it was blanched before cooking, but today's cabbage is fine to use directly.

Most of the napa cabbages were eaten raw as a *ssam* (wrap) vegetable, but for any excess or wilting cabbages, it was seasoned with *doenjang* (fermented soybean paste) and eaten as a side dish or cooked in a soup made with *doenjang* or in a clear fish soup. Each household would use their own homemade *doenjang*, and due to the differing salinity, different amounts were used. While in other Korean regions, *tojang*, a special hybrid *jang*, is often used to season cabbage, in Jeju regular *doenjang* was used.

**Preparation time: 20 minutes**
**Cooking time: 20 minutes**
**Serves: 2**

3½ oz (100 g) doenjang (fermented soybean paste)
10 oz (300 g) bomdong (spring napa cabbage/Chinese leaf)

In a large pot, combine 4¼ cups (34 fl oz/1 liter) water and the doenjang and loosen the doenjang until uniform. Bring to a boil over high heat. Once boiling, add the cabbage by hand, tearing it into bite-size pieces. Reduce the heat to medium-low and cook until the cabbage is soft and the liquid has reduced by about one-quarter. The low simmering lets the flavors of the doenjang and the cabbage marry.

Serve hot in individual bowls.

# Napa Cabbage Flower Kimchi
## Dongji Kimchi
## 동지김치

dF

*Dongji* are the flower stalks of the napa cabbage (Chinese leaf). At the end of January, when the winter cold is not yet over, flower stalks begin to sprout from the cabbages that have weathered the winter. From these stalks, yellow flowers begin to bloom for the next month or so. Just before the flowers bloom, the flower stalks are soft yet crunchy, making for a great mouthfeel. Lightly brined and made into a kimchi, its flavors are a unique taste reminiscent of the forthcoming spring, providing a long-awaited contrast to the well-ripened kimchi eaten throughout the winter. While *dongji* specifically refers to the flowering stalk of the cabbage, the whole cabbage at this stage can be used for the kimchi.

In the past, instead of the modern flour slurry, boiled barley or millet water was used.

**Preparation time:** 20 minutes, plus 1 hour brining time and 1 day fermentation
**Cooking time:** 5 minutes
**Serves:** 4

2¼ lb (1 kg) dongji (flowering napa cabbage/Chinese leaf)
⅔ cup (80 g) coarse sea salt
2½ tablespoons all-purpose (plain) flour

**For the kimchi:**
7 tablespoons anchovy jeot paste
4–6½ tablespoons gochugaru (red chili flakes)
2 tablespoons minced garlic
2 teaspoons minced fresh ginger
1 oz (30 g) scallion (spring onion), cut into 1½–2-inch (4–5 cm) lengths

In a large bowl, combine the dongji and sea salt and brine for 1 hour. Rinse with cold water and set aside.

In a small saucepan, combine ¾ cup (6 fl oz/175 ml) water and the flour and whisk well to remove lumps. Set over medium-low heat and cook, stirring constantly. Once bubbling, cook for 3 more minutes. Remove the flour paste from the heat and let cool to room temperature.

**Assemble the kimchi:** In a large bowl, combine the cooled flour paste, anchovy jeot paste, gochugaru, garlic, and ginger and mix until uniform. Add the brined dongji and scallion and mix well until uniform. Transfer to an airtight container and ferment for 1 day at room temperature before enjoying.

---

# Napa Cabbage Flower Muchim
## Dongji Namul Muchim
## 동지나물무침

dF  vE  vg  -S        [a]

When making kimchi, the base of the napa cabbage (Chinese leaf) flower can be used in full, but when making a vegetable side dish, only the tender flowering portion of the napa cabbage is used. Once the cabbage has flowered, the stalk turns tough as well, so the outer layers may be removed as needed.

**Preparation time:** 10 minutes
**Cooking time:** 10 minutes
**Serves:** 4

Salt
10 oz (300 g) dongji (flowering napa cabbage/Chinese leaf)
1 tablespoon (15 g) cheongjang (light Korean soy sauce) or doenjang (fermented soybean paste)
1 teaspoon minced garlic
1–2 teaspoons sesame oil, to taste
¾ teaspoon ground sesame seeds

Bring a pot of salted water to a boil. Blanch the dongji for 30 seconds. Rinse the dongji under cold running water to cool. Gently squeeze out excess water.

In a bowl, combine the soy sauce (or doenjang loosened with some water) and garlic. Add the blanched dongji and mix well. Finish with the sesame oil and sesame seeds and toss well.

## Rockfish & Bean Jorim
### Ureok Kong Jorim
### 우럭콩조림

dF

In Korea, the term "rockfish" refers to the Northern black sea perch, which measures over 12 inches (30 cm). But the rockfish native to Jeju is a different variety, a smaller fish (about 8 inches/20 cm) with a red or brown coloration. It has a unique shape, with its head measuring half of its body, leaving only a small amount of meat to eat. Occasionally, and rarely, a fish measuring 12 inches (30 cm) would be salted and used as a ceremonial fish.

The everyday Jeju rockfish was made into soup with seaweed or grilled, and it was commonplace to add beans to the recipes to make a hearty meal in which the beans absorbed the flavor of the fish and the seasoning. The beans used in this recipe are the native *jom-kong*, which are small beans about the size of lentils that don't need soaking before cooking.

Preparation time: 20 minutes
Cooking time: 30 minutes
Serves: 3

¾ cup (150 g) dried jom beans
7 oz (200 g) Jeju rockfish, gutted and cleaned
7 tablespoons ganjang (Korean soy sauce)
2½ tablespoons sugar
1 tablespoon minced garlic
1 teaspoon minced fresh ginger
1 tablespoon neutral cooking oil
½ teaspoon gochugaru (red chili flakes)

Rinse the beans in a sieve under running water.

In a dry frying pan, stir-fry the beans until they begin to crackle and the skins begin to crack (without the skin cracking, the beans will not absorb the seasonings). Transfer the beans to a large pot.

Add the rockfish, 1¼ cups (10 fl oz/300 ml) water, the soy sauce, sugar, garlic, and ginger to the pot with the beans. Bring to a boil over high heat. Once boiling, reduce the heat to medium-low and simmer until the fish is well cooked and the beans are tender. While cooking, constantly baste the fish with broth. Drizzle the cooking oil over the fish and garnish with gochugaru. Remove from the heat.

---

## Pearl-Spot Chromis Jeot
### Jari-jeot
### 자리젓

dF gF -5

The pearl-spot chromis, called *jari* in Jeju, is native to the northwest Pacific, from southern Korea, along the coast of Jeju Island and the southern coast of Japan. Even when fully grown, it's only the size of an adult's palm. It lives in abundance in shallow waters (16–50 feet/5–15 m deep) at 68°F (20°C), and it's in season from May through August. During this time, it's full of roe and is delicious, and it is considered a Jeju summer delicacy. Because it can be caught in abundance, it's made into many different dishes, including raw, grilled, and simmered. Even with its many cooking methods, there was often an excess of the fresh fish, so it was made into *jeotgal* (preserved seafood). While small in size, the bones of the pearl-spot chromis are hard, so a minimum of 2 months of fermentation is required to soften them before it can be enjoyed.

The Jeju *jeotgal* method follows the simplicity of the island's cuisine: The fish is rinsed in sea water and dried, then mixed with sea salt and fermented in a *hangari* (fermentation jar). For every 2¼ pounds (1 kg) of fish, about 1 cup (250 g) of salt is used, but the ideal amount is ½–¾ cup (150–200 g). In western Jeju, the fish is first crushed with a wooden spatula before fermenting, so the resulting *jeotgal* is a moist paste created as the fish loses its shape during the fermentation process. In eastern Jeju, the fish is fermented whole without any crushing, so the final *jeotgal* still retains the fish shape and its red coloration. The fish itself is slightly dehydrated and is without any liquid.

Preparation time: 10 minutes, plus 2 months fermentation time
Makes: 2¼ lb (1 kg)

2¼ lb (1 kg) pearl-spot chromis
½ cup (150 g) sea salt

Wash the pearl-spot chromis with sea water well until clean. Let dry quickly to remove all excess moisture. Combine the cleaned fish with the sea salt until well seasoned and add to a hangari or fermentation container. Cover the top with a cloth to prevent any impurities from entering and close the lid. Ferment for a minimum of 2 months.

# Tot Muchim
톳무침

Traditionally, the seaweed that the Jeju people are most familiar with is not the common *miyeok* (wakame) or *gim*, but *tot* (aka hijiki). Measured by historic records, production amounts, quality, or even usage, the *tot* is without a doubt the most representative seaweed of Jeju.

Although *tot* is also relatively widely distributed in the south and central parts of Korea, *tot* native to Jeju Island has the most robust texture, with a unique chewy taste. In other regions, it can get as big as 2 feet (60 cm) when it is fully grown, but in the ideal environment of Jeju's coastal waters, it grows to well over 3 feet (1 m). The best-quality *tot* is harvested in the cold waters from January to March, but Korean women divers (*haenyeos*) harvest the *tot* until April. Recently, the harvest has decreased by more than 90 percent compared to twenty years ago due to the reckless development of the coast and the destruction of the natural environment.

The people of Jeju traditionally dried *tot* in the open air with the sea breeze, and they used the *tot* all year-round incorporated into many dishes. It could be eaten as *namul* (vegetable side dishes), lightly seasoned, or made with rice. It is also a popular ingredient in cold soup in the summertime.

**Preparation time: 10 minutes**
**Cooking time: 10 minutes**
**Serves 4**

8½ oz (240 g) fresh tot (hijiki)
5 teaspoons doenjang
    (fermented soybean paste)
2½ teaspoons minced scallion
    (spring onion)
1 teaspoon gochugaru
    (red chili flakes)
1 teaspoon minced garlic
¾ teaspoon ground sesame seeds
2 teaspoon sesame oil
Steamed rice, for serving

In a pot of boiling water, blanch the seaweed for 1 minute. Drain and rinse under cold running water to cool. Cut the seaweed into 1½–2-inch (4–5 cm) pieces.

In a bowl, combine the doenjang, scallion, gochugaru, garlic, sesame seeds, and sesame oil and mix well until uniform. Add the seaweed to the seasoning and mix well until uniform. Serve along with rice.

# Jeong Kwan

Buddhist monk Jeong Kwan began her temple food training at the age of eighteen, when she entered the Donghwasa Temple in Mount Palgongsan in 1974. Today, she conducts events around the world to spread the knowledge and spirit of Korean temple food.

Jeong Kwan first became known as a chef through her relationship with French chef Eric Ripert, who is based in the United States and practices Buddhism. In 2014, Ripert made a documentary at Cheonjinam, her temple within the Baekyangsa Temple grounds, and she appeared soon thereafter in the series *Chef's Table*. Jeff Gordinier, a *New York Times* writer, came to the VIP banquet prepared by Jeong Kwan and wrote a moving article and, since then, Jeong Kwan has been revered as one of the most influential chefs in the world. In 2022, she won Asia's 50 Best Restaurants Icon Award, recognized for introducing Korean vegetarian culture and Korean Buddhist food culture to the world.

**Baegyangsa Temple**
1239 Baegyang-ro, Bukha-myeon, Jangseong-gun, Jeollanam-do, South Korea

## Korean Temple Food

Human life mimics the natural world in many ways. Observing the self, one coexists with the self of the past, present, and future. This can be said of all ingredients: In understanding the past, present, and future potential of an ingredient, one can create something from nothing.

Each season produces a variety of ingredients. One must understand the nature and quality of the ingredients to gain insight into how it can be best prepared. The best dishes are the result of this understanding of the characteristics of a vegetable and work to elevate its quality and maximize its potential.

## Tofu Jang
## Dubu Jang
## 두부장

dF vg vE -S

For the tofu *jang*, firm handmade tofu is the best. (If making the tofu from scratch, select soybeans that are even, hard, and shiny with clear lines.) Tofu *jang* can be used as a plant-based cheese substitute in salads and in many different dishes.

**Preparation time:** 1 hour, plus 3 months 1 week fermentation
**Serves:** 5

2 lb (900 g) firm handmade tofu
4 tablespoons jinjang (dark Korean soy sauce, aged 5 years)
1 tablespoon salt
2 tablespoons doenjang (fermented soybean paste, aged 5 years)

Soak the tofu in cold water for 30 minutes to remove any remaining bitterness. Drain.

Lightly salt the surface of the tofu and let sit for 10 minutes. Place the tofu in a cheesecloth (muslin) pouch and massage with your hands, crushing into a fine uniform mash. Transfer the tofu to a bowl and combine with the soy sauce and salt and massage well until uniform. Transfer to a small hangari or fermentation container.

Layer in the doenjang on top of the tofu and press well. Layer the top with a cloth or clean pumpkin leaves and close the lid. Ferment at 50°–60°F (10°–15°C) during the winter for 7 days. Transfer to a 50°–60°F (10°–15°C) refrigerator and ferment for 3 months. (Alternatively, store in a cool, dark place.)

---

## Steamed Vegetables with Tofu Jang
## Dubujang Chaeso Jjim
## 채소찜과 두부장

dF gF vg vE   [□]

This dish can be made using any seasonal vegetables. The combination of the tofu *jang* is particularly harmonious with steamed root vegetables.

**Preparation time:** 20 minutes
**Cooking time:** 15 minutes
**Serves:** 4

**For the vegetables:**
14 oz (400 g) mu (Korean radish), halved lengthwise and cut into half-moons ⅜ inch (1 cm) thick
3½ oz (100 g) carrots, cut into slices ⅜ inch (1 cm) thick
1 lb (500 g) napa cabbage (Chinese leaf), cut into slices ⅜ inch (1 cm) wide
5 Fischer's ragwort leaves
5 chwinamul (aster scaber) leaves
10 goatsbeard leaves
10 giant hyssop leaves

**To finish:**
2 tablespoons Tofu Jang (see above)
2 tablespoons bokbunja cheong (Korean blackberry syrup)
2 tablespoons omija cheong (red magnolia berry syrup)
2 tablespoons ganjang (Korean soy sauce)
1 tablespoon perilla oil
¼ teaspoon salt
1 tablespoon perilla seed powder

**Cook the vegetables:** In a wide pot, add 1 cup (8 fl oz/240 ml) water and all the vegetables. Bring to a boil over high heat, reduce the heat to medium, cover, and steam for 7 minutes. Set the pot aside.

**To finish:** In a small bowl, combine the tofu jang, blackberry syrup, magnolia berry syrup, soy sauce, perilla oil, and salt and mix well until uniform. Evenly add the sauce to the vegetables, set back over medium heat, and boil for 2 minutes.

Remove from the heat. Serve hot garnished with perilla seed powder.

# Gyung Kyun Shin

Gyung Kyun Shin is a traditional Korean ceramicist who has achieved global recognition as Korea's best ceramicist. His works continue the tradition of the Korean moon jar and *dawan*, Korean teacups.

He apprenticed with his father, the late Jeonghee Shin, a highly regarded ceramicist of Goryeo Dawan (called Ido-dawan in Japan), learning to use the traditional method of wheel throwing and a wood-fired kiln. In 2005, he was selected as the representative artist of the Busan APEC Summit, and in 2014 he held the first solo exhibition of Koreans at the UNESCO headquarters in Paris. During the 2018 Pyeongchang Winter Olympics, his moon jar was delivered to the German president as a national gift.

Master Shin is famous for his cuisine as much as his ceramics. With his wife, Lim Geahwa, who is an esteemed chef specializing in Korean foods, Master Shin copublished the book *To Eat Clams when the Cham Flower Blooms*, which showcases seasonal dishes along with traditional ceramics. His mantra is that to make a proper ceramic vessel, one needs to understand the food that is intended to be plated on it. Among the many ceramicists, he is regarded as a true authority of *hansik* (traditional Korean cuisine), who creates ceramic works of art that properly convey the knowledge of Korean cuisine.

Janganyo ceramics studio
24 Hajangan 1-gil, Jangan-eup, Gijang-gun, Busan, South Korea

# Korean Cuisine and Ceramics

Ceramics are the clothing of cuisine. When good cuisine is plated on good plateware, that's when the value of the food shines. As important as it is to understand Korean cuisine, it is also important to understand the history of our ceramics culture to truly understand the intent and meaning of our food.

Traditional cuisine requires continued practice through its people. Ceramics that are unused cannot be considered good ceramics, such as food that is not eaten cannot be considered good food. In the history of Korean cuisine, the ceramics that contain the food have been of utmost importance.

Korean dishes are made according to the characteristics of Korean food, so that when people enjoy food, they can experience the taste properly. Korean ceramics have evolved along with the key characteristics of Korean cuisine. *Bap* (rice), *guk* (soup), and *banchan* (side dishes) have shaped the aesthetics of ceramics and its use; the subtle beauty, the shape of nature, are all aspects of Korean ceramics that follow the psyche of Korean cuisine and its beauty.

"Food is a tool for describing pottery." Good ceramics and good food mean the same thing. The basis of good food is fresh ingredients in season. Everything must be done with sincerity and diligence to create good works. To create ceramics requires diligence, sincerity, and precision, such as is *hansik*.

# Pan-Roasted Acorn Jelly
## Dotori Muk Gui
## 도토리묵구이와 고수무침

df vg vE

Acorn jelly is made from acorns harvested in fall and is eaten fresh with vegetables. At Janganyo ceramics studio, there is a special dish made from pan-roasted acorn jelly, served with a cilantro (coriander) relish. The shape of the acorn jelly is similar to that of foie gras, and the texture is extremely charming, with the surface being crispy and the inside soft.

Preparation time: 30 minutes, plus 2 hours cooling time and 1–2 hours setting
Cooking time: 30 minutes
Serves: 4

For the acorn jelly:
1 cup (3½ oz/100 g) acorn starch powder
1 teaspoon salt
½ teaspoon sesame oil

For the cilantro relish:
1 oz (30 g) cilantro (coriander), rinsed and well dried
½ tablespoon sesame oil
1 teaspoon ganjang (Korean soy sauce)
½ teaspoon sesame seeds

To finish:
1 tablespoon perilla oil or olive oil

**Make the acorn jelly:** In a large bowl, combine the acorn starch powder and 5½ cups (44 fl oz/1.3 liters) water and mix well to get rid of any lumps. Once uniform, let set for 10 minutes.

In a heavy pot, cook the acorn jelly mixture over low heat for 10 minutes, stirring constantly to avoid burning and get rid of lumps. Increase the heat to medium and cook for 5 more minutes. Once the mixture begins to bubble, reduce the heat to medium-low and cook for 5 minutes. Add the salt and sesame oil, stir in, and reduce the heat to low and cook for 5 more minutes.

Pour the thickened acorn jelly mixture into a 4 × 6 × 2½-inch (10 × 15 × 6.5 cm) container and smooth out with a rubber spatula. Let cool at room temperature, uncovered, for 2 hours. Cover and move to the refrigerator for 1–2 hours to set.

**Meanwhile, make the cilantro relish:** In a small bowl, combine the cilantro, sesame oil, soy sauce. and sesame seeds and mix well. Set aside.

**To finish:** Cut the acorn jelly into slices ¾ inch (2 cm) thick. In a frying pan, heat the perilla oil over medium heat. Add the jelly slices and pan-roast until golden brown on both sides, about 3 minutes per side.

Plate the acorn jelly with the cilantro relish and serve.

# Janganyo Duck
## 장안덕

dFgF -5

Janganyo duck is the signature duck dish of Janganyo. In winter, when oak trees are abundant with sap, the duck is cooked in a Korean *gamasot* (iron cauldron) with oak sap. The resulting duck's skin smells like butter, and its flesh is fragrant and soft. At Janganyo, this dish marks the winter season and is served during its Christmas feast.

**Preparation time:** 20 minutes
**Cooking time:** 1 hour
**Serves:** 4

1 whole duck (6 lb 10 oz/3 kg)
6½ lb (3 kg) small oak logs, 4–5-inch (10–12 cm) pieces
3 sugar cubes, cut in half

Rinse the duck of any blood or scraps of innards left behind.

Choose a large cast-iron Dutch oven (casserole) that's big enough to hold the whole duck. Place the oak pieces upright, so that the cut surfaces are visible, filling the bottom of the pot so that there are no empty gaps. In the center, place the halved sugar cubes. Place the whole duck on top and close the lid.

Set over high heat and cook for 30 minutes. After the initial 30 minutes, the duck's fat begin to render and there should be sizzling sounds. Reduce the heat to medium-low and cook for another 30 minutes. Do not lift the lid, because you don't want the fragrance of the oak to be lost.

Serve hot.

# Index

## A
abalone 202
  abalone *juk* 402
acorn jelly
  acorn jelly *bap* 122
  acorn jelly *muchim* 225
  chilled kimchi & acorn jelly soup 225
  pan-roasted acorn jelly 479
*aehobak* (Korean zucchini) 34, 176
  anchovy broth *guksu* 365
  cod roe & tofu *jjigae* 350
  *doenjang jjigae* 346, 347
  hand-torn *guksu* 384
  Kaesong-style square *mandu* 462
  Korean zucchini *bokkeum* 257
  Korean zucchini *jeon* 236
  Korean zucchini *jeot guk* 320
  Korean zucchini *namul* 176
  littleneck clam *kalguksu* 378
  long-arm octopus & zucchini *chomuchim* 196
  mushroom *kalguksu* 377
  pomfret & Korean zucchini *jorim* 294
  *pyeonsu mandu* 391
  river snail *doenjang* & squash leaf *ssam* 212
  spicy blue crab *tang* 344
  thick *doenjang* barley *bibimbap* 107
  thick *doenjang jjigae* 348
  tofu *jeongol* 360
  zucchini *bibimguksu* 370
*aehobak bibimguksu* 370
*aehobak byeongeo jorim* 294
*aehobak jeon* 236
*aehobak jeot guk* 320
*aehobak namul* 176
*aehobak ogari* 176
*aehobak saeujeot bokkeum* 257
*aekjeot* 39, 85
agar jelly in cold soybean broth 228
aged kimchi *ssambap* 117
*agwi-jjim* 295
almonds: *ssamjang* with nuts 53
anchovies 38, 442
  anchovy broth 314
  anchovy *doenjang* perilla *jjim* 300
  *jeotgal* 84
  Korean rice balls 135
  napa cabbage kimchi 444
  radish top *doenjang namul* 182

salted anchovies 85
shishito & anchovy *bokkeum* 254
young cabbage & anchovy *doenjang jorim* 280
anchovy broth 314
  acorn jelly *bap* 122
  anchovy broth *guksu* 365
  baby jumbo shrimp & napa cabbage *doenjang guk* 327
  bean sprout *gukbap* 119
  chilled kimchi & acorn jelly soup 225
  clear cod *tang* 340
  cold kimchi *guksu* 374
  *doenjang jjigae* 346, 347
  dried pollock *gukbap* 120
  hand-torn *guksu* 384
  kimchi & bean sprout *guk* 322
  kimchi & ground soybean *jjigae* 350
  kimchi *jjigae* 348
  Korean zucchini *jeot guk* 320
  littleneck clam *kalguksu* 378
  *maesaengi* oyster *guk* 328
  raw fish in cold broth 204
  rice cake soup 408
  seafood *tang* 343
  spicy blue crab *tang* 344
  spicy cod *tang* 342
  squid & radish *guk* 326
  tofu *jeongol* 360
  young perilla *namul* 178
anchovy fish sauce: white kimchi 445
Andong 26
  Andong chicken *jorim* 288
  Andong-style *bibimbap* 99
  Andong *heotjesatbap* 99
  Andong *jjim-dak* 288
apples 36
  *ganjang*-marinated crab 86
  Gangwondo-style buckwheat *guksu* 383
  pig's feet *jorim* 290
Asian pear (Korean pear) 35
  beef short ribs *jorim* 284
  Busan-style cold wheat *guksu* 376
  chicken mustard *muchim* 200
  cold buckwheat *guksu* with *hwe* 372
  cucumber water kimchi 76
  Gangwondo-style buckwheat *guksu* 383
  green laver & radish *muchim* 188
  Hamheung-style spicy *bibimguksu* 368
  Kaesong *bossam* kimchi 460
  Korean short rib patties *gui* 270
  LA short rib *gui* 269
  onion kimchi 77
  poached Asian pear 412
  pork rib *gui* 260
  Pyeongyang-style beef *jeongol* 357

Pyeongyang-style cold buckwheat *guksu* 373
radish & green chili kimchi 71
radish & yellow pepper kimchi 70
radish water kimchi 72
raw beef *bibimbap* 104
raw beef *muchim* 198
seasoned skate *hwe* 203
stuffed cucumber kimchi 74
water kimchi 66
white kimchi 64
young summer radish kimchi 67
*yuja* punch 418
asparagus *jangajji* 82
*aspergillus oryzae* 48
azalea flowers
  azalea punch 456
  pan-fried flower rice cakes 456

## B
*Bacillus subtilis* 48
*bae* 35–6
*baechu* 33
*baechu cheonggukjang muchim* 438
*baechu doenjang guk* 467
*baechu geotjeori* 62
*baechu jeon* 232
*baechu kimchi* 60
*baechu kimchi* (Kwang Hee Park) 444
Baegyangsa Temple 472
*baek kimchi* 64
*baek kimchi* (Kwang Hee Park) 445
*baengeopo gochujang gui* 267
*baesuk* 412
*baetduri* 257
*bajirak juksun deulkkae muchim* 190
*bajirak kalguksu* 378
bamboo shoots 166, 190
  bamboo shoot & fermented soybean stew 437
  bamboo shoot & perilla seed *namul* 166
  bamboo shoot *sotbap* 138
  clams, bamboo shoot, & perilla seed *muchim* 190
*banchan* 12, 14, 15, 16, 18–19, 20, 91, 150–421, 478
*banga* 430
*bangsang* 27
*bap* 18–19, 27, 28, 30, 32, 90–149, 466, 478
  acorn jelly *bap* 122
  barley *bap* 95
  *bibimbap* 96–111
  five-grain rice 94
  green pea *bap* 94
  history of Korean food 14, 15, 16
  Korean scorched *bap* 92
  lotus leaf *bap* 95
*bapsang* 27–9
  Korean grill *bapsang* 30
barley 32
  barley *bap* 95
  thick *doenjang* barley *bibimbap* 107
bean sprout *namul* 160
  Tongyeong-style *bibimbap* 99

bean sprouts
  bean sprout *guk* 320
  bean sprout *gukbap* 119
  bean sprout *namul* 160
  bean sprout *sotbap* 137
  dried pollock *gukbap* 120
  kimchi & bean sprout *guk* 322
  kimchi & bean sprout *juk* 397
  ray with bean sprout *jjim* 300
beans 32–3
  lotus leaf *bap* 95
  peanuts & beans *jorim* 281
  red bean *juk* 399
  red bean shaved ice 414
  rockfish & bean *jorim* 470
  *see also* black beans; red beans
beef 198, 446, 448
  beef & radish *guk* 324
  beef & seaweed *guk* 322
  beef bone *tang* 334
  beef broth 315
  beef *jangjorim* 282
  beef *jeon* 238
  beef short rib *tang* 335
  beef short ribs *jorim* 284
  beef-stuffed pepper *jeon* 240
  beef *suyuk* 218
  *bibimbap* 97
  brisket & chive *muchim* 197
  *bulgogi deopbap* 143
  cabbage & beef *gukbap* 125
  cooked vegetable *ssam* 432
  cuts 259
  Diamond Cutting Technique 446–8
  *doenjang* eggplant *jjim* 298
  dumpling *jeongol* 362
  Eonyang-style *bulgogi* 275
  fish *mandu* 390
  *galbi* 268, 446–8
  *ganjang* stir-fried *tteok* 406
  Gwangyang-style *bulgogi* 272
  Hamheung-style spicy *bibimguksu* 368
  hangover *gukbap* 122
  hot stone *bibimbap* 111
  Jeonju-style *bibimbap* 98
  Jinju-style *bibimbap* 100
  *jorim* 276
  Kaesong-style square *mandu* 462
  Korean batter-fried meat patties 241
  Korean short rib patties *gui* 270
  LA short rib *gui* 269
  ox bone *tang* 335
  perilla *jeon* 237
  Pyeongyang-style beef *jeongol* 357
  *pyeonsu mandu* 391
  Pyongyang-style cold buckwheat *guksu* 373
  Pyongyang-style cold buckwheat noodles 461
  *pyunyuk* 216
  raw beef *bibimbap* 104

raw beef *muchim* 198
rice cake soup 408
Seoul-style *bulgogi* 271, 274
short ribs 268–70, 284, 446–8
snowflake *bulgogi* 451
snowflake marinated short rib 450
stir-fried beef & cucumber 257
stir-fried *gochujang* 51
stir-fried *gochujang* & lettuce *ssam* 210
beef bones
  beef bone *tang* 334
  ox bone *tang* 335
beef broth 326
  Busan-style cold wheat *guksu* 376
  hangover *gukbap* 122
  Kaesong *bossam* kimchi 460
  kimchi pork belly *jorim* 290
  Korean blood sausage *gukbap* 124
  Pyeongyang-style beef *jeongol* 357
  *pyeonsu mandu* 391
  rice cake soup 408
  seafood & soft tofu *jjigae* 352
  small intestines *jeongol* 358
beef intestines
  beef bone *tang* 334
  small intestines *jeongol* 358
beef stomach
  beef bone *tang* 334
  small intestines *jeongol* 358
beef *suyuk* 218
  Pyeongyang-style beef *jeongol* 357
beef tongue: Pyeongyang-style beef *jeongol* 357
bellflower root 34, 170
bellflower root *namul* 170
  Andong-style *bibimbap* 99
beltfish 37
*beonggeogi* 356
*beoseot* 35
*beoseot baechu jeongol* 361
*beoseot bibimbap* 106
*beoseot kalguksu* 377
*beoseot sukju deopbap* 149
beverages
  azalea punch 456
  *eumcheongryu* 411
  poached Asian pear 412
  sweet cinnamon tea 420
  sweet rice punch 420
  *yuja* punch 418
*beyongsi mandu* 386
*bibim jjolmyeon* 382
*bibim kimchi* 23
*bibimbap* 28, 96–111
  Andong-style *bibimbap* 99
  assorted sea vegetable *bibimbap* 108
  *bibimbap* 97
  cockle *bibimbap* 110
  hot stone *bibimbap* 111
  Jeju sea urchin *bibimbap* 100

Jeonju-style *bibimbap* 98
Jinju-style *bibimbap* 100
marinated crab *bibimbap* 109
mushroom *bibimbap* 106
raw beef *bibimbap* 104
raw fish *bibimbap* 102
thick *doenjang* barley *bibimbap* 107
Tongyeong-style *bibimbap* 99
*bibimguksu* 366
  *ganjang* & perilla oil *bibimguksu* 370
  Hamheung-style spicy *bibimguksu* 368
  spicy *bibimguksu* 366
  zucchini *bibimguksu* 370
*bidan-juk* 395
black beans
  black bean sauce *deopbap* 147
  five-grain rice 94
  lotus leaf *bap* 95
  peanuts & beans *jorim* 281
blood sausage, Korean 222
blue crab: spicy blue crab *tang* 344
*bokkeum* 250–7
  Chuncheon-style chicken stir-fry 256
  *ganjang bokkeum* base 250
  garlic scape & dried shrimp *bokkeum* 252
  *gochujang bokkeum* base 250
  Korean zucchini *bokkeum* 257
  roasted seaweed flakes 254
  shishito & anchovy *bokkeum* 254
  spicy pork *bokkeum* 251
  stir-fried beef & cucumber 257
  stir-fried vegetables & glass noodles 255
*bokkeumbap* 126–9
  egg & mushroom fried rice 128
  kimchi fried rice 127
  vegetable fried rice 129
bonnet bellflower root *gui* 267
*bori* 32
*bori saeu ugeoji doenjang guk* 327
*boribap* 95
brisket & chive *muchim* 197
broths 26
  agar jelly in cold soybean broth 228
  anchovy broth 314
  beef broth 315
  chicken stock 313
  pork bone broth 314
  raw fish in cold broth 204
  Seoul-style *bulgogi* 271, 274
  soybean cold broth 315
  vegetable broth 313
  *yuksu* 312–15, 442
*buchimgae* 230, 245–9
  kimchi *buchimgae* 246
  mung bean *buchimgae* 248
  shrimp & chive *buchimgae* 246

tips for making 245
*buchu* 34
*buchu gul jeon* 244
*buchu memil jeon* 231
*buchu mu jeon* 231
buckwheat 466
buckwheat flour: garlic chive & buckwheat *jeon* 231
buckwheat jelly *muchim* 226
buckwheat *muk* 224
buckwheat noodles
  cold buckwheat *guksu* with *hwe* 372
  Gangwondo-style buckwheat *guksu* 383
  Pyongyang-style cold buckwheat *guksu* 373
  Pyongyang-style cold buckwheat noodles 461
Buddhism 15, 472
*bugak* 19, 20, 424
  *gim bugak* 426
  perilla *bugak* 427
  potato *bugak* 428
*bulgogi* 258, 259, 271–5
  Eonyang-style *bulgogi* 275
  Gwangyang-style *bulgogi* 272
  Seoul-style *bulgogi* 271, 274
  snowflake *bulgogi* 451
*bulgogi deopbap* 143
Busan 242, 266
*Busan milmyeon* 376
Busan-style cold wheat *guksu* 376
butterbur leaves 209
Buyeo 14, 15
Byeok-je Galbi 446, 450, 451

C
cabbage 178, 209, 298, 327
  assorted sea vegetable *bibimbap* 108
  baby jumbo shrimp & napa cabbage *doenjang guk* 327
  black bean sauce *deopbap* 147
  cabbage & beef *gukbap* 125
  cabbage kimchi 62
  Chuncheon-style chicken stir-fry 256
  *doenjang* napa cabbage *namul* 178
  dumpling *jeongol* 362
  flat *mandu* 393
  fresh napa cabbage kimchi 62
  freshwater fish stew *guksu* 381
  Gangwondo-style buckwheat *guksu* 383
  Kaesong *bossam* kimchi 460
  kimchi pork belly *jorim* 290
  Korean blood sausage 222
  mushroom & cabbage *jeongol* 361
  napa cabbage 33, 56, 440, 467
  napa cabbage & *doenjang guk* 467

napa cabbage & fermented soybean *muchim* 438
napa cabbage *jeon* 232
napa cabbage kimchi 60
napa cabbage kimchi (Kwang Hee Park) 444
napa cabbage with chiles *jjim* 298
raw fish in cold broth 204
small intestines *jeongol* 358
spicy chewy cold *guksu* 382
squash leaf & cabbage *ssambap* 114
vegan *jang* kimchi 73
water kimchi 66
white kimchi 64
white kimchi (Kwang Hee Park) 445
young cabbage & anchovy *doenjang jorim* 280
carrots
  Andong chicken *jorim* 288
  *bibimbap* 97
  cold chicken *guk* 332
  *gim*-wrapped rice 131
  *gochujang* chicken *jorim* 286
  Jeonju-style *bibimbap* 98
  Korean-style curry rice 148
  spicy chewy cold *guksu* 382
  steamed vegetables with tofu *jang* 474
  stir-fried vegetables & glass noodles 255
  tuna *gimbap* 133
cauliflower *jangajji* 82
ceramics 476–8
*chadolbagi* 197
*chadolbagi buchu muchim* 197
*chaeso bokkeumbap* 129
*chaesu* 313
*cham gireum* 38
*cham namul* 164
*chamchi gimbap* 133
*chamkkae* 39
*chapssal* 32
chard leaves: cooked vegetable *ssam* 432
*cheonggukjang* (fermented soybeans) 437
  bamboo shoot & fermented soybean stew 437
  napa cabbage & fermented soybean *muchim* 438
*cheongjang* 45
*cheongpo muk* 228
*cheongpo muk* & *minari muchim* 228
Cheongyang chiles
  littleneck clam *kalguksu* 378
  radish & green chili kimchi 71
  radish & yellow pepper kimchi 70
  small intestines *jeongol* 358
  stuffed peppers *twigim* 306
  thick *doenjang jjigae* 348
  tofu *jeongol* 360
*cheongyang gochu baechu jjim* 298
Cheonjinam 472

Index

chestnuts
  herbal chicken *tang* 336
  Kaesong *bossam* kimchi 460
  sweet rice with nuts & jujubes 416
chicken
  Andong chicken *jorim* 288
  chicken *juk* 400
  chicken mustard *muchim* 200
  chicken *sotbap* 141
  chicken stock 313
  chicken wing *jorim* 285
  Chuncheon-style chicken stir-fry 256
  cold chicken *guk* 332
  *ganjang*-marinated chicken *gui* 264
  *gochujang* chicken *jorim* 286
  *gochujang*-marinated chicken *gui* 264
  herbal chicken *tang* 336
  Korean chicken *tang* 338
  Korean fried chicken 303
  sweet and spicy Korean fried chicken 304
chilies 34, 56, 440
  beef-stuffed pepper *jeon* 240
  brisket & chive *muchim* 197
  green chili pepper *jangajji* 81
  Korean chili flakes/powder 38
  littleneck clam *kalguksu* 378
  mackerel *jorim* 292
  napa cabbage with chiles *jjim* 298
  pomfret & Korean zucchini *jorim* 294
  radish & green chili kimchi 71
  radish & yellow pepper kimchi 70
  small intestines *jeongol* 358
  stuffed peppers *twigim* 306
  thick *doenjang* barley *bibimbap* 107
  thick *doenjang jjigae* 348
  tofu *jeongol* 360
  water kimchi 66
  young cabbage & anchovy *doenjang jorim* 280
  young summer radish kimchi 67
  *see also* Cheongyang chiles
chives
  brisket & chive *muchim* 197
  enoki & chive *namul* 183
  flat *mandu* 393
  shrimp & chive *buchimgae* 246
Cho, Hee Sook 423, 424–9
*cho-ganjang* 216
*cho-gochujang* (vinegared *gochujang*) 51, 214
  *cho-gochujang* & fresh *miyeok ssam* 214
  *cho-gochujang* & *saeng miyeok ssam* 214
  goat *suyuk* 221

parboiled octopus *hwe* 207
raw fish in cold broth 204
seasoned *hwe* 206
squid *hwe* 206
webfoot octopus & minari *hwe* 207
*chogye naeng-guk* 332
*chojang* sauce: raw fish *bibimbap* 102
*chomuchim*, long-arm octopus & zucchini 196
*chopi* 39
chrysanthemum greens 165
  chrysanthemum *namul* 165
  seafood *tang* 343
  spicy cod *tang* 342
  spring vegetable *twigim* 308
*Chuncheon dak galbi* 256
Chuncheon-style chicken stir-fry 256
Chungcheong-do 24
Chungmu 132
Chungmu *gimbap* 132
cilantro (coriander) relish 479
cinnamon
  sweet cinnamon tea 420
  sweet Korean pancakes 412
  traditional Korean donuts 418
clams 38, 190
  clams, bamboo shoot, & perilla seed *muchim* 190
  *gim* & clam *muchim* 190
  littleneck clam *kalguksu* 378
  seafood & soft tofu *jjigae* 352
  seafood *tang* 343
clear cod *tang* 340
climate 20, 22
cockles 188
  cockle *bibimbap* 110
  cockles & wild Korean chive *muchim* 188
cod 37
  clear cod *tang* 340
  fish *jeon* 244
  spicy cod *tang* 342
cod roe & tofu *jjigae* 350
communal tabletop grilling 259
Confucianism 23, 96
cookies, Kaesong honey 414
corn kernels: Gangwondo-style tadpole-shaped *guksu* 380
cow blood: hangover *gukbap* 122
cow's trotters: ox bone *tang* 335
crab
  *ganjang*-marinated crab 86
  Korean blue crab 37
  marinated crab *bibimbap* 109
  seafood *tang* 343
  spicy blue crab *tang* 344
crispy pork *twigim* 308
croaker: fish *mandu* 390
cucumber 34, 173
  acorn jelly *muchim* 225
  agar jelly in cold soybean broth 228

Busan-style cold wheat *guksu* 376
chicken mustard *muchim* 200
chilled kimchi & acorn jelly soup 225
cold buckwheat *guksu* with *hwe* 372
cold chicken *guk* 332
cold cucumber & seaweed *guk* 330
cold kimchi *guksu* 374
cold soybean *guksu* 374
cucumber *jangajji* 80
cucumber *saengchae* 173
cucumber water kimchi 76
Hamheung-style spicy *bibimguksu* 368
overripe cucumber *namul* 173
Pyongyang-style cold buckwheat *guksu* 373
Pyongyang-style cold buckwheat noodles 461
raw fish *bibimbap* 102
raw fish in cold broth 204
salt-pickled cucumbers 83
seasoned *hwe* 206
seasoned skate *hwe* 203
seaweed & squid *saengchae* 185
spicy *bibimguksu* 366
spicy chewy cold *guksu* 382
stir-fried beef & cucumber 257
stuffed cucumber kimchi 74
tuna *gimbap* 133
curry: Korean-style curry rice 148

D
*daechu* 36
*daegu* 37
*daegu maeuntang* 342
*daepa* (Korean scallion) 33
*dak gomtang* 338
*dak juk* 400
*dak-nalgae jorim* 285
*dak twigim* 303
*dak yuksu* 313
*dakbokkeumtang* 286
*dakgogi gyeoja muchim* 200
*dalgyal bansuk jangjorim* 278
*dalgyal gamja guk* 317
Damyang 436
*danhobak juk* 398
*danmuji* (yellow pickled radish)
  egg *gimbap* 134
  *gim*-wrapped rice 131
  tuna *gimbap* 133
*dasima* 20, 36, 313
  anchovy broth 314
  beef broth 315
  *dasima konjac jorim* 278
  *dasima ssambap* 113
  deep fried *dasima* 426
  vegetable broth 313
*dasima twigak* 426
*dawan* 476
daylilies 170
  daylily *namul* 170
*deodeok* 34–5, 184, 267
  bonnet bellflower root *gui* 267

*deodeok* pine nut *saengchae* 184
*deodeok gui* 267
*deodeok jat saengchae* 184
*deopbap* 142–9
  black bean sauce *deopbap* 147
  *bulgogi deopbap* 143
  *doenjang* pork belly *deopbap* 145
  Korean-style curry rice 148
  mushroom & mung bean sprout *deopbap* 149
  spicy pork *deopbap* 144
  spicy squid *deopbap* 146
desserts (*husik*) 410–21
*deul gireum* 38
*deulkkae beoseot sotbap* 140
Diamond Cutting Technique 446–8
*doenjang* (fermented soybean paste) 19, 25, 44, 46, 50, 436, 464–6
  anchovy *doenjang* perilla *jjim* 300
  baby jumbo shrimp & napa cabbage *doenjang guk* 327
  *doenjang* eggplant *jjim* 298
  *doenjang jjigae* 346, 347
  *doenjang*-marinated pork *gui* 260
  *doenjang* napa cabbage *namul* 178
  *doenjang* pork belly *deopbap* 145
  *doenjang* spinach *juk* 398
  fresh loach tang 345
  fried lotus root *doenjang muchim* 187
  goat *suyuk* 221
  *gui* dishes 258
  Korean shepherd's purse *namul* 162
  napa cabbage & *doenjang guk* 467
  pork head *pyunyuk* 217
  radish top *doenjang namul* 182
  river snail *doenjang* & squash leaf *ssam* 212
  savory *doenjang muchim* 186
  thick *doenjang* barley *bibimbap* 107
  seaweed & tofu *doenjang guk* 317
  shishito *doenjang muchim* 187
  spinach *doenjang guk* 318
  *ssamjang* 52, 209
  *ssamjang* with nuts 53
  thick *doenjang* barley *bibimbap* 107
  thick *doenjang jjigae* 348
  young cabbage & anchovy *doenjang jorim* 280
*doenjang baechu namul* 178
*doenjang gaji jjim* 298
*doenjang jjigae* 346, 347
  thick *doenjang jjigae* 348
*doenjang samgyup deopbap* 145
*doenjang sigeumchi juk* 398

484 Index

*doenjang yangnyeom*
 *dwaeji gui* 260
*dol namul* 172
*dolsot* 111, 136
*dolsot bibimbap* 111
*dongchimi* broth:
 Ganwondo-style buck-
 wheat *guksu* 383
*dongchimi guksu* 312
Donghwasa Temple, Mount
 Palgongsan 472
*dongji* 468
 napa cabbage flower
 *muchim* 468
*dongji kimchi* 468
*dongji namul muchim* 468
*Dongui Bogam* 394
donuts, traditional Korean
 418
*doraji* 34, 170
*doraji namul* 170
*dotori muk gui* 479
*dotori muk muchim* 225
*dotori mukbap* 122
*dubu jang* 474
*dubu jeongol* 360
*dubu jorim* 277
*dubujang chaeso jjim* 474
duck
 *gochujang*-marinated
 duck *gui* 266
 Janganyo duck 480
dumplings (*mandu*) 386–93
 dumpling *jeongol* 362
 fish *mandu* 390
 flat *mandu* 393
 Kaesong-style square
 *mandu* 462
 meat & tofu *mandu* 387
 *pyeonsu mandu* 391
 rolled *mandu* 392
*dwaeji chapsal twigim* 308
*dwaeji galbi* 260
*dwaeji gamja tang* 339
*dwaeji meori pyunyuk* 217
*dwaeji sagol yuksu* 314
*dwaeji suyuk* 218

E
eating like a Korean 30–31
eggplant (aubergine) 174
 cold eggplant *guk* 328
 *doenjang* eggplant *jjim*
 298
 steamed eggplant *namul*
 174
 stir-fried eggplant *namul*
 174
eggs 317
 beef *jeon* 238
 Busan-style cold wheat
 *guksu* 376
 cold kimchi *guksu* 374
 cold soybean *guksu* 374
 egg & mushroom fried rice
 128
 egg & potato *guk* 317
 egg *gimbap* 134
 fish *jeon* 244
 5-minute egg *jjim* 297
 garlic chive & oyster *jeon*
 244
 Hamheung-style spicy
 *bibimguksu* 368
 hot stone *bibimbap* 111
 Jeonju-style *bibimbap* 98
 kimchi fried rice 127
 Korean batter-fried meat
 patties 241

marinated crab *bibimbap*
 109
mushroom *bibimbap* 106
pine nut & king trumpet
 mushroom *jeon* 236
Pyeongyang-style beef
 *jeongol* 357
Pyongyang-style cold
 buckwheat *guksu* 373
raw beef *bibimbap* 104
rice cake soup 408
rolled *mandu* 392
seafood & scallion *jeon*
 242
soft-boiled egg *jangjorim*
 278
spicy *bibimguksu* 366
spicy chewy cold *guksu*
 382
enoki mushrooms 35, 183
 enoki & chive *namul* 183
 mushroom & cabbage
 *jeongol* 361
 mushroom *kalguksu* 377
 Seoul-style *bulgogi* 271,
 274
 spicy blue crab *tang* 344
*eo-mandu* 390
*eobok jaengban* 357
*eolgari myeolchi doenjang*
 *jorim* 280
Eonyang 275
 Eonyang-style *bulgogi*
 275
*eotangguksu* 381
*eumcheongryu* 411

F
fermentation 11–12, 14, 20,
 42–89
 *jangajji* 78–83
 *jeotgal* 84–9
 kimchi 54–77
fiddlehead fern 35
 dried fiddlehead *namul*
 168
 fresh fiddlehead *namul*
 168
 mung bean *buchimgae*
 248
fiddlehead *namul* 168
 Andong-style *bibimbap*
 99
 Jeonju-style *bibimbap* 98
 Jinju-style *bibimbap* 100
fish 28, 202, 442, 466
 aged kimchi *ssambap* 117
 anchovies 38
 anchovy broth 314
 anchovy *doenjang* perilla
 *jjim* 300
 assorted *hwe* 204
 beltfish 37
 clear cod *tang* 340
 cod 37
 dried pollock *gukbap* 120
 fermented flounder 89
 fish *hwe bapsang* 31
 fish *jeon* 244
 fish *mandu* 390
 freshwater fish stew
 *guksu* 381
 *ganjang*-marinated
 salmon 88
 *gochujang* whitebait *gui*
 267
 horsehead tilefish &
 radish *guk* 324

*jorim* 276
Korean rice balls 135
Korean seerfish 37
lettuce *ssambap* 116
mackerel 37
mackerel *gui* 266
mackerel *jorim* 292
napa cabbage kimchi 444
pearl-spot chromis *jeot*
 470
pollock 36–7, 194
pollock *guk* 326
pollock *hwe muchim* 194
pomfret & Korean zucchini
 *jorim* 294
radish top *doenjang*
 *namul* 182
raw fish *bibimbap* 102
raw fish in cold broth 204
ray with bean sprout *jjim*
 300
regional food 22, 23, 24
rockfish & bean *jorim* 470
salted anchovies 85
seasoned *hwe* 206
seasoned semi-dried
 pollock *twigim* 310
seasoned skate *hwe* 203
shishito & anchovy
 *bokkeum* 254
spicy cod *tang* 342
spicy monkfish *jorim* 295
tuna *gimbap* 133
young cabbage & anchovy
 *doenjang jorim* 280
fish cakes
 egg *gimbap* 134
 *gochujang* stir-fried *tteok*
 405
fish sauce 39
five-grain rice 94
5-minute egg *jjim* 297
flatfish 202
flounder 202
 fermented flounder 89
 raw fish *bibimbap* 102
flying fish roe: assorted sea
 vegetable *bibimbap* 108
fruits 35–6
*fuki* (butterbur) leaves:
 cooked vegetable *ssam*
 432

G
*gajami sikhae* 89
*gaji bokkeum namul* 174
*gaji muchim namul* 174
*gaji naeng-guk* 328
*galbi* 258, 268–70, 446–8
 LA short rib *gui* 269
*galbi tang* 335
*galchi* 37
*gam* 36
*gamasot* 136
*gamgyul* 36
*gamja bugak* 428
*gamja-chae jeon* 234
*gamja jeon* 234
*gamja kkwarigochu jorim*
 281
*gang doenjang bori bibim-*
 *bap* 107
*gang doenjang jjigae* 348
*ganghwe* 207
Gangwon-do 24, 380, 383,
 440
*Gangwondo makguksu* 383
*Gangwondo olchaengi*
 *guksu* 380

*ganjang* (Korean soy sauce)
 19, 44, 45, 50, 436, 448
asparagus *jangajji* 82
bamboo shoot *sotbap*
 138
bean sprout *sotbap* 137
cauliflower *jangajji* 82
choosing *ganjang* 46
cucumber *jangajji* 80
*ganjang* & perilla oil
 *bibimguksu* 370
*ganjang bokkeum* base
 250
*ganjang*-marinated
 chicken *gui* 264
*ganjang*-marinated crab
 86
*ganjang*-marinated
 salmon 88
*ganjang*-marinated
 shrimp 88
*ganjang* stir-fried *tteok*
 406
garlic *jangajji* 79
green chili pepper *jangajji*
 81
green tomato *jangajji* 81
Jeju sea urchin *bibimbap*
 100
onion *jangajji* 79
marinated crab *bibimbap*
 109
perilla & mushroom
 *sotbap* 140
perilla *jangajji* 83
pig's feet *jorim* 290
radish *jangajji* 80
rockfish & bean *jorim* 470
snowflake marinated
 short rib 450
vinegar *ganjang muchim*
 186
*ganjang dak gui* 264
*ganjang deulgireum*
 *bibimguksu* 370
*ganjang gejang* 86
*ganjang saeu jang* 88
*ganjang tteokbokki* 406
Gangwondo-style buck-
 wheat *guksu* 383
Gangwondo-style tadpole-
 shaped *guksu* 380
Gapyeong 397
garlic 34
 beef *jangjorim* 282
 beef short rib *tang* 335
 chicken stock 313
 cold chicken *guk* 332
 diced radish kimchi 68
 garlic *jangajji* 79
 herbal chicken *tang* 336
 Korean chicken *tang* 338
 napa cabbage kimchi 60
 napa cabbage kimchi
 (Kwang Hee Park) 444
 oxtail *suyuk* 220
 pig's feet *jorim* 290
 pork *suyuk* 218
 radish & green chili kimchi
 71
 radish water kimchi 72
 vegan *jang* kimchi 73
 white kimchi 64
 white kimchi (Kwang Hee
 Park) 445
 young summer radish
 kimchi 67
garlic chives 34
 fresh loach *tang* 345

Index 485

garlic chive & buckwheat *jeon* 231
garlic chive & Korean radish *jeon* 231
garlic chive & oyster *jeon* 244
meat & tofu *mandu* 387
rolled *mandu* 392
small intestines *jeongol* 358
white soft tofu & oyster *jjigae* 354
garlic scapes 252
  garlic scape & dried shrimp *bokkeum* 252
*gejang bibimbap* 109
*geon gosari namul* 168
*gim* (seaweed) 20, 36, 190, 318, 471
  *chungmu gimbap* 132
  egg *gimbap* 134
  *ganjang* & perilla oil *bibimguksu* 370
  *gim* & clam *muchim* 190
  *gim bugak* 426
  *gim guk* 318
  *gim*-wrapped rice 131
  roasted seaweed flakes 254
  seaweed roll *twigim* 311
  tuna *gimbap* 133
*gim jaban* 254
*gim jogaetsal muchim* 190
*gimbap* 130–5
  *chungmu gimbap* 132
  egg *gimbap* 134
  Korean rice balls 135
  tuna *gimbap* 133
*gimmari twigim* 311
Gimpo 14
ginger 34
  goat *suyuk* 221
  Kaesong honey cookie 414
  napa cabbage kimchi 60
  poached Asian pear 412
  sweet cinnamon tea 420
  sweet rice punch 420
  traditional Korean donuts 418
ginger juice: fried twists 454
ginkgo nuts
  lotus leaf *bap* 95
  pine mushroom *sotbap* 139
ginseng roots: herbal chicken *tang* 336
*gireum tteokbokki* 408
glass noodles
  seaweed roll *twigim* 311
  stir-fried vegetables & glass noodles 255
glossary 40–1
go-*galbi* 266
goat 221
  goat *suyuk* 221
*gochu* 34
*gochu twigim* 306
*gochugaru* (red chili flakes/powder) 38, 43
  brisket & chive *muchim* 197
  cabbage kimchi 62
  Chuncheon-style chicken stir-fry 256
  cold buckwheat *guksu* with *hwe* 372
  diced radish kimchi 68
  dried radish *namul* 182

dumpling *jeongol* 362
fresh napa cabbage kimchi 62
freshwater fish stew *guksu* 381
Gangwondo-style buckwheat *guksu* 383
*gochujang* 50
*gochujang* chicken *jorim* 286
*gochujang* stir-fried *tteok* 405
Hamheung-style spicy *bibimguksu* 368
Kaesong *bossam* kimchi 460
Korean chicken *tang* 338
mushroom *kalguksu* 377
napa cabbage flower kimchi 468
napa cabbage kimchi 60
napa cabbage kimchi (Kwang Hee Park) 444
onion kimchi 77
pollock *hwe muchim* 194
pork back bone *tang* 339
seafood & soft tofu *jjigae* 352
seafood *tang* 343
small intestines *jeongol* 358
spicy blue crab *tang* 344
spicy cod *tang* 342
spicy monkfish *jorim* 295
spicy pork *bokkeum* 251
stonecrop *namul* 172
stuffed cucumber kimchi 74
vegan *jang* kimchi 73
young summer radish kimchi 67
zucchini *bibimguksu* 370
*gochujang* (red chili paste) 19, 25, 30, 44, 47, 50, 96
  bonnet bellflower root *gui* 267
  *cho-gochujang* & *saeng miyeok ssam* 214
  *chojang* sauce 102
  Chuncheon-style chicken stir-fry 256
  daylily *namul* 170
  garlic scape & dried shrimp *bokkeum* 252
  goat *suyuk* 221
  *gochujang bokkeum* base 250
  *gochujang* chicken *jorim* 286
  *gochujang jjigae* 346
  *gochujang*-marinated chicken *gui* 264
  *gochujang*-marinated duck *gui* 266
  *gochujang*-marinated pork *gui* 262
  *gochujang* stir-fried *tteok* 405
  *gochujang* whitebait *gui* 267
  *gui* dishes 258, 259
  Hamheung-style spicy *bibimguksu* 368
  Korean shepherd's purse *namul* 162
  mushroom *kalguksu* 377
  parboiled octopus *hwe* 207
  raw beef *bibimbap* 104

raw fish in cold broth 204
seasoned *hwe* 206
seaweed & squid *saengchae* 185
spicy *bibimguksu* 366
spicy cod *tang* 342
squid *hwe* 206
*ssamjang* 52, 209
*ssamjang* with nuts 53
stir-fried *gochujang* 51
stir-fried *gochujang* & lettuce *ssam* 210
sweet and spicy Korean fried chicken 304
vegan stir-fried *gochujang* 52
vinegar *gochujang muchim* 186
vinegared *gochujang* 51
webfoot octopus & minari *hwe* 207
whelk & minari *muchim* 192
*gochujang dak gui* 264
*gochujang jeyuk gui* 262
*gochujang tteokbokki* 405
*godeungeo* 37
*godeungeo gui* 266
*godeungeo jorim* 292
*gogi dubu mandu* 387
Goguryeo 15
Goheung region 418
*golbaengi* 192
*golbaengi minari muchim* 192
*gomchwi* 209
  cooked vegetable *ssam* 432
*gomtang* 334
*gondeure* 172
*gondeure namul* 172
*gopchang jeongol* 358
Gordinier, Jeff 472
Goryeo Dawan 476
Goryeo dynasty (918–1392) 15, 16, 364, 458
*gosari* 35, 168
  dried fiddlehead *namul* 168
  fresh fiddlehead *namul* 168
  mung bean *buchimgae* 248
grain syrup 39
grains 14–15, 32–3, 55, 466
  see also rice
green chili pepper *jangajji* 81
green laver & radish *muchim* 188
green pea bap 94
green tomato *jangajji* 81
grills, specialized 259
*gui* 27, 258–75
  bonnet bellflower root *gui* 267
  *bulgogi* 271–5
  characteristics of Korea's grilled meat culture 259
  *doenjang*-marinated pork *gui* 260
  Eonyang-style *bulgogi* 275
  *galbi* 268–70
  *ganjang*-marinated chicken *gui* 264
  *gochujang*-marinated chicken *gui* 264
  *gochujang*-marinated duck *gui* 266

*gochujang*-marinated pork *gui* 262
*gochujang* whitebait *gui* 267
Gwangyang-style *bulgogi* 272
Korean short rib patties *gui* 270
LA short rib *gui* 269
mackerel *gui* 266
pork rib *gui* 260
Seoul-style *bulgogi* 271, 274
*guk* 16, 19, 20, 26, 27, 28, 316–33, 466, 478
  baby jumbo shrimp & napa cabbage *doenjang guk* 327
  bean sprout *guk* 320
  beef & radish *guk* 324
  beef & seaweed *guk* 322
  cold chicken *guk* 332
  cold cucumber & seaweed *guk* 330
  cold eggplant *guk* 328
  egg & potato *guk* 317
  *gim guk* 318
  horsehead tilefish & radish *guk* 324
  kimchi & bean sprout *guk* 322
  Korean zucchini jeot *guk* 320
  *maesaengi* oyster *guk* 328
  napa cabbage & *doenjang guk* 467
  pollock *guk* 326
  seaweed & tofu *doenjang guk* 317
  spinach *doenjang guk* 318
  squid & radish *guk* 326
*gukbap* 28, 118–25
  acorn jelly bap 122
  bean sprout *gukbap* 119
  cabbage & beef *gukbap* 125
  dried pollock *gukbap* 120
  hangover *gukbap* 122
  Korean blood sausage *gukbap* 124
*guksu* 364–85
  anchovy broth *guksu* 365
  Busan-style cold wheat *guksu* 376
  cold buckwheat *guksu* with *hwe* 372
  cold kimchi *guksu* 374
  cold soybean *guksu* 374
  freshwater fish stew *guksu* 381
  *ganjang* & perilla oil *bibimguksu* 370
  Gangwondo-style buckwheat *guksu* 383
  Gangwondo-style tadpole-shaped *guksu* 380
  Hamheung-style spicy *bibimguksu* 368
  hand-torn *guksu* 384
  littleneck clam *kalguksu* 378
  mushroom *kalguksu* 377
  Pyongyang-style cold buckwheat *guksu* 373
  spicy *bibimguksu* 366
  spicy chewy cold *guksu* 382
  zucchini *bibimguksu* 370

*gul baek sundubu jjigae* 354
*gul sotbap* 140
*gullim mandu* 392
*gunnamul sotbap* 137
*gwajul* 411, 452
Gwangju region 25
Gwangyang 272
  Gwangyang-style *bulgogi* 272
  *Gwangyang bulgogi* 272
*gyeban* 141
*gyeoja* 39
Gyeonggi-do 23–4, 320, 378
Gyeongnam province 266
Gyeongsang-do 23, 25–6
*gyeran beoseot bokkeumbap* 128
*gyeran gimbap* 134
*gyeran jjim* 297
*gyungwaryu ssamjang* 53

H
*haecho bibimbap* 108
*haejang gukbap* 122
*haemul pajeon* 242
*haemul sundubu jjigae* 352
*haemul tang* 343
halibut: assorted *hwe* 204
ham: *gim*-wrapped rice 131
Hamheung bibim naengmyeon 368
Hamheung naengmyeon
  buckwheat noodles
  cold buckwheat *guksu* with *hwe* 372
  Hamheung-style spicy *bibimguksu* 368
*hangari* 434
hangover *gukbap* 122
*hangwa* 452
*hansik* 11, 18–21, 430, 452, 476
Hansik Gongbang 424
*hanwoo* 446
herbal chicken *tang* 336
*hinssal* 32
history of Korean cuisine 14–17
*hobakip* & *yangbaecchu* 114
honey 38–9
  fried twists 454
  Kaesong honey cookie 414
  steamed pine nut cake 457
  traditional Korean donuts 418
*hongeo hwe muchim* 203
horse mackerel: assorted *hwe* 204
horsehead tilefish & radish *guk* 324
hot mustard 39
hot stone *bibimbap* 111
hotpots 19
  dumpling *jeongol* 362
  *jeongol* 356–63
  mushroom & cabbage *jeongol* 361
  Pyeongyang-style beef *jeongol* 357
  small intestines *jeongol* 358
  tofu *jeongol* 360
*hotteok* 412
Huh, Jung Yoo 423, 458–63
*husik* 410–21
*hwa jeon* 456

*hwachae* 411, 452, 456
*hwangtae gukbap* 120
*hwangtae mu guk* 326
*hwe* 27, 31, 202–7, 214
  assorted *hwe* 204
  cold buckwheat *guksu* with *hwe* 372
  parboiled octopus *hwe* 207
  raw fish in cold broth 204
  seasoned *hwe* 206
  seasoned skate *hwe* 203
  squid *hwe* 206
  webfoot octopus & *minari hwe* 207
*hwe bibimbap* 102
*hwe muchim* 206
*hwe naengmyeon* 372
Hyangchon 16
Hyangsi 16
*hyunmi* 32

I
ingredients 32–9
intestines: small intestines *jeongol* 358

J
*jang* 11, 12, 20, 43, 44, 49, 55, 78, 434–6
  choosing *jang* ingredients 48
  history of Korean cuisine 14, 15
  *namul* and 154
  tofu *jang* 474
  types of 45
  see also *doenjang*; *ganjang*, etc
*jangajji* 11, 19, 23, 25, 30, 43, 78–83, 440
  asparagus *jangajji* 82
  cauliflower *jangajji* 82
  cucumber *jangajji* 80
  garlic *jangajji* 79
  green chili pepper *jangajji* 81
  green tomato *jangajji* 81
  onion *jangajji* 79
  perilla *jangajji* 83
  radish *jangajji* 80
Janganyo ceramics studio 476, 479
Janganyo duck 480
*jangjori*, beef 282
*japchae*: stir-fried vegetables & glass noodles 255
*jari-jeot* 470
*jat juk* 397
*jat saesongyi beoseot jeon* 236
*jat seolgi* 457
Jeju Island 26, 216, 324, 442, 464–7, 470–1
Jeju Local Food Conservation Research Institute 464
Jeju sea urchin *bibimbap* 100
Jeju seongge *bibimbap* 100
Jeolla-do 23, 25
Jeollanam-do 110, 238
*jeon* 27, 230–44
  beef *jeon* 238
  beef-stuffed pepper *jeon* 240
  fish *jeon* 244
  garlic chive & buckwheat *jeon* 231

garlic chive & Korean radish *jeon* 231
garlic chive & oyster *jeon* 244
julienned potato *jeon* 234
kimchi *buchimgae* 246
Korean batter-fried meat patties 241
Korean zucchini *jeon* 236
napa cabbage *jeon* 232
perilla *jeon* 237
pine nut & king trumpet mushroom *jeon* 236
potato *jeon* 234
seafood & scallion *jeon* 242
*jeon-rip-tu* 356
*jeonbok juk* 402
*jeonggwa* 452
*jeongol* 19, 356–63
  dumpling *jeongol* 362
  mushroom & cabbage *jeongol* 361
  Pyeongyang-style beef *jeongol* 357
  small intestines *jeongol* 358
  tofu *jeongol* 360
*jeonju bibimbap* 98
*jeonju*-style *bibimbap* 98
*jeonyueo* 244
*jeotgal* 19, 23, 27, 56, 84–9, 442
  fermented flounder 89
  *ganjang*-marinated crab 86
  *ganjang*-marinated salmon 88
  *ganjang*-marinated shrimp 88
  salted anchovies 85
  salted shrimp 86
  salted squid 85
*jesatbap* 96
*jeungpyeon* 416, 452
*jeyuk bokkeum* 251
*jeyuk deopbap* 144
*jindallae hwachae* 456
*jinjang* (Korean dark soy sauce) 45
  cockle *bibimbap* 110
  snowflake *bulgogi* 451
Jinju *bibimbap* 100
Jinju-style *bibimbap* 100
*jinmichae muchim* 194
*jjajangbap* 147
*jjigae* 19, 27, 31, 54, 346–55, 464, 466
  bamboo shoot & fermented soybean stew 437
  cod roe & tofu *jjigae* 350
  *doenjang jjigae* 346, 347
  freshwater fish stew *guksu* 381
  kimchi & ground soybean *jjigae* 350
  kimchi *jjigae* 348
  seafood & soft tofu *jjigae* 352
  thick *doenjang jjigae* 348
  white soft tofu & oyster *jjigae* 354
*jjim* 54, 296–301
  anchovy *doenjang* perilla *jjim* 300
  *doenjang* eggplant *jjim* 298
  5-minute egg *jjim* 297
  napa cabbage with chiles *jjim* 298

pork belly & mung bean sprout *jjim* 297
ray with bean sprout *jjim* 300
*jjokpa* 34
*jjolmyeon* 382
  spicy chewy cold *guksu* 382
*jjukkumi minari ganghwe* 207
*jo* 32
*jocheong* 39
*jogae* 38
*jokbal*: pig's feet *jorim* 290
jom beans: rockfish & bean *jorim* 470
*jorim* 27, 276–95
  Andong chicken *jorim* 288
  beef *jangjorim* 282
  beef short ribs *jorim* 284
  chicken wing *jorim* 285
  *gochujang* chicken *jorim* 286
  kimchi pork belly *jorim* 290
  lotus root *jorim* 282
  mackerel *jorim* 292
  peanuts & beans *jorim* 281
  pig's feet *jorim* 290
  pomfret & Korean zucchini *jorim* 294
  potato & shishito *jorim* 281
  rockfish & bean *jorim* 470
  soft-boiled egg *jangjorim* 278
  spicy monkfish *jorim* 295
  tofu *jorim* 277
  young cabbage & anchovy *doenjang jorim* 280
Joseon dynasty (1392–1897) 16, 23, 96, 230, 356, 430
*jujubes* (Chinese red dates) 36
  herbal chicken *tang* 336
  Kaesong *bossam* kimchi 460
  lotus leaf *bap* 95
  raised rice cake 416
  sweet rice with nuts & *jujubes* 416
*juk* 20, 25, 26, 394–403
  abalone *juk* 402
  basic *juk* 395
  chicken *juk* 400
  cooking *juk* 396
  *doenjang* spinach *juk* 398
  kimchi & bean sprout *juk* 397
  mung bean *juk* 399
  pine nut *juk* 397
  red bean *juk* 399
  sweet pumpkin *juk* 398
  types of 395
*juksun cheonggukjang jjigae* 437
*juksun deulkkae namul* 166
*juksun sotbap* 138
jumbo shrimp: baby jumbo shrimp & napa cabbage *doenjang guk* 327
*jumeok-bap* 135

K
kabocha squash: sweet pumpkin *juk* 398
*Kaeseong juak* 418
Kaesong 418, 458
Kaesong *bossam* kimchi 460

Index

487

Kaesong honey cookie 414
*Kaesong pyeonsu* 462
Kaesong-style square *mandu* 462
*Kaesong yakgwa* 414
*kalguksu* noodles 377, 378
   littleneck clam *kalguksu* 378
   freshwater fish stew *guksu* 381
   mushroom *kalguksu* 377
Kang, In-hee 430
Ki, Soon Do 423, 434–9
Kim, Ji Soon 423, 464–71
kimchi 11–12, 18, 19, 27, 30, 31, 43, 54–77, 327, 348, 440, 466
   acorn jelly *bap* 122
   aged kimchi *ssam* 215
   aged kimchi *ssambap* 117
   cabbage kimchi 62
   chilled kimchi & acorn jelly soup 225
   *chungmu gimbap* 132
   cold kimchi *guksu* 374
   cucumber water kimchi 76
   diced radish kimchi 68
   fresh napa cabbage kimchi 62
   history of 55–7
   *jeotgal* and 84
   Kaesong *bossam* kimchi 460
   kimchi & bean sprout *guk* 322
   kimchi & bean sprout *juk* 397
   kimchi & ground soybean *jjigae* 350
   kimchi *buchimgae* 246
   kimchi fried rice 127
   kimchi *jjigae* 348
   kimchi *mandu* 388
   kimchi pork belly *jorim* 290
   master steps for preparing 58–9
   mung bean *buchimgae* 248
   napa cabbage flower kimchi 468
   napa cabbage kimchi 54, 60
   napa cabbage kimchi (Kwang Hee Park) 444
   onion kimchi 77
   radish & green chili kimchi 71
   radish & yellow pepper kimchi 70
   radish water kimchi 72
   regional food 20, 23
   "seasoning culture" 56, 57
   spicy *bibimguksu* 366
   stuffed cucumber kimchi 74
   types of 54, 55
   vegan *jang* kimchi 73
   water kimchi 66
   white kimchi 54, 64
   white kimchi (Kwang Hee Park) 445
   young summer radish kimchi 67
*kimchi bokkeumbap* 127
*kimchi guksu* 374
kimchi juice
   chilled kimchi & acorn jelly soup 225

cold kimchi *guksu* 374
*kimchi kongiji jjigae* 350
*kimchi kongnamul guk* 322
*kimchi kongnamul juk* 397
*kimchi muksabal* 225
*kimchi samgyupsal jjim* 290
*kimjang* 54, 216
king oyster mushrooms: mushroom & cabbage *jeongol* 361
king trumpet mushrooms
   mushroom *kalguksu* 377
   pine nut & king trumpet mushroom *jeon* 236
   tofu *jeongol* 360
kingfish 202
Kisoondo Traditional Jang 434
*kkakdugi* 68
*kkaennip* 33
*kkaennip bugak* 427
*kkaennip jangajji* 83
*kkaennip jeon* 237
*kkaennip ssambap* 114
*kkaetsun namul* 178
*kkomak bibimap* 110
*kkomak dallae muchim* 188
*kkotge* 37
*kkotge tang* 344
*kkul* 38–9
*kkwari gochu doenjang muchim* 187
*kkwari gochu* (shishito) peppers 254
   potato & shishito *jorim* 281
   shishito & anchovy *bokkeum* 254
   shishito *doenjang muchim* 187
*kkwari-gochu & myeolchi bokkeum* 254
*kkwari* peppers 187
knife work, *gui* dishes 259
*kodari gangjeong* 310
*kong* 32, 33
*kong biji* (ground soaked soybeans): kimchi & ground soybean *jjigae* 350
*kong gukmul* 315
*kong guksu* 374
*kong namul* 35
*kong namul sotbap* 137
*kongjaban ttangkong jorim* 291
*kongnamul* 160
*kongnamul gaorijjim* 300
*kongnamul guk* 320
*kongnamul gukbap* 119
konjac root: *dasima konjac jorim* 278
Korean batter-fried meat patties 241
Korean blood sausage 222
Korean blood sausage *gukbap* 124
Korean blue crab 37
Korean chicken *tang* 338
Korean cucumber peppers: stuffed peppers *twigim* 306
Korean cuisine, history of 14–17
Korean fried chicken 303
   sweet and spicy Korean fried chicken 304
Korean pear *see* Asian pear

Korean pear juice
   napa cabbage kimchi 60
   stir-fried *gochujang* 51
   vegan *jang* kimchi 73
Korean radish (*mu*) 15, 24, 34, 180, 182, 231, 276, 313
   beef & radish *guk* 324
   beef short rib *tang* 335
   beef short ribs *jorim* 284
   cabbage & beef *gukbap* 125
   clear cod *tang* 340
   cold buckwheat *guksu* with *hwe* 372
   cucumber water kimchi 76
   diced radish kimchi 68
   dried pollock *gukbap* 120
   dried radish *namul* 182
   fermented flounder 89
   garlic chive & Korean radish *jeon* 231
   green laver & radish *muchim* 188
   Hamheung-style spicy *bibimguksu* 368
   horsehead tilefish & radish *guk* 324
   Kaesong *bossam* kimchi 460
   Korean radish *namul* 180
   Korean radish *saengchae* 180
   napa cabbage kimchi 60
   napa cabbage kimchi (Kwang Hee Park) 444
   onion kimchi 77
   oyster *sotbap* 140
   parboiled octopus *hwe* 207
   pollock *guk* 326
   pollock *hwe muchim* 194
   Pyongyang-style cold buckwheat *guksu* 373
   Pyongyang-style cold buckwheat noodles 461
   radish & green chili kimchi 71
   radish & yellow pepper kimchi 70
   radish *jangajji* 80
   radish top *doenjang namul* 182
   radish water kimchi 72
   seafood *tang* 343
   seasoned skate *hwe* 203
   small intestines *jeongol* 358
   spicy blue crab *tang* 344
   spicy cod *tang* 342
   spicy monkfish *jorim* 295
   spinach *doenjang guk* 318
   squid & radish *guk* 326
   steamed vegetables with tofu *jang* 474
   tofu *jeongol* 360
   vegan *jang* kimchi 73
   vegetable broth 313
   water kimchi 66
   white kimchi 64
   white kimchi (Kwang Hee Park) 445
   white soft tofu & oyster *jjigae* 354
   young summer radish kimchi 67
Korean radish *namul* 180
   Andong-style *bibimbap* 99
Korean radish saengchae 180

Jeonju-style *bibimbap* 98
Jinju-style *bibimbap* 100
Korean rice balls 135
Korean scallion (*daepa*) 33
Korean scorched *bap* 92
Korean seerfish 37
Korean shepherd's purse *namul* 162
Korean short rib patties *gui* 270
Korean-style curry rice 148
Korean sweet potato: Chuncheon-style chicken stir-fry 256
Korean thistle *namul* 172
Korean Traditional Food Research Association 430
Korean zucchini (*aehobak*) 34, 176
   anchovy broth *guksu* 365
   cod roe & tofu *jjigae* 350
   *doenjang jjigae* 346, 347
   dried Korean zucchini *namul* 176
   hand-torn *guksu* 384
   Kaesong-style square *mandu* 462
   Korean zucchini *bokkeum* 257
   Korean zucchini *jeon* 236
   Korean zucchini *jeot guk* 320
   Korean zucchini *namul* 176
   littleneck clam *kalguksu* 378
   long-arm octopus & zucchini *chomuchim* 196
   mushroom *kalguksu* 377
   pomfret & Korean zucchini *jorim* 294
   *pyeonsu mandu* 391
   river snail *doenjang* & squash leaf *ssam* 212
   spicy blue crab *tang* 344
   thick *doenjang* barley *bibimbap* 107
   thick *doenjang jjigae* 348
   tofu *jeongol* 360
   zucchini *bibimguksu* 370
Korean zucchini *namul* 176
   Jeonju-style *bibimbap* 98
   Jinju-style *bibimbap* 100
   Tongyeong-style *bibimbap* 99
Kwan, Jeong 423, 472–5
*kyu-a-sang mandu* 386

L
LA *galbi* 269
LA short rib *gui* 269
*Lactobacillus* 48
Lee, Mal Soon 423, 430–3
lettuce 15, 30, 33, 209
   cockle *bibimbap* 110
   Gangwondo-style buckwheat *guksu* 383
   lettuce *ssambap* 116
   raw beef *bibimbap* 104
   raw fish *bibimbap* 102
   spicy *bibimguksu* 366
   stir-fried *gochujang* & lettuce *ssam* 210
Lim Geahwa 476
littleneck clam *kalguksu* 378
loach: fresh loach *tang* 345
long-arm octopus 37, 196
   long-arm octopus & zucchini *chomuchim* 196

seafood *tang* 343
lotus leaf *bap* 95
lotus root 282
    fried lotus root *doenjang muchim* 187
    lotus root *jorim* 282

M
mackerel 37, 292, 466
    mackerel *gui* 266
    mackerel *jorim* 292
*maejak-gwa* 454
*maesaengi* 328
    *maesaengi* oyster *guk* 328
*maesaengi gul guk* 328
*makgeolli* (Korean rice wine) 20
    seasoned skate *hwe* 203
*makguksu*: Gangwondo-style buckwheat *guksu* 383
*malgeun daegu tang* 340
malted barley powder: sweet rice punch 420
malted barley syrup: *gochujang* 50
Mandarin oranges 36
*mandu* 386–93
    fish *mandu* 390
    flat *mandu* 393
    Kaesong-style square *mandu* 462
    kimchi *mandu* 388
    meat & tofu *mandu* 387
    *pyeonsu mandu* 391
    rolled *mandu* 392
*mandu jeongol* 362
*maneul* 34
*maneul jangajji* 79
*maneuljong geon saeu bokkeum* 252
master artisans 422–81
meat 11
    characteristics of Korea's grilled meat culture 259
    *gui* 258–75
    Korean grill *bapsang* 30
    meat & tofu *mandu* 387
    *see also* beef; pork
*meju* 15, 44, 47, 49, 434–6
    *ganjang* & *doenjang* 50
    *gochujang* 50
*memil guksu* (Korean buckwheat noodles): *ganjang* & perilla oil *bibimguksu* 370
*memil muk* (buckwheat jelly): buckwheat jelly *muchim* 226
*memil muk gim muchim* 226
*mepssal* 32
*meyongran* (cod roe) & tofu *jjigae* 350
microorganisms 48
*mieum* 395
Mijuckgamgak 452
millet 32
    fermented flounder 89
    five-grain rice 94
*milmyeon* 376
    Busan-style cold wheat *guksu* 376
*minari* 33
    clear cod *tang* 340
    Kaesong *bossam* kimchi 460
    mung bean jelly *muchim* 228

Pyeongyang-style beef *jeongol* 357
seafood & scallion *jeon* 242
seafood *tang* 343
seasoned skate *hwe* 203
spicy cod *tang* 342
spicy monkfish *jorim* 295
vegan *jang* kimchi 73
water kimchi 66
webfoot octopus & minari *hwe* 207
whelk & *minari muchim* 192
white kimchi 64
*mit-banchan* 23
*miyeok* (wakame) 36, 185, 471
    beef & seaweed *guk* 322
    *cho-gochujang* & fresh *miyeok ssam* 214
    cold cucumber & seaweed *guk* 330
    *miyeok ssambap* 113
    seaweed & squid *saeng-chae* 185
    seaweed & tofu *doenjang guk* 317
    Tongyeong-style *bibimbap* 99
*miyeok dubu doenjang guk* 317
*miyeok ojingeo cho muchim* 192
*miyeok ojingeo saengchae* 185
*miyeok-guk* 322
*mogi beoseot* 35
monkfish: spicy monkfish *jorim* 295
moon jars 476
*mu* (Korean radish) 15, 24, 34, 180, 182, 231, 276, 313
    beef & radish *guk* 324
    beef short rib *tang* 335
    beef short ribs *jorim* 284
    cabbage & beef *gukbap* 125
    clear cod *tang* 340
    cold buckwheat *guksu* with *hwe* 372
    cold chicken *guk* 332
    cucumber water kimchi 76
    diced radish kimchi 68
    dried pollock *gukbap* 120
    fermented flounder 89
    garlic chive & Korean radish *jeon* 231
    green laver & radish *muchim* 188
    Hamheung-style spicy *bibimguksu* 368
    horsehead tilefish & radish *guk* 324
    Kaesong *bossam* kimchi 460
    Korean radish *namul* 180
    Korean radish *saengchae* 180
    napa cabbage kimchi 60
    napa cabbage kimchi (Kwang Hee Park) 444
    onion kimchi 77
    oyster *sotbap* 140
    parboiled octopus *hwe* 207
    pollock *guk* 326
    pollock *hwe muchim* 194
    Pyongyang-style cold buckwheat *guksu* 373

Pyongyang-style cold buckwheat noodles 461
radish & green chili kimchi 71
radish & yellow pepper kimchi 70
radish *jangajji* 80
radish water kimchi 72
seafood *tang* 343
seasoned skate *hwe* 203
small intestines jeongol 358
spicy blue crab *tang* 344
spicy cod *tang* 342
spicy monkfish *jorim* 295
spinach *doenjang guk* 318
squid & radish *guk* 326
steamed vegetables with tofu *jang* 474
tofu *jeongol* 360
vegan *jang* kimchi 73
vegetable broth 313
water kimchi 66
white kimchi 64
white kimchi (Kwang Hee Park) 445
white soft tofu & oyster *jjigae* 354
young summer radish kimchi 67
*mu* & Cheongyang gochu *seokbakji* 71
*mu* & yellow pepper *seokbakji* 70
*mu jangajji* 80
*mu namul* 180
*mu saengchae* 180
*muchim* 186–201, 224
    acorn jelly *muchim* 225
    brisket & chive *muchim* 197
    buckwheat jelly *muchim* 226
    chicken mustard *muchim* 200
    clams, bamboo shoot, & perilla seed *muchim* 190
    cockles & wild Korean chive *muchim* 188
    dried shredded squid *muchim* 194
    fried lotus root *doenjang muchim* 187
    *gim* & clam *muchim* 190
    green laver & radish *muchim* 188
    long-arm octopus & zucchini *chomuchim* 196
    mung bean jelly *muchim* 228
    napa cabbage & fermented soybean *muchim* 438
    napa cabbage flower *muchim* 468
    pollock *hwe muchim* 194
    raw beef *muchim* 198
    savory *doenjang muchim* 186
    seasoned *hwe* 206
    seasoned skate *hwe* 203
    *shishito doenjang muchim* 187
    vinegar *ganjang muchim* 186
    vinegar *gochujang muchim* 186
    vinegared seaweed & squid *muchim* 192

whelk & minari *muchim* 192
*mugeunji* (aged) kimchi 54
aged kimchi *ssambap* 117
*mugeunji ssam* & *suyuk* 215
*mugeunji ssambap* 117
mugwort: acorn jelly *muchim* 225
*muk* 224–9
    acorn jelly *muchim* 225
    agar jelly 226
    agar jelly in cold soybean broth 228
    buckwheat jelly *muchim* 226
    chilled kimchi & acorn jelly soup 225
    mung bean jelly *muchim* 228
*muksabal*: chilled kimchi & acorn jelly soup 225
*mul* 316
*mul hwe*: raw fish in cold broth 204
*mumallaengi* 182
*mumallaengi namul* 182
*muneo* 37
*muneo sukhwe* 207
mung bean jelly
    Jeonju-style *bibimbap* 98
    mung bean jelly *muchim* 228
mung bean sprout *namul* 160
    Jinju-style *bibimbap* 100
mung bean sprouts 35
    fish *mandu* 390
    kimchi *mandu* 388
    meat & tofu *mandu* 387
    mung bean sprout *namul* 160
    mushroom & mung bean sprout *deopbap* 149
    pork belly & mung bean sprout *jjim* 297
    *pyeonsu mandu* 391
    rolled *mandu* 392
    tofu *jeongol* 360
mung beans 33, 248
    mung bean *buchimgae* 248
    mung bean *juk* 399
    mung bean *muk* 224
mushrooms 19, 23, 35, 106, 313
    beef short ribs *jorim* 284
    *bibimbap* 97
    *bulgogi deopbap* 143
    *doenjang jjigae* 346, 347
    dumpling *jeongol* 362
    egg & mushroom fried rice 128
    enoki & chive *namul* 183
    enoki mushrooms 35, 183
    fish *mandu* 390
    *gochujang* chicken *jorim* 286
    Kaesong-style square *mandu* 462
    mushroom & cabbage *jeongol* 361
    mushroom & mung bean sprout *deopbap* 149
    mushroom *bibimbap* 106
    mushroom *kalguksu* 377
    oyster mushrooms 35
    perilla & mushroom *sotbap* 140

pine mushroom *sotbap* 139
pine nut & king trumpet mushroom *jeon* 236
Pyeongyang-style beef *jeongol* 357
*pyeonsu mandu* 391
river snail *doenjang* & squash leaf *ssam* 212
Seoul-style *bulgogi* 271, 274
shiitake mushrooms 35, 183
small intestines *jeongol* 358
*songyi* mushrooms 35, 183
spicy blue crab *tang* 344
stir-fried vegetables & glass noodles 255
thick *doenjang* barley *bibimbap* 107
thick *doenjang jjigae* 348
tofu *jeongol* 360
vegetable broth 313
wood ear mushrooms 35
mustard
  chicken mustard *muchim* 200
  cold chicken *guk* 332
  fish *mandu* 390
mustard greens
  napa cabbage kimchi 444
  white kimchi 445
*myeolchi* 38
*myeolchi doenjang kkaennip jjim* 300
*myeolchi janchi guksu* 365
*myeolchi jeot* 85
*myeolchi yuksu* 314
*myeongi namul ssambap* 116
*myeongran dubu jjigae* 350
*myungtae* 36–7
*myungtae hwe muchim* 194

N
*nabak kimchi* 66
*naeng-i namul* 162
*naengmyeon* 312
Nakdong River 25
*nakji* 196
*nakji aehobak chomuchim* 196
*namdo chueo tang* 345
*namul* 12, 19, 20, 96, 152–85, 430, 467
  bamboo shoot & perilla seed *namul* 166
  base *namul* sauces 155
  bean sprout *namul* 160
  bellflower root *namul* 170
  *cham namul* 164
  chrysanthemum *namul* 165
  cucumber *saengchae* 173
  daylily *namul* 170
  *deodeok* pine nut *saengchae* 184
  *doenjang* napa cabbage *namul* 178
  dried fiddlehead *namul* 168
  dried Korean zucchini *namul* 176
  dried *namul sotbap* 137
  dried radish *namul* 182
  enoki & chive *namul* 183
  four seasons of 154
  importance of 153–4
  Korean radish *namul* 180
  Korean radish *saengchae* 180
  Korean shepherd's purse *namul* 162
  Korean thistle *namul* 172
  Korean zucchini *namul* 176
  nutty *yangnyeom* 155
  overripe cucumber *namul* 173
  preparing *saengchae namul* 156–7
  preparing *sukchae* 158–9
  radish top *doenjang namul* 182
  seaweed & squid *saengchae* 185
  shiitake *namul* 183
  spicy *yangnyeom* 155
  spinach *namul* 166
  steamed eggplant *namul* 174
  stir-fried eggplant *namul* 174
  stonecrop *namul* 172
  sweet & sour *yangnyeom* 155
  young perilla *namul* 178
Namul People 19, 20
*namul twigim* 308
Nangpoon Bapsang 464
napa cabbage (Chinese leaf) 20, 33, 54, 56, 178, 209, 298, 327, 440, 467
  baby jumbo shrimp & napa cabbage *doenjang guk* 327
  cabbage & beef *gukbap* 125
  *doenjang* napa cabbage *namul* 178
  dumpling *jeongol* 362
  fresh napa cabbage kimchi 62
  freshwater fish stew *guksu* 381
  Kaesong *bossam* kimchi 460
  Korean blood sausage 222
  kimchi pork belly *jorim* 290
  mushroom & cabbage *jeongol* 361
  napa cabbage & *doenjang guk* 467
  napa cabbage & fermented soybean *muchim* 438
  napa cabbage *jeon* 232
  napa cabbage kimchi 60
  napa cabbage kimchi (Kwang Hee Park) 444
  napa cabbage with chiles *jjim* 298
  steamed vegetables with tofu *jang* 474
  vegan *jang kimchi* 73
  water kimchi 66
  white kimchi 64
  white kimchi (Kwang Hee Park) 445
  young cabbage & anchovy *doenjang jorim* 280
napa cabbage flowers (Chinese leaf) 468
napa cabbage flower kimchi 468
napa cabbage flower *muchim* 468
napa cabbage kimchi 60
  acorn jelly *bap* 122
  chilled kimchi & acorn jelly soup 225
  cold kimchi *guksu* 374
  kimchi & bean sprout *guk* 322
  kimchi & bean sprout *juk* 397
  kimchi & ground soybean *jjigae* 350
  kimchi *buchimgae* 246
  kimchi fried rice 127
  kimchi *jjigae* 348
  kimchi *mandu* 388
  mung bean *buchimgae* 248
  napa cabbage kimchi (Kwang Hee Park) 444
  spicy *bibimguksu* 366
*napjak mandu* 393
*neulgeun hobak* 34
*neutari beoseot* 35
*nogak namul* 173
*nokdu* 33
*nokdu buchimgae* 248
*nokdu juk* 399
noodles
  anchovy broth *guksu* 365
  Busan-style cold wheat *guksu* 376
  cold buckwheat *guksu* with *hwe* 372
  cold kimchi *guksu* 374
  cold soybean *guksu* 374
  flat *mandu* 393
  freshwater fish stew *guksu* 381
  *ganjang* & perilla oil *bibimguksu* 370
  Gangwondo-style buckwheat *guksu* 383
  Gangwondo-style tadpole-shaped *guksu* 380
  *guksu* 364–85
  Hamheung-style spicy *bibimguksu* 368
  hand-torn *guksu* 384
  littleneck clam *kalguksu* 378
  mushroom *kalguksu* 377
  Pyongyang-style cold buckwheat *guksu* 373
  Pyongyang-style cold buckwheat noodles 461
  seaweed roll *twigim* 311
  spicy *bibimguksu* 366
  spicy chewy cold *guksu* 382
  stir-fried vegetables & glass noodles 255
*nurungji* 92
nuts
  *juk* 395
  *ssamjang* with nuts 53
  sweet rice with nuts & jujubes 416
nutty *yangnyeom* 155

O
*obangsaek* 96
octopus 37, 196, 207
  Kaesong *bossam* kimchi 460
  long-arm octopus 37
  long-arm octopus & zucchini *chomuchim* 196
  parboiled octopus *hwe* 207
  seafood *tang* 343
  webfoot octopus & minari *hwe* 207
*ogari* (dried Korean zucchini): dried Korean zucchini *namul* 176
*ogokbap* 94
*oi* 34
*oi jangajji* 80
*oi miyeok naeng-guk* 330
*oi mul-kimchi* 76
*oi-saengchae* 173
*oi sobaji* 74
*oiji* 83
oil, sesame 38
*ojingeo deopbap* 146
*ojingeo hwe* 206
*ojingeo jeotgal* 85
*ojingeo mu guk* 326
*ok-dom*: horsehead tilefish & radish *guk* 324
Okjeo 15
old pumpkin 34
*omija* (red magnolia) berries 36
  azalea punch 456
*ongeun-juk* 395
onions
  beef short ribs *jorim* 284
  black bean sauce *deopbap* 147
  chicken *juk* 400
  *doenjang* pork belly *deopbap* 145
  *ganjang*-marinated crab 86
  Korean-style curry rice 148
  onion *jangajji* 79
  onion kimchi 77
  pork head *pyunyuk* 217
  radish water kimchi 72
  spicy pork *bokkeum* 251
  spicy pork *deopbap* 144
  spicy squid *deopbap* 146
  *ssamjang* 52
  *ssamjang* with nuts 53
  stir-fried vegetables & glass noodles 255
  tofu *jorim* 277
  vegan stir-fried *gochujang* 52
  vegetable broth 313
  white kimchi 64
  young summer radish kimchi 67
*ori gochujang gui* 266
overripe cucumber *namul* 173
ox bone broth: Jeonju-style *bibimbap* 98
ox bones: ox bone *tang* 335
oxtail *suyuk* 220
oyster mushrooms 35
  *bibimbap* 97
  egg & mushroom fried rice 128
  mushroom & mung bean sprout *deopbap* 149
  mushroom *bibimbap* 106
  mushroom *kalguksu* 377
  perilla & mushroom *sotbap* 140
  pine mushroom *sotbap* 139
  Pyeongyang-style beef *jeongol* 357

small intestines jeongol 358
oysters
  garlic chive & oyster *jeon* 244
  *maesaengi* oyster *guk* 328
  napa cabbage kimchi 444
  oyster *sotbap* 140
  seafood & scallion *jeon* 242
  white soft tofu & oyster *jjigae* 354

P
*paengi beoseot* 35
*paengi buchu namul* 183
pairing foods 12
pancakes
  beef *jeon* 238
  beef-stuffed pepper *jeon* 240
  fish *jeon* 244
  garlic chive & buckwheat *jeon* 231
  garlic chive & Korean radish *jeon* 231
  garlic chive & oyster *jeon* 244
  *jeon* & *buchimgae* 230–49
  julienned potato *jeon* 234
  kimchi *buchimgae* 246
  Korean batter-fried meat patties 241
  Korean zucchini *jeon* 236
  mung bean *buchimgae* 248
  napa cabbage *jeon* 232
  perilla *jeon* 237
  pine nut & king trumpet mushroom *jeon* 236
  potato *jeon* 234
  seafood & scallion *jeon* 242
  shrimp & chive *buchimgae* 246
  sweet Korean pancakes 412
*parae* 188
  green laver & radish *muchim* 188
*parae mu cho muchim* 188
Park, Kwang Hee 423, 440–5
Park, Yeong Geun 423, 446–51
Park Kwanghee Kimchi 440
*pat* 33
*pat juk* 399
*patbingsu* 414
patties, Korean batter-fried meat 241
peanuts
  Korean batter-fried meat patties 241
  peanuts & beans *jorim* 281
  sweet Korean pancakes 412
pearl barley
  barley bap 95
  thick doenjang barley *bibimbap* 107
pearl-spot chromis 470
  pearl-spot chromis *jeot* 470
peas: green pea bap 94
pepper leaves: dried radish *namul* 182

peppers
  *ganjang* stir-fried *tteok* 406
  radish & yellow pepper kimchi 70
  stuffed peppers *twigim* 306
perilla leaves 33, 178, 209
  acorn jelly *muchim* 225
  anchovy *doenjang* perilla *jjim* 300
  cooked vegetable *ssam* 432
  perilla & mushroom *sotbap* 140
  perilla *bugak* 427
  perilla *jangajji* 83
  perilla *jeon* 237
  perilla *ssambap* 114
  pork back bone *tang* 339
  spicy chewy cold *guksu* 382
  tuna *gimbap* 133
  young perilla *namul* 178
perilla oil 38
  *ganjang* & perilla oil *bibimguksu* 370
perilla seeds
  bamboo shoot & perilla seed *namul* 166
  clams, bamboo shoot, & perilla seed *muchim* 190
  fresh fiddlehead *namul* 168
  pork back bone *tang* 339
  river snail *doenjang* & squash leaf *ssam* 212
  young perilla *namul* 178
persimmon 36
pickles: quick-pickled vegetables 368, 372
  see also *jangajji*
pig's feet *jorim* 290
pine mushroom *sotbap* 139
pine nuts 397
  *deodeok* pine nut *saengchae* 184
  fried twists 454
  lotus leaf *bap* 95
  pine nut & king trumpet mushroom *jeon* 236
  pine nut *juk* 397
  poached Asian pear 412
  *pyeonsu mandu* 391
  raised rice cake 416
  steamed pine nut cake 457
  *yuja* punch 418
plant-based cuisine 11, 14
pollock 24, 36–7, 194
  dried pollock *gukbap* 120
  fish *jeon* 244
  pollock *guk* 326
  pollock *hwe muchim* 194
  seasoned semi-dried pollock *twigim* 310
  pollock *hwe muchim* 194
  cold buckwheat *guksu* with *hwe* 372
pomegranate 36
  *yuja* punch 418
pomfret & Korean zucchini *jorim* 294
pork 251
  black bean sauce *deopbap* 147
  crispy pork *twigim* 308
  *doenjang*-marinated pork *gui* 260

*doenjang* pork belly *deopbap* 145
*gochujang*-marinated pork *gui* 262
grilled pork belly 30–31
*gui* dishes 259
kimchi & ground soybean *jjigae* 350
kimchi *mandu* 388
kimchi pork belly *jorim* 290
Korean blood sausage 222
Korean-style curry rice 148
meat & tofu *mandu* 387
mung bean *buchimgae* 248
pork belly & mung bean sprout *jjim* 297
pork rib *gui* 260
pork *suyuk* 216, 218
*pyunyuk* 216
rolled *mandu* 392
spicy pork *bokkeum* 251
spicy pork *deopbap* 144
stir-fried vegetables & glass noodles 255
stuffed peppers *twigim* 306
pork bone broth 314
  Busan-style cold wheat *guksu* 376
  Korean blood sausage *gukbap* 124
pork bones
  pork back bone *tang* 339
  pork bone broth 314
  pork head *pyunyuk* 217
pork organ: Korean blood sausage *gukbap* 124
pork *suyuk* 216, 218
  aged kimchi *ssam* 215
  Busan-style cold wheat *guksu* 376
porridge (*juk*) 20, 25, 394–403
potatoes 24, 276, 281, 317
  Andong chicken *jorim* 288
  egg & potato *guk* 317
  *gochujang* chicken *jorim* 286
  hand-torn *guksu* 384
  julienned potato *jeon* 234
  Korean-style curry rice 148
  mackerel *jorim* 292
  mushroom *kalguksu* 377
  pomfret & Korean zucchini *jorim* 294
  pork back bone *tang* 339
  potato & shishito *jorim* 281
  potato *bugak* 428
  potato *jeon* 234
pots, cast-iron 15
poussin
  Andong chicken *jorim* 288
  chicken *juk* 400
  *gochujang* chicken *jorim* 286
  herbal chicken *tang* 336
  Korean chicken *tang* 338
preserved foods 466
  see also fermentation; kimchi
pumpkin leaves: river snail *doenjang* & squash leaf *ssam* 212
pumpkin seeds: lotus leaf *bap* 95

punches
  azalea punch 456
  sweet rice punch 420
  *yuja* punch 418
*put gochu jangajji* 81
Pyeongchang 440
Pyeongchang-style beef *jeongol* 357
*pyeonsu mandu* 386, 391
*pyogo beoseot namul* 183
*pyogo beoseot* 35
Pyongyang 14
*Pyongyang naengmyeon* 248, 373, 461
Pyongyang *naengmyeon* buckwheat noodles
  Pyongyang-style cold buckwheat *guksu* 373
  Pyongyang-style cold buckwheat noodles 461
*pyunyuk* 216–23
  pork head *pyunyuk* 217

R
radish *saengchae* 180
  Tongyeong-style *bibimbap* 99
radish top *doenjang namul* 182
radish water kimchi liquid: Pyongyang-style cold buckwheat *guksu* 373
radishes, Korean (*mu*) 15, 24, 34, 180, 182, 231, 276, 313
  beef & radish *guk* 324
  beef short rib *tang* 335
  beef short ribs *jorim* 284
  cabbage & beef *gukbap* 125
  clear cod *tang* 340
  cold buckwheat *guksu* with *hwe* 372
  cold chicken *guk* 332
  cucumber water kimchi 76
  diced radish kimchi 68
  dried pollock *gukbap* 120
  dried radish *namul* 182
  fermented flounder 89
  garlic chive & Korean radish *jeon* 231
  green laver & radish *muchim* 188
  Hamheung-style spicy *bibimguksu* 368
  horsehead tilefish & radish *guk* 324
  Kaesong *bossam* kimchi 460
  Korean radish *namul* 180
  Korean radish *saengchae* 180
  napa cabbage kimchi 60
  napa cabbage kimchi (Kwang Hee Park) 444
  onion kimchi 77
  oyster *sotbap* 140
  parboiled octopus *hwe* 207
  pollock *guk* 326
  pollock *hwe muchim* 194
  Pyongyang-style cold buckwheat *guksu* 373
  Pyongyang-style cold buckwheat noodles 461
  radish & green chili kimchi 71

Index 491

radish & yellow pepper kimchi 70
radish *jangajji* 80
radish water kimchi 72
seafood *tang* 343
seasoned skate *hwe* 203
small intestines *jeongol* 358
spicy blue crab *tang* 344
spicy cod *tang* 342
spicy monkfish *jorim* 295
spinach *doenjang guk* 318
squid & radish *guk* 326
steamed vegetables with tofu *jang* 474
tofu *jeongol* 360
vegan *jang* kimchi 73
vegetable broth 313
water kimchi 66
white kimchi 64
white kimchi (Kwang Hee Park) 445
white soft tofu & oyster *jjigae* 354
young summer radish kimchi 67
ramp (wild garlic) *namul ssambap* 116
ray with bean sprout *jjim* 300
red beans (*adzuki* beans) 14
  red bean *juk* 399
  red bean shaved ice 414
  steamed pine nut cake 457
red magnolia berry 36
  azalea punch 456
regional foods 22–6
relish, cilantro (coriander) 479
rice 18–19, 20, 90–149, 442, 466, 478
  abalone *juk* 402
  acorn jelly bap 122
  aged kimchi *ssam* 215
  aged kimchi *ssambap* 117
  Andong-style *bibimbap* 99
  assorted sea vegetable *bibimbap* 108
  bamboo shoot *sotbap* 138
  *banchan* dishes to accompany rice 150–421
  *bapsang* & *bansang* 27, 28, 30
  barley bap 95
  bean sprout *gukbap* 119
  bean sprout *sotbap* 137
  *bibimbap* 96–111
  black bean sauce *deopbap* 147
  *bokkeumbap* 126–9
  brown rice 32
  *bulgogi deopbap* 143
  cabbage & beef *gukbap* 125
  chicken *juk* 400
  chicken *sotbap* 141
  *cho-gochujang* & *saeng miyeok ssam* 214
  *chungmu gimbap* 132
  cockle *bibimbap* 110
  cooked short-grain white rice 92
  *deopbap* 142–9
  *doenjang* pork belly *deopbap* 145
  *doenjang* spinach *juk* 398
  dried *namul sotbap* 137

dried pollock *gukbap* 120
egg & mushroom fried rice 128
egg *gimbap* 134
five-grain rice 94
*gim*-wrapped rice 131
*gimbap* 130–5
glutinous rice 32
green pea bap 94
*gukbap* 118–25
hangover *gukbap* 122
herbal chicken *tang* 336
history of Korean food 14–15
hot stone *bibimbap* 111
Jeju sea urchin *bibimbap* 100
Jeonju-style *bibimbap* 98
Jinju-style *bibimbap* 100
*juk* 395
kimchi & bean sprout *juk* 397
kimchi fried rice 127
Korean blood sausage 222
Korean blood sausage *gukbap* 124
Korean rice balls 135
Korean scorched bap 92
Korean-style curry rice 148
lettuce *ssambap* 116
lotus leaf *bap* 95
marinated crab *bibimbap* 109
*miyeok* or *dasima ssambap* 113
mung bean *juk* 399
mushroom & mung bean sprout *deopbap* 149
mushroom *bibimbap* 106
oyster *sotbap* 140
perilla & mushroom *sotbap* 140
perilla *ssambap* 114
pine mushroom *sotbap* 139
pine nut *juk* 397
ramp *namul ssambap* 116
raw beef *bibimbap* 104
raw fish *bibimbap* 102
red bean *juk* 399
regional foods 23, 24, 25, 26
river snail *doenjang* & squash leaf *ssam* 212
short-grain rice 32
*sotbap* 136–41
spicy pork *deopbap* 144
spicy squid *deopbap* 146
squash leaf & cabbage *ssambap* 114
*ssambap* 112–17
stir-fried *gochujang* & lettuce *ssam* 210
sweet rice punch 420
sweet rice with nuts & jujubes 416
Tongyeong-style *bibimbap* 99
tuna *gimbap* 133
vegetable fried rice 129
white rice 32
rice cakes (*tteok*) 15, 24, 404–9, 411, 452
  *ganjang* stir-fried *tteok* 406
  *gochujang* stir-fried *tteok* 405

pan-fried flower rice cakes 456
raised rice cake 416
rice cake soup 408
shallow-fried *tteok* 408
steamed pine nut cake 457
rice syrup 39
rice water 312
  bamboo shoot & fermented soybean stew 437
  spinach *doenjang guk* 318
Ripert, Eric 472
river snails 212
  river snail *doenjang* & squash leaf *ssam* 212
rockfish & bean *jorim* 470

S
*saeng gosari namul* 168
*saengchae* 20, 27, 153
  cucumber *saengchae* 173
  *deodeok* pine nut *saengchae* 184
  Korean radish *saengchae* 180
  preparing 156–7
  seaweed & squid *saengchae* 185
*saenggang* 34
*saengjeot* 85
*saengseon hwe* 204
*saeu* 37–8
*saeu buchu buchimgae* 246
*saeu-jeot* 86
*sagwa* 36
salmon 202
  *ganjang*-marinated salmon 88
salt 20, 440
  *ganjang* & *doenjang* 50
  *gochujang* 50
  *jang* 48
  *jeotgal* 84
  kimchi 55
salt-pickled cucumbers 83
salt-preserved *jangajji* 78
salted anchovies 85
salted shrimp 86
salted squid 85
*samchi* 37
*samgyetang* 336
*samgyupsal* 30–31
*samgyupsal sukju jjim* 297
Samhan 15
*sangchu* 33
*sangchu ssambap* 116
sausage, Korean blood 222
saw-edged perch 202
scallions (spring onions)
  napa cabbage kimchi 444
  seafood & scallion *jeon* 242
  white kimchi 445
sea bass 202
sea bream 202
  assorted *hwe* 204
sea cucumber 202
sea pineapple 202
sea squirts: seafood *tang* 343
sea urchins: Jeju sea urchin *bibimbap* 100
sea vegetables 26
  assorted sea vegetable *bibimbap* 108
seafood 15, 36–8, 202, 466
  regional foods 22, 23, 24, 25, 26

seafood & scallion *jeon* 242
seafood & soft tofu *jjigae* 352
seafood *tang* 343
see also jeotgal and individual types of seafood
seasonings 38–9
  *doenjang* 50
seaweed 36, 209, 471
  agar jelly 226
  agar jelly in cold soybean broth 228
  beef & seaweed *guk* 322
  cold cucumber & seaweed *guk* 330
  *gim* & clam *muchim* 190
  *gim guk* 318
  green laver & radish *muchim* 188
  roasted seaweed flakes 254
  seaweed & squid *saengchae* 185
  seaweed & tofu *doenjang guk* 317
  seaweed roll *twigim* 311
  vinegared seaweed & squid *muchim* 192
Seo, Myeong Hwan 423, 452–7
*seolhwa* Hanwood bulgogi 451
*seolhwa yangnyeom galbi* 450
*seolleongtang* 335
*seongnyu* 36
*seonji* (pig's blood): Korean blood sausage 222
Seoul 16, 23, 320
  Seoul-style *bulgogi* 271, 274
Seoul *bulgogi* 264, 271
sesame oil 38
sesame seeds 39
  fried lotus root *doenjang muchim* 187
  *ganjang* & perilla oil *bibimguksu* 370
  Korean radish *saengchae* 180
  raw fish in cold broth 204
  soybean cold broth 315
  spicy *bibimguksu* 366
shaved ice, red bean 414
shepherd's purse 162
  Korean shepherd's purse *namul* 162
spring vegetable *twigim* 308
shiitake mushrooms 35, 183
  beef short ribs *jorim* 284
  *bulgogi deopbap* 143
  *doenjang jjigae* 346, 347
  dumpling *jeongol* 362
  fish *mandu* 390
  *gochujang* chicken *jorim* 286
  Kaesong-style square *mandu* 462
  mushroom & cabbage *jeongol* 361
  mushroom *bibimbap* 106
  mushroom *kalguksu* 377
  perilla & mushroom *sotbap* 140
  Pyeongyang-style beef *jeongol* 357
  *pyeonsu mandu* 391

river snail *doenjang* & squash leaf *ssam* 212
Seoul-style *bulgogi* 271, 274
shiitake *namul* 183
stir-fried vegetables & glass noodles 255
thick *doenjang* barley *bibimbap* 107
thick *doenjang jjigae* 348
tofu *jeongol* 360
vegetable broth 313
Shin, Gyung Kyun 423, 476–81
Shin, Jeong-hee 476
Shinan region 440
*shishito doenjang muchim* 187
shishito peppers 254
  potato & shishito *jorim* 281
  shishito & anchovy *bokkeum* 254
  *shishito doenjang muchim* 187
shrimp (prawns) 37–8
  baby jumbo shrimp & napa cabbage *doenjang guk* 327
  *ganjang* marinated shrimp 88
  *jeotgal* 84
  Kaesong *bossam* kimchi 460
  Korean zucchini *bokkeum* 257
  napa cabbage kimchi 444
  salted shrimp 86
  salted shrimp (Kwang Hee Park) 442
  seafood & scallion *jeon* 242
  seafood & soft tofu *jjigae* 352
  seafood *tang* 343
  shrimp & chive *buchimgae* 246
  white kimchi 445
shrimp, dried
  *doenjang* spinach *juk* 398
  garlic scape & dried shrimp *bokkeum* 252
*sigeumchi* 33
*sigeumchi doenjang guk* 318
*sigeumchi namul* 166
*sikcho* 38
*sikhye* 411, 420
*silpa* 33
*siraegi doenjang namul* 182
*Siuijeonseo* 176
skate 203
  seasoned skate *hwe* 203
snowflake *bulgogi* 451
snowflake marinated short rib 450
*so yuksu* 315
*sogalbijjim* 284
*sogogi gochu jeon* 240
*sogogi jangjorim* 282
*sogogi miyeok guk* 322
*sogogi mu guk* 324
*sogogi oi baetduri* 257
*sogogi suyuk* 218
*sokkori suyuk* 220
*soju* (Korean clear spirits): goat *suyuk* 221
*somyeon* (thin wheat flour noodles)
  anchovy broth *guksu* 365

cold kimchi *guksu* 374
cold soybean *guksu* 374
spicy *bibimguksu* 366
zucchini *bibimguksu* 370
*songyi beoseot* 35
songyi mushrooms 35, 183
  pine mushroom *sotbap* 139
*songyi sotbap* 139
*sot* 316
*sotbap* 136–41
  bamboo shoot *sotbap* 138
  bean sprout *sotbap* 137
  chicken *sotbap* 141
  dried namul *sotbap* 137
  oyster *sotbap* 140
  perilla & mushroom *sotbap* 140
  pine mushroom *sotbap* 139
soups (*guk*) 16, 19, 20, 26, 27, 316–45, 466, 478
  baby jumbo shrimp & napa cabbage *doenjang guk* 327
  bean sprout *guk* 320
  beef & radish *guk* 324
  beef & seaweed *guk* 322
  beef bone *tang* 334
  beef short rib *tang* 335
  chilled kimchi & acorn jelly soup 225
  clear cod *tang* 340
  cold chicken *guk* 332
  cold cucumber & seaweed *guk* 330
  cold eggplant *guk* 328
  egg & potato *guk* 317
  fresh loach tang 345
  *gim guk* 318
  herbal chicken *tang* 336
  horsehead tilefish & radish *guk* 324
  kimchi & bean sprout *guk* 322
  Korean chicken *tang* 338
  Korean zucchini *jeot guk* 320
  *maesaengi* oyster *guk* 328
  ox bone *tang* 335
  pollock *guk* 326
  pork back bone *tang* 339
  rice cake soup 408
  seafood *tang* 343
  seaweed & tofu *doenjang guk* 317
  spicy blue crab *tang* 344
  spinach *doenjang guk* 318
  squid & radish *guk* 326
soybean cold broth 315
  agar jelly in cold soybean broth 228
  cold soybean *guksu* 374
soybean sprouts 35, 320
  Andong-style *bibimbap* 99
  bean sprout *gukbap* 119
  bean sprout *namul* 160
  bean sprout *sotbap* 137
  *bibimbap* 97
  clear cod *tang* 340
  hangover *gukbap* 122
  Jeonju-style *bibimbap* 98
  Jinju-style *bibimbap* 100
  kimchi & bean sprout *guk* 322
  kimchi & bean sprout *juk* 397

seafood *tang* 343
spicy cod *tang* 342
spicy monkfish *jorim* 295
soybeans 14, 33
  bamboo shoot & fermented soybean stew 437
  fermented soybeans 437
  *ganjang* 45
  *jang* 44, 48, 434
  *meju* 49
  soybean cold broth 315
  *tojang* 47
  see also *doenjang*; *gan jang*, etc
spicy *bibimguksu* 366
spicy blue crab *tang* 344
spicy chewy cold *guksu* 382
spicy cod *tang* 342
spicy monkfish *jorim* 295
spicy pork *bokkeum* 251
spicy pork *deopbap* 144
spicy squid *deopbap* 146
spicy *yangnyeom* 155
spinach 33, 166
  *bibimbap* 97
  *doenjang* spinach *juk* 398
  *gim*-wrapped rice 131
  spinach *doenjang guk* 318
  spinach *namul* 166
  stir-fried vegetables & glass noodles 255
spinach *namul* 166
  Andong-style *bibimbap* 99
  Jeonju-style *bibimbap* 98
  Jinju-style *bibimbap* 100
  Tongyeong-style *bibimbap* 99
spring vegetable *twigim* 308
squash: sweet pumpkin *juk* 398
squash leaves 209
  river snail *doenjang* & squash leaf *ssam* 212
  squash leaf & cabbage *ssambap* 114
squid 202, 206
  bean sprout *gukbap* 119
  *chungmu gimbap* 132
  dried shredded squid *muchim* 194
  raw fish *bibimbap* 102
  salted squid 85
  seafood & scallion *jeon* 242
  seafood & soft tofu *jjigae* 352
  seaweed & squid *saengchae* 185
  spicy squid *deopbap* 146
  squid & radish *guk* 326
  squid *hwe* 206
  vinegared seaweed & squid *muchim* 192
*ssam* 30, 31, 112, 208–15, 259, 430, 467
  aged kimchi *ssam* 215
  *cho-gochujang* & fresh *miyeok ssam* 214
  cooked vegetable *ssam* 432
  Korea's *ssam* culture 209
  river snail *doenjang* & squash leaf *ssam* 212
  stir-fried *gochujang* & lettuce *ssam* 210
*ssambap* 112–17
  aged kimchi *ssambap* 117

lettuce *ssambap* 116
*miyeok* or *dasima ssambap* 113
perilla *ssambap* 114
ramp *namul ssambap* 116
squash leaf & cabbage *ssambap* 114
*ssamjang* 30, 52, 209, 464
*gui* dishes 259
*ssamjang* with nuts 53
*ssukgat* 33
*ssukgat namul* 165
starch 442
stews (*jjigae*) 19, 27, 31, 54, 346–55, 464, 466
  bamboo shoot & fermented soybean stew 437
  cod roe & tofu *jjigae* 350
  *doenjang jjigae* 346, 347
  freshwater fish stew *guksu* 381
  kimchi & ground soybean *jjigae* 350
  kimchi *jjigae* 348
  seafood & soft tofu *jjigae* 352
  thick *doenjang jjigae* 348
  white soft tofu & oyster *jjigae* 354
stir-fries
  Chuncheon-style chicken stir-fry 256
  Korean zucchini *bokkeum* 257
  stir-fried beef & cucumber 257
  stir-fried eggplant *namul* 174
  stir-fried vegetables & glass noodles 255
stock, chicken 313
stone bream 202
stonecrops 172
  stonecrop *namul* 172
straw: *meju* 49
stuffed cucumber kimchi 74
stuffed peppers *twigim* 306
*sujebi* 384
*sujeonggwa* 411, 420
*suk-jangajji* 78
*sukchae* 20, 27, 153
  preparing 158–9
*sukchae ssam* 432
*sukju namul* 35
Sunchang region 25
*sundae* (Korean blood sausage) 222
  Korean blood sausage *gukbap* 124
*sundae gukbap* 124
*sungnyung* 92, 411
*suyuk* 216–23
  beef *suyuk* 218
  goat *suyuk* 221
  oxtail *suyuk* 220
  pork *suyuk* 218
sweet & sour *yangnyeom* 155
sweet and spicy Korean fried chicken 304
sweet cinnamon tea 420
sweet Korean pancakes 412
sweet potatoes 442
  Chuncheon-style chicken stir-fry 256
sweet pumpkin *juk* 398
sweet rice punch 420
sweet rice with nuts & jujubes 416

## T

tang 316–45
  beef bone *tang* 334
  beef short rib *tang* 335
  clear cod *tang* 340
  fresh loach *tang* 345
  herbal chicken *tang* 336
  Korean chicken *tang* 338
  ox bone *tang* 335
  pork back bone *tang* 339
  seafood *tang* 343
  spicy blue crab *tang* 344
  spicy cod *tang* 342
taro stems
  fresh loach *tang* 345
  freshwater fish stew *guksu* 381
tea, sweet cinnamon 420
temple food 472–5
tofu
  bamboo shoot & fermented soybean stew 437
  clams, bamboo shoot, & perilla seed *muchim* 190
  clear cod *tang* 340
  cod roe & tofu *jjigae* 350
  *doenjang jjigae* 346
  kimchi *jjigae* 348
  kimchi *mandu* 388
  Korean batter-fried meat patties 241
  Korean zucchini jeot guk 320
  meat & tofu *mandu* 387
  perilla *jeon* 237
  pollock *guk* 326
  river snail *doenjang* & squash leaf *ssam* 212
  rolled *mandu* 392
  seafood & soft tofu *jjigae* 352
  seaweed & tofu *doenjang guk* 317
  small intestines jeongol 358
  spicy cod *tang* 342
  steamed vegetables with tofu *jang* 474
  stuffed peppers *twigim* 306
  tofu *jang* 474
  tofu *jeongol* 360
  tofu *jorim* 277
  white soft tofu & oyster *jjigae* 354
tofu *jang* 474
  steamed vegetables with tofu *jang* 474
tojang 47
tomatoes: green tomato *jangajji* 81
Tongyeong 99
  Tongyeong-style *bibimbap* 99
*Tongyeong bibimbap* 99
tot (hijiki) 471
  tot *muchim* 471
trout 202
tteok 15, 24, 404–9, 411, 452
  *ganjang* stir-fried *tteok* 406
  *gochujang* stir-fried *tteok* 405
  pan-fried flower rice cakes 456
  raised rice cake 416
  rice cake soup 408
  shallow-fried *tteok* 408

  steamed pine nut cake 457
*tteok galbi* 270
*tteokbokki* 404
  *ganjang* stir-fried *tteok* 406
  *gochujang* stir-fried *tteok* 405
  shallow-fried *tteok* 408
*tteokguk* 404, 408
*ttukbaegi* 316
tuna
  aged kimchi *ssambap* 117
  assorted *hwe* 204
  lettuce *ssambap* 116
  tuna *gimbap* 133
*twigak* 96, 424
  deep fried *dasima* 426
*twigim* 302–11
  crispy pork *twigim* 308
  Korean fried chicken 303
  seasoned semi-dried pollock *twigim* 310
  seaweed roll *twigim* 311
  spring vegetable *twigim* 308
  stuffed peppers *twigim* 306
  sweet and spicy Korean fried chicken 304
twists, fried 454

## U

*uegoji* 20
  baby jumbo shrimp & napa cabbage *doenjang guk* 327
  cabbage & beef *gukbap* 125
  fresh loach *tang* 345
  hangover *gukbap* 122
  Korean blood sausage 222
  pork back bone *tang* 339
*ugeoji sogogi gukbap* 125
*umutgasari kongguk* 228
*umutgasari muk* 226
*ureok kong jorim* 470
*urung doenjang & hobakip ssam* 212

## V

vegan *jang* kimchi 73
vegan *yak-gochujang* 52
vegetable broth 313
  bean sprout *guk* 320
  egg & potato *guk* 317
  gim *guk* 318
  kimchi pork belly *jorim* 290
  mushroom *kalguksu* 377
  rice cake soup 408
  seaweed & tofu *doenjang guk* 317
  vegetables 11, 23–4, 30, 33–5, 466
  *banchan* 19, 259
  cooked vegetable *ssam* 432
  *juk* 395
  kimchi 54, 55
  *namul* 143, 153, 430
  *namul* seasoned vegetables 152–85
  preparation of 20
  quick-pickled vegetables 368, 372, 373
  spring vegetable *twigim* 308

  *ssam* 112, 208–15, 430
  steamed vegetables with tofu *jang* 474
  stir-fried vegetables & glass noodles 255
  *twigim* 302
  vegetable broth 313
  vegetable fried rice 129
  *see also individual types of vegetable*
vinegar 38
  vinegar *ganjang muchim* 186
  vinegar *gochujang muchim* 186
  vinegared *gochujang* 51
  vinegared seaweed & squid *muchim* 192
  vinegared *gochujang* 51
  goat *suyuk* 221
  parboiled octopus *hwe* 207
  raw fish in cold broth 204
  seasoned *hwe* 206
  squid *hwe* 206
  webfoot octopus & minari *hwe* 207

## W

walnuts
  *ssamjang* with nuts 53
  sweet Korean pancakes 412
*wandu kong bap* 94
wasabi
  assorted *hwe* 204
  squid *hwe* 206
water: *jang* 48
water kimchi 66
webfoot octopus & minari *hwe* 207
whelk & minari *muchim* 192
white kimchi 54, 64
white kimchi (Kwang Hee Park) 445
whitebait: *gochujang* whitebait *gui* 267
wild Korean chives: cockles & wild Korean chive *muchim* 188
*wonchuri namul* 170
*wonmi-juk* 395
wood ear mushrooms 35
  stir-fried vegetables & glass noodles 255
wraps *see* ssam

## Y

*yak-gochujang* 51, 210
*yak-gochujang* & sangchu *ssam* 210
*yaksik* 416
Yang, Yong-jin 464
*yangbaechu* kimchi 62
*yangjo ganjang* 46
*yangnyeom*
  nutty *yangnyeom* 155
  spicy *yangnyeom* 155
  sweet & sour *yangnyeom* 155
*yangnyeom dak twigim* 304
*yangnyeomjang* 202
*yangonseo* 15
*yangpa jangajji* 79
*yangpa* kimchi 77
yeast 48
yellowtail 202
Yeoju 14

*yeolmu* (young radish):
  young summer radish kimchi 67
*yeolmu* kimchi 67
*yeomso suyuk* 221
*yeoneojang* 88
Yeong-dong 24
*yeongeum twigim doenjang muchim* 187
*yeongeun jorim* 282
Yeongsea 24
Yongsusan 458
young summer radish kimchi 67
Gangwondo-style tadpole-shaped *guksu* 380
yuja (yuzu) 36
  yuja punch 418
  yuja-hwachae 418
*yuk won jeon* 241
*yukhwe* 98
  Jinju-style *bibimbap* 100
  raw beef *bibimbap* 104
  *yukhwe bibimbap* 104
  *yukhwe muchim* 198
*yukjeon* 238
*yukjeot* 85
*yuksu* 312–15, 442
  anchovy broth 314
  beef broth 315
  chicken stock 313
  pork bone broth 314
  soybean cold broth 315
  vegetable broth 313
Yukuijeon 16
yuzu 36
  yuja punch 418

## Z

zucchini, Korean (*aehobak*) 34, 176
  anchovy broth *guksu* 365
  cod roe & tofu *jjigae* 350
  *doenjang jjigae* 346, 347
  dried Korean zucchini *namul* 176
  hand-torn *guksu* 384
  Kaesong-style square *mandu* 462
  Korean zucchini *bokkeum* 257
  Korean zucchini *jeon* 236
  Korean zucchini jeot guk 320
  Korean zucchini *namul* 176
  littleneck clam *kalguksu* 378
  long-arm octopus & zucchini *chomuchim* 196
  mushroom *kalguksu* 377
  pomfret & Korean zucchini *jorim* 294
  *pyeonsu mandu* 391
  river snail *doenjang* & squash leaf *ssam* 212
  spicy blue crab *tang* 344
  thick *doenjang* barley *bibimbap* 107
  thick *doenjang jjigae* 348
  tofu *jeongol* 360
  zucchini *bibimguksu* 370

## Authors' Acknowledgments

### From Junghyun Park

I would like to thank my father, Byunggeun Park, and mother, Jinok Oh, who have always supported me on my journey, which began in my childhood. I am always grateful for my life partner, wife, and eternal love, Ellia Park. Thank you for teaching me true love; you are my inspiration and greatest gift in my life. Without the understanding and support of my restaurant family, I would not have been able to complete this work, and I extend my gratitude to each member for making this personal project possible.

As we continue on, I will work tirelessly to become someone who can speak to, and converse about *hansik*, to and with the world.

### From Jungyoon Choi

I am most grateful for my father, Kyungjae Choi, my utmost role model now looking over me from heaven, for planting the roots of cuisine and culture in my life. I am endlessly thankful for my grandma Taesoo Noh and mother, Younghee Hwang, who never fails to comfort me with her warm food, and my best friend in life, my beloved sister Jooyeon Choi and nephew Jihwan Park.

Master Mal Soon Lee, who has been my respected teacher, made me realize the identity of *hansik* as a chef. I have since kept it in my heart in every aspect of work that I do. I have continued to consider the importance of remembering the uniqueness of the identity of *hansik* and have strived for it during the writing of this book.

I thank my mentor and teacher, Toni Massanés, the General Director of Fundació Alícia, who guided me to become a culinary research chef from being a kitchen cook. I am forever grateful for Jinsun Park, the CEO of Sempio, who created the joyous opportunity to research Korean fermentation and *hansik* as my career, and to each and every researcher at Sempio who are on this path together.

### Joint Acknowledgments

This beautiful book would not be complete without the spectacular work by photographer Jinju Kang and her studio team at aostudio, along with the food stylists of the Seven Doors team, Min Deul Re and Min Song i. Thank you to Baki and Matty, who joined us for the final shoot models. The heartfelt work was palpable at each photo shoot, and we learned so much from the dedication of these two teams' work to create a lasting body of work for the culture of *hansik*.

Together as a team, we also thank the 101 architects, Rakkojae and Rereplay, for their generosity in allowing us to access beautiful spaces for the photos, as well as E J-yong who helped us scout the most beautiful locations. Our deepest gratitude goes to artists of the beautiful ceramics and tableware that elevated the food: Namhee Kim, Kihwan Rah, Janganyo, Sui57atelier, Area plus, Bareunugi, Chapter1, Choeunsook gallery 1250°C.

Lastly, we are grateful for Jinah Rhee who took on the meaningful project with us to deliver *hansik* to the world. A special thank you to Phaidon commissioning editor Emily Takoudes, who supported us from before the very beginning.

## About the Authors

**Junghyun Park** is an acclaimed chef born and raised in Seoul. With his wife, Ellia Park, he runs three restaurants in New York—Atoboy, Naro, and Atomix (2 Michelin stars, 3 stars from the *New York Times*). In 2022, Park received the Art of Hospitality Award from The World's 50 Best Restaurants, as well as reaching #33 for Atomix (the highest rank of an American restaurant).

**Jungyoon Choi** is a chef, culinary researcher, and writer with 25 years of experience working in Spain, Australia, and Korea. Over the past decade, she was trained at Fundació Alícia and El Bulli in Spain and now is executive R&D chef of the Korean Culinary and Fermentation Research Center at Sempio Foods. She is Academy Vice Chair of Korea & China for World's 50 Best Restaurants.

**Recipe Notes**

Butter is salted butter, unless otherwise specified.

Eggs are US size large (UK size medium), unless otherwise specified.

Herbs are fresh, unless otherwise specified.

Salt is fine sea salt, unless otherwise specified.

Sugar is white granulated or table sugar, unless otherwise specified.

Individual vegetables and fruits, such as carrots and apples, are assumed to be medium, unless otherwise specified, and should be peeled and/or washed unless otherwise specified.

Metric, imperial and cup measurements are used in this book. Follow one set of measurements throughout, not a mixture, as they are not interchangeable.

All tablespoon and teaspoon measurements given are level, not heaped, unless otherwise specified. 1 teaspoon = 5 ml; 1 tablespoon = 15 ml. Australian standard tablespoons are 20 ml, so Australian readers are advised to use 3 teaspoons in place of 1 tablespoon when measuring small quantities.

When no quantity is specified, for example of oils, salts and herbs used for finishing dishes or for deep-frying, quantities are discretionary and flexible.

Cooking and preparation times are for guidance only. If using a convection (fan) oven, follow the manufacturer's directions concerning oven temperatures.

When deep-frying, heat the oil to the temperature specified, or until a cube of bread browns in 30 seconds. After frying, drain fried foods on paper towels.

When sterilizing jars for preserves, wash the jars in clean, hot water and rinse thoroughly. Heat the oven to 140°C/275°F/Gas Mark 1. Place the jars on a baking sheet and place in the oven to dry.

Exercise a high level of caution when following recipes involving any potentially hazardous activity including the use of high temperatures and open flames and when deep-frying. In particular, when deep-frying, add food carefully to avoid splashing, wear long sleeves and never leave the pan unattended.

Some recipes include raw or very lightly cooked eggs, meat or fish, and fermented products. These should be avoided by the elderly, infants, pregnant women, convalescents and anyone with an impaired immune system.

All herbs, shoots, flowers, and leaves should be picked fresh from a clean source.

Do exercise caution when foraging for ingredients, which should only be eaten if an expert has deemed them safe to eat. In particular, do not gather wild mushrooms yourself before seeking the advice of an expert who has confirmed their suitability for human consumption.

As some species of mushrooms have been known to cause allergic reaction and illness, do take extra care when cooking and eating mushrooms and do seek immediate medical help if you experience a reaction after preparing or eating them.

Phaidon Press Limited
2 Cooperage Yard
London E15 2QR

Phaidon Press Inc.
111 Broadway
New York, NY 10006

phaidon.com

First published 2023
Reprinted 2024 (twice)
© 2023 Phaidon Press Limited

ISBN 978-1-83866-754-2

A CIP catalogue record for this book is available from the British Library and the Library of Congress.

All rights reserved. No part of this publication may be reproduced, stored in a retrieval system or transmitted, in any form or by any means, electronic, mechanical, photocopying, recording, or otherwise, without the written permission of Phaidon Press Limited.

Photography by Jinju Kang

Commissioning Editor: Emily Takoudes
Project Editor: Clare Churly
Senior Production Controller: Gif Jittiwutikarn
Translator: Jinah Rhee
Design: Associate Studio

Printed in China

Phaidon would like to extend special thanks to Jinah Rhee for her work as translator and project manager. Thanks also to Jin Auh, Theresa Bebbington, Vanessa Bird, Ken Deegan, Brankica Harvey, Julia Hasting, Minjae Heo, Jinju Kang, Young-Jun Lee, Pedro Mendes, João Mota, Kate Slate, Ellie Smith, Tracey Smith, and Caroline Stearns for their contributions to the book.